C H I N A

Black R.

Clear R.

Red River

Ha Giang

Cao Bang

Lao Cai

Bac Kan

Lai Chau

Lang Son

Dien Bien Phu

Thai Nguyen

Yen Bai

Son La

Haiphong

Hanoi

Nam Dinh

Burma

NORTH

GULF

Luang Prabang

Thanh Hoa

VIETNAM

of

Kiungshan

Mekong

TONGKING

Kainan

Vientiane

Vinh

L

Ha Tinh

A

Thakhek

Dong Hoi

Lakhon

17ᵗʰ PARALLEL

O

Quang Tri

HUÉ

Da Nang
(Tourane)

S

Mekong

Hoi An
(Faifo)

THAILAND

Quang Nga.

(SIAM)

Pakse

Qui Nhon

Angkor
Siem Reap

SOUTH

Bangkok

Stung Treng

VIETNAM

Battambang

Kratie

TONLE SAP

Nha Trang

CAMBODIA

Phnom Penh

Da Lat

Phan Rang

Bien Hoa

Phan Thiet

GULF

Chau Doc

CHO LON

Saigon

of

Ha Tien

Long
Xuyen

Vinh Long

Ba Ria

SIAM

Rach Gia

Soc Trang

Bac Lieu

THE SMALLER DRAGON

TU DUC (1829–1883)
Emperor of Vietnam 1847–1883.

the
smaller
dragon

A Political History of Vietnam

by

JOSEPH BUTTINGER

FREDERICK A. PRAEGER, NEW YORK

The jacket was designed by ROBERT FABIAN

*The drawing of the emperor Tu Duc was made
by* TRAN TAN THANH, *Saigon, after an illustration by*
L. RUFFIER, *which appeared in La Dépêche Coloniale,
Paris 1909*

The maps and photographs were executed by
HERBERT DASSEL, *Ottawa*

Composition by THE POLYGLOT PRESS, *New York*

BOOKS THAT MATTER

To CONNIE

Table of Contents

Table of Maps

List of Illustrations

Foreword

AT THE beginning of 1954, when the serious plight of the French in Indochina revived the danger of a third world war, Vietnam suddenly became the area of greatest concern to all people determined to maintain the fragile peace of our time without abandoning further millions of human beings to totalitarian communism. The general fear of a new world war led to the Conference of Geneva, which opened on April 26, 1954. The fall of Dien Bien Phu on May 6 reduced the influence of those people in France who wanted to continue the struggle for Indochina; at the same time, it strengthened the few among the French leaders who knew that the West's cruel and costly colonial wars could no longer be won. These men were able to make the French parliament see and accept a truth it had so far refused to face: that Vietnam, which had already been lost to Japan in 1940 and then recovered by the Vietnamese people themselves in 1945, was now lost to France forever. On July 21, the government of Mendès-France signed the historic Geneva Agreement, which ended the Indochina war and at last brought full independence to Vietnam, Cambodia, and Laos. And the Geneva Agreement also removed the threat of a world conflict that had arisen shortly before French power in Asia collapsed.

But for peace in Indochina and for improved prospects of world peace, a heavy price had to be paid. France paid with the loss of her "richest colony," after having wasted on the Indochina war over seven billion dollars of her own money and more than four billion received in American aid. The

1

Vietnamese people were forced to accept a division of their country, which was accompanied by the displacement of almost one million persons from the North to the South; and the nations opposed to the spread of communism had to reconcile themselves to a *de facto* recognition of a Communist state in the northern half of Vietnam.

This was not all. The price of peace included a revival of the dreary conviction that the West had no policy for Asia to counteract the attraction of communism, and that communism would continue to advance there. But even people who did not hold this conviction shared a deeply defeatist mood in regard to Vietnam. It is a historical fact, easy to ascertain, that after July, 1954, there were in England, France, and the United States not half a dozen editorial writers, columnists, and foreign correspondents who believed that the anti-Communist government of South Vietnam, led by today's President Ngo Dinh Diem, could last. The overthrow of Diem's regime by the Communists was generally considered a certainty, and optimists could be distinguished from pessimists only by their view that the inevitable event would take place not in one year but in two. As to the consequences of this event, opinions were unanimous. The fall of South Vietnam would greatly accelerate the Communist drive to conquer the whole of Southeast Asia, and would thus take on the proportions of a global disaster for the anti-Communist nations of the world.

It was at this time, about two months after the signing of the Geneva Agreement, that I became interested in Vietnam and concerned with the political situation in the South. Early in October, 1954, the International Rescue Committee asked me to go to Saigon to set up a program of assistance for students, professors, and other intellectuals among the refugees from the now Communist North. The International Rescue Committee is an American voluntary agency engaged primarily in relief and resettlement for leaders and intellectuals from totalitarian countries. Its activities started in the early 1930's, in response to the need created by Hitler's persecution of German democratic leaders and intellectuals; but since the end of the Second World War, the Committee's work has been concerned mainly with escapees from behind the Iron Curtain. These purposes explain a lively interest in political events on the part of its Board of Directors. and chairman, whose exhortations prompted the organization to extend its activities to Vietnam. As deeply concerned with politics as a fire brigade is with fire, the Committee still pursued only its traditional humanitarian aims when it added a relief operation in Vietnam to the many it maintained in Europe.

This is not the place to speak about the work of the International Rescue Committee in Vietnam, which I directed only from October through December 1954. I mention the Committee, first because I want to make clear that those who sent me to Saigon are not responsible for the political and journalistic activities concerning French and American attitudes toward Vietnam in which I engaged after January, 1955, when I was back again in the United States. And I speak of my mission in Saigon in order to explain how I became interested in the Vietnamese problem and eventually felt called upon to write a history of Vietnam. The reader has a right to know that I am hardly a professional historian, and certainly no experienced guide in the dark labyrinth called Asian history. Moreover, when I decided to write a book on Vietnam, and even after I had written most of the first chapter, *The Smaller Dragon* was not the book I intended to produce. I meant to write about Vietnam as a vital problem of present-day international politics, not about its past. My book was designed to answer the question of whether the South was really doomed to be conquered by the Communists, or whether it could develop democratically after checking the Communist threat. Such were my inclinations, and if I now tell the reader how radically my first

3

two weeks in Saigon changed my political views, he will understand why I felt urged to write about Vietnam.

But first I have to make a confession. I went to Vietnam firmly convinced that the South could not survive, and in fact I went chiefly because of this conviction. I wanted to see Saigon before it became a Communist city—something that I, like almost everyone whose judgment I valued, believed would happen in less than two years.

A few weeks after my arrival in Saigon, Ngo Dinh Diem began his fight for control of the army by dismissing its French-appointed Chief of Staff, General Nguyen Van Hinh. This was only one of the many occasions on which the world press predicted almost unanimously that the "inexperienced, rigid, and inept" leader of the South was himself digging his country's grave. At this point, however, I was no longer in harmony with the mood behind these predictions, and expressed angry disagreement with everyone who still believed, as I myself had done when I came to Saigon, that South Vietnam was doomed. Now I felt that I had never been more wrong than when I anticipated an early Communist victory over Ngo Dinh Diem. By November 15, I was convinced that his regime would not succumb to the post-Geneva pressures of the Communists, internal and international; that the Premier was a match for all French intrigues; that the armed politico-religious sects would have to submit to the national government or be defeated; and that the projected elections to unify North and South Vietnam would not be held, or if held, would certainly not produce a Communist majority in the South. And communism, I suddenly realized, was not irresistible in Asia either.

My change of mind was so total and rapid that it had something of the quality of a conversion. It was therefore accompanied by an irrepressible urge to communicate to others what had been revealed to me. However, there was nothing mysterious about the manner in which I had acquired my new

4

convictions, nor anything startling in the arguments in support of my new views. In fact it was all very elementary. I looked around and listened, more to the Vietnamese than to the French, and I was apparently not too keen to protect my preconceptions about the dismal fate of South Vietnam by closing my eyes. The two facts I learned and regarded as politically decisive were: (1) that the people were no longer interested in supporting the Communists, because they had supported them only to free themselves of the French more quickly; and (2) that South Vietnam had the leadership needed in her struggle to survive. I regarded Ngo Dinh Diem as a man of exceptional political talent, and expected his very shortcomings to turn into assets during the critical early period of his regime.

Perhaps I should add here what I fully realized only much later: that my political experience during my early weeks in Saigon was coupled with the unexpected emotional impact that so many Westerners feel when they first come in contact with the Vietnamese people. The impression that the strength, charm, and intelligence of the Vietnamese made on me remains unforgettable. This is certainly one of the reasons why, ever since I returned from Saigon in December, 1954, I have concerned myself almost exclusively with Vietnam, with the Vietnamese people, and with the question of whether some of their modest expectations can be fulfilled before despair kills their present abhorrence for a Communist dictatorship.

The reader will now understand why I would have preferred to write a book on the Vietnam of today and tomorrow to one telling the story of her past. Of Vietnam's past I was quite ignorant, whereas I flattered myself that I had some knowledge of the forces that would shape her future, and therefore felt justified in making my views known. I was not eager to teach anyone a lesson, but rather to show how much I had been in need of one myself and what had enabled me to learn it. And I felt strongly that the subject was of unique importance. Might not Vietnam's future somehow also reflect what the future held in store for the entire world? Might not political and economic frustration lead the Communists to use force against the South and thereby unleash the horrors of a new world war? Furthermore, if South Vietnam, as I was sure, had nothing to fear from the Communists for several years, might not an ill-advised policy of the West, as for instance an American refusal to aid in a rapid development of small and badly needed industries, create entirely new premises for a revival of the Communist danger a few years hence? And had South Vietnam really been saved, or had it only been spared by the Communist powers until a more opportune time to resume their forward march in Asia?

These were some of the questions I meant to answer when I conceived the idea of writing a book on Vietnam. If the reader is sorry that he gets *The Smaller Dragon* instead, I can honestly say that I am sorry too. But no matter how true it is that *The Smaller Dragon* is not the book on Vietnam most obviously in demand, I still believe it to be a book for which there exists a patent need.

Indeed, before this preface turns into a mere apology for the shortcomings of my book, I am going to advance a claim that may well justify in the reader's eyes my decision to write *The Smaller Dragon*. Quite a few books are available in English on North and South Vietnam today, and on the country's recent past. In America and England, there is no lack of highly qualified articles discussing Vietnam's prospects for the future, and I also know that a number of books on the problems of contemporary Vietnam are being written in English at this time. On the other hand, neither my own doubts nor the most severe criticism by professional historians can deprive *The Smaller Dragon* of one distinction: it is the first, and so far the only, book in the English language that can be called a history of Vietnam.

FOREWORD

Of the curious fact that one cannot find a history of Vietnam, many people must have become aware in recent years. I know that I was not the only one who attempted to increase his understanding of present-day Vietnam through a study of its history. Ever since I realized that ignorance of Vietnam's political past was one of the reasons for my misjudgment of her prospects in 1954, I have been searching the libraries and bookshops of three continents for an English history of Vietnam, only to learn that it cannot be found, and to conclude therefrom that such a book does not exist. During the last fifty years several excellent English histories of Burma, Thailand, and other Southeast Asian countries have been written. But of the history of Vietnam, an English reader will find only the most cursory treatment in a few histories of Southeast Asia, or brief surveys in introductory chapters of a number of books on French Indochina and Asia as a whole. D. G. E. Hall's recent *History of South-East Asia* and Brian Harrison's *South-East Asia* exemplify well the deplorable state of knowledge of Vietnamese history among the leading Western specialists on this important region of the world. These books, which in the parts dealing with other Southeast Asian countries are to my knowledge based on impeccable scholarship, contain unbelievably poor, inaccurate, and incomplete versions of Vietnamese history, in respect to both the older, unexplored periods and the more recent precolonial and colonial times. The reason for this can only be that these distinguished authors capitulated before the difficulties of independent thinking about and research in Vietnamese history. They relied, instead, on the few well-known French authorities on Indochina, such as Maybon, Maspéro, Chassigneux, Aurousseau, Gosselin, Cordier, Pasquier, Cadière, and Masson, whose works are all dated, if not actually unreliable because of their author's willingness to compromise with the demands of French colonial policy and propaganda.

7

This being the state of affairs, it is not at all surprising that most references to Vietnam in encyclopedias, travel books, and magazine articles reflect a general ignorance of Vietnamese history that is serious enough in France and Vietnam, but truly appalling in all other Western and Eastern countries. What Ellen Hammer says in the foreword to her book *The Struggle for Indochina* is unfortunately true, not only of books written about the colonial period and the present time, but also of most works on all other periods of Vietnamese history: "I have reluctantly had to recognize in the course of preparing this book how inadequate, inaccurate, and often untrue the printed word has been in regard to Indochina and its people."

When I began to write what later turned into *The Smaller Dragon*, a modern and factually reliable history of Vietnam did not exist even in French. French literature on Vietnam is copious, but of the major works almost nothing has been translated into other languages, and most of the really important studies are unavailable in the libraries outside of France. Moreover, this whole literature suffers from a conspicuous lack of works dealing with Vietnam as a single and separate entity with a history of its own; and very few books have been written by French scholars in which the Vietnamese are treated as a unified and homogeneous people whose cultural and political development began well over two thousand years ago. Anyone attempting to familiarize himself with Vietnamese history is likely to be defeated by the many monographs by French scholars on prehistory, ethnic minorities, religion, art, language, literature, agriculture, ancestor worship, law, education, or other aspects of Vietnamese society and culture, as well as by the studies concerned only with special regions of the country or with a particular phase of the history of Vietnam. This tendency to break history up into many subjects unrelated to an all-embracing whole is unfortunately strong also among the few Vietnamese historians themselves, whom French

8

training did not prepare for a more synthesized approach to their own past, and who, up to the coming of the French, had not yet overcome the peculiar limitations characteristic of the older Chinese historical writings.

Under these circumstances, which make it difficult for the expert and quite impossible for the layman to acquaint himself with the mere facts of Vietnamese history, I was understandably relieved when a book by a Vietnamese scholar appeared that can rightly be called the first modern history of Vietnam. However, *Le Viet-Nam, histoire et civilisation,* by Le Thanh Khoi, which was published in Paris in 1955, exists only in French, and has several drawbacks that make it of doubtful value even for the English and American student familiar with the French language. Its chief merit lies in its being the best summary of the accumulated knowledge of Vietnam's past and in its many references to the existing sources. To the author must also be credited a first attempt to establish a modern pattern of history for Vietnam by breaking away from the antiquated frame of reference in which decisive political and social events were subordinated to dynastic chronology. But Le Thanh Khoi's study betrays a very definite pro-Communist bias, which makes the portions of his book dealing with more recent events highly unreliable. And in spite of some passages of great power and real beauty, the book is written in a most cumbersome way. Of its many purely narrative passages, very few can be understood by a reader not already familiar with the story the author is trying to tell.

The reader I had in mind when I first considered writing an English history of Vietnam is unlikely to benefit directly from Le Thanh Khoi's pioneering efforts, because his book will probably never be published in English. Its existence therefore has not lessened in the least the need for a generally available history of Vietnam in the English-speaking world.

Of this need I became strongly aware while studying Viet-

9

namese history in preparation for the book I planned to write
on contemporary Vietnam. But if I wrote *The Smaller Dragon*
instead, I did it not in order to fill a strangely persistent gap
in the historical literature on Southeast Asia which sooner or
later someone was bound to fill. My original motives for writing about Vietnam were not primarily those of a scholar;
concern over the political consequences likely to result from
the ignorance in regard to Vietnam, rather than scholarly aspirations led to my decision that *The Smaller Dragon* was the
book I had to write.

Once my studies had reached a certain point, this decision
became quite easy. The more closely I looked at Vietnam, the
more it seemed to me that the survival of the South, which
some people were already beginning to call a miracle, was
really a puzzle—in fact, one of the great political puzzles of
our time. Political logic showed that the Communists should
have taken over South Vietnam soon after the Conference of
Geneva, just as military logic had shown earlier that the French
should have won the Indochina war. On the other hand, the
Communists should never have been able to capture the leadership in this peasant nation's war of independence, and Ho
Chi Minh should never have been able to deceive so many
anti-Communists about the nature of his relations to Moscow
and about the true aims of the Vietminh. And how could a
leader of Ngo Dinh Diem's present stature develop in spite
of his refusal, maintained for twenty crucial years, to accept a
responsible position in the government of his country? Or how
could he become internationally famous for his "incapacity"
precisely while he was accomplishing a feat for which it is hard
to find a parallel in contemporary history?

The student who seeks an answer to these questions by
probing into Vietnam's past soon learns that the history of
this country is full of similar puzzles. He will find many secrets
and surprises, linking the problems of today to the problems

of the past in an unbroken chain, and he will also discover
that Vietnamese history is full of "miracles." Some of these
are greater than today's miracle of the survival of the South.
In fact, the very existence of Vietnam as a separate country,
and the survival of the Vietnamese as a distinct people, must
be regarded as a miracle, for which scores of historians have
so far tried vainly to find a satisfactory explanation. The power
of circumstances, both geographical and historical, should
indeed have made the absorption of Vietnam by the Chinese
empire and the complete Sinization of the Vietnamese people
an inescapable fate.

In order to survive as a separate people, every Vietnamese
had to be ready at all times to sacrifice his life in the many
wars against the Chinese armies of invasion or occupation.
But in order to fight the Chinese successfully, Vietnam had
to adopt many of the Chinese social and technical inventions.
How to benefit from the more advanced Chinese civilization
without becoming Chinese themselves was already the main
question in the life of this people when Vietnam emerged as
a separate state more than two thousand years ago. It was
never easy for the smaller dragon to survive and lead his own
life, next to the bigger dragon. Will Vietnam, after a millenium
of independence from China, again become a satellite of her
gigantic neighbor in the north? A touch of eternity, as it were,
distinguishes this question from all others concerning the survival of Vietnam. Other questions may have been more burning
at certain times, but surviving the dangers from the north has
now again become Vietnam's main problem. As so often in the
past, there is again—this time due to the existence of a separate
Communist state of Vietnam—an element of ambiguity in the
relationship between Vietnamese and Chinese, the effect of
which on the future of the whole country is difficult to measure.
One would like to know what made the Vietnamese accept
and cherish Chinese philosophical ideas and political concepts

in the past, in order to evaluate their degree of susceptibility to Chinese influences today. For the same reason, one would like to know what made them fight so fiercely against all attempts by China to take them into her fold. Can Ho Chi Minh change the attitude of the Vietnamese toward China? Fear of China, rather than the experience of French colonial rule, may be the key to the intense nationalism of this people; if this is the case, nationalism, once the source of strength of the Communist movement, may now become an element of its early disintegration. This could mean that China, if she should ever again attempt to subjugate the Vietnamese people, would fail again, as she failed so many times during the last thousand years. But without a close study of Vietnamese history, any answer to this question so vital for the future of Southeast Asia must remain a mere guess. He who has no insight into the forces that shaped this nation's mentality, and no knowledge of the circumstances that enabled the Vietnamese to survive, will be as surprised at the next turn of events as were the best-informed observers at least half a dozen times since the end of the Second World War. They knew all the facts, but not their meaning.

There are probably readers who do not believe that ordinary political facts can have a hidden meaning that a study of history may be able to reveal. Perhaps such readers are willing to accept another explanation for my writing about Vietnam's political past: whoever engages in a study of Vietnamese history is likely to succumb to the challenge of its many unsolved problems, just as a Westerner who goes to Vietnam is likely to be captivated by the racial and national characteristics of the Vietnamese.

As to the kind of book I decided to write once I had determined its purpose and become acquainted with the existing material, I would like to say that I wanted *The Smaller Dragon* not only to be a useful book for the student and scholar, but also one that would hold the attention of people who are interested in Vietnam for purely political reasons. This resulted in my writing a relatively brief narrative supplemented by an unusual quantity of notes. The sources of Vietnamese history are rich but little known, poorly explored, and not easily accessible, although their full exploration does not require a knowledge of the Vietnamese language. Nothing of consequence has been written in Vietnamese that has not also been published in French. The only exception I know of is a history of Vietnam by the renowned scholar Tran Trong Kim, which was translated into English for my benefit by Vietnamese friends in Saigon.

Some of my notes are not just references to sources but are concerned with controversial points of minor interest to the general reader. Many also give factual information and additional narrative material that would overburden the main text with details not essential for an understanding of the principal events. However, the critical reader and the student of Vietnamese history, whether he knows French or not, will welcome these additions, most of which are from books that have never been translated into English. They often contain the views of French authors with whom I disagree, and whose books are either not available at all in this country or hard to obtain. Without these notes most readers would find it difficult to check my facts, examine my sources, evaluate my views, and compare my approach to Vietnamese history with that of the older authorities in the field.

I was not only fortunate in the timely appearance of Le Thanh Khoi's *Le Viet-Nam, histoire et civilisation,* but also benefited greatly from the most recent French work on Indochina: the two volumes of documents, many of them never printed before, that George Taboulet published in Paris in 1955 and 1956, under the title *La geste française en Indochine.* Much of the literature on Indochina, and almost everything dealing with Franco-Vietnamese relations in the eighteenth and nineteenth centuries, has been made obsolete by Taboulet's publication.

I must add that I regard my book as the first volume of a projected two-volume history of Vietnam. The second volume is intended to describe in detail the events that are outlined at the end of this book under the title "Vietnam since 1900." It will bring me back to the subject about which I originally planned to write. However, I expect *The Smaller Dragon* to lead a life of its own, as I believe that the present lack of anything in English dealing with the periods I cover justifies its publication as a separate book.

Pennington, N. J.
October, 1957

14

The Dragon

Of the four symbolic animals that are engraved and painted on many objects, or otherwise represented in Vietnamese houses and public places, the dragon is the most important (the others are the unicorn, the tortoise and the phoenix).

The dragon, a fabulous animal of Sino-Vietnamese mythology, is usually shown with the head of a camel, the horns of a buck, the eyes of a demon (protruding from their sockets), the ears of a buffalo, the neck and body of a snake, the scales of a carp, the claws of an eagle and the paws of a tiger. Hanging from both sides of its mouth is a long barbel, and under the dragon's tongue there is hidden a precious stone. The top of its head shows a decorative protuberance, which is the mark of intelligence, and along the backbone a crest of eighty-one extra large scales runs from the neck to the end of the tail.

The dragon can live under the ground, in the water, or in the air; it spits a dangerous kind of vapor, which it can turn into fire or water at will.

Dragons are immortal. There are not many, but their number increases because another fabulous animal, a reptile half lizard, half snake, can become a dragon at the age of one thousand years.

In spite of its frightening appearance, the dragon is not a representation of an evil spirit. On the contrary: both in China and Vietnam, the dragon has always been the symbol of nobility and power. It thus became the principal attribute of the Vietnamese emperor, or Son of Heaven.

(After Thai Van Kiem, from *Times of Viet nam*, Saigon, September 21, 1957)

Chapter I

Introducing Vietnam

1.

VIETNAM, as more and more people are beginning to know, is an Asian country lying within the region for which the term Southeast Asia has recently come into general use. By Southeast Asia we mean the peninsula jutting out from the Asian mainland between India and China, and the vast archipelago south and east of it which includes Indonesia and the Philippines.[1]

Vietnam belongs to the mainland part of Southeast Asia, the so-called Indochinese peninsula. Of the six countries on this peninsula, the three larger ones occupy more than eighty per cent of its surface. They are Burma in the west and northwest, Thailand in the center, and Vietnam in the east.[2] Cambodia and Laos are squeezed between Vietnam and Thailand, in contrast to Malaya in the south, which seems to be running away from the mainland on a long and narrow peninsula of its own.[3]

A variety of names have long been in use for the Indochinese peninsula. The German-speaking geographers call it *Hinterindien,*[4] in accordance with the French scholars who have written about *l'Inde extérieure,* but *Hinterindien* means the Indochinese peninsula as a whole, while the French term is applied only to the "Indianized" western part of the peninsula. For its eastern part the French have generally used the name Indochina (*Indochine*) or French Indochina, the latter a term of purely political origin and now of no more than historical usefulness. An English equivalent of *l'Inde extérieure* is Further India,[5] with Little China as counterpart, in order to distinguish the region of Chinese cultural and political penetration from the Indianized parts of the peninsula. This, however, does not correspond with the French distinction between *l'Inde extérieure* and French Indochina. Of French Indochina, Little China is evidently no more than a part.[6]

Although some of these terms are no longer in general use, there is still much confusion about the name of the peninsula of which the Vietnamese people occupy the whole eastern coast line from the Chinese border down to the Gulf of Siam. This confusion is due in part to the fact that during the so-called Indochinese War the word Indochina became almost synonymous with French Indochina, the French-controlled former association of the three states of Cambodia, Laos, and Vietnam.[7] Prevailing usage, in short, sees Vietnam as a country of Indochina, but Indochina only as the eastern part of the Indochinese peninsula, with several other names current for either its western or eastern half but with none that is universally accepted for the peninsula as a whole.

A simple way of avoiding this confusion is to follow the authors who have applied the term Indochina to the entire peninsula. Geographical, ethnological, and historical reasons make the name Indochina for this part of the world as accurate and useful as such names ever can be.[8] The peninsula is inhabited by peoples who are neither Indian nor Chinese. It lies between India and China, geographically connected with both, and as close to the one as to the other. This is true despite the fact that the whole territory is really a southern extension of the Chinese land masses. Over the whole width of Indochina's northern boundary the mountain ranges of southern and south-western China run down into the peninsula from north to south. Their narrow river valleys have forever been migration routes of the peoples who populated Southeast Asia, descending from southern China and Tibet into the peninsula and proceeding onto the islands of Indonesia and beyond, under the pressure of a never ending stream of new arrivals.

China's geographical intimacy with the peninsula, however, is largely neutralized, as history has proved, by the easy approach by sea that India enjoys to the whole western coast of Indochina in addition to a land connection in the northwest. The sea, unlike some massive mountain formations on the Asia mainland, does not separate the countries of Asia, but rather connects them with each other and with the rest of the world. Indochina, as a result, has always been subject to the influence of her two gigantic neighbors to an almost equal degree. Indian traders and priests have contributed to the development of Indochinese civilization as much as Chinese moral philosophers, Chinese conquerors, and Chinese political administrators. Religion, philosophy, art, and political organization show the cultural predominance of either India or China over this territory for some two thousand years—without, however, making the cultures of Indochina into mere copies of Chinese or Indian culture. They evolved as individual adaptations of either the one or the other and to a minor degree as adaptations of both, which is precisely what makes them Indochinese and why the territory of their pre-eminence may properly be called Indochina.

Of Indochina as a whole, therefore, French Indochina was never more than its smaller and only partly Indianized eastern portion, a creation of the age of Western imperialism, and as a separate entity it was wholly unrelated to the geographical, racial, and cultural factors that have shaped the Indochinese world.

19

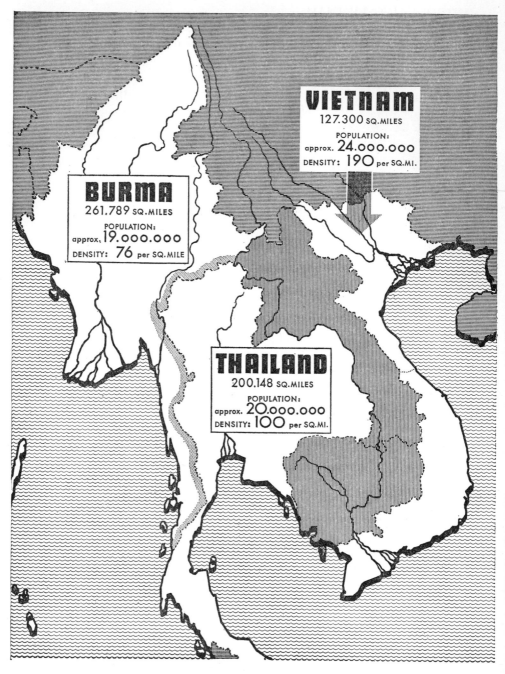

VIETNAM
127.300 SQ. MILES
POPULATION:
approx. 24.000.000
DENSITY: 190 per SQ. MI.

BURMA
261.789 SQ. MILES
POPULATION:
approx. 19.000.000
DENSITY: 76 per SQ. MILE

THAILAND
200.148 SQ. MILES
POPULATION:
approx. 20.000.000
DENSITY: 100 per SQ. MI.

Map I.—BURMA, THAILAND, VIETNAM
In territory, Vietnam is considerably smaller than Thailand and only about half the size of Burma, but
24,000,000 inhabitants make it the strongest in population of all the Indochinese states

2.

Western intervention in Indochina has been the cause of another terminological difficulty, concerning, however, only the state of Vietnam. This difficulty was encountered by many a student of international affairs after the outbreak of the so-called Indochinese War in 1946. If a newspaper reader attempted to obtain background information about Vietnam he was frustrated by the fact that most encyclopedias did not contain the word Vietnam. His atlas, too, if it was not of the latest edition, seemed to ignore the existence of a country by that name. All but the most recent dictionaries and maps were indeed thus defective.[9] They showed and they spoke about French Indochina; and if they were explicit, or if one succeeded in finding a book on the subject, one would have learned that French Indochina consisted of Tongking, Annam, and Cochinchina, in addition to the kingdoms of Cambodia and Laos. These were described as three more or less different sections of a country that at the time when the French first intervened, in 1858, was said to have been under the nominal rule of the emperor of Annam.

The land that, in the wake of French political and military intervention in Indochina, generally became known as the kingdom or empire of Annam (of which Tongking and Cochinchina were somehow regarded as having been parts) had in reality long been a highly centralized state, ostensibly called Vietnam by official proclamation in 1802. Under the inverted form of Nam Viet, this name was already used to designate the regions inhabited by the ancestors of the Vietnamese in the third century B.C. The word Viet has appeared, in one form or another, in the name of the country ever since Vietnam regained its independence, after more than one thousand years of Chinese domination, in the year 939. Vietnamese patriots have therefore expressed themselves, not unjustly, with the statement that their people and their country were known under their present name long before France ceased to be the country of the Gauls.

Vietnam lost its name, together with its unity and political independence, in a series of colonial wars inflicted upon the country by France between 1858 and 1883. Thus it came about that the maps, the dictionaries, the reference books, and the whole literature on Indochina give only the three names adopted by the French for the three parts into which they divided Vietnam: Cochinchina, a French colony since 1863, for the South; Annam, which became a French protectorate twenty years later, for the Center; and Tongking, another French protectorate since 1883, for the North.[10] The leaders of the various national movements of Vietnam, in fighting the colonial disruption of their country, have always rejected these foreign designations, but only by regaining their national independence have the Vietnamese succeeded in regaining also their country's traditional name.[11]

The names Tongking, Annam, and Cochinchina, however, will have to figure in a study of Vietnamese history of which the colonial period of less than a century is likely to be a large part—just as in a history of the German Reich the use of names like Prussia, Bavaria, and Saxony could not be avoided. But for the Germans, these names will always remain a genuine part of their national tradition, in contrast to the Vietnamese, whose political independence was violated by the imposition of a tripartite government from abroad, and whose national tradition was falsified by calling the North of their country Tongking, the Center Annam, and the South Cochinchina.[12]

3.

In territory, Vietnam is considerably smaller than Thailand and only about half the size of Burma, but 24,000,000 inhab-

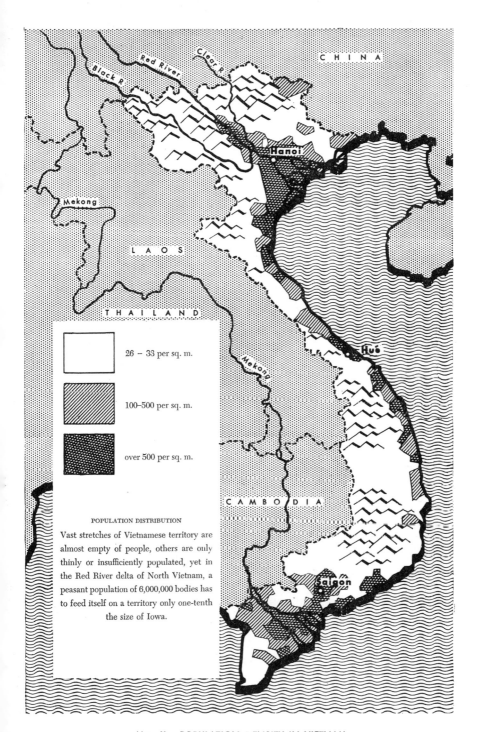

POPULATION DISTRIBUTION

Vast stretches of Vietnamese territory are
almost empty of people, others are only
thinly or insufficiently populated, yet in
the Red River delta of North Vietnam, a
peasant population of 6,000,000 bodies has
to feed itself on a territory only one-tenth
the size of Iowa.

26 – 33 per sq. m.

100–500 per sq. m.

over 500 per sq. m.

Map II.—POPULATION DENSITY IN VIETNAM

itants make it the strongest in population of all the Indochinese states.[13] There are in Vietnam, in addition to an estimated 21,000,000 Vietnamese,[14] over 2,000,000 people belonging to different ethnic minorities, and about 1,000,000 foreigners, of whom the more than 700,000 Chinese are the largest group.[15]

Twenty-four million inhabitants on a territory three-fourths the size of France—about the same as New England together with New York and New Jersey—do not add up to a very high density of population. It is about 190 people per square mile,[16] which means less than half the density of Italy, a country somewhat smaller than Vietnam with twice as many people. Japan, which is not much larger, has almost four times as many inhabitants as Vietnam.

A relative underpopulation is indeed a main feature of the whole Indochinese peninsula. More pronounced in Burma and Thailand, it is characteristic also of Vietnam, in spite of the well-known fact that the country has long been plagued by a problem of local overpopulation. This is easy to explain: roughly eighty per cent of the population live on only twenty per cent of the land. Vast stretches of Vietnamese territory are almost empty of people, others only thinly or insufficiently populated, yet in the Red River delta of North Vietnam, a peasant population of 6,000,000 bodies has to feed itself on a territory only one-tenth the size of Iowa. In one of the northern provinces the density of the rural population reaches 1,000 people per square mile.[17]

This uneven distribution of the inhabitants of Vietnam has many historical and economic causes, but it is determined above all by a few basic geographical facts. Geographically, the country shows a number of highly significant features, some of which have influenced the historical destiny of Vietnam to an unusual degree. One of them is the contrast between the mountain regions and the plains. The former are extensive territories of jungle or inferior forests, largely insalubrious and

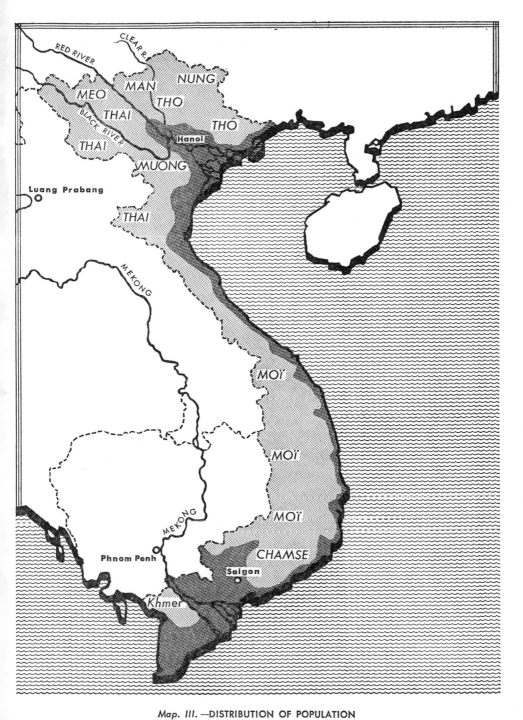

Map. III. —DISTRIBUTION OF POPULATION

Geographical distribution of ethnic minorities in
Vietnam (the territories in darker shade are occupied by the Vietnamese)

only sparsely dotted with cultivable land; the plains are fertile river deltas given to intensive cultivation, but even after the conquest of the great Mekong delta in the South by the Vietnamese, the rich plains formed hardly one-fifth of the territory of Vietnam.

The contrast between the low and the mountainous parts of Vietnam is underlined, in addition, by the racial and cultural differences of the people in the higher regions from those in the plains. The thinly spread mountain population consists almost exclusively of the various ethnic minorities, while the Vietnamese themselves, ever since their existence was first recorded by Chinese historians over two thousand years ago, have always crowded the valleys and deltas and refused to settle in higher altitudes, in spite of their need for continuous territorial expansion.

The people of the higher regions, like their mountainous country with its diversity of appearance and hospitality, present a bewildering mixture of racial and linguistic groups in different stages of civilization. Their number is as yet not fully determined and their classification still far from complete. At a congress of Vietnamese minorities held under Communist auspices in September, 1953, delegates of twenty "nationalities" were said to have participated, some of them no doubt representing only small tribes consisting of less than one hundred families.[18]

The Vietnamese, on the other hand, are not only the overwhelming majority of the population; they show a remarkable cultural unity, possess a high degree of civilization, speak the same language in the remotest North and the farthest South, and are of an almost identical physical constitution all over the country. It is not the people of the plains but the minority groups in the mountains who constitute the chaos of races, civilizations, and languages characteristic of Vietnam no less than of the whole of Southeast Asia.

26

4.

There is no way of looking at these minority peoples without, at the same time, unfolding the whole panorama of Vietnamese history and prehistory, projected against the geographical, racial, and historical background of the peninsula as a whole.

There are in Indochina, to begin with, about a million Mois, aborigines of great dissimilarity and a low level of civilization, of whom the majority inhabit the highlands of central and southern Vietnam. A study of the Mois underlines the well-established fact that, prior to the later Mongolian immigrations, the population of Vietnam and probably of the whole Indochinese peninsula was of Indonesian stock. Of the races that preceded the Indonesians—peoples akin to the Australian aborigines and the Negroid Papuans of Melanesia—very little, aside from the evidence of archeology, is left in Vietnam. However, the racial diversity of the Mois, whose skins may vary from tanned white to the darkest black, has supported the view that the original Austro-Negroid population was not altogether displaced but partly absorbed by the people of Indonesian stock—immigrants from southwest China and Tibet themselves, like their Austro-Negroid precursors, but already old settlers in Indochina when the Mongolian peoples began to move in the same direction.

Among these peoples were the Thai. The Shans of Burma, the Siamese of Thailand, the people of Laos, and the various Thai tribes of North Vietnam are all descendants of a racial group whose movement out of southern China was part of this Mongolian migration, presumably the third great human wave to reach Indochina from the north.[19] Whenever this last migration started—probably less than three thousand years ago—it has never come to a complete halt, and it is likely to continue in the future in one form or another.

27

According to Chinese historical annals, the Thai were already on the move in the sixth century B.C. They advanced into Indochina along the rivers and through the valleys in a slow and usually peaceful manner, with massive and violent outbursts against Vietnam and northern Burma occurring once during the ninth century and again at the end of the thirteenth, when the Thai, harassed by the Mongols in China under Kublai Khan, pushed into the center of the peninsula, where they began to develop one of the major Indochinese states.

The arrival of some Thai in Vietnam dates probably as far back as the appearance in history of the Vietnamese themselves. Their influx continued even after the main stream of Thai penetration began to move down the middle of Indochina toward the Gulf of Siam. At least one Thai tribe, the Nungs, settled in Vietnam as late as the sixteenth century.[20] Today the Thai are the most important, though racially quite heterogeneous, minority group of Vietnam, different also from many Thai people in other parts of Indochina. The name Thai is in fact hardly more than a linguistic classification.[21]

5.

In their customs and their degree of civilization, though not in their language, the Thai of Vietnam resemble their neighbors the Muongs, who dwell in the lower mountain regions around the Red River valley. The Muongs number about 250,000.[22] Unlike the Mois in the center and south, whose Indonesian character survived the Mongolian racial onslaught, the Muongs are probably the outcome of a series of racial mixtures, in which the preponderance of the Mongolian element emphasizes also the lateness of this important contribution. In this respect the Muongs can be likened to the Vietnamese. They are, in fact, the only minority group whose speech is closely related to the Vietnamese language.[23] The

28

Muongs share also most of the basic religious concepts and primitive religious practices of the Vietnamese, and their social organization has often been described as a replica of Vietnamese society before the conquest of Vietnam by the Chinese.[24]

If the Muongs, as seems likely, represent a racial and cultural transition from some vanished Austro-Indonesian tribe to the ancestors of the Vietnamese, the emergence of the Vietnamese people can be determined fairly accurately on the basis of the available scientific evidence. Non-Chinese Mongolian immigrants into the Red River valley, by mixing with and gradually absorbing the prevailing Austro-Indonesian stock, produced a number of new racial mixtures, in a process that must have lasted several hundred years. These new peoples were of unequal power to resist the continual dangers of absorption or annihilation that threatened them from the north. Some have disappeared; others, like the Muongs, barely survived after being pushed out of the valley into the surrounding mountains. Only the ancestors of the Vietnamese, who must have been of greater vitality than the others from the beginning, were able to survive in the country of their origin and eventually to develop the distinctive features of a separate and homogeneous nation. They are now considered specifically to result from a racial union in the Red River valley of the original Indonesian inhabitants with an early wave of Thai and one branch of the so-called Viets, another non-Chinese people from the regions south of the lower Yangtse.[25] These Viets were probably moving into southeast China and toward the Indochinese peninsula at some time between 500 and 300 B.C. The many Viets who failed to reach the Red River valley were soon afterward taken into the expanding Chinese empire and eventually absorbed by the Chinese. Only their cousins who traveled a little farther, and by uniting with other races added to their own strength, have not entirely disappeared from the family of man. They continue to exist as one of the parts that went into the making of the Vietnamese people.[26]

29

6.

If a study of the Mois, the Thai, and the Muongs throws light on the great migrations into Indochina, the racial basis of the Indochinese peoples, and the origin of the Vietnamese, an investigation of the Chams in the South will bring into relief a significant line of events in the history of Indochina and notably of Vietnam.

The Chams in Vietnam number no more than twenty thousand.[27] They live in miserable villages and resemble some of the primitive Moi tribes in their dialects, their matriarchal tribal organization, and their customs. They also belong to the Indonesian group of peoples who once dominated the whole peninsula and have given to the present diversified population of Indochina the one racial element common to all. But the Chams are not primitive for the same reasons as the Mois, who were pushed into the mountains by stronger peoples before the rise of Indochinese civilization, which took place in the fertile plains and along the narrow coasts. The state of the Chams is one of decline. They are the deteriorated remnants of a highly civilized nation conquered and almost exterminated in endless wars with the Cambodians and the Vietnamese.

The kingdom later to be known as Champa probably came into existence at the end of the second century of our era.[28] It appears to have originated, and for a time centered, in the province of Quang Nam, just below Hué, but soon extended over two hundred miles south to the Bay of Cam Ranh, and west beyond the Annamese mountain chain into the Mekong valley of present-day Cambodia and southern Laos. The first report of Cham activities is contained in a memorial addressed to the Chinese emperor in the year 280 by the governor of the Chinese provinces inhabited by the Vietnamese—the Red River valley and the coastal lands down to the so-called Gate of Annam near the eighteenth parallel, then, and for a long time after, the southern border of Chinese imperial expansion.[29]

In his memorial to the emperor, which speaks of attacks by the Chams on Chinese-held territory, the governor also complained about the fact that the Chams were supported by raiders from a kingdom called Funan, located south and west of Champa and apparently allied with the Chams against the Chinese. At the time of the governor's writing, however, the existence of this kingdom was no longer news at the Chinese imperial court. China had already sent a diplomatic mission to Funan, after having received one from there, somewhere between 245 and 250 A.D.

The kingdom of Funan, which may be described as a precursor of the kingdom of Cambodia, was only one of a number of early Indochinese states fated to disappear in the struggles caused by the slow but steady pressure of the later Mongolian immigrations.[30] Little is known of the origin of these states, of which Funan was probably the first and certainly the most powerful, but there can be no doubt that their emergence was primarily due to Indian cultural penetration of the peninsula prior to the earliest Chinese contacts with these countries. The first Chinese account of Funan dates from the middle of the third century A.D. At that time Funan was already a highly developed state. The Chinese were astonished to find walled cities and great palaces, and even books and archives, when they first arrived in Funan. A powerful fleet seems to have impressed the visitors from the north as much as the Funanese taxes, which were collected by the state in gold, silver, perfumes, and pearls.

In the south, Funan extended over the whole Mekong delta, which is now a vital part of Vietnam. But this does not establish any significant historical connection between Vietnam and Funan. The conquest of the Mekong delta by the Vietnamese did not begin until the end of the seventeenth century, whereas Funan had already disappeared at the end of the sixth. The significance of this state for the history of Vietnam lies in the fact that the knowledge derived from Chinese historical annals

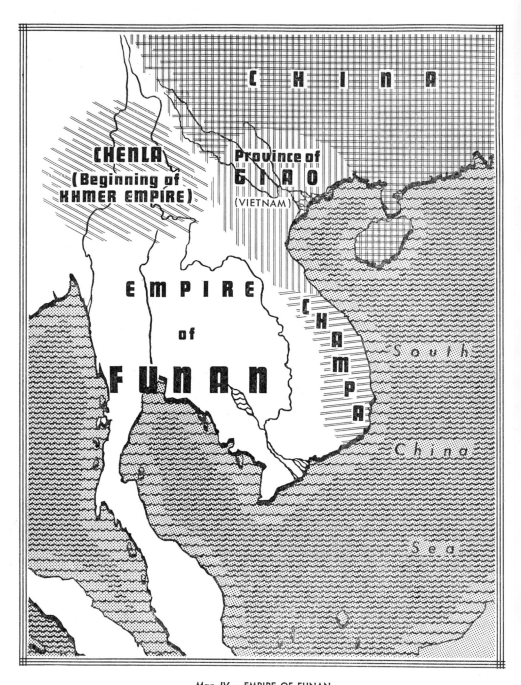

Map IV.—EMPIRE OF FUNAN

Approximate extension of the Funan empire before its disappearance during the sixth century A.D.

of the people and the history of Funan applies largely also to Champa and the Chams, whose part on the stage of Vietnamese history was second only to the part played by the Chinese. No contemporary Chinese description of early Champa and Cham customs exists—the oldest such document is a travel report from the thirteenth century—but the racial and cultural affinity of early Champa and Funan, of which their Chinese contemporaries were quite aware, is fully corroborated by evidence from later periods, such as archeological and epigraphical findings belonging to the fifth century, and by the more recent historical chronicles of the Vietnamese.

At the time of their first recorded contacts with Funan, the Chinese found the great mass of the people still in a very uncivilized state. This was no doubt equally true of Champa, which was probably the younger of the two states. Chinese reporters described the people as black, ugly, and naked, practicing only a primitive kind of agriculture but enjoying engraved ornaments and widely using the chisel to produce small works of art. The envoys of a higher civilization found it also remarkable that these simple people were apparently not at all "given to theft."[31]

The Chinese, however, have also emphasized the highly developed organization of these states and the coexistence of these primitive conditions with a remarkable culture, of which in the case of Champa considerable evidence has survived.[32] There seems to be no doubt among the historians as to the nature of the impulse that brought these states and cultures into being. Lively commercial relations with India, in which the seafaring Indochinese were probably as active as the Indians themselves, must have led to the adoption of Indian customs, Indian religious practices, and Indian art, and to the development of a layer of Indian culture among an upper class of these peoples long before the kingdoms of Funan and Champa appeared on the horizon of Indochinese history. When at the beginning of our era the first organized states

33

emerged on the peninsula, they turned out to be essentially a product of Indian cultural penetration. Their formation was not due to Indian military conquest nor to a mass emigration from India to Indochina, although it may have been preceded by an influx of Indian priests and literati, whose influence would account for the adoption of Sanskrit as the sacred language of these states. But Indian priests and literati, and the Indian officials whom the first Chinese emissaries to Funan claimed to have seen, were soon to become Indochinese, and neither they nor their superior culture were ever the instruments of Indian political domination.

7.

Things were quite different in the northeast of the peninsula, a region subject not to Indian but to Chinese cultural penetration. To the territories north of Champa, where the ancestors of the Vietnamese prevailed, the advantages of a higher civilization came as a consequence of Chinese military expansion and the establishment of Chinese political rule. The Indianized states of Funan and Champa never became colonies of the country whose cultural stimulus had brought them into existence; the Sinized northeast of Indochina made its appearance in history as an object of conquest on the road of Chinese imperial expansion.[33] In the eyes of their rulers in the north, the Vietnamese people were simply the somewhat troublesome inhabitants of the Red River valley and a vaguely determined region farther south, both usually referred to by the Chinese as their southern border province of Chiao Chi. Seven hundred years had to elapse from the time of their first diplomatic mission to the kingdom of Funan in the third century before the Chinese were ready to recognize an independent kingdom of Vietnam.

A few years after this important event, in 982, the first major

Vietnamese expedition against Champa was already under way, inaugurating the process of territorial expansion that lasted over eight hundred years and spread the Vietnamese people from the Red River valley all the way down the east coast of Indochina to the Gulf of Siam.

One aspect of this process was the downfall of Champa. When Vietnam became independent in the middle of the tenth century, Champa showed no signs of decline and was as capable of vigorous aggression as it had been during the centuries of Chinese rule over the Vietnamese. A naval expedition against the Red River valley, into which the Chams had been persuaded by refugees from Vietnam, was in fact the immediate cause of the first Vietnamese invasion of Champa. Five hundred years later, after a cruel Cham defeat in 1471, Cham power was broken, and soon afterward Champa came to an end. However Vietnamese territorial expansion continued, now at the expense of Cambodia, a kingdom that had arisen as the successor of Funan after the middle of the sixth century and had reached its summit of power and artistic achievement at at the end of the twelfth century.[34] Three hundred years later, at the time of Champa's fall, the Indianized kingdom of Cambodia itself had traveled far on the road of decline. Threatened also from the north by the ever advancing Thai, the Cambodians were unable to prevent the Vietnamese from infiltrating into their rich but thinly populated provinces in the South. The rice of the vast and fertile Mekong River delta was grown by Vietnamese hands, and many villages administered by Vietnamese elders were flourishing in Cambodian provinces not yet annexed, before the intervention of France in Indochina put an end to Vietnamese territorial expansion.[35] The Cambodians who remained in the Mekong delta region, which had still been part of their own country less than 250 years earlier, are now only another minority group of South Vietnam. Their number is 350,000.[36]

8.

Viewed against the unquiet mosaic of races and cultures on the peninsula and against Indochina's shifting historical scene, the main feature of Vietnamese history, from its pre-Chinese past to the present day, reveals itself to be its unity and continuity for over two thousand years. The development of the Mois was arrested at the dawn of history, that of the Muongs in early historical times; of the Chams, who appeared later in history than the Vietnamese and were never conquered by China, very little is left; of the great kingdom of Funan, nothing at all; and even the once powerful inheritor of Funan and the center of Indochinese culture long before Vietnam had consolidated her own independence—Cambodia—was rapidly declining when European intervention changed the course of history on the peninsula a hundred years ago. Of all these peoples, only the Vietnamese, whose beginnings in separate statehood preceded all higher political organization in Indochina, either vanished or extant, have remained on the scene; and they have become the strongest of all Indochinese nations.

If the disappearance of a state or the regression of a people is not entirely ascribed to accidents of history impervious to human investigation, the survival and present strength of the Vietnamese must be at·least partly due to a vitality of theirs that was lacking in the peoples whom they defeated, displaced, or absorbed. As to the sources of this vitality, not much can be said without resorting to speculation or to presumptuous doctrines about the factors that determine the history of man. The strength and durability of the Vietnamese people, in comparison with their vanished or weakened neighbors, could be largely the result of a fortunate racial mixture—the Mongolian addition to a predominantly Indonesian stock; but Chinese military protection against Cham and Thai attacks may well have been more decisive for the survival of the Vietnamese

36

people, and was doubtless important in getting it through its infancy and youth.[37]

The removal of the Chams, however, and the retreat imposed upon the Cambodians by the advancing Vietnamese, can also be looked upon as a clash between the civilizations of India and China, in which the Sinized Vietnamese stopped the advance and reduced the extent of Indian cultural penetration of the peninsula. Under this aspect, the advantages displayed by the later Vietnamese in the struggle for survival might be credited to the qualities of Chinese moral and political indoctrination and to the early adoption of Chinese technical skills, both resulting for Vietnam in a greater economic and social stability, the main condition for the strength and the increase in numbers of a people. A high population density must indeed have developed in the Red River valley at a very early time.

But the strength gained through the adoption of Chinese technics and Chinese moral concepts enabled the Vietnamese to do more than advance in Indochina at the expense of peoples and powers in the sphere of Indian culture penetration. Before they could set out on their own, the Vietnamese had to throw off the yoke of the Chinese and to possess the will and the energy to prevent its reimposition.

These facts lead to one of those curious contradictions in which the poorly explored history of Vietnam[38] seems to abound: the military subjection and the successful education of the early Vietnamese by the Chinese turned out to be the main reasons for China's failure to establish herself permanently on the Indochinese peninsula. Once China had lost her foothold with the advent of an independent Vietnam, her attempts at reconquest were all defeated by the skill and tenacity of Vietnamese resistance.

Thus the main features in the development of the Vietnamese people from their pre-Chinese past to the present time can be described as follows: A Mongolian racial contribution and

37

a willingness to absorb the higher culture of the Chinese gave to the inhabitants of the Red River valley an early advantage over their roving neighbors in the surrounding mountains and their piratical Indonesian cousins farther south. In spite of a permanent threat by the peoples who kept coming through the mountains in the north and northwest, the Vietnamese held on to the valleys and deltas that were their original homes.[39] They broke the power of the Indianized kingdoms to their south and carried Chinese civilization as far as the Gulf of Siam, never losing their own character as a non-Chinese people during this process, asserting their right to a separate national existence against the Chinese, the Mongols under Kublai Khan, and the later European invaders with equal determination, and remaining in all likelihood the strongest barrier against a Chinese advance into Southeast Asia to this very day.

9.

Historians probably will forever disagree about the causes of Vietnamese territorial expansion, and certainly will long argue about the methods employed in different periods of time. But there is little room for controversy over the reasons for the direction taken by the expanding Vietnamese, and none at all about the kind of country—in purely geographical respects—that this historical movement eventually produced.

The Vietnamese started to spill over the confines of the Red River valley and a few smaller deltas farther south soon after they had won their independence, in the middle of the tenth century. Their expansion was as much the result of peaceful penetration as of military conquest. It was a slow advance that lasted over eight hundred years, carried on primarily by a type of peasant soldiering for which this people seems to have developed an aptitude at a very early time. The peasant became a soldier whenever an enemy approached either for plunder or to drive the Vietnamese from a newly settled territory. The Vietnamese armies employed in the wars against the Chams and Cambodians were of importance only in consolidating gains achieved in this historic tide. Besides, they were composed also of peasants, landless as a rule, and ready to change their status from soldier to settler whenever a war had ended in the acquisition of cultivable land.[40]

However, expansion could proceed only in one direction. In the North, population pressure and Chinese military power, even in periods of Chinese dynastic degeneration, were much too strong, and the country was not nearly attractive enough ever to tempt the Vietnamese into seeking an outlet for their surplus population in southern China. Moving eastward, they would quickly arrive at the sea, from which their remotest settlements in the valleys had never been very distant. Looking west they saw only mountains. These they knew to be infested by insects and wild beasts, populated by primitive people, and unprovided with the fertile lands of the valleys and deltas that were the sole object of all Vietnamese peregrinations. Like any other people addicted to the firm habits of rice growers on the basis of irrigation, the Vietnamese had their backs turned to the mountains whenever they were in search of new land.

Land that would respond to the specific labor that the Vietnamese peasant was always willing to lavish upon it could be found only by moving down from the Red River valley along the coast, into the territories held by the still partly nomadic and predominantly seagoing Chams. Thus the Vietnamese began to march south, looking for new plains behind every new row of mountains,[41] pushing along the narrowing flatlands between the mountains and the sea, proceeding on water where the mountains went directly into the ocean, and settling in valley after valley, with every new delta as a new base, until they finally reached the open spaces of the Mekong River delta, deeper and wider than the Red River delta itself, their point of departure eight hundred miles to the north.

39

This was the famous "March to the South" of the Vietnamese people, through which their country grew to its present size and took on its present extraordinary shape. With the cession by Cambodia of the two regions of Sadec and Chaudoc, exactly two hundred years ago, the territorial growth of Vietnam came to an end.[42]

10.

The very unusual shape of Vietnam, one of its many geographical particularities, has always commanded immediate attention. The length of the country is 1000 miles, which is approximately the distance from Leningrad to Odessa, or from Milwaukee to Houston, Texas. In the North, between the coast near Haiphong and the remotest mountain crossings into the Chinese province of Yunnan, Vietnam reaches a depth of over 250 miles, but from the nineteenth parallel down to the sixteenth near the city of Tourane, the average width of the country is only 40 miles. At one point just south of Hué, if there were a modern highway from the coast to the Laotian border, a car could run across Vietnam in less than thirty minutes. The southern half of the country down to the Gulf of Siam is a little wider—from about 90 miles to a maximum of 120; but the mountains, absent only in the Mekong delta region of former Cochinchina, reduce the living space of the Vietnamese again to a slender coastal strip of plains and small deltas, even narrower, over a distance of 400 miles, than the plains in the provinces north of Tourane.

This configuration of the country is vividly illustrated in a renowned comparison. The two large deltas, in the North and the South, and their extended connection of narrow coastal lands are depicted as two baskets of rice attached to the two ends of the bamboo pole used by the Vietnamese peasant to carry his load.

The preservation of Vietnamese racial and cultural unity in this long and narrow country with its enormous difficulties of inner communication accentuates again the assets for survival with which this people is evidently endowed.[43] These assets must be biological as well as social, but while the former are likely to remain a secret, the role of the latter will become easily apparent in a history of Vietnam not limited to dynastic or military events. Geography, economy, and the accident of a specific historical environment—the Chinese empire with its pioneering civilization—have all contributed to the shaping of the Vietnamese people and to the survival of their unity over the centuries of their protracted coastal descent. In this mechanism of complex historical causation, the early development of a solid social organization is no doubt an element of the greatest importance. Its basis is economic, but its rapid emergence and continuing stability are unthinkable without the impact of Chinese technical civilization and Chinese civil and moral law.

The culture of rice entails a definite rhythm of economic activity. There is much to be done at a given time, which makes the demand for hands that may be idle later always higher than the supply; and the care for a large number of underemployed people is an economic necessity. The size and cohesion of the Vietnamese family, the basic working unity of the country, is rooted in this fact.

Rice in sufficient quantities to feed the Vietnamese people, however, would never grow in the Red River valley without a continuous effort to irrigate the fields, and the crops would invariably be destroyed either by inundation or drought without the necessary measures to regulate the flow of water, with which nature supplies Vietnam abundantly though in a most erratic way. No single Vietnamese family, whatever its size and the working ability of its members, was ever in a position to cope with these tasks. Economic survival required cooperation on a wider basis and of a higher order—that of the village, the province, and the state. The need for a complex system of dams, canals, and other hydraulic provisions thus led to the early formation of social organizations and administrative bodies fit to undertake these works; it is also the main reason for the stability of Vietnamese social institutions in the midst of events tending to destroy their substance together with their form.

The conditions for economic survival peculiar to Vietnam have always been reflected in the customs and religious ideas of the Vietnamese, as well as in their civic code and their philosophy of state. The general validity and compelling nature of these conditions is emphasized, moreover, by a willingness of the people to accept their consequences for individual life as moral law. Administrative hierarchy gained an early religious sanction, and the philosophical glorification of bureaucracy imported from China was locally endorsed long before the powers of heaven were mustered for the glory and might of the Vietnamese kings. But at the same time there was probably never a culture with stronger bonds among the members of one family, or with a higher degree of solidarity among the people belonging to the same village.

All of this made the Vietnamese a profoundly social, a strikingly nonindividualistic race. Not that Vietnamese society was ever lacking in opportunities for individual courage or outstanding work by the gifted and strong; nor was this people ever poorer than any other in men and women willing to use such opportunities and capable of excelling in personal bravery and through individual achievement. But to leave his family and native village in search of land all by himself was something else, something inconceivable for a Vietnamese of the year 1000 or 1500; this would have conflicted with his emotional needs of existence as much as with the conditions of economic success, or even of mere physical survival, of such a venture.

The historic "March to the South" of the Vietnamese people

was a series of displacements, voluntary and enforced, of large groups of individuals and families, sufficient in number to found communities similar to the ones they had left behind. The need for protection by the state, under whose auspices territorial expansion usually took place, left little room for prolonged political independence of any newly won territory; the gradual nature of the whole process, permitting full administrative integration of every new province into the Vietnamese state, was equally favorable for the preservation of a unity that was apparently threatened only by distance and by the absorption of racially different people whom the Vietnamese met on their way. This danger, however, was small for settlers who arrived always with their social, political, and cultural equipment intact—their higher technics, their unified language, their deeply rooted customs and beliefs, and especially their functionaries—altogether enough to explain why every new settlement in every new delta and valley became a link between North and South, over a distance of seven hundred miles of narrow coastal lands. The unity of Vietnam, as one imaginative observer graphically put it, is indeed like the "unity of a chain."[44]

11.

The Vietnamese, in addition to being among the world's most inveterate rice growers, have also been known since the earliest times of their recorded history for their skill in handling all kinds of vessels on river and sea. The English agents of the East India Company who visited Vietnam during the seventeenth and eighteenth centuries described the Vietnamese as the best sailors in the Far East.

A close union with the sea is indeed almost inevitable for a people whose preferred living spaces are the points of junction between river and ocean—the deltas created and continuously enlarged by the rivers at the expense of the sea.[45] In the case of Vietnam, the maritime character of the country is enhanced by the unusual length of its coast in relation to its total surface and by an extraordinary number of rivers connecting every populous region directly with the sea. The vast majority of the Vietnamese, moreover, live less than fifty miles from the ocean. This means not only that salt and fish, which play a vital role in the diet of the Vietnamese, are easy to come by; the proximity of the ocean to all important centers of population also compensates largely for the difficulties of long-distance communication by land. The sea, therefore, has been another promoter of Vietnamese unity. When at the end of the eighteenth century, after a long period of partition and civil war, political unity was re-established in a contest between North and South, the victory of the South was largely due to its maritime transportation facilities.

But the sea not only unites the various sections of Vietnam, it is also the major means of contact between Vietnam and the outside world. Over a distance of twelve hundred miles, the country exposes itself to the advantages as well as to the dangers coming from the sea. Vietnam was once called a "balcony to the Pacific," at a time when it was less perilous than of late to live under its sun; but the dangers inherent in the country's topography and geographic location are much older than her troubles of the last decades. The length of the coast, together with the fact that it is running close to the sea route connecting India with China and China with the main islands of Indonesia, is the reason why Vietnam has always been more vulnerable to attack from the sea than either Burma at the western or Thailand and Cambodia at the southern coast of Indochina. A number of excellent harbors and attractive bays seem to invite aggression, in spite of the generally forbidding nature of the coast. The Chinese tried to subdue the Chams through maritime expeditions against this coast as early as the fifth century A.D. Naval attacks by the Malayans and the Javanese were frequent during the eighth century,[46] and were again undertaken from the north in the thirteenth century, when China was in the hands of the Mongols. Even French intervention in the middle of the nineteenth century had much to do with the fact that the coast of Vietnam offered convenient stopping places for the French vessels supporting the British during the Chinese wars. The harbor of Tourane was attacked, and the town bombarded and taken, on September 1, 1858, by a French fleet returning from action in China. Five months later, the same fleet continued its voyage down the coast and started the conquest of Vietnam by France in earnest with the shelling and storming of Saigon, a city lying quite close to the ocean, on a river navigable for ships of any size. This, to be sure, was not the only time when the slight depth of the country, along with its extended coast and geographic position, underlined for Vietnam the danger of being overpowered by invaders from the sea.

There is, however, a positive side to these natural drawbacks, though one of doubtful advantage to the Vietnamese themselves. Being conveniently joined by ocean with the rest of Southeast Asia, and lying exactly where it does, Vietnam occupies an important strategic position at a crossroad of the Asian world. The ocean route between China and India was controlled by the fleets of Funan and Champa as long as the power of these kingdoms was unimpaired. Operating from the Bay of Cam Ranh in South Vietnam, a strong fleet even today could control the whole China Sea from Singapore to Formosa and from Manila to Haiphong. The invasion routes of the Chinese into the Red River valley are just as many avenues for counteraction against China from the south, and the open spaces of the lower Mekong valley are as passable for an army advancing through Cambodia toward Thailand and Burma as they are for invaders of South Vietnam coming from the north or west. The Japanese, in order to be ready for a campaign that was to carry them swiftly through the whole of Southeast Asia, moved into Vietnam fifteen months before the attack on Pearl Harbor revealed the actual scope of their military ambition.[47]

To extol Vietnam as a "balcony to the Pacific" is no doubt poetic and even fitting in a limited sense, but neither the French nor the Japanese came to Vietnam for a rest or to enjoy an ocean view; Vietnam is also an important transportation hub of Southeast Asia, and may very soon become either a dam against aggression from the north or a bridge serving the Communist block to transform the countries of the Indochinese peninsula into satellites of China.[48]

12.

Among the remaining conditions of human existence set by nature along the east coast of Indochina, the climate is by far the most important. It determines the seasonal shift from high economic activity to underoccupation, the rhythm of work and rest, the people's state of health and the nature of their diseases, the material and style of their houses and clothing, as well as the kind of food that is at their disposal and to their taste. But this is not all: the abundance of plant life and the poverty of the fauna, the occurence of certain rare animals and the complete absence of others,[49] the types of catastrophe that nature holds in store for the Vietnamese, and even the seasons of warfare in times of trouble, are all either entirely or largely the result of the country's climate.

The whole of Vietnam lies within the tropical zone.[50] The latitude of the point farthest to the north would be, if in the Western Hemisphere, halfways between Miami and Havana; the Point of Camau at the southern end of Vietnam lies almost as close to the equator as the tip of India—at less than nine degrees north latitude. The climate, therefore, is tropical, in the North as well as in the South, of the variety prevailing in all Asian countries subject to the monsoon—the seasonal winds of the Indian Ocean and Southeast Asia.

46

The alternation of these winds determines the length and character of the seasons. There are only two, and their distinguishing mark is neither the difference in temperature, which is slight,[51] nor a definite cycle in the vegetation of the country: at no time of the year is plant life in Vietnam suspended. The two seasons differ from each other mainly by being dry or wet, depending on the two directions of the monsoon. In the summer the wind blows from the southwest; the warm air is saturated with the vapors of the ocean, and a depressingly constant daily round of showers pours down on Vietnam from April to October. Between October and April the monsoon of the summer gives way to dry and cool winds from the Asian mainland. This is the dry season, during which little or no rain falls in Vietnam.

The basic regularity of this alternation between a dry and a rainy season, however, is modified to some extent by a number of geographical factors, such as the difference in latitude between North, Center, and South, and the effect of the relief on the movement of the air, and consequently on the periods and the amounts of local precipitation.[52] These amounts may differ considerably from one region to another, as is shown by the extremes of a low yearly average of less than three feet at the Cape of Padaron and a high of almost ten feet in the Atonat mountain region southwest of Hué.

Of much greater consequence than these local differences in rainfall are the changes likely to occur at the same place from one year to another. Saigon and Hanoi, for example, have an average rainfall of six feet, which means that three times the amount that is falling in Paris in twelve months comes down in these cities in the rainy months. But there were years when Saigon and Hanoi had less than four feet of rain and others when they had more than eight.

As the volume of the rivers is entirely governed by the alternation between a dry and a rainy period every year, this irregularity of precipitation has forever been one of the main causes of human distress in the valleys and deltas inhabited by the Vietnamese. It would be hard to say whether the people of the Red River valley have suffered more from the armies of invasion that have descended on them from the north or from the furious waters of the Red River in the many seasons of excessive rainfall, often followed by an equally murderous period of drought. In fact, not until they reached the delta of the giant and benign Mekong River[53] were some of the Vietnamese freed from the seasonal burden of work and fear inflicted on many by nature's peculiar threat to their lives in the northeast of Indochina: the high and low water levels of its rivers beyond the two points of danger, one spelling flood, the other drought, and both inevitably leading to famine.

This cruel alternation has always been most intense in the valley of the Red River,[54] the cradle of the Vietnamese people and to this very day the most populated region of Vietnam. The Red River, after receiving the waters of the Black and Clear Rivers about thirty miles above Hanoi, carries an average of 4,000 cubic meters (141,000 cubic feet) per second all through the delta over its hundred miles from Viet Tri to the coast.[55] This amounts to twice the volume of the Rhône, in a bed not nearly as wide. During a dry year the volume of the Red River may go below 700 cubic meters (24,600 cubic feet) per second. Its waters are then no longer able to reach the rice fields already scorching under a merciless sun and thirstier even than the feverish peasant himself when his malaria prevents him from leaving his sleeping mat before the sun comes over the horizon. Only one sight is sadder for him in these times of desperation than the melancholy spectacle of his perishing crop: the faces of his children, whose knowing eyes express the pain of hunger even before hunger strikes again.

But deliverance from this agony by the rains that must some day begin to fall gives to the Vietnamese peasant not more than a renewal of hope. He knows that the very means of his salvation is fraught with new dangers fatal not only to

48

his crop but even to himself. The waters, so often either insufficient or too unpunctual to work a yearly miracle of the two rich and safe crops, can also become too plentiful for the good of the struggling rice plants and too unruly for the safety of the toiling people, whose dread of inundation returns whenever an early wet season relieves them of the terror of drought.

The country of the upper Red River retains little of the waters carried by the monsoon from the Indian Ocean to the barren heights of North Vietnam. Excessive rainfall, therefore, is immediately followed by an inordinate rise in the water level of the Red River. But how high can this river rise without flooding the whole delta when the delta itself lies only several yards above the level of the sea?[56] The Red River has often increased its volume of a dry season ten, twenty, and forty fold—from 700 cubic meters per second to 30,000. In 1926 its water level reached the plus 12.30 mark at Hanoi, a city whose more unfortunate districts at such critical times lie six to eight meters below the level of the turbulent stream. Why, then, was it possible for the Vietnamese to settle the Red River valley and to continue to exist, if the waters of this river suffice to transform the whole delta periodically into one vast lake married to the sea?

Only a Promethean reaction against the cruel heavens and their annual threat to livelihood and life could safeguard the survival of this people and create the conditions of the growth of the civilization of Vietnam. The destructive powers of the river had to be channeled and put to beneficial use; the waters attempting to roll toward the ocean over the delta's entire width had to be forced down the valley in a line identical with the bed of the river, and some of its harmful surplus saved for the time when water would again become rare. This the Vietnamese accomplished through a system of dams, dykes, and canals, designed to control the rivers and to regulate the flow of water both when there was too little and when there was too much. The Red River now flows through the delta between two gigantic dykes, suspended, as it were, above a watchful and apprehensive population, flooding the fields, as a rule, only to the extent determined by human regulation, and spreading ruin and death only at nature's exceptional cataclysms or in consequence of human neglect.[57]

Some of the hydraulic works in the Red River valley must have been started long before the formation of an independent Vietnamese state, perhaps even before the arrival of the Chinese.[58] The dykes have now reached a length of sixteen hundred miles. Their size along the Red River is most impressive. Sixty feet wide at the base, they rise to a height of twenty feet wide at the top. Along the tops of these dykes some of the oldest roads connect village with village and province with province, as do the many smaller rivers and canals.

Such were the circumstances of life and the conditions of survival for the Vietnamese people. It seems fitting, therefore, at the beginning of a history of Vietnam, to visualize these people performing their most essential collective task. Swarming along both banks of the rising Red River, they carry baskets and buckets full of heavy soil; they are engaged in a breathless race with the mounting waters; they must beat the roaring river by strengthening and raising the old embankments, in order to save their crops, their villages, and perhaps their lives. The sturdier ones have already labored two days and two nights with little interruption; their strength may be exhausted, but their courage will last as long as the bonds of their families and the brotherhood of their villages remain intact. A heavier burden of work and sorrow than any man can carry alone awaits them if they fail. So they stick together at these crucial times in their lives, for better and for worse.

Thus did the dykes of the Red River grow. Built by the hands of the Vietnamese peasant, they rise above the flat lands of the delta in higher praise of man than the pyramids along the Nile—true ramparts of civilization, if anything ever deserved such a name.

50

Notes to Chapter One:

1. For other definitions, see John Kerry King, *Southeast Asia in Perspective*, New York, 1956, p. XIII: "Southeast Asia may be defined roughly as the area of continental Asia and the offshore Philippine and Indonesian archipelagoes which lies south of China and east of India." And Santha Rama Rau, *View of the Southeast*, New York, 1957, page 3: "Southeast Asia, which is probably more accurately described as Central-South Asia, is that stretch of the earth's surface that extends from the eastern borders of India across the Asian mainland to the Chinese frontier and the far coast of Indo-China. It includes the islands that are scattered in a graceful curve across the equator from Ceylon through Indonesia and north to the Philippines."

2. Burma has an area of 261,789 square miles, Thailand 200,148 square miles, Vietnam 127,300 square miles. (The New International Yearbook, 1956.)

3. The Malayan peninsula is separated from the Indonesian island of Sumatra by the Strait of Malacca, only 35 miles wide at the narrowest place. In prehistoric times the archipelago was connected with the mainland of Asia.

4. Cf. *Der Neue Brockhaus*, Leipzig, 1937, *Neuer Weltatlas*, Zurich, 1949, and Goldmann's *Grosser Weltatlas*, Munich, 1955. *Der Neue Brockhaus* uses Hinterindien synonymously with Indochina, whereas Goldmann's *Grosser Weltatlas* uses the term Indochina only for French Indochina, as does the new edition of *Der Grosse Brockhaus*, Vol. V, Wiesbaden, 1954.

5. Sir Hugh Clifford, *Further India*, London, 1904. Some British authors refer by this term to the eastern part of the peninsula only, e.g., J. G. Scott, *France and Tonkin: Narrative of the Campaign of 1884 and the Description of Further India*, London, 1885. For another use of Further India for the Indochinese peninsula, see the map in C. B. Norman's *Tonkin, or France in the Far East*, London, 1884. Greater India is also used—H. G. Quaritsch Wales, *The Making of Greater India*, London, 1951. One American source, *Webster's Geographical Dictionary* (1949), also uses Farther India for Indochina.

6. The culture of Cambodia, which is part of French Indochina, is "Indianized," in contrast to the Sinized culture of Vietnam. See Bijan Raj Chatterji *Indian Cultural Influence in Cambodia*, University of Calcutta, 1928. For a very recent use of the term Little China by an Eng-

lish author see Alan H. Brodrick, *Little China; The Annamese Lands,* Oxford University Press, London-New York, 1942.

7. The map inside the cover of Brian Harrison, *South-East Asia,* London, 1954, names Vietnam, Cambodia, and Laos together simply "Indo-China." Winburn T. Thomas and Rajah B. Manikam, *The Church in South East Asia,* New York, 1956, in a survey on p. XVII, use the word "Indochina" without a breakdown in its three parts, thus ignoring not only the fact that "Indochina," in the sense used, no longer exists, but never existed at all. Indochina, even while still French Indochina, consisted always of the three countries Vietnam, Cambodia, and Laos —except for the French, who after splitting Vietnam up into Cochinchina, Annam, and Tongking, spoke of five countries. Cf. Ch. Lemire, *Les cinq pays de l'Indochine française,* Paris, 1899.

8. "French Indochina is only a part of the geographical bloc called Indochina, a well-chosen name which seems to have been first used in France by Malte-Brun at the beginning of the last century."—Charles Robequain, *The Economic Development of French Indochina,* London, 1944, p. 9. See also *Der Neue Brockhaus* (1956) and *Webster's Geographical Dictionary* (1949), which both accept this definition. One of the few authors who have followed this advice is Alan Houghton Brodrick, who says that by Indochina ". . . here and in the body of this book, is meant geographical Indochina, that is Burma, Siam and French Indochina with, subsidiarily, Malaya." Cf. his *Beyond the Burma Road,* p. 10. In contrast to Robequain and as an explanation of the conflicting uses of the term Indochina, see Roger Levy, who in *Regards sur l'Asie,* p. 95, note 1, says: "Vietnam, Cambodia, Laos are for us, the French, Indochina. The peninsula also contains Burma, Thailand, and Malaya. But let us, according to our tradition, continue to write 'Indochina,' without adding the epithet 'French' in the Anglo-Saxon manner." An example of the existing confusion concerning the term Indochina is contained in the *Thorndike-Century Senior Dictionary* (1941). A map of Indochina shows the whole peninsula but gives two definitions. One is more or less correct: "Southeastern peninsula of Asia, comprising French Indochina, part of Burma, Siam and the Malay peninsula." The second definition, however, reads: "Country in SE Asia under French control. . . . Also called French Indochina."

9. The word Vietnam (also Viet-Nam and Viet Nam) can be found only on maps and in dictionaries that appeared after 1946.

10. Most authors say the word Cochinchina is of Portuguese origin, meaning Cochin in China, as distinguished from the Portuguese colony of Cochin in India. For details and sources of this explanation see Ch.

IV, note 10. On the other hand, Jean Chesneaux, *Contribution à l'histoire de la nation vietnamienne,* Paris, 1955, p. 11, note 1, says that the origin of the word Cochinchina is obscure. The early French colonists applied the designation to the central part of the country (Annam) while what later became Cochinchina was then named Lower Cochinchina (Basse-Cochinchine). Between 1870 and 1880, without any apparent reason, the designation was changed. After that the southern part of the colony was called Cochinchina and the center Annam. This is a Chinese word, meaning Peaceful South or Pacified South. (See Ch. II, note 66.) The north always was called Tonkin by the Europeans, (in English spelling usually Tongking). This was the ancient Chinese name for the city of Hanoi, meaning literally Capital of the East. The name was later applied to the part of Vietnam which the Vietnamese called the North. "The name Tongking does not even exist in the Annamese language," says J. L. de Lanessan in *La colonisation française en Indo-Chine,* Paris, 1895.

11. It is rather astonishing that a modern author like Brian Harrison, whose history *South-East Asia* appeared as late as 1954, still uses the term Annam instead of Vietnam, with very few cross references to Vietnam. (*Op. cit.,* pp. 220, 250, 255; see also map inside cover.) Cf. note 7 of this Chapter.

12. By the Vietnamese, the North (Tongking) is called Bac Bo, the Center (Annam) Trung Bo, and the South (Cochinchina) Nam Bo.

13. The reader should be aware of the fact that the population figures of most oriental countries will not be the same in the different dictionaries or reference books he may consult. The latest and most reliable figures seem to be those of the Statesman's Year Book, 1957. They are for Burma an estimated population of 19,242,000 for the year 1954. The United Nations estimated population for Burma, as given in the New International Yearbook, 1956, was 19,434,000 for the year 1955. For Thailand, the Statesman's Year Book, 1957, gives 20,227,000 for the year 1955 against a figure of 22 million in the New International Yearbook, 1956, the latter probably also an estimate referring to 1955. Concerning Vietnam, the uncertainties are more pronounced. The Statesman's Year Book, 1957, has an estimated population of 12 million for the Southern half for the year 1956 and of 12,963,900 for the Northern half for the year 1943. The New International Yearbook, 1956, gives the south "about 12 million" and the north "over 12 million." The Statistical Year Book, 1955, issued by the United Nations, mentions for the whole of Vietnam an estimated population of 18,972,000 for 1937, and of 26 million for 1954. For the years between 1937 and 1954 one could quote

53

any figure between 18 and 26 million from the various authors of whom very few give the same figure for a given year. See note 14 below.

14. There are no official data available for the last years, and the experts differ in their estimates. Le Thanh Khoi, *Le Viet-Nam*, Paris, 1955, p. 35, gives the figure of 22,635,000 for 1943; Brian Harrison, *op. cit.*, p. 220, 23,000,000 for 1940. The official census in French Indochina was based on estimates by French officials, using figures furnished by the more than 17,000 villages of the country. The villages reported the number of men between eighteen and sixty who were liable for a personal tax, and for the purpose of the census this number was multiplied by a certain coefficient. The villages had the tendency to report a lower number of people obliged to pay taxes. Le Thanh Khoi, *op. cit.*, p. 34, believes that the official census yielded figures ten to fifteen per cent below the actual population. The same opinion is to be found in G. Kherian, "Le problème démographique en Indochine," in *Revue Indochinoise Juridique et Economique*, 1937, I., 6-8. According to this author, the total population of Vietnam would be between 24,000,000 and 25,000,000.

15. The non-Vietnamese population of Indochina consists of different aboriginal tribes of various degrees of civilization and of "foreigners." Among the foreigners the Chinese are the strongest (712,000) and oldest group, the first Chinese immigration dating back to the time of the Manchu conquest (1644). The Chinese are mostly artisans, traders, and moneylenders. Their number has increased rapidly during the last decade. There were only 217,000 Chinese in Vietnam in 1936 and about 300,000 in 1940. More than 400,000 immigrated to Vietnam from China during the Sino-Japanese War and the civil war. A New York *Times* report of May 14, 1957, from Saigon by Greg MacGregor says "that the total of Chinese in Vietnam . . . is about 600,000. Many other qualified observers, however, believe the correct figure is nearly double this estimate." (Cf. Le Thanh Khoi, *op. cit.*, p. 54ff.). Thirty-five thousand French were counted at or near the peak (1937) but their number has greatly decreased. Of the French inhabitants, 52.6 per cent belonged to the armed forces, 18.9 per cent were civil servants, and only 28.5 per cent were active in trade, industry, and the professions. (*Annuaire statistique de l'Union française outre-mer*, B–91, and *Annuaire statistique de l'Indochine*, 1937–1938.) Besides the French, the official statistics mentioned more than 7,000 other Europeans and assimilated Asians (européens et assimilés). Among them are also counted 257 Americans (in 1952, according to H. Lanoue, "Activités économiques américaines en Indochine," *Cahiers Internationaux*, No. 36, May, 1952, p. 86.). The

number of Britains was 140 in 1952. Finally, about 4,000 Indians are to be listed among the inhabitants of Indochina. For the non-Vietnamese aboriginal tribes cf. note 18 of this Chapter.

16. It compares with a density of population of 76 persons per square mile in Burma, 100 in Thailand, 137 in China, 144 in Indonesia, 314 in India, 592 in Japan, 724 in Belgium, and 900 on the island of Java. These figures are based on material in the 1953 edition of *Encyclopedia Britannica* and the 1955 edition of the *New International Year Book*.

17. Tongking has a density of 207 inhabitants per square mile. In the mountainous regions of the North only 32 people live on a square mile, while in the delta the density is 1,295, equal to that of the most populated region of Java, Bengal, Japan, and China. The density reaches 2,150 in the lower delta. P. Gourou, *L'utilisation du sol en Indochine française,* Paris, 1940, p. 99, and *Les paysans du delta tonkinois,* Paris, 1936. p. 154, by the same author.) In Annam the density in the mountainous region is 26 persons per square mile, compared with 974 in the fertile costal stripe. Cochinchina has an average density of 241 inhabitants per square mile (Le Thanh Khoi, *op. cit.,* p. 34ff.).

18. Cf. the map on p. 36 of Chesneaux, *op. cit.,* showing the distribution of the national minorities, Méo, Man, Nung, Tho, Thai, Moi, Muong, and Cham. The classification of the non-Vietnamese population of Indo-China leads to different results, depending on whether one approaches the problem from the ethnographical or the linguistic angle. The following survey is from Robequain, *L'Indochine,* Paris, 1952, pp. 33ff.:

A. The *Muong.* They number about 200,000 and inhabit the hills around the Red River delta in Tongking and northern Annam. See note 22 of this Chapter.

B. The *Thai.* This is a linguistic classification, comprising many tribes speaking Thai or Thai dialects. These tribes are, however, very different in their bodily features and in civilization. About 1,500,000 Thai-speaking people live in former French Indochina (mostly in Tongking and Laos). They are not aborigines but migrated to Indochina from southern and central China.

C. The *Man* and *Méo.* They are the rear guard of an immigration from southern China. The Man and Méo live in the hills and high plateaus around the Red River valley in Tongking. They are divided in numerous subtribes, some of them comprising less than one hundred families. The immigration of the Man into Indochina did not begin before the sixteenth century and was absolutely peaceful. They often signed contracts with the inhabitants of the regions where they settled. The Man are 100,000 strong, of whom 50,000 live in Tongking and the other half in Upper

Laos and northern Annam. The Méo are an aboriginal tribe of southeast China. From there they penetrated into Tongking and northern Annam not before the nineteenth century. Unlike that of the Man, their invasion was far from pacific. There are less than 100,000 Méo in Indochina.

D. The *Moi*. A primitive people, ethnically related to the Indonesians. They do not have a written language and are very superstitious and shy when meeting foreigners. Their language resembles that of the Cham and Khmer. They number more than 1,000,000.

E. The *Khmer* and *Cham*. Remnants of the two highly civilized nations of southern Indochina. The Cham were conquered and almost exterminated by the Vietnamese. The Khmer form the population of the kingdom of Cambodia and are now usually referred to as Cambodians. Some Khmer inhabit parts of Cochinchina. About the latent hostility between Vietnamese and Khmer and about the Cham people, see note 35. About national minorities in general, see also Le Thanh Khoi, *op. cit.*, pp. 43-54.

19. "This 'drive to the South' is a recurrent theme in South-east Asian history. The succession of broad human groups which moved down into the region in prehistoric times seems to have been: Australoid, Negrito, Melanesian and Indonesian (Austronesian)."—Harrison, *op. cit.*, p. 4. The theory that all the races now inhabiting Southeast Asia came from southern China and Tibet originated with two Austrian anthropologists, Father F. W. Schmidt and R. von Heine-Geldern. Cf. also D. G. E. Hall, *A History of South-East Asia*, New York, 1955, pp. 3ff. The Negroid (Australoid) migration belongs to the mesolithic period, a transitional stage between the Old and New Stone cultures. The Indonesians, arriving between 2500 and 1500 B.C., represent the so-called age of "polished stone" (neolithic or New Stone Age). The appearance of the Mongolians introduced the Bronze Age (about 300 B.C.), followed by an iron culture. This whole period is named Dong Son culture in Vietnam, after a village in Center Vietnam, where evidence of the bronze industry was first discovered. Associated with this metal culture was a new megalithic culture which lasted until the first centuries of the Christian era. A good brief account is found in Harrison, *op. cit.*, pp. 6ff.

20. Some authors think the Nungs are not really a Thai tribe. The Diem government of South Vietnam was accused by its critics of having employed only Nung troops of the Vietnamese army to fight the sect rebellions in March and April, 1955.

21. For the languages spoken in Indochina and the whole of Southeast Asia see Robequain, *L'Indochine*, third ed., Paris, 1952, pp. 33 ff., and Harrison, *op. cit.*, p. X f. "Linguistically," Harrison says, "South-east Asia

. . . does not form a natural unit. Three of the great linguistic groups or families of Asia are represented in the region: Malayo-Polynesian, Austro-Asiatic, and Tibeto-Chinese. Languages of the Malayo-Polynesian family —one of the most widespread linguistic families in the world—are spoken in the Malay Peninsula and throughout island South-east Asia including the Philippines. Languages with a common Austro-Asiatic basis are spoken in parts of Burma, Siam, Indo-China (Cambodia and Annam), and Malaya (among the Senoi). Burmese and Siamese are included in the Tibeto-Chinese family."

22. Here again the figures given by different authorities conflict. According to Le Thanh Khoi there are 260,000 Muongs in Vietnam (*op. cit.*, p. 48), according to Robequain (*op. cit.*, p. 43) only 200,000.

23. Both the Vietnamese language and the Muong dialects are based on a Mon-Khmer (Cambodian) vocabulary. The words for the numbers, family relationships, and domestic animals are of Mon-Khmer origin. Cambodian is a monotonic language of the Austro-Asiatic group. On this monotonic base the variotonic Thai languages have exerted their influence, again both on Vietnamese and the Muong dialects. Finally, the Thai elements became predominant. Chinese domination of Vietnam has enriched the vocabulary with Chinese administrative, military, literary, and philosophical terms. (Cf. Le Thanh Khoi, *op. cit.*, p. 90f.; Meillet and Cohen, *Les langues du monde,* second ed., Paris, 1953, articles by H. Maspéro and J. Przyluski.) According to Hall, *op. cit.*, p. 169, Vietnamese is predominantly a Thai language but contains so many Mon-Khmer elements that some theorists have attempted to place it in the Mon-Khmer group.

24. L. Aurousseau, "Notes sur les origines du peuple annamite," *Bulletin de l'Ecole Française d'Extrême Orient,* vol. XXIII, p. 263f.; J. Cuisinier, *Les Muong, Géographie humaine et sociologie,* Paris, 1948; Le Thanh Koi, *op cit.*, pp. 49, 81.

25. Le Thanh Khoi, *op. cit.*, pp. 88ff., is more careful, stating only that the ancestors of the Vietnamese were related to the Melano-Indonesians and the Thai. He does not commit himself to a clear racial distinction of Thai, Viets, and Chinese, but leaves the question open as to what group of Mongolian people mixed with the original Austro-Melano-Indonesian population of the Red River valley. Hall, *op. cit.*, p. 169, is of the opinion that the Vietnamese have been "the result of intermarriage between the local tribes already settled in Tongking and a mongoloid people, who may represent the third prehistoric migration to reach Indo-China—in their case via the Yangtse valley and what are now the Chinese provinces of Chekiang, Fukien, Kwangtong and Kwangsi." This would not seem to be

the Thai, but rather a branch of the Viets, or Yue, as the Chinese call them. The earliest archeological evidence too shows the Vietnamese culture as a Mongolian-Indonesian mixture already influenced by China.

26. This contradicts the theory of Ed. Chavannes, who was the first to suggest (in his monumental work, *Mémoires historiques de Se-ma T'sien*, six vols., Paris, 1895–1905) that the Vietnamese were descendants of the pre-Chinese kingdom of Yue in the lower Yangtse valley. This opinion was supported by L. Aurousseau, *op. cit.* The Chavannes-Aurousseau theory, based more on speculation than on evidence, has now been abandoned. Cf., Le Thanh Khoi, *op. cit.*, pp. 85ff. Hall, *op. cit.*, p. 169, leaves the question of the geographical origin of the Vietnamese undecided and points only to prehistoric Chinese influence upon their culture. Cf., also Masson, *Histoire de l'Indochine*, Paris, 1950. The origin of the Vietnamese people is discussed further in chapter II, section 3.

27. This figure is given by Robequain, *op. cit.*, p. 40. Le Thanh Khoi, *op. cit.*, p. 52, places their number at 35,000. (These figures refer only to the Chams living within the boundaries of Vietnam; some Chams are settled in Cambodia.) About 6,000 of the Chams in Vietnam are Mohammedans; the rest practise a degenerate Brahmanism. Cf. also J. Leuba, *Un royaume disparu: Les Chams et leur art*, Paris, 1923; G. Maspéro, *Le royaume de Champa*, Paris, 1928; M. Ner, *Les Musulmans de l'Indochine française*, Paris, 1941.

28. The name Champa was not in use before the beginning of the seventh century A.D. The Chinese referred to the kingdom first as Lin-yi and changed that designation to Huan-wang in the middle of the eighth century and to Chang-cheng in the ninth century. (Hall, *op.cit.*, pp. 27, 159f.)

29. The kingdom of Champa is first mentioned in Chinese annals (under the name of Lin-yi) between 220 and 230 A.D. A Chinese official, K'iu Lien, took advantage of the weakness of the Han dynasty to carve out a kingdom for himself in the south of China in 192 A.D. One of his descendants sent a mission to the governor of Kwangtong and Tongking between 220 and 230. It is in the record of this mission that the name of Lin-yi appears first, together with Funan, a state allied with Champa. Both Lin-yi and Funan waged protracted border wars with the Chinese empire in the third century. Hall, *op. cit.*, pp. 24ff. Cf. also G. Coedès, *Les états hindouisés d'Indochine et d'Indonésie*, Paris, 1948.

30. According to Chinese sources Funan was founded by a Brahman, Kaundinya (in Chinese transcription Hun-t'ien) in the first century A.D. In the principal port of its territory, Oc Eo (now in eastern Cochinchina), a gold medal of the Roman emperor Antoninus Pius, dated 152 A.D. was

found. Funan was intersected with channels and was an important station on the great maritime highway between China, India, and the Roman empire. Its people were Indonesians, strongly under Hindu influence in culture and religion. They spoke a pre-Khmer Austro-Asiatic language, though at the end of the Funan period they seem to have exchanged it for Old Khmer. Hall, *op. cit.*, pp. 14, 23ff. For the history of Funan see Coedès, *op. cit.*

31. Hall, *op. cit.*, p. 26.

32. Most important are the collection of Cham art in the museum of Tourane and the ruins of a Cham city in the province of Quang Nam. Cf., H. Parmentier: *Les sculptures chames au musée de Tourane* Paris, 1922; Jeanne Leuba: *Un royaume disparu: Les Chams et leur art*, Paris, 1923.

33. Some Vietnamese might object to this statement, as it seems to imply that no independent Vietnamese state existed before the beginning of recorded Vietnamese history, which starts with China's conquest of the Red River valley. This question is discussed thoroughly in Chapter II.

34. Evidence of these achievements are the world-famous ruins of Angkor. The first city of Angkor was built by Yasovarman I (889–900) and named, after him, Yasodharapura. It covered a considerably larger area than the later and more famous Angkor Thom, constructed, together with the Bayon, under Jayavarman VII, between 1180 and 1200. The Bayon was a pyramidal temple crowned by a tower of gold, bearing four gigantic human faces. Its decorations were among the finest in Khmer architecture, its architectural motif one of the most striking in the world, but it is now in a worse state of ruin than almost any of the other great Angkor temples. (Hall, *op. cit.*, pp. 96, 108.) Angkor Wat, built about fifty years earlier (between 1130 and 1150) by Suryavarman II, is the largest religious building in the world. Of all the Khmer monuments it is the best preserved. For a plan of the Angkor group see *ibid.*, p. 109. Cf. also E. Aymonier, *Le Cambodge,* Vol. III (*Le groupe d'Angkor et l'histoire*), Paris, 1904; J. Y. Claeys and M. Huet, *Angkor,* Paris, 1948; G. Coedès, *Pour mieux comprendre Angkor,* Paris, 1924; E. Lunet du Lajonquière, *Inventaire descriptif des monuments du Cambodge,* four vols., Paris, 1902-1911. There seems to be no end to the long list of books on Angkor that have appeared ever since the ruins were discovered by European travelers. Here is a partial list: P. Jeanerat de Beerski, *Angkor/Ruins in Cambodia,* London, 1923; Helen Churchill Candee, *Angkor/The Magnificent,* New York, 1924; George Groslier, *La sculpture Khmère ancienne,* Paris, 1925; Philippe Stern, *Le Bayon d'Angkor et l'évolution de l'art khmèr,* Paris, 1927; Princess Murat, *The Ruins of*

Angkor, Shanghai, 1927; George Groslier, *Les collections Khmères du Musée Albert Saurraut à Phnom-Penh*, Paris, 1931; Editions "TEL": *Angkor*, Paris, 1931; Geoffrey Gorer, *Bali and Angkor*, London, 1936; Henri Parmentier, *L'art Khmèr classique*, two vols., Paris, 1939; Gilberte de Coral Remusat, *L'Art Khmèr/Les grandes étapes de son évolution*, Paris, 1951; Henri Marchal, *Les temples d'Angkor*, Paris, 1955; Bernard-Philippe Groslier, *Angkor/Hommes et Pierres*, Paris, 1956; Henri Marchal and Oscar Miestchaninoff, *Sculptures khmères*, Preface by Henri Gourdon, Paris.

35. Robequain, *op. cit.*, pp. 33ff.; Masson *op. cit.* Cf. also note 18 of this Chapter. Robequain, *op. cit.*, pp. 39ff., claims that the French have saved the Khmers from extinction. The old Cambodian-Vietnamese controversy was recently revived by a letter written by Sim-Var, prime minister of Cambodia, to the editor of *Le Monde*, published March 1, 1956. According to this letter, King Ang Duong of Cambodia asked Napoleon III for help against the Vietnamese in 1853. During the campaigns of the French in Cochinchina between 1858 and 1867, the French army drove the Vietnamese out of Cambodia. Later France drew the present frontier between her protectorate of Cambodia and her colony of Cochinchina. Cambodia protested to no avail. Since then Cambodia has always claimed Cochinchina as part of her territory. She protested also against the reunion of Cochinchina with the rest of Vietnam in 1949 and, at the conference of Geneva in 1954, again reiterated her right to Cochinchina, with as much effect as a Mexican demand for the return of Texas might have.

36. According to Le Thanh Khoi, *op. cit.*, p. 53. However, Sim-Var in his letter to *Le Monde* quoted above, says that the part of Cochinchina claimed by Cambodia is inhabited mostly by Phuong and Stieng, mountain people of the Khmer race, or, as he puts it, "faithful subjects of the Kingdom of Cambodia."

37. The present Chinese province of Yunnan was inhabited by Lolo and Thai peoples, first split into six principalities but, after the middle of the seventh century, united in the kingdom of Nam Chieu or Nan Chao. This kingdom invaded Vietnam in 846. Shortly afterward the king of Nam Chieu adopted the title of emperor and changed the name of his country to Dai Le or Ta Li. He invaded the Red River delta again in 860 but retreated before Chinese reinforcements. A third invasion in 862 led to the complete occupation, in the following year, of the territories that later became Vietnam. The Chinese now started a counteroffensive under General Lao Pien and reconquered the Red River valley in a ten-year war. The kingdom of Nam Chieu, reduced to its original size, kept its

independence until the middle of the thirteenth century, when it was destroyed by the Mongols. The victorious General Lao Pien was appointed high commissioner of Chiao Chi (Vietnam) and restored the prosperity of the country by building roads and making the rivers navigable. Cf. Le Thanh Khoi, *op. cit.*, pp. 125-127; C. A. J. Sainson, *Histoire particulière du Nan Tchao*, Paris, 1904, pp. 42-46.

38. Huard and Durand, *Connaissance du Viet-Nam*, Paris and Hanoi, 1954, p. 7, say the sources of Vietnamese history are numerous, but unexploited. French scholars have done extensive research on Indochina but concentrated on prehistory, archeology, and art. They were dependent, morally and financially, on the French administration. In accordance with French colonial policy they consistently ignored the reality of Vietnamese nationalism. Therefore, the French historians never produced a study of the peasant revolts in ancient Vietnamese history, or of the progress of the merchant class before the conquest, the economic and social repercussions of the colonization, the evolution of the peasantry, the decadence of the artisans, the difficulties of the middle class, the birth of the proletariat, or the development of nationalism under the colonial administration. In short, they ignored the development of the forces that they had to fight after 1945. The historians of the young Republic of Vietnam will have to fill this gap. See J. Chesneaux, *op. cit.*, pp. 7-9. Cf. also his bibliography on pp. 313-316, and Le Thanh Khoi, *op. cit.*, pp. 65-68.

39. Vietnamese myths and legends abound in factual and symbolical references to the conflict between the peoples of the mountains and those of the plains, a conflict that must have been strong in prehistoric and early historical times.

40. There was, however, an element of feudal aggression nourished by greed—a desire of the landlords to increase their holdings—that modified the picture. See Chapters II and III.

41. The Annamite mountain chain, down the length of the country, has branches running across in an almost west-east direction all over central Vietnam, reaching to the ocean at several places. The erosion working in these mountains on material of different thickness and resistance has created a rugged, picturesque scenery full of charm, which resembles, in its union of mountains and ocean, the landscape of Scandinavia. Robequain, *op. cit.*, pp. 23, 28.

42. Only the region of Soctrang, on the very tip of the country beyond the Mekong River, had not been occupied by the Vietnamese before 1840. Vietnamese penetration into Laos and Cambodia continued and led even to a temporary annexation of Cambodia by Vietnam from 1834 to 1841, but this was already a phase of the power struggle between Viet-

nam and Siam. Cf. Masson, *op. cit.,* p. 42; Chesneaux, *op. cit.,* pp. 52ff.; Le Thanh Khoi, *op. cit.,* pp. 333-338; Hall, *op. cit.,* pp. 400ff.; Adhémère Leclerc, *Histoire du Cambodge,* Paris, 1914, p. 422.

43. Most French writers on Indochina have tried to minimize this obvious racial and cultural unity of the Vietnamese people, responding consciously or unconsciously to the French political aim of holding off Vietnamese national aspirations. See P. Gourou, *The Future of Indochina,* Paris, 1947; Huard and Durand, *Connaissance du Viet-Nam,* Hanoi, 1954; A. Masson, *Histoire de l'Indochine,* Paris, 1950; C. Robequain, *The Economic Development of French Indo-China,* London, 1944; C. Robequain, *L'Indochine française,* Paris, 1948. In particular L. Finot, in his writings for the Colonial Exposition in 1931, claims that the different regimes established by the French in Tongking, Annam, and Cochinchina "conform to the realities of Vietnamese history, which also shows three countries of different formation." One of the few French writers to emphasize the racial and cultural unity of the three parts of Vietnam is Ch. Gosselin (*L'empire d'Annam,* Paris, 1904, pp. 7f.). He says he found in Indochina the most uniform population, from the high mountains of Tongking to the frontiers of Cambodia. This, he stresses, refers to the ethnic point of view as well as to the political and social. Climatic influences might have changed some physical traits. The inhabitants of Tongking are, generally speaking, taller than those of Cochinchina. But this is only a nuance frequently found in Europe or other parts of the earth among people of the same race. "We found ourselves confronted with the most unified people imaginable," wrote Captain Gosselin.

44. Paul Mus, *Vietnam: Sociologie d'une guerre,* Pairs, 1952.

45. The delta of the Red River in Tongking covers an area of about 5,800 square miles. In prehistoric times there was a deep gulf which has been filled and is still being filled by the deposits of the river at a rate of up to 100 yards a year. New villages are springing up on this newly created land, especially in the Tongkingese provinces of Nam Dinh and Nin Binh. The mass of reddish silt it carries gives the river its name. The delta of the Mekong River in Cochinchina extends over 8,500 square miles. Its deposits surpass those of the Red River. In the course of millennia they have transformed a former bay into a peninsula that juts out into the calm waters of the Gulf of Siam. The growth of that peninsula is more marked toward the west than to the east. Le Thanh Khoi, *op. cit.,* pp. 19-22; A. Agard, *L'union indochinoise française ou l'Indochine oriental,* Hanoi, 1935, p. 46; Robequain, *op. cit.,* pp. 29-31; Chesneaux, *op. cit.,* pp. 14f.

46. Cambodia was conquered by King Sanjaya of Java in the middle

of the eighth century and liberated by King Jayavarman II, the founder of the Angkor dynasty, shortly after 800. The Javanese also invaded Tongking in 767 and raided Annam in 774 and 787. Cf. Harrison, *op. cit.*, pp. 27–29; Hall, *op. cit.*, p. 91; Lawrence P. Briggs, *The Ancient Khmer Empire*, Philadelphia, 1951, pp. 60–69.

47. "By its geographic position alone the colony was the key to Japan's southern expansion. In 1942 it was Japan's military entrepôt—the center of the starfish-shaped pattern of successful Japanese drives into the Philippines, Malaya, Netherland India, Burma and South China." C. Robequain, *The Economic Development of French Indochina*, London, 1944, p. 351.

48. It is interesting to note that a French Communist historian of Vietnam, Jean Chesneaux (*op. cit.*), minimizes the strategic importance of the country by stressing that it is not situated on one of the important crossroads of the earth. He even accepts the characterization of Vietnam as a "balcony toward the Pacific" (coined in 1931 by Albert Sarraut, Governor-General of Indochina, Minister of Colonies and Prime Minister of France) as more realistic than the recent view of Vietnam as an important strategic base and a bolt for closing access to Southeast Asia. The view of the present leadership of South Vietnam on the subject was expressed by President Ngo Dinh Diem on a television program in Sidney, Australia, on Sept. 6, 1957: "In its geographic position, Vietnam occupies a key position on the classic route of invasion to Southeast Asia."

49. Vietnam's domestic animals are the elephant, the horse, the water buffalo, the goat, the pig, different kinds of fowl, and the silkworm. The use of the water buffalo is limited by its abilities. Elephants and horses are rare and expensive. Buffalo meat, pork, and chicken are only occasional additions to the daily diet, which consists mainly of rice and fish. (Chesneaux, *op. cit.*, p. 18; cf. also Huard and Durand, *op. cit.*)

50. It reaches from 8°30' to 23°24' north latitude.

51. There is, of course, a great difference of temperature between the plains and the mountains. In the mountains of Tongking the thermometer drops to 31°F. in December and January. As winter coincides with the dry season, snowfall is rare. The 3.5 inches recorded on December 5, 1922, are an exception. In the South the difference between winter and summer temperatures is very small. In Saigon, e.g., the winter average is 79°F., compared with a summer average of 86°F. In the North the difference between winter and summer is more marked. Hanoi has an average of 85°F. in June and of 62°F. in February. (Le Thanh Khoi, *op. cit.*, pp. 24f.; Robequain, *op. cit.*, p. 16.)

52. The rainy season in the center around Hué (Annam), e.g., begins, as a rule, only late in fall.

53. The Mekong arises from the highland of Tibet at an altitude of 15,000 feet. Its length is about 3,300 miles, but it descends slowly through the Chinese province of Yunnan, then forms the frontier between Laos and Thailand, crosses Cambodia, and enters Cochinchina split into two major branches, the Tien Giang and the Han Giang. The Han Giang itself is ramified into numerous smaller branches. The immensity of the Mekong basin, its moderate slope, and the influence of the large lake of Tonlé Sap and the "bengs," depressions along its course in Cochinchina, make it a benevolent river. It rises but slowly in the rainy season and reaches its summit in October and November. The inhabitants of the Mekong's banks are not in for surprises and can plan their work without fear of inundation. They do not have to build dykes. All along the banks of the Mekong there are fertile rice fields. The conditions on the lower course of the Mekong permit the irrigation of these rice fields and favor an extensive traffic of junks and sampans. Cf. Robequain, *op. cit.*, pp. 29–31; Le Thanh Khoi, *op. cit.*, pp. 19–22. Etienne Aymonier, an official in the administration of Cambodia and later director of the Ecole Coloniale in Paris, wrote an important book on Cambodia, a country that he explored as a geographer and archeologist—*Le Cambodge,* Paris, 1900. He compares the role the Mekong River plays for Cambodia with that of the Nile for Egypt, ancient and modern. Both rivers have created their countries, and both keep them fertile by inundations. The Mekong overflows Cambodia left and right. Only the trees are visible along its banks. Communication between the villages, even between houses, is kept up by barges. Numerous natural ditches allow the water to penetrate into the interior of the country. In the first days of October the inundation stops, and in January the river is back to its normal shape. But in the natural ditches, if they are deep enough, the water remains the whole year. The more shallow ditches dry out, however. They serve as ways of communication, being used by carriages in the dry season and by barges during the inundation.

54. The English name, Red River, and the French name, Fleuve Rouge, are derived from the mass of red silt it carries. Cf. note 45. In Vietnamese it is popularly called Song Cai, Great River. Other names, more literary, are Nhi Ha and Hong Ha. Its source is in the Chinese province of Yunnan. Its length is about 800 miles. Its principal tributaries are the Black River (Rivière Noire, Song Da) and the Clear River (Rivière Claire, Song Ngan). According to Vietnamese folklore the red color of the river is caused by the blood of its guardian dragon. (Le Thanh Khoi, *op. cit.*, p. 19; Robequain, *op. cit.*, pp. 24ff.; Chesneaux, *op. cit.*, pp. 12f.)

55. The volume of the Red River varies between 20,000 cubic feet a

64

second in the dry season and 850,000 cubic feet a second in the rainy season. Cf. Le Thanh Khoi, *op. cit.*, pp. 19f., and Robequain, *op. cit.*, p. 29. The two authors agree about the figure in the dry season (700 cubic meters, equal to 20,669 cubic feet) but differ slightly about the volume in the rainy season, Le Thanh Khoi giving 28,000 cubic meters (826,762 cubic feet), Robequain 30,000 cubic meters (885,816 cubic feet). In the Red River delta man has had to fight inundations since prehistoric times. Vietnamese annals mention a dam for the first time in 1108. It was erected at Co Xa to protect Thang Long, the capital of the Ly monarchs. There is no doubt, however, that dykes were built long before along the Red River. Today there are about 600 miles of dams along its course.

56. In the rainy season the Red River frequently reaches cote +10.30, whereas some parts of Hanoi are situated as low as cote +4. Vast inundations therefore often occur in spite of the dykes constructed in these regions. (Le Thanh Khoi, *op. cit.*, p. 20.)

57. The Vietnamese have been great builders of dams and canals since time immemorial. Pierre Pasquier (*L'Annam d'autrefois: Essai sur la constitution de l'Annam avant l'intervention française*, Paris, 1930, pp. 289-316) compares them in this respect with the Dutch in Europe. According to this author, the public works of Vietnam are as valid witnesses of an ancient civilization as are the still existing highways of the Roman Empire. The Vietnamese peasant was forced to devote 60 to 120 days a year to labor on public works, which, in the last analysis, were to his own advantage, protecting the fields he worked and lived on. In the Red River delta 1,500 miles of so-called "great" dykes have been erected. For 1,500 miles of such dykes 4.5 billion cubic feet of earth had to be moved. Parallel to the main dyke, a counterdyke of somewhat smaller size was usually constructed. The ditch in between is filled with water and forms both an artificial canal and a water reservoir for times of drought. Security guards are posted along the dykes in periods of danger. They alarm the population by beating drums. People from the neighborhood come to the rescue by filling in ratholes in the dykes (one of the most frequent reasons for their bursting), support them with bamboo poles, and fill ruptures with straw. The bursting of a dam is a catastrophe for the surrounding country. The waters of the Red River and the canals between dyke and counterdyke join to form a vast lake with only palm trees and roofs of houses showing on the surface. In pre-French times the mandarins were obliged to inspect all dams in their territory, but the law exempted them from punishment if the bursting of the dam was caused by excessive accumulation of water.

Canals to connect different rivers have also been built since antiquity. Such a system of canals made travel by boat from the capital of Hué to Tongking possible. Some canals near the coast have locks that are constructed so as to allow the fresh water to flow into the ocean and to arrest the penetration of the salt water into the interior.

58. All authorities agree that dams were built in the earliest period of Vietnamese history, but they were recorded for the first time in 1108. (Le Thanh Khoi, *op. cit.*, p. 20.) See also E. Chassigneux. *L'irrigation dans le Delta du Tonkin.* Paris, 1912, and A. A. Pouyanne: *L'hydraulique agricole au Tonkin,* 2 vol., Text and Atlas, Hanoi, 1931.

Chapter II

One Thousand Years of Chinese Rule

1.

THERE is a legendary period of Vietnamese history, during which the first Vietnamese state and dynasty emerge out of a collection of myths characteristic for a hunting, fishing, and agricultural people with totemistic and animistic beliefs.

The mythical nature of the first Vietnamese dynasty is well established by its miraculous longevity. According to the Vietnamese legends, whose literary elaboration, however, was undertaken after only the thirteenth century of our era, Vietnam began as a kingdom called Van Lang (or Van Tang, "the Country of the Tattooed Men") over which a dynasty by the name of Hong Bang ruled for more than 2,600 years—from 2879 to 258 B.C.[1] In 258 B.C., the last of the Hong Bang was overthrown. Van Lang was conquered by the king of Thuc, an aggressor from the north who allegedly united his own country with Van Lang and became the founder of the second Vietnamese kingdom, known under the name of Au Lac. This semilegendary creation existed only fifty years. Its disappearance in the year 207 B.C. under a flood of armies coming down from southeast China marks the beginning of authentic Vietnamese history.

This patriotic edifice of a Vietnamese history old enough to compete with the legendary past of China itself[2] collapsed as soon as it was touched by historical research. A kingdom of Van Lang seems to have existed,[3] but whether it was rather large or of modest size, and whether it extended from the lower Yangtse to the Red River, or was confined to the neighborhood of Hué, are questions likely to remain unanswered. The country was not known to the ancient Chinese geographers. What knowledge there is of Van Lang, apart from the legendary texts of the Vietnamese, is extracted from later Chinese reports describing the countries between the Yangtse and Center Vietnam before their conquest by China. None of these reports were written before the fourth century A.D. What they say about the people of this region, of which Van Lang must have been a part, is now largely confirmed by the accumulated archeological and ethnographical evidence. But it does not fit the third or second millennium B.C. It fits the last few centuries before the incorporation of these territories into the Chinese empire, which took place during the third and second centuries B.C. Thus, if there was a Van Lang, and if it was the earliest kingdom of the Vietnamese, it certainly did not come into existence before the year 1,000 B.C., and very likely only after 500 B.C.[4]

The king of Thuc who is said to have conquered Van Lang and founded the short-lived kingdom of Au Lac[5] has caused more trouble to scholars of Vietnamese history than the eighteen legendary kings of the Hong Bang dynasty together, because he is generally regarded as a historical figure. It seems impossible to locate his former kingdom with certainty. Some see it as a large country that is known to have existed in the present Chinese province of Szechwan, others as a small state close to Van Lang. The former, however, was already liquidated by the Chinese in the year 316 B.C. and could hardly have conquered Van Lang fifty-eight years later; the latter simply cannot be found. This gives credit to those among the older historians who believed that Thuc[6] was the name, not of another kingdom but of a powerful family in Van Lang itself, one strong enough to have overthrown the last king of the old dynasty, whom legend obligingly depicts as a loafer and drunkard: unable to rise from his bed in good time for the defense of his invaded capital, the sleepy king, on hearing the shouts of victory from the ranks of Thuc's army, threw himself into a well.[7]

2.

The myths relating the emergence and downfall of the kingdoms of Van Lang and Au Lac, often rich in poetic beauty, and meaningful on many different levels if examined in the light of ethnographical and archeological knowledge, reveal a common drift of great significance for the origin of the Vietnamese people. They are symbolic tales of the meeting of different races, of the struggles that accompanied their attempts to live together, of the bloody clashes preceding and following separation when these attempts failed, and of the painful process of fusion whenever circumstances favored a common lot for originally dissimilar people, either settled or on the move.

Of the latter, Asia has always had more than the rest of the world. This has made Indochina into a meeting- and fighting place of different races and peoples since the dawn of man. New ones were forever moving from north to south, clashing most fearfully in the valleys where nature suggested a halt, and in the deltas where the ocean imposed one.

The most significant aspect of these clashes in prehistoric Indochina is related to the geography of Asia, in particular of southern China and Tibet, where all major migrations into the peninsula originated. During the millennium preceding our era, which includes the centuries when the Vietnamese people was ethnologically formed, the new arrivals from the north were not only racially different from the Austro-Melano-Indonesian settlers occupying the valleys and deltas; the Mongoloid tribes descending from Tibet, Yunnan or Kwangsi all came from higher altitudes and mountainous regions, which caused the conflicts resulting from their incursion to develop into a permanent antagonism between the people of the mountains and those of the plains and borderlands of the sea.

This antagonism is the basic theme of the myths surrounding the legendary origin of the kingdoms of Van Lang and Au Lac, a theme, moreover, that recurs in the folklore of all the Southeast Asian peoples, who share "a mythology imbued with a cosmological dualism of mountain *versus* sea, winged beings *versus* water beings, men of the mountains *versus* men of the coast."[8]

The end of Au Lac as a separate kingdom in the year 207 B.C., although an unquestionable historical event, is also the subject of a myth which shows the Vietnamese people under the protection of a supernatural creature from the sea—Kim Quy, the Golden Turtle. A claw attached to the King's bow made him invincible, but when he was robbed of the magic gadget—his own beautiful daughter, married to his enemy's son, cooperated in the theft—the king was defeated and chased to the coast. However, before his pursuers arrived, he had time to chop off his daughter's head and depart from this world by following the Golden Turtle into the sea.

Historically, this was the subjugation of Au Lac by the former Chinese general Trieu Da, then governor of a large province in southeast China populated mostly by Viets and only recently conquered by the Chinese. Exploiting the crisis that led to the fall of the first imperial Chinese dynasty of the Ch'in, Trieu Da, who had adopted the customs of the Viets, killed all Chinese loyal to their emperor, enlarged the territories under his control to the north and south, and proclaimed himself the ruler of an independent new state named Nam Viet. The capital of the new kingdom was located near

Map V.—NAM VIET

**The approximate borders of Nam Viet before its conquest by the Han empire in 111 B.C.,
the date when the territories inhabited by the Vietnamese became a Chinese province**

the present site of Canton; the southern provinces of Nam Viet were the territorities of Au Lac. Au Lac ceased to exist when Nam Viet came into being during the year 207 B.C.

The old Vietnamese historians, anxious to assert the identity of their people against the perennial danger of absorption by the Chinese, looked at the kingdom of Nam Viet as their Prussian colleagues of the nineteenth century regarded the Franco-Germanic empire of Charlemagne—as an early historical realization of separate statehood by their people. But this is only another example of patriotic self-deception, of which the Vietnamese are as capable as any nation in the world. If the kingdoms of Van Lang and Au Lac, as these same historians assert, were genuinely Vietnamese, the advent of Nam Viet must be regarded not as another realization but rather as a blackout of whatever separate statehood the Vietnamese had achieved by the end of the third century B.C.

Nam Viet, which was neither Chinese nor Vietnamese, held out against imperial China for almost one hundred years. It succumbed to the armies of the powerful new dynasty of the earlier Han, in the year 111 B.C., the first of the more than thousand years of Chinese rule over the Vietnamese.

3.

Historical research has not only reduced the three thousand years of legendary Vietnamese history to a prehistory of several unexplored centuries; it has recently also done away with the most authoritative theory of the origin of the Vietnamese people. This theory, which regarded the early Vietnamese as belonging "to the great ethnic family of the Chinese," [9] was formulated by outstanding scholars of the French School of Far Eastern Studies.[10] They identified the people of Au Lac with one tribe of the so-called Viets.

72

The Viets were the people with whom Trieu Da founded his kingdom of Nam Viet. No one seems to know whether they were closely or distantly related to the Chinese. They are known to have inhabited during the third century B.C. large portions of southern China and are believed to have come from the lower Yangtse Valley, where a Viet kingdom was destroyed by the rising Chinese empire in 333 B.C.

There were several major and many minor tribes of Viets. According to French schoolbooks still used in Vietnam a few years ago, one of these tribes, the Viet Lac or Au Lac, were the ancestors of the Vietnamese. They were thought to have penetrated into the Red River valley and to have driven the original inhabitants farther south and into the mountains. They presumably also founded the kingdoms of Van Lang and Au Lac. Although they shared the historic fate of all other Viets —of being first overpowered by China, then made subjects of Nam Viet, and finally taken into the Chinese empire—the Viet Lac apparently were the only Viets who somehow managed to save their ethnic identity under Chinese rule.[11]

This theory is now abandoned. The Viets have probably participated in the making of the Vietnamese, but they do not qualify as their only ancestors. As Mongolians, they were akin to the Thai and the Chinese. In spite of the customs of tattooing their bodies and cutting their hair, the Viets did not belong to the Austro-Indonesian racial group, whereas the Vietnamese represent a racial mixture of Austro-Indonesian and Mongolian elements. All recent scientific investigations emphatically confirm this thesis. The Vietnamese originated through a relatively late Mongolian attribution to an older Austro-Indonesian stock.[12]

The claim for a mixed ancestry of the Vietnamese is also supported by a rich harvest of ethnological research. Some of it is the reward of the study of the Vietnamese language. The blending of Mon-Khmer (monotonic Indonesian) with Thai (variotonic Mongolian) elements parallels the somatic picture

73

of the Vietnamese people to perfection. The totemistic beliefs of the early Vietnamese, the customs of tattooing their bodies and of chewing the betel nut, common all over Southeast Asia, show them to have remained close relatives of the Austro-Melano-Indonesians;[13] their earliest social organization, on the other hand, as well as many of their religious customs, are clearly recognized as a heritage from the Mongolian side of their ancestry—the Viets and Thai of whatever branch they were that contributed to the making of the Vietnamese.[14] Some Thai in the mountains between the Red River and Laos have conserved an early form of social organization that is amazingly close to the Chinese descriptions of the type of feudal society prevalent among the early Vietnamese.

The sciences probing the past cannot yet fix a very definite point in time for the birth of the Vietnamese, but they can circumscribe rather accurately the area to which their earliest ethnic evolution was confined. Austro-Indonesian tribes may have gone north into the modern Chinese provinces of Kwangsi and Kwantung and mixed with some Mongoloid forerunners of the Viets; the earliest Thai or some other installment of the Mongolian migration into Indochina may have descended far down the coast of Vietnam and lost their racial identity among the Indonesians in the hot deltas; the center of the whole process was the Red River Valley, no matter what segments of the Vietnamese people originated farther north or south.

4.

What kind of societies were the kingdoms of Van Lang and Au Lac, and what state of civilization had the Vietnamese reached before their destiny was changed and their development accelerated through contact with the higher civilization of the Chinese? To answer these questions with certainty is

74

still impossible, but what knowledge there is suffices for a description that is probably not too far from the truth.

Life in the Red River valley up to the last century B.C. must have been that of a primitive agricultural people whose cereal diet was supplemented by hunting and fishing. The valley was still largely jungle, abounding in beasts such as elephants, rhinoceroses, and tigers, and the no less dangerous insects that have survived. The rice fields were temporary, won from the jungle by fire, a practice that still survives among the Mois and other mountain people in Vietnam,[15] but the fields already yielded two crops a year under the care of a people that was slowly developing the qualities of physical and spiritual endurance characteristic of the peasantry of Asia. They knew an early technique of irrigation: the use of the ocean tides that affected the water levels far into the flat delta. Their main working tool was a field hoe of polished stone[16]—ploughs and water buffaloes were first introduced by the Chinese—but bronze was already known to these early Vietnamese and was used for the points of their poisoned arrows. The possession of an artistically decorated bronze drum for ceremonial purposes connects them with the so-called Dong Son civilization of Southeast Asia,[17] but in the Red River valley the New Stone Age was only beginning to give way to the Age of Bronze when Chinese imperial expansion suddenly thrust the Vietnamese onto a higher level of civilization.

The advantages of a sedentary existence for rice growers in a fertile delta must have become evident to the Vietnamese soon after they began to practice some technics of irrigation, that is before their contact with the Chinese. The more sedentary they became, the faster grew the number of stable habitations. But once a substantial number of people were settled in villages, the need for a fixed relationship between the cultivable land and the people whose existence depended on its product became imperative. To whom did the land "be-

75

long"? How much could a family use without interfering with the livelihood of others? Was it "owned" forever or was it only for temporary use? Who would protect the weaker against the stronger, or the whole village against strangers trying to plunder or drive the settlers from their land? In answer to these questions, the development of the earliest social organization of the Vietnamese began.

It appears to have resulted very soon in a strictly feudal society, remnants of which are still found among the Muongs, the only surviving relatives of the early Vietnamese.[18] In such a society, the principal human relationship is one of vassalage, or dependence of the lower groups on the next higher of smaller size, reaching through several stages from the great numbers at the base to the head of the feudal order, the king. Dependence is rooted in the power of the higher ranks to dispose of the available land, a power always formalized as right, with a claim to some supernatural sanction. Among the early Vietnamese too, all land, although it belonged theoretically to the people, was in trust of the king. The king divided the country among his brothers and sons, of which there were always many,[19] and among others elevated into the upper ranks of nobility. These feudal lords were the heads of provinces; they subdivided their domains among the lower nobility, whose members were the chiefs of villages or of groups of villages. Their charges and privileges, like those of the higher nobles, were hereditary; they were civil, military, and religious authority in one. As such, they administered justice, led in war, presided over local festivals and religious ceremonies, and were in effective control of all the land. Their privileges and powers may originally have been derived from merit, most likely of the military kind, for which defensive wars against nomadic mountain people offered enough opportunities; the social vice that made their position and powers hereditary, however, must have devaluated such claims in ancient Vietnam as quickly as in other feudal societies.

Although control over the land and the exercise of power were highly decentralized in this hierarchical setup, the common people had no share in either. For them, the times of Van Lang and Au Lac were certainly no Golden Age. They brought them the advantages of a higher form of social organization—some degree of security and protection, some measure of order and justice, and the rites and celebrations of communal life that heighten the joys and lighten the miseries of individual existence; but their lives were hard, and what hopes of a better future they were given by their prophets remain still unfulfilled after a sorrowful history of two thousand years.

5.

During the first of these two thousand years, Vietnam was a Chinese province. As such, it figures in the Chinese annals under the name of Chiao Chi.[20]

When the Chinese entered the flaming capital of Nam Viet in the year 111 B.C., the twilight of Vietnamese history ended, the time of recorded and verifiable events began. But the texts that mark the beginning of authentic Vietnamese history, in contrast to the ones dealing with its legendary period, are not from Vietnamese hands; they were written by those who were now also the makers of Vietnamese history—the conquering and scholarly Chinese. The verifiable history of Vietnam begins as part of the imperial history of China.

This, however, is not the main reason why the nature of Vietnamese history has been so largely determined by China. The Chinese have not only written and dominated Vietnamese history; they have also participated in the making of the Vietnamese people and in fact completed the process in historic times. Only when Chinese imperial expansion reached the Red River valley did the last and decisive phase in the evolution of a separate Vietnamese people begin: the cultural formation, which was entirely governed by the civilization of ancient China. The singular and salient features of Vietnamese history, therefore, will not become properly visible nor reveal their real meaning unless they are seen against the background of Chinese history and Chinese civilization.

6.

The China of which Vietnam became a part at the end of the second century B.C. was quite new as an empire. A systematic policy of establishing Chinese rule over non-Chinese people was started only under Han Wu Ti,[21] the most famous emperor of the Han dynasty, whose reign began in the year 140 B.C. Even China proper, comprising all the regions inhabited by Chinese people in a single and unified state, was less than a century old when Han Wu Ti inaugurated the policy of imperial expansion. The subjection of all Chinese lands under a powerful monarch at the head of a centralized state came about in 221 B.C., after a century filled with wars of mutual extermination known in Chinese history as the "period of the warring kingdoms." Chinese national unity was completed when the northwestern kingdom of the Ch'in, which in the year 316 B.C. had won the first of these terrible wars, also won the last.[22]

But new as was the China that unification and expansion had created, the Chinese who came to the Red River valley during the last century B.C. were the product of a civilization at least fifteen hundred and possibly more than two thousand years old.

The ancient Chinese historians, whose picture of their country's venerable and glorious past was drawn during the first millennium B.C., claimed an even higher age for Chinese civilization. But the deeper traditional Chinese history reached into the past, the more it turned into pseudo history, and eventually into a set of legends and myths. A succession of gifted rulers of the third millennium B.C., these legends say, taught the Chinese how to make fire, fish with nets, rear domestic animals, plant new crops, build brick houses, observe the stars, control the floods, and write official history. According to the old historians, the first Chinese dynasty, that of the Hsia, came to an end, through depravity and corruption, in 1765 B.C., after 450 years of rule.[23] The Hsia are now regarded as entirely legendary. They were replaced by the semilegendary Shang, who were supposed to have lasted until 1122 B.C., when they in turn were overthrown by the more rugged Chou from the Chinese northwest. But even the events of the earlier Chou, whose nominal reign actually reached into the third century B.C., are not entirely historical. The facts of early Chinese history remain tightly woven into the pattern of legend up to the ninth century B.C.[24]

But no matter how unreliable all traditional Chinese history dealing with events prior to the first millennium B.C. is known to be, the view that Chinese civilization antedates the fifteenth century B.C. is now well established and can do without the testimony of historians who were as wanting in facts as they were rich in fiction. It rests on the solid ground of archeological findings and scholarly work. The exact century when Chinese civilization began to develop can still not be determined; it remains also uncertain whether the first impulse came from the outside or from an indigenous source.[25] But a highly developed civilization is now known to have existed in northern China before the twelfth century B.C. This civilization was of a degree that must have required several centuries of preliminary stages, from its inception to the stage it had reached before some accident of history put the evidence of its existence in the great storehouse of later archeological research.

It was a Bronze Age culture located in the North China plain and the adjacent valleys. The Chinese of this period made beautiful pottery on the wheel, built solid houses erected on tamped earth, had weapons cast as skillfully as bronze techniques permitted, and used strong chariots for warfare—warfare apparently being a Chinese occupation almost as old and permanent as the tilling of the soil. They also grew wheat and millet, as they do in these regions today, and had most animals given to domestication. They probably even had books. In any case writing, as is shown by the characters they used, was not a recent invention, but rather an art presupposing a long period of gradual evolution. This and similar evidence may not suffice for the scholar to fix the exact date for the beginning of Chinese civilization, but that this date lies somewhere before the fifteenth century B.C. seems now beyond dispute.[26]

7.

The birthplace of this civilization is much easier to determine than its age. It lies in the north of China, along the middle and lower course of the Yellow River, China's great provider and perennial curse. This was the part of China where the natural fertility of the soil first invited man to become a settler, confirmed him in his agricultural inclinations, and by rewarding his labors with a product in excess of his immediate needs enabled him to build his civilization.

For her conditions of early civilization, China is no less indebted to the Yellow River and its tributaries than Egypt to the Nile or Mesopotamia to the Tigris and Euphrates, in spite of the different manner in which the Yellow River performed its work. There is in the northwest of China an immense region of high country covered entirely by a thick layer of yellow earth, which has been deposited there for many millennia by desert winds from the west. This mixture of clay, sand, and limestone, piled up to depths that reach several hundred meters, is of an inexhaustible fertility—provided it receives the necessary water to activate its dormant wealth. The rainfalls, however, are on the whole insufficient in these zones —less than two feet per year. The yellow earth, therefore, could display its virtues and tempt some early nomads into exploiting its treasures only where natural conditions for irrigation existed. These the Yellow River provided, though profusely over only a relatively short stretch of its middle course, in the valleys between the plateau in the northwest and the plain in the east, where the main stream, after being joined by the Wei and Foen, flows no longer south but east. This is the precise area where Chinese civilization was born.

But the Yellow River did more. It created the great plain of Northeast China, larger than England and Ireland combined; formerly part of the Yellow Sea, this plain has now been one of the most fertile regions of the whole world for over three thousand years. Its rich alluvial soil is none other than the famous yellow earth, carried by the river to which it gave its name from the northwestern highlands toward the low territories in the east, forever increasing, and incessantly nourishing the soil in which Chinese civilization is rooted.[27]

8.

From its original area, whose center lies where the present provinces of Honan, Shensi, and Shansi meet, Chinese civilization was spread by pioneering peasants north and east over the great plain, southwest and south into the "Alps" of present Szechwan and down the Han River toward the valley of the Yangtse,[28] and finally west and northwest: up the valley of the Wei and into the higher regions of the yellow earth.

These vague and changing territorial confines circumscribe the stage for the first millennium of Chinese history. The time was mainly that of the dynasty of the Chou, from 1200 to 221

B.C., but comprised also the semihistorical phase of the later Shang, going back perhaps to 1500 B.C. This period ended toward the third century B.C., when the vaster China known from all later history began to emerge under the rising Ch'in, who unified and simultaneously enlarged what had been China during the preceding thousand years.

This old "Kingdom of the Middle," which began to exist when some of its hunting, fishing, and roaming inhabitants became permanent agricultural settlers, produced not only the archetype of the peasant but also that of the warrior, the vaga-bond,[29] the social philosopher, and the pirate. They came about, as it were, in preparation of that unique product of Chinese civilization known as the mandarin, the archetype of the bu-reaucrat, durable as the Chinese empire itself and combining, again like the empire, something of the peasant, vagabond, pirate, warrior, and philosopher, the qualities with which this people and this everlasting society managed to survive.[30]

The successive emergence and re-emergence of these classes and groups is the main theme of Chinese history, and in their close correlation lies the key to the secrets of Chinese society from its origin to modern times. At the beginning was the peasant, but almost like his twin brother emerged the warrior, a state as compatible with human nature as that of the peasant or the saint, but one that in prehistoric China clearly came about in response to a social need. In this wild country filled with roaming people in different stages of primitive life, the early centers of agricultural civilization were in danger of destruction from the very hour of their birth. The precious earth, the rich crops, the stable settlements had to be defended against people of other races and nomadic ways of life. The necessary guardians and fighters developed into specialists, the specialized warriors into a permanent institution. Their leaders wielded the power inherent in the warrior's social function, and because no other sources of power exist for societies at this stage, power was a monopoly of the military

82

chiefs. In order to make a monopoly of government too, as it developed beyond the sphere of war, they had to acquire possession or control of land. This they did. When their charges and possessions became hereditary, the primal form of Chinese feudalism was born: a single master at the head of a small state.

This early stage of feudalism was to remain the Chinese form of government from the origin far into historic times; it lasted in fact through the eighth century B.C. To be sure, Chinese civilization in the meantime had grown tremendously, in quality as well as in scope. The territory it covered in the eighth century B.C. was many hundred times larger than the regions along the Yellow River and at the edges of the Great Plain where the first organized states were formed. But the states themselves, whether of the twelfth or the eighth century B.C., were by and large still the same small territorial units. Instead of growing in size, they had merely increased in numbers.[31] The old Chinese historians, who said that there were at one time seventeen hundred Chinese states, may not have been far from the truth; there is no doubt that many hundreds still existed during the ninth and eighth centuries B.C.

They had long been city-states reminiscent in many respects of those of early Greece and parts of medieval Europe. Their centers were the castles of the lords, erected in the middle of cities that housed the whole population and were surrounded by walls. The outlying country, comprising the cultivated fields, was as a rule walled in too, to facilitate its defense against the ever-present "barbarians"—nomadic strangers in the west and north, but elsewhere largely the still "uncivilized" masses of the Chinese, those who had not yet settled down and taken up agriculture on the basis of irrigation. The rulers in charge of defense had also important economic functions, such as directing the deforestation of new country and the construction of the works that were to protect the fields against floods and insure their irrigation. The lords also controlled the allocation of land to all families according to their size, which took place at regular intervals. In order to provide for the rulers, their retinues, and other needs of the state, some fields were set aside and groups of families were charged with their cultivation. "Vagabonds" and pirates were still unknown, but the mandarin and the social philosopher already had an embryonic existence—the former in the multiple administrative functions of the chiefs and their assistants, the latter in their efforts at semireligious and ideological indoctrination. Those in control of the existing state of affairs appeared in need of some moral or religious sanction for it at an early time. They sought to derive it from philosophical concepts describing Chinese society as in basic harmony with the immutable order of the universe, and from legends showing it as conforming to the will of the mythical emperor-founders, whose beneficial activities had made China the only civilized country and center of the world.[32]

9.

It is in this context that some of the peculiarities of ancient China become as plausible as such secrets of old societies will ever be: the "religion" of ancestor worship, long restricted to the ruling classes; the continuity of the Chou emperors in an almost sacred position totally devoid of power over the individual states; and also the early emergence of the social philosopher, partly in place of the priest, for the purpose of elaborating a universal code of ethics designed to solidify and perpetuate the *status quo*. Stability, these early Chinese rulers felt, was synonymous with order, for which society had a perfect model in the universe. An order would function properly and continue forever if the fixed relationship of its parts and the basic regularity of its movements remained undisturbed. In the social sphere, however, the ideal of order, because it depended on human behavior, was difficult to achieve; stability and perma-

84

nence were constantly threatened by the moral vacillations of man. The effectiveness of the ethical code, therefore, had to be heightened by a system of reinforcements. A technic of behavior, it was thought, could make up at least partly for man's insufficiency of virtue. Important acts of private and public life were strictly formalized, and the performance of hard duties was tied up with a complex and rich ceremonial, intended both to give satisfaction and to act as a safeguard against unpredictable and disorderly behavior. Order, it was said in every one of these states, was the road to perfection; from this maxim it followed logically that society could improve only by always remaining the same. Confucianism was indeed born a thousand times before its great prophet walked the "good earth" during the sixth and fifth centuries B.C.[33]

But all existing things are subject to eternal transformation, as a Chinese Heraclitus was soon to preach—not, however, before the seemingly frozen political order of ancient China entered a period of drastic changes. As the regions of cultivated land grew and the territories of previously isolated states became contiguous over vast expanses, a process of political concentration set in. The small city-states became parts of larger units. Of the many hundreds still in existence in the eighth century B.C., only a few dozen were left in the fifth. The former rulers of the small states were made the vassals of those lords whose initial strength or better strategic position had helped them to become rulers of the larger and more powerful new territorial combines. These men were the creators of the next form of Chinese political organization, the genuinely feudal principality or kingdom under an imperial figurehead, a form that dominated in China between the seventh and third centuries B.C.

During this time China went through the most vital and fruitful phase in the history of her civilization. Chinese culture, born in small independent city-states and reared under the rivalry of their ambitious lords, was ready for its "classical" age when the rise of large kingdoms with their accumulation of wealth and skills furnished the means and the stimulus for new thought and creation. The seventh, sixth and fifth centuries B.C. were China's great time of philosophy, artistic originality, and literary perfection. They were also a time of technical inventiveness, which put Chinese civilization at the head of mankind for many centuries to come.[34]

Before this prodigious period started, the Chinese had already gone through a hard training for life in the rough school of their nascent civilization. The overpopulated valleys, the shrinking allocations of land, the dangerous rivers, the perpetual struggle of small states against the surrounding "barbarians" had made them thrifty, hard-working, tough, and resourceful. They had learned how to face catastrophe and how to endure and survive the endless hardships of their existence. Now they began to develop their astounding qualities of social sophistication, their refined politeness, their art of concealing what they thought and felt, their high concept—moral, worldly, and esthetic alike—of civilized humanity. No other race or time has produced human specimens of greater cultural refinement than the Chinese during the "classical age" of their civilization.

This great age, however, ended in one of the bloodiest periods of Chinese history. At the end of the fourth century B.C., Chinese society was ready for a new transformation. The sixth, fifth, and fourth centuries were also the time when social evolution and technical progress created the conditions, recognized by philosophy and statecraft, for the next stage in the political development of Chinese society, the unified and centralized national state. Born of misery and bloodshed, it was to be only a brief transition to the final form of Chinese political organization: the vast empire created by the Han, whose armies destroyed Nam Viet in 111 B.C., annexed Korea less than ten years later,[35] and were already looking at the Pamir mountains, two thousand miles west of the center of China, long before the soldiers of Caesar looked at the Thames.

86

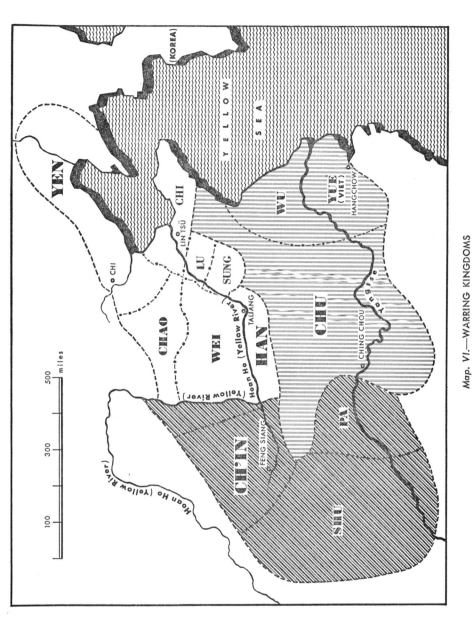

Map. VI.—WARRING KINGDOMS

400 B.C.—The approximate borders of the Chao, Wei, Chu, and Wu kingdoms before their conquest by
Ch'in, the unifier of China

10.

The social and political forces that produced a unified and centralized state of all the Chinese began to stir during the fourth century B.C. In the earlier kingdoms situated along the Chinese "frontier," the old methods of warfare based on the battle chariot of the feudal war lord[36] proved more and more inadequate against the growing number of "barbarians" who invaded China from the north and west. These nomadic aggressors were the warlike Mongols of the central Asian steppes, later known in Europe as the Huns. In order to cope with these masses on swift-moving horses, a new kind of army, made up of a new type of warrior, had to be created: a cavalry as mobile and large in numbers as the armies of the Huns, with mass armies of supporting foot soldiers to garrison and defend outlying places of strategic importance. The border kingdoms in the north and west were the first ones to develop such armies.[37] They gradually replaced the old armed forces composed of the feudal lords and their suites, which were now as obsolete as the feudal battle chariot. When the military function of the feudal lords expired, their social and political position deteriorated also, while the power of the kings, who were in direct control of the new armies, increased.

The kingdom of the Ch'in, by responding more vigorously than all other Chinese states to the new requirements of military technics, became the Prussia of the rising Chinese empire.[38] There, social conditions had been created which made the formation of mass armies not only possible but quite imperative as a remedy for one of the most fearful and persistent diseases of Chinese society: the existence of masses of landless people, whose status in an agricultural society is that of the "vagabond," and who for more than two thousand years have been the reservoir for the hosts of Chinese pirates, private armies, and the armies of the state. The social process responsible for the mass production of the Chinese "vagabond" was started by the Ch'in themselves, whose many revolutionary measures were probably adopted under the pressure of circumstances but perhaps also with a consciousness of great purpose not unusual in Chinese history: the Ch'in were the first Chinese rulers to establish the principle of private property in regard to land.

Under the old order of periodical distribution of land among all families according to size, the possibility of separating any part of the people from the land did not exist. The lots grew smaller as the population increased, but the right of everybody to a share was never questioned. The peasant, therefore, could not lose his land for the simple reason that he did not own it; but as owner he could, and he very quickly did. The complex causes behind the concentration of landed property in ancient Rome and Tudor England operated also in ancient China, with the same disastrous results, at least from the peasant's point of view. The multitudes who lost their land were swelled by the superfluous members of growing families for whom the original lot no longer provided enough food.[39] Judging by the size of the armies that were thrown against each other at the time of the "warring kingdoms," the number of Chinese whom their rulers regarded as expendable must already have been enormous around 300 B.C. The army of the Ch'in, after defeats inflicted on three neighboring states between 293 and 260 B.C., chopped off 240,000 heads in the kingdom of Han, 150,000 in Wei, and more than 400,000 in Chao. In the year 234 B.C., when the first emperor of unified China was twenty-five and only king of Ch'in, he received a birthday present from one of his generals consisting of no less than 100,000 enemy heads.[40]

Thus did the unity of China come about. The first Ch'in emperor, after victory was completed in 221, reorganized the whole of China, applying the autocratic principles on which his family had founded the power of their kingdom.[41] Feudalism was attacked at the root. The powers and functions formerly held by the lords were divided and given to provincial military commanders and civil administrators appointed by the emperor. The lords themselves were made attendants at the imperial court. Ch'in also "was in great need of works of irrigation. This it was which strengthened the central State power at the expense of the smaller feudal lords, and one may say that the process of replacement of feudalism by feudal bureaucratism had its beginning in the State of Ch'in." [42]

The Ch'in imposed many great and lasting reforms. China received a single script, a unified system of measurements and weights, and a road net connecting all parts of the country with the capital. Instead of the many walls between the former kingdoms, which were torn down, one Great Wall was built against the Huns and other nomadic invaders along the northern frontier. Regionalism was ruthlessly fought by mass deportations and mass exchanges of populations. In fact, the regime of Ch'in was a perfect totalitarian dictatorship. The citizens of China were already organized in small groups and instructed to spy on each other 2,100 years before the leaders of Communist China were born, by a government whose ideology and economic policy could hardly be called "socialistic."

These and other drastic methods of political rule did not fail to arouse strong discontent and even a political opposition that was as constructive as any regime could wish to have. It was expressed by the Confucian scholars, whose influence as literati, teachers, philosophers, and men of science had long been considerable. But the head-chopping first emperor of China called the demand for more liberal forms of government "utopian dreaming"; he forbade the scholars to preach their doctrines and had many of them executed or exiled. Upon the advice of a "renegade" from Confucianism in the service of the state, the emperor ordered all books of the scholars that were not purely technical to be burned. [43] This *Realpolitik*, however, was successful only as long as the first Ch'in emperor was alive. After his death in the year 210 B.C., the political edifice erected by the Ch'in collapsed within a few years.

The main cause for the general breakdown, which occurred during 208 B.C., was the growing number of "vagabonds" created by the agrarian policy of the Ch'in after it had been introduced all over China. The masses of landless peasants exceeded by far the need of the state for soldiers. Huge armies were employed beyond the Yangtse to conquer southern China, and all "vagrants" were at one time rounded up and sent off to colonize these new lands, but as nothing was done to remove the cause of the evil, it spread and eventually entered the critical stage. The "vagabonds" became pirates; private armies recruited from their ranks overthrew provincial governments; and in a general condition of anarchy during which the central power vanished, the empire returned to the former state of kingdoms at each others' throats.[44]

The restoration of Chinese feudalism, however, lasted only five years. A capable general and politician, who had appropriately started out as a leader of pirates, reunited China in 202 B.C. and founded the famous dynasty of the Han.[45] The Han resumed and completed what the Ch'in had begun, proceeding more cautiously and achieving permanent success.[46] Fifty years of Han rule finished all resistance to a unified and centrally governed China. The new dynasty won the support of the scholars, whose philosophical and religious teachings supplied a lasting ideological foundation for the new society. When the scholars took up active service for the state, the mandarins were permanently established as a class that did more than any other to perpetuate the social and political structure of the China built by the Han.

But to maintain themselves during the earlier phases of their dominion, the new rulers also had to mitigate the problem of the landless, that recurrent calamity for which Chinese society apparently never provided a cure. In this the Han

91

dynasty succeeded, at least temporarily, by resuming the Pan-Chinese policy of territorial aggrandizement through military efforts, by systematically colonizing newly conquered regions, in particular the enormous and still thinly populated South, and by adopting a far-reaching policy of imperial expansion, the policy that brought the Chinese into Vietnam under Han Wu Ti. When the reign of Han Wu Ti ended in 87 B.C., the Chinese empire stretched "across Central Asia to Western Turkestan, across the Korean peninsula to the heights of Seoul, and across Indo-China to the approaches of Hué." [47]

11.

The first annexation of Vietnam by the Chinese was a bloodless event of little immediate consequence for either the Vietnamese people or their political chiefs. In 207 B.C. the founder of Nam Viet had divided Vietnam into two provinces, but had left the local lords in control of the population, under the supervision of a royal delegate at the head of each province. After the fall of Nam Viet in 111 B.C., these two delegates submitted to the victorious Chinese general, and on behalf of the Vietnamese people pledged allegiance to the Chinese empire. By confirming them both in their former functions, the Chinese rulers made themselves the overlords of the Vietnamese lands.

The country was soon divided into several military districts directed by Chinese prefects under a Chinese governor,[48] but in the purely Vietnamese provinces no interference with local political institutions took place. The feudal chiefs, who, with only one exception, had offered no resistance to the Chinese, continued in their old positions, but ruling with a somewhat heavier hand, as they now had to extract from the people the tribute demanded by the Chinese. This regime lasted over a century, during which Vietnam was no more than a leniently governed protectorate of China.

A policy of local interference that eventually led to the establishment of a direct Chinese administration was adopted only after the beginning of our era. It was accompanied by intensive efforts to teach the people of the Red River valley the ways of life of the Chinese. Profiting from their indirect relations with the Chinese during the era of Nam Viet, the Vietnamese had already acquired a modicum of Chinese culture and Chinese technics before the first century B.C. When their contact with Chinese civilization became direct, it became also increasingly active. The plough was introduced, working animals were imported, new tools and materials became known, while Chinese customs and learning were spread by the growing number of officials, soldiers, colonists, and fugitives from China. The latter in particular became quite numerous during the first three decades of our era, when China went through a period of economic disaster, civil war, and changing political regimes.[49] Many of these new arrivals were former state officials and Confucian scholars—the intellectuals of old China, who were among the first to become political refugees whenever the evil of agricultural unemployment undermined the existing order and led to chaos, revolution, or successful invasion from abroad.[50]

To the Chinese governor who headed the Vietnamese provinces from the year 1 to 25 A.D., these refugees were doubly welcome: as political allies against the successor of the former Han dynasty, whom he and many other provincial commanders refused to recognize, and as agents of the new policy of local interference and rapid Sinization of the Vietnamese. He created schools to spread the language, the art of writing, and the ideas of the Chinese, and he made the introduction of their higher technics, their more civilized customs, and even their social rites a main object of Chinese policy. As powerful people with an advanced civilization generally do, the Chinese regarded it as an act of charity on their part to dispense their knowledge and skills to the Vietnamese and to make them as much like the Chinese as possible.

This policy of the empire, which made so many regions of the Asian mainland fully and permanently Chinese, met with a curious fate in the southern provinces of former Nam Viet. Marvelously successful in one respect, it was a complete failure in another. The people of the Red River valley were quite willing and certainly gifted enough to learn what the Chinese could teach them; but the more they absorbed of the skills, the customs, and the powerful ideas of the Chinese, the smaller appeared the chances of their ever becoming a mere part of the Chinese people. In fact, it was during the many centuries of intensive efforts to make them Chinese that the Vietnamese completed their ethnological formation as a separate people, with a beginning of political and cultural aspirations of their own.

It is not difficult to see why the Chinese were so successful in transplanting their culture from the North China plain and the Yellow, Foen, and Wei River valleys to the valley of the Red River. There is in all of China south of the Yangtse no plain or valley as rich in alluvial soil and as suitable to the original methods of Chinese agriculture as the Red River delta. No one, therefore, could have been better suited than the Chinese to bring to the people of this delta the advantages of a higher technical civilization. Their better methods of irrigation, of treating the soil, of making tools, weapons, and pottery, were not just those of a people more than one thousand years ahead; they had been developed in response to the same needs, and under economic conditions almost identical with those existing in the Red River valley. Moreover, as agriculturists and irrigators whose crops and lives were forever threatened by invading nomads and the unpredictable furies of the rivers, the Chinese and the early Vietnamese were bound to develop a fundamentally similar outlook on life. This made it as easy

94

for the Chinese to implant their ideas in the Red River valley as it was for them to impart their higher technics. They were the perfect and accepted leaders of the Vietnamese, in the sphere of the practical as well as in all fields not directly related to the physical needs of existence.[51]

In spite of these advantages, and their military, administrative, and propagandistic efforts of fifteen hundred years notwithstanding, the Chinese failed completely in their attempted assimilation of the Vietnamese. This is the more astonishing as so many other peoples less disposed than the Vietnamese to accept Chinese civilization, once they were taken into greater China, ended by becoming Chinese.[52]

One reason why the people of the Red River valley survived both the attraction and the coercion tending to make them a subgroup of the Chinese must have been a prehistory long enough for the development of distinctive ethnological features in the Vietnamese: the roots of their culture probably reached deeper into their pre-Chinese past than the paucity of scientific evidence permits one to affirm. Another reason why the Vietnamese did not end as one more addition to the ethnological composite known as the Chinese is purely geographical. Lying at the periphery of the empire, Vietnam always had a chance to free itself from China whenever Chinese military power declined in times of dynastic decadence or inner strife. The mere difficulties of reconquest would grant the Vietnamese a period of independence if they succeeded in breaking Chinese rule; with luck, these difficulties might one day keep the Chinese as rulers away forever.[53]

But a mere element of hope for success in case of action would never have aroused the Vietnamese to fight Chinese domination, as they have done so often, had it not been that they were driven by compelling motives to end the state of political affairs created by the Chinese. It is the story of Chinese rule, therefore, that must contain the final explanation for the ethnic durability of the Vietnamese. Subject to coercion and attraction alike, and destined to become Chinese through education and governmental pressures, the Vietnamese, when they finally broke out of the Chinese mold, had forever passed the stage when a people could become anything other than its own riper self.

12.

One of the earliest concerns of the Chinese in Vietnam was the construction of roads, waterways, and harbors to facilitate communication with China and to insure administrative control and military defense of the country. They also built stronger dykes and introduced better methods for their upkeep and supervision. These and most other technical innovations, as well as the spread of Chinese learning and the introduction of some of their customs and rites, were tasks of the state for which the indigenous feudal regime was ill equipped. The Chinese governors adapted the old order to the needs of a state in process of "modernization" by creating an administrative setup of their own, filling new posts as a rule only with Chinese, whom they may have considered politically more reliable, and whom they certainly knew to be more competent for the task of introducing Chinese-inspired reforms.

The benefits derived by the Vietnamese people from these reforms, however, were not to be had without a price. The Chinese governors needed Vietnamese labor, higher tributes, and soon also recruits for armed forces under their command. The cost of progress imposed from above was high, and the Chinese no doubt had occasion to bewail the ungratefulness of the Vietnamese, among whom discontent soon interfered with their original acceptance of Chinese innovations. But whatever discontent may have existed among the Vietnamese peasants, opposition as an active political force and a conscious negation of Chinese rule developed first in the ranks of the feudal lords.

After more than one hundred years of Chinese noninterference with their rule, the hereditary local chiefs began to feel their position seriously endangered by the new Chinese policy of reform and *Gleichschaltung*. The revenues they were able to extract from their peasants may have been affected, but the main cause of their unrest was the loss of power and prestige. The number of officials not subject to their control increased steadily; the growing necessity for centralization disturbed them in their own functions and hurt their particularisms; the dissemination of Chinese religious ideas and the practice of Chinese rites damaged their authority as spiritual heads of the people; while the levying of Vietnamese troops under Chinese command threatened to rob them of their basic function, that from which all their powers and privileges sprang: defense of the country.

Feudal resentment against the Chinese turned into opposition, which hardened the more the lords realized that the basis of their position was being ground away. Opposition led to repression, with open rebellion as the only answer left for the lords. Threatened with extinction, like so many feudal classes before and after, the hereditary chiefs of the Vietnamese decided to fight.

The first Vietnamese uprising against the Chinese occurred in the year 39 A.D.[54] A new Chinese governor, by adding to the repressive measures of his predecessors the simple and common device of brutality, provided the atmosphere as well as the occasion that unleashed the furies of armed revolt. The insurrection was started by a dauntless noblewoman whose husband had been killed by the Chinese in order to frighten the restive lords back into submission. Led by the lady Trung Trac and her equally fearless sister, the lords and their vassals attacked and defeated the Chinese forces at the governor's residence, stormed most of the fortified places in the hands of Chinese,

97

and proclaimed the Trung sisters queens. Their kingdom, founded in 40 A.D., comprised all three provinces inhabited by the Vietnamese; it reached down to Hué[55] and probably also into southern China,[56] but it lasted little more than two years. The Chinese sent a strong army, led by one of their oldest and best generals, to reconquer the lost provinces.[57] The well-trained and experienced Chinese troops quickly defeated the Vietnamese army led by their queens; hopelessly beaten, the Trung sisters jointly committed suicide by throwing themselves into a river.[58]

Vietnamese historians have always been very kind toward the Trung sisters, whose ill-fated uprising was probably also ill-advised. When Vietnam became independent, they were both proclaimed national heroines. But the historians who now call them two Joans of Arc willing to sacrifice their lives for the liberation of their country seem not to know at all what the Vietnamese people felt, did, or suffered during these events. There is little evidence that the people participated in the struggle.

The circumstances of foreign rule, if seen in the light of later developments, were bound to distort the true nature of this first Vietnamese "national revolution." There was no "nation" of Vietnamese, and even their evolution as a separate people was still far from being completed when the Chinese were chased from the Red River valley for the first time, by two women to boot. The revolt of the Trung sisters was primarily an attempt by the indigenous chiefs to preserve their inherited privileges and powers, and their battles were fought by and for the feudal minority whom Chinese interference threatened with political extinction.[59]

With the defeat of the old feudal class, which was total, the long period in the history of Vietnam called Sino-Vietnamese began. The progress of Sinization was no longer retarded by the fears and obstructions of the traditional local rulers. The majority of the lords had been killed in battle. Of the survivors,

98

some fled south. Those who remained were demoted, and hundreds of families were deported to China. Only the lower grades were left in their positions, surrounded by increasing numbers of Chinese officials and equally subject to the autocratic central government, headed usually by the commanders of the Chinese troops. These troops were spread all over the country, stationed at fortified places considered strategically sound. Vietnam, in brief, was made a colony destined to become a Chinese province, governed henceforth without local intermediaries by the Chinese themselves, under a harsh regime disinclined to relax. With only brief interruptions, this new order was to last nine hundred years.

13.

During the first few centuries of our era, Chinese civilization penetrated not only higher up the Red River valley and farther down the Vietnamese coast, but also deeper into the social body of Vietnam, producing changes in its structure that greatly affected Chinese rule and became of decisive importance for the future of the Vietnames people.

Both the organizational frame and the spiritual foundations of Vietnamese society were altered by the incessant waves of technical, social, political, and religious innovation that followed the establishment of direct Chinese rule. Whether the individual Chinese governors were lenient or cruel, enlightened or just murderous experts of power, they were all "progressive" by virtue of their task. They had to, and desired to, reproduce the civilization of China, the only one they knew, and knew to be rational and superior to any other, granted there were others as well as their own. Some favored books and objects of art, others material means of comfort or military inventions; but whatever the Chinese possessed in skills, arts, rules of poetry, codes of law, philosophical ideas, and administrative experi-

99

ence, they now gradually brought into the Red River valley, for their own enjoyment as well as to manage and transform the Vietnamese.

Thus opened the final and decisive phase in the evolution of the Vietnamese people. In its genesis as a future *nation,* the first few centuries of our era are the time of its prenatal growth. They contain the great secret in the history of this people—how they were able to avoid becoming Chinese.

The process as a whole, to be sure, was one of tangled social interaction, in which the spheres of accident, blind force, and conscious direction cannot be distinguished from each other by the feeble light of present historical knowledge. But the result is there—the Vietnamese people, with a national character of its own. To know the Vietnamese and to understand their national character may well be the key to the secret of their ethnological survival, a secret that neither their own nor the Chinese historical annals completely reveal.

14.

After the ephemeral kingdom of the Trung sisters was crushed, the Chinese created a completely new kind of administration. Their aim was to replace the old feudal chiefs on all levels with a more modern, more competent, and more reliable type of local and provincial administrator. He was to be no longer an independent ruler over his territory but rather a servant of the centralized state.

The policy of employing Chinese—colonists, fugitives, officers, generals, imported scholars, and officials—was intensified. To hold these people in the country and on their jobs, they were given large portions of land—some newly opened, some appropriated from the defeated nobles or expropriated at the expense of the villages. But these people were not the only ones thus employed or rewarded. In accordance with their aim of

100

eventually making a Chinese out of every local inhabitant, and in need of officials who knew the people and the customs of the country, the Chinese retained the subdued remnants of the old local aristocracy. Soon they also employed such Vietnamese as they had educated, trained, and induced to accept Chinese ways of life. However they recruited them with great caution and used them only in minor posts, preparing the Vietnamese, as it were, for the distant future when the same policy was practiced on them by the French.[60]

It did not take long before these high and low officials, provincial and local commanders, and scholars in the service of the state, constituted a privileged new upper class. They were all either Chinese or native allies of the Chinese made fit for their functions and raised in their status by the culture and the training received from the Chinese. The role this class played was progressive and oppressive at the same time. Most of its members may have been solid experts, and well intentioned, but both their way of life and their official duties opposed them to the people whose ascent to Chinese civilization they were to promote. To rule and administer, alas, meant to exploit and hold down the masses of the peasants, whose labor was still almost the only source of wealth at the stage of development Vietnamese society had reached.

After this Chinese-created new upper class had taken shape and deepened its roots in Vietnamese society, it revealed three main characteristics, which together determined the curious political role it was to play during the many centuries of Chinese domination. It was semifeudal because its members acquired more and more land and succeeded in making their privileges quasi-hereditary; it was semimandarinal because of the many officials whose position depended on their scholastic degrees; and it was to a large extent foreign. Although the number of Vietnamese increased steadily even in higher positions, the class as a whole remained predominantly Chinese. It had a Chinese culture, and it was constantly replenished with Chinese appointees: refugee intellectuals mainly, who arrived again in great numbers before and after the fall of the second branch of the Han dynasty in 220 A.D.[61]

15.

The fall of the Han, like all major convulsions in Chinese history, had repercussions in the extreme south of the empire that suddenly opened a new line of development in the political history of Vietnam. As a direct consequence of the empire's declining military power, a "barbarian" state arose on Sino-Vietnamese territory north of Hué. It called itself Lam Ap. Founded in 197 A.D., it became the nucleus of Indianized Champa, Vietnam's dangerous contender for supremacy along the east coast of Indochina.

More important still was what happened in the heart of the Vietnamese provinces while the Han dynasty declined and after it had run its course. Under the governorship of Che Sie,[62] who ruled in the Red River valley from 187 until 226, the Vietnamese territories became virtually independent from China. Che Sie continued to pay what tributes he owed the capital, he welcomed the scholars and officials who fled from the parts of the empire torn by civil war, and he vigorously pursued the policy of Sinization. But he ruled in the manner of a sovereign king over a state that was to be Chinese without being subject to the orders of a distant imperial court. When toward the end of the Han dynasty China was split into three contending kingdoms, Che Sie established his merely formal relationship of subordination with the heads of Wu, who ruled all of southern China from Nanking. Che Sie died in 226. Before the court of Wu had a chance to act, Che Sie's son proclaimed himself his successor, and on hearing that Nanking would not confirm him as governor, made military preparations to defend the provincial autonomy his father had achieved. He was quickly defeated by an army of the Wu and lost not only his position but also his life.

As proponents of an autonomous policy calculated perhaps to end in independence, Che Sie and his son, although Chinese, should be recognized as forerunners of the first true champion of Vietnamese independence since the destruction of the old aristocracy, the great Ly Bon.[63] The rebellion he led broke Chinese domination in 542, half a millennium after the rise and fall of the Trung sisters, and he was emperor of an independent Vietnam about as long as they had been queens.[64] But Ly Bon was not only a leader of the ruling class which was Chinese-created and still essentially Sino-Vietnamese; he himself was a descendant of a family of Chinese refugees. What had made him a Vietnamese? How did he become a rebel against China and the initiator of an enterprise doomed to failure for another four hundred years?

16.

In the millennium of Vietnamese history under the Chinese, the fraction of time when Ly Bon rose, triumphed, and went under is like the instant of lightning in a long and dark night: the outlines of the world become visible for a moment and can be fixed forever if the proper instruments are at hand.

The Sino-Vietnamese upper class that replaced the old indigenous aristocracy had slowly changed its composition and character during the five centuries between the Trung sisters and Ly Bon. If its Vietnamese members became somehow Chinese by virtue of their training and their culture, its Chinese members became more and more Vietnamese. The class as a whole developed common interests entirely rooted in their local position, interests that were different from and became increasingly opposed to the interests of the Chinese empire in Vietnam. Why should their wealth be tribute, their laborers be soldiers, their profits from international trade be revenue for China instead of remaining in the country?

When the Chinese extended their conquests into the peninsula, they had a motive as modern as any imperialist power that penetrated into Indochina in more recent times. Desirous to advance their trade with Southeast Asia and India, and via India with the West, they tried to establish a trade route that was easier and safer than either the famous "Silk Road" through Central Asia or the old "Burma Road" to the Bay of Bengal by way of the Irrawaddy River.[65] This great project, conceived by the emperor Han Wu Ti, was indeed largely realized through the annexation of the southern provinces of Nam Viet. After the first century A.D., the delta of the Red River developed into an important center of inter-Asian communication and international trade.

One further effect of these foreign contacts was important besides the material advantages of lively Sino-Indian trade. The merchants, scholars, and Buddhist pilgrims who arrived in great numbers in the delta soon added an Indian touch to Vietnamese upper-class culture, whose Chinese form and substance, moreover, was being modified all along by the stubbornly persisting local customs and beliefs from the country's pre-Chinese past. The language, for instance, although greatly enriched by a vocabulary imported from China together with Chinese objects, inventions, and ideas, remained the language that was spoken before Nam Viet was conquered by Han Wu Ti. Chinese was used only for official business. There is no doubt that the many new and special features developed by Chinese culture on Vietnamese soil assisted in the gestation of a prenationalist mood among the Sino-Vietnamese upper class. But the driving force behind all the efforts to secure autonomy or independence was the lure of material gains uncurtailed by the needs and demands of the empire.

Che Sie, consequently, was not the only governor tempted to rule as independently from China as Chinese imperial conditions permitted. He and others, in order to assure themselves of local support for their semiautonomous regimes, strongly favored the Vietnamese element of their administration. His policy, moreover, far from splitting the Sino-Vietnamese upper class, rather convinced the permanently settled Chinese colonists and administrators that their interests too were tied up more closely with the prosperity of Vietnam than with the welfare of China. The whole class, therefore, stood behind every governor who defended their local interests against Chinese imperial demands and interference, and opposed the many more governors who felt that looking after the interests of China was the best way of looking after their own.

The new upper class, in fact, staged its first insurrection in 248 A.D., three hundred years before the brief episode of independence under Ly Bon, and shortly after a Chinese army had overthrown the son of Che Sie and reintroduced a strictly Chinese-controlled regime. The revolt was a glorious failure, but it enriched Vietnamese patriotic history with a third Joan of Arc, the young Trieu Au, who met the enemy in golden armor high on her elephant, and killed herself, at the age of twenty-three, after the Chinese had cut down her army of only one thousand men.[66]

The small size of Trieu Au's army underlines sharply the main feature of all earlier Vietnamese uprisings against Chinese rule. They were primarily upper-class revolutions in which the people had very little part. This is one of the reasons why they failed. When success came in the tenth century, it was due not only to China's inner troubles but also to the fact that the struggle for independence was no longer hampered by the limits of a narrow social base. Instead of being the concern only of the rich and an elite engaged in administration and rule, it had gradually taken on the character of a national revolution.

Between the second and tenth centuries A.D., that is before the movement for independence had broadened enough to promise permanent success, a Vietnamese rebel obviously was

105

neither a confirmed "nationalist" nor necessarily a man of local descent. He was an inhabitant of the northeast of Indochina who possessed Chinese culture and Chinese administrative experience but wanted to get rid of Chinese political rule. Ly Bon, who is regarded by many as the founder of the first historical Vietnamese dynasty,[67] was the perfect example of such a man.

But there is a negative aspect in this description of a Vietnamese revolutionary that is even more important than its positive content: it does not fit the Vietnamese peasant at all, and the peasants made up ninety per cent of the people, then as now. What happened to the Vietnamese peasant during the ten centuries between the fall of Nam Viet and the dawn of independence, and how was his village affected by the spread of Chinese civilization and the fact of Chinese rule? Only an answer to these questions can fully reveal why the inhabitants of northeast Indochina graduated from their thousand-year course of Sinization as a separate people with national aspiration that opposed them to the Chinese.

17.

Chinese technical civilization revolutionized the economic basis of Vietnamese life quickly and with lasting effects. The metal plough, the water buffalo, the more sweeping and more permanent provisions for irrigation wiped out the remnants of a preagricultural way of life. The spaces of rice land widened, the yield increased, and not only the population but also the wealth of the country grew faster than in any other Chinese territory south of the lower Yangtse.

This economic prosperity, however, was accompanied by a social, political, and cultural transformation as costly and unbeneficial to the peasant as the progress of civilization in an agricultural society could possibly be. The country grew rich, the peasant remained poor. The material needs of the ruling and civilizing minority and the swelling demands of the state took more from his table than Chinese technical innovations had added to the product of his fields.

This fact is a crucial one for the understanding of this people's ethnological survival under Chinese rule. The Vietnamese peasant had probably no desire to discard his new tools and give up his new methods of cultivation, but his new masters, it is safe to assume, he would rather have exchanged for those of some distant "good old time." The Golden Age of the Vietnamese, the existence of which must be as doubtful as that of any other people, was certainly not the time when the Chinese installed their busy and costly officials. In the legends and myths that survived in the villages through oral transmission, the better times of the Vietnamese lay far in their pre-Chinese past.

Vietnamese dynastic and patriotic history stresses the role of armed rebellion against Chinese rule in the emergence of a national community strong enough to resist its absorption by China. Fighting the Chinese in a dozen or so uprisings between the years 39 and 939 must indeed have contributed much to the growth of national sentiments, not only among the actively engaged but also among the merely suffering part of the people. The peasant, in particular, could only have longed for an end of conditions that were harder on him than on anyone else, as every return of the Chinese was bound to increase his burden of misery and exploitation. His interests conflicted more sharply with Chinese rule than those of the rebellious upper classes. He, too, wanted to get rid of foreign rule, from which he endured much, profited little, and learned to expect only worse at every turn of events. If for so many centuries he did not engage in active resistance, it was not only because of the cultural barrier and the clash of social and economic interests that set him against his rich and administrating compatriots; it was mainly because he lacked their consciousness of self-interest, as well as the possibility of organized action that existed for the ruling class. But when the century of decision aproached, it became clear that the peasant's passive resistance to Chinese rule had contributed more to the survival of the Vietnamese people and its national consolidation than the moods and traditions engendered by all the upper-class revolts.

After a millennium of Sinization aimed at assimilating another tribe into the great family of the Chinese, the villages of the Red River valley and those three hundred miles down the coast were still inhabited by a people essentially unchanged since the Chinese subjected them to their domination. Chinese culture had not pentrated into the masses of the Vietnamese. The peasant clung to his pre-Chinese customs and religious ideas, and he would cling to some of them to this very day, under an outer cloak woven of later importations. He continued with his un-Chinese habit of chewing the betel nut. He kept his hosts of village genii and spirits of the house, of the rivers, and of the mountains. He rejoiced in his ceremonies and festivals that originated in a pre-Chinese past. He stuck to his special form of ancestor worship. And he even preserved the memories of Van Lang and Au Lac, into which he poured his yearning for a life of peace and plenty, free from the vexations of foreign rule. He was, in fact, more of a Vietnamese in the year 900 of our era than he had been in the first century B.C.

If Sinization, while creating a new Sino-Vietnamese upper class, transformed only a small fraction of the Vietnamese people, this was by no means due to an innate unwillingness of the peasants to consent to any innovations from abroad. Endowed with inquisitive minds that helps to explain the lust for knowledge in the later Vietnamese, these stubborn villagers accepted a great deal that was new, either freely or under compulsion; but they transformed what they accepted by adapting it to their own likings and needs.

There was, however, another and more fundamental reason why the Vietnamese villages preserved their originality and

108

became the breeding places for a nation apart. Once the elementary advances of Chinese agriculture had been introduced, the villages were neither in need nor intrinsically capable of radical transformation. As in China itself, all innovation on the village level was limited by the nature of its essentially static economy. Neither the Chinese overlords, who knew something about the dangers of agrarian reform, nor the local Sino-Vietnamese elite had a desire to interfere with the basic productive institution of the country, its only permanent and reliable source of wealth.

Seen from this viewpoint, the complex pattern of motives and causes behind the birth of this nation reveals at last a few clearly perceptible and unbroken lines. But such are the intricate ways of history that the two principal currents toward national independence ran for centuries counter to each other and away from their goal. The members of the upper class developed the ability to govern and the ambition to rule without the Chinese through a training, a world of ideas, and a way of life imported by the Chinese. The interests and aspirations that made them revolt against China and strive for Vietnamese independence were precisely what estranged them from those who had refused to become Chinese: the masses of the Vietnamese peasants. The peasants, on the other hand, who were the ones that remained basically Vietnamese, developed a hostility that for centuries was directed primarily against the members of the local upper class—Chinese-educated, but nevertheless pioneers of Vietnamese national independence.[68]

It was only during the ninth and tenth centuries that these conflicting trends gradually converged. The village, to be sure, emerged as the great source from which the national spirit drew its strength, but it was in the ranks of the upper class that this spirit had come to life. Members of the upper class now awakened the peasant to an awareness of national interests related to his wants. They voiced his growing national aspirations and harnessed his forces for action against the Chinese. Inspired by ambition and a generosity not uncommon in the struggle for national liberation, the upper-class rebels began to look at the peasant no longer as a mere object of exploitation; they recognized him as an indispensable ally if their long war of independence were ever to end in success.

The Sino-Vietnamese upper-class leaders mobilized the peasant by appealing to that which they had in common with him and which separated them both from the Chinese. To this end, they had to speak the language of the villages and extol it as a common treasure, together with the peasant's native ways and his memories of the pre-Chinese past. But they could not preach the national gospel without simultaneously transforming themselves into something more genuinely Vietnamese than they had theretofore been.

The evolution of the Vietnamese people toward national separateness thus reached its concluding phase. The end product, the Vietnamese as he became known to all later centuries, would soon compete in the arena of history in his own name. There his national character would receive a few final touches, but its basic features, those that distinguish the Vietnamese as a separate member within the family of man, were fully developed when the thousand years of Chinese rule came to an end. He had not only preserved his pre-Chinese culture. By locally modifying and even slightly "Indianizing" whatever Chinese elements he added to the cultural heritage of his own past, the Vietnamese made something new out of both. One day the world would recognize him as the truest son of Indochina, enduring and indomitable for many reasons, but perhaps mainly because he derived his strength from more than one source.

110

Notes to Chapter Two:

1. The origin of this legendary dynasty is a confusing story, which, however, has some bearing on many aspects of Vietnamese prehistory and on the origin of the Vietnamese people, as the reader will see later on. According to the oldest Vietnamese annals, the first ancestor of the Hong Bang was a descendant of Than Nong, (in Chinese, Chen Nong), or, as he usually is called, Viem (in Chinese, Yen). Viem's descendant was named Kinh Duong Vuong. (We omit the numerous accents this name requires, thus making the spelling senseless for the Vietnamese —a fact that is true for the spelling throughout this book but is of no consequence for the English reader). Legend does not consider Kinh Duong Vuong a Vietnamese national ruler. His empire, Xich Qui ("Land of the Red Demons," some authors think) was somewhere south of the Yangtse. One day, Kinh Duong Vuong went to the Palace of the Waters, where the Dragon ruler of the water lived. There he married the Dragon's daughter, with whom he had a son named Sung Lam, who became his successor under the title Lac Long Quan ("Dragon Lord of the Lac" is the usual translation). Lac Long Quan is regarded as the civilizing hero of the people from whom the Vietnamese descended. His reign in Xich Qui was said to have been a golden age, perhaps because he retired to the Palace of the Waters and left the country without a chief. Trouble coming from China, however, forced him to return; but the invading Chinese emperor Lai died, leaving a daughter by the name of Au Co. Peace and prosperity were restored, Lac Long Quan married Au Co, who gave birth to a sack of flesh containing one hundred eggs. After five or six days, the eggs hatched one hundred boys. Lac Long Quan and Au Co thereupon decided to part. This myth is quoted in Le Thanh Khoi, *op. cit.*, p. 83, as translated from Toanthu, Ngoai Ky I, 16-2a (the Vietnamese annals written between the thirteenth and seventeenth centuries). The king and queen divided their children, fifty of whom went with their father to the Kingdom of the Waters in the South; the other fifty followed their mother into the mountains, to a region that legend has localized somewhere near Viet Tri, twenty miles north of Hanoi. There the oldest of Au Co's sons was elected king, under the name of Hong. He became the founder of the Hong, the first dynasty recognized by legend as genuinely Vietnamese. See P. Huard and M. Durand, *op. cit.*, pp. 7-8. Also Le Thanh Khoi, *op. cit.*, pp. 82-3. Mme. Ngo Dinh Nhu, in an address before the International Women's Association at the Independence Palace in Saigon on October 29, 1956,

pointed out that a woman, Queen Au Co, is thus the first well-known personage in Vietnamese history, and that this and other legends give support to the thesis that the Vietnamese people, at the time of Van Lang, were still under the influence of matriarchy. See the *Times of Vietnam,* March 9, 1957.

2. Chesneaux, *op. cit.,* thinks that its elaboration was largely dictated by a desire of Vietnamese historians to provide their country with a past as venerable and as illustrious as that of China. For an extended study of ancient Chinese history see H. C. Creel, *The Birth of China,* London, 1936, O. Lattimore, *Inner Asian Frontiers of China,* London, 1940, and O. Franke, *Geschichte des Chinesischen Reiches,* Berlin, 5 vols., 1930-1947; for a shorter treatment, K. S. Latourette, *The Chinese, Their History and Culture,* New York, 1945, Chapters II and III, and C. P. Fitzgerald, *China: A Short Cultural History,* third completely revised edition, New York, 1950, pp. 13-18. Fitzgerald aptly characterizes the history of the first Chinese dynasty as "little more than a pedigree occasionally adorned by an anecdote" (p. 15). Cf. also Latourette, *A Short History of the Far East,* New York, 1951, pp. 78-82, and Joseph Needham, *Science and Civilization in China,* Cambridge, 1954, Volume I, Historical Introduction.

3. It is, however, mentioned only in Vietnamese sources and is unknown to Chinese authors. From that fact H. Maspéro ("Le royaume de Van Lang," in BEFEO, XVIII, Nos. 3 and 4) deduces that it was identical with the ancient kingdom of Ye Lang or Da Lang in southern China, the name of which was incorrectly transcribed as Van Lang in Vietnamese. There was another kingdom of Van Lang in north-central Vietnam. It seems that Vietnamese writers have confounded the two states. See Pierre Huard and Maurice Durand, *Connaissance du Vietnam,* Paris and Hanoi, 1954, p. 8.

4. The great authorities on the early period of Sino-Vietnamese history are: E. Chavannes, *Mémoires historiques de Se-ma Ts'ien,* 5 vols., Paris, 1895-1905; L. Aurousseau, "La première conquête chinoise des pays annamites," in *Bulletin de l'Ecole française d'extrême-Orient* (usually abbreviated BEFEO), Vol. XXIII (1923), pp. 137-264; H. Maspéro, *Le royaume de Van Lang,* BEFEO, Vol. XVIII (1918) Nos. 3, 4. All these outstanding works are dated in many respects.

5. The name of *Lac* was the first ethnic denomination by which the Vietnamese became known to the Chinese. Chavannes, *op. cit.,* Vol. I, p. 38; Le Thanh Khoi, *op. cit.,* p. 86; Huard and Durand, *op. cit.,* pp. 12f.

6. The name of the king of Thuc was Thuc Phan. The story of his conquest of Van Lang (also written Van Lan) is completely legendary.

112

Huard and Durand (*op. cit.*, pp. 10f.), who believe that Thuc Phan was a historical personality, also think he was a feudal chief residing in the north of Van Lang. The capital of Au Lac was Co Loa, of which three ramparts are still preserved. Cf. Le Thanh Khoi, *op. cit.*, pp. 84f.; G. Domoutier, *Etude historique et archéologique sur Co-loa*, Paris, 1893; R. Despierres, *Co-loa, capitale du royaume d'Au Lac*, Coh. Soc. Geogr., Hanoi, 1940.

7. Drowning seems to have been the traditional form of royal suicide in Vietnam. Thuc Phan himself, after having been defeated by the Chinese, walked into the ocean; his son jumped into a well; the Trung sisters, who in 40 A.D. overthrew Chinese rule for a short time, threw themselves into a river when they were defeated; the last of the Tran rulers, Guy Khoach, jumped into the sea from the boat that took him to China; etc.

8. Hall, *op. cit.*, p. 8, quoting Coedès, *op. cit.*, pp. 25-6. This antagonism is to be found in the whole of Indochina and in other Southeast Asian countries as well. A very good example of a legend that illustrates this antagonism is the story of the marriage of My Nuong, daughter of a king of the legendary Hong Bang dynasty: "The 18th king of Hung Vuong, the first royal dynasty of our history, had a daughter by the name of My Nuong. At the age of twenty, My Nuong had a rare beauty and found numerous young princes from different neighboring countries rushing at her door. But they were all refused by the King. One day, two young men happened to arrive at the Palace at the same time. The one introduced himself as Son Tinh (God of the Mountain) and the other, Thuy Tinh (God of the Water). The King's embarrassment was great since the two suitors were equally handsome and powerful. After much thinking, he decided to grant his daughter's hand to the one who would arrive first the next day with his wedding presents. It was Son Tinh the Mountain's God who arrived first. He brought quantities of presents entirely composed of jade, ivory, gold and silver works the King himself had never seen before. Keeping his promise, he allowed Son Tinh to take My Nuong off to his home in the Tan Vien Mountain, located in the province of Son Tay (North Viet Nam). When Thuy Tinh the Water's God in his turn arrived, with no less strangely precious objects, the beautiful princess had gone. The angry Thuy Tinh swore to ravish by all means the lovely young person from his adversary. And when a god, particularly a god of the water, acts under the sting of jealousy, you know what can happen to things on earth. Upon his first roaring, the elements burst out from everywhere, whirlwinds sweeping the space, rainfalls and tides flooding immense areas. Amidst the

113

fury, sea fauna suddenly turned themselves into soldiers marching against the Mountain of Son Tinh. But the Mountain's God was not less powerful. He also transformed the whole highland's fauna into warriors. Dreadful battles then took place to the detriment of men dwelling in the area, which is now the delta of the Red River. The number of victims of the two gods' love conflict and the damage to immense ricelands were uncalculable. The war dragged on for weeks and there seemed to be no possible issue since the higher Thuy Tinh raised his water, the higher Son Tinh raised his mountain. The former was finally discouraged and withdrew his forces towards the sea. Unfortunately, the grudge did not fade away in the heart of the Water God, and thus every year his floods and thunder continue to plague the people of the North Delta area." Taken from *The Times of Vietnam*, Aug. 3., 1957.

9. Quoted from the official textbook by Duong Quang Ham, *Leçon d'histoire d'Annam à l'usage des élèves des cours moyen et supérieur des écoles franco-annamites,* Hanoi, 1927 (first edition), p. 13.

10. See L. Aurousseau, "Les origines du peuple annamite," BEFEO, Vol. XXII; L. Aurousseau, "La première conquête chinoise des pays annamites, IIIe siècle avant notre ère," BEFEO, Vol. XXIII; René Grousset, *Histoire de l'Extrême-Orient,* Paris, 1929, Vol. II, pp. 599f.

11. See Duong Quanh Ham, *op. cit.,* pp. 13ff. According to Aurousseau and Chavannes, three of the four most important Viet tribes settled within the frontiers of China proper (near Wenchou, Foochow, and Canton, respectively) and were absorbed by the Chinese. The Lac Viet or Au Lac are supposed to have settled south of the Chinese province of Kwangsi before 300 B.C. and to have entered Tongking and Annam at the beginning of the third century B.C. These scholars denied emphatically that there was a proto-Vietnamese population in the Red River valley before the fourth century B.C., i.e. before the arrival of the inhabitants of the Viet kingdom on the lower Yangtse conquered by the Chinese. This theory was first attacked by H. Maspéro in *T'oung pao,* December, 1924, p. 393. Le Thanh Khoi, *op. cit.,* p. 86, says that the theory of the Viets being the ancestors of the Vietnamese rests on flimsy evidence and is no longer valid. In spite of this refutation by their most learned historian, the Vietminh leadership still holds on to this outmoded theory and elaborated on it in a popular history of Vietnam published in Hanoi as late as 1955. See note 59, Ch. III.

12. Five races made up the prehistoric population of Indochina: Melanesians, Indonesians, Negritos, Australoids, and Mongoloids. The present inhabitants are of Indonesian and Mongoloid stock. The Indo-

nesians are represented by the Mois, the Kha, and certain Tho and Man. The mass of the Vietnamese population is formed by a later addition of Mongoloid blood to Indonesian stock. Huard and Durand, *op. cit.*, pp. 39-43; Huard and Bigot, "Les caracteristiques anthropo-biologique des Indochinois," Tr. Inst. Anat. V. Hanoi, 1938; Le Thanh Khoi, *op. cit.*, p. 90; L. Malleret, *Groupes ethniques de l'Indochine*, Saigon, 1937.

13. In Indochina, the custom of tattooing goes back to prehistoric times. A mythical king is supposed to have ordered the fishermen of his realm to tattoo sea monsters on their arms. It was believed that this would protect them against being attacked by crocodiles. The rulers of Vietnam up to Tran Anh Tong (1293) were tattooed with images of a dragon, considered to be their ancestor. The crocodile was the totem animal of both China and Vietnam. In the imagination of the people it was transformed into a dragon. According to H. Maspéro, "Le royaume de Van Lang," BEFEO, Vol. XVIII, nos. 3, 4, tattooing as a protection against crocodiles, chewing of betel, and the blackening of the teeth were common in Indochina before the Chinese conquest. Cf. Le Thanh Khoi, *op. cit.*, pp. 81, 87ff. The betel nut played an important role in the social and religious life of old Vietnam. A marriage proposal had always to be preceded by presents of betel nuts and leaves. Betel chewing is known in the whole of Southeast Asia. Blackening of the teeth is also practised in the Chinese provinces of Fukien and Kwangtung, in Indonesia, and in Japan. (P. Huard, "La coutume du noircissement des dents en Asie orientale et en Indochine," in the magazine *Indochine*, March 25, 1943; M. Durand in the magazine *Dan Viet Nam*, No. 3, pp. 105-106.)

14. The name Thai, it should be remembered, is a linguistic, not an ethnographic, classification. The Thai-speaking people comprise a variety of Mongoloid tribes related to the Chinese but very much differing in their bodily features and in civilization. See Chapter I.

15. The mountain tribes of today first cut all trees on the selected territory and then burn the brush and underwood. Many forests in Indochina show traces of gigantic fires. Especially in February, the height of the dry season, one can see the smoke rising in the mountains. When the fire is burned out and the soil all covered with ashes, rice, corn, and cotton are planted. The soil, enriched by the ashes, can yield a better crop than the irrigated fields, if there is abundant rainfall. In dry years, the crops are a failure; unfortunately, dryness occurs very often. When rainfall is sufficient, the crops grow but so do the weeds, and soon the jungle has recovered its loss. Therefore, this primitive form of agriculture

could not, in the long run, compete with the more advanced form of irrigated fields. Even if everything turns out to the best, a host of guards has to be on the alert to protect the crops against invaders from the surrounding jungle: birds, monkeys, boars, and especially rats that multiply excessively in some years and are killed with bamboo sticks. The tribes that create their rice fields by forest fires are nomads or semi-nomads. When their fields are exhausted, they break off their encampment and look for other places where they again settle temporarily. This change usually takes place after three or four years, sometimes even after a single crop, and only rarely after five or six years. (Robequain, *op. cit.*, pp. 78-80.)

16. Some Moi tribes in the central plateau of Annam still use such hoes. Le Thanh Khoi, *op. cit.*, p. 87, note 59.

17. The Dong Son culture is not only characterized by bronze; the people who introduced the use of metal to Indochina were ironworkers also. The expression Dong Son culture was coined by R. von Heine-Geldern after a place in Tongking where the most interesting specimens of this early civilization were found. Their bronze work was of a very high quality. The present-day inhabitants of Pulo Nias, off the west coast of Sumatra, show the Dong Son culture still in its living stage. Hall, *op. cit.*, pp 7f. For a more detailed treatment of the Dong Son culture see: V. Goloubew, "L'âge du bronze au Tonkin et dans le Nord-Annam," BEFEO, XXIX (1929), pp. 1-46; V. Goloubew, *L' archéologie du Tonkin et les fouilles du Dong-Son*, Hanoi, 1937; R. von Heine-Geldern, "L'art prébouddhique de la Chine et de l'Asie du Sud-Est et son influence en Océanie," in *Revue des Arts Asiatiques*, XI (1937), no. 4, pp. 177-206; Paul Lévy, *Recherches préhistoriques dans la région de Mlu Prei, accompagnées des comparisons archéologiques*, Hanoi, 1943; H. Mansuy, *Le préhistoire en Indochine*, Paris, 1931.

18. The Muongs call their feudal lords *quan-lang*, which was the title of the sons of the legendary king of Van Lang, Hong (Le Thanh Khoi, *op. cit.*, p. 87, note 58). According to the Vietnamese historians of the fourteenth and fifteenth centuries, Van Lang was a feudal but decentralized state. Its inhabitants reached a certain level of civilization. They created arable land by burning the forests and worked the soil with the hoe. They lived on rice. They knew the use of bronze. The inhabitants of Van Lang were both fishermen and seafarers. They tattooed their bodies with pictures of crocodiles, dragons, snakes, and sea animals. They chewed betel and probably also blackened their teeth. (Huard and Durand, *op. cit.*, pp. 8-10; Le Thanh Khoi, *op. cit.*, pp. 82f.)

19. One of the reasons for polygamy among feudal rulers is their wish

to have as many sons as possible to be put at the head of provinces and fiefs. About polygamy in Vietnam generally, see La Giang: "La polygamie," in the review *Indochine*, March 16, 1944.

20. Emperor Wu Ti annexed Tongking and Annam together with the rest of Nam Viet, and divided it into three military districts, Giao Chi (Tongking), Chu Chen (Than Hoa) and Jenan (North Annam). Giao is often spelled Chiao. The reader will have to keep in mind that place names differ, depending on whether Chinese or Vietnamese designations are used. There is also a discrepancy in spelling in English and French (e. g. Tongking and Tonkin).

21. The Chinese word *ti* means emperor. Han Wu Ti means literally The Mighty Emperor. Like the Japanese rulers of today, the Chinese emperors had two names. They used one as long as they were alive, while the second was a posthumous epithet. Under their *miao-hao* or temple name they became known in history. The nomenclature of Chinese emperors changed slightly with the dynasties. The word *ti* was added to the temple name only until the Tang dynasty (seventh century A.D.). The transcription of Chinese names is even more difficult than that of Vietnamese names. Many ways of so-called "Romanization" of the Chinese script have been invented. They are, however, meaningful for the scholar only. The general reader would only be confused by them. This book, therefore, endeavors the simplest rendering of Chinese and Vietnamese names.

22. The kingdom of Ch'in, also rendered Chin, Tsin or Ts'in, (to which Needham in his *Science and Civilization in China* adds the spelling Chhin), gave the whole nation the name of Chinese, exclusively used by foreigners. The Chinese call themselves "The Sons of Han," after the dynasty that reigned over the country from 202 B.C. to 220 A.D. The Chinese refer to their country as Chung-kuo, the "Middle Kingdom."

23. In ancient Chinese history, dating is difficult and uncertain. According to Latourette, *A Short History of the Far East*, p. 82, the Hsia dynasty came to an end and the Shang dynasty began in 1765 B.C., but the author admits that this "traditional" date might be in error by several centuries. Grousset believes that the Shangs took the place of the Hsias in 1558 B.C. For the Shangs the "traditional" dates according to Latourette are 1765–1122 B.C., while Grousset assigns to the second dynasty the years from 1558 to 1050 B.C., qualifying his statement with a question mark. (*Op. cit.*, p. 16.) For an extended treatment of the Hsia and Shang dynasties see H. C. Creel, *op. cit.*, and O. Lattimore, *op. cit.* Needham, *op. cit.*, Vol. I, p. 78, gives still different dates: Hsia c. 2000 to c. 1520, and Shang c. 1520 to c. 1030.

24. "Everything that took place before 841 B.C. has to remain undated." (Paul Marcel Granet, *La civilisation chinoise*, Paris 1929). For a detailed account of the Chou period see O. Franke, *op. cit.*, Vol. I, parts 1 and 2; O. Lattimore, *op. cit.*

25. Skeletal remains of a very primitive form of man (*Homo Pekinensis*) have been discovered near Peking. It is, however, not yet proved that the Peking man was the ancestor of the present Chinese. But it is established that a neolithic culture flourished in northern China and Manchuria before the dawn of history. Between one branch of this neolithic civilization and historic China some continuity has been proven. The Hsia dynasty is identified with this neolithic culture, while the Shangs developed a rich Bronze Age civilization. Bronze was used earlier in western Asia than in China. The use of that metal might therefore be an importation. On the other hand, the bronze technique of the Shang period is different from any used outside of China. So are the designs and forms of writing. The question remains open whether Chinese bronze culture is of native origin or came to China by known overland routes from the west or south. All three theories, that of Chinese origin, that of a western, and that of southern importation, have their followers among scholars. Some authors believe that both the Chinese and the Sumerian civilization in the Euphrates-Tigris valley have a common origin in an ancient culture located in the oases of the Tarim basin. Latourette, *Short History of the Far East,* pp. 79ff; Louzon, *La Chine: Ses trois millénaires d'histoire, ses cinquante ans de révolution,* Paris, 1954, p. 15. See in particular Needham, *op. cit.*, Vol I, Historical Introduction.

26. Important discoveries were made at An Yang in 1934 and 1935 which threw new light on early Chinese history and civilization. An Yang was the capital of China in the later years of the Shang dynasty (twelfth century B.C.). The excavations testify to an advanced material civilization already at its height, but give little information about the beginning of Chinese culture. Cf. Grousset, *The Rise and Splendor of the Chinese Empire,* Berkeley, 1953, pp. 18ff.

27. As the mud the Yellow River carries year after year has raised its bed, the riverside dwellers have been obliged to build up their embankments proportionately, with the result that the river has ended by flowing in a great gutter above the level of the plain. "A paradoxical situation," Grousset calls it, "and one fraught with extreme danger" (*op. cit.,* p. 9). The Yellow River valley is frequently exposed to the most terrible inundations, ravaging hundreds of square miles of cultivated soil. After such an extended inundation, the Yellow River sometimes changes its course. In historical times, since about 1000 B.C., the Yellow River has changed its

118

bed completely four times, not to count the many small changes occurring almost yearly. The latest great change was recorded in 1887, when the Yellow River temporarily became a tributary of the Yangtse Kiang. The location of the mouth of the Yellow River has shifted over three hundred miles in historical times. (Louzon, *op. cit.*, p. 10).

28. The Yangtse, called the Blue River or the Long River by the Chinese, is less liable to inundation than the Yellow River. Also, the southern climate of its valley is more favorable than that of the Yellow River in the north. The northern river challenged the Chinese to become the great builders of dams, while other difficulties they encountered in the north made them the industrious people they are. Whenever China was strong, its power centered in the north; whenever it was weak, its center of gravity was in the middle or the south. (Luzon, *op. cit.*, pp. 18ff.)

29. About the use of the term "vagabond" by ancient Chinese historians for the landless, vagrant population and for the turning of these "vagabonds" into a soldier class during the unification of China by the rulers of the principality of Ch'in (fourth and third centuries B.C.), cf. Luzon, *op. cit.*, pp. 29f.

30. The Chinese is now also widely known for his talents as a merchant, but these are qualities he acquired later and, as it were, reluctantly. Confucianism is an antitrade philosophy. In Confucius' teachings the scholars (mandarins) took the first place, followed by farmers and artisans, the traders being fourth in rank, having precedence only over the fifth and lowest class, the soldiers. Soon after Confucius, who lived in the sixth century B.C., commerce began to prosper during the wars of unification and the merchants acquired prominence. In fact, the rise of the trader class went hand in hand with the rise of the army. To supply the armies made many rich, though they were first not highly respected and were forbidden to acquire land (Latourette, *op. cit.*, pp. 84f.). For the relationship between Chinese philosophy and Chinese social structure cf. also Y. L. Fung, *History of Chinese Philosophy*, Peiping, 1937, and E. R. Hughes, *Chinese Philosophy in Classical Times*, London, 1942.

31. In the Chou period, China was split into many small states. The Chou king, whose title was *wang*, was vested with ritual functions which none of the other princes was allowed to perform. But his authority was small; the real power was held by the heads of the various states. These states were bound together by the tie of a common culture. Latourette (*op. cit.*, p. 84) calls them a kind of league of nations. Warfare was regulated and restricted by custom. In the relations between higher and subordinate princes Chinese feudalism resembled European feaudalism.

119

Grousset (*op. cit.*, p. 22) speaks of "Chou barons" and voices the opinion that ancient China from the eighth to the third century B.C. could provide Western students of the Middle Ages with material for a comparative study of feudal systems (p. 24). At the height of the Chinese feudal age, seventeen hundred such small states were counted. Their number was reduced to a few hundred in the eighth, and to about fifty in the third century B.C.

32. About Chinese intellectual history and the impact of Chinese civilization upon the peoples of Asia cf. the monumental seven-volume work by Joseph Needham, *Science and Civilization in China*. Two of the projected seven volumes are already published by the Cambridge University Press in England. Volume I contains, on pp. 73-149, an up-to-date, excellent introduction to Chinese history with a most complete bibliography. Maps on pp. 113 and 121 show how far Chinese domination extended into the Indochinese peninsula in different periods.

33. Confucius was born, according to tradition, in 551 B.C. The date usually given for his death is 479 B.C. (Latourette, *op. cit.*, p. 88). For a thorough study of Confucius and Confucianism see Y. L. Fung, *op. cit.*; H. G. Creel, *Confucius, the Man and the Myth*, New York, 1949; W. E. Soothill, *The Analects of Confucius*, Yokohama, 1910; A. Wiley, *The Analects of Confucius*, New York, 1939. For a good short treatment see Grousset, *op. cit.*, pp. 28ff. Louzon (*op. cit.*, p. 12) gives a Marxist's view of Confucius. He calls his philosophy "petite-bourgeoise" and his morals "utilitarian," comparing him with Benjamin Franklin and Bentham.

34. "By the −6th century we are indeed entering the greatest period of intellectual flowering of ancient China. The 'hundred schools' of philosophers were at their height between −500 and −250." (Needham, *op. cit.*, p. 95.)

35. There is some uncertainty about the precise date of the first conquest of Korea by the Chinese. Le Thanh Khoi (*op. cit.*, p. 96) puts it at 108 B.C., Louzon (*op. cit.*, p. 32) at 102 B.C. Latourette (*op. cit.*, p. 102) refrains from giving an exact date.

36. Many good representations of chariots are preserved on bas-reliefs of the Han period. A chariot, harnessed for four horses, consisted of a short narrow frame, open at the rear and mounted on two wheels. The Chinese war chariot carried three men: the driver, a lancer on the right, and an archer on the left. The charioteers wore breastplates, armlets, knee pieces, all three made of oxhide, and shields painted in brilliant colors. The attacks by Chinese war chariots were probably very similar to those of the Assyrians and early Greeks, as described in Homer's *Iliad*. Like the Greeks and Trojans in the famous epic, Chinese war lords of

120

the Chou period exchanged boasts before opening battle. Sometimes they drank together and even exchanged weapons before fighting. Warfare was carried out in conformity with a strict code of courtesy. The vanquished were spared if they had given proof of their bravery. (Grousset, *op. cit.*, pp. 25ff.)

37. For a good short treatment of this period in Chinese history see Fitzgerald, *op. cit.*, pp. 55-73. This book contains also two maps on pp. 54 and 68, showing the location of the different warring states of the feudal period. The transition from battle chariot to cavalry was first accomplished in the state of Chao in 307 B.C. The kingdom of Chao was situated in the northern portion of the modern province of Shansi and was often invaded by the Huns of Mongolia. The war chariots of Chao proved to be too slow against the Hun horsemen and were therefore replaced by mounted archers. The art of warfare made progress with the invention of siege machines, movable towers, and catapults, which constituted a veritable artillery. At the same time warfare became unbelievably cruel. Grousset (*op. cit.*, p. 39) gives some hair-raising examples. About the Chinese feudal age and its warfare cf. also Louzon, *op. cit.*, pp. 22-24.

38. The state of Ch'in enjoyed a great advantage because of its geographical situation. From the high valley of the Wei it dominated the rich plains of Honan, the chief prize in all this rivalry. (Grousset, *op. cit.*, p. 39.) The historian Ssu-ma Ch'ien (or Se-ma Ts'ien), the Herodotus of China, who died about 80 B.C., drew attention to this: "The country of Ch'in was a state whose position alone predestined it to victory. . . . With twenty thousand men it could hold back a million spearmen . . . " (Cf. Chavannes, *op. cit.*). Another factor was the military fitness of the people of Ch'in, whom Grousset calls a race of pioneers and soldier-farmers (id.). A minister or regent, Wei Yang, is credited by an annalist of the year 359 B.C. with having introduced order, authority, and discipline in the state of Ch'in. He later became a victim of the discipline he introduced and was cruelly executed by the new king, whom, as an heir to the throne, he once reprimanded.

39. "Since the advent of Chinese autocracy the latifundia had increased and the class of small landowners had diminished, thus adding to the numbers of dependents and slaves. In times of famine especially, the poor people were reduced to selling all their patrimony, and even to selling themselves and their children into slavery."—Grousset, *op. cit.*, p. 64. A Chinese usurper who had made himself emperor in A.D. 9, Wang Mang, sought to combat this enslavement of the rural population. "One sees," he said, "the fields of the rich stretching in hundreds and

121

thousands, while the poor have not land enough to plant a needle. Furthermore, slave markets have been established where men are sold like horses and cattle . . . " (About Wang Mang's reforms and their collapse see Grousset, *op. cit.*, pp. 65f.; O. Franke, *op. cit.*, Vol. I; Latourette, *op. cit.*, pp. 104f.)

40. At the onset of the "period of warring kingdoms," the territory of Ch'in was about identical with the modern province of Shensi. In 331 B.C., the kingdom of Wei was conquered (today the province of Shansi). In a series of wars waged with the utmost cruelty the other rivaling principalities were destroyed. The work of unification was accomplished by King Chang, who ascended the throne of Ch'in in 264 B.C. at the age of thirteen. In 221 B.C. he completed the forceful unification of China at the age of thirty-eight and assumed the title Huang Ti (Supreme Ruler or Emperor). He is also known in Chinese history as Ch'in Shih Huang Ti, i.e., first Emperor of the Ch'in Dynasty. Grousset, *op. cit.*, calls him a Chinese Caesar. For a more detailed treatment of the First Emperor and his period (Ch'in dynasty) see: D. Bodde, *China's First Unifier: A Study of the Ch'in Dynasty as Seen in the Life of Li Ssu*, Leiden, 1938; E. Chavannes, *op. cit.*; O. Franke, *op. cit.*, Vol. I, pp. 223-267; O. Lattimore, *Inner Asian Frontiers of China*, London, 1940.

41. "It is entirely fitting that our word China as a designation of a thus unified empire should be derived historically from Ch'in, the dynasty whose rulers first applied to so much of the land the principles on which the subsequent realm rested."—Latourette, *op. cit.*, p. 96.

42. Needham, *op. cit.*, pp. 96-7. Reference should be made in this context to the fundamental study of "oriental" (and especially Chinese) society by Karl A. Wittfogel: *Oriental Despotism, A Comparative Study of Total Power*, Yale University Press, 1957. Wittfogel describes state-created, large hydraulic works as the basis of total power in the hands of a centralized bureaucracy.

43. This renegade from Confucianism was the philosopher Li Ssu, minister of the First Emperor, Shih Huang Ti. He is one of the outstanding figures of earlier Chinese history and much of the credit that went to Shih Huang Ti for the creation of a unified China is due to him. He had been in the service of the Ch'in king since 247 B.C. Confucian philosophy and morals seemed to Li Ssu to be useless for the Ch'in ruler. His need was for an ideology and a theory both Machiavellian and totalitarian. This was supplied by the so-called Realists or School of Law. "One of the principles of Realist government was mutual espionage. The people were to be organized into groups who were mutually responsible for each other and even obliged to denounce each other's crimes. A

122

member of the group who failed to do this was to be punished as though he had himself committed the crime."—Arthur Waley: *Three Ways of Thought in Ancient China*, Doubleday Anchor Book, p. 152.

44. This state of disintegration made it possible for General Trieu Da, who was governor of a new, large southern province, to proclaim its independence and to establish the state of Nam Viet in 207 B.C. He is the same Chinese general who conquered the kingdom of Au Lac. According to tradition, this took place in 208 B.C., one year before Trieu Da's defection from the Chinese Empire. According to Maspéro (*op. cit.*), however, Au Lac recognized Trieu Da's suzerainty only in 181 B.C. Trieu Da's kingdom extended into Vietnam, but its bulk was situated in southern China with the capital near the site of present-day Canton.

45. Re-unification of China under the Han dynasty took place in February, 202 B.C. Historians, however, usually date the Han dynasty from 207 B.C. to 220 A.D., including the five years that form the transition from the Ch'in to the Han. For a detailed treatment of the Han dynasty see O. Franke, *op. cit.*, Vol. I, pp. 268-431; R. Grousset, *China*, New York, 1934, ch. I; O. Lattimore, *op. cit.*; Pan Ku, *The History of the Former Han Dynasty*—a critical translation with annotations by H. H. Dubs, 2 Vols., Baltimore, 1938 and 1944.

46. "Never in human experience has so extensive an area with so large a population been held together culturally and politically over so long a period of time."—Latourette, *op. cit.*, p. 96.

47. Grousset, *op. cit.*, p. 60. Emperor Han Wu Ti, after whom the Chinese call themselves "sons of Han," reigned from 140 to 87 B.C.

48. There were originally nine military districts. In 48 or 46 B.C. two were abolished. The remaining seven formed the Chinese province of Giao Chi. The name of Giao Chi, which referred originally to the whole southern territory, comprising the Chinese provinces of Kwangtung and Kwangsi, as well as Tongking and northern Annam, was later, 264 A.D., applied only to the Vietnamese part of the territory. Cf. Le Thanh Khoi, *op. cit.*, pp. 98-100; E. Gaspardone, "Matériaux pour servir à l'histoire d'Annam. La géographie de Li Wen-Fong," BEFEO, XXIX, pp. 63-105; Aurousseau, *op cit.*, pp. 205, 242; Cl. Madrolle, "Le Tonkin ancien," BEFEO, XXXVII, pp. 1ff.; H. Maspéro, "L'expédition de Ma Yuan," BEFEO, Nos. 3, 11.

49. Economic conditions of China had deteriorated during the first century B.C. Property became more and more concentrated in a few hands while the number of landless peasants grew. Slavery, unknown to China before the Han, was first tolerated and later legalized. Emperor Han Wu Ti tried several measures to stop the accumulation of landhold-

123

ings. He forbade the use of funds derived from commerce and industry for the purchase of land. He even decreed that no family could possess more land and more slaves than a fixed maximum that varied with the size of the family. These laws were never obeyed. The Han dynasty was overthrown by Wang Mang (3 A.D.), who tried to introduce a sort of state capitalism into China and declared soil and slaves inalienable. His reforms were a complete failure. In A.D. 14, dams broke, vast areas were inundated, the harvest was destroyed, and famine gripped the land. This caused the revolt of the Red Eyebrows, the overthrow of Wang Mang, and the restoration of the Han in 22 A.D. In these years of trouble, many Chinese left their country and went to Vietnam in search of a new home. Cf. Louzon, *op. cit.*, pp. 40-43; K. A. Wittfogel and Feng Chia-sheng, *History of Chinese Society*, Philadelphia, 1949. See note 50 below.

50. "Under the usurper Wang Mang, many families of Han officials and scholars came to Tich Quang (or Si Kuang, governor of Vietnam from 1 to 25 A.D.) in order to seek refuge. These new arrivals certainly encouraged and helped the governor in his efforts to introduce Chinese civilization."—Maspéro, "Etudes d'histoire d'Annam," BEFEO, Vol. XVI. Cf. also Le Thanh Khoi, *op. cit.*, pp. 99f. Si Kuang forced the inhabitants of Vietnam to follow Chinese rites in their wedding ceremonies and to wear shoes and caps in Chinese fashion.

51. The inhabitants of the Vietnamese province of Cuu Chan erected a temple in honor of the Chinese governor Jen Yen for the technical and administrative innovations he introduced during his governorship (29 to 33 A.D.). (Le Thanh Khoi, *op. cit.*, p. 100; C. Sainson, *Mémoire sur l'Annam*, Peking, 1896.) The building of this temple might, however, have come about like the erection of the Stalin monuments in Budapest and Vienna.

52. For instance, the Ye Lang, the Tien, and the Nan Chac.

53. Another striking example for the advantage of the geographical position on the fringe of an empire is Korea. To a lesser degree, the rule also applies to Burma and Thailand.

54. In China, meanwhile, the "usurper" Wang Mang had been defeated by the "legitimists" and the Han dynasty had been re-established (29 A.D.). The Han moved their capital from the Wei valley to the east and therefore became known as the Eastern Han. The governor of Vietnam, Ten Jang, recognized the new regime. The revolt was staged against his successor, Su Ting (To Dinh in Vietnamese). See Le Thanh Khoi, *op. cit.*, p. 100.

55. The three parts are referred to as Cuu Chan, Nhat Nam, and Ho Pho. None of the old historians of this period seem to know what name

the Trung sisters gave to their country; they devoted much space to that
episode but said nothing about the reaction of the Vietnamese peasantry
to the Chinese occupation.

56. Huard and Durand, *op. cit.*, p. 13. It is almost impossible to ascertain the exact borders of states and provinces at that time. It probably
cannot be done for any period prior to the coming of the Europeans. In
these times of eternal warfare, borders were subject to continual changes,
as e.g., between Vietnam and Champa.

57. Ma Yuan (in Vietnamese Ma Vien), then over seventy years old,
was assigned the task of reconquering Vietnam by the Han emperor
Kwang Wu in 41 A.D. He fulfilled his task in A.D. 43. During his campaign
he also subjugated the Yi Chou, a tribe in present Yunnan, who threatened
the first Chinese-Burma Road, which led from the capital of Lo Yang
through the provinces of Szechwan and Yunnan to the Irrawaddy River,
at the mouth of which the Chinese met traders from India. For the
Chinese reconquest of Vietnam and the defeat of the Trung sisters see
Le Thanh Khoi, *op. cit.*, p. 101; M. Kaltenmark, "Le dompteur des
flots," in *Han Hiue*, 1948, Vol. III, fasc. 1-2; Maspéro, *op. cit.*, p. 15;
E. Gaspardone, *Les pays du Sud et la Chine des derniers Han et des
trois royaumes*, Cours, 1950-1951 of the Collège de France.

58. The Trung sisters, Trung Trac and Trung Nhi, are celebrated in
Vietnamese history as the first heroines of the independence of their
country. Two pagodas have been erected to honor them, the Pagoda of
the Two Sisters (Hai Ba) in Hanoi, and the Hat Mon Pagoda in the
province of Sontay. (Huard and Durand, *op. cit.*, p. 13.) "A comrade in
combat of the sisters was Phung Thi Chinh, wife of Dinh Luong of Phu
Nghia (Province of Son Tay). Intelligent and very astute, she commanded the army of the center with the title of Thi Noi Tuong Quan,
enjoying the complete confidence of the two sisters. When the troops of
Ma Vien attacked her, she was pregnant but leading the battle all the
same. Surrounded, she delivered at the front itself, after which, putting
the newborn baby on her back and brandishing a sword in each hand,
she opened a bloody route in the ranks of the enemy and escaped.
Learning later that the vanquished queens had committed suicide, she
followed their example."—Quoted from an address by Mme. Ngo Dinh
Nhu before the International Women's Association in Saigon, October
29, 1956. Reprinted in *The Times of Vietnam*, March 9, 1957.

59. The Vietnamese Communist historian Than Luong, following the
Stalinist pattern in World War II, emphasizes the national aspects of
Vietnamese history to the ridiculous extent of identification with dynastic
history. Dealing with the Trung sisters, he writes, "In 39 A.D. a great

movement of popular discontent broke out against the Chinese authorities represented by the cruel To-Dinh. This first *national* uprising was led by two women, the sisters Trung-Trac and Trung-Nhi, scions of the indigenous nobility. . . . The grateful people later built a temple in memory of these two first *national* heroines." (Than Luong, *Histoire résumée du Viet-Nam*, Hanoi, 1955, p. 6.)

60. In the first years after the Chinese reconquest, higher education was withheld from the Vietnamese in order to hinder the development of a class of officials able to administer their own country. Even well-educated Vietnamese were barred from entrance into the civil service. Only under the emperor Ming Ti (58–75) did a Vietnamese, Truong Trong, become prefect of Kin Cheng. Toward the end of the Han dynasty another Vietnamese, Ly Tien, was even appointed governor of the whole province of Giao Chi. About the same time or somewhat later, several Vietnamese filled high posts in the administration of China proper. Ly Cam served in the palace guard, and two other Vietnamese were sub-prefects in two Chinese provinces. The appearance of a class of Vietnamese civil servants coincides with the decadence of the Han rule. At this time, many Vietnamese students excelled at institutes of higher learning in China, as some did seventeen hundred years later in French universities (Le Thanh Khoi, *op. cit.*, p. 106; R. des Rotours, *Nouvelle histoire des Tang*, Paris, 1932; Sainson, *op. cit.*, pp. 505f.).

61. The fall of the Han dynasty split the Chinese empire into three parts, Wei in the north, Chou, which covered approximately the present province of Szechwan, and Wu in the lower Yangtse valley. Vietnam became part of the kingdom of Wu. In 264, the kingdom of Chou was conquered by the rival state of Wei, which shortly after changed its name to Tsin (or Ch'in). In 280, Tsin also absorbed Wu and thus for a short time re-established Chinese unity. The years from 221 to 264 (or 265—dating is still unprecise in Chinese history, even at this time) are known as the period of the Three Kingdoms, celebrated by the most famous of Chinese historical novels, *The Romance of the Three Kingdoms*. (Le Thanh Khoi, *op. cit.*, pp. 113-115; Latourette, *op cit.*, p. 116.)

62. The Vietnamese version of his name is Si Nhiep. His life story has been somewhat obscured by legends and he even became an object of a veritable religious cult (Chesneaux, *op. cit.*, p. 25). He is credited especially with the introduction of Chinese classical studies in Vietnam (Duong Quang Ham, *op. cit.*, p. 24).

63. Also Ly Ban (other versions of his name are Li Bi and Ly Bi). He was a descendant of a Chinese family. After his revolution had triumphed he made himself ruler of Vietnam (544) under the title Ly Nam

126

De. Whether he is to be styled as king or as emperor is a matter of taste and interpretation. The Vietnamese word for king is *vuong*, ostensibly derived from the Chinese term for ruler, *wong* or *wang*. Ly Bon's kingdom covered the whole of Tongking and Annam, but its independence lasted only about three years. Ly Bon was defeated by the Chinese general Chen Pa Sien and fled to Laos, but the then half-savage Laotians cut off his head and sent it to the Chinese general. The story of further Vietnamese resistance against the Chinese after 547, connected with a lieutenant of Ly Bon, Trieu Quang Phuc, was proved by Maspéro to be legendary (Grousset, *op. cit.,* p. 603; Duong Quang Ham, *op cit.,* p. 25; Maspéro, *op. cit.,* BEFEO, Vol. XXII).

64. Some authors consider Ly Bon's short-lived kingdom as the cradle of the future Vietnamese state and Ly Bon as the founder of the first truly historical Vietnamese dynasty (Le Thanh Khoi, *op. cit.,* p. 119; H. Maspéro, "La dynastie des Ly antérieur," BEFEO, XVI, pp. 1-26). Thai Van Kiem, in *Viet-Nam d'hier et d'aujourd'hui,* Saigon, 1956, p. 46, even speaks of "several Vietnamese dynasties" between 544 and 601, calling them "ephemeral and sometimes rival," and admitting that in this "very confused period" the Chinese were always able to maintain themselves in Vietnam. See note 67 of this Chapter and section 6 and 8, Chapter III.

65. A land route from India through Assam and Upper Burma to the Chinese province of Yunnan was in use as early as 128 B.C. This predecessor of the modern Burma Road was already known to Ptolemy about 200 A.D. Cf. G. Coedès, *Textes d'auteurs grecs et latins relatifs à l'Extrême-Orient depuis le IVe siècle av. J.-C. jusqu'au XIVe siècle,* Paris, 1910. The connection between China and India via Assam and Burma was constantly threatened by the Thai. Historically and economically more important was the Silk Road, connecting western Asia with China through the oases of the Tarim basin. It was opened in the first century of our era. The Silk Road served not only trade but also the exchange of ideas. Buddhist missionaries entered China via the Silk Road. It reached the summit of its traffic under the Mongol domination of China and lost importance when the Ming built a great fleet. After that, commerce between Europe and East Asia followed the sea route around India. Sea trade was, of course, important since earliest antiquity. In the time of the Mongols, when Marco Polo visited China, that country exported silk, satin, gold brocade, and sandalwood to India and received in return pepper, ginger, musselin, cotton fabrics, pearls, and diamonds.

66. Shortly after the repression of the Trieu Au revolution, the name of Annam appeared for the first time in reference to the country of Vietnam. It was originally the title of a Chinese marshal who "pacified"

Indochina. The word, used for the first time about 264, means "Pacifier of the South," and was transferred later from the marshal to the country. "Pacifying," of course, then had the same meaning as sixteen hundred years later, when Admiral Bonard "pacified" Cochinchina for the French in 1863. In the third and fourth centuries, when the word Annam came into use, the word Giao was applied only to the territory of the former kingdom of Au Lac, i.e., North Vietnam or Tongking, and a part of Central Vietnam, which the French later called Annam.

67. French historians enumerate fifteen dynasties in Vietnamese history, of which four held power before independence was permanently established. See notes 2 to 6, Chapter III. For a full list of all Vietnamese rulers see Hall, *op. cit.*, pp. 754-758. The nomenclature of Vietnamese rulers offers the same difficulty as that of Chinese and Japanese emperors. They assumed another name when they ascended the throne, and were spelled differently by Vietnamese, French, and English authors.

68. Le Thanh Khoi (*op. cit.*, p. 113) oversimplifies the historical situation by stating that the Sino-Vietnamese ruling class and intellectual elite fought in isolation from the people, and by adhering to the romantic viewpoint that national consciousness was born in the village. His only argument for this theory is that the village population "preserved not only its racial individuality but also its language."

Chapter III

Nine Hundred Years
of Independence
and Growth

1.

THE country of Vietnam was reborn as an independent state after its one thousand years as a Chinese province during the tenth century of our era. One of the many bloody encounters between Chinese imperial and Vietnamese rebel soldiers in the Red River valley took place in the year 939. The Vietnamese, as often before and after, were both brave and lucky. They defeated the armies of their oppressors on land and water, drove them out of the country, and thus broke Chinese rule over territories that had once been, and were destined to become again, those of an independent non-Chinese state.

After the battles of 939 were over and the Chinese thrown out, the winners celebrated their triumph with customary abandon. But they could hardly have known the full significance of their victory for the history of Vietnam. Twice before in their lifetime, in 906 and 931, the older ones had fought and defeated the Chinese and rejoiced in the humiliating departure of the enemy, only to see him return and reimplant his hated regime. Indeed, it took the valor of their sons and grandsons to secure for the Vietnamese fighters of the year 939 their unique historical fame. By defeating China's subsequent attempts to retake the Red River valley, they changed 939 from simply another year of Vietnamese military triumph into the founding year of a new Vietnamese state. The smaller dragon had at last become strong enough to refuse obedience to the bigger.

2.

Although by no means internally secure and out of danger from the Chinese, Vietnam, as a separate and independent state, had become a historical reality by the year 940. It was to exist as such, with only one brief interruption, for well over nine hundred years, ending in 1883, the year France succeeded in terminating her twenty-five-year struggle for the domination of the country.

The one interruption of Vietnam's nine centuries of independence was another period of Chinese rule. The Chinese, soon after Vietnam had fought herself free, made several attempts to regain what they called their former province of Giao.[1] Their invasions failed in the tenth, the eleventh, and no less than three times in the thirteenth century, while Vietnam's powerful northern neighbor was ruled by the Mongols under Kublai Khan. The country's extraordinary power of resistance against the Chinese was broken at the beginning of the fifteenth century, and Chinese rule was restored in 1407. But it lasted only twenty years and ended in such an upsurge of Vietnamese national vigor that the history of Vietnam, after 1427, can be said to have taken a new course.

3.

This Chinese interregnum divides the nine centuries of Vietnamese independence into two periods of almost equal length. The difference in the character of Vietnamese history of these two periods makes such a division not only convenient but also meaningful. Between 940 and 1400, Vietnam, after a painful beginning marred by civil wars and conditions close to chaos, developed a stable and efficient political regime. The central power of the state, built around a hereditary monarchy, was normally supreme, and medieval Vietnam, even in times of crisis, always was united under one government. The country went through many phases of disgraceful dynastic corruption and consequent political debility, but was always strong enough to repel all invasions from the north and to hold her own against vigorous aggression from her southern neighbors Champa and Cambodia. Yet in spite of her unity, her highly developed political organization, and her military strength, up to the fifteenth century, Vietnam as an independent state remained in size what it had been as a Chinese province. It consisted of the Red River valley, its mountainous back country, and a narrowing coastal strip running south like a spear into Champa, toward an uncertain border that moved back and forth with victory and defeat between the seventeenth and sixteenth parallels. When the Chinese retook Vietnam in 1407, ninety per cent of the territories that make up the present state of South Vietnam had not yet become Vietnamese.

4.

But the growth of Vietnam to her present size is not the only new feature of Vietnamese history after the Chinese interregnum of the fifteenth century. Champa had hardly been eliminated by the advancing Vietnamese when during the sixteenth century their growing country suffered its first political division. It lasted over fifty years. And the Vietnamese, in their historic "March to the South," were still far from the

Gulf of Siam when around 1620 their state, only thirty years after the first reunification, was split again into two contending halves. This second division of Vietnam lasted over 150 years, of which the first 50 were filled with fruitless attempts to reunite the country through war. A great nationwide revolution, whose slow but irresistible course started soon after 1770, succeeded briefly in making the two Vietnams into one. But unity became permanent only in 1802, after a long civil war won by the South with foreign technical advice and military assistance.

The unity of the country, which as a oneness of language, culture, and national feeling had existed even during long periods of political separation, was one of the most striking features of nineteenth-century precolonial Vietnam. Only the spokesmen of French imperialism, in order to facilitate French conquest and domination of Vietnam, disregarded this historical fact. As a result, the French, while putting an end to the nine centuries of Vietnamese independence, decided also to deny the unity of Vietnam and made every effort to destroy it. For the first time in Vietnamese history, and in violation of its own well-founded pattern, the country was divided into three parts: Tongking, Annam, and Cochinchina.

5.

The course of Vietnamese history from the exit of the Chinese in 939 to the coming of the French is also reflected in the history of Vietnam's ruling houses, which, for many centuries and up to a recent date, was the main subject of all Vietnamese historical writing. To this very day, dynastic names and dates have remained, as it were, the student's chief guideposts of chronological orientation. Such names and dates therefore cannot be dispensed with in a modern history of Vietnam either.[2] But in order to fill the empty frame of dynastic succession with substance and meaning, these names and dates must be related to great and decisive events.

The first period of Vietnamese independence up to the year 1010 was a time of successive crises. Native institutions of state power unsustained by foreign garrisons evolved slowly and under stress and strain. During these seventy years Vietnam used up three dynasties.

This contrasts strongly with the long period of almost four hundred years after the achievement of political consolidation. From 1010 to 1400 Vietnam had only two ruling houses, each one lasting approximately two hundred years.

The depth of the crisis that brought the Chinese back to Vietnam in 1407 is confirmed by the fact that the dynasty whose glory had been the defeat of the Mongols could be pushed from the throne by a high official of the court. The reign of the usurper ended with the coming of the Chinese.

The greatest of all Vietnamese dynasties was born in 1427 out of a war of liberation that lasted ten years. This dynasty remained in possession of the throne for more than three and a half centuries and survived both partitions of Vietnam in impotent glory. During the first partition, which was brought about by the rise of another usurper, the legitimate dynasty headed only the smaller half of Vietnam, but during the second, its emperors were recognized as the nominal heads of the country both by the two houses actually ruling and by the subjects of divided Vietnam. The end of this dynasty came only during the thirty years of civil war that preceded the country's reunification in 1802.

After 1802, a member of the family that had ruled the South during the hundred-and-fifty-year period of political division became the founder of the last dynasty of Vietnam.

6.

Of the many questions of dynastic history a Vietnamese student is still expected to answer, those relating to the dynasties before the establishment of independence in 939 should be dismissed forthwith. These dynasties are either legendary or not authentically Vietnamese.[3] The history of the Vietnamese dynasties should begin with the known history of Vietnam as an independent state.

Because the great rebel Ly Bon, after his successful uprising against the Chinese, had proclaimed himself emperor in 544, he is usually also regarded as the founder of a Vietnamese dynasty listed under the name of the Earlier Ly. However, this not only increases the existing confusion about the number of authentic dynasties; it also raises the question of whether the independence of Vietnam was not already established long before the generally accepted date.[4] Ly Bon had indeed proclaimed the country's political independence, but the four years of its precarious existence weigh little against the following four hundred during which the Chinese, with only short interruptions, continued to oppress Vietnam.[5] Dynastic history, therefore, should begin only with the year 939, when history is no longer legend and independence has become an unquestionable historical fact.

7.

This view reduces the Vietnamese dynasties to a small and wieldy number and also permits one to attach meaning to dates and names.

There were, to begin with, the three dynasties of the troublesome first seventy years of independence. Their names were the Ngo, the Dinh, and the Earlier Le.

Against these ephemeral three should be set the three dy-

nasties to whose names the Vietnamese historians have unanimously attached the adjective "great." They were the Ly,
the Tran, and the Later Le. Together, they covered a time
span of more than seven hundred years. The Ly consolidated
the new state after 1010 and headed it until 1224. The Tran
effectively ruled and defended Vietnam during most of the
succeeding two centuries. The Later Le started out most vigorously after freeing Vietnam from the Chinese in 1427, but their
strength did not last. Although every Vietnamese emperor
from 1427 to 1787 was a descendent of the first great Le, after
the Le had been on the throne about one hundred years the
country was governed by two powerful feudal families, who
eventually divided Vietnam into two separate states. The rulers
of the North were the Trinh, those of the South the Nguyen.

Only two usurpers broke this long line of dynastic continuity. The first one, Ho Qui Ly, lasted from 1400 to 1407.
The second, Mac Dang Dung, who took the throne in 1527,
had not yet achieved uncontested control of the entire country
when the Le and their later masters, the Trinh and Nguyen,
began the war that was to eliminate the Mac in 1592.

The end of the Le, as well as that of the Trinh in the North
and the Nguyen in the South, came in the course of Vietnam's
great revolution of the 1770's and 1780's. For a brief time it
looked as if the victorious leaders of the revolution, three
brothers named Tay Son after their native village, had given
Vietnam the new dynasty required by a new age. But they
succumbed to Nguyen Anh, a lone survivor of the family that
had ruled the South.

Nguyen Anh was the man who in 1802 founded the last
Vietnamese dynasty. The Nguyen emperors led Vietnam into
hopeless isolation from the West and headed her ineffective
resistance against the French; they ended in resentful acceptance of the colonial regime. The dynasty expired only with the
dismissal of Bao Dai in October, 1955.

8.

To this bare outline of Vietnamese dynastic history the objection may be raised that it disregards the earlier brief periods of independence established by a number of successful revolts. But if there is merit in accepting Ly Bon or others as rulers of an independent Vietnam, it lies only in the suggestion that independence was not the result of one victorious battle nor of that series of battles won by the Vietnamese between 906 and 939. The struggle for independence lasted almost as long as the rule of the Chinese. It began with the revolt of the Trung sisters in the year 39 of our era and undoubtedly came closer to permanent success under Ly Bon in 544 than at any other time before the beginning of the tenth century.

Ly Bon's uprising was not the only one rewarded with temporary success. Of the ten major rebellions on record,[6] at least three produced a functioning Vietnamese administration whose armies kept the Chinese out of the Red River valley for several years. But their leaders all lacked the support of a united and fanatically determined population, without which the small country was unable to cope with the overwhelming military strength of the returning Chinese.

It appears that the first two revolts with a measure of popular support were those of Mai Tuc Loan in 722 and of Phung Hung in 791. But the condition necessary for success, as well as the spirit of the people, needed another century and a half to ripen.

9.

The most important one of these conditions—a weakening of Chinese imperial power—came about through the fall of the Tang dynasty at the beginning of the tenth century. The reign of the Tang had lasted almost three hundred years.[7] After centuries of decline, China had recovered under their rule through imperial conquests and agrarian reforms, and had reached its apex of power, culture, and material civilization. The end of the Tang was caused by the same social evil that had undermined the power and glory of the Han—the uncontrollable increase in great landholdings, perennial producer of landless and starving millions who threatened the existence of the empire more often than any enemy from abroad.[8] As in the case of the Han, it was a chief of bandits who destroyed the power of the Tang, and another bandit leader who took the emperor's throne in 907 and occupied it for sixteen years, after first removing and then murdering the last of the Tang, a boy of thirteen. Acting under the same necessity as the rulers of the declining Roman Empire, the Tang had called on barbarians from the North to sustain the unity and order of imperial China, already ravaged by agrarian revolts since 874. But the presence of these barbarians[9] inside the Great Wall only increased the political chaos that spread during the agony of the Tang. In southern China alone, seven kingdoms arose after 902, and five different dynasties succeeded one another in the North within fifty years. Only after 960, when the dynasty of the Sung assumed power, did order and imperial unity slowly return.

By that time, however, Vietnam had already been independent for over twenty years. Independence was achieved through a series of upheavals that had started in 906 and prompted the Chinese to send big armies into the rebellious Red River valley on two occasions. But when the Vietnamese leader Ngo Quyen defeated and expelled the Chinese in 939,[10] they decided to give up, at least for the time being. Ngo Quyen became the founder of the first authentic Vietnamese dynasty.

137

10.

However it soon became apparent that the Vietnamese chiefs and nobles were not at all able to keep abreast of these events. Nor did most of the earlier rulers show themselves equal to the greatness of their task. The days of triumph after the struggle against the common enemy had hardly passed when an outbreak of general disorder, manifestly inspired by the greed and ambition of the local nobles and provincial chiefs, threatened the unity and security of the young state. Ngo Quyen himself was a capable ruler, but he died in 944 without having subdued the forces tending to split the territory of Vietnam into private domains of feudal families. His heirs all lacked the mettle to succeed where he himself had failed. The Ngo dynasty, fortunately, lasted only thirty years, but during twenty of those years the new kingdom offered the sad spectacle of political murder, dynastic intrigue, feudal effrontery, and royal emasculation. By 966, when the dynasty of the Sung began to reassemble the shattered Chinese empire, the Red River valley had no less than a dozen autonomous rival chiefs, omnipotent within their domains, powerless beyond them, and unfit to take care of the needs or impose the duties of a national administration—needs and duties the neglect of which would spread famine irrespective of local powers and provincial borders established by the feudal lords.

It was a peasant by upbringing, the old annals say, who saved Vietnam in 968. His name was Dinh Bo Linh. He overthrew the last feeble Ngo and reunited the country under the name of Dai Co Viet by defeating the countless provincial potentates. For this he was called the "king of the thousand victories." He became the founder of the second Vietnamese dynasty, that of the Dinh. After Bo Linh had beaten the lords, he established a hierarchy of civil and military officials in order to strengthen the central authority of the state against local interference and obstruction. The prospect of being either boiled in oil or fed to the king's tigers, the old historians think, helped enormously to re-establish a public order that had so unexpectedly collapsed when Chinese power over Vietnam was broken. A couple of assassinations, however, reduced the second Vietnamese dynasty within twelve years to a six-year-old king in the hands of a divided court. The year was 980. The Sung in China had just retaken the whole Chinese south, and two of their armies advanced toward the Red River valley, one by land and one by sea, ready to complete the imperial reorganization of China by reconquering Vietnam.

11.

If history could teach anything to those who live it, the Vietnamese of the tenth century might have learned a great deal from the events that surprised and dismayed them after they had shaken off the Chinese yoke. The feudal chiefs, it seemed, had fought the Chinese only for selfish goals. Their personal desire to be free of all restrictions in dealing with their own subjects proved to be stronger than the wish to assert the claim of the country to its whole produce and the right of the Vietnamese to their own way of living and of settling their public affairs. The structure of Vietnamese society created by the Chinese was obviously quite to the liking of the semifeudal and semimandarinal local bosses once the central authority of the state was removed. Their main objection under the Chinese had been to the taxes required for a national administration, and to interference with their local rule in the interest of national economy and defense. But this was precisely what aroused them also against their own monarchs after the Chinese had left, and why they created a state of political anarchy fraught with dangers that were greater for Vietnam than another century of Sinization.

Ngo Quyen and Dinh Bo Linh, therefore, did what the Chinese governors had done when the old local chieftains opposed them during the first century A.D. They fought their feudal antagonists, and if they fought them at times with less success than the Chinese, they certainly fought them with more justification.

When the new state was eventually stabilized under the following dynasties, Vietnam's advanced social and political organization was saved. But even under the strongest future kings, unity and order rested on a compromise between the needs of centralization represented by the monarchy and the interests of the local chiefs and provincial nobles.

Much progress toward a stable central administration was made by Le Hoan,[11] the founder of the so-called Earlier Le dynasty, who himself ruled during twenty-five of the twenty-nine years his dynasty was to last, from 980 to 1005. He had been head of the army under Bo Linh. With the Chinese at the gates in 980, his partisans succeeded in making him king in place of the six-year-old boy, the last of the preceding dynasty. Le Hoan defeated the Chinese in 981. A peace that brought formal Chinese recognition of Vietnamese independence was concluded with the Sung emperor. Le Hoan then reduced the danger of invasions from the South in a campaign against Champa.[12] He was the first Vietnamese monarch to replace Chinese currency with Vietnamese money, and he was also a great builder, like all strong leaders. By putting his many sons at the head of important provinces, he hoped to strengthen the monarchy without destroying the traditional organization of the state inherited from the Chinese. But royal power and the necessary degree of central administration became secure against feudal infringements only under the

140

dynasty of the Ly, whose successful reign lasted from 1009 to 1225.

Although the old chroniclers say little or nothing about the life of the people in these times, it is easy to see why the brisk pace of Vietnamese history during the tenth century created conditions of exceptional misery for the peasant. For him, things did not improve at all after the Chinese were out. He had fought the foreign masters in many battles between 906 and 939, but his hope for a change, more inspiring to all fighting peasants than the promises of their leaders, had been dashed by feudal greed and permanent warfare. Yet it was the peasant who again and again defended the country against the Chinese at the behest of his unloved local and distant national rulers. He may have been fighting reluctantly, but he certainly fought well, as almost a thousand years later he would fight against the French, behind the city intellectuals who then had become the national leaders, and even behind the Communists who were allied to the Chinese. It was again the promise of change that made the peasant accept this leadership and wage a bitter war against his foreign rulers, whose presence in Vietnam had always aggravated and had long been the symbol of his misery and humiliation.

12.

With the year 1010, when the reign of the Ly dynasty began, the Vietnamese monarchy at last entered the stage when all its energies were no longer absorbed by the mere struggle for survival. The first of the Ly kings ruled eighteen, the second twenty-six, the third again eighteen, and the fourth, Ly Nhan Ton, no less than fifty-five years. Although all later Ly rulers were said to have been "sapless and feeble," and the last one was a psychopath who abdicated in favor of his seven-year-old daughter, the dynasty lasted 215 years. This alone shows how political stability had increased after the strife-torn first century of Vietnamese independence, during which the vitality of three dynasties—the Ngo, the Dinh, and the Earlier Le—had been exhausted within seventy years..

The change inaugurated by the Ly becomes even more striking if the life-span of the first three dynasties is compared with that of the three later ones—the Ly, the Tran, and the Later Le—who together were on the throne, though not always in effective political control of the country, for more than seven hundred years.

There is no doubt that the long life enjoyed by the great Vietnamese dynasties had a common basis in a vital function of the monarchy, of which both the Ly monarchs and their successors were keenly aware. It consisted in the construction and supervision of dykes to protect the cultivated valleys and deltas against floods, in the building of canals and other provisions to insure the irrigation of the rice fields,[13] and in the no less important task of increasing the available rice land through administrative action—such as deforestation and the requisition of unused plots—and in particular through military means. The young nation's survival required not only that nothing impair the use and productivity of the existing land; new land had to be added to the old to feed an increasing population and to supply the material means for upper-class cultural advancement and meet the growing demands of a "progressive" state.

The social and political implications of these tasks were many and tremendous. One was a loss of feudal autonomy on the provincial level and the ensuing consolidation of the central authority of the state. Both their limited field of action and the insufficient means at their disposal prevented the local rulers from effectively performing most functions on which the economic survival of the country depended. In this, as in the field of national defense, feudal ambition as a rule could only obstruct the execution of the necessary large-scale measures. Perhaps the Vietnamese and their rulers after

142

all had learned something during the tenth century, when the hated order of the Chinese was followed by political anarchy and economic distress, both obviously fruits of feudal dissension. However that may be, it was the people's good fortune —a rare thing in the history of Vietnam—to have a number of rulers with both the vision and the energy to discharge the vital economic tasks of the state.

Much was accomplished in this sphere during the eleventh and twelfth centuries. Although dykes and canals had in fact been in existence for over a millennium, the old annals, in order to praise the Ly dynasty, claimed that it was Ly Nhan Ton who in 1108 constructed the first major dyke. It was to protect the capital of Vietnam from the intemperate Red River. The Ly had moved the seat of the government from a higher region of the valley into the economic center of the country and thus re-founded Hanoi.[14] Better supervision of the dykes and quicker local repairs were promoted through small peasant cooperatives of ten families, and even military service was adapted to the needs of agriculture: the soldiers could return to their work in the villages for six months every year. In 1224, Thai Ton, the founder of the Tran dynasty, ordered the Red River dykes to be extended all the way down to the ocean.

As promoters of agriculture, the first Tran rulers were surpassed only by the fifteenth-century monarchs of the Le dynasty, in particular by Le Thanh Tong, who conquered most of Champa and headed the state of Vietnam from 1459 to 1497. His famous code contained innumerable and quite meticulous legal provision designed to assure the proper care of all hydraulic installations. The Le created a permanent staff of dyke inspectors, set up a commission to fix compensations for landowners on whose fields the state built dykes, and confiscated all idle fields for the benefit of anyone willing to put them to use. In times of peace the army was employed to increase the surface of the rice land. The soldiers had to clear

143

jungles, drain swamps, build dykes, roads and canals, and were even sent south into the territories wrested from Champa, both to defend and to colonize the fertile regions of Center Vietnam.

The role of the monarchy as a promoter of active agricultural policies had long been unequivocally expressed in the development of a special cult. The different seasons and phases of agricultural life became the occasions for numerous ceremonies and festivals, in which the emperor figured as the high priest of agriculture and the first tiller of Vietnamese soil.[15]

13.

Together with their promotion of agriculture,[16] the better monarchs of the Ly and Tran dynasties were forever trying to find new sources of dynastic strength. To this end they created all sorts of national institutions under their control. Their aim was a well-organized state with a strong central administration, for which the China of imperial unity and order was their model.[17] After this model they established a fixed hierarchy of state officials in 1089, with nine degrees of civil and military mandarins.[18] A college for the training of civil servants, and an imperial academy, had already been created in 1076, both schools that were destined only for children of officials and for young princes and nobles. Examinations for public office were made compulsory in 1075, and literary competitions to determine the grade of an official were introduced soon afterward.[19] The Ly ordered textbooks to be written, imported classics from China, and used the elite of the Buddhist clergy as leaders in education and for the highest administrative and diplomatic posts.[20] As early as 1044 they had started the construction of roads between their principal cities and had founded a postal system for quick communication with all parts of their state.[21] The Tran, in 1225, were the first to see the need for an officers' training school. General military service, however, already had been introduced under the Ly,[22] who created an army that was no longer composed of the semiautonomous hosts of princes and local nobles.[23] The armies of the Ly, the Tran, and the Later Le were raised by the monarchy and were led by officers and generals who derived their authority and livelihood directly from the monarch, as did all officials in economic, religious, educational, and administrative functions. The state, in short, was no longer held together by military force alone, but rather by the much more reliable institution of a specialized, well-trained, and stable bureaucracy. The great Le monarchs of the fifteenth century, Thai To and Thanh Tong, who were in many respects ahead of their royal contemporaries in Europe,[24] completed the work of the Ly and Tran. Vietnam became the most advanced and strongest of all Indochinese states.

14.

The economic and administrative measures of these dynasties counteracted political anarchy more effectively, no doubt, than Bo Linh's boiling oil and hungry tigers; but the task of holding down the many ambitious smaller men of power remained hard. The times were many when this task was beyond the resources and abilities of the monarchs. In fact Vietnam, even after it had won the long struggle for independence, hardly ever enjoyed a decade of complete inner peace. The country was always plagued by feudal dissension and ravaged again and again by civil war.

The reason for this was a basic conflict in Vietnamese society: its survival required a progressive and centralized state, but its essentially agrarian economy allowed for no ruling class free of feudal economic interests and feudal political aspirations.[25] No matter how often the monarchy dispossessed the factious lords and smashed the power of ambitious local administrators, within the limits of Vietnam's agrarian economy the social basis of a local type feudalism was constantly reproduced.

The first Ly, the early part of whose reign was marred by a long struggle against provincial separatism, replaced the defeated nobles with members of his family. The harvest of this policy was most disappointing. When his death raised the question of which one of his sons should succeed him on the throne, the royal family, whose members individually controlled most of the country's armed forces, decided to settle their differences through civil war. The winner, Ly Thai Thong, thereupon dropped his father's policy of basing dynastic strength on family ties. More and more people with ability and training were needed for high central offices and at the head of the many provinces. The new ruler felt there must be a safer way of attaching all these people to the monarchy. But what could that be in a society where all wealth, power, and prestige derived from the possession or control of land? Ly Thai Thong paid his officials for their services and rewarded his servants for their loyalty with large domains of rice land. This meant either the right to pocket the taxes that could be extracted from the peasants on these lands or a title of ownership for life. In the latter case, more frequent when success in the wars against Champa provided the state with much new land, the beneficiaries were usually given prisoners of war and families of criminals to work on their estates. They could also make a temporary slave out of any person who was unable to repay the expensive loans that the wealthy mandarins and landowners habitually provided for peasant families in distress.[26] These privileges were granted to active or retired generals, high civilian officials, provincial administrators, Buddhist monasteries, and deserving heads of the clergy, as well as to mere friends and personal servants of the monarch.

The descendants of these people theoretically could not inherit these domains. But this in no way diminished the danger of these landholdings developing into centers of feudal interest and local power. Their growth would sooner or later threaten the authority of the monarchs and the unity of the state. Frequent royal edicts against the increase and the illegal acquisition or transfer of these domains did not check the evil; they proved, rather, how widespread the abuse had become. As in China, the growth of these landholdings, in addition to transforming a great number of peasants into serfs, made many of them landless. But restrictions imposed by some monarchs[27] and measures to prevent excessive exploitation of the peasants could only enhance the predilection of the great landholders for more local political autonomy and exasperate them against interference from above.

There were times when the landholders, who were after all a large part of the ruling class, modified dynastic policy drastically to their own advantage. One of the Tran rulers, for instance, invited the provincial nobles in 1266 to round up all "vagabonds" and unemployed and use them as slaves on large landholdings created by deforestation. There were other times when a monarch felt that the peasants and the country could be saved from economic ruin only through a radical limitation of the rights, possessions, and powers of the land-owning nobles and officials. The very frequency of such interventions, however, proved their ineffectiveness. But if a monarch was weak or a dynasty at the point of collapse, there followed inevitably a breakdown of order and a period of civil war, resulting as a rule from rebellious action by powerful and dissatisfied members of the ruling class. The greedy ones would add to their possessions by killing a few neighbors or rivals —robbery being the only quick way of increasing one's wealth in a precommercial and preindustrial society; the politically ambitious would strengthen their local rule and try to extend it over vaster areas. And even the just would often rise in such times to defend their honor or their lives against an imbecile or a madman on the throne: it is a melancholy fact that, in

147

addition to a number of great monarchs, Vietnam had more than one Nero, Richard Third, and Ivan the Terrible.[28]

At such times some local chief or high official might assemble enough supporters to check his rivals, overthrow an incompetent or cruel monarch, and found a new dynasty; or the old dynasty might produce a capable chief who would defeat, dispossess, and usually also kill most of the rebels. But whoever came out on top would replant the seed of Vietnam's special brand of feudalism, simply by rewarding his followers and loyal officials with wealth and status, in the manner determined by the economic and social foundations of the state: they received land or control over land and over the people who cultivated it. The power inherent in the public functions of these people was thus increased to a degree that eventually became again dangerous to the central authority of the state.

15.

As a consequence of the monarchy's active agrarian policy, the country's wealth grew at a most satisfactory pace. The amount of construction that some of the monarchs indulged in would alone suffice to prove that economic prosperity was by no means a rare condition. The Ly, Tran, and Le built not only dykes and roads but also fleets and fortifications, parks and palaces, and too many Buddhist pagodas and Confucian temples, if we may believe the great Le Thanh Tong (1459-1497), who decreed that no new ones should be added. There was much gold and glitter at the court and in the great pagodas, and the luxurious lives of many mandarins and nobles expressed the normal economic conditions of the country as graphically as did the progress in arts and letters. The country was able to feed quite an army of Buddhist monks, among whom could be found not only the greatest scholars but also the greatest Vietnamese loafers of the age.

Who paid for these achievements that were attended by so much waste? There was only one permanent and inexhaustible supply of wealth for the rulers of Vietnam: the product of the land, extracted by the labor of the peasant. To this the gains from trade, the exploitation of mines, and the booty of warfare never added a significant amount. But expensive as a cultural progress remained that throve on the luxury of the few and smothered the talents of the many, the Vietnamese peasant could have paid for it with relative ease if this had been the whole of his burden. However, there were also the devastations and the costs of civil and foreign wars.

The first few Ly monarchs had hardly overcome the difficulties of political reconstruction and recovered from two expeditions against the Chams (in 1044 and 1069) when the rulers of China decided to attempt a reconquest of their former province of Giao. Rather than wait until the advancing enemy armies poured into the Red River valley, the Vietnamese, in 1057, met them on Chinese soil. Four years of war and a series of costly Vietnamese victories were required to make the Chinese accept a new peace and recognize Vietnamese independence for the third time.[29]

In the South, trouble was permanent during the reign of the Ly. Both Champa and Cambodia invaded the southern provinces while the Vietnamese fought off the Chinese in the North. A successful invasion of Champa in 1104, provoked by a series of Cham raids into Vietnamese territory, netted much booty but did not bring peace. The Cambodians attacked Vietnam by land and sea in 1128, and again four years later, together with Champa. Their attacks failed, but Cambodia was at the height of her power, and her rulers refused to believe that they could not succeed where the mighty Chinese had failed: they staged five more major invasions of Vietnam between 1138 and 1216, some even with the help of Burmese and Siamese contingents.

The advent of the Tran dynasty in 1225 was preceded by

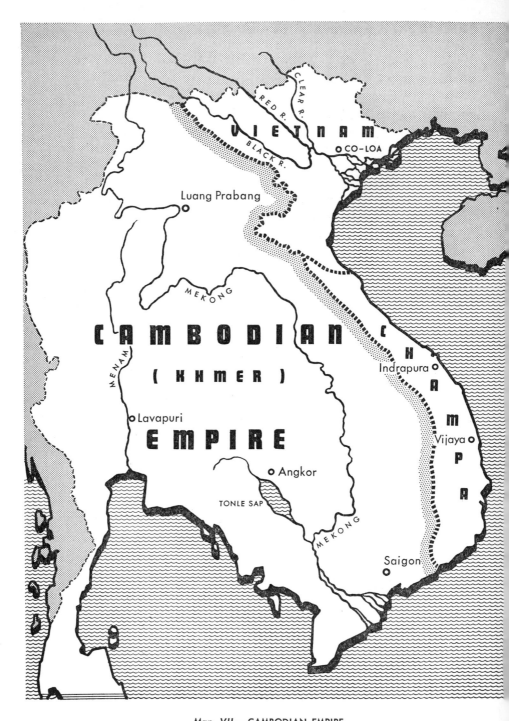

Map. VII.—CAMBODIAN EMPIRE
Approximate borders of Vietnam, Champa, and of the Cambodian empire at the height of its power durin
the twelfth century A.D.

twenty years of feudal arrogance, dynastic confusion, and civil strife. The first Tran monarch had barely restored order and revived prosperity when the conquest of China by the Mongols threw a shadow over the Red River valley that almost ended in a blackout for the Vietnamese as a separate people in a country of their own. Even before the Mongols had overpowered the last ruler of the Sung dynasty who held out in the South, they invaded Vietnam in 1257, sacked Hanoi, and would probably have taken the whole country if heat and disease had not forced them to retire under heavy Vietnamese attacks.

Master of an empire greater than any the world had seen before,[30] Kublai Khan, grandson of Genghis, resumed the Chinese imperial policy of Han Wu Ti after eliminating the Sung in 1276. He pursued it with greater power and stronger economic motivation. The Mongolian empire needed a maritime route to its western outposts connecting East Asia with India, Persia, and the Mediterranean; it wanted control of the spice routes through the Indonesian archipelago; and it required positions of strength against the Mohammedan kingdoms that had spread over India into the Southeast Asian world. Like others before and after, Kublai Khan immediately recognized the strategic importance of the Indochina east coast for the execution of his great schemes. Champa was occupied and Cambodia briefly invaded in 1282, after the Mongols had reopened the old land route through Yunnan and northern Burma, subjecting or destroying the states they met on the way.[31] But to supply, maintain, and extend his footholds in Indochina, Kublai Khan had to eliminate the main obstacle to control of the peninsula by the Chinese empire. This obstacle was the existence of a strong and independent state anchored around the Red River valley. Kublai Khan therefore decided to take Vietnam, and perhaps also to punish the Vietnamese, who had stubbornly refused to let the Mongolian armies pass through their territory for conquests farther south. Five hundred thousand sturdy Mongolian warriors, the annals

151

say, crashed into the Red River valley in 1284, the darkest year in the history of Vietnam.

The small country was not unprepared. It had built up an army of 200,000, led by one of those extraordinary geniuses of locus and circumstance that a human crisis sometimes brings forth.[32] The battles were bloody, the devastations frightful, the skill of the Vietnamese commander and the valor of his troops beyond comparison. But victory needed more. It was achieved because the whole people threw itself body and soul against the foreign armies on Vietnamese soil. The Mongolian invaders met with greater disaster in Vietnam than in their attempts to conquer Korea and Japan. They were beaten again when they returned with an army of 300,000 in 1287. The proud words of a Vietnamese general who sang at the royal victory banquet in 1285 had thus taken on the quality of an inspiring historical truth: "This ancient land shall live forever."

16.

The same general—a minor poet as were so many Vietnamese officials and rulers—had also proclaimed that "peace is the sole object of our efforts and pains." In these pursuits, however, the leaders of the Vietnamese people remained sadly unsuccessful. The war with Champa was resumed even before Vietnam had recovered from the ravages of the Mongol invasions. Champa was made a feudatory state of Vietnam in 1312, but freed itself again in 1326, and was even capable of invading the Red River valley and pillaging Hanoi in 1371.[33] By that time the Tran dynasty had long lost the vigor of its earlier rulers and spent the credit gained during the Mongol wars. Vietnam was weakened by Thai minority insurrections, by defeats suffered from a small kingdom in the west that was to become Laos, and by renewed Cham attacks that ended in Vietnam's loss of provinces previously wrested from Cham-

152

pa. During the half-century from 1350 to 1400, hardly a year went by without either an invasion by or of Champa.

Military efforts and royal incompetence finally led to an economic crisis such as Vietnam had never known before. It hastened the end of the Tran dynasty, which was accompanied by widespread famine and innumerable local revolts. As in the case of the Ly dynasty, the last of the Tran rulers was a child. His regent, the ambitious and capable Ho Qui Ly, had long recognized that only a policy of radical reform could restore economic welfare and political order. Such higher motives, he claimed, were the reason why he usurped the throne in 1400. But before his efforts could bear fruit, an even greater catastrophe than the Mongol invasions of the preceding century befell Vietnam. A huge Chinese army descended on Vietnam, sent by the new dynasty of the Ming, who had ousted the Mongols from China in 1368 but not broken with their imperialist policy.[34] Under the pretext of restoring the legitimate dynasty overthrown by Ho Qui Ly, the Ming invaded Vietnam in 1406. A year later Vietnam was again under Chinese rule.

17.

Why could the Ming accomplish in one campaign what the Mongol rulers of China had failed to bring about in three? Their success was due neither to luck nor to greater military strength. They won because Vietnam had lost both the power and the will with which it had fought and destroyed the armies of Kublai Khan.

During the crisis that enabled Ho Qui Ly to establish his own brief dynasty, all the elements of social decomposition operated at their fullest strength. The permanent war against Champa ruined the monarchy's treasury. Taxes became as hard to extract from the impoverished villages as recruits for the army or the labor force for the few necessary and the many wasteful public works.[35] Some of the later Tran rulers accelerated the ruin of their dynasty by building not only luxurious palaces in times of war and famine, but also huge parks with artificial lakes and hills and other provisions for royal amusement. The loose court life invited a thorough corruption in the upper ranks of the nobility and administration. Monarchs and mandarins no longer possessed either the will or the means to relieve the misery of the people whenever harvests were destroyed by droughts, floods, insects, or typhoons.[36] In order to survive, the landowning peasants sold their small plots, and sometimes even their wives and children, to the rich mandarins and the owners of big estates. Those who left the villages because they were unable to feed themselves or to pay their taxes were joined by the thousands who wanted to escape from the ever extending terms of military and labor service. Many of the small landowners became either serfs or tenants of the great, many simply vagabonds. As such they would sooner or later join groups of pillaging bandits, or the rebel armies of powerful lords who were driven by greed and ambition to exploit, or by anger to try to remedy, the deplorable state of public affairs.

The weakened condition of the country, which was only partly overcome in 1406, was no doubt an important reason why the Ming succeeded in defeating Vietnam. But it was not the main reason. Ho Qui Ly was a first-rate general. It was he who had stopped Cham aggression while he was still governing the country in the name of the Tran, and he was now well prepared against the Chinese. Some think that under his regime Vietnam's armed forces were greater than at any time before or after.[37] The Chinese, however, in addition to a mighty army, possessed an extra weapon that proved more potent than the speed and fury of the Mongol hordes. Well aware of the social and political conflicts in Vietnam, they successfully practiced psychological warfare and created an effective fifth column against Ho Qui Ly.[38]

154

It would have been very surprising, in view of China's advanced intellectualism in the business of power, if the Ming had not exploited the condition of national discord that existed in Vietnam. From the beginning of his career, Ho Qui Ly had shown himself as bold in his reforms as he had been reckless in his struggle to achieve supreme power. With some of his more drastic innovations, such as those in the fields of finance and education, he was singularly ahead of his time.[39] As men of such vigor under such regimes usually do, he made more enemies for himself than he could possibly kill. The surviving members of the old dynasty and their retinue of rapacious courtiers had appealed to China for help against Ho Qui Ly even before the Ming started their expeditions against Vietnam. But they constituted only a fraction of those whose privileges the new dynasty had attacked or annulled.

Like some of the great reformers who arose in China whenever the empire crumbled, Ho Qui Ly knew perfectly well what had emasculated the monarchy and subverted the power of the state. It was the increase, in numbers as well as in size, of the big landholdings, perpetual producers of feudal power, universal destroyers of a sound village economy, and main preoccupation of all Vietnamese monarchs who preferred a life of hard work to one of brute lechery or refined debauch. Only a flourishing village economy, Ho Qui Ly knew, could reduce the causes of social unrest, and only a taxable peasantry could supply the means to revitalize the monarchy and restore the power of the state.[40] This it was that made him decree a radical limitation of all landholdings—not love for the people or hatred for the upper class.[41] All land beyond the limits fixed for one family was distributed to the landless peasants, for a small rent payable to the state. However, the taxes that all holders of public land were forced to pay soon made Ho Qui Ly's regime unpopular among the poor, as his law against big landholdings made it hated among the rich. The peasants were quick to realize that the new ruler had reinstated them as masters of their own produce because he intended the state to get the lion's share. Therefore their willingness to die for their country was not very great when the Chinese launched their attack.

Soon after the Ming armies had entered Vietnam, a dangerous movement of national defection got under way. From the beginning, the Chinese were supported by the Tran family, whose right to the throne the Ming had recognized and promised to respect. Chinese propaganda against Ho Qui Ly, however, was effective mainly because large segments of the ruling class sided with the Tran, hoping that the restoration of the old dynasty would restore also the privileges they had lost.

The Tran and their followers paid a heavy price for their lack of political foresight. The Chinese promises were not kept. After Ho Qui Ly was beaten, the Ming made all Vietnamese officials and nobles sign a request for the return of Vietnam to the fold of the empire—as the old Chinese province of Giao. China speedily complied with this request. The Tran were dropped in favor of a direct Chinese administration.

Embittered against their Chinese allies, whose treachery had triumphed over their own, the Tran called on the country to rise once more against foreign rule. But neither their reputation nor their abilities could make them a serious threat to the Chinese. For several years they kept up a local movement of resistance in a number of provinces, until the exasperated Chinese killed or captured the leaders and drowned the whole movement in Vietnamese blood.

18.

The rule of the Ming was probably worse than anything Vietnam experienced either before or after. Economically, the country was exploited to the utter limit. Masses of forced labor were driven into mines and forests, and even to the bottom of the ocean, to extract whatever treasures Vietnam possessed for shipment to China. But metals, precious stones, rare woods, pearls, elephant tusks, and spices were only an addition to the main booty. This was collected in the form of high taxes on all products and all economic processes of the country.

Economic exploitation was accompanied by radical measures to denationalize the Vietnamese. Schools were permitted to teach only in Chinese. All local cults were suppressed in favor of Chinese rites and Chinese religious ceremonies. What national literature the Vietnamese had so far produced was confiscated and shipped to China. The Vietnamese women were made to dress like the Chinese, to which they probably objected as much as did the men to the order that forced them to wear long hair. Even old customs like the chewing of the betel nut or the blackening of teeth were declared to be illegal. Experts in the field of government and in managing unruly subjects, the Ming governors also issued identity cards for every citizen of Vietnam, to help control a people that was not famous for obedience to the Chinese.

The Vietnamese, who had profited much during the millennium of previous Chinese rule, now gained nothing at all as political satellites of the Ming, save perhaps some improvements in the technics of civil administration. But they learned how to live with a burning and swelling hatred, and how to conceal their wrath and their intentions until the time was ripe for revenge.

19.

Vietnam's most powerful movement of national resistance started in the province of Thanh Hoa, just south of the Red River valley, in the year 1418. It was led by a rich, aristocratic landowner, whose family was said to have numbered over one thousand heads. This was Le Loi, the celebrated first ruler of the Later Le, the dynasty that was to outlast all others through its life of 360 years. The annals compiled under this dynasty relate that Le Loi spent most of his wealth to alleviate the condition of the poor. Stirred by their misery, and outraged by the degrading spectacle of collaboration with the enemy offered by members of his own class, Le Loi proclaimed himself "Prince of Pacification" and embarked upon the stupendous project of evicting the Chinese from Vietnam.

If the greatness of a leader in an enterprise of such scope can be expressed in terms of individual merit, Le Loi deserved much of the acclaim that five centuries of patriotic history and national propaganda have lavished upon him. His achievements in the war of liberation against the Chinese cannot even be devaluated by today's praise by the Communists, for whom Le Loi as a national leader is second in greatness only to Ho Chi Minh. Le Loi was indeed an "architect of national unity" and a "pioneer in the art of guerilla warfare." He was a man who seemed never to have lost courage in a war that lasted over ten years—two years longer than Ho Chi Minh's war against the French.

The Chinese, who had lost most of the country by 1427, hung onto the fortress of Hanoi for almost a year. But after Le Loi had defeated two armies dispatched by the Ming to relieve their beleaguered forces in Hanoi, the Chinese capitulated and evacuated the country early in 1428.[42] To say that they had learned a lesson may have been a naive interpretation of history by the happy and proud Vietnamese. However, the Chinese did not return for 360 years. They made their last unsuccessful attempt to conquer Vietnam in 1788, during the great Vietnamese crisis that also brought the long life of the Le dynasty to an inglorious end.

20.

Le Loi, who adopted the name Le Thai To, ascended the throne shortly after the Chinese had evacuated the country.[43]

One of his first measures as monarch was another attempt to solve the problem of the landless. Their number had grown again under Chinese rule and during the war. Le Thai To knew that the peasant's ability to make a living for himself had to be restored, if only because there was no other way of providing for the needs of the state.[44] The new monarch therefore ordered a general repartition of land among the whole population. Everybody from the highest mandarin to the poorest peasant, women and children included, had a right to a share. However these shares were not equal. Furthermore, the available land did not suffice to meet all needs. The members of the new royal family, for instance, wanted to be taken care of. In addition there was the crowd of deserving generals and faithful followers of Le Loi, who had to be rewarded and lifted to the status of princes, lords, and high officials of the state. All these people received land or control of land sufficient for an income that corresponded to their elevated positions.

Of the existing great landowners, only those who had collaborated with the Chinese were expropriated.[45] Some land for redistribution came from owners who had died during the war, some from devastated districts where land had fallen into disuse, and some from villages whose population had been decimated by epidemics or slaughtered by the Chinese. But the relief Le Thai To's policy provided, great as it was, kept too many peasants in their former miserable state. No plot of land was left for them, not even one big enough to serve as standing room for themselves and their lean wives and children.

However the problem of the landless with all its disastrous consequences became less acute for longer periods of time under the better monarchs of the fifteenth century. This was no doubt due to both their economic and their military policies. Le Thanh Tong, whose reign of thirty six years ended in 1497, made the remaining community lands inalienable and untransferable, in order to protect them against further inroads by the great landowners. But if the population increased, the land that was available for periodic redistribution among all peasants became insufficient even in the best times, when the monarchy was strong enough to make the landlords and mandarins respect its measures.

The conquest of Champa, virtually completed by Le Thanh Tong in 1471, brought a timely respite.[46] Masses of superfluous people were absorbed by the army. Of these, quite a few were settled in military colonies and on great landholdings of the state. Even before Champa was defeated, mandarins and nobles had long sent "vagabonds" and landless peasants into the fabulous South, where land was presumably just waiting to be taken. Under the monarchy's protection, new Vietnamese villages of small landholders, with enough communal lands for everybody, sprang up all the way down the coast of Center and South Vietnam; but the number of private estates grew equally fast. In fact, under Le Thanh Tong especially deserving officials for the first time were rewarded with lands that were not supposed to be returned to the state when the beneficiary died. This could only increase the tendency toward property concentration that the same monarch had made such efforts to check. Vietnam became stronger and wealthier, but its social organization was not affected by this growth. The feudal forces of Vietnamese society remained alive and continued their destructive work.

The social conflicts and political struggles under the Le consequently remained essentially what they had been under the Ly and Tran, except that everything ran in higher gear. The monarchy climbed to greater heights but also plunged to lower depths. Periods of remarkable achievement and of bottomless decline followed each other at a bewildering pace. Some of the Le monarchs were the best and the strongest, others the most depraved and politically most impotent rulers of Vietnam. In keeping with the spirit of national renovation generated during the war against the Chinese, Le Thai To imposed a strictly puritanical regime on his country in order

160

to speed up the process of reconstruction. Under his penal code even laziness and gambling became major crimes. He forced many a Buddhist monk and Taoist priest to give up his sheltered monastic existence and begin a wearisome life of personal responsibility and work. But only ten years later Le Thai To's young successor died of exhaustion from uninterrupted pleasures, at a time when the hand of a peasant was still lawfully cut off if he were caught in the act of gambling.

21.

It would be tedious to describe in detail what happened to the Le dynasty during the following two and a half centuries. It was permitted to exist as a semicorpse but not allowed to die. The history of its perpetual expiration was on the whole only a repetition, in sharper outlines, of everything that accompanied the decline of the Ly and the Tran: political ineptitude and moral debasement of the monarchs, feudal impertinence and usurpation of royal power, occasional vain efforts to secure economic stability by coming to the aid of the peasants, and interminable bloody civil strife. The periods of general prosperity and peace were brief and few.

However, there was one great difference between the time from 1500 to 1750 and the preceding five hundred years. With Champa eliminated and China resigned to leaving Vietnam alone, the country was free from major foreign wars for these later 250 years.

Why was this long period not a great time of peace and prosperity for Vietnam? Why were the valleys and coastlands, the deltas and even the mountains of this unhappy country drenched with Vietnamese blood during these centuries of untroubled relations with the surrounding world?

Instead of enjoying peace and progress, Vietnam suffered from palace intrigues and their sequels of court assassinations;

161

from local and national uprisings provoked by dynastic mis-management and royal folly; from minority rebellions and peasant revolts caused by economic distress and administrative terror;[47] and last but not least, from an explosion of feudal lust for power that brought on the climax of political madness in the eyes of the Vietnamese: the split of the country into two discordant halves.

The feudal cancer in the social body of Vietnam had been allowed to grow until it became a threat even to the survival of the Vietnamese as a homogeneous nation in a single and unified state. The country was torn apart twice, in the first half of the sixteenth century and again almost a century later, and each of these divisions was followed by more than fifty years of civil war between the North and the South.

22.

If those who believe that history repeats itself studied the crisis that led to the first division of Vietnam, they would easily find new confirmation for their old view. But they could also discover a much greater historical truth: the same events do occur again and again, but, in the context of a different time, they neither have the same meaning nor do they produce the same results.

With Hien Tong, who died as a young man in 1504, the capacity of the Le dynasty for virtue and work was apparently exhausted. His successors, if they were not children, were mur-derers and pleasure-hungry weaklings. Vietnam had no less than eight different rulers during the following twenty-five years. Six of these were assassinated either by royal relatives or by ambitious lords who fought all others for control of the disintegrating state.[48] One of them emerged on top, as Ho Qui Ly had done 130 years earlier, when the debility of the last Tran rulers permitted the eruption of a similar state of social unrest and political chaos. The new victor was Mac Dang Dung, the second great usurper in a dynastic history of 750 years. From his position as governor of Hanoi, Mac built himself a staircase of lordly and royal corpses right up to the throne, which he reached in 1527.[49] But as in the case of Ho Qui Ly, it took less than ten years before another Chinese army was assembled at the border of Vietnam.

But Mac and his Vietnamese opponents, although in the same positions and facing the same dangers and tasks, acted in a manner totally different from their precursors, whom the power of the Ming had jointly eclipsed in 1407. Ho Qui Ly had been ready with his armies to battle the Chinese,[50] with whom his enemies, the deposed Tran and their followers, made common cause. Mac, on the other hand, although in a greater hurry to meet the invaders than Ho Qui Ly had been, did not meet them at the head of his troops. He rushed to the border loaded with presents for the Chinese generals, and he even offered China a portion of Vietnam in exchange for a promise not to touch his country and his regime. He was as successful with his diplomacy as he had been in transforming his personal crimes into acts of state. The Chinese went home, and Mac soon received Peking's recognition for his new dynasty.[51]

The Le, unlike the Tran, did not side with the Chinese,[52] perhaps only because they lacked the energy to pursue high treason systematically. After some hesitation, the Le dynasty followed Nguyen Kim, another ambitious Vietnamese leader, who planned to overthrow the Mac and take their place. A refugee in Laos since the Mac had come to power, Nguyen Kim in 1532 set up a government in exile nominally headed by a descendant of the Le, and with the help of the Laotian king prepared to wrest Vietnam from the Mac. The fight began in 1540. Five years later Vietnam was divided into two states headed by two governments and dynasties at war with each other. In the name of the Le, Nguyen Kim had won the southern half of the country up to Thanh Hoa, at the edge of the Red River delta. But when Nguyen Kim was murdered in 1545 the Mac were still firmly in control of the North. In fact, it took almost sixty years of war before the servants of the Le, who in the meantime had become their masters, were able to drive the Mac out of Hanoi and put the Le back at the head of a reunited Vietnam.[53]

23.

This costly reunification, which came about in 1592, was only a brief interlude in a long history of division and armed conflict between North and South.

After the defeat of the Mac, all power in Hanoi was in the hands of another family, the Trinh, whose chiefs had conducted the wars and the government of the Le ever since Nguyen Kim's untimely death. The first of the Trinh was a general with an appetite for power that Nguyen Kim had vainly tried to satisfy by making the man his son-in-law; Nguyen Kim's early death made Trinh also his heir. To be sure of the future, Trinh soon eliminated the oldest of Nguyen Kim's two sons. When the Mac were beaten and the Le again installed in Hanoi, the Trinh family formalized their position as actual rulers of Vietnam. They left the Le on the throne but made themselves hereditary princes in charge of government.[54]

However, there remained the younger of Kim's sons, Nguyen Hoang, who had managed to avoid his brother's fate. First he had feigned madness. Later, in 1558, he had persuaded the Trinh to let him leave the Le court. He was appointed governor of a troublesome and little-developed region farther south. During the remaining forty years of struggle against the Mac, the territories under Nguyen Hoang's administration not only increased in size and wealth; they also became virtually independent of the war-torn North. When the war was over, the Nguyen family controlled all of Vietnam south of the seventeenth parallel.

Nguyen Hoang was called to Hanoi, where he found it difficult to stay alive. He had remained loyal to the Le and also supported the Trinh against the Mac. But after he succeeded in leaving Hanoi for his own residence, he felt neither in the mood nor under any necessity to add to the power of the Trinh by letting them rule the South also. When death ended his long and successful rule in 1613, Nguyen Hoang transmitted the government of the South to his oldest son. From then on, the Nguyen family ruled the South as autocratically as the Trinh ruled the North. Although both the Trinh and the Nguyen continued to recognize the Le monarchs as the only legitimate heads of the whole country, Vietnam was again divided into two separately governed rival halves.

24.

The Trinh made a first unsuccessful attempt to oust the Nguyen in 1620, whereupon the latter discontinued all payments previously made to the government in Hanoi. The first major offensive by land and sea against the South was launched in 1627. Its failure enabled the Nguyen to counterattack and slightly increase their territory to the north, but as a rule the South remained on the defensive. Aggression came from the much more powerful North. However, by skillfully relying on the narrowness of the coastal plain, the South was able to repel northern armies two to five times as strong as its own. The Nguyen built two enormous walls, one six, the other eleven miles long.[55] In seven great campaigns, of which some lasted over many years, the Trinh never succeeded in breaking through both of these walls. It took them fifty years of useless effort to realize that military conquest of the South by the

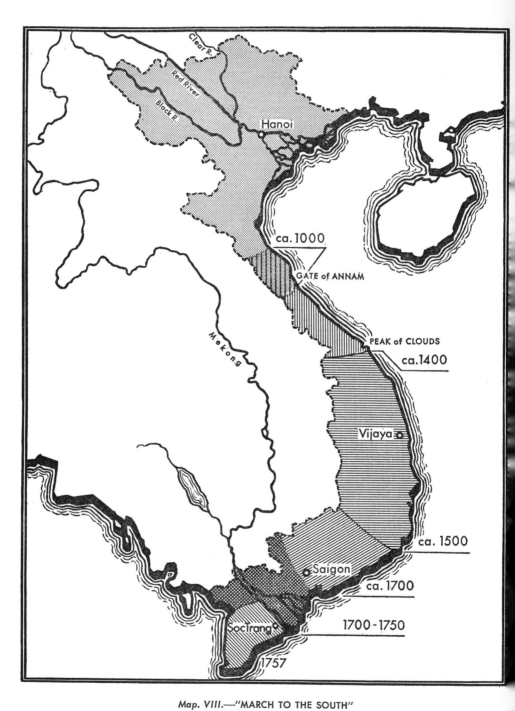

Map. VIII.—"MARCH TO THE SOUTH"

Through the "March to the South," the Vietnamese eliminated Champa and advanced to the Gulf of
Siam at the expense of Cambodia

stronger North was not the right method of unifying a divided Vietnam.

As soon as the Trinh stopped their attacks in 1673, the war between North and South was over. The fifty-year struggle between the two rival houses was followed by a hundred-year truce. When this truce was broken in 1774—again by the North —an entirely different movement of national reunification, directed against both the Nguyen and the Trinh, was already under way.

During the century of peaceful coexistence between the two halves of the divided country, the Trinh and Nguyen never ceased to pay homage to the idea of Vietnamese unity. Unity was represented by the Le, who continued to be recognized as the one legitimate dynasty of Vietnam by both sides.[56] Even the war had been fought under their banner. The North claimed to have no other war aims than the return of the dissident South to the authority of the one monarch, whereas Southern propaganda stressed the duty of the Nguyen to free the Le dynasty from the harsh tutelage of the Trinh. But neither family, once it was convinced that force could not subject the whole country to its rule, made any other effort to reunite Vietnam.

25.

The 150 years when North and South Vietnam led a separate political existence under the Trinh and Nguyen have supplied the Vietnamese with an inexhaustible source of patriotic controversy and intellectual speculation. Why did the Trinh fail to overcome the Nguyen, if the population of the North was really at least three times that of the South?[57] Did weakness or statesmanship determine the Trinh's hundred-year policy of noninterference with the administration of their Southern opponents? What enabled the South not only to exist without the North but even to continue more vigorously than ever the traditional Vietnamese policy of territorial expansion? And thanks to what forces did the unity of Vietnamese culture and national sentiment survive the long separation and struggle between North and South?

The Trinh were not only stronger than the Nguyen; they were for a long time also supported by the Dutch, whose attempt to get a foothold in Vietnam was part of their effort to oust all their European rivals from Southeast Asia. This had brought about their sharp conflict with the Portuguese, who consequently sided with the Nguyen. Regular shipments of modern weapons from Portugal and instruction in their use enabled the Nguyen partially to offset the numerical superiority of the Trinh. As early as 1615 the Portuguese had equipped the Nguyen with a foundry for the local production of heavy guns.

These military assets, together with the South's geographical advantages, were no doubt important in defeating the Trinh policy of unification by force. But they were not decisive, and they certainly do not explain how a separate Vietnamese state, on the territory that had so recently belonged to the powerful state of Champa, could survive, expand, and remain wholly Vietnamese in absolute independence of the North—the Red River valley and its surroundings, whence Vietnam's vitality had sprung for almost two thousand years.

Starting out from these regions, the Vietnamese had worked and fought their way south for many centuries. But the new territories they had occupied by the end of the sixteenth century, if compared with the great delta in the North, looked like a long handle on a wide pan: six hundred miles of coastlands and valleys, but altogether hardly a fifth of the population, and even less of the wealth, that remained concentrated in the North. The South could never have become more than an awkward annex to the North had it not been for a distant region that the Vietnamese only now began to touch: the

168

enormous Mekong River delta, owned by Cambodia when the first Vietnamese arrived, but poorly exploited by a people that had long reacted with inertia to the demands of an insatiable state.[58]

The discovery and settlement of this real South, through which the former South became the future Center, was a turning point in the history of Vietnam. Its role during the seventeenth and eighteenth centuries has often been likened to that of the West of the United States—a valid comparison if taken in the limited sense in which any comparison may serve to demonstrate a truth. The Vietnamese pioneers, once they had reached the Bay of Phan Thiet, could contemplate from the last hills near the coast vaster and more empty spaces than they or their ancestors had ever seen before. They must have stopped and looked with awe and wonder before they took to work. The obstacles in their way were great, but so were the opportunities. The South became the region of Vietnamese national growth. It attracted not only the needy and the desperate, but also those who were bold enough and strong enough to wrestle with the difficulties of a frontier life.

This was the positive side in the long history of Vietnamese national disunion. The weaker Nguyen could resist the power of the Trinh and then get along without the North because they headed a country that solved its problems by growing. The constant need for new land could be satisfied, with larger shares for peasant as well as for lord. There were fewer candidates for desirable positions and more open places for those with ambition to learn in order to rule—for the Nguyen too, in 1632, had introduced the Chinese method of recruiting officials through literary examinations. A steady stream of immigrants and refugees from the North enriched the state of the Nguyen in population and skills. Some left the North because they were tired of war, others were looking for land, but many also fled from the tyranny of the Trinh in search of greater personal safety and public peace. Neither the methods nor the principles of government were different in the South, but there were wider spaces to move into, with greater chances for unrestricted activity and for the unmolested private existence that must have been the ideal of freedom of the age.

Even the wars of the Nguyen were short, inexpensive, and not entirely devoid of sense from the peasant's point of view. Between 1650 and 1770, South Vietnam waged no less than a dozen wars. All but the last one were fought against Cambodia, a weak opponent whom both Vietnam and Thailand threatened to absorb, and every one of these wars ended with improved protection for Vietnamese villages in Cambodian territory, if not with substantial gains of new land.[59]

26.

The merits of the Nguyen in settling and organizing the Vietnamese South were evidently great. However, there is also a negative side to the story of their historic success. After the South had received its new social and political organization, the domain of the Nguyen was only a copy of the state and the society that had developed within the narrow confines of the Red River valley. Three hundred years of territorial expansion changed neither the social structure nor the political organization of Vietnam, both of which were based on an apparently immutable economy.

For centuries Vietnamese dynastic power had been rooted in, and at times also restricted to, the Red River valley. Beyond this valley and its great delta, on which the river had imposed an early administrative centralization, provincial autonomism had always been strong. It derived its unfortunate vigor from an economy that could prosper locally no matter what happened ten miles away. The farther south the country extended, the larger became the regions not subject to the forces of centralization that were still operating along the Red River.

170

Hanoi had long ceased to be the center of Vietnam. With the expansion of the country, therefore, provincial separatism was constantly gaining new strength.

The great landowners and local mandarins had always been opposed to national institutions not subject to local control. But their position was equally threatened by economic activities that were not rooted in the villages or provinces under their control. Any kind of economic activity, such as small manufacture and trade, encountered the hostility of the great landowners and money-lending mandarins if it originated or developed beyond the spheres where their power was supreme.[60] Such activities, they knew, could only strengthen the central authority of the state, in addition to creating a class of rich merchants and urban centers of political power that would be difficult to rule or exploit by local mandarins and lords. Their privileges and powers were obviously more secure if the existing economic order remained unchanged.

These were the reasons why Vietnam's economy was not permitted to rise from its village level in spite of the country's fantastic growth. The elements of health and stability in this economy secured Vietnam's somewhat miraculous survival; territorial expansion somehow solved the problem of population increase; Vietnam no doubt possessed the most advanced native administration in all of Southeast Asia;[61] but the peculiar feudal components in its social structure prevented all economic and social development beyond a point it had long since reached. The mandarins opposed economic progress, even when it became clear that the only alternative to such progress was stagnation and military impotence in the struggle against the West.

This, however, explains only what the country's ruling classes wanted, and not why their interests could block the economic development of Vietnam. They succeeded because the well-being of all upper class families, the existence over the whole country of an adequate administration, and even

171

the minimum subsistence of the peasant masses, were compatible with a static economy restricted to the village level. To safeguard the traditional ways of life and to secure the survival of the Vietnamese did not require the development of a national market. The country could get along with a modest amount of provincial trade. Consequently there was no need for a national system of transportation. In short, no kind of economic necessity broke the semifeudal, bureaucratic, and ideological chains around the social body of Vietnam. After having fought the central authority of the state for centuries, the semifeudal and bureaucratically anchored forces of separatism could even break up the unity of the state without substantially changing the conditions of life for any group of the people and without striking a death blow to Vietnam.

27.

The mighty Vietnamese lords, together with the locally prosperous mandarins, accomplished what no foreign power had been able to achieve. They split the country and interrupted the development of the Vietnamese people as a unified national community for almost two hundred years. Family quarrels among both the Trinh and the Nguyen frequently threatened to dismember the state even further. The Mac, after their defeat in 1592, managed to retain a small principality near the Chinese border for another eighty-five years, while several other feudal families were able to rule minority regions in virtual independence of Hanoi.

What prevented this feudal dismemberment of the state from destroying the unity of Vietnamese culture and national sentiment? The same forces that had prevented the Vietnamese from becoming Chinese—the forces rooted in the Vietnamese village. Vietnam's national unity survived in the peasant's way of life, which was immutable like the economy of the Vietnamese village and identical all over the country. The forces of the village, inexhaustible as the fertility of the Vietnamese soil, were forever mending what the lords, the mandarins, and the rulers were tearing apart.

The near identity of the geographical and climatic conditions for agriculture all over the country helped to make the Southern villages close copies of the villages in the North. But there was a more important reason why the peasants who settled the coastlands of the Center and the plains of South Vietnam remained fundamentally like their brothers who stayed behind. They always came in large groups, or rather groups of large families. The draining of swamps, the clearing of jungles, the building of dams and waterways for the fields and of bamboo walls for the settlements[62] called for pioneers with firm habits of social life and cooperative work. Vietnamese penetration into non-Vietnamese lands was a movement of small communities composed of people with common beliefs. The farther they went from the lands of their ancestors, the more tenaciously they clung to their own ways of life. Wherever they settled, there was Vietnam, because Vietnam, as a totality and continuity of human existence, was the Vietnamese village.[63] To the peasants therefore must be credited the two most extraordinary achievements in the history of independent Vietnam: the territorial growth of the country and the preservation of its national unity.

How were the peasant's labors and his constancy rewarded? An old sad song, which the Vietnamese have long been singing with every justification, describes his condition and expresses his feelings better than either the sympathetic reports of early missionaries or the most compassionate lines of Vietnam's great national poets.[64] "I am always bathed in sweat," the song goes, "and of my torn garments only the collar survives."

Nourished by a provincial economy that no territorial expansion or dynastic policy was able to overcome, the local feudal and bureaucratic powers continued to produce human misery and social disorder. The laws for the protection of the peasants were as numerous under the Trinh and Nguyen as they had been before[65] and quite as ineffective. Especially the Trinh, who were more plagued by population pressure, were forever issuing decrees to check the greed of the great landowners and provincial mandarins. Most of these decrees remained on paper. The central authority of the two states, in need of strong local arms, again and again gave to the lords and the local mandarins a free hand in the exploitation of the Vietnamese peasants. The number of landless, of semislaves, and of vagabonds kept growing, and so did the financial difficulties of the state. There were times when the majority of the peasants owned no land at all and were consequently unable to pay taxes. "You are being exploited and suppressed by your masters the Nguyen," said the Trinh to the people of the South during the war. "They ruin you with their heavy taxes, and in order to build walls and wage a senseless war, they prevent you from studying and doing useful work."

The accusations of the Nguyen against the Trinh were similar. The Trinh themselves reached a low point of public morality for a country that had always recruited its officials from the learned on the basis of impartial tests: in 1730 administrative positions were sold to the highest bidder, a practice that made examination for public office only another exercise in corruption.

Under such conditions, there was of course no hope that Vietnam would ever recover its lost unity through any action of its two existing governments. Both the Nguyen and the Trinh had trouble enough to hold their respective domains together. The degree of provincial dissidence and the number of local revolts increased again during the eighteenth century. But there was one difference. More and more uprisings occurred in which the blind forces of peasant rebellion were stronger than the elements of upper-class political ambition.

174

However, even if despair drove him into rebellion, the peasant could never develop political aims of his own. He pillaged to eat, and he fought to defend and avenge himself. If he raised any demand at all, it was for the return of the land that he had once either owned or rightfully used. He had no choice of leaders. As a rule, his aimless action quickly led either to catastrophe or to local success. But success in the end would only strengthen the power of a provincial war lord who, if he did not come from the ranks of the peasant's oppressors, would soon enter them.[66] Thus, after feudal greed had created enough misery for an explosion of violence, it was again feudal ambition that exploited the forces of revolt, to the detriment of the people and against the central authority of the state. Although these rebellions led nowhere and only increased the misery of the peasants, hardly a year went by without at least one peasant insurrection, in the South as well as in the North. Vietnam was simply too crowded with people—as some missionaries and at least one French historian observed—"who had nothing and were ready for everything."[67]

28.

But the day was approaching when this cycle of hopelessness would begin to break. By the middle of the eighteenth century, when the West was on the verge of the American and French revolutions, new social forces, however feeble, had entered the Vietnamese historical scene. One local rebellion, at first not very different from the others, spread until it had reached the proportions of a national revolution. It started in the South, in the year 1772, and it was led by three brothers whose name in history became that of their native village—Tay Son.[68]

Both the French and the historians of the last Vietnamese dynasty have tried hard to depict the Tay Son brothers as bandit leaders, although some of the French at least recognized the youngest, Hué, as a military genius of Napoleonic stature. But more important than the personal motives and talents of the Tay Son were the social forces that led their movement to national success. The Tay Son were not only followed by the masses of the landless and the miserable peasants, they were also financially supported by the small class of merchants that somehow had developed by that time.

The Tay Son rebellion very quickly became fatal for the Nguyen, the masters of the South. They fell in 1777. But the Trinh too, who had tried to exploit the difficulties of the Nguyen and invaded the South in 1774, were marked for doom. As soon as the Tay Son were in solid control of the South, they decided to march north into the Red River valley. When Hanoi fell to the new regime of the South, Vietnam was at last reunited. The Trinh were driven out in 1786. A year later the Tay Son abolished the decrepit Le monarchy also. In 1788 the Vietnamese, under the competent military leadership of the Tay Son, defeated another Chinese attempt to penetrate into the Indochinese Peninsula.

The rule of the Tay Son was brief, but the unity of Vietnam survived when the last of their rulers was overthrown in 1802, again by forces that moved up from the South. This, however, is part of another story: when the Tay Son fell, the destinies of Vietnam were already influenced by the forces that had intruded into Asia from the West.

Notes to Chapter Three:

1. The first Chinese attempt to reconquer Vietnam after independence was established took place in 981, the second almost one hundred years later, in 1075. The Chinese gave up in 1076 only after fifteen months of murderous warfare. See note 29 of this Chapter. Under the Mongolians, three invasions of Vietnam were undertaken, in 1257, 1284-85, and 1287. The Ming invaded Vietnam in 1406 and sent two armies of relief in 1427. An attempted invasion in 1540 was prevented under the Mac dynasty by the cession of six border provinces to China. The last Chinese attempt to take the Red River valley was defeated under the Tay Son dynasty in 1789. Before the establishment of independence in 939, the Chinese sent big armies against every major Vietnamese rebellion, of which there were at least ten. See note 6 of this Chapter.

2. Even a modern author like D. G. E. Hall (op. cit., pp. 754-758) supplies long and supposedly correct and complete lists of historical and legendary dynasties.

3. The Hong Bang, who are said to have ruled the Vietnamese kingdom of Van Lang from 2879 to 258 B.C., are unconnected with known history. The Thuc, who perhaps ruled from 257 to 258 B.C., might have to be taken more seriously if the existence of their kingdom Au Lac were a more certain historical fact. The Trieu, who undoubtedly headed Nam Viet from 207 until its annexation by China in 111 B.C., were Chinese by origin, and Nam Viet a country of which the Vietnamese inhabited only the southern provinces.

4. At least one French author lets Vietnam become independent only after the Chinese interregnum of 1407 to 1427, "After a long time of changing fortunes, during which the country was either a vassal or a province of China, Annam definitely gained her independence in 1427 after Christ." F. Romanet du Caillaud, Histoire de l'intervention française au Tong-King, Paris 1880, p. 14. This curious date is also given for the founding of independent Vietnam, under Annam, by the New Century Cyclopedia of Names, New York, 1954.

5. None of the revolts before the tenth century established Vietnamese rule for more than four years.

6. Ten rebellions against Chinese rule occurred between the first and the tenth century:

   (1) The revolt under the leadership of the Trung sisters (39–43), as described in the text.
   (2) Trieu Au, another woman, led about one thousand partisans to fight the Chinese in 248.

(3) Lo Tuan raised the banner of revolt in the Red River delta in 411. He drowned himself in the Red River after his junks were burned by the Chinese with flaming arrows. This revolution is treated in Sainson, *Mémoire sur l'Annam,* Peking, 1896, pp. 507ff., and Maspéro, "Le protectorat général d'Annam sous les T'ang," BEFEO, Vol. X., p. 574.

(4) More successful was Ly Bon, also called Ly Bi, who began his revolt in 541. A detailed description of this uprising is to be found in Maspéro, "La dynastie des Ly antérieure," BEFEO, Vol. XVI., pp. 1-26. See also notes 63, 64, Chapter II.

(5) In 589 and 590 Ly Xuan brought the whole Red River delta under his domination (Maspéro, *op. cit.,* p. 22).

(6) Ly Phat Tu revolted in 602, was defeated the following year, and died in Chinese captivity (Maspéro, *op. cit.,* p. 25).

(7) Mai Thuc Loan proclaimed himself emperor in 722. He was of dark complexion and became known as Mai Hac De, the Black Emperor. Defeated by the Chinese, he continued resistance in the mountains. It is not known when he died. Where he had his citadel, called Van An Thanh (the City of Eternal Peace), a shrine has been preserved until today.

(8) About Phung Hung and his son, see Le Thanh Khoi, p. 124.

(9) A partly successful revolution was staged by Khuc Thua Du in 906. The Tang emperors of China confirmed him in power. He died in 907, the same year the Tang dynasty was overthrown. His son, Khuc Hao, ruled from 907 to 917. He established a well-functioning administration. But Khuc Hao's son and successor was defeated in 923 and Chinese rule re-established. See note 10 of this Chapter.

(10) A lieutenant of Khuc Hao, named Duong Dien Nghe, raised the banner of revolt again in 931. He was assassinated in 936.

(11) Ngo Quyen's successful uprising, which drove the Chinese out definitely, started in 939. It is treated in the text.

7. The Sui dynasty re-established the unity of China in 588. It was a dynasty of "barbarian" origin, followed in 618 by the Tang dynasty of pure Chinese blood, which ruled the "Middle Kingdom" until 907. Under the Tang China reached a new height of civilization. It was the golden age of Chinese poetry (Li Po, Tu Fu) and painting. Silk weaving was perfected and beautiful glazed earthenware (china) was produced. The Tang also introduced the consumption of tea. Printing was invented at that time. Under both the Sui and the Tang the frontiers of the empire were extended in all directions. The Sui conquered Manchuria, Mongolia,

and Turkestan. Under the Tang the Chinese invaded Tibet, penetrated even into India, and defeated the ruler of Delhi (647), but soon they retreated from the subcontinent. Since the seventh century the Chinese never have attacked India again, neither has India ever waged war against China. The Tang also established a protectorate over Korea and crossed the Pamir plateau, imposing their suzerainty on different states in the Tarim basin, almost three thousand miles from their capital. Beyond the Pamir the Chinese met the new expanding nation of the Arabs. They were defeated by Islam in 751 and lost all their conquests in the Tarim basin. Their defeat by the Arab horsemen provoked a series of revolts on the fringes of the empire. Yunnan and Tibet were lost. Finally the Chinese emperor had to ask for the help of the Mohammedan Turks against the Tibetans, who had invaded the provinces of Kansu and Szechwan. With the end of the Tang dynasty at the beginning of the tenth century the Chinese empire began to crumble again. The fall of the Tang empire was accompanied by a great economic and social crisis. About the reasons for this crisis, see note 8 of this Chapter. For the history of Sui and Tang China cf. Grousset, *The Rise and Splendor of the Chinese Empire,* pp. 117-177; Latourette, *op. cit.,* pp. 121-126.

8. Under the Tang dynasty there existed a mixed system of land distribution and ownership. The state remained theoretically the sole owner of the land, but in practice it acted only as the distributor. On attaining manhood, every peasant received an allotment of village land. These grants made the peasant liable to payment of a land tax, to forced labor, and to service in the militia. When he died his allotment reverted to the community. Officials, however, could not only acquire larger estates but also keep them in their families through inheritance. The small peasant holding based on the life grant of a plot of land suddenly disappeared in the eighth century. Taxes, forced labor, and military service became too heavy to bear. Debts grew so pressing that most of the peasants, despite the laws that forbade such transactions, sold their land to the large landowners and became tenants or agricultural laborers, little better than serfs. At the end of the eighth century the landowning families represented no more than five per cent of the total population. Instead of a prosperous peasantry, China now had only a sort of agricultural proletariat. This description follows Grousset, *op. cit.,* pp. 171f. Cf. also Louzon, *op. cit.,* p. 58.

9. The first "barbarian" tribe to be invited into China in order to help bolster the Tang rule was a Turkish horde from the Gobi desert, named Tchól in Turkish and Sha To in Chinese. They settled in northern Shansi in 878. Their chieftain, Li Ke-yung, was the most powerful personality

of the China of his day. He served the Tangs faithfully and saved them from numerous rebels and enemies. As a compensation for his services he was given the province of Shansi as a fief, to which later the north of Hopei was added. In the course of a few decades the Sha To were completely absorbed by the Chinese. The second "barbarian" tribe to invade China, at the time of the downfall of the Tang dynasty, were the Chi Tan, also called Kitan or Khitai. They were a Mongolian people living in what is now Manchuria and Inner Mongolia. A Chinese general, Shih Ching-tang, appealed to them for assistance in 936. They helped him to found a new imperial dynasty at Kaifeng. They were recompensed for their assistance with the northern parts of the provinces of Hopei and Shansi, including the city of Peking (963). This important part of northern China was held by Mongol tribes until 1368. After the Kitan came the Ju Chen and then the Mongols of Genghis Khan. But Chi Tan or Kitan was the name used for all these Mongol peoples, for the territory they occupied, and even for large parts of China. Marco Polo uses the name of Cathay for North China, and the Russian designation for China is Kitay to the present day. Chinese historians call the period from 907 to 960, when the Sung dynasty was established, the time of the Five Dynasties. Politically it was an era of chaos, but culturally China remained on a high level. Printing was further developed, painting continued. The way was prepared for another outstanding period in Chinese history (Grousset, *op. cit.*, pp. 174-177; Latourette, op. cit., p. 126). For a more thorough study of Chinese-Mongol relations, see H. H. Howorth, *History of the Mongols from the Ninth to the Nineteenth Century,* London, 1876-1888.

10. In 906 the population of the protectorate of Annam revolted, expelled the Chinese governor and put Khuc Thua Du, a rich landowner "respected for his virtuousness and his charity," in his place. The helpless Tang ruler confirmed his nomination. The following year, 907, saw both the downfall of the Tang dynasty and the death of the aged Khuc Thua Du. He was followed by his son, Khuc Hao (907-919). During his tenure the Chinese governor of Canton rebelled against the imperial court and proclaimed his province an independent kingdom, Nan Han. Khuc Hao and his son and successor, Khuc Thuc My, refused to accept the suzerainty of the new king of Canton. Therefore the ruler of Nan Han invaded Annam in 923 and made Khuc Thuc My a prisoner. After eight years (931) a former aid of Khuc Hao, named Duong Dien Nghe, led another revolt and chased the Chinese out of the country. He was assassinated in 937 by one of his officers, Kieng Cong Tien. His son-in-law, Ngo Quyen, avenged him by killing the usurper. Before his

180

death, Kieng Cong Tien had appealed to the king of Canton for help. Ngo Quyen defeated the Cantonese army and navy in 939 and secured the independence of Vietnam from China. Le Thanh Khoi, *op. cit.*, p. 134. The original source for the victorious revolution of Ngo Quyen is *Kham-dinh Viet-sir* (*The Imperial Annals of Annam*), translated into French by Abel des Michels, Paris 1892.

11. Like Dinh Bo Linh, who eliminated the last Ngo, Le Hoan had to eliminate the last Dinh in order to establish the dynasty of the Earlier Le, whose life span of twenty-nine years was as short as that of the Ngo, though longer than that of the Dinh, who ruled only from 968 to 980.

12. The Vietnames stormed and burned Indrapura, the capital of Champa. They took as prisoners a troupe of royal dancers who are believed to have exercised a lasting influence on Vietnamese music. See Le Thanh Khoi, *op. cit.*, p. 140, and Thai Van Kiem, *La princesse Huyen Tran et l'influence sino-chame sur la musique classique viet-namoise,* Saigon, 1950.

13. "A relatively stable central government became necessary very early in Vietnam, at a time when the first French kings of the house of Capet had difficulty in making their orders obeyed between the Seine and Loire. . . . This fact is explained by the necessity to maintain irrigation canals and dykes to protect the . . . results of the progress agriculture had made under Chinese domination."—Chesneaux, *op. cit.*, p. 28.

14. The city of Hanoi was founded during the Chinese occupation of Vietnam. The Chinese called it Dong Kinh (Tongking) i.e., Capital of the East, a term later erroneously applied to the entire province. After independence had been achieved in 939, Ngo Quyen transferred the capital upstream to Co Loa, where some of the ancient rulers were supposed to have resided. Economic reasons and their policy of expansion at the expense of Champa induced the Ly kings to move their capital again to Hanoi, which was then named Thang Long, but was renamed Dong Kinh by Le Loi after his victory over the Chinese in 1428 (Masson, *Histoire de l'Indochine,* Paris, 1950, p. 31).

15. Twice a year the ruler performed the rite *tich dien* by ploughing the first furrow and by harvesting the first fruit. In 1048 the Xa Tac Dan, a temple of the gods of the earth and the harvest, was erected. There the emperor sacrificed four times every year, to each of the four seasons, and prayed for rain and fertility. New Year's Day according to the lunar calendar was the holiday marking the rejuvenation of nature and therefore the greatest festival of the monarchy (H. Maspéro, *Les religions chinoises,* Vol. I., pp. 19-47; Le Thanh Khoi, *op. cit.*, pp. 147, 149).

16. Hien Tong (his name is sometimes also given as Hien Ton), who

reigned from 1497 to 1504, introduced mulberry trees and silkworms into Vietnam; he built canals and roads and allotted fallow land to peasants willing to work it (Le Thanh Khoi, *op. cit.*, p. 232).

17. Chinese remained the language of government and, for a long time, of the literary life of Vietnam. Only in the latter part of the fourteenth century did the Vietnamese develop their own script, a less difficult form of Chinese characters. Soon afterward a national literature written in the new script began to appear, but did not replace Chinese language and script at once. Almost one hundred years after the introduction of a Vietnamese script and the appearance of a national literature, the annals composed by order of Le Thanh Tong were still written in Chinese (Latourette, *op. cit.*, p. 273).

18. To the civil mandarins (Quan Van) all administrative functions were reserved. They were chosen from the educated class and had to pass severe examinations. Their social standing was far higher than that of the military mandarins (Quan Vo). The Confucian doctrine of the inferiority of the military career had been absorbed by the Vietnamese during the Chinese occupation. Both the civil and the military mandarinates were divided into nine degrees, and each degree was subdivided into two classes. The military mandarins also had to pass an examination that was rather a physical than an intellectual test. They had to carry two balls of lead, each weighing sixty pounds, over a distance of sixty yards; they had to prove their ability with different weapons such as swords and halberds. Only after having passed these and similar physical tests were they subjected to an examination in military tactics, military history, and the institutions and history of their country. The ninth and eighth degrees of the military mandarinate could be awarded without an examination to soldiers who had excelled in bravery. For the seventh degree and all higher ranks examinations were prescribed. The seventh and sixth degrees were conferred on company commanders, the fifth and fourth degrees on colonels, the third and second on generals, the first degree on marshals and the admiral of the fleet. Only the commander-in-chief (called Marshal of the Center) was a military mandarin of the first class of the first degree. In the civil mandarinate the first class of the first degree was only seldom conferred. The cabinet ministers and governors of the large provinces were mandarins of the second class of the first degree; the governors of the small provinces were mandarins of the second class of the second degree. The mandarins were not only civil servants but priests of the official religion. The symbol of their office was a seal they always had to carry with them. The theft of a mandarin's seal was punished by decapitation. The same

182

punishment was applied for the forgery of an official's seal. The civil mandarinate brought various privileges not only to the holder of the office but also to his family. The sons of mandarins of the first, second, and third degrees were exempt from military service, taxes, and labor service; all sons of mandarins of the fourth degree were exempt from military service, so was one son of mandarins of the fifth degree and the first class of the sixth degree (Pierre Pasquier, *L'Annam d'autrefois: Essai sur la constitution de l'Annam avant l'intervention française*, Paris, 1930, pp. 119-165). About the studies of the mandarin, the examination system, and the manadarinal regime in general, see Chapter V.

19. In China the Grand College for training of civil servants in Confucian orthodoxy was founded by the emperor Wu-ti in 124 B.C. After A.D. 6, examinations were required for all officials.

20. During the Chinese rule Vietnamese ports had been frequented by Indian merchants, and some Indian colonies sprang up. The Indian visitors introduced both Hinduism and Buddhism. Hinduism never made an impact on the Vietnamese; Buddhism did. An Indian named Vinitaruci is credited with having introduced Buddhism to Vietnam around A.D. 580, after having done missionary work for his religion in China since 574. Thai Van Kiem, *op. cit.*, p. 12, says Buddhism was introduced into Vietnam by Chinese refugees from the second century A.D. on. However, several centuries passed before the Buddhist clergy gained influence on the monarchy and government of Vietnam. Under the Ly dynasty (1009-1224) cooperation between the rulers and the Buddhist hierarchy reached a high point. The pagodas acquired large domains, mostly through royal grants. The Ly rulers were ardent Buddhists, who often sent embassies to China to collect and copy holy scriptures. Under the reign of Ly Nhan Tong (or Li Nhon Ton), 1072-1127, the empress Linh Nhan often assembled Buddhist monks in her palace for religious disputation. See Latourette, *op. cit.*, p. 273; Le Thanh Khoi, *op. cit.*, pp. 127-130, 142f., 147f., 152-155; Tran Van Giap, "Le bouddhisme en Annam dès origines au XIIIe siècle," BEFEO, Vol. XXXII, pp. 191, 256.

21. It was also under Ly Thanh Ton that the agrarian cult was introduced. Cf. note 15 of this Chapter.

22. They surrounded themselves also with an elite troop of two thousand men for the protection of their person. See Le Thanh Khoi, *op. cit.*, p. 146.

23. Ly Thai Thong (1028-1054) introduced military conscription for the whole population. Every community had to register all male inhabitants in the following five categories: 1. princes of the blood and manda-

rins; 2. professional military men; 3. special professions (priests, physicians, actors); 4. all other men between eighteen and sixty; 5. male inhabitants over sixty, the sick, and the absent. Each of these categories was separately entered in rolls bound in material of different color. Category 4 had, of course, the largest number of persons. It was bound in yellow covers and gave the whole institution the designation "Yellow Roll." Princes of the blood and mandarins were exempt from military service. So were some sons of mandarins. (See note 18 of this Chapter.) Teachers also were not obliged to serve in the army even if they had no mandarin degree (Le Thanh Khoi, *op. cit.*, pp. 146.; Pasquier, *op. cit.*, pp. 125ff).

24. After having ascended the throne, Le Thai To (1428-1433) initiated a series of far-reaching reforms. His main interest was directed toward the peasantry. During the Chinese occupation the lot of the peasants had deteriorated and the greater part of the soil had come into the hands of large landowners. Le Thai To confiscated the holdings of families who had collaborated with the Chinese and distributed them among the rural masses, together with virgin soil and with the property of persons who died without heirs. During the Chinese war robber bands had established themselves all over the country. Le Thai To exterminated the brigands and introduced a new penal code to fight crime more effectively. It is interesting to note that gambling, that eternal vice of Indochina, was punished by cutting off one hand. Furthermore, Le Thai To democratized education by admitting children of the people to the colleges along with sons of mandarins. He even extended his reforms to religion. Monks had to pass examinations to prove their knowledge of theology, otherwise they were forced to leave the monasteries and choose useful occupations. Another great ruler of the dynasty, Le Thanh Tong (1459-1497), created an administration of a character very advanced for the fifteenth century, including a cabinet with a prime minister and ministers of rite, interior, finance, army, justice, and public works. He built dykes, appointed supervisors for their maintenance, forbade landowners to leave their fields fallow under penalty of confiscation, and systematically extended cultivation into virgin areas. Communal property was declared inalienable and was divided periodically among needy peasants. Far ahead of his times, Le Thanh Tong founded numerous hospitals where patients were treated at state expense, and he also organized a service to fight epidemics. He tried to imbue his subjects with the moral ideals of Confucianism, forbade the building of more temples, which he considered to be places of superstition, and published a moral code in twenty-four articles regulating

184

the duties and privileges of state and family. In accordance with the Confucian code, he decreed the separation of sexes and—a most original measure—fixed a maximum time limit for the period between engagement and marriage. Le Thanh Tong is also credited with one of the most advanced legal codes of older times—an almost complete codification of the civil law. A remarkable feature of this code was that it decreed women's equality with men in almost every respect. Marriage became valid even without parental permission. Daughters were granted equal rights with sons to the parental inheritance. In the field of education Le Thanh Tong enlarged the National College by building a Temple of Literature, where the students prostrated themselves before the image of Confucius on the first day of every month. He also founded an academy (Tao Dan) where twenty-eight court dignitaries competed in composing poetry. *The Nine Songs of the Garden of Red Jade* originated from these contests. In Le Thanh Tong's reign the folklore of Indochina was collected and the arts flourished. His achievements were upheld and even enlarged under his son, Hien Tong (1497-1504). (See note 16, above) Hien Tong improved the administration of justice by introducing a direct appeal to himself against a judge's sentence.

25. The term "feudal" is here used in a somewhat looser sense than by Karl A. Wittfogel, who tries to show that "hydraulic societies," as he describes and discusses them in his latest book, are not feudal societies. See Karl A. Wittfogel, *Oriental Despotism*, Yale University Press, 1957.

26. This kind of slavery was legally abolished in 1403 for persons entered in the Yellow Rolls of military conscription, but the right of a creditor to seize a debtor and hold him in bondage until he had paid off his debt through labor was still a provision of the progressive code of Le Thanh Tong in the fifteenth century. Cf. Le Thanh Khoi, *op. cit.*, pp. 148, 225f.; R. Deloustal, *La justice dans l'ancien Annam*, Hanoi, 1911.

27. Foremost of them was Le Thai To (see note 24 above), although his land distribution program did not create equal holdings; nor did it touch the possessions of all proprietors, because that might have caused a revolution. But communities with extensive landholdings were forced to abandon a certain part of them in favor of poorer villages. These reforms were taken up and enlarged upon by Le Thanh Tong, who enforced the law against neglect and disuse of farm land, and set up military colonies on virgin soil. The settlers were peasants in time of peace and soldiers in time of war (Le Thanh Khoi, *op. cit.*, pp. 217f., 224f.; Deloustal, "Resources économiques et financières de l'état dans l'ancien Annam," *Bulletin des Amis du Vieux Hué*, 1932, no. 2, p. 155; Deloustal, *La justice dans l'Annam*, Hanoi, 1911, pp. 217-232, 265;

Vu Van Hien, *La propriété communale au Tonkin,* Paris, 1939, pp. 24f).

28. They were to be found especially among the sixteenth-century rulers of the Later Le dynasty, beginning with Le Uy Muc (or Le Ui-Muc De) who reigned from 1505 to 1509. He spent his nights in orgies, and the next morning he strangled the women whom he had debauched the night before. He was murdered by Prince Gian Tu, who proclaimed himself king under the name of Tuong Duc or Le Tuong-Duc De (1509-1516). After some effort to reform the administration, he fell into the wicked ways of his predecessor. He was murdered by a high dignitary whom he had ordered whipped for having given him un-solicited advice. This dignitary, Trinh Duy San, led a successful revolt against Tuong Duc and put him to death. One of the most confused and bloody periods in Vietnamese history followed. Another general, Ngu-yen Hoang, revenged Tuong Duc and burned the capital. King followed king in quick succession, and each ascendance to the throne was the result of regicide. For a detailed description of these confused periods of Vietnamese history, see Le Thanh Khoi, *op. cit.,* pp. 233ff.

29. Chinese recognition of Vietnamese independence had already been extended previously to the Dinh and then to Le Hoan. It was granted for the third time to Ly Thuang Kiet in 1077 in exchange for five border districts. In 1079 these districts were returned to Vietnam which, in compensation, released Chinese prisoners of war. In 1084 the Chinese-Vietnamese frontier was delineated by a mixed commission and normal relations were restored. In 1174 the Chinese also recognized the ruler of Vietnam, styled until then king of Giao Chi, as king of Annam (Annam Quoc Vuong). Cf. Le Thanh Khoi, *op. cit.,* pp. 162f.; Ma Touan Lin *Ethnographie des peuples étrangers à la Chine,* Geneva, 1876-1883, Vol. II, pp. 343f.; Hoang Thuc Tram, *Lich su xa hoi Vietnam* (published 1950 in the Vietnamese language). There is some dispute among scholars about the correctness of the date of 1174 for the recognition of the king-dom of Annam by the Chinese. See Le Thanh Khoi, *op. cit.,* p. 163, note 69.

30. Kublai Khan's empire stretched from European Russia, Iran, and Iraq in the west to the China Sea in the east, from the Mongolian-Siberian border in the north to Vietnam in the south. His capital, Cam-baluc, was probably present-day Peking. Over much of this territory Kublai's control was only nominal. Cf. Latourette, *op. cit.,* H. Yule, *Cathay and the Way Thither,* London, 1913; H. Yule, *The Book of Ser Marco Polo,* London, 1921.

31. Kublai also attacked Burma and Indonesia without being able to secure complete control over these two regions. However these wars

had a lasting historical effect. Through the destruction of the ancient Indianized kingdoms in Burma and Indonesia, the Mongols paved the way for the rise of Thailand (Siam) in the Menam valley. A Thai group, the "Siamese," became independent from the Khmer empire in the middle of the thirteenth century and flourished under a famous king, Rama Kamheng, toward the end of the thirteenth century (Le Thanh Khoi, *op. cit.,* pp. 189f.; Coedès, *Les états hindouisés d'Indochine et d'Indonésie,* Paris, 1948, pp. 327ff.; H. Maspéro, *Le royaume de Champa,* Paris, 1928).

32. The victorious general, Tran Hung Dao, is one of the most venerated heroes in Vietnamese history. Many Buddhist pagodas have been erected in his honor. The cult of Tran Hung Dao has not come to an end yet. When the Communist general Giap started his offensive against the so-called Delattre line in 1951, he quite officially put his action under the patronage of Tran Hung Dao (Chesneaux, *op. cit.,* p. 30). Tran Hung Dao is credited with having defeated 500,000 Mongols with his army of 200,000. At the beginning of the Mongol invasion he assembled 10,000 old men from all over the country and asked them for advice whether to risk a fight against superior forces or to submit to Mongol domination. All 10,000 shouted "War." Tran Hung Dao's warriors are reported to have tattooed the slogan *"Death to the Mongols"* on their arms. For a detailed report on the Mongol invasion of Vietnam, see Le Thanh Khoi, *op. cit.,* pp. 183-189. Tran Hung Dao's proclamations to his officers and soldiers are a classic of Vietnamese literature. *Ibid.,* p. 176.

33. King Che Bong Nga (ca. 1360-1390) restored the power of Champa for a short period. He landed with a fleet in the Tongking delta and pillaged Hanoi (1371). King Tran Due Ton of Vietnam (also called Kham Hoang) thereupon invaded Champa but was ambushed and massacred with all his troops (1377). In the same year Che Bong Nga attacked Hanoi again from the sea, retook the previously lost Cham provinces, and even conquered the Vietnamese province of Thanh Hoa. In 1383 he attacked Hanoi again, this time overland. When he marched against Hanoi for the fourth time, in 1390, he was killed in battle. With his death Champa's decline as a sovereign state began. The Vietnamese conquered all territories down to and beyond Tourane. What remained of Champa soon became a satellite of Vietnam (Grousset, *Histoire de L'Extrême-Orient,* Paris, 1929, Vol. II, pp. 609f.).

34. In 1368 the Mongol rule over China (Yuan dynasty) was overthrown by a Buddhist monk, Chu Yuang-chang, who made himself emperor and founded a new dynasty, the Ming. This word means "bril-

liant" in Chinese. The name that Chu Yuan-chang gave his dynasty proved to be prophetic. China reached new heights under his successors, both in power and in civilization. The third emperor of the Ming dynasty, Chu Yuang-chang's second son, Yung Lo (also known as Yung Le-ti), who ruled from 1403 to 1424, undertook naval expeditions to Vietnam, Cambodia, Thailand, Sumatra, Java, and Ceylon. He forced a prince who ruled over part of the island of Ceylon to pay tribute to him. Never before and after had Chinese domination reached so far. Chinese fleets visited India, the Persian Gulf, and the Red Sea. For an important naval power, Vietnam with the Tongking delta was a useful base. In 1404 an adventurer, Tran Thiem Binh (also called Tran De-Qui or Tran Gian-Dinh De), revolted against Ho Qui Ly (1400-1407). Tran asked the Chinese emperor for help. Yung Lo gladly interfered in 1406. After having conquered Vietnam in 1407, he deposed both pretenders to the throne and annexed the country to China, declaring that Annam was a part of the former Chinese province of Giao. A detailed description of the Ming conquest of Vietnam is to be found in Le Thanh Khoi, *op. cit.*, pp. 203-209. Cf. also Grousset, *The Rise and Splendor of the Chinese Empire,* Berkeley, 1953, pp. 258-264; Latourette, *op. cit.*, pp. 135f. The Chinese naval expeditions of the fifteenth century are treated by J. L. Duyvendak, "The True Dates of the Chinese Maritime Expeditions in the Early 15th Century," in the periodical *T'oung Pao,* Vol. XXXIV, 1938, pp. 341ff., and in the same author's *Chinese Discovery of Africa,* London, 1950.

35. These public works were achieved through the institution of an obligatory labor service, called *corvée* by French authors. The Vietnamese peasant was forced to devote 60 to 120 days a year to labor on public works. Cf. Chapter I, note 57.

36. When in 1290 famine broke out and many peasants were not only forced to sell their rice field but also their children into slavery, the king (Tran Nhon Ton, 1278-1293) cancelled all taxes and distributed alms. In 1343, when an unusual drought spoiled the harvest, the king (Tran Du Ton, 1341-1369) reduced taxes by fifty per cent. In spite of the tax reduction peasant revolts broke out. Cf. E. Chassigneux, *L'irrigation dans le delta du Tonkin,* Paris, 1921; Chesneaux, op. cit., p. 33.

37. After the Tran dynasty was overthrown by Ho Qui Ly in 1400, the usurper introduced numerous administrative, military, economic, and even cultural reforms. He enlarged his army to one million (?) men, repressed the interior troubles, and consolidated the finances of the country by introducing a personal tax and paper money. In spite of all his

reforms he was unable to prevent the conquest of Vietnam by the Chinese. Peasant revolts continued under the Ming occupation and ceased only after Le Loi started his rebellion against the Chinese in 1418. The Communist historian Thanh Luong (*op. cit.*, pp. 17-19) is strongly partisan against Ho Qui Ly but praises Le Loi as the national liberator. In the eyes of present-day Communists, Le Loi, who restored the independence of Vietnam in 1427, is the great hero of the medieval period.

38. Knowing that a part of the population did not acknowledge the Ho dynasty as legitimate, the Ming plastered the country with posters and let pieces of wood with inscriptions float down the rivers. In these "leaflets" they declared that they came only to restore the legitimate dynasty, and exhorted the population to assist them in this task. Many officers and soldiers, fooled by the Chinese propaganda, laid down their arms. (Le Thanh Khoi, *op. cit.*, p. 204; cf. also note 34, Chapter III.)

39. While still regent of the country, Ho Qui Ly introduced banknotes in Vietnam in 1396. These banknotes (*Hoi Sao* in Vietnamese) were marked with different designs for each value, as algae, clouds, turtles, phoenixes, dragons, and others. The population was forced to exchange all metal money in their possession against these banknotes. Illegal possession of coins was declared punishable by death. (In Europe banknotes were introduced by Palmstruch, founder of the Bank of Sweden, in 1656.) Ho Qui Ly was also much interested in education. He reformed the public examinations and facilitated school attendance by poor children by introducing free instruction in the capitals of all provinces (Le Thanh Khoi, *op cit.*, pp. 197-200).

40. Only the domains and communal land were taxed. Personal holdings were free of taxes until 1723 (ibid., p. 224).

41. In 1397 Ho Qui Ly decreed that nobody, with the exception of princes and princesses of the blood, might hold more than 10 *mau* of land, about 8.8 acres. (*Ibid.*, p. 199).

42. Le Loi won his decisive victory over the Chinese in 1426 by using elephants against their horsemen. The Chinese lost all their artillery and were restricted to a few fortified places. In order to produce new cannons, the Chinese melted the bells of Quy Dien and the bronze urn of Pho Minh, two of the four "wonders" of Vietnamese antiquity. After all attacks of the beleaguered Chinese had been repulsed, their general Wang Tong looked for a way to save his army and also to save face. He remembered that the Chinese had pretended, in 1407, to have come in support of the Tran dynasty. He therefore offered to give up Vietnam if the Tran dynasty was restored. Le Loi, though wanting the throne for himself, agreed in order to spare his country further bloodshed. He suspended the siege,

whereupon Wang Tong sent messengers to China for reinforcements. Le Loi intercepted them and continued to fight against the Chinese. Wang Tong finally capitulated. Le Loi gave him and all his troops permission to retreat to China; he even supplied him with five hundred junks to facilitate his return (*ibid.*, pp. 210-216).

43. During his negotiations with Wang Tong, Le Loi had put Tran Cao on the throne. Now the king had lost his usefulness. Le Loi deposed him and made himself ruler of Vietnam, thus founding the Later Le dynasty. The dates of the beginning and end of the various dynasties vary with different authors. This is not due to uncertainty of information but rather to the interpretation of events. Some historians, e.g., date the Later Le dynasty from 1428, the year in which Le Loi proclaimed himself king; others put the beginning at 1418, when Le Loi started his successful revolt against the Chinese (Hall, *op. cit.*, pp. 171-175; Le Thanh Khoi, *op. cit.*, pp. 203ff., 231f.; Duong Quang Ham. *op. cit.*, *pp.* 57f., 72; Maspéro, "Etude d'histoire d'Annam II: La géographie politique de l'empire d'Annam sous les Le, les Tran at les Ho (Xe-XVe siècles)," BEFEO, Vol. XVI, no. 1.).

44. The taxes extracted from the peasants were almost the only source of income for the Vietnamese state.

45. Cf. note 27, above. The collaborators were also executed as traitors.

46. Toward the end of the fifteenth century the kingdom of Champa disappeared. Several small principalities sprang up on its territory. They were gradually absorbed by Vietnam in the seventeenth and eighteenth centuries. The details of this piecemeal final absorption of the remnants of Champa by Vietnam are described in Le Thanh Khoi, *op. cit.*, pp. 264ff. For the conquest of Champa by Vietnam see especially the following works: C. Maybon, *Histoire moderne du pays d'Annam,* Paris, 1920; Trinh Hoi Duc, *Histoire et description de la Basse-Cochinchine,* Paris, 1863; L. P. Briggs, *The Ancient Khmer Empire,* Philadelphia, 1951; G. Maspéro, *L'empire khmer,* Phnom Penh, 1904; A. Leclerc, *Histoire du Cambodge,* Paris, 1914; P. Boudet, "La conquête de la Cochinchine par les Nguyen et la rôle des émigrés chinois," BEFEO, Vol. XLII, pp. 115-132.

47. Revolts of the ethnic minorities, the Tho, the Nung, the Thai, and the Muong, occurred as often in the fifteenth century as in previous times. The tribute imposed on these peoples by the government in Hanoi always lay heavy on them. In the first ten years after the foundation of the Le dynasty, 1430 to 1440, five rebellions of the Muong, two of the Thai north of the delta, and one each of the Thai south of the delta and of the Nung are recorded. The Red River delta was again the scene

190

of a revolution after the death of Le Thanh Tong. In 1516 Tran Cao raised the banner of revolt in the immediate vicinity of Hanoi. He posed as an incarnation of Buddha, dressed in black, and ordered his soldiers to shave their heads. The Le dynasty of the fifteenth and sixteenth centuries was unable to keep in check either the peasants of the plains or the minorities of the mountains. (Chesneaux, *op. cit.*, p. 42.)

48. Hien Tong died, still a young man, through a grave illness. His oldest son, Tuc Tong, reigned only six months (1504-1505). He was followed by his brother Uy Muc (1505-1509), the first of a series of cruel and depraved rulers. About him and his successors, see note 28 above.

49. Mac Dang Dung's rebellion started in 1524 and ended in 1527 with his ascending the throne. He ordered the execution of the legitimate ruler, known under different names: Le Hoang De Xuan, or Le Hoang Thung, or Cung Hoang De, or Le Cung Hoang. The mother of the young ruler was also assassinated. The annals enumerate all the mandarins who remained faithful to the Le dynasty and refused to collaborate with the usurper. They were either beheaded or committed suicide by jumping into rivers or killing themselves at home. Mac Dang Dung abdicated in favor of his son, Dang Doanh, in 1529, retired to his native village occupying himself ostensibly with fishing, but in reality administered Vietnam from retirement (Le Thanh Khoi, *op. cit.*, pp. 235f).

50. He had tried hard to secure peace with the Mings but had failed. Cf. *ibid.*, pp. 202ff.

51. Mac ceded six districts (*dong*) to China: Ta Phu, Kim Lac, Co Xung, Lien Cat, La Phu, and An Luong. They were mostly inhabited by non-Vietnamese mountain tribes. The rest of Vietnam he was to rule under Chinese protection. This agreement was reached in 1540. Cf. Le Thanh Khoi, *op. cit.*, p. 236; C. Dévéria, *Histoire des relations de la Chine avec l'Annam-Vietnam du XVIe au XIXe siècle,* Paris, 1880; L. Aurousseau in BEFEO, 1920, no. 4, pp. 98-102.

52. The Le actually did send a mission to Peking by sea in 1532 to denounce Mac and to ask help against the usurper. The Ming, glad to have an opportunity to interfere in Vietnamese affairs, pretended to be agreeable to the demands of the legitimate dynasty, and massed an army on the frontier of Tongking. However, they finally accepted the arrangement with Mac that brought them six districts and the protectorate over the rest of Vietnam.

53. The Mac dynasty came to an end with Mac Kinh Hoan (or Mac Kinh Vu), who reigned from 1638 to 1677. The Mac enjoyed a certain protection by the Ming and, after 1644, by the Manchu rulers of China.

Only when Mac Kinh Hoan sided with a rebellious governor in southeast China against the Manchu emperor, was protection withdrawn and the Trinh allowed to do away with the Mac (Le Thanh Khoi, *op. cit.*, p. 251).

54. There exists in English a contemporary report by a traveler in the Far East on the seventeenth century division of Vietnam. This report, although highly inaccurate in respect to the historical events that led to the cession of the South, is very significant as far as it describes the relationship between the Le monarchy and the Trinh rulers of North Vietnam. The reader will find this description in William Dampier's *Voyages and Discoveries* (The Argonaut Press, London, 1931), which is a new edition of a work that was published in 1699 as the second volume of Dampier's *New Voyage Round the World,* which appeared in 1697. The first part of *Voyages and Discoveries* consists of a detailed account of Dampier's adventures in Tongking in the year 1688. Dampier describes the existing division of power in Hanoi in the following paragraphs from chapter IV, entitled "Of the Government, Kings, Soldiery, and Mandarins," pp. 50-51. His description will become very clear if the reader, wherever Dampier speaks of the *Boua,* reads "the Le emperor," and if he substitutes "the Trinh ruler" for the *Choua:*

"This Kingdom is an absolute Monarchy, but of such a kind as is not in the World again; for it has two Kings, and each supreme in his particular way: The one is called *Boua* [Le], the other *Choua* [Trinh]; which last name I have been told signifies 'Master.' The *Boua* [Le] and his Ancestors were the sole Monarchs of Tonquin; tho' I know not whether as independent Sovereigns, or as Tributaries to China, of which they have been thought to have been a Frontier Province, if not a Colony: for there is a great Affinity between them in their Language, Religion, and Customs. These two kings they have at present, are not any way related in their Descent or Families: nor could I learn how long their Government has continued in the present Form; but it appears to have been for some Successions. The occasion is variously reported; but some give this account of it.

"The *Boua's* [Le] or ancient King's of Tonquin, were formerly Masters of Cochinchina, and kept that Nation in subjection by an Army of Tonquinese constantly kept there, under a General or Deputy, who ruled them. When Cochinchina threw off the Tonquinese Yoak, the King had two great Generals, one in Cochinchina, and another in Tonquin itself. These two Generals differing, he who was in Cochinchina revolted from his Sovereign of Tonquin, and by his Power over the Army there, made himself King of Cochinchina: since which these two Nations have always

192

been at Wars; yet each Nation of late is rather on the defensive part than on the offensive. But when the General who commanded in Cochinchina had been thus successful in his Revolt from under the *Boua* [Le], the Tonquinese General took the Courage to do so too; and having gained the Affections of his Army, deprived the King his Master of all the Regal Power, and kept it with all the Revenues of the Crown in his own hands: yet leaving the other the Title of King; probably, because of the great Zeal the People had for that Family. And thus the Kingdom came wholly into the Power of this Tonquinese General, and his Heirs, who carry the Title of *Choua* [Trinh]; the *Boua's* [Le's] of the Ancient Family having only the shadow of that Authority they were formerly Masters of. The *Boua* [Le] lives the Life of a kind of Prisoner of State, within the old Palace, with his Women and Children; and diverts himself in Boats among his Fish-ponds within the Palace Walls, but never stirs without those Bounds. He is held in great Veneration by all the Tonquinese, and seemingly by the *Choua* [Trinh] also; who never offers any violence to him, but treats him with all imaginable respect. The People say they have no King but *Boua* [Le] and seem to have sad Apprehensions of the Loss they should have, if he should dye without an Heir: and whenever the *Choua* [Trinh] comes into his presence, which is 2 or 3 times in the Year, he useth abundance of Compliments to him, and tells him that his very Life is at his Service, and that he governs and rules wholly to do him a Kindness: and always gives him the upper Hand. So also when any Ambassadors are sent from the Emperour of China, they will deliver the Message to none but the *Boua* [Le], and have their Audience of him. Yet after all this Pageantry, the *Boua* [Le] has only a few Servants to attend him, none of the Mandarins make their Court to him, nor is he allowed any Guards: All the Magistracy and Soldicry, Treasure, and the ordering of all Matters of Peace or War, are entirely at the *Choua's* [Trinh's] disposal; all Preferment is from him, and the very Servants who attend the *Boua* [Le], are such only as the *Choua* [Trinh] places about him. Besides these Servants, none are ever suffered to see the *Boua* [Le], much less Strangers: So that I could learn nothing as to his Person. But as to the *Choua* [Trinh], I have been informed that he is an angry, ill-natured, leprous Person. He lives in the second Palace, where he has ten or twelve Wives; but what Children I know not. He governs with absolute Authority over the Subjects, and with great Tyranny: for their Lives, Goods, and Estates are at his Command. . ."

55. The first was called the wall of Dong Hoi, the second the wall of Tran Ninh or Truong Duc. They were about twenty feet high. For a

detailed description of these walls see L. Cadière, "Le mur de Dong-hoi, étude sur l'établissement des Nguyen en Cochinchine," BEFEO, Vol. VI., pp. 95ff. Cf. also Le Thanh Khoi, *op. cit.*, pp. 246f., and Masson, *op. cit.*, p. 37.

56. The Nguyen made an attempt to obtain recognition from China but did not succeed.

57. This is a rough estimate. Reliable population figures are not available for the two parts of the country. All authors dealing with this period are vague in this respect. The relative strength of the Nguyen and the Trinh is difficult to assess because the frontiers between the two states were fluctuating and because both extended their territory during the 150 years of their war. There is agreement among the authors that the Trinh had a numerically superior army and navy. Thai Van Kiem, in an article in *The Times of Vietnam* entitled "The Origin of the Vietnamese Army" says about the Nguyen Navy: "The armed forces included also 15,000 sailors scattered on 500 well-painted galleys having three cannons, one at the head and two at the stern. Twenty-five rowers stood at each board, facing the head of the galley. The rest were fighting sailors." According to reports of Christian missionaries, the army of the Trinh was 100,000 strong, that of the Nguyen only 50,000. The Nguyen troops were, however, better trained and equipped with modern artillery, which they had procured with the help of the Portuguese João da Cruz. They were therefore able to resist the onslaught of the Trinh forces. Another reason for the successful resistance of the smaller Nguyen state was the fact that the Trinh were continually bothered by the rivalry of the Mac, at least in the first phase of the secession (Cadière "Le mur de Dong-hoi," BEFEO, Vol. VI., p. 234; Hall, *op. cit.*, p. 355; Huard and Durand, *op. cit.*, pp. 27ff.; Le Thanh Khoi, *op. cit.*, pp. 250ff).

58. Speaking of the wonderful buildings of Angkor in the Mekong River delta, Hall, *op- cit.*, p. 111, says, "A programme such as this was far too heavy for a people already exhausted by the burden of wars and the buildings of Suryavarman II. Thousands of villages were assigned for the upkeep of the great temples, while tens of thousands of officiants and hundreds of dancers were employed in their service, not to mention the army of laborers. Jayavarman VII . . . impoverished his people with heavy taxation and insatiable demands for forced labor and military service." Coedès, *op. cit.*, pp. 176-210, calls him a megalomaniac whose foolish prodigality was one of the causes of the decadence of his country.

59. A dynastic crisis in Cambodia in 1658 gave Vietnam the pretext to interfere and to force its suzerainty upon that country. Another war in 1674 resulted in the conquest of Saigon and Phnom Penh. In 1679 a

fleet of fifty Chinese junks arrived at Tourane. The sailors of that fleet, remaining loyal to the defeated Ming dynasty and unwilling to serve the Manchus, offered their services to Vietnam. They were settled in the recently conquered South. In 1688 Cambodia revolted against Vietnam but was defeated again. At the beginning of the eighteenth century the dominion of the Nguyen reached the Gulf of Siam. There were more wars against the remnants of Cambodia in 1717, 1739, 1747, 1755, and 1757, and several campaigns against Thailand, which also wanted to share in the dissolution of Cambodia, the last one in 1772. The Nguyen, who moved their capital to Hué in 1687, organized their conquests administratively and settled the annexed territory with colonists. A detailed description of these wars is again to be found in Le Thanh Khoi's standard work, *op. cit.*, pp. 264-275. Other books dealing with this period and the conquest of Cambodia by the Vietnamese are: Maybon, *Histoire du pays d'Annam*, Paris, 1920; L. P. Briggs, *op. cit.*; F. Garnier, "Chronique royale du Cambodge," in *Journal Asiatique*, 1871-1872; G. Maspéro, *L'empire khmer*, Phnom Penh, 1904; Leclerc, *Histoire du Cambodge*, Paris, 1914; P. Boudet, "La conquête de la Cochinchine par les Nguyens et la rôle des émigrés chinois," in BEFEO, Vol. XVII; W. A. R. Ward, *A History of Siam*, Bangkok, 1933.

60. The mandarins had always been hostile to commerce. This hostility is strongly expressed in the teachings of Confucius who considered commerce a contemptible occupation.

61. Hall, *op. cit.*, pp. 359f., dealing with the administration in both parts of Vietnam, says, "[The Trinh] had inherited an administrative system which functioned adequately and was well in advance of any other native administration in South-East Asia. But they did much to improve it. Trinh Cuong (1709-1729) commenced a cadastral survey of land and renovated the taxation registers, thereby reforming the collection of revenue from the products of the soil and the mines. . . . He also improved the penal code. His successor, Trinh Giang (1729-1740), carried through further financial reforms by regulating the salt trade and the exploitation of the mines. . . . In the south the Nguyen, unlike the Trinh, had to create a new administrative system in order to unify their diverse territories. As might be expected, it was very similar to the one which had grown up under the Le dynasty. . . . The Nguyen organized their territory into twelve provinces (*dinh*) with a governor (*tran-thu*), treasurer (*coi-bo*) and judge (*ki-luc*) at the head of each."

62. Cf. the penetrating first chapter on Vietnamese geopolitics in Paul Mus, *Vietnam: Sociologie d'une guerre*, Paris, 1952.

63. Pasquier, *op. cit.*, pp. 55ff., gives the following idyllic and some-

what overromanticized description of a Vietnamese village, stressing that the modern community is hardly different from that of ancient periods: "The villages are of various size, some of them counting 15,000 inhabitants. Inside the community, the houses are separated from each other by hedges, underlining the individualistic character of the people. Inside the village everything is clean, discreet and calm. The tea plants are well kept and the houses beautifully adorned with sculptures of bizarre fishes and grinning dragons. Black pigs and dogs are roaming in the streets. They are never confined to the houses. A stranger, especially if he speaks the native idiom, is received with politeness. If a stream flows through the village, fishermen are sitting on its banks with picturesque fishing tackle. In other communities artisans are weaving silk, producing paper and lacquer wares. The artisans form a caste and the son always takes up the trade of his father. But whether it is an agricultural village or an artisan community, life always follows the same pattern."

64. See especially *Chinh phu ngam,* the song of a woman whose husband went to war, a poem of melancholy beauty, containing discreet social criticism and voicing sympathy with the suffering poor (Le Thanh Khoi, *op. cit.,* p. 276). In Nguyen Du's famous epic *Kieu* one finds the following lines (591-598):

> The whole day was spent begging and asking for mercy, but the crying and pleading made the men only deaf, and their cruel hands continued to beat. On the beam of the house they hung a rope for the torture of the innocent. A lifeless stone would have felt pity at this spectacle, but did it move these people? . . . Against injustice the victims have no resort but to cry to Heaven. Heaven, however, is too high to hear. One day suffices for the vengeance of the mandarins that causes irreparable ruin for nothing but a little money.

(Rendered into English after a French translation, from the Vietnamese, by Nguyen Van Vinh, Saigon, 1951.)

65. The Trinh reduced the power of the mandarins by forbidding them to create villages under their own exclusive feudal jurisdiction. They preferred to give them pensions instead of land. In the South, Hien Vuong (1648-1687) set up a bureau of agriculture which classified cultivated lands and encouraged cultivation of virgin soil (Hall, *op cit.,* p. 395f).

66. The embittered subjects "may kill some local officials. They may defeat the government's men in arms. They may even overthrow a tottering dynasty. But eventually they will only revive—and rejuvenate—the agromanagerial despotism whose incompetent representatives they eliminated. The heroes of China's famous bandit novel, the Shui-hu-Ch'uan, could think of nothing better to do than to set up on their rebel island a

196

miniature version of the very bureaucratic hierarchy which they were so fiercely combating."—Wittfogel, *Oriental Despotism*, p. 135.

67. Maybon, *op. cit.*

68. The great-grandfather of the Tay Son brothers took part in one of the wars between the Trinh and the Nguyen on the side of the former, was captured by the latter and sent to a newly created village, Tay Son, on the Ankhe plateau in Cochinchina. Under the name of their native village the three brothers, Nhac, Lu, and Hué, became known in history. They themselves adopted the famous name of Nguyen as family name. It seems that the oldest brother, Nguyen Nhac, was first a sort of Vietnamese Robin Hood who took to the woods in 1771 as the head of a band of outlaws, robbing the rich and aiding the poor. The peasant masses followed him in the hope of a social revolution. His army swelled to such a size that he defeated Trinh Sam (1767-1782) in 1776 and proclaimed himself emperor in 1778 under the title Thay Duc (1778-1793). A civil war followed in the North and South. Saigon was taken, lost, and retaken several times until, in 1783, Nguyen Anh, the leader of the anti-Tay Son forces gave up and fled to Thailand. Now the Tay Son turned against the North. The youngest brother, Hué, took Hanoi in 1786. The rival dynasties of the Nguyen and the Trinh were both deposed by the Tay Son brothers. Hué formally installed the ancient Le dynasty and married the daughter of Le Hien Toang, the last of the Le. Meanwhile the high mandarins of the old regime, afraid of the social implications of the Tay Son victory, asked the Manchu rulers of China for help. A Chinese army of 200,000 men invaded Vietnam but was routed by Hué in 1789. For a brief time the Tay Son were masters of the whole of Vietnam. Hué died in 1792, Nhac in 1793. Hué's son, Nguyen Quan Toan, became emperor. He succumbed to the influence of the mandarins, discontinued the assistance to the villages his father and uncle had introduced, lost the sympathy of the peasantry, and was defeated by Gia Long in 1802. Sociologically the Tay Son episode is difficult to assess. The Tay Son revolution was to some extent rooted in the small merchant class. The followers were recruited from the villages and there was also strong religious support, both Buddhist and Taoist. The Tay Son period is the first event in Vietnamese history that was described by contemporary European eyewitnesses, especially Pigneau de Béhaine, Bishop of Adran. Nevertheless, the history of the Tay Son is still poorly explored. A biography of the Tay Son brothers is available only in Vietnamese (in Liet Truyen, *Chinh Bien*, XXVII and XXXX). Cf. Le Thanh Khoi, *op. cit.*, pp. 296-302; Chesneaux, *op. cit.*, pp. 59-63. (More about the Tay Son revolution in Chapter IV, especially note 85.)

Chapter IV

Missionaries, Merchants, and Conquerors

1.

AT THE beginning of the sixteenth century, Portuguese explorers and conquerors started an entirely new chapter in the history of the world: prodded by merchants and missionaries, they became the pioneers of Western imperialism in the Far East. The Portuguese consequently were the first Europeans to establish permanent contacts with Vietnam.[1]

Their arrival in Vietnam in 1535, however, was only a minor and belated event in the history of Portuguese exploration and conquest in Asia. Long before Columbus had been so fantastically successful through failing to reach his goal, the Portuguese had been sailing down the west coast of Africa in hopes of reaching the "Indies" by sea. Their aims were primarily mercantile. They wanted to break the monopoly of the Venetians and Arabs as intermediaries in all trade between the Far East and the West. When the great Vasco da Gama reached India in 1498, after sailing around the Cape of Good Hope,[2] the West had at last found a route for direct penetration into the Asian world.[3]

The Portuguese immediately settled a number of places on the coast of India and started to fight the Arabs for control of the surrounding waters. They quickly succeeded in cutting the old trade route from the East via Alexandria to Venice by blocking the entrance to the Red Sea. Only five years after da Gama's first landing in India, European merchants could buy pepper in Lisbon at a fifth of its price in Venice. Lisbon became the main European depot for all Oriental products.

From India the Portuguese rapidly penetrated farther east under the leadership of Admiral Albuquerque. In 1510 Albuquerque made Goa the first Asian stronghold of the Portuguese and the capital of all their Indian possessions. In order to open the Strait of Malacca for his ever advancing fleets, he attacked and ruined Arab shipping in the Bay of Bengal. Malacca itself, which was the center of a budding Mohammedan empire on the west coast of Malaya, was conquered and made another Portuguese stronghold in 1511. This gave Albuquerque control of the routes into the Gulf of Siam, the South China Sea, and the waters of the vast Indonesian archipelago. Without waiting a moment, the Portuguese pushed up toward Siam and China and down into the Java Sea. They swarmed over Asia "in a spirit of frank brigandage," [4] convinced that the worlds they discovered were created only to make Portugal strong and rich.

It was toward the home of the clove tree and the sources of nutmeg and mace that Albuquerque most eagerly dispatched his best captains and ships. From the very year when they conquered Malacca, the Portuguese stretched their hands out toward the spice treasuries of the distant Ceram and Molucca Islands. The Javanese traders who shipped these spices to the Malacca market were attacked as fiercely as was Arab navigation between Malacca and the Red Sea. The Portuguese also fought the Spanish, who intruded into the Moluccas from the east after the first voyage of Magellan.[5] In order to secure for themselves the high prices they had resented so much when the products of the East could be had only in Venice, the Portuguese drastically reduced the supplies of spices by establishing a monopoly of purchase as well as of shipping and sale. Their trading methods were such that "even their own historians were ashamed of their crimes in the Moluccas."[6] According to Saint Francis Xavier, who arrived in Amboina in 1546, the knowledge of the Portuguese was restricted to the conjugation of the verb *rapar,* in which they showed "an amazing capacity for inventing new tenses and participles."[7] Such talents naturally limited the effectiveness of the Christian missionaries who attempted to prevent the conversion of the whole of Indonesia to the Moslem faith.[8] But the unhappy Portuguese marriage between Christian zeal and naked greed nevertheless became a pattern of colonial behavior for several other nations.

The efforts required to make the spice islands their exclusive domain did not prevent the Portuguese from sailing all over East Asia between Malaya and Japan. Their progress was nowhere else as quick or spectacular as in India and in the spice-filled and politically divided island world of Indonesia, but they opened the doors of most Eastern capitals for contact with the West in a single tremendous push. A Portuguese was the first European to visit Ayuthia, the capital of Siam, and another Portuguese was most likely the first Westerner to see the spectacular ruins of Angkor. Soon after Malacca had fallen into their hands, the Portuguese were able to secure for themselves trading concessions in both Thailand and Burma. They landed on the Chinese coast near Canton in 1513 and reached Japan in 1542. However, a regular base for trade between these remoter countries and the West was established only when the Portuguese settled Macao, in 1557, almost three hundred years before the English became their close neighbors by acquiring Hong Kong.

Roaming the sea between Malaya and southern China, Albuquerque's lieutenants had long been attracted by the inlets and harbors of the east Indochina coast. One of his captains, Antonio da Faria, entered the Bay of Tourane in 1535.[9] He had no trouble finding and acquiring what he was looking for —a suitable bay, less than fifteen miles south of Tourane, where he himself decided on the site of Faifo as another possible center of Portuguese trade and shipping. His plan to make Faifo a stronghold like Goa or Malacca did not materialize, but by 1540 Faifo was the main port of entry for foreign goods into "Cochinchina," which was the name given by the Portuguese to Vietnam [10]

During the sixteenth century the Portuguese controlled Western trade with Vietnam as effectively as Western trade all over Asia. From their strongholds of Macao, Malacca, and Goa, to which they added Colombo and Diu,[11] they dominated Asian waters and were able to hold off all competitors until almost the close of the century. The sixteenth was indeed the century of Portugal's maritime greatness. Her unmatched power at sea was based on the wealth that her conquering merchants derived from the discoveries of her indefatigable explorers and sailors.

2.

However, Portugal's very success shortened the time of her undisputed dominion of the Asian seas. Both her control of Far Eastern shipping and her monopoly on the European spice market were challenged by the English and the Dutch. A Lisbonian Cassandra could have discovered the first omens of Portuguese decline long before the sixteenth century ended.

Holland and England, at war with Portugal and Spain,[12] were forbidden to enter the Lisbon market. Anger and envy were sufficient to explain why they started to do to the Portuguese what the Portuguese had done to the Arabs and Venetians. But the Dutch and the English were also inspired by the more respectable motives, economic and others, that had prompted the Spanish and Portuguese to sail the seas in search of new routes and new worlds. The spirit of adventure and enterprise possessed them as much as their Latin rivals. Besides, to best Philip II of Spain, who occupied also the Portuguese throne after 1580, meant for the Dutch the crowning of their long war of independence.

During the first years of their trade war against the Portuguese, a phase that ended around 1600, the English and Dutch were allies in intention as well as in fact. They both started out by demonstrating that the methods of piracy, as practiced by Malayan and Portuguese raiders in the East, were as compatible with Protestant ethics as they had proved to be with the spirit of Mohammed or the moral code of a Catholic merchant. The destruction of the Spanish Armada in 1588 had strengthened the position of the English and Dutch as powers on the sea. But not until the last two years of the outgoing century, and against the unrelenting opposition of their Portuguese predecessors, did the English and Dutch begin to set up their own trading stations in the Far East. At the turn of the century the two Protestant powers, who would one day possess the two largest colonial empires in Asia, were still not the permanent owners of a single square inch of Asian land. But their determination to rise at the expense of Catholic Portugal and Spain had long been perfectly clear.

Although the reduction of Portuguese power in Asia was a common aim of the English and Dutch, their European alliance against Portugal and Spain never developed into joint action in the Far East. On the contrary, in Asian waters the Anglo-Dutch alliance quickly deteriorated into an Anglo-Dutch struggle over their respective shares in the profitable business of buying and selling spices. It was a struggle as bitter as were the separate trade wars of the English and Dutch against the Portuguese, and as sorry a display of human greed and violence as the world had ever seen. If the peoples of Southeast

Asia had accepted the religion of these intruders, they would certainly have been convinced that Satan had unleashed the hounds of hell.

As it turned out, England's rise to colonial supremacy was still a century away. Neither China nor India was ripe for European conquest. The seventeenth century, as far as Asia was concerned, was to be the century of the Dutch. They were wealthier than the English, and more experienced in navigation and international trade. They became the heirs of the Portuguese chiefly by concentrating their efforts on Southeast Asia.

The English, though deeply engaged between Sumatra and the Moluccas, committed the error of first vying for the Indian positions of the Portuguese. They founded an East India Company in 1600, two years before the Dutch, but in India itself they had made no progress at all by 1610. Only after defeating a Portuguese fleet in Indian waters in 1612 were they able to acquire their first trading concession on Indian soil. By that time, however, their trading stations in Southeast Asia had already been under heavy attack from the aggressively operating Dutch for several years.

When the Dutch founded their East India Company in 1602, they only amalgamated a number of existing companies that had been operating for many years, each on its own smaller scale. At the very outset, the capital of the United Dutch Company was almost ten times as large as that of the English.[13] No less than fifteen Dutch fleets had sailed to the East Indies both around the Cape and through the Strait of Magellan during the four years prior to the founding of the new company. The incentive for these voyages was ordinary and unusual at the same time: Cornelius de Houtnam and others in his wake had shown, between 1595 and 1597, that with daring and luck profits up to four hundred per cent could be made on such expeditions.[14] The Dutch knew how to preserve the advantages they had gained over the English from the start. By 1605 they had visited every major port in Southeast Asia and set up their "factories" [15] all over the archipelago from Malaya to New Guinea.

But less than ten years later the directors of the Dutch Company made a shocking discovery. The gains of the Company, far from fulfilling their original expectations, showed a dangerous tendency to decline. The days of a profitless future could be predicted by the dullest of the many merchants put on canvas by Frans Hals.

One reason for this sorry state of affairs—dividends were not higher than forty, and sometimes as low as ten per cent —was the high cost of military operations, along with the losses suffered in the struggle against the Portuguese. The Portuguese, who had as much to lose as their opponents had hoped to gain, put up a determined fight. At the beginning of the struggle, the Dutch benefited much from the hatred of the native rulers and the island populations for the Portuguese, who were, after all, also the pioneers of Western colonial brutality and corruption. But the ruthlessness and duplicity of the Dutch, who "chastised with scorpions," whereas the Portuguese only "chastised with whips," [16] soon caused unexpected local trading difficulties and unforeseen expenses for aggressive military action as well as for defensive military installations to protect Dutch factories and ports.

This was not all. While the costs of extracting and shipping the spices climbed higher and higher, the prices they brought kept sinking from year to year. The Dutch directors, who were as willing to invest as they were ready to condone the "appalling frightfulness" [17] of the Company's agents, diagnosed the growing competition of the English as the main cause of their unforeseen troubles.

From the outset, the Dutch had made difficulties for the English wherever they could. They tried to prevent them from entering any place the Dutch considered their own by virtue of their earlier arrival. Political considerations vital to their

204

position in Europe forced the Dutch to tolerate the English in Asia, but they did all they could to prevent them from getting more than a small fraction of the Oriental trade. By 1615, however, the leaders of the Dutch became convinced that these considerations had to be dropped. Profits declined, they said, because their policy against the English had not been sufficiently aggressive. And they added that their own venture was bound to ond in failure unless the Dutch Company secured for itself a monopoly of the Asian trade.

The father of this theory was Jan Pieterzoon Coen, one of the many political visionaries of Western colonialism—men whose greatness, as a rule, derived from their ability to make money out of blood. When Coen was appointed governor general of the Netherlands Indies in 1618 the Dutch Company also endorsed his program of action. Coen's task was to fight the Portuguese more energetically, to stamp out the trading activities of the local rulers, to drive the Spanish from the Moluccas even if this meant an expedition to Manila, and above all to ruin English trade and shipping in the archipelago. The English had to be fought in Asia, regardless of all truce negotiations and agreements concluded between the two Companies in Europe.

As behooved a great man of action, Jan Pieterzoon Coen started out by demanding more money in order to conduct the many wars that followed from the application of his program. Very soon he also had two important revelations. One concerned the English. He decided they could only be gotten rid of by destroying their factories and ships and by assassinating their agents. The other revelation was that for the spice trade to remain profitable under all circumstances, the elimination of all competitors was not enough. The motto of the Company was not only to sell dear but also to buy cheap. Local resistance to Dutch buying practices had to be broken, and complete Dutch control over all existing supplies had to be secured. However, this could be achieved only through territorial conquest and the establishment of direct Dutch rule over the spice-producing islands. Higher dividends required the spending of more money and the shedding of more blood.

If the Company would provide the money, Jan Pieterzoon Coen was quite willing to shed the blood. He was neither the first nor the last of the great in business and politics who believed in the maxim that the end must justify the means, without raising the question of whether the end—in this case the Company's desire for higher profits—was not itself in need of justification. Coen's policy, which led to a long and costly struggle, set a pattern of behavior in the colonies that was unfortunately imitated not only by some of his Dutch successors but also by colonial leaders from other Western nations. But even a historian on whose scale of judgment the victims of history have no weight at all would find it difficult to prove that these men and their methods had at least the excuse of being successful. In the case of the Dutch, the results were dubious even from the Company's narrow and selfish point of view. Some individuals became rich, the capital of the Company increased constantly, but the expenses for military and punitive action ate up the Company's resources, while the exploitation and enslavement of the natives impoverished the countries on whose wealth the Dutch had hoped to thrive. The high dividends that kept up the credit of the Company could soon be paid only through the floating of enormous loans. After declining steadily during the whole eighteenth century, the bankrupt Dutch East India Company had to be taken over by the state.[18]

But in spite of the Company's permanent financial difficulties, and also in spite of the commercial origin and the purely commercial nature of their colonial expansion, the Dutch succeeded in replacing the Portuguese as the dominant colonial power of Asia. By 1668, fifty years after Jan Pieterzoon Coen had first taken office, the Portuguese were definitely defeated. They were able to hang on to Goa and Diu in India and to

Macao on the Chinese coast, but Portugal's possessions between India and China and her control of Far Eastern navigation had gone. The Dutch had the Cape of Good Hope. In India they had the Malabar and Coromandel coasts, as well as Ceylon. They also had Malacca, which they had taken from the Portuguese in 1641. In the archipelago Dutch power was supreme. After the Portuguese and Spanish, the English had given up too. Among the spice islands of eastern Indonesia the Dutch had wiped out the independence of every single state. Places they could not permanently control were regularly visited for the purpose of destroying spice trees: the Dutch had to make sure that no sources of supply existed for anyone willing to pay higher prices in Asia and still sell cheaper in Europe than they. They were also the only ones who were permitted to trade with Japan after all Westerners had been expelled by the Japanese in 1641. Between 1642 and 1661 the Dutch even conquered and held Formosa. It would indeed have been surprising if they had not gone into Vietnam too.

3.

The Dutch appeared in Vietnam exactly one hundred years after the Portuguese. They established their first factory in 1636, in the southern half of the country ruled by the Nguyen. But when the rulers of the North, only one year later, gave them permission to set up a factory in Pho Hien,[19] the Dutch instantly directed their main trading activities toward the richer half of Vietnam: the North, governed by the Trinh.

The Trinh, anxious for Western support of their war effort against the Nguyen, soon allowed the Dutch to establish themselves also in their capital.[20] For a price, both the South and the North could enlist European help. The Nguyen had bought weapons and technical assistance from the Portuguese long before they received any offers from the Dutch. Relying on the strength of the North, the Dutch, in their support of the Trinh, went so far as to risk the hostility of the Nguyen.[21] Nourished by Portuguese intrigues, this hostility forced the Dutch in 1654 to retire from the South altogether.

In conformity with the pattern of Western penetration in the East, the next to appear at the gates of Vietnam were the English. But their great time in Asia had not yet begun. They had so far failed in India and Indonesia, and they were not very lucky in Vietnam either. An early English attempt to enter Faifo, in 1613, met with disaster.[22] Later exertions to get a foothold either in the South or the North were blocked by the Portuguese and Dutch. Only in 1672 were the English able to open an office in Pho Hien, which they later moved to Hanoi, hoping for business that would justify the trouble they had taken to get into Vietnam.

In the meantime another rival, the French, had appeared on the scene. The French had founded their own East India Company in 1664, more than sixty years after the English and Dutch.[23] In 1676 they acquired the site of Pondicherry, on the east coast of India south of Madras. In the teeth of the Dutch, they also managed to set up a factory at Bantam, on the western tip of Java. A French ship had gone up the Red River in 1669,[24] but the first regular trading office of the French in Vietnam was not opened until 1680. It too was located in Pho Hien, where the English had started out 8 and the Dutch 43 years earlier. And Portuguese merchants had been in Vietnam 140 years when the French opened shop in Pho Hien. The French came in spite of many warnings by their greatly concerned Western competitors who were already established. Trade with Vietnam, they were told, was bad and was manifestly declining. More unwelcome to their European rivals than to the Vietnamese, the French went to Vietnam at the risk of having their ships sunk by Dutch saboteurs, their agents murdered as a result of Portuguese intrigues, and their merchandise as well as their reputation as traders slandered by the English. The French, of course, were ready to fight back.

But the ugly commercial practices that had created the Portuguese and Dutch monopolies in Indonesia remained unrewarded in Vietnam, as all European traders would eventually learn. Conditions were such that no single member of this discordant European quartet could outplay the other three. What they all needed was a general increase in the volume of business between the West and Vietnam. Their contentious actions, however, strengthened Vietnamese opposition against any closer relations with Europe. This in turn could only add to the existing difficulties for trade with the West. When the French arrived, trade with Vietnam was in fact about to become unprofitable.[25]

It took only a few years for the pessimists among the French to cry out that they had boarded a sinking ship. When the Dutch, in the wake of their conquests on Java, drove both the French and English out of Bantam,[26] the isolated French trading position in Vietnam was doomed. The only comfort of the French was that their stronger rivals suffered the same fate. The English closed their Hanoi factory in 1697, the Dutch theirs in 1700. Only the Portuguese were able to continue their old exchanges between Macao and Vietnam, though on a smaller scale.[27]

When the English East India Company tried to re-enter Vietnam in 1822, after a century of rough treatment for everyone in the subcontinent of India, it warned its agents against a repetition of the abuses committed by the Europeans, blaming them for the failure of all previous trading ventures in Vietnam.[28] The counsel was no doubt wise, but the diagnosis revealed only part of the truth. Before 1672, which was the year the English started to trade with Vietnam, the Dutch and the Portuguese had not done too badly, although their tactics in fighting each other had always been fierce and foul. If their business subsequently declined, this was due largely to the fact that 1672 was also the year when the long war between

North and South Vietnam came to an end. Military equipment, which had been the main item in the list of Western goods imported by Vietnam, was no longer in urgent demand. Peace among the Vietnamese did more to ruin Dutch and Portuguese trade with Vietnam than did European knavery or English and French competition. And peace in Vietnam was followed toward the end of the seventeenth century by a series of long European wars with damaging effects on intercontinental traffic and trade.[29]

However, there were other and more fundamental reasons why the West failed to make trade with Vietnam as simple and profitable a business as with other parts of Asia. The methods of piracy and plunder, for instance, could not be employed. Both South and North Vietnam had strong governments, big armies, and even respectable fleets to defend themselves against brigandage disguised as trade. Vietnam's educated upper class was as experienced in war as in administration and was determined to remain in solid control of the country's wealth. Pirates from the sea, invaders from the mountains, and armies of occupation had again and again been defeated by this firmly entrenched ruling class. It had always been ready to fight and able to mobilize the people when the possessions it managed to extract from them were threatened by foreign hands. As long as the blood and the sweat of the peasants were at their command, the rulers of Vietnam would be able to handle all dangers from abroad.

To treat Vietnam as the Portuguese and Dutch had treated the island populations of Southeast Asia would have been possible only if the West had had the strength to vanquish the Vietnamese. But for the time being this was too costly and too difficult a task. For a conquest of Vietnam the Portuguese were already too weak, the French not yet strong enough, and the Dutch and English too busy holding each other's throat at too many other places. In addition, nobody was quite sure whether

Vietnam was worth the high cost of invasion and rule by force. The country's wealth was certainly not lying at its shores waiting to be picked up by well-armed and ill-intentioned European raiders. Even if her Western intruders had not fought one another in true pirate fashion, Vietnam at the end of the seventeenth century would probably have had no difficulty in holding off a European attack.

In order to add Vietnam to their money-making Asian ventures, the seafaring nations of Europe had to forego their customary method of applying brute force. They decided that trade, by hook or crook, was for the time being the only key to whatever treasures the country possessed. Therefore, fighting one another in order to get the largest share of the existing trade, and trying to cheat the inexperienced natives, were the ways in which the nations of the West became known to the Vietnamese. The English and French made their efforts probably at considerable expense to themselves. They were slow to recognize that Vietnam would be as disappointing a country for trade as it appeared to be difficult for military conquest. They tried hard to do business but failed dismally. Although rich enough potentially, Vietnam was economically not ready at all for genuine trade on a large and profitable scale. Only the state and the small group of the rich were in the market for goods from Europe. "The people," as the French historian Maybon remarked, "had no part in this trade, and without the people solid and lasting commercial relations were impossible."[30] Ruse was of no help either. Most of the tricks that the Portuguese and Dutch had successfully practiced in India and Indonesia were quite ineffectual in Vietnam. It was true that the mandarins, whose status and power were rooted in land and learning, were inexperienced in trade. But if the business of trading was made an exercise in violence, theft, and corruption, these philosophical bureaucrats were likely to be a match for the boldest and most unscrupulous Europeans.

211

Vietnam, in short, was not yet ripe to be exploited by Western greed or victimized by the white man's lust for adventure.

4.

Mercantile penetration of Vietnam had failed, and conquest by force would evidently have been ill advised. The year 1700, therefore, might well have marked an end of all contacts with Europe and of Western influence on the Vietnamese had it not been for an entirely different kind of Western activity in Asia, one as old as Portuguese penetration into the Far East. This was the missionary work of the Catholic Church. After the last European traders had left Vietnam in 1700, Holland and England were definitely out. However, Portugal and France remained represented, because most of the missionaries in Vietnam were either Portuguese or French.

The beginnings of Catholic religious propaganda in Asia are inseparable from the history of Portuguese Far Eastern trade and territorial expansion. When Pope Alexander VI in 1493 divided the world between Portugal and Spain for the purpose of spiritual and territorial conquest, the Portuguese, already wordly masters in the East, somehow managed to seize Asia as their spiritual domain also.[31] Missionaries who went to Asia had to embark in Lisbon and get their "clearance" from the Portuguese authorities in Goa. They worked under Portuguese supervision, which was political as well as ecclesiastic.[32] The Portuguese watched over their exclusive right to organize the transformation of Asian heathens into Christians as jealously as over their monopoly to transform pepper into gold, and they defended it more successfully: it survived their trading monopoly by more than half a century.

The story of the Catholic missions in Asia is a story of many hopeful beginnings and some astonishing recoveries from

212

deadly blows; but, comparing the results with those in Central and South America, it must be regarded as one of failure rather than success. This general truth applies also to Vietnam, in spite of the fact that the Catholic Church was more successful with the Vietnamese than with any other Asian people except the Filipinos.

Very little is known about missionary work during the sixteenth century in Vietnam, in contrast to Indonesia, China, or Japan.[33] According to the Vietnamese annals,[34] a certain Ignatio entered Vietnam and preached in the province of Nam Dinh in 1533, but he was obviously the one proverbial swallow that never made a summer. More is known of a Spanish Dominican by the name of Diego Adverte. But he arrived in Vietnam only in 1596. For a while he was allowed to preach freely, but the appearance of Spanish warships soon after his arrival made the authorities suspicious. They chased Adverte from the pulpit onto one of these unwelcome ships.[35]

Organized religious propaganda began only twenty years later, after Portuguese merchants trading in Faifo had invited a group of reluctantly idle Jesuits in Macao to come to Vietnam. These Jesuits from Macao, who built up the first Vietnamese mission in 1615, already knew a great deal about the hazards and rewards of missionary work in Asia. Most of them had lived through the changing fortunes of their mission in Japan. Founded by Saint Francis Xavier in 1549, the Japanese mission had done extremely well for over thirty years. In 1587, however, the missionaries were ordered to leave Japan.[36] They were not persecuted immediately, and as obedience to anyone but their own superiors was never a Jesuit virtue, the expulsion order, which was repeated several times, remained ineffective for twenty-five years. It was enforced only in 1612. By 1614 the Japanese mission had almost ceased to exist.

The expulsion of the Jesuits from Japan could hardly be called an act of Asian religious intolerance. It must be regarded, rather, as the beginning of the Japanese policy that led to the exclusion of all Westerners from Japan after 1640. This anti-Western attitude was primarily due to internal political preoccupations of the ruling cliques, which however were intensified in the case of the Jesuits by the scheming of Spanish Dominicans who had intruded into this Portuguese sphere around 1585. The Dominicans told the Japanese that the Jesuits were more interested in preparing Japan for Portuguese domination than in saving Japanese souls. Back in Macao from where they had started, the expelled missionaries were waiting either for another assignment or for an early return to their work in Japan.

The Italian Buzomi and the Portuguese Carvallo[37] were the first to exchange their lives of comparative inactivity at the Jesuit Training College at Macao for a chance to make new converts in a new land. They arrived in Tourane in January, 1615, and at once founded the "Cochinchinese Mission" at Faifo. Among the many who hurried to join the new mission was also Christoforo Borri, the first European author on Vietnam and the Vietnamese. As such, he was also the first to succumb to the charms of the Vietnamese, whose "natural kindness and hospitality" he praised beyond measure. Borri regarded the Vietnamese as superior to the Chinese in intelligence and courage, and to all other Asian peoples in friendliness, good manners, and a native craving for knowledge.[38]

But Father Borri was soon overshadowed, as an author as well as in every other capacity, by a Frenchman from the papal city of Avignon, the famous Monsignor Alexander of Rhodes. Rhodes was a gifted, strong, and dedicated man. Only six months after his arrival in Vietnam he had mastered the language and started to preach in Vietnamese.[39] He wrote the first catechism in Vietnamese and also published a Vietnamese-Latin-and-Portuguese dictionary. Moreover, these works were the first to be printed in Quoc Ngu, a truly revolutionary invention, which enabled the Jesuits to write for their converts in Latin letters and freed the Vietnamese themselves from

214

ALEXANDER OF RHODES (1591–1660)
A gifted, strong, and dedicated man.

CATHECHISMVS
in octo dies diuisus.

Dies Primus.

SVppliciter petamus ab optimo Cœli Domino vt adiuuet nos ,ad hoc vt intelligamus probè legem Domini [b] *intelligendum autem ad hoc est neminem esse in hoc sęculo qui diù viuat,* [c] *vix enim pertingitur ad septuagesimum aut octogesimum ætatis annum quęrendus est igitur à nobis modus vt possimus diù viuere,* [e] *hoc est, vitam sempiternam adipisci* [f] *hoc enim verè prudentis est* [g] *cætera omnes huius mundi artes quamuis diuitÿs acquirendis sint aptæ,* [h] *minimè tamen eripere nos poterunt ab ignobilitate & miseria ; quin tădem in eam inci.*

Phép giảng tám
ngày

Ngày thứ nhít.

Ta cầu cử đức Chúa blời giúpsức cho ta biét tỏ tưẵng đạo Chúa là nhưẵng naò [b] vì bậy ta phải hay ỏ thễ nẵy chảng có ai sóu lâu ; [c] vì chưng kẻ đén bảy tám mươi tuẻi chảng cò nhềo. [d] vì bậy ta nên tìm đàng nào cho ta được sỏu lâu, [e] là kièm hàng sỏu bậy: [f] thật là vie người cuẻn tử. [g] khác phép thễ gian nẵy, dù mà làm cho người được phú qúi : [h] saú le chẳng làm. được cho ta ngày sau

First page of Alexander of Rhodes' catechism in Latin and Quoc Ngu, printed in Rome, 1649.

CATHECHISMVS

Pro ijs, qui volunt suscipere

BAPTISMVM

In Octo dies diuisus.

Phép giảng tám ngày cho kẻ muắn chiụ phép rứa
tọi, ma ꞗểào đạo thánh đức Chúa bltò̀i

Ope Sacræ Congregationis de Propaganda Fide
in lucem editus

Ab Alexandro de Rhodes è Societate IESV,
eiusdemque Sacræ Congregationis
Missionario Apostolico.

ROMÆ, Typis Sacræ Congregationis de Propaganda Fide
Superiorum permissu

Title page of Alexander of Rhodes' catechism in Latin and
Quoc Ngu, printed in Rome, 1649.

FRANÇOIS PALLU, Apostolic Vicar of Tongking (1626-1684)
Msgr. Pallu in a memorandum to the East India Company: In
Indochina there would be "as many promoters of the Company's
progress as there will be bishops, priests and believers."

the difficulties of written communication inherent in their ideography derived from the Chinese.[40] Quoc Ngu was the result of collective efforts by Portuguese and Italian Jesuits, but it was Rhodes who perfected and consciously employed it as a weapon in the battle that was about to begin between the Catholic missionaries and the Confucianist mandarins for the souls of the Vietnamese.[41]

In 1627 Rhodes was sent to Hanoi. He was well received by the court and instantly successful with the people. The rich presents he gave to the Trinh rulers, however, had far less value than the precious gifts he himself possessed as a diplomat, a preacher, and an organizer of the church.[42] According to his own meticulous accounts, he baptized 6,700 persons in less than two years. He made Catholics of many nobles and even converted a princess and seventeen relatives of the ruling Trinh.

At this important juncture, Rhodes was a man of thirty-seven. He was to live another thirty years and to remain active to the last beat of his heart, but the climactic moments of his existence were his first years in Vietnam. He would relive them, but only as memories of an unforgettable past.

Rhodes' active life was like a mirror that reflected the agitated history of the missions in Vietnam. He was expelled from the North in 1630, at a time when the Nguyen in the South too began to wonder what this new religion might do to the moral foundation of their state. As long as the war between the South and North lasted, the policy of tolerance was interrupted only rarely by edicts against the "false doctrines" from abroad. Both the North and the South were lenient in applying their anti-Catholic measures for fear that the ships with their precious cargoes of weapons and ammunition might never return, as the Jesuits frankly declared, if the missionaries were not permitted to stay.

After his expulsion by the Trinh Rhodes continued to work for his cause, in the fashion of the eternal political refugee,

Over a distance in time of two hundred years, it ignited a conflagration in Indochina whose consequences, a full century after it occurred, may still become the cause of a cataclysm for the entire world.

How close the French marriage between trade and religion was when France made her first efforts to enter Vietnam could be seen from an observation made in a contemporary letter from Hanoi. Its author was an agent of the local English factory, and he wrote his letter long before the French started their own quite unprosperous factory in Pho Hien in 1680. The puzzled Englishman remarked: "The French have a house in town, but we cannot make out whether they are here to seek trade or to conduct religious propaganda." [44]

This surprising inability to recognize the difference between French efforts to make money and French attempts to save souls had a very good reason. The French house in Hanoi had been founded ostensibly to organize Franco-Vietnamese trade, but it was in reality inhabited by missionaries disguised as French merchants. Some trade was conducted, but mainly as a cover for "underground" proselytizing.

The clash of two different lines of action, quite unrelated to each other in their beginnings, had created this curious state of affairs. One originated in France. Churchmen and businessmen, encouraged by a proselytizing and mercantilistic state, had recognized that in their struggle for a French share of the Asian pastures, an intimate cooperation between missionaries and merchants was a condition of success for both. A maritime trading company created at Rouen in 1660, for instance, made precise statutory provisions for the free transportation and feeding and the establishment of missionaries and their servants in "Tonkin" or China, in exchange for clearly specified services by the missionaries as the company's Asian buyers, sellers, and bookkeepers.[45] And François Pallu, one of the two apostolic vicars appointed by Rome to direct the Vietnamese missions, was even more blunt than the money-making maritime merchants who were the first to provide for his voyage to the East.[46] They could be sure, he told the directors of the French East India Company in a report on Indochina submitted in 1667, that they would have "as many promoters of the Company's progress as there will be bishops, priests and believers."

Pallu had stated the principles of this cooperation between business and Church immediately after his appointment as head of the Tongking mission in 1658. Although these voyages to the Far East, he said, were undertaken for the glory of God and for the conversion of souls, their practical side must not be neglected; however, in order to realize profits of three hundred per cent and more it was necessary to know the conditions under which they could be made.[47] Pallu must have devoted as much time to the study of these conditions as to his work for the Church. When the French started to compete with the Portuguese, English, and Dutch, no Frenchman knew better how to go about organizing Western trade with Asia, nor was anyone more active in spreading his knowledge among interested circles than the apostolic vicar François Pallu. He was forever writing reports and submitting projects for new trading ventures to the East India Company and the French Minister Colbert, and he even advised Colbert and the Company as to the best military measures to be taken against the Dutch.[48]

When Pallu and his French colleague Monsignor Lambert de la Motte tried to resume the work that Rhodes and his Jesuit colleagues had been forced to abandon in the 1640's, the obstacles in their way greatly strengthened their alliance with business—into which they had entered, however, long before either of them had seen Vietnam. These obstacles resulted from the actions that the two Vietnamese governments had been taking, ever since 1630, against the missionaries as organizers of a Catholic community in Vietnam. Although the missionaries were not yet persecuted, their activities were made illegal and they themselves could enter the country, North or South, only clandestinely. To get their assistants into Vietnam, Pallu and de la Motte chose the method of disguising them as merchants and of using them as promoters of Franco-Vietnamese trade.[49]

But trade with the West no longer flourished in Vietnam after 1672. The fate of the missions, therefore, would ultimately depend on the degree of acceptance or rejection of their religious activities by the Vietnamese.

6.

The Jesuits and their Catholic competitors in Asia apparently were not at all averse to the writing of letters, and many have also recorded their experiences and observations in voluminous books. This whole literature confirms the fact that the missionaries were well received in Vietnam, unmolested by the authorities at the beginning, and quite successful with the people whom they were able to reach. Father Borri's description of the way in which these strangers were gently forced to answer hundreds of questions and civilly persuaded by the poorest to share their modest meals testified as eloquently to the immediate popularity of the missionaries as Monsignor Rhodes' impressive statistics and hopeful prognostications.

But in spite of some claims made by Rhodes and several others, conversions were rare within the circles of the educated, the ruling, and the rich.[50] The early converts came from among the poor and downtrodden, very much as in the Roman Empire sixteen hundred years earlier. Those who were poorest were most eager to listen to the Christian gospel of universal love and human equality in the eyes of God. They were also more in need of the presents and the medical help that the missionaries were often in a position to give.

When trouble started—and in the North it started after only three years—it was neither because of the effrontery of the Jesuits, whom some people thought "little scrupulous about the means so long as they effect the end in view," [51] nor was it due to a refusal on the part of the Vietnamese to accept the religious ideas and the advanced scientific knowledge imported by the West. As to the latter, there was never a time when the courts of the Trinh and Nguyen did not harbor some Jesuit physician, astronomer, mathematician, or military expert, whose honored position contrasted oddly with that of their preacher-colleagues in hiding or in jail.[52]

But in religious matters too, the Vietnamese people had always been more open-minded, and their rulers more tolerant, than any of the nations and governments engaged in converting them to their own beliefs. During the same seventeenth and eighteenth centuries, when the European missionaries were forbidden to enter the country and the Catholic communities were constantly molested and at times persecuted, Vietnam willingly admitted Buddhist preachers and scholars from China.[53] Vietnam's synthetic religious ideology was in fact reaffirmed at this very time through another revival of Buddhism, which, however, eliminated neither the old indigenous practices and beliefs of the people nor a widespread Taoism that existed in many perverted forms.[54] Even the steadily petrifying Confucianist pseudo religion of the state was once more assured of continuity by the very process of its further dilution and temporary contraction.

As was the case in Japan, the conflict between the Vietnamese governments and the Catholic missions was essentially not of a religious nature. It was a political conflict whose two most obvious aspects underlined the nonreligious motivation behind all Vietnamese measures against the Catholic Church. In the first place, the Vietnamese as a rule found that those Westerners devoted to spiritual goals were in alliance with the agents of worldly conquest. Between the Portuguese rape

that the individual Christian conscience was guided as much by authority as the actions of a Vietnamese youth who obeyed his strictly Confucianist father. Besides, the conscience of a Vietnamese Christian was obviously shaped by the doctrines of a public institution that took its orders from abroad. Therefore to be a Christian, according to the Confucianist mandarins, was not only immoral but also an act of subversion against the state.[58] The standard accusation against the missionaries, in fact, was that the existing social order was being corrupted by their work.

Consequently the Catholic Church was treated by the two Vietnamese governments as a "foreign" political party might be treated in a modern democratic state. It was forbidden to operate, and the leaders were often put in jail; its foreign agents, the missionaries, were deported. In the course of the two hundred years of their illegal activity a number of missionaries and Vietnamese Catholics paid for their unwavering zeal with their lives.[59] But in spite of occasional outbreaks of violence for which, as in the case of the Nazi pogroms, the initiative always came from above, the Catholic communities of Vietnam were never in danger of extinction. Subject to a policy of containment rather than extermination, they were strong enough two hundred years after the expulsion of Rhodes in 1645 to provide a pretext for Western military intervention in Vietnam.

7.

Shortly before France's fiasco in Siam, the Indochinese aspirations of the French had been hurt also by an order from Rome. After 1682, missionaries who went to Asia were forbidden by the Pope to engage in trade. This was a triumph of the Portuguese faction at the Vatican over the French Society of Foreign Missions. By 1693, the position of the French Society had become so weak that the Oriental vicarship was given to the Spanish. In Indochina, this did not advance the work of the missionaries either, but rather intensified the quarrels that had always been going on between the many missionary societies over their respective rights in the various countries. A commission of inquiry sent by Pope Clement XII in 1738 assigned definite zones to the competing groups. North Vietnam was given to the Jesuits, which left the French Society with only the territory of the Nguyen. But as both the Nguyen and the Trinh refused to relax their proscription of the Catholic faith, neither group was able to make any progress in Vietnam.

As the eighteenth century unfolded, it became clear that Western penetration of Vietnam had become a movement in reverse. The work of the missionaries, if it failed to show progress in numbers of converts or impact on Vietnamese thinking, had at least the animation of a struggle for a great cause. It was quite different in the field of trade. Exchanges between Vietnam and the leading Western powers grew constantly smaller in volume, rarer in frequency, and soon barren of interest to all but a few Portuguese traders in Macao. What foreign trade there was remained largely in the hands of the Chinese colony at Faifo.

In the eyes of some forward-looking Western colonial politicians, this state of affairs was regrettable more from a Vietnamese than from a European point of view. They regarded Vietnam as a steppingstone to China, and if Vietnam's markets and seaports and navigable rivers remained closed to European trade and shipping, the country would one day have to be opened, inevitably, by force.[60] The question was only which one of the two contenders for supremacy in this area, England or France, would possess the necessary strength when military intervention in Vietnam became opportune.[61]

It was this Anglo-French rivalry, however, and England's determination to destroy the Indian positions of the Portuguese and Dutch, that gave to Vietnam her long respite from Euro-

turn Vietnam into a worth-while object of exploitation or even open her doors wide enough for gainful trade, as most of these people soon found out. The story of French intervention in Indochina, therefore, became largely the story of the efforts of individual promoters who tried to engage the man power, the funds, and the prestige of the state for their particular private schemes.

The fruitless endeavors of these men make up the eighteenth-century story of Franco-Vietnamese relations. As in the preceding century, the missionaries were again prominent among the advocates of intervention. But before the whole matter was taken up by the Bishop of Adran, in 1778, the voice of the traders was louder, and the proposals and urgings of the missionaries appeared timid beside the projects and actions of some captains in the Asian waters and commanders in Pondicherry.

Outstanding among the latter was Dupleix himself, France's first great colonial statesman and soldier. From his position in India, he tried again and again to open the ports of Vietnam for French commercial vessels and to trick the Vietnamese rulers into giving him a military base along the east Indochina coast. He used the Irish baron Jacques O'Friell, his cousin by marriage and source of information, to reopen French contact with Vietnam. This Irish adventurer, from his trading post in Canton, had taken several trips to Vietnam and become one of the rare Europeans of the eighteenth century who knew the country and the people. At another time Dupleix sent a missionary, Monsignor Bennetat, to the "King of Cochinchina" with a load of presents such as no independent Vietnamese ruler was ever again to receive from an official of France.[66] They were not given in vain. Permission to trade was granted, as it had been to O'Friell and would again be granted to other envoys of France.

The Vietnamese kings and officials, although they had long become alert to the dangers of Western infiltration, were as a

228

rule still ready to talk and to trade and to receive what the West had to offer, sometimes "at the point of the spear." The efforts of Dupleix and others came to naught mainly from lack of support by France. No number of memoranda and no amount of persuasion by missionaries, traders, travelers, and colonial officials could stir either the French government or the French East India Company into action on a significant scale.

Premature and ineffectual as it was, this early colonial propaganda was nevertheless remarkable for a concreteness and frankness that all later French talk about Indochina lacked. The rich vocabulary did not contain the words "civilization," "cultural mission," "honor of France," "obligations toward the natives," or the like. Even the word "religion," so prominent in the propaganda of the seventeenth and nineteenth centuries, rarely appeared in the documents of the eighteenth. If they took the island of Condore, wrote one agent of the East India Company in 1755, they would not only have their own flourishing Asian trade but also be in a position to ruin the trade of the English and Dutch. And one overenthusiastic Abbé de Saint-Phalle exclaimed: "They have gold in their mines and rivers, and even in the excrement of their ducks, and there is hardly a country in Asia where labor is cheaper than in Cochinchina." [67]

But the abbés and agents, as well as the traders and officials, were truthfully told by the French government and the East India Company that the money to send ships and soldiers simply could not be found; or that France could not risk widening her Asian conflict with England and Holland; or that it was more important to defend what had been acquired in India than to disperse the available strength along the distant and still not fully known coast of Cochinchina.

The lifework of Pierre Poivre from Lyon, one of the pioneers of French Indochina, reflects most vividly the ineffectiveness of all eighteenth-century attempts to overcome France's incapactiy for action in Vietnam. A man with the irrepressible temperament of a trader, Poivre nevertheless missed not one of the roles that a promoter of French colonialism could play in his time. He started out in 1720 as a missionary in Vietnam, but while still in his first field of action switched back to the vocation of his father, who had amassed a fortune by buying and selling silk. He spent two years trading in Canton and then lost his right arm in a sea battle with the English on his return trip to France. After another two years devoted to intensive propaganda for trade with Vietnam, Poivre returned to Cochinchina as an envoy of France and the East India Company with a cargo of goods and rich presents for the Nguyen king. He was determined to build for France a commercial position that would put an end to the hated spice monopoly of the Dutch. The trader had by now become a politician and diplomat of the very first order. But while it was easy for him to get rid of his presents, he had trouble finding buyers for his cargo of goods. Although Poivre was able to see that the poverty of the people was one of the reasons for his commercial failure, he blamed the crookedness of the mandarins for his losses and decided that the military power of his nation should come to the rescue of its persecuted trade. This he concluded, although he had been granted the Vietnamese royal license for trading. Poivre was also permitted by the Nguyen rulers to set up an office for the East India Company in Tourane. But it was all to no avail. The license was used by Dupleix for some minor transactions between French India and Vietnam, but because of lack of interest in France no action whatever was taken to exploit Poivre's initial success. His subsequent efforts in Paris and later as governor of the Mascarene Islands all met with a similar fate.[68]

To the effects of their operations on the Vietnamese these bold and observant Frenchmen were as blind as their many successors of the nineteenth and twentieth centuries, of whom quite a few were as well-intentioned as a white man in the colonies could humanly be. They reacted with the utmost indignation whenever the mandarins succeeded in doing to them what the foreigners had come to do to the Vietnamese, totally ignoring the impact that two hundred years of European crimes had made upon Asia, and always speaking of treachery when they learned that the Machiavellianism of Asia was superior to their own. A European in Asia, after the year 1600, was universally regarded as a thief who would not hesitate to commit murder. To rob him, if possible, was an honorable deed. Poivre's fury at the Vietnamese mandarins only revealed the white man's fateful moral blindness in Asia. In a setting that lacked a common code of ethics, he found every Asian immoral who employed a cunning for which a Westerner's mentality was unprepared.

The behavior of the mandarins, of whom many were probably as crooked as Poivre thought, was determined not only by the white man's deeds of the past but also by his intentions for the future. The mandarins judged these intentions correctly, and consequently treated Poivre as they would have treated one Count D'Estaing, whose idea of Franco-Vietnamese relations, conceived in 1758, remained unfortunately popular with quite a few people for almost two hundred years. This noble gentleman, a captain of the king, worked out an elaborate plan to invade Hué for seventy-two hours in order to rob the imperial palace of all its treasures and gold. The military feat was to be followed by a commercial transaction in the Philippines and China, where the greatest possible financial benefit from the Count's patriotic coup could be expected.[69]

D'Estaing's project was officially approved by the governor of French India, Lally-Tollandal, who only insisted on "a share in the benefits." The expedition got under way in October, 1759, but the Count's uncontrollable desire to exercise his piratical vocation also on the English trading posts along the west coast of Sumatra ruined the entire scheme. D'Estaing, who had lost many of his men through fighting and disease, missed the monsoon that was to carry his ships to Hué; the ships were damaged, most of their officers were seriously ill, and with a bleeding heart (*"la mort dans l'âme"*) the Count returned to Port-Louis and eventually to Paris.

Nine years later, in 1768, Count D'Estaing, whose thinking had now "matured and hardened,"[70] proposed an enterprise that was said to have differed from his earlier piratical concepts by being at once "serious and durable." Under the leadership of Pierre Poivre, three thousand soldiers were to have landed in Tourane, fortified the port, and made it the backbone of a vast commercial and political operation. The aim was to ruin the English and make France the dominating power in the Far East. But if the French government had had the money for an expedition of such a size, it would have sent three thousand men to its possessions in India. The fate of Pondicherry in case of a new conflict with England was a concern of the French court that overshadowed all its colonial aspirations and prevented all action in any other Asian sphere.

Thus France also missed the greatest of all opportunities for an eighteenth-century conquest of Vietnam, one that was offered to the West by the Vietnamese themselves. In 1778 the Tay Son rebellion had broken the power of the Nguyen in the South. Both circumstances and the Nguyen's dynastic aspirations called for the one thousand soldiers and two hundred guns that would have sufficed for a foothold strong enough to realize the boldest of all eighteenth-century French schemes. Look how little it would cost, wrote Commander Chevalier of Chandernagor to his superior in Pondicherry, to raise French power and increase French commerce, and prevent the English from getting Indochina too! By aiding a prince in distress, France could get "one of the richest commercial branches of the Indies" and make herself the master of Cochinchina. But "we always lack the funds, and if we had them, wouldn't you be restrained by the fear of blame for having acted without an order from the Court?"

A few days after Chevalier had written this letter, he

PIERRE POIVRE (1719–1786)
He missed none of the roles a promoter of French colonialism
could play in his time.

PIGNEAU DE BÉHAINE, Bishop of Adran (1741–1799)
"I shall make the Revolution in Cochinchina alone."

learned of the arrival in Calcutta of a delegation of Cochin-chinese mandarins, led by the Portuguese Jesuit Loureiro from the unlucky Nguyen Court. The English were already discussing the prospects of an intervention in favor of the Nguyen, for which their company agent Chapman pleaded after his return from a special mission to war-torn Vietnam. But Chevalier somehow succeeded in bringing Loureiro into the French camp and in shipping him to the governor of Pondicherry with the outlines of a treaty by which "the king of Cochinchina," in return for rather modest military support, would enter into a defensive and offensive military alliance with France and would cede a province of France's own choice, in addition to granting complete freedom of trade—a "small beginning," as Chevalier remarked, but one that would "no doubt lead our nation into erecting a great empire." [71]

Probably no moment in the whole eighteenth century was less propitious for Chevalier's plan than the spring of 1778. The circumstances of the time made his knowledge, ability, and perseverance totally ineffective. France was about to enter into her new war with England on the side of the United States. By September, 1778, the English had occupied both Chandernagor and Pondicherry.

The year of Chevalier's failure, however, was also the year of Pigneau de Béhaine's first major success. The Bishop of Adran and his sixteen-year-old protégé Prince Nguyen Anh had opened their long war against the Tay Son and had temporarily regained Saigon.

9.

Pigneau de Béhaine was not quite twenty-five years old when the Society of Foreign Missions sent him to the Far East. After a few waiting periods of several months, some of which he spent in Macao,[72] Pigneau entered the province of Hatien, at the southwestern corner of Vietnam, in March, 1767.[73] There the preacher was instantly ordered to become an educator. For two and a half years Pigneau headed a seminary that had only shortly before received asylum from the governor of Hatien after being driven from Siam by a Burmese invasion. But political trouble in the wake of a Siamese invasion of Hatien led to the destruction of the seminary in 1769. Pigneau, who had already spent two months as a political prisoner in a horrible Hatien jail, was forced to flee Vietnam. After many hardships he reached Malacca, together with some of his pupils, on a Chinese junk.

In 1770 the hapless seminary was reopened in French India, and its twenty-nine-year old head and rescuer appointed Bishop of Adran.[74] Pigneau humbly, or perhaps wisely, deferred his consecration until 1773.

From India, where he had also become a scholar and completed a Vietnamese dictionary, the young bishop, in the footsteps of Alexander of Rhodes, returned to Macao, published a new Vietnamese catechism, and waited as eagerly as his illustrious predecessor for the day when his work in Vietnam could be resumed.

In 1775 Pigneau was back in Hatien. A twenty-year-old ban against the Christian religion had been lifted by the last of the Nguyen kings, shortly before the Tay Son revolution put an end to both the power and the lives of the ruling family of South Vietnam. But the king's sixteen-year-old nephew Nguyen Anh escaped the royal massacre when the Tay Son caught up with the fleeing Nguyen court. By hiding him from his pursuers and by helping him to the safety of an island in the Gulf of Siam, the Bishop of Adran probably saved the young man's life.

Pigneau's act of Christian duty, however, was also a consciously taken political step. This preacher, organizer, educator, and scholar discovered his true vocation only after his encounter with Nguyen Anh. To attain the fullness of human activity and the total exercise of all his talents, Pigneau had to

234

become a politician, and he became one who was as passionate as he was great. From the day of his first meeting with Nguyen Anh, Pigneau ceased to be the ardent missionary he had been during the previous ten years. But the humble French churchman became not only a forward-looking politician; this truly devout priest[75] was to end as a first-rate leader in the many fields of preparing and waging war. Ten years of his remaining life he spent in an extraordinary individual effort to bring about French military intervention in Indochina. During the last remaining decade of his life, the Bishop of Adran, whose talents his own country had been unable to use, became one of the greatest statesmen and generals in the history of Vietnam.

As a true politician, who would always rather dominate the present than know what the future held in store, Pigneau no doubt ignored how effectively he had interfered with the destinies of Vietnam when he rescued a young prince in 1777: twenty-five years later Nguyen Anh had conquered the whole of Vietnam, in turn exterminated all surviving members of the ruling Tay Son family, and founded the last dynasty of his reunited country.

In order to secure their possessions against the Trinh in the North, the Tay Son moved the bulk of their armies back to Center Vietnam after subduing the distant South. They had hardly left the South when their sixteen-year-old antagonist, Nguyen Anh, reappeared in the country, rallied the followers of the old regime, hired Cambodian mercenaries and Chinese pirates, and in a series of lightning victories conquered several provinces together with the city of Saigon. He ruled the far South as "king of Cochinchina" for fully four years. In 1782, however, the Tay Son descended on him by sea and shattered his army as thoroughly as his tough and efficient young administration. Once more the Tay Son left and Anh returned, but this time for only six months. When another attempt, for which the king of Siam had provided an army of twenty thousand, also ended in disaster, the fate of Nguyen Anh seemed definitely sealed. By the end of 1784 he was a refugee in Thailand, pondering the question whether he might not be able to reverse the tide of events with European military help.

To seek such help, and to seek it from France, was the advice Pigneau had been offering Nguyen Anh ever since he had rejoined the new king in Saigon in 1778. If he appealed to the "generosity" of the king of France, he kept telling the reluctant young ruler, he would be able to defeat his enemies and become master of the whole of Vietnam in a very short time. Nguyen Anh, in fact, considered the help of the English, the Dutch, and the Portuguese; he even tried to negotiate with the Spanish in Manila. But only the French had a permanent advocate on the spot—Pigneau de Béhaine, whom the young ruler liked and admired, and who was his equal in political sagacity and determination. In November, 1784, Nguyen Anh requested Pigneau to negotiate the price for which France would be willing to support his aspirations to the Vietnamese throne. When the Bishop returned to Pondicherry in February, 1785, he arrived as a fully empowered ambassador, authorized to offer what the "king of Cochinchina" was ready to concede to France in exchange for adequate military assistance, and in possession of credentials that strongly expressed the king's confidence in Pigneau: the exiled ruler let the bishop take not only his royal seal but also his five-year-old son, Nguyen Canh.

On the French authorities in Pondicherry, however, Pigneau's unusual credentials made as little impression as his audacious military and political proposals. The men in charge of the remnants of French India lacked both the means and the courage for action on the scale envisaged by Pigneau. For fifteen months Pigneau struggled to overcome their fear of responsibility and their unwillingness to make an effort beyond their accustomed routine. It was a time of cruel and mounting frustration, during which Pigneau, for once in his life, was driven to the brink of despair. Sabotaged by his compatriots in Pondicherry and denounced for his project by the Spanish

Franciscans in Rome, he offered his royal pupil, together with his political mandate, to the Portuguese. Siamese opposition and perhaps also Nguyen Anh's confidence in Pigneau weighed heavily against the chances of the Portuguese, who, at the beginning of 1787, were ready to come forward with a fleet of fifty-six ships. In the meantime Pigneau had reconsidered his act of desperation and decided to submit his project directly to the government in Paris. He left Pondicherry for France in June, 1786.

10.

The month of June, 1786, when Pigneau and little Prince Canh left Pondicherry for Paris, was a crucial one in the history of Vietnam for another reason also. The Trinh rulers of the North, who had exploited the Tay Son uprising to invade the South in 1774, were driven out of Hué and their armies chased back into the Red River valley. In a brilliant campaign lasting less than four weeks, the youngest of the Tay Son brothers marched from Hué to Hanoi to put an end, simultaneously, to the Trinh regime and the division of Vietnam. Both had lasted more than two hundred years. From the Gulf of Siam to the borders of Yunnan and Kwangsi, the power of the Tay Son was unchallenged and supreme for a brief moment in the bloody history of their rise and fall.

Six months later, as Pigneau reached France after an absence of more than twenty years, another battle for Vietnam started. It opened in Paris, where it was waged in the salons of the aristocracy, across the tables of several ministries, and in the antechambers of the king. In this battle, which lasted from February to November, 1787, Pigneau, in a role he had never played before, revealed himself as a true genius of public relations. He charmed the whole female nobility with his seven-year-old exotic pupil,[76] and seduced the technicians of military action with his precise instructions as to the conditions of warfare in Indochina and the equipment needed for his proposed campaign.[77] If they acquired a few fortified positions along the east Indochina coast, he told the lovers of power and military exploits, France would be able "to dominate the seas of China and of the archipelago." And to the traders and the troubled custodians of public finances he promised secure French control "of all commerce in this part of the world." [78]

The year 1787 became one of triumph for the Bishop of Adran. By November he had vanquished all opposition and apparently reached his goal. Pigneau's persuasiveness and public pressure misled a reluctant government and king into signing an agreement they were unable to keep.[79] The Bishop was both given the authority and promised the means for the execution of his plan. He arrived at Pondicherry in May, 1788, as "Royal Commissioner of France for Cochinchina" with a treaty of alliance between the King of France and the "King of Cochinchina." France agreed to supply four ships with 1650 men, as well as a stated number of guns and other needed equipment. Nguyen Anh agreed to give France the port of Tourane and the island of Condore, and in addition to many other privileges the right of free trade in all parts of Vietnam, to the exclusion of all other European nations.[80] Missing among the many concessions the Bishop had extracted from Nguyen Anh was permission for the free exercise of the Christian religion.

Pigneau's triumph in Paris, however, was like the victory of a salesman who had succeeded in persuading a beggar to buy an estate. The Bishop learned, unfortunately too late, that propaganda can only exploit and improve, but not create, the conditions for political success. Thus it came about that the keenest of all French minds engaged in the affairs of Indochina was more deceived than any other at the very moment when he had accomplished his greatest feat. Only four days after the signing of his precious treaty, the agreement was virtually annulled by the instructions the minister of foreign affairs sent to Governor Conway of Pondicherry.

Conway was to provide the ships and troops for Pigneau's expedition. He was known as an opponent of further French expansion in Asia, and even advocated the liquidation of French India, which he believed France was too weak to exploit and defend. He was secretly instructed by Paris that it was up to him to decide whether Pigneau's expedition to Cochinchina should take place immediately, at a later date, or not at all. Conway probably decided nothing, but let the difficulties of the project, for which he lacked the necessary means, delay all action indefinitely.

Unaware of the government's duplicity,[81] Pigneau fought the most furious personal battle of French colonial history against Conway, who was apparently both a lover of intrigue and a giant of inaction. Although the Royal Council decided in October, 1788, to approve Conway's refusal to act, Paris told Pigneau only in April, 1789, that the "expedition could not take place."[82]

This was the moment for the Bishop of Adran to develop the full strength of his political determination. "I shall make the revolution in Cochinchina alone," he is reported to have said.[83] After rejecting an offer by the English to do for him what his own country had refused, Pigneau raised money from the French merchants in the Mascarene Islands and India, acquired and equipped two ships, bought weapons and ammunition, hired volunteers and deserters from the French Navy, and left Pondicherry for Vietnam at the head of his privately organized expedition on June 19, 1789—four weeks before the storming of the Bastille set the pace for the French Revolution.[84]

Pigneau sailed directly to Vietnam because he knew that his royal protégé was back again in Saigon. A conflict among the three Tay Son brothers in 1787, and a Chinese invasion of North Vietnam in 1788, were opportunities for Nguyen Anh that a man of his acumen was not likely to miss. He had returned to Hatien in August, 1787, and soon afterward he relighted the fires of war that were to burn in Vietnam for another fifteen years. When Pigneau joined him at the end of July, 1789, Saigon and the southern provinces of Cochinchina had been in the hands of Nguyen Anh for almost a year.

While Pigneau fought his political battles in Pondicherry and Paris, the Tay Son revolution had passed through a phase that was both its apex and the starting point of a rapid decline. The movement had not fulfilled the hopes of the people. The spirit of reform, instead of growing, expired through the effort of innovation,[85] and the social impulses that were the secret of its initial success produced no change in the structure of Vietnamese society. If the movement had had a task in the history of Vietnam, it was completed after the fall of the Trinh. Against the Chinese invaders, whom the last monarch of the old Le dynasty treacherously invited into the Red River valley, the Tay Son could still arouse the spirit that had saved the country on so many previous occasions.[86] But the stakes in the war against Nguyen Anh were of little importance to the people of Vietnam. The peasant's interest in peace began to favor Nguyen Anh as soon as the king of Cochinchina showed signs of being able to defeat his opponents.

The war between Nguyen Anh and the heirs of the Tay Son brothers consequently deteriorated into a mere struggle for power between two families whose differences in social outlook and in technics of political rule were slight. Vietnam would probably have progressed more rapidly if the Tay Son regime had survived. The regime founded by Nguyen Anh was strictly conservative; for his successors, a policy of innovation was identical with giving in to the aggressively advancing West. To keep the windows of Vietnam closed against the din and the lure of a feverishly changing world was an obsession with them, of which the Tay Son had never shown any sign. But the military superiority of Nguyen Anh, whose French assistants provided him with the advanced technics of European warfare, tipped the scales in favor of the South.[87]

For Pigneau's French companions the war was a slow and disappointing business. Most of them were young adventurers who had joined Pigneau in hopes of making great fortunes in a very short time. Only a handful remained after two or three years.[88] Pigneau himself was quite ready to drop his political and military career on several occasions. Because Nguyen Anh was determined to take no unnecessary risks and had actually no reason to be in a hurry, his French advisers believed him to be timid, unenergetic, and probably incapable of achieving victory for his cause. It took more than a dozen campaigns before Nguyen Anh was able to land his troops in the center of the country near Hué. But once Hué had fallen, Hanoi fell quickly too, both in 1802. When the Tay Son had lost Hanoi they had also lost the war.

The victor, who proclaimed himself emperor of Vietnam under the name of Gia Long, was now quite happy that France had defaulted on Pigneau's treaty of 1787.[89] He was grateful and generous toward the Frenchmen who had helped him to reach his goal. On the surviving members of the Tay Son family Gia Long took bestial revenge,[90] but the Bishop of Adran, even before he died, was officially praised and revered as was no foreigner in Vietnam either before or after him.

As to the true aims the Bishop had pursued in Vietnam for thirty-two years, fate had decided to leave his superhuman effort unrewarded. Pigneau had fought and suffered for the glory of the Church and the advancement of his religion. The real dream of his life was not to give France an empire in Asia but to give Vietnam a Catholic ruler in the person of his beloved pupil Prince Canh. But Pigneau failed to make the boy a Christian, and even had he succeeded, he would still have lost his stirring political gamble: the young prince was fated to die nearly twenty years before his father.[91]

Gia Long himself never favored the Christian religion,[92] but for obvious political reasons practiced a policy of tolerance as long as he needed his French collaborators, and also abstained from persecution after he was able to do without his Christian friends—no doubt in honor of the memory of his great friend Pigneau. But even this meager result of the Bishop's titanic exertions was smaller than it looked to his admirers in France. They did not know that the number of Christians in Cochinchina, which was estimated at 100,000 at the beginning of the war, was probably less than 30,000 when Pigneau, in 1799, expired during one of Nguyen Anh's seasonal campaigns.[93]

11.

The Bishop of Adran, if judged by his attempt to shape the destiny of Vietnam, was doubtless a great believer in the historical effectiveness of human planning and individual determination. In his private writings, however, he appeared in a totally different light. Pigneau strictly adhered to a religious interpretation of history. Behind all events he believed in a purpose that would forever remain incomprehensible to the human mind. Both the miseries of his life and the unwanted consequences of his actions he regarded as determined by divine providence, and as tests of his faith and punishments for his sins.

In this manner he would certainly have accepted the ultimate outcome of his political endeavors also, if he had lived another twenty-five years to witness the desolate state of affairs that developed between France and Vietnam, as well as between his Church and the Vietnamese regime he had promoted.

Vietnam moved toward isolation from the West even under Gia Long, who respected and honored his French collaborators but had little or no confidence in any of the European powers that were active in the East. His alleged friendship for France, which became a schoolbook item in Vietnamese history through

French colonial propaganda, was never put to the test. During the wars of Napoleon and the first years of the Restoration, France made no serious political or mercantile efforts to exploit the advantages it was said to have possessed under the reign of Gia Long. The last two of Pigneau's assistants left the court of Hué only a few years after Gia Long died, and relations with France were again reduced to the contacts of the Frenchmen engaged in missionary work.[94]

However, a policy of open opposition against the West was adopted only under Gia Long's successors. Their attitude toward France was largely determined by the new tide of European aggression that rolled over India, into Malaya and Burma, and gradually up along the Chinese coast.[95] Vietnam's policy of isolation, therefore, could be likened to a fox's refusal to face his hunters outside his hole. Gia Long himself, who foresaw the trend of European policy in Asia, took a final stand on the issue by appointing a successor hostile to the West.[96] Five years after his death the missionaries were again treated as agents of a subversive movement. In an imperial edict of 1825, the "perverse religion of the European" was officially accused of "corrupting the hearts of men."[97] Between 1833 and 1838 seven missionaries were sentenced to death and executed. The existence of the Church was more seriously threatened under Gia Long's successors than at any time since the Catholic missions had been founded in Vietnam. The lifework of Pigneau was undone.

In the meantime the forces of Western imperialist aggression were growing stronger from year to year. During the reign of Gia Long, Vietnam was still quite unaware of the approaching threat to its independence. The danger became visible only under Gia Long's immediate successor Minh Mang, who died at the age of fifty after ruling Vietnam as an absolute monarch from 1820 to 1841. The threat increased, not without Vietnamese provocation, during the brief rule of Thieu Tri, who was one of the forty-nine sons of Minh Mang. The final clash occurred under Tu Duc, the last emperor of Vietnam as an independent state.

Tu Duc headed his unfortunate country from 1847 to 1883. The first of his thirty-six agitated years as emperor was also the year of the first French attack in the harbor of Tourane. When Tu Duc died in 1883, the North and the Center of his country were in the process of becoming the two French protectorates of Tongking and Annam. The South, which was torn away from Vietnam by France between 1859 and 1867, was already known to the world as a French colony under the name of Cochinchina.

The nine hundred years of Vietnamese independence thus came to an end.

Notes to Chapter Four:

1. Relations between Indochina and the West were established long before the Portuguese arrived. The visit of a Roman to Indochina in 166 A.D. is recorded in Chinese annals. Another Roman, most probably a trader, visited the court of the Wu in Nanking in 266 (F. Hirth, *China and the Roman Orient*, Leipzig, 1885, pp. 173, 306). Roman coins with the images of the emperors Antoninus Pius (133-162) and Marcus Aurelius (162-180) were found in Vietnam. There was extended intercourse with the Persian State of the Sassanides and with the Arab Caliphate. Marco Polo probably visited Champa on his way to China in 1285. So did the Franciscan missionary Odoric de Pordenone between 1318 and 1324 (Le Thanh Khoi, *op. cit.*, p. 284; Hall, *op. cit.*, pp 186-194).

2. He was the first to reach India via the Cape, not the first to sail around it. The Cape of Good Hope was discovered by Bartholomew Diaz in 1488.

3. See the stirring account of Vasco da Gama's first voyage around the Cape of Good Hope in Sir Hugh Clifford's *Further India*, London, 1904, pp. 45-48.

4. *Ibid.*, p. 48.

244

5. The Spanish-Portuguese rivalry over the newly discovered territories was settled by a papal bull of 1493 that divided the spheres of interest along a line drawn between the North and South Poles one hundred leagues to the west of the Azores. This decision, as later amended by agreement, gave Brazil to Portugal and the rest of America to Spain, but left the possession of the newly discovered lands in Asia in doubt. In a treaty between Spain and Portugal concluded in 1530 the Spaniards agreed to halt their explorations seventeen degrees east of the Moluccas. This treaty, however, was broken by the Spaniards in 1570, when they annexed the Philippines and founded Manila (Hall, *op. cit.*, p. 201).

6. *Ibid.*, p. 206. For an account of Portuguese cruelties in their colonies in the sixteenth century cf. also Reinhold Schneider, *Iberisches Erbe*, Olten, 1949, first part, "Das Leiden des Camoes," esp. pp. 39ff.

7. Quoted from Hall, *op. cit.*, p. 202.

8. The rapid spread of Islam constituted a serious setback to the plans of the Christian missionaries. By 1535 the whole coast of Java had become Mohammedan. The Catholic missionaries, unable to convert the followers of the Prophet, concentrated mainly on the pagan and Hindu population. The fortunes of Christianity depended almost entirely on the military strength of the Portuguese. Christian converts mostly fell away when threatened by the Mohammedans. For the ups and downs of Portuguese missionary activities see Hall, *op. cit.*, pp. 202-205. According to Harrison, *op. cit.*, p. 75, Christianity was considered as a badge of submission by the East Asian peoples and became rooted, in the Protestant form, only after the Dutch had taken over from the Portuguese.

9. In 1516 Fernando Perez and in 1524 Duarte Coelho reconnoitred the Indochina coast in preparation of da Faria's landing (Le Thanh Khoi, *op. cit.*, p. 285). For this period cf. also H. Cordier, "L'arrivée des Portugais en Chine," in *T'oung Pao*, 1911, pp. 483ff.; A. Kammerer, "La découverte de la Chine par les Portugais au XVIe siècle et la cartographie des Portulans," supplement to *T'oung Pao*, Vol. 1944; P. Huard, "Les Portugais et l'Indochine," in *Bulletin de l'Institut Indochinois pour l'Etude de l'Homme*, 1940.

10. The Portuguese gave the name of Cochinchina first to the region at the mouth of the Mekong, but after the seventeenth century it referred to the whole country ruled by the Nguyen. The Portuguese form of the name is Cauchichina. The first part, "Cauchi," seems to be derived from the Chinese name of Vietnam, "Giao Chi," possibly first heard by the Portuguese in the Malayan form of "Kutchi." The second part, "China," was added to distinguish Cochinchina from Cochin in India, another Portuguese settlement. Cf. Pelliot, "Le Fou-non," BEFEO, Vol. III, p.

299, note 1; L. Aurousseau, "Sur le nom de 'Cochinchine'," BEFEO, Vol. XXIV, pp. 563-579. About the Portuguese port of Faifo in Cochinchina see A. Sellet, "Le vieux Faifo," in *Bulletin des Amis du Vieux Hué*, 1919, pp. 501-519; Nguyen Thien Lan, "Le port et la ville de Faifo au XVIIe siècle," in *Cahiers de L'Ecole Française d'Extrême Orient*, 1942, p. 11. About the name Cochinchina see also note 10, Chapter I.

11. The Portuguese landed on Ceylon as early as 1505. They founded the capital of Colombo, named in honor of Christopher Columbus, in 1517. Goa was acquired in 1510, Diu in 1535. Both places, the latter on the west coast of India, 170 miles northwest of Bombay, are still Portuguese colonies, the cessation of which has been energetically demanded by India since she gained independence.

12. In 1556 the Dutch possessions of Spain, having accepted Protestantism, revolted against the Spanish. England supported their rebellion, became involved in a war with Spain, and defeated the Grand Armada in 1588. Portugal, after dynastic troubles, was incorporated into Spain eight years before this event. The defeat of the Armada, therefore, not only deprived the Spanish but also the Portuguese colonies of much of their protection. Holland and England now entered the race for the possession of Southeast Asia, Africa, and America.

13. The United East India Company or Vereenigde Oostindische Compagnie (V.O.C.) was founded on March 20, 1602, by a decree of the Dutch government, the States General. It was granted the monopoly of trade in the regions between the Cape of Good Hope and the Straits of Magellan. The United East Indian Company was entitled to conclude treaties, build forts, maintain armed forces, and install officers of justice. The initial capital was six and a half million guilders. For details see Hall, *op. cit.*, pp. 233f.

14. Jan Huygen van Linschoten, after having spent four years in Portugal and five in Goa, spread word in his writings that Portuguese rule in the East was rotten and that their relations with the native peoples were so bad that other traders had a splendid opportunity. He pointed to Java as an excellent center of trade, as the Portuguese seldom went there. Cornelius de Houtnam, who also had spent some years in Portugal, led the first Dutch expedition to Java in 1595. In 1597 he revisited the island. Though he was a bad commander and lost 145 of his 249 men on his first voyage, he opened the way for further expeditions. One of his successors, van Warwijck, who treated the natives with tact, brought back four ships fully laden with pepper. Another Dutch trader, van Neck, made a profit of four hundred per cent, but none of the later expeditions made such a gain; some even suffered great losses.

Dutch merchantmen also visited Sumatra, Borneo, Siam, the Philippines, China, and Japan. There was hardly an important port in East Asia that the Dutch did not reach (Hall, *op. cit.*, pp. 230-232).

15. Factory, in this sense, is a trading post in a colonial country.

16. This biblical comparison between kings Solomon and Rehoboam is used by Hall, *op. cit.*, p. 287.

17. *Ibid.*, p. 248, uses this expression in describing the treatment of the inhabitants of the Bandanese Islands by the agent of the Dutch East India Company, Jan Pieterzoon Coen, in 1621. The islanders were first supported by the English against the Dutch but later abandoned to their fate. Coen thereupon rounded up all inhabitants, destroyed their huts and boats, and removed them from their settlements. Many were sold as slaves to Java, tortured, or executed. Other settlers were brought to the Bandanese Islands. Thousands of rebelling Bandanese died in the mountains from starvation rather than surrender to the Dutch. The cultivated land in the islands was parceled out to the company's employees to be worked with slave labor. Coen's ruthlessness shocked even the company, and he was reprimanded by its directors. A full account of the British-Dutch rivalry in the Far East and Coen's part in it is to be found in Hall, *ibid.*, pp. 224-251. For the incident of the Bandanese Islands see H. T. Colenbrander, *Koloniale Geschiedenis*, 3 vols., Hague, 1925, Vol. II, p. 117, and F. W. Stapel (ed.), *Geschiedenis van Nederlandsch-Indie*, 5 vols., Amsterdam, 1939, Vol. III, p. 151.

18. The Dutch East India Company came to an end when the armies of the French Revolution under General Pichegru overran Holland in 1795. The governor general, William V, fled to England and ordered the Dutch East India officials to place the Company's possessions in British hands as a safeguard against the French. Under this agreement the English took over the Cape of Good Hope, Ceylon, and Malacca, which they never returned in spite of their promises, and Sumatra and other islands of the Indonesian archipelago, which later came again under Dutch rule. Meanwhile the States General was replaced by the Batavian Republic, which abolished the College of Directors of the Dutch East India Company and replaced it with a Committee for the Affairs of the East Indian Trade and Settlements. In 1798 it was decided to liquidate the Company. Its assets and debts were taken over by the state. The charter of the Dutch East India Company expired on December 31, 1799. Its debts then stood at 134 million guilders. Hall, *op. cit.*, pp. 281f.

19. Pho Hien was situated near present-day Hung Yen. It attracted traders from China, Malaya, Thailand, and Japan, and soon became the most important city of Vietnam next to the capital of Kecho (Hanoi).

Cf. Le Thanh Khoi, *op. cit.*, pp. 286f.; Hall *op. cit.*, p. 358. For a more detailed treatment of the Dutch settlements in Indochina see G. Dumontier, "Le comptoir hollandais de Pho-hien," in *Bulletin Géogr. Hist. et Desc.*, 1895; W. J. M. Ruch, "La Compagnie des Indes Néerlandaises et l'Indochine," in BEFEO, Vols. XXXVI and XXXVII.

20. Kecho (also called Cacho), meaning "The Market" or "The Fair," was the name used for Hanoi in the seventeenth century. Kecho was then the capital of the northern part of Vietnam under the Trinh. The city was visited by the French traveler Samuel Baron, who wrote a vivid account, *Description du royaume de Tonquin,* published in 1685 and reprinted in *Revue Indochinoise,* 1914-1915. There he says that Kecho compared favorably with many Asian cities and surpassed most of them in number of inhabitants. On the first and fifteenth day of each month a market was held. On such a day the streets were filled with buyers to such an extent that a visitor could not make more than a hundred steps in half an hour.

21. In 1638 the Dutch East India Company suffered a damage of 25,000 guilders when some of its ships were captured by the Nguyen and their crews sold into slavery. In June, 1642, a Dutch fleet joined the Trinh in their expedition against the Nguyen. This fleet could not effect a junction with the land army of the Trinh. Both were defeated and the Dutch naval commander, Van Liesvelt, died in action. In the following year another Dutch fleet under Pieter Baeck met total disaster in a naval combat against Nguyen galleys commanded by Nguyen Phuoc Tan (July 7, 1643). To take revenge for their defeat by the Nguyen, the Dutch raided the Vietnamese coast and beheaded every peasant they caught. See Chassigneux, in *Histoire des colonies françaises,* by G. Hanotaux and A. Martineau, Paris, 1932, Vol. V, pp. 311-598. After their second defeat the Dutch withdrew their support from the Trinh but kept their factory in the North until 1700. The war between the Trinh and Nguyen was resumed in 1648 without Dutch participation. Nguyen Phuoc Tan, who had defeated the Dutch, again secured victory for the South (Le Thanh Khoi, *op. cit.*, pp. 248f.; Ruch, *op. cit.*, p. 183).

22. The chief of the British East India Company's factory at Hirado in Japan, Richard Cocks, made an attempt to open the Nguyen territory to British trade. He sent Walter Carwarden to Faifo with a letter and presents from James I to Nguyen Hoang, ruler of South Vietnam, who resided in Hué. But as soon as Carwarden and his interpreter landed, they were murdered by the local population. A few years later the Hirado factory sent a trading expedition to the Trinh, but this too was a failure (Hall, *op. cit.*, p. 358; C. Maybon, *Histoire moderne du pays d'Annam,*

Paris, 1920, p. 69; P. Villars, "Les Anglais au Tonkin," in *Revue de Paris,* 1903, pp. 262-286).

23. While both the English and the Dutch East India companies were private ventures, the French East India Company (*Compagnie des Indes Orientales*), founded in 1664, was a state enterprise. It directed its main efforts toward Thailand. Cf. Harrison, *op. cit.,* pp. 123f., 147ff.

24. The first European ship to reach Hanoi was the Dutch boat *Ryp* in 1638.

25. Toward the end of the seventeenth century the European market for Asian goods declined also, partly as a result of uninterrupted warfare.

26. The French had their only factory in Indonesia at Bantam; the English had three: in Macassar, in Bantam, and in Bencoolen on the west coast of Sumatra. They first lost Macassar. In 1682 both the English and the French were driven from Bantam. The British were able to remain in Bencoolen until 1824. The Dutch finally became the unquestioned masters of the Archipelago. Hall, *op. cit.,* p. 265.

27. In 1696, the Englishman, Thomas Bowyear, asked the government of Hué for permission to open a factory in Faifo. His demand was politely denied. Chesneaux, *op. cit.,* p. 57.

28. The instructions given by the British East India Company to its agent, Crawfurd, in 1821, read partly as follows: ". . . a very general fear and distrust of Europeans . . . is predominant; resulting, it is too much to be feared, from the violence, imprudence, and disregard of national rights, which occasionally characterized the conduct of all the European nations in the earlier periods of their intercourse. . . . Upon a dispassionate review of our commercial transactions in former times, the Council is disposed mainly to attribute to the effect of the unpopular privileges so obtained, and to the indiscreet exercise of them, of which so many examples are recorded in the history of that period, the subsequent extinction of our commerce, as well as that of other European nations, or its arbitrary restriction . . ." John Crawfurd, *Embassy to Siam and Cochinchina,* London, 1830, Vol. II, appendix, pp. 443, 445.

29. The two great European wars of this period were that of the League of Augsburg (1688-1698) and the War of the Spanish Succession (1701-1714). In these wars France was finally defeated by a coalition of England, Holland, and Austria. In the peace treaties following the War of the Spanish Succession, the Dutch were cheated of their part in the spoils in spite of their heavy efforts. As a result England emerged as the most important colonial power of the world.

30. C. Maybon, *op. cit.,* p. 163.

31. At this time the Vietnamese did not clearly distinguish between

different European nations. They called the Dutch "Hoa Lang," a Vietnamese transcription of Holland, but they used the same word for the Portuguese as well. They also did not distinguish between Catholics and Protestants (Ch. Gosselin, *L'empire d'Annam,* Paris, 1904, p. 90). The Europeans, at the same time, called Vietnam "Cochinchina."

32. H. Chappoulié, *Rome et les missions d'Indochine au XVIIe siècle,* Paris, 1943, Vol. I, pp. 42ff.

33. The Portuguese missionaries first tried to Christianize Japan. Their Japanese mission was set up by Francis Xavier in 1549, and worked successfully until Spanish Dominicans landed in 1585 and intrigues between them and the Portuguese Jesuits set in. When they were expelled by the Japanese they turned their attention to other countries, the Spanish Dominicans to the Philippines and the Portuguese Jesuits to Vietnam. However the missionary work in Vietnam was not done exclusively by Portuguese. Italian and French Jesuits came to that country as well. According to Chassigneux, *op. cit.,* p. 328, there were twenty-one Jesuits at Faifo during the five years from 1615-1620, ten Portuguese, five Italians, five Japanese, and one Frenchman, Alexander of Rhodes. See also Le Thanh Khoi, *op. cit.,* pp. 288ff.; G. B. Sansom, *Japan: A Short Cultural History,* London, 1952; G. B. Sansom, *Japan and the Western World,* London, 1950.

34. *Kham Dinh Viet Su Thong Giam Cuong Muc,* meaning literally *Text and Explications Forming a Complete Mirror of Vietnamese History Compiled by Imperial Order,* published in numerous volumes between 1856 and 1884. It is usually quoted as *Cuong Muc.* A French translation was published in Hanoi in 1950. Reference to the Portuguese missionary Ignatio is to be found in Vol. XXXIII, 6 b. His name is rendered in Vietnamese as I Ne Khu.

35. Adverte was literally chased out of the country. He had to embark under a hail of arrows and was wounded by two hits (Gosselin, *op. cit.,* pp. 89ff).

36. Toyotomi Hideyoshi, then a sort of prime minister or major domo and the real ruler of Japan, whose emperor had been reduced to a mere figurehead, sent a mission to Europe to study conditions among Christian nations. This commission came back with reports about the burning of heretics by the Inquisitions and about Christians hunting Negroes in Africa in order to sell them as slaves. Hideyoshi used this report to justify his first order to expel all Christian missionaries from Japan in 1587. See Le Thanh Khoi, *op. cit.,* p. 288. Hideyoshi's study mission to Christian countries is usually omitted by authors connected with missionary work. Cf. Latourette, *op. cit.,* pp. 233ff.

37. Christianity reached Indochina early in the sixteenth century, notwithstanding the report of Alexander of Rhodes, who claims that missionary work started only at the beginning of the seventeenth century. As early as 1533 an edict promulgated in Tongking proscribed a religion preached by a certain I Ne Khu (Ignatio) who probably came to Vietnam from Malacca. Beginning with 1550 and especially after 1580 several Franciscans, Dominicans, and Augustines of Portuguese, Spanish, and Italian nationality stayed in Indochina or at least passed through the country (Taboulet, *op. cit.*, p. 10; Romanet du Caillaud, *Essai sur les origines du christianisme au Tonkin et dans les pays annamites*, Paris, 1915; Boniface, *Les débuts du christianisme en Annam dès origines au début du XVIIIe siècle*, Hanoi, no date, probably published in 1930). For a more thorough study of Christian missionary work in Vietnam, consult, E. Louvet, *La Cochinchine religieuse*, Paris, 1885; H. Chappoulié, *Rome et les missions d'Indochine au XVIIe siècle*, 2 vols., Paris, 1943-1947; A. Launay, *Histoire générale de la Société des Missions Etrangères*, 3 vols., Paris, 1894; A. Launay, *Histoire de la mission de Cochinchine*, Paris, 1920.

38. Borri wrote that the "Cochinchinese" were friendlier and more polite toward the Europeans, though they had a high opinion of their own personal value. They believed that giving vent to anger was degrading. While all other Oriental nations considered the Europeans to be profane people whom they hated and at the sight of whom they ran away, the situation was very different in Cochinchina. There crowds gathered at the arrival of Europeans, asked thousands of questions, invited them for dinner, and treated them with courtesy and familiarity. This is taken from a report Borri published in Rome in 1631. It was reprinted three hundred years later in *Bulletin des Amis du Vieux Hué;* July-December, 1931, p. 308, under the title "Les Européens qui ont vu le Vieux Hué: Cristoforo Borri."

39. "When I arrived in Cochinchina [he writes] and heard the inhabitants of the country, especially the women, speak together, I had the impression of listening to twittering birds, and I lost all hope ever to learn their language. After four months I knew enough to understand confessions, and after six months I preached in the language of Cochinchina."—Alexandre de Rhodes, *Voyages et missions,* Lille, 1884, Chapter III, pp. 66-67.

40. The Vietnamese not only borrowed the ideography from the Chinese, but their older literature was also written in the Chinese language. Only toward the end of the thirteenth century was the national language, Chu Nom, accepted for writing prose and poetry. It used Vietnamese

words, which were, however, transcribed by a simplified set of Chinese characters. Even after the missionaries had invented Quoc Ngu, Chinese script was exclusively used in Vietnamese literature. Only in the second half of the nineteenth century did some authors begin to publish their works in the Latin letters of the Quoc Ngu. Cf. Huard and Durand, *op. cit.*, pp. 267ff.

41. Quoc Ngu was not invented by Alexander of Rhodes, as most French authors say, but by Italian and Portuguese missionaries, two of whom, Gaspar de Amaral and Antonio de Barbosa, were the authors of the first Portuguese-Vietnamese dictionary. (Portuguese was then used by all Europeans in their relations with the Vietnamese.) Alexander of Rhodes perfected their system of transcription. It was no easy work, for words in Vietnamese, as in Chinese, have a different meaning if pronounced in a different tone. It was therefore necessary to add signs to the words to indicate their tone. Quoc Ngu was extensively used by the Communists of Northern Vietnam to fight illiteracy. They have simplified the writing of the Latin letters and have replaced the traditional alphabetic order (a, b, c) by arranging the letters according to the difficulty of writing them. The Viet Minh alphabet now goes like this: *i, t, u, n, m,* and so on. The Communists say that 3,491,900 persons have been taught reading and writing in North Vietnam between the beginning of 1947 and mid-1948 (Le Thanh Khoi, *op. cit.*, p. 292; *ibid.*, p. 263).

42. Among the presents Rhodes brought to the court at Hanoi was, characteristically, a complex technical instrument-toy, a clock with a powder case, and a beautifully gilded book on mathematics. The Jesuits of the seventeenth century were masters in that highly valued science. Their knowledge of mathematics and mechanics opened to them many courts in the Orient, the most important of which was that of the Manchu in Peking (Le Thanh Khoi, *ibid.*, p. 290).

43. Alexandre de Rhodes, *Divers voyages et missions*, Paris, 1653. Other works by Rhodes on Vietnam were *Relations des heureux succès de la foi au royaume de Tonkin*, (1650) and *Histoire du Tonkin*, (1652). The latter, as well as *Divers voyages*, was reprinted several times. Rhodes also published a "Carte du royaume humaniste" (1650).

44. Quoted in Maybon, *op. cit.*, p. 75.

45. This statute is reprinted by H. Cordier in his standard work, *Histoire générale de la Chine et de ses relations étrangères depuis les temps les plus anciens jusqu'à la chute de la dynastie Mandchoue*, Paris, 1920-1921, 4 vols. (in Vol. III). For the cooperation between French trade and Church in Indochina cf. also A. Launay, *Histoire générale*

de la Société des Missions Etrangères depuis sa foundation jusqu'à nos jours, Paris, 1894, 3 vols.; P. Kaeppelin, *La Compagnie des Indes Orientales et François Martin,* Paris, 1908.

46. Pallu reported regularly to Colbert, Minister of Finance under Louis XVI and founder of the French East India Company, about conditions in Indochina. His reports contained, of course, political and commercial and not religious information. When his ship was wrecked on the Philippine coast, a paper was found on him, called *Project of an Establishment of the Royal East Indian Company in the Kingdom of Tongkin.* Cf. Le Thanh Khoi, *op. cit.,* p. 293; Launay, *op. cit.,* Vol. I., p. 234; Chappoulié, *op. cit.,* Vol. II., passim. See also Chassigneux, who is most revealing on the subject of commerce and religion in the seventeenth century, and on Pallu. He says the missionaries paved the road for commerce. Through them, France was henceforth present in Vietnam. About the draft of a letter by the king of France to the "kings of Cochinchina, Tonkin and China," Chassigneux says that it "contained not the slightest allusion to the conversion of the unbelievers." He praises Pallu in that he pursued "religion, commerce and the glory of the king" at one and the same time, unlike the Dutch, English, and Portuguese, whose "brutal rapaciousness" and "knavery" Chassigneux condemns, *op. cit.,* pp. 332-338.

47. These opinions are taken from a proposal to organize a French trading company for the Far East. The complete text is printed in Cordier, *op. cit.,* Vol. II.

48. Cf. his letter to the Minister of Finance Colbert, dated January 2, 1672, which contains the following paragraph; "I beg you, sir, in the interest of the Faith, on which depends that of the Company, and for the honor and glory of His Most Christian Majesty, to order the general managers incessantly to make all preparations to establish an office in this kingdom, or at least to undertake a voyage there. This business could be only very advantageous to the Company. By doing so, it could provide for a Christian population of 300,000 who would be in great peril if we would be too slow to support it." Reprinted by A. Launay in *Revue de l'Histoire des Missions,* Vol. I., pp. 213f., and in George Taboulet, *La geste française en Indochine,* Paris, 1955, Vol. I., pp. 82f.

49. See Pallu's letter to Colbert, quoted in note 48. "M. de Bérythe . . . succeeded in obtaining from the king a permission for two of his priests, disguised as merchants, to stay there and build a house, for which a beautiful site was assigned, in the hope that the Company will be able to set up an establishment there. He wrote to the general managers and sent them very instructive memoranda about the deals they could

make there." Pallu fought over thirty years under the banner of commerce and religion. He got his appointment as apostolic vicar for Vietnam in 1658, after he had seen Pope Alexander in 1657. He went to the East without going to Lisbon in 1662, returned to Europe in 1665 with new projects for the French king and the pope, and was back again in Siam in 1673 with letters from Pope Clement IX and Louis XIV. He was shipwrecked and thrown on the Philippine coast the same year, when he tried to sail from Siam to Tongking. He was imprisoned by the Spanish, sent to Mexico and Spain, and was released only in 1677. He was back in Siam in 1682, but never reached Vietnam. He died in 1684 in Fouhien, China.

50. The early Jesuits tried to reconcile Christianity with Confucianism by tolerating ancestor worship, its most prominent feature. They declared ancestor worship to be an admissible, though exaggerated, fulfillment of the Fourth Commandment. This changed in 1774 when Pope Benedict XIV condemned ancestor worship as idolatry. From then on the missionaries lost contact with the educated classes. Gosselin, *op. cit.*, p. 49, claims that Christian missionaries were able to convert members of the illiterate class only. This statement seems somewhat exaggerated. In the permanent conflict between colonial administration and missionaries, Gosselin was a decided partisan of the administration, to which he belonged as government commissioner for Laos.

51. See Hall, *op. cit.*, p. 558, quoting from a letter of March 13, 1847, by the English governor of Singapore, Butterworth.

52. At the court of the Nguyen in Hué the Czech Jesuit John Koeffler served as personal physician to the king and was retained in service even after the mass expulsion of missionaries in 1750. He wrote a history of Vietnam in Latin, *Historica Cochinchinae Descriptio*. This work was published in a French translation in the *Revue Indochinoise*, 1911. Other Jesuits serving at the court of Hué were the Portuguese geometrician Xavier de Monteiro and the naturalist Juan de Loureiro, also a Portuguese, and author of a *Flora Cochinchinae* (1790). Monteiro was appointed director of physical science at the court of the Nguyen. Loureiro pleased the rulers of the South by constructing fire-fighting equipment. The Trinh in Tongking also employed a Czech physician, Palecek, who arrived in Hanoi in 1748, and five "mathematicians and artillery experts" (Le Thanh Khoi, *op. cit.*, p. 294; Chesneaux, *op. cit.*, p. 56). The most prominent of these Jesuit scholars was Koeffler. Maybon published a monography on Koeffler in *Revue Indochinoise*, 1912, pp. 539ff.

53. In Vietnam, Buddhism combined with a cult of local benefactors to whom pagodas were erected. It was especially favored by the Earlier

Ly and some of the Tran rulers. Taoism, the mystical teaching of the Chinese sage Lao Tze (fifth century B.C.), came to Vietnam during the Chinese conquest but never attained the influence of Buddhism or Confucianism. Buddhism was persecuted in the fifteenth century under the influence of a militant Confucianism but had a short renaissance in the seventeenth century. The Earlier Trinh restored ancient Buddhist pagodas and places of pilgrimage. Buddhist scholars traveled to China in search of religious writings. The Nguyen erected the famous Buddhist pagoda of Thien Mu west of Hué in 1601. Chinese bonzes, emigrating from their country after the Manchu conquest, were favorably received in the South. Many Vietnamese scholars were attracted by Buddhism and entered monasteries. While the Nguyen remained benevolent to Buddhism, The Trinh, in 1662, reversed their attitude and proscribed all Buddhist books together with those of Taoism and Christianity (Le Thanh Khoi, *op. cit.,* pp. 104f., 127-130, 279-282, 293; Gaspardone, "Bonzes des Ming refugiés en Annam," in *Sinologica,* Basle, Vol. II, no. 1, 1949; and Gosselin, *op. cit.,* pp. 47f).

54. Apart from the social reasons that had earlier accounted for the success of Buddhism, there was in Vietnam the absence of a firm and dogmatic set of religious beliefs. The Vietnamese absorbed new religious concepts without giving up their old notions and practices; they were totally free from religious fanaticism, and the masses were often hostile to the official Confucianist religion, which sanctioned the abuses of the system under which they suffered.

55. Singapore, an island on the southern tip of the Malaya peninsula, was for centuries considered the ideal site for a naval base to dominate the whole of Southeast Asia. This myth was exploded when the Japanese conquered Singapore with ease from the land during World War II (February, 1942). Singapore was first occupied by the Portuguese, then by the Dutch, and during the Napoleonic wars was conquered by the British. The English empire builder, Stamford Raffles, founded the city and naval fortress of Singapore on the island. (Hall, *op. cit.,* p. 296; Hall, "From Mergui to Singapore, 1686-1819," in *Journal of Siam Society,* Bangkok, Vol. XLI, no. 1, July 1953, pp. 1-18; Makepiece, Brooke, and Bradell, *One Hundred Years of Singapore,* London, 1921.

56. See the dramatic account of this episode in Hall, *op. cit.,* pp. 302-314. Cf. also E. W. Hutchinson, *Adventures in Siam in the Seventeenth Century,* London, 1940; Simon de la Loubère, *Du royaume de Siam,* 2 vols., Paris, 1691 (considered the best contemporary report on Siam); Hall, "From Mergui to Singapore, 1686-1819." See also the French version of Chassigneux (*op. cit.,* pp. 338-341), who blames the Jesuits,

255

not Pallu, for the misconception about the attitude of the Siamese and their king.

57. The abyss between Christianity and Confucianism was created by the later's ancestor worship. Cf. note 50 of this Chapter. Alexander of Rhodes was very much impressed by the veneration the Vietnamese showed for their ancestors. He wrote in his report, "The piety they have for the souls of their dead parents surpasses everything we can think of in Europe; they take incredible pains to find suitable places for their tombs; they think that the whole well-being of a family depends on the respect shown to its dead; they do not spare word or money, neither their own nor that of their friends, to offer a feast to those who just passed away, and again on the anniversaries of their death,, and they do that to all their ancestors as far back as the eighth or even tenth generation." Rich families built pagodas to their ancestors, but even the poorest inhabitants of the river junks put up ancestral tablets, in front of which they offered food to the deceased. The meal, however, was finally eaten by the family. This cult was reserved for the paternal ancestry, the maternal ancestors being excluded. In every village a pagoda was erected to the souls who had no descendants. Cf. Gosselin, *op. cit.*, pp. 48-51. Gosselin is of the opinion that Pope Benedict XIV, by condemning the cult of ancestors and Confucianism in 1774 (cf. note 50), did more harm to the Catholic religion in Asia than all persecutions (*op. cit.*, pp. 48f). About the conflict between Confucianist ancestor worship and Catholicism, see also note 75 of this Chapter, describing the position of the Bishop of Adran, Pigneau de Béhaine, and note 14, Chapter V, describing Gia Long's position. On ancestor worship, see also Le Van Dinh, *Le culte des ancêtres en droit annamite*, Paris, 1934, and Tran Van Trai, *La famille patriarcale annamite*, Paris, 1942, Livre III, Chapitre IV.

58. Trinh Tac (1657-1682) proclaimed an Instruction on Moral Reform in 1662 in which he flatly declared, "A subject owes all his allegiance . . . to the state and his sovereign." His successor, Trinh Con (1682-1709) pronounced in 1696, "The Catholic religion is contrary to natural principles, blights reason, and confounds the mind of the people." In accordance with these views, Trinh Cuong (1709-1729) prohibited preaching by Catholic priests in 1712. The Nguyen in the South took analogous steps. Catholic books were burned and the missionaries banned from the country. These periods of persecutions, however, were interrupted by spells of tolerance (Le Thanh Khoi, *op. cit.*, pp. 293f.; Deloustal, *La justice dans l'ancien Annam*, pp. 152-158; H. Chappoulié,

Rome et les missions d'Indochine au XVIIe siècle, 2 vols., Paris, 1943-1947).

59. Alexander of Rhodes was sentenced to die in 1645 but was released after twenty-two days of imprisonment and was expelled from the country. He described his persecution in *Divers voyages et missions,* pp. 318-344. Of nine missionaries who accompanied him, two were beheaded and the seven others were condemned to have a finger cut off. See Taboulet, *op. cit.,* pp. 21f. Father Feret died in prison in 1700. Several missionaries were killed during at least seven persecutions in 1694-1696, 1706, 1712-1713, 1721, 1736-1737, 1765, and 1773. Contemporary reports on these persecutions are reprinted in Taboulet, *op. cit.,* pp. 96ff. More martyrs' deaths occurred in the nineteenth century. From 1833 to 1857 altogether ninty-five victims were counted in the whole country (*ibid.,* p. 398). Cf. also Montezon and Estève, *Mission de la Cochinchine et du Tonkin,* 1858.

60. Before the end of the seventeenth century the French East India Company propagated the idea of a French stronghold on the coast of Vietnam. In 1686 one of its agents, Véret, recommended the occupation of the island of Poulo Condore, opposite the mouth of the Mekong River. This suggestion was taken up by the British, who tried unsuccessfully to turn the island into a naval and commercial base in 1702. The French Company then conceived a new plan: the occupation of Tourane. This place seemed best suited because it was a central point between China, the Philippines, and Malacca. It sent one of its agents, O'Friell, to explore this possibility in 1744. It was on the basis of O'Friell's study and a previous voyage by himself that Pierre Poivre of Lyon was sent to Indochina in 1749 with the instruction to set up a factory and to wrest from the Dutch their monopoly in the spice trade.

61. Both French and British eyed the island of Poulo Condore as an ideal base for their Eastern commerce. The British occupied it in 1702 to forestall a French seizure. They garrisoned the island with native troops from Macassar. In 1705 these troops, annoyed at being kept there beyond the term of their contract, mutinied and massacred all British on Poulo Condore. Only two escaped in a boat. The French East Indian Company sent an agent to the island in 1723. His report advised against occupying it, and when it became known that England had no intention to reoccupy Poulo Condore, the Company dropped the plan (Hall *op. cit.,* p. 364).

62. With the weakening of the Mogul empire in India, the leading European naval powers tried to carve up the subcontinent. The Dutch

had no success there, the Portuguese were finally reduced to a few places they still hold. Two rivals remained in the field: Britain and France. Both enlisted the help of some Indian princes and waged an almost continual war in the second half of the seventeenth century and throughout the better part of the eighteenth century. The British had their bases in Madras, Calcutta, and Bombay, the French in Pondicherry and Chandernagor. During the War of the Austrian Succession (1740-1748), when the French and British were also fighting in Europe, the able French governor Dupleix captured Madras, but the place was restored to England by the peace treaty. A few years later French-British warfare was resumed. Dupleix dreamed of building a French empire in India and sought to enlist the help of the native princes to oust the English. During the 1750's the French gained in the Deccan but lost to the British in the southeast of the subcontinent. Dupleix' dream came to an end when he was recalled to Paris in 1754. In the Seven Years' War (1756-1763) the French were decisively defeated and practically eliminated from India. The way was now open for the founders of the British Raj in India, Robert Clive (1725-1774) and Warren Hastings (1732-1818). Immediately after their expulsion from India, the French began looking to Vietnam in search of compensation for their losses. Indochina would also be the ideal strategic position to interrupt British trade between India and China. Foreign Minister Vergennes sent a ship to Vietnam in 1778 to explore the situation. The report he received said that "the situation in Cochinchina offered a splendid career there for the French nation." At this time the Tay Son brothers had unfurled the banner of revolution in Vietnam. This gave both the French and the English a golden opportunity to meddle in the internal affairs of Vietnam. Neither nation, however, pursued the project very energetically, for both were engaged in fighting elsewhere at this time: they had chosen opposite sides in the American War of Independence (Latourette, *op. cit.*, pp. 298ff.; Hall, *op. cit.*, pp. 364ff.; Maybon, *Histoire d'Annam moderne*, p. 170; Henri Blet, *L'histoire de la colonisation française*, 3 vols., Grenoble and Paris, 1946, 1948 and 1950; P. Lehault, *La France et l'Angleterre en Asie*, Paris, 1892).

63. In 1778, the year the French decided to support the thirteen colonies, the British governor general of India, Warren Hastings, sent Charles Chapman to Indochina to examine the prospects of opening Vietnam to British trade. Chapman returned to Calcutta in 1779 with an optimistic report. He advised supporting Nguyen Anh against the Tay Son brothers and pointed to Tourane as a prospective base. If the English were forced to abandon Canton, they could buy Chinese goods

cheap enough in Tourane. Chapman also pointed to the strategic value of the Bay of Tourane and said that it offered a splendid shelter for ships and a useful base to operate against enemies. He also warned of French plans to gain influence in Vietnam. Chapman left a written record of his voyage to Indochina, "*Narrative of a Voyage to Cochin-China in 1778*," which is, however, available only in a French translation, "Relation d'un voyage en Cochinchine en 1770," in *Bulletin de la Société des Etudes Indochinoises de Saigon*, New Series, XXIII (1948), no. 2, pp. 15-75. A detailed account of Chapman's mission to Indochina is to be found in Maybon, *op. cit.*, pp. 175-182.

64. Between 1753 and 1778 several projects of commercial penetration and even of colonial settlement in Vietnam were aired in France. Taboulet, *op. cit.*, p. 141, says that at least six such projects found consideration, some of them put forward by merchants with the prospect of substantial profits, others by civil servants desirous to establish France as a maritime power in the Far East. Also France's intellectual life became aware of the existence of Indochina. The country is mentioned in the writings of both Diderot and Voltaire.

65. The Mascarene Islands are an archipelago due east of Madagascar.

66. Among these presents were a gilded coach worth 24,000 pounds, a golden belt adorned with diamonds and rubies, a clock, gilded walking sticks, gold and silver brocade, muslin, linen, handkerchiefs, pistols, and guns (Taboulet, *op. cit.*, p. 138, note 4).

67. Charles Thomas de Saint-Phalle spent the years from 1732 to 1741 in Indochina as a missionary. Between 1747 and 1753 he wrote a series of memoirs about Vietnam to influential people in France. The memoir from which the enthusiastic sentences in the text are taken was written to the Lord Privy Seal (minister of justice), M. Silhouette, on February 24, 1753. Saint-Phalle's memoirs were never published though they are excellent source material, especially for their economic analysis. They were, however, extensively used by the Abbé Richard for his *Histoire naturelle, civile et politique du Tonkin,*, Paris, 1778, 2 vols. (Cf. Archives France-Outre-Mer, Correspondance général de la Cochinchine, Vol. III, folios 69-76, reprinted in Taboulet, *op. cit.*, pp. 142f.)

68. Poivre collected three hundred trees and useful plants during his stay in Indochina and brought them to Paris in 1750. "A company wishing to establish itself in Cochinchina and to lay solid foundations for advantageous commerce, has to start by making itself feared and respected. It will find the means in the general situation of the country and in the Bay of Tourane especially, which is a place that can easily be fortified." When Poivre departed, he kidnapped a Vietnamese in-

terpreter, whereupon the Nguyen ruler Vo Vuong (1738-1765), also called Nguyen Phuc Khoat, expelled all missionaries (1750). Two years later the interpreter was returned, the missionaries readmitted, and the French East India Company allowed to open a factory in Tourane. After that time the idea of establishing French colonial rule over Vietnam never died. Cf. Le Thanh Khoi, *op. cit.*, pp. 294f.; M. Gaudart, "Les archives de Pondichéry et les entreprises de la Compagnie des Indes en Indochine au XVIIIe siècle," in *Bulletin des Amis du Vieux Hué*, 1937, no. 4, pp. 353ff.; Launay, *Histoire de la mission de Cochinchine*, Paris, 1920, Vol. II, pp. 344f. Poivre himself wrote extensive reports on his experience in Indochina. They were published by J. Cordier in the *Revue d'Extrême Orient*. In the volume for 1883 appeared "Mémoire sur la Cochinchine (1774)," "La description de la Cochinchine," and "Journal de voyage de Pierre Poivre." In 1894 Cordier reprinted "Voyage de Pierre Poivre en Cochinchine." About Poivre's kidnaping of Michel Cuong, see his letter to Msgr. Lefèbvre, dated Canton, October 26, 1750 (Arch. Miss Etrang., Vol. 743, p. 359, repr. in Launay, *Hist. Miss. Coch.*, Vol. II, pp. 326-328, and Taboulet, *op. cit.*, pp. 131-133.) Chassigneux, *op. cit.*, pp. 344-345, underlines some negative aspects of Poivre's character and achievements. Based on research by Maybon, he says Poivre was expelled from the mission for "serious reasons."

69. As such it was indeed presented in a fantastic memorandum to René de Magon, governor of Ile de France and Bourbon. This memorandum is undated and was probably composed by the Count d'Estaing during a voyage from Pondicherry to Ile de France in December, 1758, or January, 1759. It was published for the first time by Taboulet, *op. cit.*, pp. 145-151. Taboulet characteristically recognizes the "good motives" of the Count, who was also driven by a desire to alleviate the financial difficulties of the East India Company. D'Estaing proposed that half of the booty should go to the commander of the expedition and the other half to the Company.

70. Taboulet, *op. cit.*, p. 146. D'Estaing later distinguished himself as an admiral in the American War of Independence and died on the guillotine during the French Revolution (April 28, 1794).

71. For the foregoing see the correspondence between Chevalier, commander of Chandernagor, and M. de Bellecombe, governor general of Pondicherry, dated February 12 and February 15, 1878. Arch. France-Outre-Mer, Corr. Gen. Coch., Vol. III, folios 161-172, and Archives de Pondichéry, nos. 2647 and 2648, published by E. Gaudart, *Bulletin des Amis du Vieux Hué*, 1937, pp. 353-380, and Taboulet, *op. cit.*, pp. 156-160.

72. The Society had had its headquarters in that Portuguese colony since 1732 (Taboulet, *op. cit.*, p. 164).

73. Hatien, in the seventeenth century a part of the kingdom of the Khmer and a meeting place of merchants and pirates of all nationalities, was settled by a Chinese refugee, Mac Cuu, who had left his country after the Manchu conquest. By permission of the Khmer ruler he founded seven cities which soon became prosperous places. But Mac Cuu soon realized that Cambodia, torn by dynastic troubles, could not protect the new settlements sufficiently. He therefore offered the Nguyen suzerainty over Hatien. Mac Cuu died in 1735 but his son Mac Thien Tu continued his work. After having received permission from the Nguyen to coin his own money, Mac Thien Tu set up a civil and military administration, erected fortresses, built highways, and organized trading fairs. The province flourished continually under the Nguyen, though the rule of Hué over Hatien was energetically challenged by Siam (Le Thanh Khoi, *op. cit.*, pp. 268-272; Gaspardone, "Un Chinois des mers du Sud, le fondateur de Ha-tien," in *Journal Asiatique*, 1952, fasc. 3, p. 363).

74. The Catholic Church distinguishes between residential bishops, who have jurisdiction over a certain territory, and titular bishops. The latter, also called bishops *in partibus infidelium*, are assigned a bishopric in a part which once was Christian but, in the course of history, was lost to the "infidels." Thus Pigneau became bishop of Adran or Adrana, an ancient city in Bythinia (Asia Minor), at the time of his consecration a part of the Mohammedan Turkish Empire. However, the pope could have made Pigneau a residential bishop of Indochina. He refrained from doing so lest he offended the Portuguese, who still claimed the country for themselves. For the life story of Pigneau consult the following works: A. Faure, *Les français en Cochinchine au XVIIIe siècle: Mgr. Pigneau de Béhaine, évêque d'Adran,* Paris, 1891; E. Louvet, *Mgr. d'Adran, missionnaire et patriote,* Paris, 1900; Cl. E. Maitre, "Documents sur Pigneau de Béhaine," in *Revue Indochinoise*, 1913; G. Taboulet, "La vie tourmentée de l'évêque d'Adran," in *Bulletin de la Société des Etudes Indochinoises*, 1940, Nos. 3/4, pp. 9-42.

75. Pigneau's letters to his parents show his happiness emanating from his imperturbable faith in God in times of despair. "If I stayed in France, I might have attached myself to the despicable goods of this world. Instead I came to this country [Vietnam] and here I am happy in the invaluable necessity to rely on nothing else than God Himself" (July 3, 1767). In June, 1768, he was imprisoned and put into the *kang*, a wooden and iron frame fastened around hands and legs weighing eighty pounds. "Bless the Lord a thousand times [he wrote to his parents on

261

June 23, 1768] that He has done such an honor to your family. Thank Him, for me; pray to Him to let me soon re-enter my mission and suffer for His holy name." When his parents pressed him to return to France in 1772, he refused. "Do you want me to abandon the salvation of so many souls for a pleasure that can last but a few years? . . . Is it not better to sacrifice a few years to the glory of God and the salvation of so many abandoned souls?" (October 1, 1772) See Arch. Miss. Etrang., Vol. 746, pp. 124, 430, 738, 943; Launay, *Hist. Miss. Coch.*, Doc., Vol. II, p. 387; Taboulet, *op. cit.*, pp. 165-168. It strangely contrasts with Pigneau's profound faith that when his religious beliefs came into conflict with his politico-diplomatic plans, he was apt to compromise the former. This is clearly shown in the change of his views on ancestor worship. He first took the papal ban so strictly that he influenced his pupil, Prince Canh, to refuse saluting the altars of his ancestors, a behavior that greatly shocked the prince's father, Nguyen Anh. But Pigneau changed his opinions later and proposed to consider ancestor worship as a civil ceremony, a simple manifestation of respect to the deceased. It was ridiculous, he wrote in a letter to M. Boiret dated June 15, 1798, to consider ancestor worship as idolatry. The apostles were tolerant of the usages of the countries where they preached. "Are we more capable than they were?" he asks. To go too far, he said characteristically, would endanger the propagation of the faith. In the last years of his life, the Bishop of Adran showed great tolerance in questions of ritual and had vivacious controversies with more intransigeant collegues, like Msgr. Saint-Martin, the Apostolic Vicar of Szechwan. On his deathbed he pleaded with M. Lelabousse for indulgence toward ancestor worship. One of his biographers thinks that he might have converted the Holy See to his convictions, had he had a chance to travel to Rome. Cf. Launay, *Histoire de la Mission de Setchouen*, Vol. II., appendix, pp. 21-28; Emile Tavernier, "Mgr. Pigneau de Béhaine, évêque d'Adran, quelques aspects de sa vie politique et religieuse," in *Bulletin de la Société d'Enseignement Mutuel du Tonkin*, Vol. 14 (1934); Henri Bernard, "Le conflit de la religion annamite avec la religion d'Occident à la cour de Gia Long," in *Bulletin Général de l'Instruction Public*, Hanoi, January, 1941; Taboulet, *op. cit.*, pp. 226ff., where an interesting letter of Pigneau to Letoudal (dated August 17, 1789) is reprinted.

76. The world of fashion made a pet of the young prince."—Hall, *op. cit.*, p. 369.

77. Faure, *op. cit.*, p. 86, quotes a memorandum by Pigneau, called "Some Observations," about a campaign in Indochina. There the bishop gives his opinion about the pieces of artillery best suited for this kind

of warfare. He recommends that shiploads of biscuits, flour, grain, and liquor be sent to Indochina, for he anticipated that the French soldier would not be satisfied with the native rice. He suggests that one or two experienced engineers be employed with the expeditionary forces. Pigneau also lists other items to be included in the supply of the attacking army: tents, hatchets, engineering tools, pharmaceutical articles, surgical instruments, and gauze. Finally he estimates the necessary strength of the expeditionary corps at approximately fifteen hundred men and the navy required at three frigates, one corvette, and three auxiliary craft. Excerpts from this memorandum are also reprinted in H. Cordier, *Correspondance générale*, pp. 31f., and Taboulet, op. cit., p. 184f.

78. Memorandum to Count of Montmorin, entitled *Notes sur la Cochinchine*. (Cordier, *op. cit.*, pp. 37-43; Faure, *op. cit.*, pp. 78-85; Taboulet, *op. cit.*, pp. 182-184).

79. "France was tottering on the brink of national bankruptcy which was to bring on the Revolution."—Hall, *op. cit.*, p. 369.

80. The complete text of this Treaty of Offensive and Defensive Alliance, dated November 28, 1787, and signed for France by the Count of Montmorin and the Bishop of Adran, is published in Arch. Miss. Etrang., Vol. 801, p. 155, and reprinted in Launay, *Hist. Miss. Coch.*, Vol. III., pp. 168-171, and Taboulet, *op. cit.*, pp. 186-190.

81. In a letter dated December 2, 1787, Montmorin informed the Chevalier d'Entrecasteaux, governor of Ile de France and Bourbon, that the king had left the decision about the expedition against Indochina to Count Conway. But he added, "I beg you not to mention to the Bishop of Adran that the king left to M. de Conway to suspend or postpone the expedition." Conway, born in Ireland in 1733, was a very controversial figure. Lafayette, under whom he fought in the American War of Independence, called him an "ambitious and dangerous man." Taboulet *op. cit.*, p. 196, says he was an intriguer and a bad character. King Louis XVI had hardly a better opinion of him. During his farewell audience with Pigneau he warned the bishop that Conway might wreck his whole expedition. Louis XVI also confided to Pigneau that he had appointed Conway commander-in-chief in India for no other reason than to get rid of him in France. Only to please Pigneau (who ostensibly had asked for it) would he promote Conway to lieutenant-general (Cordier, *op. cit.*, pp. 96-99; Faure, *op. cit.*, p. 128).

82. He received the information in a short, and extremely cool letter from Count de la Luzerne, dated April 16, 1789, which reads, "Sir, I received the letters you kindly wrote to me last August 28, concerning the slowness of the measures taken in connection with the expedition to Co-

chinchina. I can only refer to the letter in which I indicated to you that this expedition will not take place. I authorized the Count de Conway to supply you with the means to return to France, if you so desire" (Cordier, *op. cit.*, p. 226; Taboulet, op. cit., p. 209).

83. In a letter to M. de Saint-Riveul. See Taboulet, *op. cit.*, p. 210.

84. Most authors on French colonial history claim that the outbreak of the French Revolution in 1789 interfered with Pigneau's plans for a conquest of Indochina. Faure, the biographer of the Bishop of Adran, denies this categorically. According to him the whole "shame" fell on the government of Louis XVI. If the French government had given more support to Pigneau, the protectorate over Annam could have materialized at the end of the eighteenth century. See Faure, *op. cit.*, pp. 186ff. On the other hand Gosselin, *op. cit.*, pp. 96ff., claims that, if France had not been engaged in the revolutionary and Napoleonic wars in Europe between 1789 and 1816, she would not have forgotten her colonial expansion and could have compensated her loss of India in Vietnam. It would have been easy, according to Gosselin, to establish the French in Indochina by a treaty with the young ruler who owed his throne to French support.

85. Vietnamese sources of this time are too scant to allow the historian to determine exactly the reasons for the Tay Son rebellion. It seems that the Tay Son brothers translated a mute and deep discontent into action. Taboulet, *op. cit.*, pp. 168-170, quotes from letters written by the Coadjutor of the Bishop of Adran, M. Labartette, to M. Boiret, director of the seminary of the Rue de Bac, in 1775 and 1776, which illustrate the desolate conditions of the country. "This country [he writes], once so rich and fertile, is now almost totally ruined and lacks everything. . . . War and famine have caused such ravages that half of the inhabitants of the country have perished. . . . Whole families take poison in order to die immediately and to avoid slow death by starvation. Mothers eat their babies. One often sees human flesh sold in the market." Cf. also Arch. Miss. Etrang., Vol. 745, p. 749; Launay, *Hist. Miss. Coch., Doc.*, Vol. III, pp. 104-108. Gosselin, whose sympathies are entirely on the side of Nguyen Anh, calls the followers of the Tay Son "malcontents, smugglers, bandits of all sorts" (*op. cit.*, pp. 97ff). But these designations are commonly used for revolutionaries by the adherents of the existing order. More characteristic for the Tay Son leaders were their actions against the Chinese settlers of Vietnam. When they entered Saigon in March, 1782, they burned and pillaged the Chinese shops of Cholon and massacred more than ten thousand Chinese of that city. Their intention was to destroy the commercial monopoly of the Chinese

settlers in Vietnam (Le Thanh Khoi, *op. cit.*, p. 300; J. Bouchot, "Note historique sur Cholon," in *Extrême Asie,* no. 23 (1928), pp. 581-585). The Tay Son ruler Quang Trung was more tolerant toward the Catholic religion than Nguyen Anh, and at the same time hostile to Buddhism. Christian missionary work made some progress under his rule (Le Thanh Khoi, *op. cit.,* p. 310; *Nouvelles lettres édifiantes des Missions de la Chine et des Indes Orientales, p.* 214). The three Tay Son rulers were Nguyen Van Nhac (or Thäg Duc), the eldest of the three brothers (1778-1793), Nguyen Van Hué (or Quang Trung), the youngest brother (1788-1792); and Nguyen Quang Toan, son of Quang Trung (1792-1802). The reign of the two brothers overlaps as they divided the country between themselves. Quang Trung created a completely new administration in which, for the first time in Indochinese history, the military had precedence over the civil power. Under the threat of heavy fines, he ordered the recultivation of all fallow land and encouraged commerce. His reforms were intelligent and realistic, though somewhat limited. But Quang Trung was unable to solve Vietnam's social contradictions, and this brought about the downfall of the Tay Son dynasty. The peasantry expected from him a reduction of taxes and forced labor and a distribution of the rice fields concentrated in the hands of the landlords. Quang Trung disappointed them in all respects. If the old bureaucracy was replaced by a new one, this produced no change for the peasants. The merchants who had financed the Tay Son rebellion lost their best market when the South was reconquered by Nguyen Anh. The country found neither peace nor unity. Soon Quang Trung lost all support in the nation, and only the prestige of his army saved the dynasty for a while. To divert from his internal troubles, Quang Trung planned to regain the two Kwangs (the two Chinese provinces of Kwangsi and Kwangtung that had formed, together with the Red River valley, the ancient Nam Viet). He sent an embassy to the court of Peking, proposing to marry a Manchu princess and asking the two provinces as a dowry. Before the embassy reached Peking, Quang Trung died at the age of only forty in 1792. (Le Thanh Khoi, *op. cit.,* pp. 304-313; Chesneaux, *op. cit.,* pp. 58-64; Huard and Durand, *op. cit.,* pp. 32f).

86. The Chinese invasion of Vietnam took place in 1788 with a force of 200,000 men. Quang Trung defeated the Chinese with an army of 100,000 men and 100 elephants. After his victory Quang Trung sent an embassy to the Chinese Emperor Kien Long with precious presents and vows of a lasting peace. The last Le king of Vietnam, Le Hien Tong, at whose instigation the Chinese had invaded Tongking, died in Peking in exile in 1793 (Le Thanh Khoi *op. cit.,* pp. 306-309; G. Deveria, *Histoire*

des relations de la Chine avec l'Annam-Vietnam du XVIe au XIXe siècle, Paris, 1880, pp. 24ff).

87. Authors disagree about the number of French soldiers and sailors who fought under the banner of Nguyen Anh. Faure, who thoroughly studied the records of the French ships that sailed to the Far East in 1788 and 1789, lists the names of 369 officers, sailors, soldiers, and workmen who left their ships during the voyage. He assumes that most of them entered the service of Nguyen Anh. Taboulet, *op. cit.,* p. 240, disputes this theory and points to the fact that there were always many casualties and desertions during a long voyage in the age of the sailing ships. Vannier (as quoted by Taboulet, *ibid.*) gives the number of Frenchmen fighting in Nguyen Anh's forces as 14 officers and 80 men. This would agree with information contained in a letter of Pigneau, dated July 18, 1794, who mentions 40 Europeans serving in the Vietnamese army, exclusive of those having joined Nguyen Anh's navy. Taboulet estimates the number of Frenchmen who enlisted with the Vietnamese forces at about 100. Cf. H. Cosserat, "Notes biographiques sur les français au service de Gia-Long, in *Bulletin des Amis du Vieux Hué* 1917, pp. 165-206; 1920, pp. 137-176; L. Cadière, "Les français au service de Gia Long," in the same periodical, 1926; H. Berland and B. Taboulet, "Le cimetière français de Cangio," in *Bulletin de la Société des Etudes Indochinoises,* 1944, pp. 9-16.

88. Many French officers and enlisted men left Nguyen Anh's service in 1791 and 1792. Typical is the fate of the French colonel Raymond Olivier. His testament, addressed to the Bishop of Adran on March 6, 1799, is reprinted in Taboulet, *op. cit.,* pp. 246-248. For Nguyen Anh's victory over the Tay Son, see Le Thanh Khoi, *op. cit.,* pp. 313-316; Maybon, *op. cit.,* pp. 301-347.

89. Nguyen Anh had hesitated a long time before he accepted Pigneau's offer of help. The Bishop of Adran had to convince the young ruler that France was mighty and generous and that King Louis XVI was good and sympathetic toward the unhappy. Only after long deliberation did Nguyen Anh accept French intervention and refuse similar offers of the British and the Dutch.

90. Nguyen Anh was not of a cruel disposition but he wanted to frighten his enemies and to avenge his uncle, who was executed by the Tay Son in 1777. In August, 1802, the surviving members of the Tay Son family and the leading generals of their army were executed, together with their whole families, at the imperial palace of Hué. A French missionary, Pierre Jacques Lemonnière de la Bissachère (1764-1830) witnessed the horrible scenes and left a vivid description of them. The

skeletons of King Quang Trung and his queen were exhumed, the bones were put into a basket, and soldiers of Nguyen Anh's army urinated on them in the presence of the last Tay Son king, Nguyen Quang Toan, son of Van Hué. The king was then bound to four elephants, which were driven in different directions and thus tore the young ruler into four pieces. (A similar cruel form of execution, with horses taking the place of elephants, was used in France for Ravaillac, tho murderer of Henry IV, and for Damiens, who attempted to kill Louis XV.) The torn limbs of Van Hué were then fed to the ravens. Cf. Taboulet, *op. cit.,* pp. 265-267; Maybon, *La relation sur le Tonkin et la Cochinchine de M. de la Bissachère* (1807), Paris, 1919, pp. 117-121.

91. Pigneau died October 9, 1799, at the age of fifty-seven, of dysentery which he contracted as far back as 1788. He was buried on December 16 in the presence of the crown prince, all mandarins of the court, the king's bodyguard of twelve thousand men, and forty thousand mourners both Christians and pagans. King Nguyen Anh (Gia Long) composed a funeral oration, which was read by a court dignitary at the funeral. In it he called the Bishop of Adran "the most illustrious foreigner ever to appear at the court of Cochinchina." Father Lelabousse of the Seminary of Foreign Missions wrote a report on the funeral, which was published in the *Archives of Foreign Missions* under the date of April 24, 1800. (Vol. 746, p. 839. Launay, *Hist. Miss. Coch., Doc.,* Vol. III, pp. 374-382; Taboulet, *op. cit.,* pp. 230-236, also about the illness and death of Pigneau.) The king's funeral oration was published, in a French translation by Pham Quynh, in *Bulletin des Amis du Vieux Hué,* 1936, pp. 107-119. It was written in Chinese characters on a piece of silk and handed to Pigneau's successor as Bishop of Adran, Mgr. Labartette. The original was kept in the bishop's palace at Saigon.

92. M. Lavoué, in a letter to M. Letoudal, dated Lai Thieu, June 16, 1792, writes, "Though the King does not persecute the faith, he shows at every opportunity that he is not pleased when somebody accepts it, and it does not seem probable that he will ever become a Christian." (Arch. Miss. Etrang., Vol. 801, p. 436; Launay, *Hist. Miss. Coch., Doc.,* pp. 222-229; Taboulet, *op. cit.,* p. 235.)

93. In an epitaph written in Chinese characters on a stele in front of Pigneau's tomb, the following sentences are to be found: "In more than twenty years he helped us commanding our armies and organizing the administration of our country. His actions deserve to be transmitted to posterity. The prompt restoration of our kingdom is due in large part to the indefatigable efforts of the Grand Master. In 1799 he followed the army that was to march on Qui Nhon; on the eleventh day of the

ninth month, at the age of fifty-seven, he succumbed to an illness amidst the troops encamped in front of the mouth of the Thi Nai. In the tenth month a royal decree appointed him Preceptor of the Prince Royal and raised him to the rank of a duke. The place chosen for his grave is to the north of the town of Giadinh, the place where he built his religious edifice." The epitaph was translated into French by Truong Vinh Tong, son of the famous Vietnamese writer Petrus Truong Vinh Ky. It is reprinted in Taboulet, *op. cit.*, p. 235.

94. After the death of Pigneau only four Frenchmen remained at the court of Hué: the Duke of Chaigneau, Vannier, Forsans, and Despiau. Gia Long granted them the rank of mandarins and gave them a body-guard of fifty men. He also exempted them from the customary five prostrations before the throne. Their influence at court was strong enough to forestall a settlement of the British East India Company in Vietnam. The annexation of Singapore by the British disturbed Gia Long, and when dying he recommended to his son and successor, Minh Mang, to treat all Europeans well, especially the French, but not to grant them any position of preponderance. Chaigneau was appointed consul of France in 1821 and charged with concluding a treaty of commerce. Minh Mang refused to sign such a treaty. Commerce was open to all nations according to Vietnamese law, he declared. Thereupon Chaigneau returned to France on November 15, 1824. The only Europeans to remain were now the missionaries (Le Thanh Khoi, *op. cit.*, pp. 338-341; Michel Duc Chaigneau, *Souvenirs de Hué;* H. Cordier, "Le consulat de France à Hué sous la Restauration," in *Revue de l'Extrême-Orient,* 1883, pp. 139, 267; Taboulet, *op. cit.*, pp. 310f).

95. Raffles acquired Singapore for the British in 1819. The first British-Burmese War broke out in 1824 and ended two years later with the annexation of two large Burmese provinces by England. The Opium War (1839-1842) opened China to European trade and turned the Chinese city of Hong Kong into a British crown colony. It was followed up by a second British war against China (1856-1860) in which France joined. Their victory made the Celestial Empire a helpless object of European exploitation (Hall, *op. cit.*, pp. 430, 515-518; Latourette, *op. cit.*, pp. 368-378).

96. The order of succession in Vietnam was not fixed by unalterable rules. Until 1816 it was generally assumed that the son of Prince Canh (the king's eldest son, who had accompanied Pigneau to France) would become his successor. Gia Long, however, chose prince Chi Dam, oldest son of his first concubine, as the future ruler. Chi Dam, born in 1791, ascended the throne in 1820 under the dynastic name of Minh Mang.

Gia Long chose him for his strong character and his deep aversion against the West. Even before he became king, on May 17, 1819, Msgr. Labartette reported to the French ministry of foreign affairs, "He praises the Japanese for having abolished the Christian religion in their country. His maxim is that it is not good to have two religions in one country." On June 18, 1822, Msgr. Labartette wrote to M. Baroudel, Procurator of the Foreign Mission in Macao, "The king hates all commerce with the Europeans. . . . He threatens to chase us from his country at the smallest complaint against us. Since he ascended the throne, our holy religion has made little progress" (Arch. Miss. Etrang., Vol. 747, pp. 737, 855; Launay, *Hist. Miss. Coch., Doc.*, Vol. II, p. 434; Vol. III, p. 438; Taboulet, *op. cit.*, pp. 294f).

97. Minh Mang forbade the entry of missionaries into Vietnam in February, 1825. French boats entering the ports of Indochina were ordered to be searched with scrupulous attention. All entries into the country were to be watched "lest some masters of the European religion enter furtively, mix with the people and spread darkness in the kingdom" (Louvet, *La Cochinchine religieuse*, Vol. II, pp. 41f; Taboulet, *op. cit.*, p. 322).

Chapter V

The Flight into Isolation

1.

THE nineteenth century began not at all badly for Vietnam. A thirty-year period of civil wars came to an end. The country was again united and was now larger in territory and population than ever before. It had shown its vitality by steadily growing at the expense of Cambodia, even while the war between the Tay Son and Nguyen Anh used up much of its strength. Cambodia was in fact no longer a fully independent country but rather a vassal of Vietnam.[1] For the first time, food promised to become plentiful for every Vietnamese, once the new territories in the South were settled and the new lands put to full use. Vietnam's independence was respected by China, and her new borders were in little danger of attack by her Indochinese neighbors, all of whom were inferior to Vietnam in population and weaker in military strength.

Moreover, during the first two decades of the nineteenth century, Vietnam was under no military or political pressure from the West. The new dynasty had risked the hazards of a military alliance with a European power but had gone through this experience with unprecedented luck. Because the Bishop of Adran had adequately made up for the failure of France to keep her treaty obligations, Gia Long was able to enjoy the benefits of European military assistance without having to pay

270

the customary suicidal price. The treaty of 1787 would have allowed France to move into Vietnam peacefully sixty years before she actually started her costly and protracted Indochinese campaigns. But Gia Long's need for foreign help had ended long before France could think of reconsidering her withdrawal and of belatedly fulfilling her part of the deal.

Thanks to the effectiveness of the Bishop's political and military operations, Vietnam was also able to avoid the dangers of an alliance with any of the other Western powers that were ready to acquire a Vietnamese harbor by supplying Nguyen Anh with soldiers and ships. Both the English and the Portuguese were prevented by Pigneau from exploiting the weakness of France by rendering the help for which the young prince had made the alarming concessions of the 1787 treaty.[2] When Gia Long proclaimed himself emperor of Vietnam in 1806, he could consider himself the ruler of a truly independent Asian country.[3]

Gia Long's good fortune in regard to the West continued to favor his policies after victory was achieved. From the turn of the century on, Asia enjoyed a long period of relief from vexation by Europe, as a direct result of the Napoleonic Wars.[4] For fifteen years these wars drastically reduced European commercial and political activities in Asia and almost extinguished Western interest in Vietnam. Gia Long was virtually unmolested by proposals for trade with the West. He was obviously convinced that such trade was not vital for Vietnam, and clearly opposed to the granting of special trading privileges to any European country. The English, well ahead of all other nations in the new search that was on for overseas markets, tried to obtain such privileges from Gia Long in 1804. The attempt, which remained unsuccessful, was notable mainly because it was the only one made within a period of more than thirty years. It was not repeated until 1822.[5]

At the beginning of the nineteenth century France represented no danger whatever for Vietnam. Of the many projects that were conceived in French circles during the whole eighteenth century, only the echoes of worn-out slogans were audible after the year 1800. To be sure, some of the people who had pleaded for action in Asia during the preceding century were still alive, and also still enamoured of their old projects, and Napoleon himself was quite willing to sacrifice French man power and wealth for an empire in the East.[6] However, his continental policy of conquest forced him again and again to waste on the battlefields of Europe what he would have needed to realize his Asian dreams. France was the only European country with permanent spokesmen in Vietnam during the whole reign of Gia Long. The majority of the missionaries were French, and two of the surviving companions of Pigneau, Chaigneau and Vannier, had become high mandarins at the court of Hué.[7] These men may have strengthened Gia Long's reluctance to grant commercial privileges to the English and Dutch,[8] but French trade did not benefit from their presence in Vietnam: the France of Napoleon had neither commercial nor political contacts with Vietnam or any other Indochinese country.

French interest in Indochina reawakened only after the Restoration.[9] From 1817 on, French vessels began to reappear in Vietnam. The first traders were well received, although their cargo was of no use to the Vietnamese. Gia Long even invited them to return with more suitable merchandise; he set up no obstacles against the exchange of goods between France and Vietnam, but he granted the French no special favors either, and he politely rejected an attempt to establish official relations and negotiate a trade agreement with France.[10]

The greatness and happiness of Vietnam, Gia Long felt, could be preserved only through a policy of strict noninvolvement with any of the Western powers. France was not excepted, as Gia Long had no reason to believe himself obligated to anyone in France but the late Pigneau. This obligation he fulfilled by tolerating the Christian religion, but he would never

272

have tolerated any political interference by the missionaries or by France. To make sure that Vietnam would not deviate from this course, he chose as his successor a man whom he knew as an opponent of close contacts with the West.[11]

2.

The death of Gia Long no doubt deprived Vietnam of a very great ruler, but with the policies he practiced, he would have failed as disastrously as his less fortunate successors had he lived for the showdown between his country and the West.

Gia Long's attitude toward the West was based on a simple formula. He tried to secure friendly relations with every power by granting favors to none. If Western activity in Asia had remained as restricted after 1820 as it had been during the preceding thirty years, this policy of noninvolvement with Europe would have given as much satisfaction to Gia Long's successors as it did to himself. Western policy, however, turned toward active interference in Asia soon after the Napoleonic Wars had come to an end. Interference became military aggression, and against military aggression the negative principle of noninvolvement was politically inoperative. This made Gia Long's policy as inadequate diplomatically as was the country's technical equipment for a military struggle with the West.

Gia Long, therefore, has been wrongly acquitted of guilt for Vietnam's failure to cope with the dangers that threatened Asia from the West after 1820. Among French historians of Vietnam, it has become almost a dogma to put all blame for Vietnam's conflict with the Catholic missions on Gia Long's immediate successor Minh Mang, who ruled Vietnam from 1820 to 1841. Even the armed intervention of France, although it started eighteen years after Minh Mang's death, has been described as an inevitable consequence of his so-called break with Gia Long's policy in regard to the West.

The great fault of Minh Mang was not that he abandoned the allegedly pro-Western course of his father; it was rather his inability to recognize that, after 1820, noninvolvement had become obsolete as a defensive policy against the West. In an entirely new world of international activity, and against previously unknown dangers that threatened Asia from the West, Vietnam's policy toward Europe remained in fact fundamentally unchanged. What Gia Long had preached while France was nonexistent as a political and military factor outside of Europe, Minh Mang and his successors, Thieu Tri and Tu Duc, tried to practice against a France that soon was able to destroy Vietnamese harbors and warships at will.[12]

Through the very firmness of his character, Minh Mang became more quickly and hopelessly imprisoned by the narrow concept of this policy than either Thieu Tri or Tu Duc. To compromise on the issue of national survival appeared criminal to his strong but all too rigid mind. Consistent and fearless in the exercise of power, he boldly confronted the dangers he sensed for his policy in the presence of foreign missionaries and in the influence of a Western religion on the Vietnamese mind. His first edicts were mild, and although they were not heeded by the missionaries, no force was used to bring about their observance.[13] Only after he had become convinced of foreign-inspired Catholic plots against his regime did Minh Mang begin his policy of persecution. This was his most serious political error; it underlined his courage and determination, but also his inability to act without passion and fear.

But between Gia Long's passive hostility toward the Christian religion and Minh Mang's measures to outlaw the Catholic cult, the difference of policy was not very great.[14] On the basis of Gia Long's political principles, Minh Mang's edicts against the "foreign religion" became almost inevitable shortly after Gia Long died. The West had resumed its penetration into Asia and become a military threat on the Indochinese peninsula itself. The first English invasion of Burma in 1824 clearly

274

demonstrated the impotence of Gia Long's passive method to achieve noninvolvement. Minh Mang knew that he had to fight. Precisely because he remained in the footsteps of his father, he could now hardly do less than adopt a policy of determined isolation, of which the ejection of all foreigners was a necessary part. Under Thieu Tri and Tu Duc, who were already subject to French military action, it was probably no longer possible to reverse this policy. To change would have meant to give in to French pressure and to capitulate without a fight.

3.

The policy of noninvolvement with the West had thus led Vietnam to a dilemma from which none of the Nguyen emperors was able to extricate his unfortunate country. The more they felt threatened, the higher they built the walls that were to isolate Vietnam from the West. But no walls were high enough to keep out the Western aggressor. The more boldly France advanced, the more helpless became a Vietnamese policy that would not even compromise with a Western power for the sake of diplomatic counteraction. Vietnamese hostility toward the West strengthened and incited the forces of Western aggression; Western threats and demands, on the other hand, fortified the resolve of the Nguyen emperors to eradicate all foreign influence within the borders of their state. They may have overrated the aggressiveness of French policy toward Vietnam before 1850, but they could point to the examples of India and Burma, and after 1840 they experienced also the shock of English and French intervention in China. Unable to learn the proper political lesson, they continued to persecute, but they did it out of their own growing fear of being persecuted.

For Minh Mang, Thieu Tri, and Tu Duc, the fight against

275

the missionaries was always an inseparable part of their struggle against Western political interference. But these intellectuals on the throne were subject to a common ideological aberration. They saw the moral and material forces of the West as a single hostile totality, against which the East had to react with a total negation of all ideas, intentions, and approaches from the West. English and American attempts to negotiate trade relations were as negatively treated as those of the French;[15] Portuguese and Dutch interests in trade with Indochina were as much neglected as those of all other powers that had misgivings over France's designs on Vietnam and might have opposed French military intervention. The rulers of Vietnam were equally incapable of exploiting the currents of French opinion against military action in the East. Strong waves of opposition kept arising in France while intervention was being prepared and during the twenty-five years it took to complete the actual conquest. This opposition was either ignored or misunderstood by the Vietnamese rulers, whose anti-Christian policy, to be sure, made it almost impossible for them to mobilize Western sympathy for their country. When Minh Mang in 1840 made a lukewarm attempt to submit his case to influential circles in Paris, the Society of Foreign Missions had no trouble in preventing his envoys from achieving their goal.[16]

By that time the leaders of the Catholic missions had long made up their minds about the Nguyen regime. The missionaries might have become the best allies of Vietnam in her struggle against foreign oppression and exploitation. Instead, they became active proponents of French military intervention. It was Minh Mang's policy of indiscriminate opposition to all men and ideas related to the West that transformed most of the servants of the Roman church into unhappy agents of French imperialism. As victims of persecution, they were indeed the only Europeans with a legitimate case against the government of Vietnam. But at the height of the crisis their cause was degraded into a mere pretext for the West's wholly unjustified military intervention. As a result of French military action, the missionaries became politically privileged and the emperors and mandarins politically persecuted.

But in the crimes of power the victims are seldom free of guilt. Although terrorized by people whose military forces were superior to their own, the nineteenth-century rulers of Vietnam were nevertheless responsible for the success of colonial aggression against their country. Their earlier errors and omissions in the field of international relations were as fatal for Vietnam as their later weakness at every instant of a military test. Vietnam's anti-Western policy under the Nguyen emperors, in short, must be recognized as one of the causes of the country's colonial dismemberment and loss of political independence.

The failure of the Nguyen dynasty to develop an adequate policy of defense, however, was not a mere accident of history that would never have happened with better men in high office and on the throne. Vietnamese dynastic policy from Gia Long to Tu Duc was deeply rooted in the social structure of the country and was determined to a considerable degree by the historical evolution of Vietnamese society and intellectual life. The attitude of the Nguyen emperors, whose talents as rulers no observer denied,[17] did not result from an intelligent anticipation of their country's beclouded future. On the contrary, the strongest of the many forces that shaped the thinking of these men were the forces of Vietnam's past, newly consolidated and more hostile to change and progress than ever. Gia Long's desire to avoid international involvements was conceivable as a policy only because of the country's persistent economic immobility. Minh Mang's rigidity of thought and dogmatic Confucianism mirrored faithfully the growing stagnation that characterized Vietnam's thinking in regard to social change. When Tu Duc ascended the throne that Thieu Tri had occupied from 1840 to 1847, it was apparently too late for any Vietnamese ruler to take his country on a new road. The future was now in the hands of the "barbarians from the West," as Minh Mang had called them, and imperial action had become only another element of the tragedy that was in the making for the Vietnamese people.

4.

How could the Nguyen emperors remain in power in nineteenth-century Vietnam with policies of economic and social immobility that were essentially those of medieval Vietnam? And how was it possible for them to lose Vietnam without first losing their throne? The answers to these questions lie in a curious and unique development of the Vietnamese state at the beginning of the nineteenth century.

Gia Long, who revived the authority of a single monarch over the whole country, was too cautious to risk economic and social innovations and too conservative to desire them.[18] Consequently his victory, although achieved with advanced technical means, brought Vietnam no economic and technical progress. The military science of the present had served merely to restore the absolute power of a monarch who looked for political guidance only to the past. Gia Long's greatest concern, once the war was over, was to refurbish the ideological armor of medieval Vietnam.

In one important respect, however, Gia Long and his successors were willing and able to go beyond a mere restoration of Vietnam's *ancien régime*. To rule the reunited country effectively, and to administer it again from one capital in the name of one holder of divine rights, called for a stronger central authority than the greater and reunited Vietnam had ever had before. It was not enough to re-establish the social and political basis of the great ancient dynasties. The country had grown immensely, in territory as well as in population, since the lords' love of power had split it in two at the beginning of the seventeenth century. The new dynasty could hold Vietnam together, perform its functions, and assure its own survival only if it was equipped to cope with all regional dissidence and to suppress every type of feudal political aspiration. In this the new monarchs were undoubtedly successful.

There were several reasons why the Nguyen dynasty, whose later military impotence against the West became notorious, survived every threat to its power from within. One was Vietnam's temporary cooperation with the West. Through it Gia Long acquired a well-trained army, a competent navy, a system of provincial fortifications, and such modern equipment as enabled him first to defeat the Tay Son and later to doom any local rebellion in advance.

But more important for its stability were some of the new dynasty's political and administrative reforms. A program to reorganize the state, cautiously launched by Gia Long, was energetically pursued and completed by Minh Mang. His administrative ability and passion for absolute power created a strictly centralized monarchy with strong and unified national institutions.

But decisive for the stability of the Nguyen dynasty became the one social reform that has to be credited to Gia Long and his immediate successor. It consisted of a series of measures designed to eradicate the old bastions of feudalism. Thus was removed from the Vietnamese historical scene an evil that had plagued the older dynasties ever since the country had broken away from Chinese rule.

Vietnam's peculiar brand of feudalism was attacked at the root when Gia Long abolished all large landholdings by princes, nobles, and high officials. Gia Long also gave up the eight-century-old practice of paying officials and of rewarding or endowing nobles with a claim to the taxes from a village or a group of villages. In 1839 Minh Mang decreed with finality the end of this practice, through an administrative measure that was as simple as it was radical for the Vietnam of his

279

time: the salaries, pensions, awards, or unearned means of subsistence for princes and nobles, as well as for officials of all degrees, were henceforth to be paid only in money and rice.[19]

5.

While these reforms strikingly reduced the old struggles for power through which the former dynasties had so often come to grief, they did little to alleviate the misery of the people from which the Tay Son rebellion had derived its overwhelming popular support. Feudalism as a threat to dynastic power was abolished, but feudalism as a feature of peasant exploitation remained. Vietnam still had its rich landowners on the one side, and on the other the peasants with no land or with holdings too small to feed themselves and their families. But even a more equal distribution of land could not have removed the causes of peasant misery completely.[20] There was one problem far more basic for social conditions in Vietnam than the unfortunate relation between small and big landholdings: the growth in population exceeded the increase in cultivable land.

Answering to the same pressures as the great monarchs of the Ly, Tran, and Le dynasties, the Nguyen too made constant efforts to gain new rice fields in order to narrow the gap between population and land that even the best of the rulers never quite succeeded in closing. They used again the old device of creating military and penitentiary colonies to open up new regions; they built dykes and drainage canals to increase the surface of cultivable land; they endorsed the general attitude that held the creator of a new village in higher esteem than the winner of a battle; they legalized permanent ownership of small holdings given to the landless from newly won land. The old dynastic efforts in favor of the small landowners

280

and landless peasants were resumed too. The Nguyen ordered land illegally taken by the rich from the communities to be restored for periodical distribution, and forbade all sale or other forms of acquisition of communal lands; they decreed the periodic repartition of these lands to take place every three instead of every six years, and even insisted on lots of equal size for every member of the community.[21] But under the existing social and political system, neither the good intentions nor the administrative energy of the Nguyen rulers produced the desired result.

Some of the reasons why all these efforts failed to improve the lot of the people were as old as Vietnam. As had always been the case with Vietnamese agrarian reforms, quite a few of these measures remained on paper. Their execution, which formerly had depended in too many instances on the great landholders and other provincial potentates, was now entrusted to the so-called notables or village councils.[22] The astonishing administrative independence of these bodies, which made the Vietnamese community a democratic institution in relation to the state,[23] unfortunately did not diminish their character as local oligarchies. Imperial measures favoring the small or landless peasants were seldom applied faithfully, and often not at all, if they hurt the interests of the notables, whose strongest members were customarily the mandarins and the rich.[24]

The emperors themselves did much to defeat the purpose of their own social measures. "It is sad to observe the great number of people whom the state employs for absolutely unproductive work," one visitor, an English doctor, remarked in 1822, confirming the testimony of Gia Long's French mandarin Chaigneau[25] and adding to that of the many missionaries who wrote movingly about the misery of the Vietnamese people. Public works, as for instance the fortifications that were erected all over Vietnam under Gia Long and Minh Mang, required such masses of forced labor that even some of the existing rice land frequently fell into disuse.[26]

6.

But more disastrous for Vietnam was the inability of the Nguyen monarchs to recognize economic progress as the only effective way of fighting the people's misery and of increasing the country's strength. Gia Long and his successors knew quite well that spear and arrow had ceased to be adequate weapons of war, but against their country's economic ills they still fought only with the medieval remedy of enlarging the surface of cultivable land. An agriculture that had made no technical progress for centuries had been Vietnam's basic economy in 1500; it was equally basic, and technically still unchanged, in 1850, in spite of the three hundred years during which Vietnam had been subject to the influence of Western ideas and the temptations of international trade, and in spite of the country's territorial growth.

The leaders of precolonial Vietnam, to be sure, were not entirely unacquainted with the dangers of a stagnant national economy in an explosively developing economy-minded world. Besides, the voices of forward-looking men who knew what the country needed grew more insistent as these dangers became more visible, in particular after the South was lost to France.[27] It was necessary to employ the surplus population in fields other than agriculture, these men urged. The need was to exploit mines and forests, found small industries, develop the old village handicrafts beyond the traditional restricted scope, increase internal communication and exchange, favor international trade, take part in inter-Asian shipping, and spur economic progress by importing the technical knowledge and the machinery available in the West.

Why were the voices of these men not heeded? None of the Nguyen rulers was lacking in intelligence, and if their good intentions were distorted by the values and concepts of a moribund past, they were nevertheless evident in many of their actions. Even Minh Mang, whose arrogant Confucianism forever interfered with his better judgment, recognized and tried to use the West's advanced scientific knowledge,[28] and Tu Duc went so far as to admit that a country was actually moving backward if it refused to move ahead.

Indeed, whatever shortcomings these men had, Vietnam's falling into the abyss of colonialism was not simply a result of their errors and omissions, nor even of their basic misjudgment of the West. They themselves and their actions were only one aspect of Vietnam's failure to escape colonial rule. This failure had more general and deeper causes, though none of them too deep to be penetrated by the better Vietnamese minds of the time. There were enough Vietnamese who understood that their country was being victimized by the West because it was incapable of social change and technical progress. And they also knew that change and progress were prevented by the men who exercised power on all levels of the Vietnamese state: the mandarins who, after the reforms of Gia Long and Minh Mang, were the only people to possess and exercise political power in precolonial Vietnam.

7.

The absence of any group of people other than the mandarins who exercised power or had means to influence the government's decisions was indeed one of the most striking features of Vietnamese society prior to French intervention.

Under the Nguyen dynasty, Vietnam had no people who took part in shaping the country's policy, either directly or indirectly, because they had more than an average share of the available economic wealth. Wealth had a certain political weight only on the community level, where the rich as a rule had all the power, but a power that was limited to local affairs. Less than ever before in history did Vietnam now suffer from a class of wealthy people who owned the state. Large-scale landholdings by princes and high officials had been abolished, and Vietnam was still practically devoid of all other means of production and possible economic sources of power. There existed no capitalists, and even their precursors, the rich traders, were exceedingly rare. The mores of the country, rooted in its primitive and static economy, did not favor a systematic accumulation of wealth. The rich man's mark of distinction was not power based on possessions but rather ostentatious consumption, of which the ruinous pomp of funerals or expensive weddings was generally more characteristic than a steady train of luxurious living.

Absent also from the structure of Vietnamese society after 1800 was an aristocracy with significant social privileges or specific political rights. Titles of nobility were bestowed as mere honors.[29] The nobles and many members of the imperial family no longer constituted part of the class of great landholders that had formerly played such an important economic and political role. Nobility gave a man status, but not automatically also an income or a public function.

Vietnam, moreover, was spared the doubtful blessings of being ruled by the military. Vietnamese society had always been one of the few that did not permit political power to become the prerogative of the professional soldier. As a matter of fact, a separate military caste such as developed in most civilizations and ruled most countries at one time or another never existed in Vietnam. A Vietnamese general was a high official with the soul of a soldier only when he discharged his military duties in times of war. Not one of the prominent generals in Vietnamese history looked upon military exploits as a possible vocation for an entire human existence. In the official hierarchy, the military mandarins ranked lower than the civilian, and the wisdom of the people always recognized the difference between a successful general and a really great man. For a Vietnamese army commander to be honored as a great man it was not enough to excel on the field of battle; he had

284

to distinguish himself also in the fields that were traditionally considered the testing grounds of genius—philosophy, poetry, knowledge of history and literature, moral leadership, and the conduct of public affairs. If he did, a general could enjoy uncommon political authority, to which his military achievements would contribute decisively only in times of national crisis due to prolonged wars.

This society without feudal landowners and industrial capitalists, in which the nobility had no political influence and the army no chance to rule, was also lacking in a body of men with power derived from religion. For reasons that were older than its independence as a state, Vietnam had never developed an organized church. These reasons were the variety of beliefs and their eclectic character; the performance of much ceremonial inside the family and without the assistance of a priest; the local nature and purpose of most religious activities, which made them independently conducted village affairs; and the semireligious functions assumed by the state. To be ruled by a priestocracy was as remote a danger for the Vietnamese peasant as to have his crops ruined by a frost. The weight of religious oppression fell on him only when the state exercised its function as religious authority by interfering with popular attitudes and beliefs: the emperor of Vietnam was also the country's only "pope."

The role of the emperor as supreme religious authority dated as far back as the founding of the Vietnamese state. It did not result from an original totalitarian disposition that was never rectified in later times, but was rather an indispensable attribute of a political order based on Confucianist views. In a society to which these views were applicable at all, the authority of the emperor had to be as absolute and all-inclusive as the authority of a father. Just as a Vietnamese family fell apart if the father's orders were disobeyed, opposition to the emperor was bound to bring chaos and ruin to the state. Better to have a dynasty that was no longer able to command obedience replaced by force than to question its authority or to apportion its supreme power among several different hands. The Vietnamese emperors were not only the chief administrators but also the only lawmakers of Vietnam. As Confucianist philosophers of state, they would have regarded the so-called "division of powers" as an absurdity—like a family run on a parliamentary basis, or an Almighty God with no right to dispense justice. The emperor was the first judge of Vietnam for the same obvious reasons that required him to be the commander-in-chief of the country's armed forces.

8.

But imperial authority, no matter how absolute it became and how undivided it remained, was always different from parental authority in one important respect. It could not be wielded over all subjects of the country in the direct and personal manner in which parental authority guided and compelled all members of a Vietnamese family. The emperor's subjects were too many, and the territories over which they were spread too vast. To fulfill both the variety and multiplicity of his governmental functions, the emperor had to delegate his powers to an army of agents who operated in his name. These were the mandarins.

There was, of course, nothing unusual in the emperor's need of such agents to discharge his various duties on all levels of government. Only in the smallest and most primitive societies are the rulers not subject to this need. A Vietnamese mandarin under Gia Long or Minh Mang, however, was something quite singular among public officials.

To begin with, these officials were responsible only to the emperor, who alone had the power both to appoint them and to deprive them of their functions or degrees. Vietnam had no local authorities or national institutions that could either nominate a mandarin or control what he did.[30] On the community level, the notables appointed and supervised a man with a number of functions akin to those of a village sheriff and mayor.[31] But all real officials, no matter how high or low, were mandarins, which meant employees of the state and responsible only to the emperor. Private officials of any kind did not exist.

But the power of the emperor to make and unmake all officials, exclusive as it was, was subject to one significant limitation. The emperor could make a mandarin only out of a certain type of man—the educated, or "man of letters," as he was called at the time. And even the educated could become a mandarin only if he passed a number of officially prescribed tests. This system, a Chinese invention,[32] had been in operation in Vietnam ever since the Ly dynasty had introduced it in the year 1075. Study in order to qualify, and competitive examinations to determine a candidate's degree of knowledge and resultant official rank, were the roads for a Vietnamese to a public career. The Nguyen emperors, and in particular Gia Long and Minh Mang, recruited all their officials from the educated through competitive tests. This resulted in a curious sociological and unique historical fact: if only the educated could enter the ranks of the mandarins, and if the mandarins had a monopoly on political power, the educated minority of Vietnam was in fact the country's "ruling class."

9.

There can be no doubt that the mandarins, whose authority derived from the acquisition of knowledge, were the country's only wielders of power, nor that as a class they were firmly opposed to technical progress and social change. Thus, if it is true that Vietnam could have avoided the loss of her independence by changing and progressing, the mandarins must be held largely responsible for the failure of Vietnam to defend herself against the West.

The mandarins have indeed been blamed by their critics for almost everything that went wrong in nineteenth-century Vietnam. Vietnam's alleged intellectual stagnation, social immobility, and suicidal policy of isolation from the West were directly ascribed to the conservative attitudes of the mandarins, and to a governmental system that gave them control of the state. Western observers in particular, ever since they began to study Vietnam's strictly mandarinal system of government, have concentrated on discovering and exposing its flaws. They saw that mandarinal mentality rejected the idea of change and progress, and they consequently connected the mandarins' intellectual habits with the state of stagnation in which they found Vietnam. The mandarins' peculiar intellectual training, which was responsible for their habits of mind, was diagnosed as the whole system's basic fault. In a manner quite typical for the mandarins' own intellectual predisposition, Vietnam's economic backwardness and political inflexibility in the face of colonial aggression were explained by the intellectual matter that fed, and the educational methods that formed, the mandarins' minds. After a century of such criticism, the word "mandarin" has now become a term of abuse.[33]

Although some aspects of Vietnamese life became quite plausible through this approach, as they would in every effort to show the correlation of mind and society, this Western theory has also done a great deal to obscure the realities of social and intellectual life in nineteenth-century Vietnam. It stresses only one element in a complex pattern of causes, and uses as an explanation what needs to be explained. To say that the mandarins' intellectual formation contributed to Vietnam's state of social immobility is no doubt correct; but even this is an insight of little value without an answer to the question of why Vietnamese society lacked the forces, and the man-

darins themselves the motives, to break the mold of an antiquated mind.

10.

The rule of the mandarins could hardly have lasted for so
many centuries if the system had not been adapted to the
social structure of the country, and if it had not also had some
virtues to recommend it to so many generations of the educated
Vietnamese. It consequently found also its apologists, who
would not allow these virtues to remain forever obscured by
the views of Western critics, which were at least in part due
to a desire to destroy mandarinal Vietnam. By exploiting the
nationalist sentiments of a later time, some Vietnamese thinkers
have actually succeeded in making these virtues more attractive to the intellectuals of their country than the mandarins
themselves could have known them to be a century ago.

The mandarinal system of government, its modern de-
fenders proclaimed, allowed for a maximum of democracy in
a precapitalist civilization and was free of the universal evils
that go with all class and caste rule. The mandarins were not
a closed and self-perpetuating group, or selected only from
one level of the people, as are most ruling classes in other
civilized societies. They were recruited from the whole people,
and recruited in one manner only, to which every aspirant for
office was compelled to submit: in order to become a mandarin,
a young Vietnamese had to go through the required studies
and pass the prescribed number of official tests. No other road
to public office existed in Vietnam, and no dispensations from
the labor of study and the trials of examination were granted
either to the wealthy and noble or to a mandarin's own sons.
The office of mandarin was neither hereditary nor for sale, and
since education was always free in Vietnam, the mandarinate
was equally accessible to the poor and the rich. The selection

of the country's officials, in short, was based on a democratic principle long before anyone in the West could ever dream of such governmental progress.

This view, which as a weapon of anticolonial propaganda became quite popular among Vietnamese nationalists,[34] does not agree too well with the evidence of history produced by modern research. The realities of Vietnamese social life, as less romantically inclined Vietnamese thinkers have pointed out, gave to the rich and the poor no equality of chances to become officials, and the sons of mandarins enjoyed advantages that even the law acknowledged in various forms.[35] Besides, the power of appointment was always reserved to the emperor, and the emperor was never obliged to appoint a man merely because he had passed his tests. But neither social injustice nor temporary abuse, such as the sale of offices at some times under the Trinh, could quite nullify the principle of access to the mandarinate for all. The mandarins obviously were not an economically anchored ruling class, or even a firmly closed group of Vietnamese society, but rather a group of changeable composition with all the main features of a so-called elite.

11.

The mandarins' character as a governing elite was emphasized both by the nature of the training they received and by the tests they had to undergo. These tests, which were competitive and strictly impartial,[36] made sure that only the fittest among all students received their diplomas as "men of letters," and that the best of these men, in terms of the established criteria, could obtain the highest official degrees. But before a Vietnamese youth could compete for the highest honors, the years of study and the passing of preliminary examinations might well have made him a middle-aged or elderly man. Only the very brilliant were able to get to the summit as young men, after absorbing no less than all the knowledge that existed, or was recognized as existing under the prevailing Confucianist views.

Thus it came about that the country's ruling class, after the seedbeds of feudal power were destroyed, became identical with the country's educated minority. Vietnam was administered and ruled by its intellectuals, and no Vietnamese intellectuals existed who were not either members or associates of the country's ruling elite.[37]

Indeed, a closer examination of Vietnamese society during the first half of the nineteenth century reveals a surprising historical phenomenon: a state had come into being in which the ancient dream of a government by philosophers was literally fulfilled; the training of the mandarins was philosophical in the fullest sense of the word. There were no special courses in administration. No instruction in any kind of technical skill was required for the official tests.[38] The subjects to be mastered were exclusively literary, and the skills to be acquired purely rhetorical and scholastic. The bulk of the curriculum consisted of ancient Chinese philosophy, with history and poetry as mere handmaidens of Confucianism. The aim of all studies was to absorb the accumulated wisdom of the past, in order to achieve the moral perfection that qualified a man to rule. Minh Mang himself, the most scholarly of the Nguyen emperors, expounded these views in his remarkable political and poetic writings.[39] He was the truest mandarin-emperor Vietnam has known, a king who based his own qualifications for government and his right to exercise absolute power not on royal blood but on his role as moral philosopher and head of the nation's intellectual elite.

12.

Minh Mang's views on government, which had been part of mandarinal ideology since the system had been in force, came close to answering the question of why a philosophical education was regarded as essential for all governmental tasks. To be the emperor's prolonged arm on the lower levels of administration, and to exercise local political power in the name of the state, did not depend on special knowledge or a training in particular skills. The functions of government in Vietnam's pre-industrial and pre-mercantile society were still too simple to require the kind of abilities that only a technical training could provide. The mandarins, apparently, were men who studied for their vocation as no government officials studied ever before them or after, but what they learned was hardly related to their specific tasks. These were essentially political, and in the field of politics, teaching was never of tangible use.

What the mandarins needed was not technical proficiency for complicated governmental functions but a claim to authority that no one would dare to attack. To give them such authority was the purpose of their endless studies and difficult tests. This made the mandarins' seemingly quite irrelevant intellectual training as practical a preparation for the exercise of power as ever was designed. It was more than a systematic ideological indoctrination. It was above all a profound and immensely successful system of justification of governmental authority, erected upon the only universal and indestructible foundation for any man's claim to be obeyed by other men: intellectual and moral superiority, demonstrated in impartial tests that only a man who was thoroughly learned could pass. And the learned alone, Confucius had established, traveled the roads of wisdom, which were also the roads that led to the moral perfection of man. Only the wicked would dare to object to a system of government under which the wisest and best of men were given the highest positions.

The possession of knowledge became thus inseparably connected with the right to exercise authority, and intellectual capacity became the only sure basis for a man's claim to an office of the state.

13.

In this close association of knowledge and power, the prestige of learning was always greater than that of mere force. To acquire knowledge, after all, was the only generally accessible gateway to power; knowledge, at least in principle, also determined official degree, which was the measure of status in Vietnamese society. This alone could explain why intellectual achievement became the yardstick of individual greatness and posthumous fame. But there were other reasons. The country's restricted economic activity kept the number of wealthy and the size of their fortunes unusually small. The contrast between the misery of the masses and the luxury of the few was less odious than in other civilizations, and the difference in status between the wealthy and the poor was smaller than that between the plain citizen and the official. Besides, public office led as safely to the modest material welfare that was customary for the upper classes as did the pursuit of wealth through economic activity. Elsewhere the ambitious wanted to be rich; in Vietnam they preferred to become officials. It was easier for a mandarin to extract a favor from a man of wealth than for the wealthy to make a mandarin bow to his wishes. And even as a beggar among beggars, the mandarin was still the beggars' king.

For a Vietnamese mandarin or even a mere "man of letters," it was indeed quite possible to combine the condition of a beggar with the standing and dignity of a king. The best of this class never abused their powers to add material comfort to the enjoyment of status. The moral authority of these people was great, and it has transmitted a puritanical streak to their political grandsons of the twentieth century that is as noticeable in the Communist Ho Chi Minh as it is in the Catholic Ngo Dinh Diem. The mass of the mandarins, however, was a plague to the people such as only a bureaucracy with too much power and not enough pay could ever become.[40]

Under the first Nguyen emperors, whose dogmatic Confucianism promoted a strictly mandarin-made scale of social values, the main feature of mandarinal ideology reached its most extreme form. Its undeniably positive expressions were numerous, such as the low esteem for force compared to knowledge; the incomparable prestige of the teacher and professor; the pride and joy of families and villages if one of their own passed a difficult test; the honors bestowed by the state upon the great thinkers of the nation; and the high status of the scholars, or "men of letters," even if they preferred a life of study and teaching to the advantages of a mandarinal career. Knowledge indeed had a social value in Vietnam for which it would be hard to find a parallel in the history of civilization. Here, for once, knowledge was power in a literal sense.

The concept of power as a derivative of knowledge, however, was not as exclusively mandarinal as it appeared in these extreme manifestations during the final phase of Vietnam's Confucianist regime. Nor is it an exclusively Asian concept, as was the mandarinate itself, but rather a basic and universally recognized human insight. All children are convinced that to know means to be powerful, and so are all primitive people. Moreover, no supreme being was ever conceived by human minds as omnipotent without also being conceived as omniscient. If the missionaries, in presenting their own supreme being to the Vietnamese people, had not been able to present God as the highest, the wisest, and therefore also the most powerful of all mandarins, they would not have converted so large a number of their listeners to the Christian faith. And the mandarins would not have opposed the Christian religion with such acrimony if the concept of God introduced by the West had not undermined their authority as custodians of all knowledge. To know more than a mandarin was a challenge to his right to rule; to introduce and spread the knowledge of the West was therefore no less than an attack upon the foundations of Vietnam's Confucian society.[41]

14.

When the French reappeared in Vietnam in the first half of the nineteenth century, there occurred a clash between Western and mandarinal mentality, which preceded by more than thirty years the clash of arms that brought about the end of the mandarinal state. In this duel of minds, which continued after Western arms had triumphed over Eastern philosophy, both sides had sharp eyes for their opponents' moral conceit and intellectual errors, but they had little understanding for each others' motives and none at all of the social forces behind their colliding actions.

What is the use of all these mental exertions, the men from the West would ask the mandarins, if the purpose of study was only to possess the knowledge of the past, if the learned would admit no previously unknown ideas, pursue no scientific investigations, strive for no new insights into nature, and decline to experiment and invent?

Some people in Vietnam were deeply disturbed by these questions, but to the mass of the mandarins they made very little sense. "Our country has maintained itself in its present condition for a long time," they contentedly retorted, "and we hope that it will continue to maintain itself also in the future." [42]

Vietnam had indeed survived every threat to its existence and grown bigger and stronger during the many centuries of mandarinal rule. Their training, the mandarins felt, had always prepared them adequately for their functions, which for the vast majority were local and purely political, so that they saw no reason at all to acquire new knowledge in order to fulfill their changeless tasks. Only one kind of training could properly qualify these men for their governmental functions, and that was the Confucianist indoctrination a mandarin had to receive before he was able to pass his tests. The prevailing philosophical ideas and moral maxims about family and state were indispensable for the maintenance of the existing order; they were as meaningful for the mandarins under Tu Duc in the 1860's as they had been to their predecessors in the 1460's under the Emperor Le Thanh Tong. This was the reason why the mandarins held their old knowledge in higher esteem than all the scientific ideas and technical skills developed in the West. Even before they realized how profoundly Western ideas and inventions would affect the society they ruled, considered to be perfect, and wanted to maintain, the mandarins had had only contempt for an educated Vietnamese who desired his country to imitate the West's unnatural craving for innovation. They sensed evil in a spirit that would not stay at rest.

The men from the West, whom the explosive forces of early industrialism had propelled to the shores of Asia, encountered this mandarinal immobility primarily as an obstacle to their commercial and political projects. How easy it would be, the traders and political adventurers exclaimed, to initiate the economic activities necessary for a transformation of this country into a haven of profitable business! The centers of population lay close to the ocean and could be quickly reached by river from the many harbors along the coast. There were the neglected mines, the forests waiting to be exploited. There were spices and exotic fruits, and no doubt also other treasures of nature not yet discovered that could be extracted by Vietnamese labor, which was cheap, willing, and abundant. The existing material conditions, these Westerners thought, would have made economic progress almost inevitable if the mandarins had not opposed all trade and economic innovation.[43]

For the Westerners of adventurous disposition who traveled or traded in Asia during the first half of the nineteenth century, the attitude of the Vietnamese mandarins was senseless enough to make them believe there was something basically wrong with the "Eastern mind." It was "stagnant" and "petrified," said many of the learned visitors from Europe, and mortally afraid of any kind of innovation or change. The country, it was generally thought, did not participate in the world's technical and economic progress because the mandarins had imposed their own intellectual immobility upon the social body of Vietnam. "Intellectual sterility," in brief, became the accepted explanation for the technological and economic backwardness of the Asian world.[44]

The Frenchmen who roamed Asia between 1820 and 1860 soon convinced themselves that this evil was greater in Vietnam than in China itself, where Confucianism was born and a literary training for public office had been required long before the Vietnamese could read and write. But in China political power had never become a monopoly of the bureaucrats trained in Confucian scholastics. The reasons for this difference between China and Vietnam were many. One was the size of China, which created the need for an intercontinental system of communication, as well as the old and permanent Chinese interest in foreign trade; another was the changes produced in China's political structure by barbarian invasions, which as a rule led to the replacement of the established ruling groups. Rich traders and mighty landlords often became the centers of local political independence, and there was seldom a time when China was without men of great military power whom the civilian mandarins were in no position to subdue. Mandarinal rule in China, consequently, never reached the classical perfection that distinguished the system under the Nguyen dynasty in nineteenth-century Vietnam. To the frustrated French promoters of trade and progress, the damage caused by the mandarins' alleged intellectual sterility therefore appeared infinitely greater in Vietnam than in the country where the mandarinal system was invented.[45]

As to the causes of this obnoxious mandarinal mentality, however, there was general agreement that the Confucian training imported from China had ruined the Vietnamese mind. The basic vice of this training was correctly diagnosed. It stemmed from the notion that knowledge was an existing quantity of established historical facts and philosophical truths. To know them all, interpret them well, apply them faultlessly, and transmit them to the next generation of the learned were the signs of a well-trained and therefore superior mind. The main function of such a mind was not to invent or produce, but rather to absorb the accumulated knowledge, which was regarded as sufficient and impossible to improve upon. A great mind might at best think up some new reason why individual and social perfection depended on the wisdom of the past. But the young man "most likely to succeed" was one with an unusual memory, great rhetorical skill, and a capacity for verbal analysis and abstraction. Originality and creativeness were obviously no advantage for a mandarinal career. A spirited independence of thinking or an everlasting curiosity of mind were not praised as virtues but condemned as vices. In the offices of the Vietnamese state, new ideas by inventive and experimentally disposed individuals could only be an element of political disturbance, and no individual mandarin could advance himself by either learning or trying to do something new. "In order to have knowledge," Confucius had said, "one has to read about the past." Learning thus became memorizing the old and venerable Confucian books. The curriculum for the training of a Vietnamese mandarin therefore remained always up to date, but after centuries of mere verbal exercise, the minds of the mandarins certainly did not crave novelty and adventure.

The mind, which most thinkers in the West had come to regard as the motor of all historical progress, could apparently also become inert and unproductive. This, the philosophers of European industrialism and colonial expansion concluded, is what had happened to the "Eastern mind." A deteriorated mind was the cause of Asia's much lamented refusal to progress along Western lines. From this premise the philosophers of Western expansion in Asia derived a melancholy insight into the relationship of society and mind. If the mind could somehow become an obstacle to all progress, a government of philosophers was manifestly more pernicious than one dominated by men with economic interests, and perhaps even worse than the rule of naked force.

15.

In reply to such presumptuous views about the causes of Asian stagnation, the mandarins were quick to point out what the East had achieved before the year 1000 A.D., when the West, in relation to China, was technologically backward and intellectually in a state of inaction. But this made as little impression on the men from the West as Western praise of science, industry, and trade made on the mandarins whenever white visitors argued with them on board their unwelcome ships. The men from the West were not interested in the early achievements of the mandarins. What they resented was the mandarins' opposition to Western ideas and proposals, and what they could not understand, and did not learn from the mandarins either, was why the system was able to survive in nineteenth-century Vietnam. A mind apparently could be as closed as an oyster, and as content to be sterile as a well-fed mule. But how was it possible for people with such minds to remain in power?

If the traders from France had been free of all Western ideological indoctrination, they would no doubt have discovered the right answer to the question of why the Vietnamese mandarinal system continued to exist. But the thinkers from the West confused them forever with their complex reasoning about the peculiarities of the "Eastern mind." Clearly, the "closed mind" of the mandarins was not just a deplorable result of antiquated intellectual training. It was the right kind of mind for an antiquated society, the only permissible kind of mind if the mandarinal system should continue to exist, and a fully adequate mind for the functions of an elite within the social structure of Vietnam.

The secret of its adequacy and durability was Vietnam's primitive economy. It generated little impulse for social change. The weak forces aspiring after change were easily suppressed by the mandarins, whose position was founded in the social immobility of Vietnam. No Western system of intellectual training could have produced mandarins eager to promote a transformation of Vietnamese society; asking the mandarins to promote a transformation of society was asking them to cooperate in the liquidation of their rule. Ruling classes are not in the habit of abdicating, and even less are they disposed to question the moral and intellectual values on which their power rests. They have to be overthrown by force or replaced in a long process of gradual social transformation.

But Vietnam did not have what it needed to break the rule of the mandarins and thus to revitalize its thinking and open its mind for the knowledge of the West: a class of people interested in the development of industry and trade. The old order consequently continued to exist, and within this order the mandarins and their training were as sufficient for the tasks of government as was the water buffalo as working animal and power supply within the economy of Vietnam.

16.

But if the training of these men was functional, and if they succeeded in preventing an inner development that would have threatened their monopoly of rule, their minds could not have been as inferior as Western criticism of their immobility implied. They were certainly closed against most ideas from the West, but from their own point of view they closed their minds to these ideas for very good reasons, and in their praise and defense of the existing order they were far from "immobile," "sterile," or "inert." On the contrary, it is doubtful whether any ruling class has ever been more successful than the Vietnamese mandarins in justifying the present by praising the past, and in holding off economic and social developments detrimental to their monopoly of political power.

For the mandarins, therefore, social immobility was a condition of survival, and one task of their clever minds was to invent reasons why this immobility was also a condition for the survival of Vietnam. In this they succeeded, in spite of the pressures and temptations to which they themselves and their country had been exposed in more than three hundred years of contact with the West. They succeeded even in the nineteenth century. From the time of Gia Long to the fall of Vietnam, the mandarins' intellects, keen and active as ever, fully upheld the Vietnamese *status quo* against a people as ready for new social activities and intellectual adventures as any in the West.

When the pressure for change became serious, it unfortunately also became quite easy for the mandarins to show that change was a greater evil for Vietnam than the preservation of existing economic conditions. The pressure for change came from the West, and to give in to the West, most Vietnamese knew, meant to become a victim of the West. The West might destroy the prison in which the mandarins held the bodies and minds of the Vietnamese people, but it would replace it with one stronger and more dreadful than all their prisons of the past. Fear of the West thus became the strongest weapon of the manadarins in their struggle against the forces aspiring to social and political innovation.

When the blows of the imperialist aggressor began to fall on the country, the mandarins as a class were still in undisputed control of Vietnam. But their policy of isolation and their refusal to permit social change accelerated Vietnam's loss of independence, and with independence lost, the mandarins were doomed as Vietnam's ruling class. It took the superior military forces of the West to unseat the Vietnamese mandarins, who were truly one of the world's most enduring political elites.

When the conquest of Vietnam was completed, the mandarins were faced with a bitter choice. Many finished their careers, and even their lives as determined opponents of the colonial regime; what survived of the whole system gradually became a tool in the hands of Vietnam's new foreign masters.

17.

The mandarin's most fateful political error was to lead Vietnam into a position of hostility toward and isolation from the West. This policy was based on Gia Long's conviction that Vietnam's refusal to get involved could contain the dangers coming from the West. Minh Mang found out that his father had been mistaken, but after walking in his footsteps during the twenty years of his rule he discovered, just before dying, that certain errors of policy can never be undone.

From the beginning of his reign in 1820, the mandarin-emperor Minh Mang had worked hard to bring about Vietnam's complete isolation from the West. By 1832 he had almost reached his goal. The only remaining generators of Western ideas in Vietnam were the missionaries. They were not many, and they had no hopes for spectacular progress. If Minh Mang had granted them freedom of propaganda, they might have become his best allies against any Western power that threatened Vietnam's independence. Why did he try to put an end to their activities, expel them from Vietnam, and undo their work with a program of moral and political re-education for Vietnamese Catholics? If he was right in treating them as men of politics, how could he neglect the fact that a missionary's loyalty was always divided between his church and his country of origin, and that many, in addition, had adopted Vietnam as their second country and permanent home?

302

Minh Mang was neither stupid nor mean. His actions against the missionaries are understandable only as actions of a man in a serious political dilemma. After he had achieved isolation and was left alone even by France, his fear of the West subsided. Catholic religious propaganda could not really frighten him. What he was truly afraid of was his own people. Minh Mang was one of the few Vietnamese emperors who were always aware of the miserable conditions in which eighty per cent of the people lived. Frequent local rebellions reminded him of their plight whenever he was in danger of forgetting it. Although his faults were many, they did not include indifference. He hated and denounced the West, he was ruthless and addicted to the exercise of absolute power, but he loved the Vietnamese people and worked for them as passionately as he fought his enemies. But his measures to improve the lot of the peasants excluded economic progress in nonagricultural fields and remained as ineffective as those of his father.

Minh Mang was not a man to close his eyes when he saw an unwelcome fact. He knew how easy it was for a capable leader to arouse his desperate people with no other prospect than the mere hope for a change. Descendants of the old Le dynasty made trouble for him in the North, appealing not only to the miserable peasants but also to the persecuted Christians, and seeking support from abroad with promises to the missionaries to grant them freedom of religious propaganda. Local leaders in the South, whose relative political autonomy Minh Mang's administrative reforms destroyed, were ready to exploit the existing discontent among both the poverty-stricken masses and the Christians, many of them wealthy landowners, whom the mandarins could vex and squeeze without fear of retaliation. If some leaders in the South did not already conspire with the missionaries to win foreign help for an insurrection, as Minh Mang firmly believed, his policy of repression was bound to induce them to adopt such a course sooner or later. When an uprising actually occurred in Saigon in 1833, both sides felt justified in taking steps that led Vietnamese policy toward the West into a truly tragic impasse.[46] The rebels appealed to the Christians to fight against Minh Mang, and sent Catholic emissaries to seek help abroad; furious, Minh Mang thereupon switched in his anti-Catholic policy from administrative vexation and educational measures to bloody persecution.

The first French missionary to be executed was Father Gagelin, who died at the age of thirty-four on October 17, 1833, through strangulation;[47] the second was Father Marchand, who was cut to pieces, together with the leaders of the Southern rebellion, on September 30, 1835. Father Marchand's role in the rebel camp has remained obscure,[48] but he was caught with the rebel leaders when the citadel of Saigon finally surrendered, in September, 1835, after a siege that had lasted over a year.[49] Between 1835 and 1838 five more missionaries were executed, as well as an unknown but certainly higher number of Vietnamese Catholics.

After 1838 Minh Mang contented himself again with his former policy of mere administrative vexation and anti-Catholic propaganda, but the damage was done. The missionaries began to clamor for protection by their home countries, and the French Society of Foreign Missions started to advocate a policy of force against the new "Nero" in the Far East. When Minh Mang took the initiative for an improvement of relations between Vietnam and the West, it became clear that the Society of Foreign Missions and the spokesmen of French political Catholicism had decided that military intervention alone could save the missionary cause in Vietnam.

Minh Mang's successors, Thieu Tri and Tu Duc, were unable to escape from the impasse that the policy of isolation and hostility toward the West had reached after 1840. Exposed to increasing French demands supported by threats of military action, they became more and more convinced that isolation from the West was the only way to preserve their country's political independence. But the walls they erected between

304

1840 and 1858 proved too weak for the guns that the West was producing during the same time.

The mandarins' refusal to permit social change and technical progress, which was at the bottom of the policy of isolation from the West, was also the reason why the Vietnamese people lacked both the means and the will to defeat colonial aggression when the West was ready to attack.

The flight into isolation had only shortened Vietnam's life as an independent state.

Notes to Chapter Five:

1. The conquest of Cambodia by the Vietnamese began about 1600. The Nguyen, who always looked for extension of their territory toward the south, established their suzerainty over Cambodia in 1658. A detailed description of the conquest of Cambodia by Vietnam is to be found in Le Thanh Khoi, *op. cit.*, pp. 264-271, 273, 299-301, 321f., 333-336; and in Maybon, *op. cit.*, pp. 113-134. In the eighteenth century Cambodia was for all practical purposes incorporated into Vietnam, forming the three provinces of Tran Bien, Phien Tran, and Long Ho, with a governor administering each of them. Nevertheless a king of Cambodia, a ruler by name only, resided in Phnom Penh all the time, with the exception of a short period between 1796 and 1802. (Hall, *op. cit.*, pp. 737ff., gives a complete list of the Cambodian monarchs.) Siam repeatedly championed the cause of Cambodia, and there were several wars between that kingdom and Vietnam in the seventeenth, eighteenth, and nineteenth centuries. When Gia Long established the unity of his country in 1802 he held Cambodia in firm control. King An Chan of Cambodia (1802-1834) consented in 1807 to pay a tribute to the court of Hué every four years. However this did not settle the Vietnamese-Cambodian relations for good. A war between Siam and Vietnam over Cambodia broke out under the reign of Gia Long (1810), another under Minh Mang (1833-1834), and a third under his successor, Thieu Tri (1841-1848). In the first two of these three wars the Vietnamese were victorious, the third ended with a compromise. In 1847 King Ang Duong was invested in his capital by both Vietnam and Siam. From this year on, the two countries exercised

a kind of common protectorate over Cambodia. (Cf. J. Moura, *Le royaume du Cambodge,* Vol. II, p. 129.) This situation prevailed until the conquest of Cochinchina by the French.

2. It is astonishing that none of the rival European powers tried to get into Vietnam by siding with the Tay Son. The reasons for this were never properly explored in the many studies devoted to this period. Some French authors refer to Gia Long's alleged friendliness toward the West, and speak of the Tay Sons' hostility toward Europeans. However, the former is doubtful, to say the least, and for the latter there is hardly any evidence. On the other hand, colonial powers prefer to deal with established conservative monarchies rather than with revolutionary leaders.

3. At the beginning of the nineteenth century Vietnam was a truly independent state, in spite of the fact that Gia Long sought the recognition of his reign by the Chinese emperor, to whom he dispatched several embassies between 1793 and 1819. Maybon, *op. cit.,* pp. 374-379, gives a detailed description of these embassies, quotes the humble, almost humiliating language of Gia Long's letter to the emperor of China, and enumerates the gifts and tribute brought to Peking. In one of these letters Gia Long calls himself "a little neighboring vassal of your empire." This, however, was flowering Oriental oratory rather than an expression of reality. Gia Long spoke like a vassal and paid his tribute, but otherwise he acted as an independent ruler. Chinese Emperor Kia King recognized Gia Long as king of Vietnam and sent him the seal of a satellite ruler. This seal was made of gilded silver and had the picture of a camel, the symbol of vassalage, engraved on it. At this time the same seal of vassalage was conferred by the emperor of China on the kings of Burma, Siam, Laos, and the Ryukyu Islands. In a decree issued simultaneously (1803), Emperor Kia King gave the country its modern name of Vietnam. About the etymology of the word Vietnam, cf. Maybon, *op. cit.,* p. 377, note 1. Some French authors do not mention that Gia Long sought China's recognition and contrast him in this respect, quite wrongly, with his son, Minh Mang.

4. John F. Cady, *The Roots of French Imperialism in Eastern Asia,* Ithaca, N. Y., 1954, p. 15, summarizes the situation as follows: "During the turmoil of the French Revolution, the successive French governments were too preoccupied in Europe to do anything about the Far East. They were openly hostile to missionary endeavors. Governmental allowances previously paid to missionary personnel lapsed. . . . Napoleon's Egyptian campaign and his anti-British intrigues marked the limit of France's capabilities in eastern Asia. The French consulate at Macao closed in 1800. In 1802, when Napoleon heard of Pigneau's death, he contemplated

appointing a successor as Bishop of Adran, but again nothing came of it.
. . . The question of Annam was examined for the first time and without
decision by Napoleon's Ministry of Marine in 1812. Meanwhile missionary interest in France reached a low ebb. The director of the Paris
Missionary Society had fled the country in 1792. The Society was revived only temporarily from 1805 to 1809, and not until 1820 was it
permanently re-established."

5. During the war between Nguyen Anh and the Tay Son, British firms
in Madras and Calcutta, especially Abbott & Maitland, had supplied arms
to the future Emperor Gia Long. Nguyen Anh had bought on credit, and
the settlement of his debts necessitated protracted negotiations. These
negotiations and the desire to break the French influence in Vietnam
revived British interest in Indochina. In 1804 the British East India
Company sent an agent, J. W. Roberts, from Canton to Hué. He was
received in an unfriendly way, no commercial privilege was granted to
the Company, the presents he brought to Gia Long were not even
accepted. Roberts left Vietnam after having complained in a letter to
the Emperor, dated August 14, 1804, about the "proud and arrogant
behavior" of the monarch. However, it seems that it was rather the agent
of the East India Company who behaved arrogantly. He demanded not
only the exclusive right to trade with Vietnam for his company, but also
the cession of the island of Cham, near Faifo, to Great Britain. Cf. the
letter written by the French agent G. Jaussand to Count Molé, Minister
of Marine and Colonies, dated November 15, 1818, reprinted in Taboulet,
op. cit., pp. 276ff. After Gia Long's death, another British envoy, John
Crawfurd, appeared at the court of Minh Mang in 1821-1822 but was
not more successful than Roberts. See John Crawfurd, *Journal of an
Embassy from the Governor-General of India to the Courts of Siam and
Cochin China*, London, 1828. (Also note 28 of Chapter IV.)

6. Napoleon was much more interested in East Asia than the French
kings of the eighteenth century. His thinking was not economic but
military. In India and East Asia he looked for the bases from which he
could destroy the British Empire. But European entanglements hindered
him from realizing his "Indian dream." Shortly before he attacked Russia,
on January 29, 1812, he asked his Minister of Marine for information
about the mission of the Bishop of Adran in 1788. The archivist of the
ministry prepared two volumes of files for the Emperor, but Napoleon
probably did not find time to peruse them. Only after the restoration of
the Bourbons did the "question of Cochinchina" come up again as an
object of French policy (Taboulet, *op. cit.*, pp. 272f).

7. Jean-Baptiste Chaigneau, a cousin of the French poet René de

Chateaubriand, came to Vietnam in 1794. He lived in the house of Pigneau, who "loved him like a son." In 1802 he married a Christian Vietnamese girl and bought a house in the vicinity of Hué. He held at the same time the ranks of a Vietnamese mandarin, first class, and of a consul of France. He sat in the council of King Gia Long. His reports to Paris show a high degree of perspicacity. He observed the discontent and the poverty of the Vietnamese people, suffering under taxes, forced labor, and the arbitrariness of the mandarins. Chaigneau took a dim view of the prospects of the Vietnamese monarchy. Cf., e.g., his letter to M. Letoudal, dated May 12, 1808. (Arch. Miss. Etrang., Vol. 801, pp. 1238-1267, repr. in BEFEO, 1912, p. 60.) Philippe Vannier, soldier, sailor, and participant in the American War of Independence, came to Vietnam in 1789 by the invitation of the Bishop of Adran. In 1802 he was appointed a mandarin, first class. He returned to France only in 1825, after having spent thirty-six years in Indochina (Taboulet, *op. cit.*, pp. 254f., 261, 277, 283; L. Cadière, "Les diplômes et ordres de service de Vannier et de Chaigneau," in *Bulletin des Amis du Vieux Hué*, 1922, pp. 147-149).

8. Dutch and especially British attempts to penetrate Vietnam economically were frustrated by the influence of Chaigneau and Vannier. These men were probably responsible for the complete failure of the mission of J. W. Roberts of the British East India Company in 1804. Cf. notes 5 and 15 of this Chapter, and Edouard Chassigneux in *Histoire des colonies françaises et de l'expansion de la France dans le monde*, Paris, 1932, Vol. V. (L'Inde, l'Indochine), p. 362. It is interesting to note that the first United States diplomatic mission in the Far East was sent to Vietnam, not to China. Edmund Robert, who was given this mission by President Jackson, tried twice unsuccessfully, in 1832 and 1836, to contact Minh Mang. (Huard and Durand, *op. cit.*, p. 52, note 2.) The first American citizen to see Saigon was apparently John White (see note 15 of this Chapter), whose mission failed not because of Vietnamese resistance but rather for lack of American interest in the limited commercial possibilities Vietnam offered.

9. Between 1815 and 1818 numerous memoirs were presented to the Bourbon court asking for the reopening of the Vietnamese market to French commerce. The arms manufacturers of Bordeaux sent ships to Vietnam on their own account but were not successful. They suffered serious losses through shipwrecks and met strong Chinese competition. But the main reason for their failure was the fact that the only commodity Vietnam was able to offer in exchange for arms was sugar, which could not compete with the product of the Antilles, favored by tariffs. The French government sent three vessels to Vietnam, in 1818, 1822, and

1825, and appointed Chaigneau consul of France, but failed to establish friendlier relations with Vietnam (Taboulet, *op. cit.*, pp. 282-287; Cordier, "Bordeaux et la Cochinchine sous la Restauration," in *Toung Pao*, series II, Vol. V, 1904, pp. 516-521; Cordier, "Le Consulat de France à Hué sous la Restauration," in *Mélanges d'histoire et de géographie orientales*, Vol. III, 1922, pp. 214-216).

10. Towards the end of 1817 the French Prime Minister, Duke de Richelieu, dispatched the *Cybèle*, a frigate of fifty-two guns, under the command of Captain Kergarion to Vietnam. The captain was ordered not to mention the treaty of 1787 but only to show French sympathy and to assure Gia Long of the benevolence of the King of France. Kergarion landed at Tourane, was friendly received, but was refused an audience with Gia Long by reasons of protocol: he did not carry with him a letter from the King of France to the King of Vietnam. With his mission unaccomplished, Kergarion returned to France in January, 1818 (Taboulet, *op. cit.*, pp. 288-290; P. de Joinville, *La mission de la* Cybèle *en Extrême-Orient*, Paris, 1914). Chesneaux, *op. cit.*, p. 93, makes the erroneous statement that Kergarion asked for the application of the treaty of 1787 and the cession of the island of Poulo Condore.

11. The biographer of Gia Long's successor, Marcel Gaultier, (*Minh Mang*, Paris, 1935, pp. 71f.) stresses the conformity of Gia Long's and Minh Mang's policies: "When he was only hereditary prince, Minh Mang had uttered opinions about the policy to be followed in the interest of Annam concerning foreigners and Catholic priests. Gia Long seems to have tacitly approved the projects of his son, and the recommendations he formulated on his deathbed confirm this hypothesis. He did not recommend to his successor to maintain the current situation in the way he had tolerated it in memory of Pigneau de Béhaine, but he advised him always to protect the French whose kind feelings were so precious to the dynasty. Minh Mang always respected this wish, though with repugnance."

12. There was much less difference between the policy of Gia Long and that of his three successors than most French historians claim. A very typical example for the contrasting picture French authors used to paint of the kings of the Nguyen dynasty is to be found in Philippe Devillers, *Histoire du Viet-Nam de 1940 à 1952*, Paris, 1952, pp. 18f. and 24. There Gia Long appears as the enlightened monarch, inspired by European ideas, reforming his administration, codifying the laws, building roads, bridges, canals, dams, granaries, fortresses, and harbors; whereas Minh Mang, Thieu Tri, and Tu Duc are characterized as impregnated with Chinese culture, despising the "Western Barbarians," imitating the Manchu emperors' policy of isolating their subjects from contact with

foreigners and meeting European imperialism by retreating into their own shell.

13. Minh Mang started his fight against Catholicism with a shrewd move. He deprived the faithful of their priests by calling the French missionaries to Hué under the pretext that he had no interpreters after the departure of Chaigneau and needed them to translate Occidental books for him. Minh Mang gained their reluctant cooperation by conferring high grades of the mandarinate upon them. However, the fight was on when a new missionary, Father Régéreau, arrived in the country. Now Minh Mang signed the first of several anti-Catholic edicts, forbidding further entry of missionaries into Vietnam (1825). In this edict he spoke of the "perverse religion of the Europeans" and used language very similar to earlier proclamations by Vietnamese rulers against Christianity in the seventeenth and eighteenth centuries. (Cf. note 58, Ch. IV.) The edict was followed by a wholesale arrest of missionaries. Le Van Duyet, vice-king of Cochinchina, an old intimate of Gia Long, pleaded with Minh Mang to revoke the edict. The king refused but agreed to free the imprisoned priests under the condition that they go straight to Tourane and embark for France. None of the missionaries obeyed. They returned to their parishes and resumed their work. Minh Mang showed great restraint in view of the constant violation of all his orders. At this time a Catholic priest, Father Jaccard, gained some influence over Minh Mang and was even permitted to recite prayers on the monarch's birthday (Gaultier, *op. cit.*, pp. 90-94). Minh Mang's biographer is of the opinion that he was more generous toward the Christians than his father, whose religious policy was never questioned (*ibid.*, p. 97).

14. Gia Long was an adherent of the cult of ancestors and of Confucianism. He disliked Buddhism and withstood the influence of his entourage, especially of the ladies at the court, who were in favor of the Buddhist bonzes. He disliked Christianity even more because he considered it to be a revolutionary doctrine. Out of gratitude to the Bishop of Adran, he never persecuted the Christians; but, on the other hand, he never stopped the petty vexations of the missionaries by his mandarins. Gia Long would have been more tolerant toward the Christians if the Pope had not condemned the cult of ancestors, the cornerstone of the king's religious creed. He said so expressively in a conversation with Pigneau in 1789: "I wish that the cult of the dead could be conciliated with Christianity. . . . I believe in the cult of parents. . . . It is the base of our education. . . . I beg you to give your attention to this fact and to allow the Christians to get nearer to the remainder of my subjects . . . " —Report of the missionary M. Boisserand, dated August 11, 1789. Under

Gia Long's reign there were very few conversions and the total number of Vietnamese Christians decreased. The letters of Chaigneau in the years 1806 and 1808 are full of anxiety lest the king give up his neutrality and start a persecution of Christians. Gia Long, however, kept his cool neutrality until his death. In 1819 Vannier reported that no harrassment had taken place so far "out of regard to the two of us" (meaning himself and Chaigneau) but that the heir presumptive (Minh Mang) was openly talking about the persecution of the Christian religion under his coming reign. See Chassigneux, *op. cit.,* pp. 362f., 372; Taboulet, *op. cit.,* pp. 224-226, 278; Launay, *Hist. Miss. Coch., Doc.,* pp. 222-229; Henri Bernard, "Le conflit de la religion annamite avec la religion d'Occident à la Cour de Gia-Long," in *Bulletin Général de l'Instruction Publique* (Hanoi), January, 1941.

15. The first American to make contact with Vietnam was a Captain White, whose ship arrived in Saigon in 1820. Minh Mang, then in the first year of his reign, was willing to sign a contract, but the only merchandise he was willing to buy were pieces of artillery, firearms, uniforms, and—books. This offer to buy "technical equipment" did not seem advantageous enough to Captain White from a commercial viewpoint. See the interesting account by John White, "Lieutenant in the United States Navy," in his book, *History of a Voyage to the China Sea,* originally written as a memoir to be deposited in the archives of the East India Marine Society of Salem, but then published in Boston by Wells and Lilly, Court Street, 1823. Another American approach, the Roberts mission, in 1832, was also completely futile. Two British endeavors to open Vietnam to foreign trade—Roberts in 1804 and Crawfurd in 1822—are described in note 5 of this chapter. Crawfurd was allowed to land in any Indochinese port except in Tongking, but was unable to exact any concessions from Minh Mang (Le Thanh Khoi, *op. cit.,* p. 339; Chesneaux, *op. cit.,* pp. 93ff.; Crawfurd, *op. cit.*). On the American Roberts mission of 1832, see *Bulletin des Amis de Vieux Hué,* 1937, no. 1, p. 62.

16. Immediately after the outbreak of the Opium War, Minh Mang, aware of the danger that an attack by European powers on China could mean for Vietnam, sent a mission to Paris and London. This mission consisted of two mandarins of lesser degree and two interpreters. Why Minh Mang selected second-rate ambassadors remains obscure. They were received in Paris by Prime Minister Marshal Soult and Minister of Commerce Cunin-Gridaine, but not by King Louis-Philippe. Not only the Society of Foreign Missions and individual French prelates, but also the Pope, had urged this rebuke for an "enemy of the religion." Gaultier

(*op. cit.*, p. 240) remarks that Minh Mang's diplomacy failed "through the intransigeance of the French government, which was maneuvered by a Catholic party blinded by hatred." Louis-Philippe's policy is hard to understand. Now had come the opportunity for which the French had waited so long: an offer of commercial relations. The Vietnamese envoys, after their rebuff in Paris, went to London, where they did not accomplish anything either, though no religious question troubled their relations with Protestant England. The ambassadors reached Hué only after the death of Minh Mang. A detailed description of this interesting though futile mission, and also of the endeavors of the Catholic Church in France to make it a failure, is contained in Delvaux, "L'ambassade de Minh-mang à Louis-Philippe," in *Bulletin des Amis de Vieux Hué,* 1928, no. 4. For a good short summary see Taboulet, *op. cit.*, pp. 347-349. Many noted French authors do not mention the Vietnamese mission to Paris in 1840 at all (Gosselin, Chassigneux, Maspéro).

17. Gia Long was an able administrator who tried to restore the economy of Vietnam after a devastating civil war. He repaired the highways and built new ones, especially the famous Mandarin Route from Saigon to Langson. On these highways he organized an efficient postal service. Gia Long also constructed public storehouses to alleviate the suffering of the people after bad harvests. He is credited with a successful monetary reform and attempts at a social agrarian policy. Finally, Gia Long was the author of a legal code that took the place of the ancient Le code, which had become obsolete. (About the Code Gia Long, see note 18 of this Chapter.) Taboulet, *op. cit.*, p. 267, gives a short sketch of his achievements. Lelabousse characterized him as firm but not cruel (*ibid.*, p. 268). Contemporary writers also praised his frankness and contrasted him with the shrewd Minh Mang, who, on the other hand, had more understanding of the suffering of his subjects. In a letter to M. Baroudel, Chaigneau reports under the date of June 25, 1822: "The old king was more frank and one could rely on what he said, whereas the present king does not say what he thinks. . . . He [Minh Mang] rules his subjects rather well. There is less forced labor than in the time of his father. He is generous to his soldiers and mandarins but very exacting in his demands on their service." Gosselin, *op. cit.*, p. 110, calls Minh Mang erudite and imbued with the science of the Orient. Though he disdained Western knowledge, he was well informed about it. Minh Mang was of a rare intelligence and animated by a sincere devotion to his country. He was a domineering character. Le Thanh Khoi, *op. cit.*, p. 324, gives credit to Minh Mang for having been one of the best legislators Vietnam ever had. This is what his biographer, Gaultier, has to say about him: "Minh Mang

remained, first of all, the tender literate his teachers had tried to make of him. . . . He was prepared for the vocation of a poet. . . . He was generous, ambitious with a morbid desire to impose on everybody the fear and respect of his sovereign power. He possessed a feminine instinct in the service of a male character. . . . The attention Minh Mang devoted to the most intimate details of the administration astonished his contemporaries. The emperor ruled directly, and the official annals show how he penetrated into every detail in regulating the existence of his subjects" (*op. cit.*, pp. 13f., 17f). In his biography of Minh Mang, Gaultier wanted to do justice to a king who had found no other historians than official court annalists and a few Europeans who completely misunderstood his policy, which Gaultier characterizes as the expression of robust and generous thoughts (*ibid.*, p. 21). Thieu Tri was a sensible and peace-loving ruler who, immediately after he ascended the throne, ended the war against Siam over the domination of Cambodia and was satisfied with an honorable compromise. (Cf. note 1 of this chapter.) But the aggressive behavior of France made Thieu Tri even more hostile to foreigners than his predecessor. After the Opium War he decreed that every European caught on the territory of Vietnam should be executed without a trial. But no missionary was executed under his rule. Like Minh Mang and Tu Duc, Thieu Tri was a poet of renown (Le Thanh Khoi, *op. cit.*, pp. 335, 343, 347). The last independent ruler of Vietnam before the French conquest, Tu Duc, was "intelligent, well educated and of a sweet disposition" (Gosselin, *op. cit.*, p. 124). Léopold Pallu de la Barrière, in *Histoire de l'expédition de Cochinchine*, Paris, 1864, gives the following character sketch of Tu Duc: "He was represented, and is still represented, as a kind of wild and bloodthirsty beast; for this is a method that small men use, and complacent men imitate, in order to degrade an enemy. But by the Annamite people he is not considered to be a harsh and inhumane prince. Quite to the contrary, it seems that his mild and conciliatory character very soon attracted the attention of his father, the emperor Thieu Tri, and induced him to drop an elder son who had become notorious for acts of rage and authoritarianism. An Annamite who lived at the court of Hué has supplied this information in Latin, at that time the common language, and he has characterized the opinion of the Annamites about their emperor: *pertinax et tenax*, penetrating and thoughtful." This is what another French author, Gabriel Aubaret, (*Histoire et description de la Basse-Cochinchine*, Paris, 1863) has to say about Tu Duc: "I talked with this Oriental potentate for more than an hour and I received an excellent impression. . . . I expected a terrible character and I saw a refined and distinguished personality. Tu Duc has a pale, oblong face, and his black eyes are of a remarkable profundity. . . . His hands . . . are the most charming one can imagine. This type of physiognomy is often to be found in Cochinchina, but seldom in such a purity as in this king; he reminds you really of the types of Egyptian antiquity."

18. Even his legal code was only a careful modernization of the old Le code without any far-reaching changes. Le Thanh Khoi, *op. cit.*, p. 330, calls it "an instrument to consolidate the new monarchic order after thirty years of civil war." The preamble to the code shows that clarity of codification was attempted above all. Gia Long and his legal advisors, believing in Confucious' maxim that man was basically good, thought that a clear distinction between moral and immoral behavior would finally abolish crime. Somewhat naïvely the preamble says: "We gave orders to high mandarins to examine all existing codes with scrupulous attention . . . and to create a law that We Ourselves have examined and are promulgating now so that everybody may know what is allowed and what is forbidden, that our laws and regulations may be clear like the light of the sun or the moon. . . . Every mandarin will have to know the laws included in this code; the ignorant people will know them too, will change their behavior and will become good, so that education will take the place of punishment." In spite of the assertion of the preamble that the king ordered a scrupulous study of all existing laws before the codification, Gaultier, *op. cit.*, p. 40, criticizes Gia Long's code for having been compiled with undue haste. The Gia Long Code was promulgated in 1812. It consisted of 398 articles arranged in 22 books. A French translation was published by P. Philastre in two volumes (Paris, 1876).

19. See Le Thanh Khoi, *op. cit.*, p. 327.

20. Chaigneau wrote to M. Letoudal on May 12, 1808: "All the people live in great misery. The king forces the people to work for him without feeding or paying them. Furthermore, he raises all contributions and exempts nobody from the taxes. The mandarins torment and rob as much as they can. In lawsuits they do not pass a sentence before they have ruined both parties. Therefore the kingdom is in a condition of crisis which cannot last for long. . . " (Arch. Miss. Etrang., Vol. 801, pp. 1236-1267, reprinted in BEFEO, 1912, p. 60.) Taboulet, who republishes this letter (*op. cit.*, p. 278), takes exception to part of its contents, especially the statement that no tax exemptions were granted. He points to the fact that Gia Long had reduced the rice tax by one-half in 1806 "for once." Chesneaux, *op. cit.*, pp. 59f., quotes the report of a Spanish missionary, Diego de Jumilla, for an earlier period (1773), about the misery of the peasantry and armed revolts as a consequence of it.

314

21. Le Thanh Khoi, *op. cit.*, pp. 358-360, deals extensively with these agrarian reforms. A detailed treatment of the measures taken by Minh Mang is to be found in Gaultier, *op. cit.*, pp. 253-271. Minh Mang decided in 1830 to give fallow soil, uncultivated fields, and even forests to everybody who asked for them. Tu Duc granted mandarin rank to people who recruited colonists to till virgin land. However, if the colonizer abandoned his project within three years, he was deprived of his rank and whipped in public. Agrarian colonies were set up by paupers and vagabonds under the instruction of special officials. Military colonies with a similar purpose were founded by soldiers, prisoners of war, and banished criminals. In 1840 it was decreed that rich landowners had to return one-third of their holdings to the communities. Minh Mang's activities in dyke building and irrigation surpassed anything achieved in the French colonial period, Chesneaux believes (*op. cit.*, p. 90). A last effort at extending the cultivated area was made by Tu Duc in 1849. He employed soldiers stationed in the South to till virgin soil. Villages created by their effort were tax-exempt for seven years. These new villages were especially frequent in western Cochinchina. Their settlers played an important part in organizing the resistance against the troops of Napoleon III in the 1860's. But all these reforms did not heal the permanent agrarian crisis in Vietnam. In the wake of famine and inundation, peasant revolts broke out. One of them engulfed the North in 1826 and 1827. It was led by Nguyen Han (an old comrade-in-arms of the Tay Son emperor Quang Trung), who had lived in exile in China since 1802. His professed aim was to bring back the better times of the Tay Son dynasty. Another revolt of 1833 took place in South Vietnam. It was led by Le Van Khoi, an adopted son of the protector of the Christians, Le Van Duyet. (See note 13 of this Chapter.) He succeeded in conquering the whole of Cochinchina before he was defeated. Several other peasant uprisings occurred between 1833 and 1848.

22. The rural life of Vietnam in the nineteenth century was dominated by the "community." This term is not synonymous with "village" or "township." The community was the basic administrative unit in Vietnam. It not only administered itself, but had a voice in the distribution and collection of taxes, organized its own public works, and looked after its own safety. The organ through which all this was done was the council of notables. The notables of the village were chosen among the rich landowners, to whom one or two poor old men of great respectability were frequently added. The village chief or elder presided over the council of notables. He was the justice of peace and the distributor of the village treasury. In addition to the village chief, each community had an official

315

in charge of relations with the higher authority. This official was called *ly truong,* which the French, perhaps not quite correctly, translated as *maire* (mayor). He was chosen by the notables. The notables also acted as judges. Only major crimes were dealt with by the mandarins. After the conquest this village organization impressed even some French observers, who used to refer to it as a masterwork of peasant democracy. Le Thanh Khoi, *op. cit.,* p. 360, refuses to give the epithet "democracy" to the Vietnamese village organization but speaks instead of an oligarchy where all the power belonged to the notables. According to him, the notables ran the village in their own interest and exercised an authority without control. In the same vein the French administrator Ory, toward the end of the nineteenth century, called it an instrument in the service of the rich landowners, in the hands of a few wealthy families, who administered it at their will and did everything to assure a continuity of existing conditions. For a descripton of the institution of the Vietnamese community from different points of view, cf. Pasquier, *op. cit.,* pp. 41-65; Le Thanh Khoi, *op. cit.,* pp. 353-361; Chesneaux, *op. cit.,* pp. 69-73; P. Ory, *La commune annamite au Tonkin,* Paris, 1894; P. Kresser, *La commune annamite au Cochinchine,* Paris, 1935; Camille Briffaut, *La cité annamite* Paris, 1909 and 1912. See also the chapters concerned with "le village" or "la commune" in André Dumarest, *La formation des classes sociales au pays annamite,* Lyon (probably 1936), and Colonel E. Diguet, *Les annamites,* Paris, 1906.

23. The Vietnamese state did not take cognizance of the existence of individuals but dealt exclusively with the communities.

24. In a letter written in 1807, Chaigneau comments: "The rich can attack the poor without fear of punishment because he can be sure that with money justice will be on his side." (Repr. in BEFEO, 1912.)

25. Quoted by Chesneaux, *op. cit.,* p. 85.

26. The conditions under which these slave laborers had to work were truly appalling. Many died from sheer exhaustion. Working hours extended over the whole day and part of the night. Sometimes the forced laborer had to stand on guard for the rest of the night. No respite was given in rain and bad weather. The slave laborer had hardly time to eat. These descriptions are based on missionary reports as published in *Nouvelles lettres édifiantes et curieuses,* edited by Le Clerc, 1818-1828, Vol. VIII., and in Cadière, "Documents sur l'époque Gia-long," in BEFEO, Vol. XII, no. 7.

27. About the middle of the nineteenth century some Vietnamese intellectuals traveled abroad, studied the immense transformations the world was going through in these years, and made sound proposals

about a modernization of Vietnam. None of these men was listened to. The most important of them, Nguyen Truong To (1825-1871), a Catholic who accompanied French priests to Italy and France, presented fifteen memoirs to the court of Tu Duc. He proposed cooperation with all Western powers, separation of the executive and judicial branch of government, teaching of the exact sciences, replacement of the Chinese alphabet with a modern script, and publication of newspapers. He further recommended that European experts be invited to Vietnam to modernize agriculture, to develop industry, commerce, and mining, and to reorganize and re-equip the army. Tu Duc was at first impressed by Nguyen Truong To and sent him to France in 1866 to buy machinery and recruit experts for Vietnam. But the occupation of Cochinchina by the French in 1867 brought his mission to a sudden end. The mandarins were hostile to Nguyen Truong To's plans for a modernization of the country and succeeded in persuading Tu Duc to dismiss all reform plans. They also isolated the king from other innovators, like Dinh Van Dien who, in 1868, asked for scientific methods in agriculture, exploitation of the gold mines, construction of railroads, and establishment of international economic relations. The mandarins were even able to induce Tu Duc not to receive ambassadors to Asiatic courts coming home to report and thus kept him ignorant about the latest developments in Siam, Japan, and China. This was the case with Nguyen Hiep returning from Bangkok in 1879, and with Le Dinh, who visited Hong Kong in 1881. Another reformer, the academician Phan Liem, presented a plan to develop commerce and mining in 1881 but was ignored as his predecessors had been. (Le Thanh Khoi, *op. cit.*, pp. 363-365; Nguyen Lan, *Nguyen Truong To*, Hué, 1941; Dao Dang Vy, "Page historique: Nguyen Truong To et son temps," in *La Patrie Annamite*, no. 221.)

28. This is proved by his interest in modern Western medicine. Minh Mang heard about vaccination against smallpox and asked Vannier, his French mandarin, first class, to help him introduce this innovation into his kingdom. Vannier brought the French surgeon Jean-Marie Despiau to the king. Minh Mang gave Despiau a house on the palace grounds where he could vaccinate the whole day. All the king's children, among them the future ruler Thieu Tri, were vaccinated against smallpox by Despiau. See Taboulet, *op. cit.*, p. 296; Vannier's letter to Baroudel, July 13, 1820 (Arch. Miss. Etrang., Vol. 801, p. 1489, reprinted in BEFEO, 1912, p. 64.); Despiau's letter to Baroudel, July 28, 1821 (*Arch. Miss. Etrang.*, Vol. 800, p. 1529, reprinted in *Bulletin des Amis du Vieux Hué*, October, 1926, p. 428).

29. Vietnamese aristocracy was not a class completely isolated from

other groups of society. The emperor continually added to its members by granting titles that were not automatically hereditary. There were five grades of nobility in the nineteenth century: *cong, bau, ba, tu,* and *nam.* They were translated into English as duke, marquess, count, viscount, and baron, respectively. Each member of the aristocracy was entitled to a landholding, which, however, became so small under Thieu Tri (1841-1848) that it was an extended plot for the ancestral tombs rather than an estate. A duke received ten maos, a marquess eight, and the lesser degrees smaller lots. These allotments for the nobility were abolished in 1883 by Tu Duc and converted into an annuity in cash. The titles did not give any political prerogative. They represented an honor and nothing else. Here is the difference between the nobility and the mandarinate. The former was an amorphous group of distinguished citizens without any real power or importance, the latter another group of distinguished citizens with a certain formal education and with the exclusive right to all posts in the administration of Vietnam. The mandarins would probably constitute a "class" in the judgment of a sociologist. They enjoyed certain privileges that other classes did not. In addition to their monopoly to the administration, they were exempt from taxes, military service, and forced labor; their sons had precedence over other youths in entrance to colleges. A detailed description of the institution of the mandarinate, civil and military, of its ranks and privileges and the examinations they had to pass, is contained in Pasquier, *op. cit.,* pp. 119-181. Cf. also A. Laborde, "Les titres et grades héréditaires à la cour d'Annam," in *Bulletin des Amis du Vieux Hué,* 1920, pp. 395ff.; Le Thanh Khoi, *op. cit.,* pp. 353-357; and Gaultier, *op. cit.,* pp. 245f. See also Diguet, *op. cit.,* Chapter III. On the Vietnamese nobility, see Robert Petit, *La monarchie annamite,* Paris, 1931, which contains also an excellent bibliography.

30. "Political power was concentrated in the hands of the emperor. Between him and the people there was nothing, no feudal class, no aristocracy, no parliament, nothing but the functionaries, who were pure instruments of imperial power." Devillers, *op. cit.,* p. 19.

31. For a description of his functions and his curiously subordinate position, see E. Diguet, *op. cit.,* p. 87.

32. See Chapter III, p. 144 and note 18. In order to pass an examination, the future mandarin had to master the Chinese language with the knowledge of at least five thousand characters which were necessary to read Chinese classics. This necessity of knowing Chinese separated the educated class from the common people.

33. The word "mandarin" is of Sanskrit origin. In that language *man-*

trin means a councilor or minister of state. From Sanskrit it was taken over into the Malayan language. The Portuguese adopted the word when they first heard it in the sixteenth century. From Portuguese it was transplanted into all European languages. Neither the Chinese nor the Vietnamese have assimilated the word "mandarin." The designation for a public official is *kuan* in Chinese and *quan* in Vietnamese. There is hardly a difference in the pronunciation of the Chinese and the Vietnamese word, but only in the customary way of transcription into Latin letters.

34. See, e.g., Tran Duc Thao in *Les Temps Modernes*, February, 1946, and Tran Van Trai, *L'enseignement traditionnel en Annam*, Paris, 1942.

35. There was a special college, Quoc Tu Giam, for the sons of mandarins. While studying there they received a small allowance from the state. However, this college accepted also brilliant students who did not come from mandarin families. Sons of mandarins of the first, second, and third degrees were exempted from military and labor service as well as from taxes. All the sons of mandarins of the fourth degree and one son each of mandarins of the fifth and of the first class of the sixth degree were also free from military and labor service, but had to pay taxes. Some other privileges of the mandarins are enumerated in Pasquier, *op. cit.*, pp. 158ff. See also Chesneaux, *op. cit.*, p. 86, and Le Thanh Khoi, *op. cit.*, p. 355. In criticizing the mandarinal system, this author draws attention to the fact that the "College of the Children of the State" created in 1076 accepted only children of officials. The literary contests became open to all only at the end of a long evolution (*op. cit.*, p. 149, and note 35 of same page).

36. During these tests the students were held incommunicado until the end of the examinations. The place of their confinement was called "Camp of the Educated." The candidates were allowed to take one personal servant to their cells or tents. The examiners were a commission of mandarins especially selected and appointed by the emperor. They were very independent, and it happened frequently that sons of high-class mandarins were not able to pass. The examiners too were kept in confinement, sometimes up to five weeks. They were guarded by troops and were not allowed to receive any communications from outside. A detailed description of an examination in nineteenth-century Vietnam is to be found in Baille, *Souvenir d'Annam*. Cf. also Pasquier, *op. cit.*, pp. 174-181; Gaultier, *op. cit.*, p. 251; Tran Van Trai, *L'enseignement traditionnel en Annam*, Paris, 1942, pp. 71-103. See also Huard and Durand, *op. cit.*, Chapter VIII.

37. Some intellectuals, after having passed their examinations, did not apply for jobs in the administration but returned to their native villages, where they lived poor and honored and taught the children the rudiments of Chinese characters. They kept the spirit of Confucianism alive in the masses and thus contributed to the defense of the old monarchic order (Chesneaux, *op. cit.*, p. 88). "The 'men of letters,' whether they were officials or not, therefore constituted the ruling class." —Philippe Devillers, *op. cit.*, p. 20. Pasquier, *op. cit.*, pp. 165-174, gives a touching description of the life of the village sages: "There are no public schools in the villages but often private teachers are holding classes there, scholars with university degrees, even with the equivalent of a Ph.D. degree. They are not paid but live on gifts they receive from their students' parents. These private teachers are exempt from taxes and military service. Mostly old men with thin white beards, they enjoy a very high reputation. Even middle-aged men with successful public careers do not think it below their dignity to receive instruction from a village teacher. If the teacher dies, his pupils mourn him for three years, the same period as one mourns for a father in Vietnam. He is addressed by the honorary title of *thay* (master)."

38. The curriculum of the Vietnamese student included philosophy, with special emphasis on ethics, poetry, rhetoric, ancient Chinese and Vietnamese history, and political science. The exact sciences were excluded. This was in the spirit of Confucius, who taught that natural phenomena surpassed human understanding and that man therefore should limit his interest to his relations with his fellow men. The main subject of the studies were the five classical books written by or ascribed to Confucius. Among the other Chinese philosophers, only Mencius and Lao Tze were included in the curriculum. Instruction in literature covered poetry and the historical novel. Knowledge of a few hundred Chinese characters was essential for elementary education. So, of course, was reading and writing in Vietnamese as transcribed in the Latin alphabet (Quoc Ngu). The method of teaching, in both elementary and higher education, was a crude and unimaginative learning by heart. For the essentials of Vietnamese education, see Huard and Durand, *op. cit.*, pp. 83-86; Tran Van Trai, *op. cit.*, p. 114; Gaultier, *op. cit.*, pp. 243-253; Pasquier, *op. cit.*, pp. 165ff; Chesneaux, *op. cit.*, pp. 85-88; Le Thanh Khoi, *op. cit.*, pp. 327, 355, 362f.

39. See Gaultier, *op. cit.*, 13f.

40. Numerous foreign observers—missionaries, travelers, merchants, and representatives of European powers—reported how cruelly the mandarins treated the population. Among the foreign observers Chaigneau

was especially critical of the mandarins. (See quotation from his letter in note 20 of this Chapter.) Also, Vietnamese folk songs and satirical poems through the centuries contain bitter accusations against the mandarins and show that they were considered a plague to the people.

41. Characteristic of a mandarinal view of Christianity is a petition presented by the mandarins to Minh Mang in August, 1826. It says that Christianity is contrary to the "true doctrine." It seduces the people and abuses simplicity. It threatens the weak with the tortures of hell and lures others with the promise of the pleasures of heaven. It advertises that it is holy and that it gives dignity to its followers. But the Christians do not adore the spirit of clarity; they do not have any cult of their ancestors. (Reprinted in Louvet, *La Cochinchine religieuse*, Vol. II, pp. 504-507, and in Taboulet, *op. cit.*, pp. 323f.)

42. A captain of the French navy, Félix Favin-Lévêque, commander of the corvette *L'Héroïne*, came to Vietnam in February, 1843, in order to rescue five French missionaries imprisoned in Hué since 1841 under the most cruel conditions and awaiting execution. He succeeded with his mission. While staying in Tourane, he had a five-hour-long discussion with several mandarins, during which one of them uttered the words quoted in the text (Arch. Aff. Etrang., Mém. et Documents, Asie, Vol. 24, fol. 96-141, reprinted in *Revue Coloniale*, December, 1843, p. 572, and January, 1844, pp. 35-48). About the mission of Favin-Lévêque, see Taboulet, *op. cit.*, pp. 356-359.

43. Typical of this way of thinking is Admiral Rigault de Genouilly's description: "Saigon is destined to become the center of an immense commerce as soon as its port is opened to the Europeans. The country is wonderful, rich in products of all kind; rice, cotton, sugar, tobacco, lumber are there in abundance; and as the river is connected with the interior by numerous waterways, there will be available incalculable resources, at least for export."—Quoted in A. Thomazi, *La conquête de l'Indochine*, Paris, 1934, p. 37. Marquis R. de Courcy, a French diplomat who served as consul in Macao in the 1850's, speaks in a similar vein of the "immense wealth, so far unexploited" of Cochinchina and Tongking. This wealth would make a French expedition, which Courcy recommended, a "very useful and very profitable diversion." (Report to the Ministry of Foreign Affairs, dated Macao, December 31, 1855. Arch. Aff. Etrang., Correspondance de la Chine, Vol. 17, fol. 92/93, published in Taboulet, op. cit., p. 387.) De Courcy published reminiscences (*Souvenirs*, Paris, 1900, 3 vols.) which are highly interesting for students of the Far Eastern policy of France in the nineteenth century.

44. This is stressed by several authors. Le Thanh Khoi (*op. cit.*, pp.

361ff.) speaks of *"immobilisme intellectuel"* (intellectual immobility). Nourished for centuries with Confucian thought, the mandarins were unable to conceive another civilization than the Chinese and closed their eyes against the Western world and the great progress it had made in the scientific domain. Chesneaux, *op. cit.,* p. 106, also blames Confucian ideas for the "intellectual sterility" of Vietnam. According to Gaultier, *op. cit.,* p. 253, the exclusion of all scientific research kept Vietnam outside the great movement of universal evolution. Therefore Vietnam, in the grave hours of her destiny, met very real menaces with nothing else than formulas of sterile subtlety. Left alone with an illusory verbalism, Vietnam was helpless against the activity of the Occident. See also Francis Garnier's *La Cochinchine française en 1864,* Paris, 1864, published under the pseudonym, G. Francis; *De la colonisation de la Cochinchine,* by the same author, 1865; and *La Cochinchine, ce qu'elle est, ce qu'elle sera,* anonymous, Perigueux, 1865. Gaultier, *op. cit.,* p. 10, ascribes all the mistakes and faults the king committed to his intellectual formation by the mandarins and adds, "In a new society, Minh Mang remains the man of the old world." This is, of course, a misinterpretation of history. In fact, Vietnamese society under Minh Mang did not differ basically from that of the seventeenth and eighteenth centuries.

45. The responsibility of the mandarinal system for the downfall of China in the nineteenth century is stressed by Latourette, *A Short History of the Far East,* New York, 1946, p. 156. For Francis Garnier, the same applies to Vietnam to an even higher degree. Vietnam was the only country that completely adopted the Chinese mandarinal system during the long period of Chinese overlordship. In spite of China's overwhelming influence on Japan and Korea in the fields of language, literature, philosophy, and education, these two countries did not accept the mandarinal system. Comparative sketches of Chinese influence on Japan, Korea, and Vietnam are to be found in Latourette, *op. cit.,* pp. 195-199, 265-270, 274. Thailand also took over only part of the Chinese administrative system.

46. The death of Le Van Duyet in 1832 removed a strong defender of Christianity from the scene. On the other hand, the opposition of the Catholics changed into rebellion in spite of Minh Mang's moderate attitude. Though there was no Catholic uprising as such, the Christians in Vietnam became an element of trouble, siding with all movements against the monarch and his authority. The persecution of the Catholics reached its climax after Le Van Duyet, the protector of the Christians, had died in 1832. Minh Mang ordered him posthumously indicted. He was found guilty and one hundred lashes were applied to his grave.

According to Taboulet, *op. cit.*, p. 331, this ridiculous and disgusting behavior of the king caused great indignation among the friends of the late Le Van Duyet. A revolt broke out under the leadership of his adopted son, Le Van Khoi, in July, 1833. Le Thanh Khoi, *op. cit.*, p. 341, on the other hand, believes that the abolition of the autonomy of Cochinchina was the real reason for the outbreak of the revolt. He puts the posthumous trial of Le Van Duyet and the razing of his tomb at the end of the revolt. The revolutionaries soon brought the whole of Cochinchina under their control. Le Van Khoi proposed to dethrone Minh Mang and to proclaim a son of Prince Canh as emperor. He looked for assistance where he could find it. Khoi invited Father Marchand, who had been in hiding since the outbreak of the persecution of the Christians, to come and stay with him in the citadel of Saigon. The idea behind this move was to win over the Christianized segment of the population to his revolt. Khoi furthermore persuaded the king of Siam to send an army to his support. But the Siamese army was defeated by Minh Mang's generals, Cochinchina was reoccupied, and Khoi was beleaguered in the fortress of Saigon. He died during the siege (December, 1834), possibly poisoned by his enemies. Saigon was captured by Minh Mang in September, 1835. The four remaining leaders of the revolt, Khoi's seven-year-old son, and Father Marchand were cruelly executed. (About Marchand, see note 48.) About the Khoi rebellion, see the detailed and politically penetrating account of Gaultier, *op. cit.*, pp. 107-173, who, like Le Thanh Khoi, stresses the regional element in the uprising, the alienation between the South (Cochinchina) and the North (Annam and Tongking). Unfortunately the fascinating rendition of the events is distorted by a strange inconsistency of the author, who wants to be both an anti-Catholic defender of the Confucianist Minh Mang and a pro-French supporter of Cochinchinese separatism.

47. François-Isidore Gagelin worked as a missionary in Vietnam from November, 1821, to his death. After the edict of persecution was published, he first thought of hiding in the mountains, but finally decided that this would compromise the persons he had converted to Christianity. He gave himself up to the authorities in July, 1833, was brought to Hué, was sentenced to death by strangulation for having illegally preached the gospel, and was executed. His execution is described in a report by Father François Jaccard, who himself died a martyr's death on September 21, 1838. See Taboulet, *op. cit.*, pp. 329f.; J. B. S. Jaquenet, *La vie de l'abbé Gagelin*, Paris, 1850; Louis Crochet, *Vie du vénérable François Jaccard*, Paris, 1879, pp. 175-188.

48. It seems that Marchand had no active part in the Khoi rebellion.

According to Schreiner (*Abrégé de l'histoire d'Annam,* 2nd ed., Saigon, 1906), Khoi invited Marchand to join him in Saigon in order first to secure a rallying point for the Vietnamese Christians and later to use him as a councilor and intermediary to France. Marchand remained so passive in Saigon that he even refused to write letters to Christians in Vietnam in support of the uprising (Taboulet, *op. cit.,* p. 331). The captured leaders of the revolt, probably in the vain hope of saving their own skin, put all the blame for the revolution on Father Marchand. The death sentence was pronounced for *lèse-majesté.* Father Marchand was only thirty-two years old when he was cut to pieces by the executioner. Jacquenet, the biographer of Father Gagelin (see note 47), also wrote a monograph on Marchand (Paris, 1851). Le Than Khoi is of the opinion that Marchand aspired to a position with the rebel leader similar to that Pigneau de Béhaine had with Nguyen Anh, in the hope of creating a dissident Catholic kingdom in Cochinchina (*op. cit.,* p. 341f.), but he offers no proof for his statement.

49. All authors agree that Minh Mang's troops slaughtered everybody they found in the citadel, combatants as well as noncombatants. However, they disagree about the number of killed. According to Le Thanh Khoi, *op. cit.,* p. 341, 2,000 "rebels" were executed. Chassigneux, *op. cit.,* p. 374, gives their number as 1,200; Gosselin, *op. cit.,* p. 117, says 1,137. Taboulet, *op. cit.,* p. 331, says that 499 persons who had sought refuge in the city were put to death, among them 66 Christians. This figure seems to cover noncombatant refugees only, while the balance of the executed was made up of the remnants of Khoi's army. The prisoners were first forced to dig a big ditch; then they were killed and buried in the ditch. The French later gave the place of the massacre the name of "Plaine des Tombeaux" (Plain of Tombs).

Chapter VI

The Conquest
of French Indochina

1.

EXACTLY forty years elapsed between the reappearance
of France in the Far East, in 1817, and the decision by
the French government, in July, 1857, to organize a military expedition against Vietnam.

This decision, as well as the circumstances in which it was
taken and the actions and forces that brought it about, belonged until 1955 to that part of French colonial history considered forbidden knowledge.[1] Some of the archives have now
been opened, and the main actors at last have become known,
yet the forces and motives behind French military intervention
in Vietnam are today as difficult to interpret as they were while
many of the facts remained a well-kept political secret.

After contacts were resumed in the nineteenth century,
French policy toward Vietnam went through three distinctive
phases prior to planned military intervention. The first of these
phases lasted from 1817 to 1831. France started out by making
diplomatic efforts to obtain trading privileges and by trying to
persuade the government of Hué to enter into close political
relations with Paris. These efforts were entirely unsuccessful.
They were politely discouraged by Gia Long and firmly re-

jected by Minh Mang, whom neither diplomatic courtesy nor the lure of goods from France could sway in his anti-Western course. Even the last two French war companions of his father, Chaigneau and Vannier, were given to understand that they were no longer welcome. They left Vietnam in 1824.[2] Three French diplomatic efforts in 1825, 1827, and 1831, failed to change Minh Mang's mind.[3] Minh Mang also refused, for the third time in 1831, to accredit a French consul for Vietnam.[4] After this last setback the French abandoned their efforts to get into Vietnam by diplomatic and peaceful means.

During the second phase of her nineteenth-century relations with Vietnam, France showed little interest in, and pursued in fact no policy toward, her future colony. Apart from the presence of French missionaries, no relations at all, either official or private, existed between France and Vietnam during the following decade. A French warship came to Tourane in 1837 and another one in 1838, but they failed to renew contacts with either the Vietnamese authorities or the missionaries.[5]

The 1830's, however, were a more crucial period for the future of Franco-Vietnamese relations than any other ten years between the arrival of Alexander of Rhodes in 1625 and the storming of Tourane in 1858, which was the first act in the conquest of French Indochina. It was during the fateful 1830's that the anti-Christian policy of Minh Mang drove the missionaries to become spokesmen of French military intervention.

2.

If the missionaries and their supporters in France still abstained from proposing immediate military action, this was due to the fact that the forces of French aggression were far from ready by 1840. The last phase of French policy prior to planned military intervention, which was the phase of open and mounting hostility toward Vietnam, unfolded slowly and culminated in aggression only after almost twenty years. Its beginning should be dated from the year 1838, when a young naval officer by the name of Fourichon revived the idea of a military coup against Tourane. But Fourichon was listened to only nineteen years later, after he had become an admiral and a member of the study commission for Cochinchina that proposed the attack of 1858.

Two years after Fourichon, in 1840, another naval officer[6] made a similar proposal and persuaded some cabinet members to submit it to the government, but the minister of foreign affairs, Guizot, who directed French policy under Louis-Philippe from 1840 to 1848, was more interested in restoring France's position in Europe than in Asian expansion, for which he felt his country still lacked the necessary strength. Besides, he was afraid that the proposed action might damage the friendly relations with England on which his whole international policy was based.

But in spite of Guizot's caution, France was deeply involved in Asia only three years later, and in exactly the kind of trouble the Anglophile Guizot had foreseen and tried to avoid. When the English broke into China during the Opium War and took possession of Hong Kong in 1841, a new era of Western expansion in Asia commenced. The main powers of the West descended on China like vultures on a corpse.[7] Since all great European nations were establishing themselves in Asia, Guizot himself now argued, it was no longer appropriate for France to remain absent from this large part of the world. As early as 1841, he sent a mission to the Far East with instructions to explore the chances for trade with China; two years later his government decided "that a naval division be henceforth stationed in the seas of China and Japan, in order to protect, and if necessary to defend, our political and commercial interests in these regions."[8] A sizable French fleet, commanded by Admiral Cécille and Captain Charner, now sailed the Asian waters, where only individual French warships had sporadically appeared before.

The French fleet, which arrived in Macao in August, 1844, brought a strong diplomatic mission to China. It had orders to secure for France the same trading privileges that England had won at the conclusion of the Opium War through the Treaty of Nanking. This object the French accomplished in December, 1844, but Guizot's secret instructions called for more. He had been persuaded that France needed one or several places in the East that would give her the advantages England enjoyed in Singapore and Hong Kong, and Portugal and Spain in Macao and Manila. Acquire a suitable place, Guizot told Cécille and de Lagrené, who was the political head of the mission to China, but abstain from any action along the coast of Vietnam. His fear of a conflict with England if France tried to establish herself along the Indochinese coast inspired him to argue that the country was unhealthy and that a position on the mainland was also too difficult to defend.[9]

Guizot was obeyed, Vietnam was given another reprieve, and France temporarily was enriched instead by the acquisition of Basilan, an island between Borneo and the Philippines, which Cécille believed would become a strong point equal to Hong Kong. Spain, however, claimed that Basilan was a Philippine dependency, and Spanish protests forced the Paris government to relinquish what her enterprising naval commanders had acquired in a bold though apparently ill-advised move.[10]

After this incident Guizot was in no mood to listen to a new proposal by his frustrated naval commanders in the East, who wanted to repair the Basilan fiasco at the expense of Vietnam. A new project was recommended to Paris by Admiral Cécille, who had had his eyes fixed on the Indochinese coast and his heart set on a Vietnamese harbor ever since he arrived in the East in 1841. Let France try to get into Vietnam by endorsing the claims to the Vietnamese throne of the descendants of the Le dynasty, Cécille proposed. According to Cécille's informants, the supporters of a Le pretender were numerous in the North and ready to rise if a minimum of military assistance were promised to their leader. Once the Le dynasty was re-installed in the North, Cécille was assured by his missionary informants, France would immediately obtain a naval base and the missionaries at last be granted full freedom for prose-lytizing.

In the meantime, however, the navy had given Guizot the trouble he feared most: France clashed with England over the island of Tahiti, which had become French through the un-authorized actions of another admiral who disliked sailing the Eastern waters without purpose and aim.[11] After almost losing his position and trembling for weeks under an English threat of war, Guizot was able to save Tahiti by compensating Eng-land financially, but he was now more than ever determined to avoid another conflict with any of his European allies, and he firmly rejected Cécille's plan for establishing France on the Indochinese coast.

3.

Guizot's unyielding attitude in regard to Vietnam greatly infuriated the naval commanders in the Far East. Their pride as Frenchmen suffered whenever they had to take their ships to Singapore, Macao, Hong Kong, or Manila, instead of going to places where French officers in Asia might find it less difficult to feel at home. What was the point to their presence in the Far East, they asked, if they were not allowed to do for France what the Portuguese, Spanish, and English navies had done for their countries? They found out that the trade they were sup-posed to protect and defend hardly existed, and soon they became convinced that it would develop only if their own actions resulted in French territorial establishments and in-creased French prestige. Besides, they added, their pointless voyages were as costly for the state as it was to employ their ships for the enlargement of France's possessions.

These views of the grumbling naval commanders in the East were enthusiastically endorsed by only two groups of Frenchmen: the missionaries in Asia and their political supporters in France. The missionaries were almost the only Frenchmen whom the naval commanders met in the Far East. The officers' desire to do something with the means at their disposal would have led them to adopt the cause of the missionaries even if the plight of the missionaries had not touched them at all. The missionaries not only "constituted the only tangible aspect of national interest with which naval officers could concern themselves;"[12] they were also the only people who knew something about the East, including the Asian languages, which made them almost indispensable in all negotiations conducted by the diplomats and soldiers. Admiral Dupetit-Thouars, for example, had been well served in his conquest of Tahiti by two missionaries of the French Society of Mary, whose knowledge of the island supplied him with the military intelligence and whose alleged mistreatment gave him the pretext he needed to intervene.

In this political coalition of soldiers and priests, the missionaries were by no means only a passive party. In China, for instance, they succeeded in committing France to the protection of their aggressive and politically embarrassing activities, over which the French government had no control. When Guizot, after de Lagrené had completed his mission, made his first diplomatic appointment for China, he warned the envoy not to support missionary requests that would create difficulties between the two countries. But the influence of the missionaries, who were on the scene of action, misled most French diplomats to deviate from the policy of their government. Moreover, the orders of the government were constantly flouted by the naval commanders, in particular by Admiral Cécille, who meddled not only in China but actually made French policy during the 1840's both in Korea and Vietnam.

The feelings of the missionaries about official French policy were well expressed by the Jesuit Father Douai, who compared French action in the Far East with the behavior of "little dogs that bark from a distance but never bite."[13] The French missionaries who came to Asia after 1820 were as a rule politically aggressive men. Unlike those who worked in the East during the preceding thirty years and who had felt isolated from and ignored by their homeland, the new men were confident that increasing numbers of the French people admired their work and supported their efforts. French interest in the missions had indeed been growing ever since the beginning of the Catholic revival that marked the political life of France under the Restoration, the July Monarchy, and the regime of Napoleon III.[14] Minh Mang's persecution of the missionaries had aroused French Catholic opinion more than any other event outside of France.

From 1840 on, Catholic propaganda openly asked for French intervention in favor of the persecuted missionaries in Vietnam. The anticlerical Guizot consistently refused such intervention. But by 1843 public pressure had become too strong for Guizot to persist in his refusal. He authorized the naval commanders whom he dispatched in growing numbers to the East "to afford protection to French missionaries threatened with personal violence, if it could be done without involving the French flag in any altercation."[15]

4.

Captain Favin-Lévêque of the *Héroïne* had acted along these lines in Vietnam six months before Guizot had given his cautiously worded permission. On hearing of the plight of five

French missionaries whom Minh Mang's successor Thieu Tri held imprisoned in Hué, Favin-Lévêque sailed from Macao to Tourane, Vietnam's main harbor near Hué. Through skillful negotiations with the mandarins, he managed to obtain the release of his compatriots, who were allowed to leave Vietnam on board the *Héroïne*. They even received money and three suits from Thieu Tri, who also took the trouble to explain his action in a letter to the French captain. He had pardoned these men, he said, because when they arrived they had probably been ignorant of his laws forbidding missionaries to enter and preach in Vietnam.[16]

In May, 1845 Admiral Cécille, whose plot to subvert the Vietnamese regime had been thwarted by Guizot, heard of another French missionary in trouble. This was Monsignor Lefèbvre, whom the Vietnamese had sentenced to death but not executed. Cécille learned of Lefèbvre's predicament through Captain Percival of the U.S.S. *Constitution*, whose own somewhat clumsy attempt to save the Frenchman had failed.[17] Captain Fornier-Duplan of the *Alcmène,* whom Cécille dispatched to Tourane, received not only the unharmed Lefèbvre but also a load of presents for himself and his crew. Thieu Tri had obviously no desire to persecute the missionaries, but only to get rid of them and the threatening French warships as quickly as he could.[18] No missionaries had been executed since Minh Mang's last outburst of fury in 1838. Thieu Tri even played with the idea of sending his own ships on trading voyages to Europe, and many missionaries began to think that peace between them and the Vietnamese emperor was not too far off.[19]

However, the naval commanders and some of the missionaries were interested in peace only on their own unacceptable terms. Whatever prospects for an agreement with Thieu Tri existed after Monsignor Lefèbvre's release were ruined completely, and ruined forever, by the action of French warships in April, 1847, in the harbor of Tourane.

It was again Monsignor Lefèbvre who started the events that led to this first act of murderous French aggression against Vietnam. The bishop tried to re-enter Vietnam illegally in May, 1846. He was caught and once more sentenced to death, but again not executed. Admiral Cécille, who had lacked a pretext for intervention in Vietnam for almost two years, eagerly seized this as an occasion to dispatch two warships to Tourane, and to demand the free exercise of the Catholic faith in addition to the release of Monsignor Lefèbvre. The expedition was commanded by Captain Lapierre, who arrived in Tourane on the *Gloire* on March 23, 1847, shortly after the *Victorieuse* under Captain Rigault de Genouilly had reached Tourane. Neither of these men knew that Monsignor Lefèbvre had been released by the Victnamese and shipped to Singapore four weeks before their arrival. In order to force the local mandarins to accept Cécille's letter to the emperor,[20] Lapierre, in a surprise move, had the Vietnamese ships in the harbor stripped of their sails. After waiting two weeks for the emperor's answer, the French captains became angry. On April 15 four Vietnamese ships seemed to approach them in the harbor. Lapierre felt threatened and decided to shoot. In seventy minutes French guns had taken a hundred times more lives than all the Victnamese governments in two centuries of religious persecution.[21]

Without bothering further about Lefèbvre's fate, Lapierre and Genouilly left Tourane, also leaving all other missionaries at the mercy of the furious Vietnamese. The *Gloire* and the *Victorieuse* sailed to Macao, and from there north to Korea. Their orders from Cécille were to smuggle missionaries into the country and to get an answer from the government at Seoul to a previously delivered letter by Cécille, demanding freedom of action for the missionaries.[22] Before Lapierre and Genouilly had a chance to repeat their Tourane performance, they ran aground in shallow water near the Korean coast.

Lapierre and Genouilly escaped punishment for losing their ships and for their unauthorized action in Tourane only because influential missionary leaders pleaded for them in Paris with high personalities, including the king and the queen. Their main defender was Monsignor Forcade, whose presence on board the *Gloire,* it was believed, was one of the reasons for Lapierre's "energetic attitude" before Tourane.[23] For this bishop, Tourane was only a beginning, and should be followed by much firmer action very soon. Forcade claimed that even His Holiness the Pope "would not disapprove rigorous measures which France could employ against the Annamite king."[24] The warmongering missionary was joined by Admiral Cécille, who, after he returned from the East in 1847, demanded that France talk henceforth to Vietnam "only with guns" and see to it that Thieu Tri be given "a good successor."[25]

Thieu Tri died shortly after the attack on Tourane, his heart filled with a stronger hatred for the West and the missionaries than he had ever shown during his whole reign. He has been accused by French colonial historians of having revived Minh Mang's policy of persecution "with even greater rigor."[26] The fact remains, however, that no missionaries were executed during the seven years of Thieu Tri's rule. Although he regarded them as agents of a foreign power whose presence in Vietnam was against the laws of the country, Thieu Tri never refused to release any imprisoned missionaries if the French came to take them off his hands.

5.

The aggressive political attitude of the missionaries and naval commanders, which produced the slaughter of Tourane, reversed the Vietnamese drift toward moderation under Thieu Tri and destroyed the last chance for a reconciliation between the Catholic Church and the Nguyen regime. Thieu Tri's successor Tu Duc, who became emperor in 1848, saw no alternative to the policy of fighting the missionaries and the Vietnamese Catholics. The missionaries clamored for more warships to visit his harbors and exert pressure on Vietnam; they supplied the naval commanders with military and political intelligence; they acted as advisers on board the threatening and shooting vessels; and their leaders in France headed the campaign for open military intervention. All this Tu Duc and his mandarins knew. But he also knew that Vietnamese Catholics had been implicated in the Southern uprising against Minh Mang and had conspired in the North with the Le pretender whom Admiral Cécille had wanted in place of Thieu Tri. Soon Tu Duc himself had on his hands a Christian-supported Northern rebellion, which aimed at putting a dissatisfied brother of his on the throne.

The new emperor, who was said to have been of a "mild and restrained" disposition,[27] decided to frighten the missionaries out of Vietnam and to terrorize the Vietnamese Catholics into submission. After he had put down the Northern rebellion in 1851, he had a French missionary executed; a year later, another one suffered the same fate.[28] Against the Vietnamese Catholics Tu Duc issued two edicts, in 1848 and in 1851. These would have destroyed the Catholic community if the mandarins had enforced them systematically all over the country.[29]

There can be no doubt that both edicts were issued under the impact of news from France. In 1848 it was the revolutionary overthrow of the July Monarchy; in 1851, the conflict between Parliament and Louis-Napoleon before his *coup d'état*, from which Tu Duc's alert mandarins concluded that France would be unable to interfere with their attempt to liquidate Christianity in Vietnam. Tu Duc's conscience in persecuting the Christians was probably as good as that of the "mild and restrained" Marcus Aurelius, who had tried the same in Rome. He certainly felt as justified in his action as any modern democratic statesman who approves of the execution of spies and

335

the forceful suppression of subversive political movements. Nothing illustrated the nature of his struggle better than the experience of Monsignor Retord, who was thrown into prison in the North during these harrowing years. He too was in danger of being executed, but by using his dialectical powers he succeeded in convincing the mandarins that as a missionary he had absolutely no interest in politics. Thereupon they let him go free, only to be sorry forever after. Monsignor Retord, it seems, was the only missionary able to talk himself out of prison. Many others were freed too, but only against substantial sums of money that went into the pockets of the mandarins.

While the mandarins did their mischievous work, the missionaries were not idle either. There were about forty of them in Vietnam at this time, mostly in hiding but secretly continuing their work. Life became considerably harder for them as a consequence of the Tourane attack in 1847. For a long time afterward, no French vessels visited Vietnam.[30] This caused a great deal of bitterness in the ranks of the French missionaries against their own country during these years. However, these were also the years during which France lived through the change from the anticlerical regime of Louis-Philippe and Guizot to the pro-Catholic Second Empire of Napoleon III.[31] One consequence of this change was that Paris after 1852 was ready to listen not only to the complaints of the missionaries but also to their proposals.

From 1851 on, these complaints became louder and the proposals for action more numerous and more urgent every year. The "unpolitical" Monsignor Retord, who had wanted no other than a strictly diplomatic intervention in 1848, now asked for negotiations backed up by military force. He would agree to a treaty with Vietnam only if France were given the right to occupy a portion of Vietnamese territory.[32] In 1852 eight missionary bishops stationed in the Far East appealed directly to Louis-Napoleon to send a strong fleet under an

336

energetic commander into Asian waters, in order to dispel the false idea that France was too weak to come to the aid of her persecuted missionaries. Peaceful and conciliatory tactics, the bishops reasoned, were no longer of any use.

6.

During the same year, 1852, missionary propaganda scored a major success by converting the key French diplomat in the Far East to its interventionist views. This was Count Bourboulon, the first duly accredited envoy of the new French regime to China. Bourboulon, who claimed to be a disciple of Fourier and liked to advertise his atheist and socialist opinions, arrived at his post in October, 1851. Less than a year later he was the main French advocate of military intervention against Korea and Vietnam. He was also the first man to use—apparently with real conviction—the new language that was to become so popular among the French profiteers, jailers, and executioners in Indochina during the subsequent thirty years of conquest and "pacification." Vigorous action against these countries, the Count said, would be "in the interest of all humanity," and all "civilized nations" would applaud if France decided to punish these "wretched and insolent barbarians." [33] In Vietnam, France must insist on religious tolerance for Christians, or at least on "complete security for French and Spanish missionaries"; as reparation for the blood of the missionaries shed over thirty years, Vietnam should cede the port of Tourane to France. If the Vietnamese should decline to accept these "reasonable conditions," which Bourboulon volunteered to present to them in "peaceful negotiations," the French navy should take possession of Tourane and the surrounding territory. In this manner, the Count affirmed, "relations of friendship and commerce" between France and Vietnam could be established "on a new liberal and equitable basis." [34]

Bourboulon's counselors and main sources of information were the procurator of the Society of Foreign Missions in Hong Kong, Father Libois, and a Lazarist missionary from southern China by the name of Huc. Neither of these men had ever seen Vietnam, but the busy Monsignor Retord supplied them so well with reports and opinions that they had no compunction in expressing even a military judgment about the harbor defenses of Tourane.

Bourboulon's suggestions were well received in Paris. The early 1850's were the years of Louis-Napoleon's honeymoon with the Catholic Church. France had secured freedom of action for the Catholic missions in China,[35] and France was being praised by Catholic leaders all over the world as the first champion of the missionary cause. Praise, of course, was coupled with admonitions for more energetic action and with prospects of rewards for France that were by no means limited to the spiritual realm. "Catholic influence in the Far East," the missionaries assured Napoleon III, "is and will always be there the measure of French influence."[36] Missionaries trust more in God than in men, they wrote to the French government from Vietnam; "however, as God also uses men to accomplish His designs, we would be proud to have Him use the arm of France, rather than that of any other nation, to bring us better days . . ." [37]

Louis-Napoleon was only too willing to use "the arm of France" wherever and whenever he saw an opportunity to strengthen his power and prestige through military exploits.[38] But in 1852 he was preoccupied with the consolidation of his newly established dictatorial regime, and in 1853 with his preparations for the Crimean War, which started in the following spring and dashed the hopes of the missionaries for French intervention in Vietnam for another three years.[39]

During this whole period the struggle between Tu Duc and the missionaries continued without pause. The year 1855 brought new anti-Christian measures, as well as a new missionary attempt to get French support for a rebellion in favor of a descendant of the Le who had adopted the Catholic faith. With remarkable fortitude, the missionaries became almost silent about their own plight, stressing instead, like Alexander of Rhodes two hundred years earlier, the numerous advantages France would gain if she established herself in Vietnam. The prospect of an uprising in favor of the Le was now presented as a "useful diversion" in case France should intervene, and the taking of Tourane no longer demanded as necessary for the continued protection of the missionaries; possession of Tourane was now a condition of "profitable commerce" and a device to get at the "unexploited riches of Cochinchina and Tonkin." [40]

The disappointment of the missionaries was great, and their anger even greater, when French intervention, after the Crimean War was over, led only to a repetition of the unfortunate Tourane attack of 1847. In M. de Montigny Paris had appointed an envoy devoted to the missionary cause.[41] The list of demands he was to submit to the government at Hué was a composite of all the proposals the missionaries ever had made. Several well-gunned warships were ordered to Tourane to help Montigny convince the Vietnamese of the seriousness of his intentions. But political and military action were badly coordinated. The first ship to arrive in Tourane, in September, 1856, was the *Catinat*. It brought a letter from Montigny, who was himself delayed in Cambodia; but the mandarins as usual refused to accept and forward the letter to Hué. Afraid of a Vietnamese attack on his ship while he was waiting for Montigny, the captain of the *Catinat*, after bombarding the harbor defenses, landed a detachment of marines in order to destroy the Vietnamese guns. A second French ship, the *Capricieuse*,

arrived in October, but the vessel with Montigny reached
Tourane only in January, 1857, after the *Catinat* had already
left for China in compliance with previous orders.

Montigny's requests for direct contact with the court of
Hué were coldly rejected. If he wanted peace, the mandarins
told him, keep the peace; if he wanted war, let him fight. As
he lacked both the means and the authority for the use of
force, the French envoy had no choice but to discontinue his
fruitless endeavors. After threatening punitive action by France
if religious persecution did not stop, Montigny left Tourane
on February 7, 1857.

7.

What the missionaries thought about the failure of the
Montigny mission was drastically expressed by Monsignor
Retord. "Our brave compatriots," he wrote, "have left us helplessly in the claws of the tiger, after exciting him properly
against us. . . . They came without having been called by us,
and they leave after compromising us. They started out with
an act of provocation and ended up with an act of coward-
ice." [42] A little later, in May, 1857, another missionary advised
Napoleon III publicly not to waste French money by stationing
ships in the East which, "as some naïve people say," are sent
to protect the missionaries. "Fine protection!" the angry priest
exclaimed. And, carried away by a zeal that could hardly be
called very Christian, he added, "Let them come and bash in
Tu Duc's head! Of words and red tape we have had enough!" [43]

But if the French missionaries, as Monsignor Retord put
it, were losing patience with their government because its half-
hearted measures had only increased their sufferings, this did
not diminish the ardor with which they fought for an interventionist policy based on force. Nor did they change the tactics
they had recently adopted. Monsignor Retord spoke now in

specific terms of the riches to be found in Vietnam, saying that Tongking had gold, silver, copper, coal, and timber. Through Count Bourboulon, whom the missionaries untiringly prodded to demand forceful action, Retord also transmitted to Paris new information of military value about the Vietnamese coast, and in particular about the defenses of Hué.[44] On October 12, 1857, Bourboulon was able to give Napoleon the good news that the Spanish were ready to support an expedition against Vietnam with a well-disciplined army of Catholic Filipinos.

The missionary efforts of more than thirty years indeed reached their climax between January and December, 1857. Two of the keenest advocates of force, the Lazarist Father Huc from China and Monsignor Pellerin from Vietnam, came to Paris in hopes of achieving through personal intercession what their pounds of memoranda had so far failed to bring about. Huc, who was received by Napoleon in January, assured the Emperor in an enthusiastic paper that the occupation of Cochinchina was "the easiest thing in the world," while the "results would be immense." The Vietnamese people, he prophesied, would receive the French "as liberators and bene-factors," and it would take "only a short time to make them all Catholics and devoted to France."[45]

More circumspect than Father Huc was Monsignor Pellerin. This bishop had suffered much in Vietnam and barely had been able to save his life by boarding one of the French ships in Tourane harbor in November, 1856. His reports now nourished the campaign that the Catholic press waged for immediate French action. He also preached movingly in the churches of Paris about the struggle of the Vietnamese Christians and the duty of France to come to their aid. In July he was received by Napoleon, whom he saw again in December after a trip to Rome, where the bishop had sought the Pope's blessing for French action against Vietnam—the blessing of God for Napoleon and his dynasty Pellerin already had promised the Emperor in July.[46]

8.

When Monsignor Pellerin returned from his audience with Napoleon in July, 1857, he was a very pleased but slightly astonished man: the Emperor had "granted more to him than he had demanded." [47] The bishop and his associates were indeed unaware of the fact that Louis-Napoleon had already made up his mind to intervene in Vietnam. He had his cabinet informed of his decision some time before July 16.[48] The missionaries continued their campaign vigorously during the second half of the year 1857, but from the perspective of today they appear like men trying to break through a door that was no longer locked.

How did France's decision to invade Vietnam come about? Had missionary propaganda and Catholic political pressure suddenly become too strong for Napoleon III, whose popular support depended largely on the approval of his regime by the Catholic Church? Only a few months before July, the missionaries' prospects of an early success still looked quite poor. Count Walewski, Napoleon's minister of foreign affairs, angrily rejected Father Huc's project for the occupation of a few Vietnamese ports, "to which France, according to the Treaty of 1787, has an incontestable right." [49] A report of the Foreign Ministry to the Emperor, dated March 20, maintained that there was no utility in military action against Vietnam, nor any necessity for it. The whole project was called inadmissible from the point of view of the existing treaties, and contrary to international right. Besides, "we have a sufficiently rough and complicated task in Algeria," and should not increase troubles and expenses by undertaking a "hazardous enterprise" in the Far East.[50] Four months later, however, Walewski had completely changed his mind. Now he endorsed a document that described military intervention in Vietnam as easy and inexpensive, French rights as sufficient to justify the use of force, and the project altogether as "honorable for our policy, useful for religion and favorable for the commerce and the general interest of the country." [51]

Walewski's reversal of opinion was no doubt primarily due to the Emperor's personal decision to intervene in Vietnam. But between March and July, 1857, the Minister of Foreign Affairs had also received a very intensive political education. The work of a "Commission on Cochinchina" had shown to the leaders of France that a drastic change in her Far Eastern policies was overdue: France had to enter the race for Asian possessions or become a European power of second rank.

By emphasizing the commercial advantages of an aggressive policy toward Vietnam, missionary proposals had largely anticipated the persuasive findings of the Commission on Cochinchina. To be sure, the economic, political, and military experts who deliberated the Indochinese problem in May, 1857 were not indifferent to the interests of religion, nor were they free from the motives of national pride and military prestige. But these interests and motives had been strong before 1857 too, without producing a French Far Eastern policy based on military intervention. Missionary and nationalistic propaganda had created the climate for such action, but planned military action was undertaken only after French economic interests in Far Eastern expansion had come into play.

Conditions in France for imperialist adventures in Asia rather suddenly became ripe through the economic upsurge of the 1850's.[52] France's rapid economic development after 1850 produced the need for overseas markets, strengthened the desire for a larger French share of Asian territories conquered by the West, and also supplied the French government at last with the means, hitherto lacking, for the execution of such a policy. The Commission on Cochinchina summed up these factors as "the force of circumstances" that "pushes the nations of the West to expand toward the Far East." "Are we going to be the only ones without possessions in the East, where the English, the Dutch, the Spanish, and even the Russians are building up their positions?"[53] By 1857, the answer of any French government to such a question could only be *No*. On November 25, 1857, the fleet in the Far East was instructed to take Tourane. The orders given to its commander were unequivocal: he was to establish himself there solidly through military force, without any further attempt to negotiate with the Vietnamese.[54]

9.

The execution of these orders was delayed by the Anglo-French action against China during the following winter[55] and by the allied negotiations for the treaties of Tientsin, which lasted until the end of June, 1858. Admiral Rigault de Genouilly, who was chosen to command the attack on Vietnam, was able to assemble his forces and set out for Tourane only during the month of August. He had fourteen vessels and twenty-five hundred men.[56] Behind the fifty guns of the flagship *Nemesis*, Monsignor Pellerin could be observed, smoking Manila cigars and arguing with the commander. The Bishop had succeeded in imposing himself on the Admiral as political and military adviser.

While the fleet was still on its way, officially inspired articles in the Paris press described Vietnam's abounding resources and splendid commercial possibilities—adding, however, that they could be exploited only if France became a naval power in the Far East by acquiring the site of Tourane.

The expedition reached the Bay of Tourane on August 31, 1858. The harbor defenses were attacked on September 1, and the occupation of the town was completed on the following day. Resistance was weak. There was, however, none of the popular rejoicing on the part of the Vietnamese, and certainly no sign of the Christian uprising predicted by missionary propaganda. Most of the Vietnamese simply disappeared. The invaders were thus deprived of the indigenous labor force with which they had hoped to transform Tourane into a vast and impregnable base for all further operations. Moreover, heat and disease almost immobilized the troops within a few days. Four weeks later the rains, which in the Center of Vietnam start in October, ruined all chances to reach the capital Hué by land. For an attack by water the French lacked the shallow-draft boats needed to go up from the ocean to Hué on the Perfumed River.

"The government has been deceived about the nature of this enterprise in Cochinchina," Admiral Genouilly wrote to Paris after he saw that he would make no progress beyond Tourane until the end of the local rainy season in April.[57] He angrily blamed Monsignor Pellerin for having misled the planners of the expedition; the Bishop in turn accused Genouilly of a lack of vigor in the execution of his military task. Pellerin demanded an attack in the North; the Christians, he said, were more numerous in Tongking than in any other part of Vietnam, and would rise against Tu Duc's mandarins as soon as the French fleet approached the Red River delta. The Admiral's answer was that he could not subordinate important strategic considerations to "more or less problematical religious interests."[58] Instead of pleasing the missionaries by going to Tongking, he decided to use the main part of his forces for an attempt to conquer Saigon.[59]

10.

Genouilly went to Saigon not only because he wanted to lay his hands on the rice that the South supplied for other parts of Vietnam and for the Vietnamese army. Saigon, he wrote to Paris later, "is destined to become the center of an immense commerce as soon as the port is opened for Europeans." Leaving only a small garrison at Tourane, Genouilly sailed south on February 2, 1859. By February 17, Saigon was in French hands. The foreign invaders were again not supported by the native Christians. Genouilly did not know whether the reason was fear of the mandarins or an inability of the Vietnamese to respond to "noble . . . and holy causes;" [61] but he was now convinced that no local support could be expected for any future military action undertaken by France.[62]

Although Spanish and French reinforcements had in the meantime increased the number of his soldiers to over three thousand, Genouilly was unable to extend his southern conquest beyond the city of Saigon. Soon he found that not even all of Saigon could be held. The end of the rainy season and news of incessant attacks by the Vietnamese forced the Admiral to come to the aid of his encircled garrison at Tourane. Leaving only part of his army in a strong and well-supplied position at Saigon, Genouilly returned to Tourane in April, 1859. What the rains had prevented him from doing in the autumn he hoped to achieve during the dry months of spring.

Tourane, however, turned out to be as miserable a place for the French soldiers in spring and summer as it had been in fall and winter. For every one killed in action against the Vietnamese, at least twenty died of tropical diseases. In June a cholera epidemic killed over two hundred in less than three weeks. In July typhus broke out. An average of one hundred soldiers per month died from disease between May and December. While cholera and typhus reduced the numbers and the fighting power of the invader at an alarming rate, Vietnamese resistance grew stronger from month to month. In spite of the arrival of another thousand soldiers from France, Genouilly recognized that he would not be able to extend his foothold with the troops at his disposal, let alone take action that would force the Vietnamese emperor on his knees.[63] His hopes for more substantial reinforcements from France had vanished completely when he had learned of Napoleon's wanton declaration of war against Austria in May, 1859.[64] Unable either to defeat the Vietnamese or to make them accept his demands in negotiations, the embittered and discouraged Admiral asked to be relieved of his command.[65]

Genouilly's successor, Admiral Page, arrived in Tourane on October 19, 1859. He could not help seeing that the only territory firmly occupied by the French after a year of fighting was the cemetery of the many soldiers who had died of disease. Page's efforts to obtain from the Vietnamese through negotiations what military action had failed to produce remained as unsuccessful as those of Genouilly, although Paris had in the meantime decided to drop the demand for territorial concessions. Tourane, it became clear, had to be abandoned. The first steps for an orderly evacuation of all troops and supplies were taken in February, 1860. Several weeks later, on March 22, the last French soldiers left the harbor.

11.

During the year 1860 France made no progress at all in Vietnam. French military strength in the Far East was absorbed in a new Anglo-French attack on China,[66] where Admiral Page's forces were sent after the evacuation of Tourane. The isolated garrison at Saigon under Captain Jaureguiberry[67] was able to hold out, and even managed to keep the port of Saigon open for ships from Europe,[68] but Vietnamese countermeasures made its position more precarious with every month that went by. Unless France intended to resume her policy of military intervention on a larger scale within a very short time, the effort to hang on to Saigon would turn out to have been merely a waste of lives and money.

After the Tourane fiasco, and while the Far Eastern fleet was still tied down in Chinese waters, the struggle for Vietnam shifted back to Paris, where it soon became more lively than it had been during the crucial years before the attack. Disappointed by the results of Genouilly's expedition, Napoleon himself was again undecided as to the policy he should pursue toward Vietnam. Missionary propaganda had become more restrained, and its effect on the Emperor considerably weaker, since events had shown that the Vietnamese Catholics would not rise in support of a foreign invasion and Tu Duc's empire would not fall apart because French troops landed on a Vietnamese shore. But even without the subdued voices of the missionaries, the chorus demanding a new military effort against Vietnam was now bigger and louder than in 1857. While France was failing in Cochinchina, these voices kept repeating, the English were gaining the upper hand in both Burma and China. If France should withdraw from Saigon instead of enlarging her foothold, Genouilly predicted, the English would very soon move into Vietnam. He and his fellow crusaders even began to speak accusingly of all the "French blood" that was being spent, apparently in vain, to preserve Saigon, knowing quite well that eighty per cent of the French troops under Jaureguiberry were Senegalese and Algerians.

When the outcome of the Anglo-French action in China in 1860 showed England again way ahead of France, the party in favor of going into Vietnam made many new converts. There were now more people who applauded Genouilly for his decision to take Saigon, and who found fault with the attack on Vietnam only because the forces employed had been too weak. A new crop of angry generals, worried politicians, and frustrated navy men protested a Far Eastern policy that made France a mere "satellite" of England. Behind them there was a growing number of merchants and manufacturers interested in overseas markets. There were also the many young officers longing for action and adventure in exotic lands. And there appeared in France, ahead of all other European countries, a new breed of nationalist intellectuals, torn between the use of sword and pen, who tried to convince themselves of their own superiority by proclaiming a new kind of "mission":

it was the task of France, more than that of any other nation, they aggressively asserted, to civilize the backward peoples of the world. Let her not imitate the greedy and philistine British, who tried to conquer the whole world for the mere love of money! Let France demonstrate her generosity by fulfilling the greatest of all her duties toward mankind, which was to educate and to guide the destinies of the black and yellow races.[69]

This rationalization had a tremendous effect on French thinking and attitudes in regard to Vietnam.[70] Its impact was one of the reasons why the party of aggressive imperialism grew strong enough to sway Napoleon once more. It subsequently forced every French government, reluctant or even antagonistic, to follow an interventionist policy in Indochina until the arduous task of conquering Vietnam was accomplished with the occupation of Tongking and Annam in 1883.

12.

The party of aggressive imperialism gained a decisive victory when one of its most vocal spokesmen, Chasseloup-Laubat, was made minister of marine and the colonies. Under his leadership the government decided to launch the unhinged operation against Vietnam a second time. As soon as the new peace treaties with China were signed in October, 1860, Admiral Charner, the commander of all French forces in the Far East, was ordered to prepare the new expedition. He was to go to Saigon and continue the action Genouilly had been forced to interrupt in spring 1859.

On February 7, 1861, Charner started to fight his way up the Donnai River to join the Saigon garrison of some eight hundred troops. The new expedition consisted of seventy vessels and thirty-five hundred men. Chasseloup-Laubat saw to it that Charner was soon reinforced with further contingents from China. Vietnamese army resistance was broken in a few murderous battles. By the end of June the French held the main points of three provinces around Saigon between the ocean and the Cambodian border. On July 1, 1861, Charner announced to the world that Saigon had become French.

In the eyes of the French, the Vietnamese should now have learned their lesson. The commanders in Saigon, as well as the agitators in Paris, believed that the emperor of Vietnam, in order to restore peace in his mutilated country, would now eagerly accept the terms he was offered by Charner for a treaty between Vietnam and France. Tu Duc, however, was not yet ready to relinquish three of his richest provinces for a mere promise by France to discontinue her one-sided acts of war. He knew that disease was again rampant in the French army and that Paris was becoming unhappy over the cost and the length of the operation in Vietnam. There was also hope at the court of Hué that guerilla attacks against the invaders would increase. The refusal of the local mandarins to collaborate with the French authorities, it was thought, would prevent the establishment of a functioning French administration and add to Charner's difficulties. If they held out a little longer, the mandarins in favor of resistance argued, the French would become discouraged, decide that the whole enterprise was a mistake, and go home.

When Charner was replaced by Admiral Bonard in November, 1861, these hopes were quickly drowned in new rivers of Vietnamese blood. Through indiscriminate slaughter, Bonard succeeded in suppressing all resistance in the province of Bien Hoa, east and northeast of Saigon, and in extending French control of the Mekong delta to the west. He penetrated into the province of Vinh Long beyond Mytho, but by April, 1862, the French had once more spent their offensive power, and their undermanned and widely separated positions again became targets of Vietnamese guerilla attacks. Under these circumstances, Bonard was just as eager as his predecessor to

350

obtain through negotiations what military action alone seemed unable to achieve—but definitely less hopeful.

To everybody's surprise, delegates from Hué appeared in Saigon with peace proposals before Bonard had acquainted Tu Duc with the whole list of French demands. On June 6, 1862, a treaty was signed in Saigon that would have filled the hearts of Dupleix, Poivre, and Pigneau with joy. It left France in possession of the three provinces adjacent to Saigon and of the long-coveted island of Poulo Condore; it opened three Vietnamese ports for trade with the West; it granted to the missionaries freedom of action, and to French warships free passage up the Mekong to the Cambodian border; it forbade Vietnam to cede any part of her territory to another power without the consent of France; and for the trouble Tu Duc had caused the French by opposing their invasion of his country he had to agree to pay a war indemnity of four million piasters.

13.

What were the reasons that prompted Tu Duc to ask Bonard for peace and to buy it at such an exorbitant price? One was undoubtedly the loss of the rice that Hué had been getting from the South before Saigon had fallen into French hands. Tu Duc's ability to raise and dispatch sizable armies against the invaders was considerably reduced by this loss. Another reason why Hué accepted the French terms was the delusion that a gain of time was necessarily also a gain for Vietnam. The climate and disease would weaken the French, and the growing resistance of the Vietnamese people would break their aggressive spirit. The enterprise would turn out to be much more costly than Paris had expected. Once this was clear, the elements opposed to the "Cochinchina adventure" would persuade Napoleon to drop the project altogether.

This reasoning, although by no means unrealistic, would have made a great deal more sense if Tu Duc had mobilized his country's entire resources and called on his people for an all-out war against the French instead of suing for peace. This, however, the troubled emperor of Vietnam was in no position to do. The country's resources were undeveloped, and of its insufficient economic wealth, much was wasted by mismanagement and corruption. The abuses of the mandarins and their refusal to promote economic progress had re-created the conditions of general misery from which the Tay Son revolution had derived its drive and force ninety years earlier. Absolute power and unchangeable routine had made most of Tu Duc's mandarins arrogant and inefficient. By being lazy as helpers and busy as thieves, they had created walls of hatred and indifference between the monarchy and the masses of the peasants, who had always been the monarchy's only real source of strength. After decades of isolation from the world and of estrangement from their own suffering people, the Nguyen dynasty lacked both the authority and the knowledge to successfully organize the country's defense.

Already the first landing of the French in Tourane had revealed a disgraceful incapacity on the part of Hué to take the appropriate military measures. No serious efforts were made to supply the Vietnamese soldiers with weapons more adequate than their own for fighting a Western invader. But even without such weapons, an army of fifty thousand determined Vietnamese could easily have thrown the French into the sea. The small Vietnam of the thirteenth and fifteenth centuries had been able to meet foreign invasions with armies of several hundred thousand. With his vastly extended and much more populous empire, Tu Duc, although he had had a respite of two years to prepare himself for the second French attack, still lacked the army of one hundred thousand he needed to defeat Charner at Saigon in February, 1861.

This astonishing military weakness was not the only proof

352

that the Nguyen dynasty was in a state of decline. Aside from its lack of ability for the organizational tasks of the hour, the dynasty was obviously without the moral authority to arouse in its people the will to resist the foreign intruder at any cost. Although the enemy was already on Vietnamese soil, the people were concerned only with the problems of personal survival, to which the immediate answer was to get out of the way of the French. The peasants had every reason to fear and hate the shouting and shooting intruders,[71] but they hated the mandarins hardly less, and their condition was such as to preclude the idea that even these bearded, odd-looking, and apparently always ill-tempered strangers could add to the misery of their existence. To be sure, the peasants themselves left no written evidence of the hatred they nourished against the mandarins and their deteriorating social and political order;[72] the history of the period was written either by the mandarins or by French missionaries and the highly biased conquerors and colonial administrators.[73] But the people's indifference during the first critical years of French military action, and their unwillingness to risk their lives in order to save the country, condemned the existing regime more forcefully than all the verbal expressions of grief and dissatisfaction by the few intellectuals who had discovered what was wrong with Vietnam.[74] The army had fought well enough in a number of bitter encounters, but of the spirit that had enabled Vietnam to defeat the more powerful Chinese on so many previous occasions not a trace could be found, either in the villages or among Tu Duc's ill-equipped troops.

Nor was this spirit very conspicuous at the imperial court. Tu Duc and his mandarins all over the country feared the Vietnamese people as much as the military power of the French. The success of the French had created a crisis that threatened to become deadly for the regime even if the invasion should somehow end in failure. While Tu Duc was trying to check the French in the South, his own subjects sapped his power with a rebellion in the North. Instead of rallying behind their emperor against the enemy from abroad, the Northern peasants, when given an opportunity, preferred to strike a blow at their enemies at home. Guided by missionaries who promised French military support for any insurrection, a new pretender of the old Le dynasty arose in spring 1862 to challenge Tu Duc's authority over the Red River valley. Although less than ten per cent of the Northern peasants were Christians, the rebellion quickly took on proportions that made Tu Duc almost lose his head. He and his mandarins knew what made this movement more dangerous than any previous rebellion since the Nguyen had become masters of the entire country: the misery of the people, which in the overpopulated North was like a chronic and incurable disease. But in order to justify their brutal acts of repression, they accused all the rebels, and in particular the Christian elements of the movement, of a treacherous desire to help the French.

To help the French, however, was much easier for the court of Hué than for the desperate peasants of the Red River valley. Tu Duc, out of fear of his own subjects, decided to use his full military power against the rebels in the North. This was the chief reason for his sudden willingness to talk peace with the French. Tu Duc agreed to the treaty of June, 1862, because he needed his every soldier to re-establish his shaken authority in the North. In order to reconquer the provinces he had lost to the rebels in Tongking, he decided to sacrifice the provinces he had lost to the French in Cochinchina. He made peace with his foreign enemies because he had to wage war against his fellow Vietnamese.

On the side of the French, political expediency led to a betrayal of similar proportions. The missionaries, delighted that one of their oldest predictions had at last come true, demanded French military intervention in favor of the Tongking rebels. If Tu Duc lost the North to a pro-Christian government in Hanoi, they assured Bonard, the Nguyen monarchy would

354

soon collapse in the rest of the country too. But Bonard, like Genouilly before him, put the interests of France above the interests of the Church. As long as Hué refused to accept his demands, the Admiral threatened to support the Tongking rebellion, but when Tu Duc agreed to let France have Saigon and three provinces between the ocean and the Cambodian border, Bonard gave Hué a free hand against his Christian brothers in the North.

By refusing to support the Catholics in Tongking,[75] whom the missionaries had incited to fight against Tu Duc, Bonard was by no means out of step with the policy of his superiors in Paris. For the French, "the missionary cause had long ceased to be a decisive consideration in determining governmental policy." [76] It was true that the treaty of June, 1862, promised freedom of religion for the Vietnamese Christians; but it also enabled Tu Duc to slaughter them by the thousands after he had mastered the insurrection in the North. Between 1858 and 1862, the missionaries lost many illusions about the motives and aims of French action in Indochina. But in spite of their disappointment, they would never admit in their public writings what they had learned during these years and what at least one prominent French historian expressed unequivocally some forty years later: that the missionaries had been only "the pretext for our intervention" and that they had supplied a "precious opportunity to establish ourselves in the Far East." [77]

14.

Ratification of the Saigon Treaty by the Vietnamese government was considerably delayed and for a while actually imperiled by events that frightened Bonard and made Tu Duc deeply regret the course he had chosen when the Tongking rebellion threatened his rule in the North. While the document was still on its way back to Saigon after ratification by Napoleon, the Vietnamese people surprised both their own government and the French authorities in the South with a series of powerful local insurrections.

After only a brief taste of French rule, the peasants began to lose their indifference and to support the many small armies of guerillas that sprang up all over the territories occupied by the French. The lieutenants and sergeants in whose hands Bonard had put all lower civil, military, and judiciary functions made excessive use of their unlimited power over the lives and possessions of the Vietnamese. Their many "acts of summary justice" [78] soon convinced a growing number of younger men that there was no greater danger of losing one's life by joining the guerillas than by staying in the towns and villages under French rule. During the month of December, 1862, the French were so strongly attacked at so many places at once that Bonard spoke of a general and concerted Vietnamese insurrection. [79]

On December 2, Tu Duc delivered the first installment of his war indemnity, thereby showing that he was still ready to fulfill the obligations of the June treaty. His people's growing resistance to the French, however, encouraged him shortly afterward to demand that the treaty be revised. He publicly condemned the attacks on the French, but he and his whole court secretly prayed for the success of the insurrection, and applied themselves to inventing new reasons why Vietnamese ratification of the Saigon Treaty had to be postponed.

Through "energetic action"—a euphemism for the indiscriminate slaughter of entire populations suspected of helping the rebels—the French succeeded in breaking this first wave of Vietnamese armed resistance, but only after their last African troops stationed in China were also transferred to Vietnam. Their position was further strengthened when the Tongking rebellion against Tu Duc flared up once more. By threatening again to support the rebels and to add the three southernmost provinces to the three France already held, Bonard finally extracted ratification of the treaty from Hué in April, 1863.

15.

The struggle for a French-controlled Cochinchina, however, was by no means over after the Treaty of Saigon was ratified by Vietnam. The task of making the South a secure possession of France was taken up by Admiral de la Grandière, who succeeded Bonard in May, 1863; it required another four years of military and diplomatic efforts against Vietnam resistance, during which time the proponents of French imperialism had to wage a determined campaign also against their numerous enemies and discouraged sympathizers at home.

The military difficulties of the French were due mainly to their methods of rule and their lack of restraint in organizing the country's exploitation. De la Grandière eventually mastered these difficulties, although he received little support from France during the crucial years of his rule.

More dangerous for a French-controlled Cochinchina than Vietnamese resistance were the political troubles of the imperialist faction in France. They had two main causes, one of which was Napoleon's lack of interest in Vietnam between 1863 and 1867. His ill-fated attempt to put a Catholic emperor on the Mexican throne[80] absorbed both his attention and most of the funds available for overseas adventures.[81] At this critical stage a move by the Vietnamese emperor became most embarrassing for the spokesmen of further conquests in Indochina: Tu Duc confounded Paris by an offer to cooperate with the French if they agreed to reduce their demands.

In spite of his victory over the Tongking rebels, Tu Duc's authority was rudely shaken by the military and political events of the five years since the French had first landed in Tourane.

It had become evident that the Nguyen monarchy was unable to protect the Vietnamese people against an invader from the West. In order to save their decadent regime, Tu Duc's high mandarins at the court and in Tongking had advised his shocking capitulation of June, 1862. The morale of Vietnam's ill-equipped army sank lower from year to year. The finances of the empire were shattered by the costs of war and civil war and by the loss of the rice from the South. The state of disintegration that the monarchy had reached became manifest in two disgraceful and desperate measures to replenish the empty treasury. The sale of opium, hitherto forbidden in Vietnam,[82] was granted to Chinese importers in Tongking against a heavy tax. But more demoralizing was the sale of public offices, to which a government of Vietnam had resorted only once in the more than one thousand years of independence.[83] For a sum of one to ten thousand *ligatures* anyone with money, whether qualified or not, could now buy from Hué the office of a mandarin of the three lower degrees.

By spring 1863, Tu Duc and his court realized that they would be able to check their enemies at home only if their regime ceased to be threatened from abroad. They knew of Napoleon's difficulties and sensed that he might be willing to stop French aggression in Vietnam if some of his objectives could be reached without war. Hué decided to explore the chances for a permanent peace with France. A large diplomatic mission was sent to Paris, headed by the man who had negotiated the Saigon Treaty of 1862.

Phan Than Giang, whose task was to obtain from Napoleon a revision of this treaty, was one of the oldest and probably the most capable of Vietnam's higher mandarins.[84] To get back the three provinces France had already conquered in the South was now Tu Duc's main desire. For this he was willing to pay a high price. Phan Than Giang was permitted to make concessions such as Tu Duc and his mandarins would have refused even to discuss before 1862. The old mandarin's strategy suc-

358

ceeded, but to be reinstated in his lost provinces, and for a French promise to abstain from further aggression, Tu Duc had to agree to a French protectorate over the whole of Cochinchina,[85] give up the cities of Saigon and Cholon as well as Cape St. Jacques at the mouth of the Saigon River, pay a yearly tribute to France, and open his country to French trade.

Tu Duc was far from delighted with the success of his mission to Paris, but he knew that he needed peace and a free hand against his domestic enemies if his dynasty were to survive. As his immediate aim was to save the monarchy, his gamble with the French would have made sense even if the force of circumstances had allowed him more freedom of action. It was indeed conceivable that the French as "protectors" of Cochinchina would no longer desire Tu Duc to be at the mercy of his domestic foes; to support his tottering regime might henceforth serve their interests better. Precisely because such consideration also prevailed among Napoleon's counselors, France agreed to the revision of the Saigon Treaty. A former aide of Bonard and advocate of a compromise solution in Vietnam, Lieutenant Aubaret, was sent to Hué, where a new treaty, based on Phan Than Giang's proposals in Paris, was actually signed in June, 1864.[86]

But Tu Duc and Napoleon, although still emperors of their respective countries, no longer fully determined the policies of France and Vietnam. In the eyes of the advocates of French territorial expansion in Asia, the revision of the Saigon Treaty was an unnecessary and dangerous retreat. The party that plotted the conquest of Indochina had become too strong to accept a policy of partial withdrawal from Vietnam without putting up a fight. Its most active and articulate leaders all held strategic positions, from which they were able to force Napoleon's not so firm hand. They were the men who controlled the navy, both at home and in the East. The navy had been the instrument, the captains and admirals the fighting pioneers of French imperialism in the Far East. Some of them had agitated and fought for a foothold in Vietnam for more than twenty-five years. What the navy had won in battle was now administered by its admirals, captains, and lieutenants stationed in Cochin-china. These men regarded the portion of Vietnam already in their hands only as a bridgehead for a much bigger campaign in Asia, one that was to give France "an empire as vast and flourishing as the English possessions in India."[87] From Chasseloup-Laubat, the Minister of Marine and Colonies, down to the twenty-five-year-old ensign Francis Garnier, who had fought under Charner in 1861 and become inspector of indigenous affairs in Saigon, the navy solidly opposed the main provisions of the new treaty. Lieutenants and admirals wrote erudite memoranda for the government and passionate pamphlets for the public,[88] showing not only that an isolated position like Saigon was untenable without the surrounding country; the three provinces must be retained, they added, because South Vietnam offered the only remaining chance for a French-dominated trade route into China. Garnier and others tried to show that by controlling the Mekong River up to the border of Yunnan, France could monopolize all trade with western China and thus more than make up for her weakness along the Chinese coast, where all the advantages were in the hands of the English.

The navy's struggle for retention of the occupied territories was supported by forces both old and new. The missionaries, although no longer enthusiastic over a military solution of their problem, were nevertheless outraged by the idea of a compromise with Tu Duc before their freedom of propaganda had been made invulnerable all over Vietnam. Their position was vigorously defended by the entire Catholic press. But the naval lobby besetting Napoleon was strengthened also by two types of men who had only recently begun to join the soldiers and preachers on the new colonial scene: the lovers of money, for whom the extent of French control over Vietnam determined the size of their gains, and the lovers of power, whose brief

360

PRINCE NGUYEN CANH
"The world of fashion [in Paris] made a pet of the young
prince."—D. G. E. HALL.

PHAN THANG GIANG (1796–1867)
His last demand of his sons was a promise never to collaborate
with the French.

enjoyment of unrestricted authority over the "natives" had made most of them thirsty for more. The partisans of French imperialist expansion in Asia knew what they wanted, which was something that could no longer be said of the fumbling Emperor whom they were determined to persuade. Before the year 1864 ended, the admirals and lieutenants found out that the use of ink was as important and effective for the conquest of Indochina as the spilling of blood. Napoleon gave in, the new agreement signed by his envoy Aubaret was brushed aside, and Tu Duc was warned not to go back on his word to fulfill the harsher obligations of the earlier Saigon Treaty.[89]

16.

After this triumph, the aggressive faction of French imperialism was both in an excellent position and in the right mood for driving ahead with new speed. By making Admiral de la Grandière governor of Cochinchina, the navy had given to a strong-willed and competent political schemer its most important overseas job: with secret maneuvers, the Admiral-Governor produced events designed to justify the various steps of his policy of progressive conquest. He had learned from his predecessors and the pioneers of conquest, beginning with Admiral Cécille, that the government in Paris was unequipped to deal with a naval policy of creating accomplished facts in the Far East. De la Grandière also knew better than most of his successors how to get around a distant government's inability to make up its mind. He took the steps he deemed necessary without waiting for orders or permission from Paris. French possessions were thus increased through unauthorized actions conceived in Saigon. Paris as a rule would condemn these actions, but rarely would renounce the gains they produced.

One of de la Grandière's first steps was to bully the king of Cambodia into accepting a French protectorate over his hapless country. With this action the new governor risked being repudiated by Napoleon[90] and getting involved in an armed conflict with Siam. The king of Siam effectively controlled Cambodian policy ever since Tu Duc had become too weak to continue the Vietnamese-Siamese policy of absorbing the country of the Khmer. De la Grandière claimed that France, through the Treaty of Saigon, had inherited the powers Vietnam possessed over Cambodia. But he was out of trouble with Paris only after Chasseloup-Laubat had persuaded Napoleon to ratify the Cambodian treaty in December, 1863. The danger of a conflict with Siam, however, was not removed until July, 1867, when Paris at last succeeded in obtaining Siamese consent to a French protectorate over Cambodia. The price was high, but it was not paid by France.. The new protectors forced Cambodia to cede her two old provinces of Battambang and Angkor to Siam.[91]

During the same summer, a heavier blow than any other since the attack on Tourane in 1858 was dealt by the French both to Vietnam and to Tu Duc's crumbling regime. De la Grandière occupied all of Cochinchina south and west of the three provinces already in French hands. The new invasion was secretly prepared in Saigon over many months, but at least one member of Napoleon's cabinet knew and approved of these preparations: Admiral Genouilly, who had started the conquest of the South in 1859 and had become minister of marine and colonies in January, 1867. De la Grandière attacked on June 17, 1867. One week later he could report to Paris that all of southern Cochinchina had become French. Resistance on the part of the Vietnamese authorities was weak. Their leader was the old Phan Than Giang, who had negotiated the Saigon Treaty, and whom Tu Duc, in a vain effort to restrain the French, had made viceroy of the three provinces that lay beyond the three already held by the French. The old man of peace, however, was accused by Saigon of sheltering anti-French rebels, and his alleged support of their guerilla activities served de la Grandière as a pretext for the annexation of all Vietnamese lands between the Mekong and the Gulf of Siam. Phan Than Giang preferred surrender to a struggle he considered hopeless, but he also recognized that his policy of appeasement of the French had failed. He committed suicide. His last demand of his sons was a promise never to collaborate with the French.

17.

These military and diplomatic actions in June and July, 1867, completed the conquest of the great Mekong delta by the French and made secure their protectorate over Cambodia, the little kingdom through which the unexplored Mekong River, believed to come from western China, flowed down into South Vietnam.

The annexation of the Vietnamese South had taken the French more than eight years—from February, 1859, when they made their first attack on Saigon, until June, 1867, the month they occupied the three provinces west of the Mekong. With this action the first phase of the conquest of French Indochina came to an end. Like gluttons who suffered from indigestion, the French in Vietnam, as if to recuperate from their latest exploit, abstained from further aggression for several years. Between 1867 and 1872 they made much progress in subduing Vietnamese resistance, in organizing a functioning administration under their firm control, and in getting the colony ready for large-scale economic exploitation. But all their attempts to obtain recognition from the Vietnamese emperor for their latest conquests met with failure.

Before aggression was resumed in 1873, a change of regime and of political temper occurred in France, which the spokesmen of imperialist action in Asia had every reason to bewail. Napoleon III foolishly maneuvered his country into the Franco-Prussian War of 1870; he lost his throne, and France Alsace-Lorraine, as a result of Bismarck's superior diplomacy and Prussia's greater military strength. Napoleon's fall led to a revolutionary uprising in Paris, the victory of the Paris Commune to a fearful civil war. France recovered quickly, but for a whole decade political dissension and military weakness obstructed a revival of interest in imperialist action in the East. Under President Thiers, all governmental efforts were directed toward ending the occupation and paying off the war indemnity Bismarck had imposed upon France. After the fall of Thiers in 1873, the passions of France's political leaders were engaged in a bitter struggle between republican and monarchist parties until 1879, when President MacMahon's retirement made it clear that the monarchist forces had lost out. During the whole decade nationalist sentiment was strong, but the action it favored was for the return of Alsace-Lorraine rather than military efforts to increase French colonial possessions.

The Frenchmen in Indochina, who for a variety of reasons desired that the policy of conquest be speedily resumed, had only one alternative to accepting the state of total inaction induced by these conditions in France: to proceed on their own; to act without, and if necessary also against, orders from Paris; to create, at the risk of being repudiated, accomplished facts that might compel their government into action. These tactics were not new, nor were they applied only during the decade of conquest: the administrators, military chiefs, and rich colonials in Indochina practiced them whenever France possessed a government indifferent to their aims. But no other instance revealed this aspect of French colonial policy better than the first attempt, undertaken by a handful of imperialists in 1873, to make Tongking a French possession, against the will and the orders of the government of France.

Both the scene and the main actors of this new drama

showed how Vietnam, as an object of imperialist policy, had evolved in the minds of the French during the fifteen years since the storming of Tourane. The French had come to Vietnam to protect the Christian religion, to open the country for trade, and to build for themselves a Far Eastern bastion of power to rival both Singapore and Hong Kong. Military and mercantile considerations soon made them neglect the interests of religion. Under Admiral Genouilly they began to concentrate their efforts on Saigon and the South, because the vast Mekong delta looked richer to them and easier to exploit than either the Center of Vietnam or the North. Under Bonard the cause of religion was openly betrayed. For the sake of order necessary for an undisturbed exploitation of the South, the emperor of Vietnam was offered peace and cooperation, which enabled him to beat down the Tongking rebellion and in the process take ruthless action against the Christians in the North. In the South, the rule of the French had brought to the missionaries full freedom of action, but the appeal of Christianity was greatly weakened by the policies and the behavior of the conquering Christians from abroad. Ten years of an intervention that had been justified by their plight gave to the missionaries and Vietnamese Catholics more cause for distress than satisfaction. The voice of the missionaries, therefore, was not very audible after 1870, when a new chorus of agitators demanded that France strengthen her hold on Indochina by moving into the North of Vietnam.

Before this revival of the interventionist spirit, some of the expectations the French had nourished after the taking of Cochinchina were recognized as false. One of the reasons for the strategy of concentrating on the South had been a geographical misconception concerning the Mekong River. A voyage of exploration, sponsored by the minister of marine and colonies, was organized by naval officers in Saigon under Admiral de la Grandière's governorship, in order to determine the course of the river and its assumed usability as a channel for trade with western China. The expedition left Saigon in June, 1866. It was led by Captain Doudart de Lagrée, with Francis Garnier as second in command. It brought back a wealth of geographical and other useful knowledge but robbed the builders of French Indochina of one of their greatest hopes. The mighty Mekong proved to be unsuitable for navigation. Besides, if the daring French explorers had continued their voyage to the river's forever receding source, they would not have reached some prosperous part of western China but probably would have perished in the barren wilderness of Tibet.[92]

However, the men who returned to Saigon via Hankow and Shanghai, after more than two years of incredible exertion, possessed more than one item of knowledge that lessened the shock of their negative report. And even in regard to the main object of their mission all hope was not lost. There was indeed a river connecting southwestern China with the Vietnamese coast, but it was in the North, which the French so far had neglected in favor of the South. As one member of the Mekong expedition put it in the *Revue des Deux Mondes* in 1869: "This way of communication searched for so fervently, this outlet through which we may one day expect the excess wealth of western China to flow into a French port—it is the Red River, not the Mekong." [93]

Both direction and purpose of the next phase of French aggression against Vietnam were thus fixed. For the men who had appointed themselves the builders of a French empire in Asia, the conquest of Tongking was now the most urgent task.

18.

Among the promoters of French rule over Tongking, three men dominated the scene when aggression against Vietnam was resumed in 1873. The first was Admiral Dupré, who had been governor of Cochinchina since 1871 and was an exponent of the old naval policy of expansion in the Far East. The second was Jean Dupuis, a French trader, imperialist, and explorer residing in Hankow, where he had made most of his money selling arms to the Chinese. The third was young Francis Garnier, probably the most intelligent, eloquent, and passionate champion of a French empire in Asia, and certainly the French "adventurer-imperialist *par excellence.*" [94]

The trader Dupuis and the soldier-writer Garnier first met in June, 1868, when the Mekong mission passed through Hankow on its long way back to Saigon. Encouraged by the mission's report about the course of the Red River, Dupuis, who had an arms contract with the governor of Yunnan, set out on a perilous journey to verify the theory that sizable vessels could go up into China on the Song Koi, as the Vietnamese call the Red River.[95] Warmly supported by the Yunnan authorities with official credentials, Dupuis thereupon undertook the no less perilous task of ascending the Red River without Vietnamese permission in order to deliver his cargo of heavy guns, rifles, and ammunitions to his Chinese protector and customer Marshal Ma. With skill, daring, and bribery, Dupuis overcame all obstacles between Haiphong and the Chinese border. He reached Yunnan city in March, 1873, returned to Hanoi with a cargo of tin in May, but was not permitted to take a huge cargo of salt on a second journey to Yunnan.[96] Not only was the export of salt forbidden by Vietnamese law; the Vietnamese authorities also made a belated attempt to enforce their old policy of keeping foreign shipping out of the Red River. Dupuis' next move surprised everyone who had not already recognized the adventurous merchant as a French *agent provocateur.* With his heavily armed company of 150 Asians and 25 Europeans, he occupied a section of Hanoi, hoisted the French flag, and appealed to Saigon for help..

In Saigon, Admiral Dupré had been waiting for this appeal ever since he had heard that Dupuis had reached Hanoi in December, 1872. The admiral and Dupuis had met earlier in

Paris, where the dynamic trader had vainly tried to enlist official support for his scheme to open the Red River for foreign trade through a combination of ruse and force.[97] Although driven by other and less personal motives, Admiral Dupré was as eager to go into Tongking as the impetuous trader-imperialist Dupuis. "To establish ourselves in the rich country bordering on China," Dupré wrote in spring 1873 with respect to Tongking, "is a question of life and death for the future of our rule in the Far East."[98]

The Admiral-Governor was not the only official in Saigon who adhered to this view. When Dupuis passed through Saigon in 1872 on his way back from France to China, General d'Arbaud, the acting governor during Dupré's absence, assured him that he would not be abandoned by the French in Saigon if his attempt to go up the Red River got him into trouble with the Vietnamese authorities. Dupré himself, after his return to Saigon, had generously responded to a request for financial assistance submitted to him by Dupuis. He had no scruples against using public funds for a private business venture, knowing quite well that both circumstances and personal motives made Dupuis' venture an eminently political act.

On hearing of Dupuis' brazen reaction against the Vietnamese order to leave Hanoi, Admiral Dupré cabled to Paris, on July 28, 1873, that Tongking had been opened by Dupuis, and if France did not occupy it immediately, China or some European power would deprive her of this unique route for trade. "Need no help," he added. "Can act with means at my disposal. Success assured."[99] In reply, Dupré received a warning from Paris not to create international complications for France through any action in Tongking.[100] But this warning reached Dupré only in September after he had taken the necessary measures to exploit the Hanoi incident for his own far-reaching aims in a manner designed to mislead both his government in Paris and the court of Hué.

By July, 1873, Dupré had long been persuaded that Tu

Duc's authority in the North was nearer the point of collapse than at any other time since the French first attacked Vietnam. Had the powerless emperor not been forced to abandon the Vietnamese South in order to crush his enemies in the North? But in spite of these dearly bought victories over his mutinous Northern subjects, Tu Duc was unable to master the social misery and the political chaos that drove his people into rebellion and enabled his enemies to rise again after each defeat. Economic stagnation and Hué's refusal to initiate or permit reforms had brought about conditions for which the old mandarinal order was without a cure, in the overcrowded North more than in any other part of Vietnam. As long as Tongking had too many hungry peasants and corrupt and inefficient mandarins, it would also have too many embittered Christians, rebellious mountain tribes, and plotting adherents of the old Le dynasty. For the North was also reserved, since 1866, the special plague of several groups of Chinese pirates, whom the Vietnamese authorities were unable to expel.[101] In order to restore some measure of public security and as a substitute for Vietnam's own shattered military force, the court of Hué decided to take one group of these pirates, the so-called Black Flags, into Vietnamese pay. Tu Duc no doubt knew that the Vietnamese people, in their condition of exceptional misery,[102] would hardly be willing to fight for the existing order if the French should decide to take action in the North.

The pirates in charge of security, however, contributed little to the military strength of the country and nothing at all to public welfare and civil peace. Of this the French Admiral in Saigon was no less aware than the Vietnamese emperor in Hué. Only a few weeks before Dupuis called upon Saigon to intervene in his favor, Dupré's desire to take Tongking had been aroused by one of his officers acquainted with conditions in the North. Captain Senez, who had just returned from a long "voyage of exploration," as missions of espionage were usually called, reported to the Admiral that a Vietnamese army capable of defending Tongking did simply not exist. With a few well-gunned vessels and several battalions of disciplined men, Senez prophetically asserted, the French could easily take Hanoi and control the whole Red River valley.[103]

From the beleaguered trader in Hanoi, Dupré had also received assurances that disaffected local elements were ready to support an armed intervention by the French. The Admiral, convinced that the time to get Tongking was now or never, thereupon made his first important decision in preparation of his coup. He sent for Francis Garnier, whom he had chosen to lead his projected expedition.

19.

The man whom Dupré thought better qualified than any other to execute his plan no longer held the positions on the colonial scene in which he had excelled at such an early age.[104] The young officer, administrator, explorer, and writer, after his return to Saigon as head of the Mekong expedition, had gone to Paris to prepare the expedition's enormous report for publication in two monumental and splendid volumes.[105] In 1872, when this work was completed, Garnier resigned from the navy and returned to China, apparently in a private capacity, as an explorer and to do business, thus playing out all the roles that a Frenchman of the nineteenth century could assume as a pioneer of imperialism in the Far East.

In July, 1873, Garnier was still a man of only thirty-four. He was then on his way back to Shanghai, after a voyage of three months through the interior of China.[106] In Shanghai he found Dupré's letter urging him to hasten to Saigon. Ready at all times to comply with a call to action, Garnier would probably have accepted Dupré's invitation even if he had known that it was his call to death.

370

Garnier's sensational but brief career as the hero of France's ill-seasoned first conquest of Tongking has been described too often to require elaboration,[107] but its customary French coloring needs to be supplemented with a few Vietnamese hues. This man who has been likened to Cortez and Pizarro came to Saigon, as a private citizen, in August, 1873. At the end of October, when he reached Hanoi, he was the most important French colonial leader in Asia. Admiral Dupré had entrusted him with full military and political powers, and Garnier was a man determined to use them as he saw fit.

Garnier moved into Hanoi with Tu Duc's hesitant blessing, which Dupré, on Garnier's advice, had extracted from the embarrassed emperor by holding out a promise to evict Dupuis.[108] But once in Hanoi, Garnier joined forces with Dupuis. Dupuis' armed men substantially increased Garnier's tiny army, which consisted of sixty white soldiers and the crews of three small ships.

As soon as Garnier had convinced himself of Tu Duc's calamitous local weakness, he dropped all attempts to obtain freedom of navigation on the Red River through negotiations with Tu Duc's Tonkingese mandarins. Instead, he decided to settle "the whole question of Tongking" by a bold use of force. Through his intentional arrogance and calculated brutal behavior, he created a mood of hostility on the part of the mandarins and a climate of tension in Hanoi, in which the idea that an understanding could be reached through negotiation quickly became absurd.

Having thus prepared the ground, Garnier arrogated to himself the role of Vietnamese lawmaker. On November 15, he issued a proclamation informing friend and foe that the Red River was henceforth open for international trade. He also ordered all Vietnamese customs tariffs to be suspended and to be replaced by rates more agreeable to Dupuis and other interested parties—in order, as Garnier had told his soldiers, "to safeguard the interests of civilization and France."

On November 20, after receiving small reinforcements from Saigon, Garnier bombarded and stormed the Hanoi citadel. In the manner of a Roman general at the head of a newly conquered province, he then began to issue proclamations to the people and orders to the local officials, in which he referred to himself as "the Great French Mandarin" who would punish high and low if his orders were not obeyed.

To make these orders effective the length of the whole Red River valley, Garnier began to employ his artillery against all important towns and fortified places between the ocean and Hanoi. After three weeks of terror, culminating in the capture of Nam Dinh, lower Tongking was under French military control[109] and the nucleus of a French administration established in all major cities. At this point, however, Garnier's career came abruptly to an end. On December 21, 1873, he was killed outside Hanoi, in an encounter during which he displayed both the courage through which he had risen and the contempt for the Oriental soldier that brought him to a sorry end.

Although Francis Garnier was only thirty-five when he met his fate, he was without question the most outstanding French leader in the long history of the struggle between France and Vietnam.[110]

20.

The death of Francis Garnier occurred at a moment when the forces opposed to Admiral Dupré's Tongking adventure were ready to throw their full weight against his aggressive course.

Dissatisfaction was strong in the French cabinet, which the Duc de Broglie had headed since the fall of Thiers in May, 1873. De Broglie had remained faithful to the anti-imperialist views that had inspired his opposition to the policies of Napoleon III. His position was strengthened by the cabinet's fear, which was shared by the Chamber of Deputies, of possible international complication and of expensive military action if the Vietnamese should decide to fight back. Cochinchina, in serious economic difficulties since 1872, was costly enough to administer and defend, and Paris was in no mood to weaken French rule in the South by trying to extend it over other parts of Vietnam.[111] Aroused by the events that led to the death of Garnier, the French cabinet decided to call the action off. On January 7, 1874, Paris informed Dupré in no uncertain terms that a prolonged occupation of Hanoi or any other part of Tongking was out of the question.[112]

Of equal importance for the eventual outcome of Dupré's Tongking adventure was the existence of an antiaggressive faction within his own administration and among influential French business circles in Saigon. The main interest of these circles was not a conquest of the North but a quicker economic development of the South. They strongly supported the many influential administrators who had a more lively concern for consolidating what was in their hands than for increasing their troubles by adding to France's Indochinese possessions. These people were no less devoted to the idea of a greater French Indochina than their more aggressive military colleagues. But they favored a gradual extension of French power and largely believed in success by peaceful means. Men like Luro[113] voiced their misgivings as soon as Garnier's actions revealed the Admiral's real intentions, hoping, however, that all would go well, and cautioning Garnier against letting the Vietnamese "feel the chains too much." [114]

A much firmer position was taken by M. Philastre, who was head of the colony's indigenous court administration. This officer sharply condemned the whole Tongking adventure. In a revealing letter addressed to Garnier himself, M. Philastre said: "Did you consider the shame that will fall on you and on us if what you are doing becomes known? You were sent to get rid of a businessman of doubtful reputation[115] and to work for an understanding with the Annamite officials; instead, you made common cause with this adventurer and fired, without warning, at people who had not attacked you and did not defend themselves."

Under the pressure of such local opposition, and knowing that Paris would let him down if anything went wrong, Dupré began early in December to prepare his road of political retreat. He and his predecessors back to Admiral de la Grandière had been trying for six years to replace the treaty of 1862 with one through which Hué would formally cede to France the three provinces occupied by de la Grandière in 1867. Dupré knew that both Paris and the antiaggressive faction in Saigon were as keen as he himself to obtain Vietnamese recognition of these conquests. In the manner of an unskilled political liar, the Admiral, who secretly still supported Garnier's tactics and aims, now presented his Tongking adventure as only a means of forcing Hué into signing the proposed new treaty.

For a while Dupré had better luck than he deserved. His vulnerable antagonist in Hué, who had invited disaster by asking Dupré to intervene against Dupuis in Hanoi, now invited Dupré to reopen the treaty negotiations. Instead of refusing to talk as long as a single French soldier remained in the Red River valley, the helpless emperor tried again to save the North by selling out the South.

The man whom Dupré chose as his envoy to Hué was no other than M. Philastre, the most outspoken opponent of aggressive action in Tongking at this time. Philastre left Saigon on December 7, with orders to proceed to Hanoi after fixing the terms of the new treaty. He interpreted his instructions, which were no doubt ambiguous, in the sense of his well-known political views. He regarded himself as empowered to liquidate the Tongking adventure, knowing well that without this there was no way of coming to terms with Tu Duc.

From Hué, where everything went exactly as he had ex-

ADMIRAL RIGAULT DE GENOUILLY (1807–1873)
He would not subordinate the interests of France to "more or
less problematical religious interests."

ADMIRAL BONARD (1805–1867)

ADMIRAL DUPRÉ (1813–1881)

FRANCIS GARNIER (1839–1873)
"The cause of French imperialism in Tongking suffered a serious
check in his death and acquired its most glorious martyr."
—JOHN T. CADY.

pected, Philastre set out for Hanoi with a definite purpose in mind. He arrived on December 24, eight days after the death of Garnier, whose actions he denounced as "odious aggression" and whose conquests he annulled in less than a week. He ordered all places occupied by French troops to be evacuated. This may not exactly have been what Admiral Dupré had instructed Philastre to do, but it was exactly what de Broglie in Paris wanted, whose orders reached Dupré before he received the news of M. Philastre's military coup-in-reverse.[116] The admiral's request to be relieved of his position as governor of Cochinchina was granted.

Fate, not quite as blind as usual, also caught up with Dupré's accomplice Dupuis. He had to leave Hanoi without his ships and with no hope of making the profits for which he had gone to such trouble.

The Tongking adventure of 1873 thus ended badly for the three men who had conceived and started it with great hopes for fame, promotion, and profits. One lost his position, one his money, and one his life. But France, although she failed to get Tongking, could hardly be called a loser in this affair. By putting the crimes of their aggressive copatriots to excellent use, the moderate faction of French colonialism at last gained Vietnamese recognition of all French conquests in the South.[117]

As was the case with the Saigon treaty of 1862, the main sufferers in this struggle between the decrepit mandarinal regime and the foreign aggressor were again the Vietnamese people, and in particular the Vietnamese Christians, in whose interest aggression allegedly was begun. According to some French historians,[118] twenty thousand Northern Christians were killed for "cooperation with the French" and seventy thousand were made homeless. The missionaries were once more driven into the camp of the foreign aggressor. Monsignor Puginier, their leader in Tongking, sided with the angry officers who opposed M. Philastre, and demanded that a "restrained and peaceful" occupation of Tongking be maintained.[119] His wish

375

was never fulfilled. When the occupation he demanded finally took place, it added to the rivers of Tongking one filled with blood, the only river flowing profusely also during the dry season, for more than ten years.

21.

The North of Vietnam became a protectorate of France less than ten years after Dupré had launched his ill-fated Tongking expedition. It was again a governor of Cochinchina who sent an officer with a small force to Hanoi. Captain Henry Rivière had 233 men. He was given more precise but also more cautious instructions than Garnier. Governor Le Myre de Vilers was concerned with both the dangers of military disaster and international complications, but in contrast to Dupré he was assured of his government's support. A change in outlook and mood had dissolved the opposition that ten years earlier had been strong enough to undo Garnier's work. No pretext was needed for this second attack on Tongking. Under the prevailing mood, it had become the duty of France to bring the blessings of her civilization to the backward nations of the East. By pushing ahead on his own against constant warnings from Saigon, Rivière was in fact more in step with his country and government than with his cautious superior de Vilers in Saigon.

Rivière, who was neither "restrained" nor "peaceful," reached Hanoi on April 3, 1883. Except for a more open display of contempt for the Vietnamese people,[120] he behaved exactly like Garnier. After reinforcements from Saigon had raised the number of his soldiers to over six hundred, he stormed the citadel and later, although it took a whole year, also established French control of lower Tongking by occupying all the cities Garnier had once held. And like Garnier,

Rivière too was killed by Chinese pirates, near Hanoi, on May 19, 1883.

The effect of Rivière's death on Paris was the opposite of that produced by the death of Garnier. It strengthened the forces determined to settle the "Tongking affair" through decisive military intervention. Such intervention, however, had already been decided on by the Chamber of Deputies on May 15,[121] four days before Rivière was killed—or, as one official in Vietnam put it, before Rivière had "harvested what he had sown." [122] The Chamber had voted the credits necessary for the imposition of a French protectorate over Tongking.

The reasons why the "Tongking affair" of 1883 took a different turn from the "Tongking adventure" of 1873 were written all over the face of France. During the 1870's industry had expanded enormously; the cry for overseas markets and an "outlet for surplus capital"[123] had become louder every year. All over France numerous geographical societies had sprung up, the leaders of which were among the most active spokesmen of French imperialism in the Far East.[124] Germany, Belgium, Russia, and even Japan had joined the older imperialist powers in the new race for overseas markets, from which the French government, increasingly dominated by high finance and big business, could no longer stay away. Even Bismarck wanted France to look for overseas outlets in order to direct French attention away from the continent of Europe and thus weaken French interest in a war of revenge for 1871. For the first time since the attack against Vietnam had started in 1858, France was almost entirely behind her imperialist aggressors in the Far East.[125]

In August, 1883, a strong French expeditionary corps penetrated the Red River valley and began the twelve years of slaughter that figure in history as the pacification of Tongking. At the same time a French fleet bombarded Hué to teach Tu Duc a good European lesson. But Tu Duc had already died during the month of July. The French gave no quarter, and

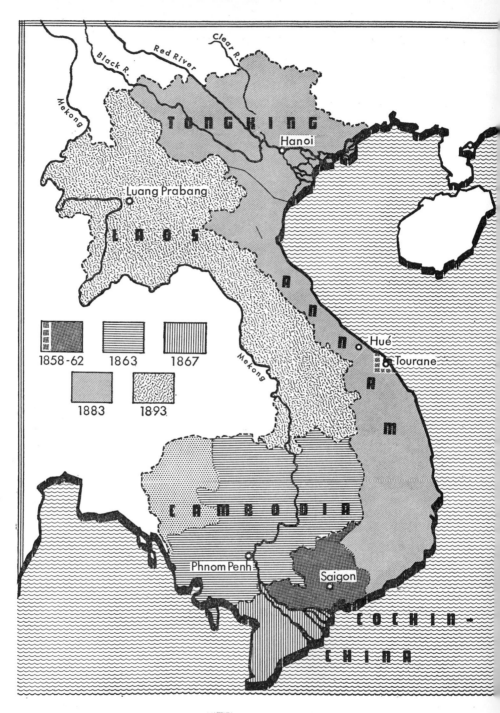

Map. IX.—THE PHASES OF FRENCH CONQUEST

1858-1893—The five phases in the conquest of Indochina by the French

their terror quickly succeeded in forcing the mandarins to submit. On August 25, 1883, they signed the Treaty of Protectorate through which the independence of Vietnam came to an end.

Much of the South had been a French colony for over twenty years when the Center and North of Vietnam became protectorates of France. When French rule ended in 1954, it had lasted seventy-one years in Hué and Hanoi and ninety-three in Saigon. In August, 1883, however, nobody could have foreseen how long the French would be able to hold Vietnam down. Only one thing was certain: neither the people nor the mandarins welcomed a foreign master or regarded his presence as an unalterable fate. In announcing the death of Tu Duc, the imperial court expressed Vietnam's will to regain her independence at the very moment independence was lost. Tu Duc, it said, "was killed by sorrow to see the foreigners invade and devastate his empire, and he died with curses against the invader on his lips. Keep him in your hearts and avenge his memory." [126]

22.

Although all of Vietnam was now under the tutelage of France, the conquest of Indochina was by no means completed after the court of Hué had been forced to agree to French protectorates over Tongking and Annam.[127]

To begin with, the French had to fight an undeclared war against China, to prevent the Chinese from annexing a portion of Tongking under the pretext of coming to the aid of the Vietnamese. The Chinese announced that a treaty involving Vietnam was invalid without their approval, and Peking ordered troops from Yunnan to occupy several bases within Vietnam. These troops clashed with the French, who advanced toward the Chinese border under General Bouet. Al-

379

though he was unable to displace the Chinese, General Bouet became famous as a commander by employing methods of warfare that portended clearly what was in store for the peoples of Indochina if they resisted being civilized by the French. "He was up against regulars, but chose to regard them as insurgents and hence beheaded all his prisoners."[128] Well aware of China's military weakness, the French refused a bargain which might have given them a "pacified" though somewhat smaller Tongking ten years ahead of the actual date. They held onto Tongking until China, in a treaty of June, 1884, agreed not to interfere with French rule in Vietnam. But the treaty displeased too many people on both sides, and a border incident revived and intensified the war. This meant another year of fighting in Tongking, during which the French navy attacked China and landed in Formosa. It all ended, ironically, in a new treaty, signed in June, 1885, that was almost identical with the one concluded a year earlier. China recognized the French protectorates over Tongking and Annam, and also consented to open her provinces adjoining Tongking to French trade.

In the meantime, the French had persuaded themselves that Vietnam and Cambodia would be more easily defendable and more accessible to economic exploitation if France could make the Mekong, between Cambodia and Yunnan, the western border of her Indochinese possessions. Thailand, which coveted the territories between the Mekong and Vietnam, and Upper Burma, which was clearly destined to be taken by England in a short time, would thus be separated by a large river from a French Indochina of much greater size. However, in order to control all of Indochina east of the Mekong River, the French had to annex the kingdom of Laos, a country almost half the size of France, though largely covered with thick forests, and even fifty years later inhabited by only one million people. Laos had several times been a vassal of Vietnam, but in 1885 the Laotian government was controlled by the king of Thailand, whom the French rightly suspected of more far-reaching designs.

The French claimed to have inherited Vietnam's rights over Laos, but this only aroused Siamese and English protest. If Laos eventually became French, this was largely due to the skill and valor of one man—Auguste Pavie, another hero of French Indochina, whose spadework enabled his country to annex Laos in 1893 at almost no cost and with little military effort.[129] Laos was made part of the so-called Indochinese Union, which the French had created in 1887.

By setting up a unified administration for their colony of Cochinchina and their protectorates of Cambodia, Annam, and Tongking, the French had in mind to coordinate from the outset all measures aiming at a systematic exploitation of their Indochinese resources. But in 1887 Vietnam was still far from being fully conquered, and not at all in a state in which long-range projects of economic exploitation could be conceived. Annam was all "blood and fire," as one contemporary authority wrote in 1887—an assistant and son-in-law of Paul Bert, the new Resident General to Annam and Tongking. Paul Bert was appointed in January, 1886, precisely in order to bring about peace and create the necessary climate for the productive activities that were so impatiently awaited by Paris. This is what he saw when he took up his post: "The capital was in our hands, but not even the immediate surroundings were safe; the revolt triumphed everywhere; we had no friends, and even the people surrounding the king, who was our creature, were not in our favor."[130]

How was it possible for such conditions to develop three years after the dreams of Garnier, Dupré, and Rivière had been fulfilled? The French forces stationed in Indochina were now larger than those that had defeated Tu Duc's armies and forced Hué to sign away the independence of Vietnam. Peking had become resigned to the presence of France in the Red River valley, and had thus freed the French forces engaged against Chinese regulars for the task of holding down the rebellious Vietnamese. But no matter how many Vietnamese guerillas were caught and summarily executed new ones turned up to replace them and to perpetuate a state of anarchy that doomed all large-scale economic projects in advance.

Slowly the French began to realize that in 1883 they had only defeated Tu Duc's inadequate armies and brought down his hated mandarinal regime, but had net yet dealt with the real potential of Vietnamese resistance, which remained unknown to them because the court of Hué had never tried to mobilize it on a national scale. It was stronger in 1883, after official Vietnam had capitulated, than at any time during the preceding twenty-five years of conquest. Now that the invader was regarded as the master of the whole country, and as such held responsible for the condition it was in, the people's dissatisfaction over the existing misery and their old hatred for authorities whose abuses no one checked turned against the French. The mandarins, to be sure, had their own special reasons for hating the foreign overlords, whom they generally regarded, if not as "barbarians," certainly as people lacking in both self-control and education. The officers chasing guerillas, and the administrators inventing and extracting new taxes from every Vietnamese, had little occasion to befriend either the mandarins or the peasants. Growing resistance led to more brutal repression. For years it seemed that there was no chance at all of re-establishing peace and of winning the cooperation of the Vietnamese. Most Frenchmen came to the desperate conclusion that because the Vietnamese could not be appeased, pacification alone could bring about order.

But order was hard to restore once the emperor of Vietnam himself, together with most of his court, had joined the camp of armed resistance. This happened in July, 1885, after the court's abortive attempt to overwhelm the French garrison at Hué in a surprise attack. In two years, the spirit of compromise that had dominated Hué's policy before 1883 had given way

382

to a fighting spirit that might well have saved Vietnam had it not come twenty-five years too late.

The emperor who joined the guerillas was not the man whom Tu Duc had designated as his successor. Tu Duc's death at the height of the crisis had led to a series of palace revolutions, in which two rival members of the Council of Regents, Nguyen Van Tuong and Ton That Thuyet, played the principal roles. On July 30, 1883, they replaced the old emperor's immediate successor—only forty-eight hours after his elevation to the throne—by one of Tu Duc's younger brothers, who, under the name of Hiep Hoa, signed the protectorate treaty on August 25. But in November, Hiep Hoa was forced by the regents to commit suicide, presumably because he favored cooperation with the French. The regents, whose anti-French policy was apparently also a screen for personal crimes, thereupon appointed an adolescent nephew of Tu Duc as emperor, only to replace him by another boy in July, 1884. This was the twelve-year-old emperor Nam Nghi, under whom the regent Ton That Thuyet, one year later, staged his unsuccessful coup to oust the French.

Nam Nghi was the last Vietnamese-made emperor. Henceforth the Vietnamese throne could be occupied only with the blessing of the French. They replaced Nam Nghi with a man willing to take their orders, but "the elevation of Dong Khanh to the throne and Nam Nghi's flight set Annam afire."[131] The six months of terror that followed did nothing to weaken Vietnamese resistance; the intensity it developed convinced Paul Bert, soon after his appointment in January, 1886, that force alone was no sure way of bringing peace and order to a French-controlled Vietnam.

Nam Nghi was caught only in November, 1888. His troops were dispersed soon afterward, but under the great scholar Phan Dinh Phung military resistance remained strong in northern Annam until 1896.[132] It continued even longer, and spread over wider territories, in the valleys and mountains of Tongking, where as late as 1897 the invincible De Tham forced the French to conclude a temporary peace with him on his own terms.[133]

23.

Eight years after the storming of Hanoi and Hué, Paris began at last to wonder whether the Vietnamese had really wanted to be freed of their mandarins by the French. Among the more enlightened French civilians in Indochina the idea gained ground that the killing of more and more Vietnamese was obviously not the speediest way of preparing the country for undisturbed economic exploitation. But not only were the military leaders powerful; they also had an argument that no civilian could ignore. You will all be killed within twenty-four hours, they were told by the officers, if we give up our vigilance for a single day.

To describe what this vigilance meant does not require the testimony of Vietnamese nationalists or of Frenchmen opposed to their country's colonial policies. One of France's most prominent colonial statesmen, de Lanessan, has said all one needs to know in a single paragraph of one of his books. As soon as he became Governor General in 1891, de Lanessan tried desperately to win the cooperation of the mandarins and to reduce the people's hatred for the French. This, he knew, could only be done if he first put an end to "the acts of incredible brutality" committed everywhere in the fight against the guerillas. "It seemed to me," he wrote after his enemies had succeeded in having him recalled in 1894, two years before his term was up, "that the burning of villages, the mass shootings, the bayonet slaughters, and the executions of notables should be replaced by other less violent procedures."[134]

After he himself had been defeated, de Lanessan sat down to show that his policy of "stopping these massacres at all

384

costs" was already producing the results he had predicted whenever some of his measures had been under attack. This the protagonists of naked force have denied to this very day, asserting instead that the first phase of Vietnamese resistance was broken exclusively by their bullets and swords. No one will ever be able to decide which policy contributed more to the change that came about after 1895. But what de Lanessan wrote about the first eight years after the fall of Tongking and Annam, the military leaders themselves have never attempted to deny: that no work of any public utility had been undertaken prior to his arrival in the year 1891.[135]

The projects de Lanessan was able to start were too modest, and Vietnamese armed resistance still was too strong during his tenure of office, to connect his name with the great change that came about a few years after his "brutal recall." [136] It was only under the Governor General Paul Doumer, who from 1897 to 1902 was a more absolute ruler of Vietnam than any of the Nguyen emperors ever had been, that the period of conquest and its terrible aftermath of pacification came to an end. Now, at the turn of the century, the French could at last show to the Vietnamese that they were capable of other than military achievements. What they accomplished during the next forty years up to the coming of the Japanese may have been more than most Vietnamese are willing to admit, but all they brought to Vietnam during the preceding forty years of conquest and pacification was death and destruction.

The new conquerors of Vietnam, like the Chinese before them, made an indelible impression on the minds of the Vietnamese. All later facts of Vietnamese history up to the present day will therefore reveal their meaning only to those who understand what this people experienced while the French were engaged in conquering Vietnam.

Notes to Chapter Six:

1. The French Ministry of Foreign Affairs has not yet—one hundred years after the event—published all the existing documents relating to the actions and forces that brought about the conquest of Indochina. Until the end of World War II these documents were kept secret almost *in toto*. Only a few scholars were given access to the archives. Documents from the French archives are used by John F. Cady, *The Roots of French Imperialism in Eastern Asia*, Ithaca, N. Y., 1954, and by the French author George Taboulet in the two volumes of his *La geste française en Indochine*, published in Paris in 1955 and 1956. A comparison of the two works seems to indicate that John F. Cady, a professor of history at Ohio University, was shown only the material in the archives of the Ministry of Foreign Affairs, whereas the material used by Taboulet points to additional documents. There are papers relating to the conquest of Vietnam in the secret archives of the Ministries of Marine and Colonies to which Cady apparently was unable to gain access (cf. the preface to his book, p. vi), and which Taboulet does not mention as source. The official documents on the conquest and its diplomatic prelude are mostly contained in Vol. 27 of Arch. Aff. Etrang., Mémoires et Documents, Asie. Before 1954 most French writers do not even mention the fact that the intervention was officially decided upon as far back as July, 1857. (See note 58, Chapter VI.)

2. Chaigneau, treated by Minh Mang with growing coolness and frustrated in all his undertakings, decided that it was time to quit. On November 1, 1823, he wrote to La Bissachère: "I hope I shall not have to stay another year in this damned country . . . " He postponed his departure, however, owing to a short war between France and Spain. Minh Mang, dissatisfied with the delay, sent Chaigneau the reproduction of a ship as a present. This the consul of France took as a more or less tactful hint that his departure was desired. Accompanied by Vannier, he left Hué on November 15, 1824. Minh Mang presented honorary diplomas to both his foreign-born mandarins, but Taboulet (*op. cit.*, p. 310) is of the opinion that their language was rather ironic and little obliging. Chaigneau arrived in France in September, 1825, and died in 1832. Cf. Cordier, *Le consulat de France à Hué,* also for the failure of the mission of J. B. Chaigneau's successor and nephew, Eugène Chaigneau.

3. In February, 1822, while Chaigneau was still in Hué, the French frigate *La Cléopâtre* visited Tourane. Her captain, Chevalier Courson

de la Ville-Hélio, sought through Chaigneau to pay his respects to the ruler of Vietnam. Minh Mang not only refused to see him but sent troops to Tourane as if he doubted the peaceful intentions of the French. In 1824, Henri, Baron de Bougainville, son of the famous explorer, was sent to Vietnam with a letter and gifts from Louis XVIII to Minh Mang. His credentials, issued by the Minister of Marine Clermont-Tonnerre, read that his mission was one "of peace and protection of commerce." Bougainville commanded a brand-new ship, the *Thétis*, equipped with 44 cannons and 300 sailors. When the *Thétis* arrived in Tourane in January, 1825, Bougainville, although received with cool correctness, was not allowed to proceed to Hué. To avoid having the letter of Louis XVIII (who had died meanwhile) presented to him, Minh Mang informed the Baron that there was no one to translate it. As many French missionaries were known to be in the country, this was a poor excuse. The reason for Bougainville's cool reception seems to have been his clandestine attempt to smuggle a Catholic missionary ashore. Bougainville wrote a book about his abortive mission—*Journal de la navigation autour du monde de la frégate* La Thétis *et de la corvette* L'Espérance *pendant les années 1824-25-26* (Paris, 1837, 2 vols.). In it he recommends a permanent French settlement in Cochinchina.

4. Minh Mang refused to recognize a French consul for fear that the British and others would demand a like representation. The younger Chaigneau, Eugène, arrived in Vietnam in 1826, but Minh Mang would not let him assume his intended official capacity and forced him to leave the country. Eugène Chaigneau returned in 1829 and was again unsuccessful (Taboulet, *op. cit.*, pp. 311-315; Cordier, *op. cit.*, pp. 338-346, 359-363; Le Thanh Khoi, *op. cit.*, pp. 339f.; Chassigneux, *op. cit.*, pp. 370f.). In 1821 Louis XVII sent the king of Vietnam a letter in which he offered a trade agreement. It was answered indirectly by a mandarin of the second grade, who wrote in a letter to the director of the French merchant marine that "our kingdom lies in the far south, France in the far west. . . . People from our country come seldom to yours. . . . If your people want to trade in our kingdom, they will have to submit to our rules—which is only reasonable." The rules Minh Mang was alluding to gave complete equality to all nations and no favored treatment to France. For the period of deteriorating French-Vietnamese relations, see: Chassigneux, *op. cit.*, pp. 367-371; Chesneaux, *op. cit.*, pp. 92-96; Prosper Cultru, *Histoire de la Cochinchine française, des origines à 1883*, Paris, 1910, pp. 29-40; Thomas E. Eunis, *French Policy and Development in Indochina*, Chicago, 1936, pp. 30ff.; Cordier, *Le conflit entre la France et la Chine*, Paris, 1883, pp. 10ff.; Cordier, *Le consulat*

de France à Hué sous la Restauration, Paris, 1884, pp. 116ff.; Cady *op. cit.,* pp. 15-17.

5. During the reign of Louis-Philippe (1830-1848) several French warships were ordered on a world cruise. One of their ports of landing was Tourane, where they were to get in touch with the French missionaries in Vietnam, the uncertainty of whose fate had caused great concern in France. First to arrive was the corvette *La Bonite* under Captain Vaillant (early 1837), followed by the *Artémise* commanded by Captain Laplace (August, 1838). Both were received with ill-disguised hostility and kept from communication with the French missionaries as well as the population proper (Taboulet, *op. cit.,* pp. 343-346; also his reprint of Vaillant's report to the Ministry of Foreign Affairs, dated March 7, 1837, from Arch. Aff. Etrang., *Mémoirs et Documents, Asie,* Vol. 27, fol. 170-210).

6. His name was Laroque de Chaufray. In 1840 he commanded the brig *Le Lancier* in a punitive expedition against pirates in Sumatra who had killed a French sailor. During this expedition he became interested in Vietnam (without, however, visiting that country) and upon his return wrote a report in which he advised that the French occupy the islands of Condore and also Cham Callao at the mouth of the Faifo River. His recommendation won the support of the Minister of Agriculture and Commerce, M. Cunin-Gridaine, and the Minister of Marine, M. Duperre, but did not convince Foreign Minister Guizot. It was formally rejected in a cabinet meeting on June 8, 1841 (Taboulet, *op. cit.,* p. 344).

7. The Opium War (the First Anglo-Chinese War) broke out in 1839 when China resisted the importation of opium from British India. It ended in 1842 with the complete defeat of the Chinese and the Treaty of Nanking, through which Britain acquired Hong Kong. China was opened to foreign trade and the rights of extraterritoriality were established. This meant that henceforth British subjects, though living in China, were under the jurisdiction of British courts. In 1844 the United States obtained the same rights from China, and in 1845 France and China concluded a treaty whereby the Roman Catholic Church was given freedom of proselytization. In 1852, Great Britain, the United States, and France won further concessions. A second war, won by Britain joined by France, gave Western powers complete access to China. The United States and Russia shared with Britain and France in Chinese concessions, Russia also acquiring the entire territory north of the Amur and east of the Ussuri. Cf. Latourette, *op. cit.,* pp. 368-376.

8. This was the so-called Jancigny-Cécille mission. Its objectives were:

388

to assay the political situation in China and the prospects of expanded French trade in the Far East; to recommend measures by which France might play a greater role in that area; to enhance French prestige by the display of the French flag. The mission was not instructed to negotiate with the Chinese authorities (Cady, *op. cit.*, pp. 33-40).

9. See the confidential instructions, dated November 9, 1843, given by Foreign Minister Guizot to the newly appointed French envoy to China, Théodore de Lagréné. Lagréné was to look for a locality suitable for a French naval base, to be to France what Hong Kong is to the British and Macao to the Portuguese. Guizot had some island in the Pacific in mind rather than a port in Vietnam, having specifically ruled out Indochina as a good choice. "What is known about Indochina," he wrote, "is too little and not specific enough for a critical appraisal." Guizot thought the islands south of the Philippines a better choice; he probably meant one of the islands of the Moluccas. These instructions (Arch. Aff. Etrang., Chine, Vol. I, fol. 216-222) were published by Guizot himself in his introduction to Laurence Oliphant's *La Chine et le Japon, la mission du Comte Elgin pendant les années 1857, 1858, 1859,* Paris, 1860, Vol. I, pp. iii-vi. It is reprinted in Taboulet, *op. cit.,* pp. 349-352, with an excellent introduction on French foreign policy under Louis-Philippe. On the Lagréné mission see also Cady, *op. cit.,* pp. 46-56; J. M. Callery, "Journal des opérations diplomatiques de la légation française en Chine," Macao, 1945; Théophile de Ferrière le Vayer, *Une ambassade française en Chine, Journal de voyage,* Paris, 1854; Angelos Grosse-Aschhoff, *The Negotiations Between Ch'i-Ying and Lagréné, 1844-1848,* Allegany, N. Y., 1950. Callery, a renowned sinologist, was the interpreter of the mission, Ferrière le Vayer the secretary to the chief of the embassy, Lagréné. About Guizot's fear of England, Cady (*op. cit.,* p. 17) comments: "British naval and commercial hegemony in the Far East, based on India, was unchallengeable, so that any move which France might contemplate within the area would have to fall within the bounds of British consent."

10. As described in Guizot's instructions, the French believed Basilan to be the ideal place for a naval base. Through a strange deal between a French physician, Dr. Mallet, and the sultan of Sulu it was acquired for the price of 100,000 Spanish piastres (February 20, 1845), but French naval authorities were either too slow or the news of their preparations for the island's occupation leaked out. Spain became suspicious and claimed her historic right to Basilan in several victorious clashes with the French. The episode is described by Cady, *op. cit.,* pp. 57f. and Taboulet, *op. cit.,* pp. 352-356. Taboulet also reprints the

pertinent official French documents from Arch. Aff. Etrang., Asie, Vol. 23, fols. 181-190, 225-234, 242-246; Vol. 24, fols. 35-38.

11. Two French missionaries, accompanied by a carpenter, landed on Tahiti in 1836 but were expelled by the queen of the island group on the advice of the British missionary George Pritchard. Pritchard, who enjoyed the queen's full confidence, also frustrated a second French attempt in 1837. In 1839 a French naval captain, Dupetit-Thouars, asked and obtained an apology and indemnity from the queen. In 1842 Dupetit-Thouars, now an admiral, declared Tahiti a French protectorate. The queen sided openly with the British, whereupon Dupetit-Thouars deposed her and annexed the island group for France. England protested, but for an indemnity recognized French possession of Tahiti (1845). See Cady, *op. cit.*, pp. 30f. and J. R. Baldwin, "England and the French Seizure of the Society Islands," in *Journal of Modern History*, Vol. X (1938), pp. 212-231.

12. Cady, *op. cit.*, p. 29.

13. Father Douai, a missionary closely connected with Admiral Cécille, in a letter to the Seminary of the Foreign Mission, dated Manila, June 18, 1843 (Arch. Miss. Etrang., Vol. 139, published by Taboulet, *op. cit.*, p. 361).

14. For an exhaustive treatment of this subject see especially Cady, *op. cit.*, Chapter II, "France under Louis Philippe," pp. 18-28, and Chapter VII, "French Policy under Louis Napoleon, 1848-1853," pp. 87-102. Cf. also: John M. S. Allison, *Church and State in the Reign of Louis Philippe*, Princeton, 1916; Ross William Collins, *Catholicism in the Second French Republic, 1848-1852*, New York, 1923; C. S. Phillips, *The Church in France, 1848-1907*, New York, 1936; H. F. Stewart and Paul Desjardins, *French Patriotism in the Nineteenth Century, 1814-1833*, Cambridge, 1933; John R. Hall, *The Bourbon Restoration*, London, 1909; K. S. Latourette, *History of the Christian Missions in China*, New York, 1929.

15. Cady, *op. cit.*, p. 32; R. P. Delvaux, "L'Ambassade de Minh-Mang à Louis-Philippe, 1839 à 1841," in *Bulletin des Amis du Vieux Hué*, Vol. XV, Oct.-Dec., 1928, p. 264; Prosper Cultru, *Histoire de la Cochinchine françaises des origines à 1883* Paris, 1910, pp. 45f.; Cordier, *"La* politique coloniale," in *T'oung Pao*, Vol. X, p. 21f.

16. Favin-Lévêque's intervention took place in February and March, 1843, not in October, 1842, as erroneously stated by Cady, *op. cit.*, p. 73. Thieu Tri's letter to Favin-Lévêque was dated March 12, 1843; the captain's report to the Minister of Marine about his successful mission was sent from Singapore on April 9, 1843. The king's letter is to be

390

found in Arch. Miss. Etrang., Vol. 749, p. 843, Favin-Lévêque's report in Arch. France Outre-mer, Cochinchine, Vol. IV, folio 106f. Both documents were published for the first time by Taboulet, *op. cit.*, pp. 356-359.

17. Dominique Lefèbvre came to Vietnam in 1835. After having learned the native language in Tongking, he preached in Cochinchina, where he lived in hiding most of the time. He became titular bishop of Isauropolis in 1841. On October 31, 1844, he was arrested and soon afterward sentenced to death by decapitation. Thieu Tri, perhaps because he was afraid of the French warships that cruised in the waters near Indochina, postponed the execution. In the spring of 1845 Lefèbvre learned, while in prison, that a foreign warship had landed in Tourane. It was the U.S.S. *Constitution,* commanded by Captain John Percival. Lefèbvre assumed erroneously that it was a French ship, and he succeeded in sending a secret message out of his prison, addressed to "the commander of the corvette" (April 1, 1845). It was delivered to Captain Percival. While he received Lefèbvre's message, three or four mandarins were on board of the *Constitution* on a courtesy visit. Percival had them arrested as hostages and threatened to keep them until Lefèbvre was released. When Thieu Tri refused to exchange the Bishop for the mandarins, Percival set the Vietnamese dignitaries free and left port with threats of reprisals. As soon as the mandarins returned to Hué they were arrested by their own government and punished for having been so awkward as to allow the American captain to take hold of them. The United States government disavowed Percival and sent its consul in Singapore to Hué to offer formal apologies. After Percival's failure Fornier-Duplan was dispatched to Tourane (June, 1845). He succeeded with his mission. See Taboulet, *op. cit.,* pp. 362-369. The journal of Fornier-Duplan was published in *Bulletin de la Société de Géographie de Rochefort,* 1908, pp. 91-115. Other works dealing with this episode in French-Vietnamese relations are J. Itier, *Journal d'un voyage en Chine en 1843-44-45-46,* Paris, 1848, Vol. II, pp. 43-140; M. C. Lavollée, *Voyage en Chine,* Paris, 1853, pp. 407ff.; Auguste Haussmann, *Voyage en Chine, Cochinchine, Inde et Malaisie,* Paris, 1848, Vol. II, pp. 372-395. Le Thanh Khoi, whose very detailed *Le Vietnam: Histoire et civilisation,* has been quoted frequently in these pages, devotes only four lines to Lefèbvre (*op. cit.,* pp. 342f.). His treatment of the preconquest period is somewhat sketchy. Chesneaux (*op. cit.,* p. 95) writes that an American warship had the doubtful privilege of committing the first act of armed intervention against Vietnam in 1845. To classify the temporary retention of some mandarins as an "act of armed intervention" is rather an overstatement. Chesneaux seems to be not too well informed about the

incident. He does not even know Percival's name but credits his behavior to "an American commander whose name history has not recorded." Bishop Lefèbvre returned to Vietnam in 1846, accompanied by Father Duclos, who died soon after they arrived in the country. Lefèbvre was again arrested and sentenced to death. As before, Thieu Tri did not confirm the death sentence but deported the bishop to Singapore (February, 1847). Three months later Lefèbvre returned for a third time and now remained in Cochinchina until after the French conquest. He returned to Europe in 1864 and died in 1865. Cf. Taboulet, "Quelques lettres de Mgr. Lefèbvre, premier évêque de Saigon français," in *Bulletin de la Société des Etudes Indochinoises*, 1943. Cady, *op. cit.*, p. 74, confuses the fates of Duclos and Lefèbvre and lets Lefèbvre die of illness at Saigon in 1846, following some French authors whom he quotes. The correct version is also to be found in Cordier, "La politique coloniale," in *T'oung Pao*, Vol. X, p. 22. For an interesting document about the incident involving Captain Percival and the U.S.S. *Constitution* in the Straits Settlements records (a letter written by Governor Butterworth of Singapore on March 13, 1847), see Hall, *op. cit.*, pp. 557f.

18. Lefèbvre's first release from prison in June, 1845, was announced to the bishop in a letter which stated: "The Emperor considers that you, a foreigner, had not full knowledge of the laws prohibiting the Christian religion. Therefore the Emperor pardons you and sends you back to your king. He even wishes to treat you with consideration and will give you clothing and money." The French historians, somehow embarrassed by this magnanimous attitude of the Vietnamese ruler, keep emphasizing that he was afraid of French warships in East Asian waters.

19. "We thought to be on the verge of peace," wrote Msgr. Cuenot on May 3, 1847. See Taboulet, *op. cit.*, p. 370.

20. Thieu Tri forbade his mandarins under penalty of death to accept any communication from Europeans. This is the reason why they refused to forward messages from French naval commanders to the emperor (Taboulet, *op. cit.*, p. 393, note 3).

21. There are two completely different versions in the French archives on what happened in the harbor of Tourane on that fateful April 15, 1847. They were never officially published and were printed for the first time by Taboulet in 1955 (*op. cit.*, pp. 371-374). The French version is contained in a letter from Msgr. Théodore Auguste Forcade to the Seminary of Foreign Missions, written aboard ship in the Red Sea on June 2, 1847 (Arch. Miss. Etrang., Vol. 568, pp. 342-345); the Vietnamese version is given in a report by Charles Géraud, a business-

man from Bordeaux, to the Minister of Agriculture and Commerce, written in Paris in February, 1849 (Arch. Aff. Etrang., *Mémoires et Documents, Asie,* Vol. 25, ff. 102-105). According to the French version the Vietnamese gathered five ships for an attack on the two French vessels in port, *La Gloire* and *La Victorieuse.* The French commander asked the Vietnamese fleet to retreat and, after the warning had been disregarded, opened the attack. Eight hundred shots were fired. One Vietnamese ship blew up, another sank, a third fled, the remaining two surrendered. According to Msgr. Forcade, the French navy suffered only two casualties, one dead and one wounded. Charles Géraud reported that the Vietnamese ("this sweet and unaggressive people") did not think of attacking the French. Their orders were for returning the fire only if the French warships started an aggression. These orders were brought to the French commander by a spy, were wrongly translated and their Oriental rhetoric misinterpreted. "Could this letter," asks M. Géraud, "pompous and quite arrogant as it was, justify the destruction of five ships and the massacre of 10,000 men?" French historians, prior to the publication of this document, never mentioned any number of killed in this battle and put the blame, more or less, on the Vietnamese. August Antoine Thomazi (*La conquête de l'Indochine,* Paris, 1934) even claims that the Vietnamese attacked first, though even Msgr. Forcade in his letter admits that *La Gloire* fired the first cannon shot. Hall (*op. cit.,* p. 558), writing as late as 1955, accepts Thomazi's extreme pro-French version that the Vietnamese opened the attack. Hall sometimes carelessly distorts recorded facts and even changes the chronological order of events to prove his point, as in the case of the second bombardment of Tourane by the French warship *Le Catinat.* Hall writes (*op. cit.,* p. 559): "In 1851-2 two French priests were put to death. M. de Montigny, the French consul to the governments of Siam and Cambodia, was thereupon ordered to lodge a very strong protest. When this was rejected . . . the *Catinat* bombarded the forts at Tourane." The Montigny mission did not take place "thereupon" but four years later. Tourane was bombarded by *Le Catinat* and *La Capricieuse* in the fall of 1856, and this was a willful act of terror, which had nothing to do with any action of the Vietnamese at that time. Cf. Taboulet, *op. cit.,* pp. 387-394. Hall's attitude toward the Vietnamese before the French conquest hardly differs from that of Maspéro and other French historians in the service of colonial propaganda. His otherwise valuable book lacks the necessary independent research and thinking in the chapters dealing with Vietnam before the establishment of French Rule.

22. Admiral Cécille had appeared off the Korean coast in September, 1846, to ask for the release of an imprisoned Korean priest, André Kim. The result of his intervention was the immediate execution of Kim. After the massacre of Tourane, Cécille returned to Korea to put some missionaries on land secretly. His ship ran aground and sank. British vessels picked up the stranded sailors and brought them to Shanghai (Cady, *op. cit.*, pp. 76; Launay, *Histoire générale de la Société des Missions Etrangères depuis sa formation jusqu'à nos jours,"* Paris, 1894, Vol. III, pp. 212-215).

23. See Taboulet, *op. cit.*, p. 373, note 1. Théodore Auguste Forcade was put ashore on the Ryukyu Islands in 1844 by Cécille in order to study a missionary approach to Japan. In 1846 he became titular bishop of Samos and apostolic vicar of Japan. In 1847 he served as interpreter to Captain Lapierre aboard *La Gloire*. Later he became archbishop of Aix-en-Provence. See E. Marbot's biography of Forcade, published in Aix-en-Provence in 1889.

24. See Cady, *op. cit.*, p. 79, note 26, and Launay, *op. cit.*, Vol. III, p. 218.

25. Cécille even offered to Guizot to lead an expedition against Hué, a proposal the French government rejected. Not all missionaries were bellicose at that time. Two priests prominent in the Far East, Bishop Pierre André Retord, apostolic vicar of Tongking, and his coadjutor, Bishop Charles Hubert Jeantet, counseled moderation. They proposed a diplomatic and mollifying approach in the form of a mission, to be led by a brother of the king and carrying presents. Such a procedure, they advised, would be of greater help to the Church than the hated appearance of warships. The two prelates presented their suggestions in a letter addressed to King Louis-Philippe, written on March 26, 1848, unaware that the French monarchy had fallen just one month earlier. The letter arrived at the Seminary of the Foreign Mission in October, 1848, and was placed in its archives without being shown to the government of the Second French Republic, possibly because of the letter's peaceful contents. The document is contained in Arch. Miss. Etrang., Vol. 703, p. 119, and was reprinted by Launay, *op. cit.*, Vol. III, pp. 219-222, and by Taboulet, *op. cit.*, p. 375f. Cf. also Cady, *op. cit.*, p. 79.

26. Hall, *op. cit.*, p. 557, in characterizing Thieu Tri, again follows blindly the prejudices of French colonial historians.

27. According to Gosselin, *op. cit.*, p. 124, Tu Duc was "intelligent, quite soft-hearted, not subject to fits of rage like his predecessor, and well educated." Bishops Retord and Jeantet reported in their letter to

394

Louis-Phillippe, cited in note 25, that Tu Duc was said to be of a "sweet and moderate disposition." For further characterizations of Thieu Tri and Tu Duc, see Chapter V, note 17.

28. In 1851 Father Augustin Schoeffler was executed—a youthful missionary, only twenty-nine years old at the time of his death—and in 1852 Father Jean-Louis Bonnard shared his fate. Bishop Retord was also imprisoned early in 1851 but talked himself to freedom by insisting that missionaries had no interest in political affairs (Cady, *op. cit.*, p. 80; Launay, *op. cit.*, Vol. III, pp. 266-269; Taboulet, *op. cit.*, p. 382; Mangenot, *Le bienheureux Augustin Schoeffler*, Nancy, 1900; Finot, *Un martyr lorrain en Extrême-Orient, La vie et la mort du bienheureux Aug. Schoeffler*, Metz 1900; X (anonymous), *Vie du vénérable Jean-Louis Bonnard*, Lyon, 1876).

29. The edict of Tu Duc against the Christian faith, dated March 21, 1851, is reprinted in Louvet, *La Cochinchine religieuse*, Vol. II, pp. 183-185, and in Taboulet, *op. cit.*, pp. 382f. An abbreviated version of both edicts is to be found in Gosselin, *op. cit.*, pp. 124-126. Tu Duc's main contention against missionaries was that they forbade the ancestor cult. The decree ordered European priests to be thrown into the sea or rivers and Vietnamese priests to be cut in half lengthwise. The mandarins were to keep the content of the emperor's edict secret. Whoever delivered a European priest to the authorities was entitled to a reward of eight silver taels and half of that missionary's property; the other half went to the king's treasury. The death sentence was to be imposed on anyone who helped hide a priest. Followers of the Catholic faith, however were not to be put to death but only to be punished by exile or prison because, so Tu Duc's first edict of 1848 reads, they were "poor idiots seduced by the priests." The edicts were not enforced, because —as most historians believe—the mandarins were open to bribes. See Cady, *op. cit.*, p. 79; Cultru, *op. cit.*, pp. 49f.; Ennis, *op. cit.*, pp. 34f.

30. The first French ship to visit Vietnam after an interval of several years was *La Capricieuse* under Captain Gaston Rocquemaurel. This vessel circled the globe via Cape Horn and on her return voyage to France made short stops in four Indochinese ports: Phu Yen, Honekone, Cam Ranh, and Cap St. Jacques. Captain Rocquemaurel was tactful enough to avoid Tourane lest the memories of 1847 be reawakened. His stay in Vietnam lasted from December 13 to 28, 1851. The ship was at first received with cold reserve, but, as the peaceful intentions of this French vessel became clear, relations gained increasing warmth. Captain Rocquemaurel's reports to the Minister of Marine are to be found both in the archives of the Ministry of Foreign Affairs and the

Ministry of Marine (Arch. Aff. Etrang., *Mémoires et Documents, Asie,* Vol. 27, fol. 262-264; Arch. Min. Marine, *Papiers de Rocquemaurel;* both published for the first time by Taboulet, *op. cit.,* pp. 379-381). The Minister of Marine complimented Rocquemaurel on the success of his mission.

31. Napoleon III was not a pious Catholic by conviction but was under the strong influence of his very religious Spanish wife, the Empress Eugénie. She had gathered the Catholic support that made possible Napoleon's *coup d'état* of December 2, 1851. During the entire life of the Second Empire clerical pressure remained strong and was responsible for the political and social reaction at home as well as for Napoleon's colonial policy, especially in regard to Vietnam and Mexico. Chassigneux, *op. cit.,* p. 377, says that Napoleon III abided by the Catholic party's suggestions throughout his entire reign. Antonin Debidour, in his *Histoire des rapports de l'église et de l'état en France de 1789 à 1870,* Paris, 1898, pp. 524f. remarks of the Second Empire: "The Church had never seen a government in France more desirous to please." Cf. also Cady, *op. cit.,* pp. 87-92; Ross William Collins, *Catholicism and the Second French Republic, 1848-1852,* New York, 1923, pp. 45-317; C. S. Phillips, *The Church in France, 1848-1907,* New York, 1936, pp. 41-57.

32. In a letter to Msgr. Forcade, dated April 14, 1851, he wrote: "A simple intervention by France, without guaranties or treaties, without occupation of some ports or islands, would do more harm than good. But if France were to obtain some territory and establish a settlement there, peace would be assured. Measures should at first be diplomatic, such as the dispatch of a high-ranking envoy, supported by military means if need be. . . ." The reason for this letter was a request by the French chargé d'affaires in China, Baron de Forth-Rouen, to Msgr. Forcade for news about the situation in Vietnam. Forcade, then residing in Macao, asked Retord for a report. Retord's letter to Forcade, in Arch. Aff. Etrang., *Correspondance politique de la Chine,* Vol. 13, fol. 279, was first published by Taboulet, *op. cit.,* pp. 384f. Taboulet thinks Retord not only gave his personal opinion but that shared by all French missionaries and Vietnamese Catholics who were tired of French half-measures.

33. Count Bourboulon was French Minister to China from October, 1851, to November, 1852, and then again from February, 1857, to March, 1862. His appeal for French intervention in Vietnam was first made in a letter to the French Foreign Minister, Drouhin de Lhuys, dated August 21, 1852 (Arch. Aff. Etrang., *Correspondance Politique*

de la Chine, Vol. 13, folio 236-241; published by Taboulet, *op. cit.,* pp. 384-386). However, the minister ignored the proposal for the time being. France was then busy with other problems—it was only a few months after the *coup d'état*—and the Vietnamese problem had to wait some more years. See also Cady, *op. cit.,* p. 98, and Cordier, "La politique coloniale," in *T'oung Pao,* Vol. X, pp. 26-30.

34. See Cady, *op. cit.,* p. 99. Cady takes his information directly from the archives of the French Ministry of Foreign Affairs, quoted by him as AEC (Affaires Etrangères, Chine), Vol. 12, fs. 256-279. Bourboulon's second and more explicit proposal of intervention, dated September 23, 1852, is not mentioned by Taboulet. It is difficult to decide whether he had no access to this particular document or whether he decided not to use it. The second alternative seems more probable. Taboulet also ignores a third message by Bourboulon (AEC, Vol. 12, f. 309-310, dated December 26, 1952) in which he indicated that Admiral Lapierre could undertake the proposed mission to Tourane, but would need an impressive force for the task.

35. The Treaty of Whampoa, (see note 7, Chapt. VI), in which China agreed to give access to the Roman Catholic Church, was negotiated by the first French envoy to China, Théodore de Lagréné. Henceforth the field was opened to missionary activities by the Société des Missions Etrangères, which was exclusively French, and by the Lazarist Society, which was predominantly so. Fourteen new vicariates were established between 1844 and 1860. According to Cady, an aggressive ultramontane spirit characterized the entire program. Dressed in native garb and subsisting on native fare, French missionaries worked unostentatiously and unremittingly. Both Protestant missionaries and non-French diplo mats testified to their devotion and effectiveness. Louis Charles de Montigny, an attaché of Lagréné's mission and later French consul in Shanghai, distinguished himself in later years in the furtherance of Catholic activities in China. About the Lagréné mission and its success, see Cady's detailed account, *op. cit.,* pp. 43-73; also Adolphe Dubois, *Les accords franco-chinois,* Paris, 1928; Cordier, *Histoire générale de la Chine et de ses relations avec les pays étrangers depuis les plus anciens jusqu'à la chute de la dynastie mandchoue,* Vol. IV, Paris, 1920; Callery, *op. cit.;* Grosse-Aschhoff, *op. cit.;* Launay, *op. cit.,* Vol. III; Brouillon, "Missions de Chine": *Mémoire sur l'état actuel de la mission du Kiamg-Nan, 1842-1855,* Paris, 1855.

36. This statement is contained in an appeal by eight Catholic bishops residing in the Far East to the then President of the French Republic,

Prince Louis-Napoleon Bonaparte, in mid-1852. The appeal was for increased French protection of the missionaries. See Cady, *op. cit.*, pp. 97f., and Cordier, "La politique coloniale," *T'oung Pao,* Vol. X, pp. 28-30.

37. These are the words of Bishop Retord in his letter to Msgr. Forcade, dated April 14, 1851, quoted in note 32 of this Chapter.

38. Napoleon III waged six major wars in the eighteen years of the Second Empire; the Crimean War (1854-1856), the war with China (1856-1860), the war with Vietnam (1858-1863), the war with Austria (1859), the intervention in Mexico (ending 1867), and the Franco-Prussian War that brought about his downfall in 1871. He also engaged in minor warfare in Syria and Algeria. In the Crimean War France was allied with Great Britain, Turkey, and Sardinia; in the war with China with Great Britain; in the Austrian war with Sardinia; in the Vietnamese campaign with Spain. All these wars were either started or provoked by Napoleon III.

39. The outbreak of the Taiping rebellion in China and the tension it created in the Far East was another reason why France could not intervene in Vietnam. A Chinese village teacher, Hung Hsiu Chuan, claimed to be the younger son of God and brother of Jesus Christ. He proclaimed himself emperor under the dynastic name of Tai Ping (meaning Great Peace) in the very year 1854 when the Crimean War broke out in Europe. He set up his capital in Nanking and declared the Manchu dynasty deposed. The Taiping rebellion was not suppressed until 1865.

40. Cf. the letter the Marquis R. de Courcy wrote to the Minister of Foreign Affairs on December 31, 1855. (Arch. Aff. Etrang., *Correspondance politique de la Chine,* Vol. 17, fs. 92/93, published by Taboulet, *op. cit.,* p. 387.) The Marquis de Courcy was French chargé d'affaires in Peking during the absence of Bourboulon. He left memoirs (*Souvenirs,* Paris, 1900, 3 vols.) throwing a very interesting light on French Far Eastern policy. See also Msgr. Pellerin's letter to Msgr. Libois of December 14, 1854 (Arch. Aff. Etrang., *Correspondence politique de la Chine,* Vol. 16, fs. 287/288), in which he asked for a French naval demonstration to halt continuing anti-Christian persecutions. Cf. Cady, *op. cit.,* p. 139.

41. Louis Charles de Montigny accompanied Lagréné to China in 1843 and sent much interesting economic information about China to Paris. He was chosen for the important post of French consul in Shanghai in 1848. In religious matters he inclined towards skepticism and was far more interested in commercial than in missionary affairs. His experience in the Far East showed him the importance of the missionaries for French political and moral influence, and he decided to support them

with all means at his disposal. Montigny was the founder of the French concession in Shanghai. Cady characterizes Montigny's role with the following statement: "When the new regime of the Prince-President Louis Napoleon eventually got around to formulating a considered policy for the Far East, Montigny's performance at Shanghai was one of the few shining examples of the enhancement of French prestige in that part of the world." See Cady, *op. cit.*, pp. 80-86; Maybon and Fredet, *Histoire de la concession française de Changhai, Paris,* 1929; Meyniard, *Le Second Empire en Indochine,* Paris, 1891.

42. Quoted in Taboulet, *op. cit.*, p. 394. Msgr. Retord had apparently forgotten his earlier request for French military intervention. See note 32 of this Chapter.

43. Taboulet, *op. cit.*, p. 384.

44. Retord's letter to Bourboulon was dated September 19, 1857. It contained hydrographic and topographic information concerning the coastal areas, rivers, anchorages, cities, and neighboring provinces. The letter concluded by urging the French to abandon half-measures, which only aggravated the plight of the missionaries. France should either strike hard or abandon the missions to their fate. Bourboulon used the information contained in Retord's letter to prepare a memorandum to the French government, in which he suggested a major expedition with the objective of permanent occupation by France of a point of territory on the Vietnamese coast. See Cady, *op. cit.*, p. 187. In dealing with this period, Cady overlooks that the French cabinet had already decided on intervention in July, 1857, and erroneously gives as date of this decision November 25, 1857, the day when the orders were issued for the expedition. Bourboulon was actually asking for things already decided upon. See note 1 of this Chapter. Le Thanh Khoi (*op. cit.*, p. 367f.) treats this period very superficially, probably because the events became clear only through the publication of hitherto secret documents in the archives of the Ministry of Foreign Affairs by Taboulet (*op. cit.*, pp. 410-418).

45. Father Huc's note, dated January, 1857, was handed to Napoleon III in person in the course of an audience. Impressed by this note, the emperor set up a "Special Commission on Cochinchina" on April 27, 1857. Taboulet (*op. cit.*, p. 406) remarks that Huc's note does not contain anything that had not been told before by others. But he had the chance to talk to Napoleon III in person and to impress him duly. Father Huc, a successful missionary in China and author of many excellent books on this country, was then too sick to go to Vietnam and be an eyewitness of the conquest. He died in Paris in 1860. His famous

note (Arch. Aff. Etrang. *Mémoires and Documents, Asie,* Vol. 27, fol. 288/289) was first published by Taboulet (*op. cit.,* p. 405f.) with a few omissions and abbreviations. One of his arguments, which probably impressed the emperor most, was that England had an eye on Tourane and would occupy it if France did not do so first.

46. Father Huc and Msgr. Pellerin were only the two most important but by no means the only missionaries and Church dignitaries who campaigned for a French war against Vietnam. Msgr. Pellerin became apostolic vicar for Northern Cochinchina in 1851 and served as an interpreter on *Le Catinat* during the attack of September, 1856 (see note 21 of this Chapter). Pellerin bombared Napoleon III with notes and was also heard by the Special Commission on Cochinchina. He used very successfully the same argument as Father Huc—that England was preparing the seizure of Tourane. (About Msgr. Pellerin, cf. Taboulet, *op. cit.,* pp. 401-406, and H. Perennes, *Un grand coeur, Mgr. François-Marie Pellerin,* Brest, 1938.) Other high Church dignitaries who strongly influenced the decision of Napoleon III to intervene in Vietnam were Cardinal Henri Boisnormand de Bellechose, Archbishop of Rouen, Father Libois, a missionary of long standing in China, and Father Legrand de la Liraye, author of many memoirs to the Emperor. (See Taboulet, *op. cit.,* pp. 401-415, and about Libois, Abbé Loiseau, *Missionnaires originaires du diocèse de Seez,* Seez 1908.) But the strongest influence was exerted by Father Huc and Msgr. Pellerin.

47. Taboulet, *op. cit.,* p. 404.

48. The story of how Napoleon III made up his mind about a war against Vietnam and how his Minister of Foreign Affairs, Count Alexandre Walewski, announced this decision to the cabinet, is told in detail by Taboulet, *op. cit.,* pp. 410-15. Walewski's letter to Napoleon III in which he reported about his announcement to the Council of Ministers, dated Etiolles, July 16, 1857, has already been published by Gaston Raindre in *Revue Française,* March 1, 1925, pp. 53f., in an article, "Papiers inédits du comte Walewski," but has escaped the attention of authors concerned with the history of Vietnam. It has been reprinted in Taboulet, *op. cit.,* p. 413f. The Council of Ministers met on the fourteenth, the fifteenth, or sixteenth of July, 1857. The decision of Napoleon III was certainly influenced by the fact that Great Britain had to suppress a widespread revolution in India and would probably not have been in a position to interfere with a French attack on Vietnam. Cf. also Taboulet, "La première évocation de la question de Cochinchine au Conseil des Ministres," in *Bulletin de la Société des Etudes Indochinoises,* 1943, pp. 69-77, and d'Ornano, *La vie passionante du comte Walewski,*

400

Paris, 1853. Walewski's letter describes in a sarcastic vein how he broached the subject of intervention in Indochina in the Council of Ministers without telling his colleagues that the Emperor had already decided on war. The members of the cabinet were all set against the occupation of Cochinchina. The Minister of Finance, Fould, even said he did not know where Cochinchina was situated and that it certainly was not worth the expenditure of six million francs. When Walewski finally disclosed the Emperor's decision, the ministers felt they had no choice but to vote in favor of intervention. So they did, unanimously.

49. See Father Huc's note to Napoleon III of January, 1857, as quoted in note 45 of this Chapter.

50. This statement is contained in a note edited by the Ministry of Foreign Affairs on March 20, 1857. The note, according to Taboulet (op. cit., p. 407) was unsigned but probably reflected the opinions of Count Walewski. Cady, quoting the same note (*op. cit.*, p. 179) ascribes it to Pierre Cintrat, keeper of the archives of the French Ministry of Foreign Affairs. The wording of the note, with the warning that France already had enough interests abroad to engage her energies without throwing herself into a hazardous and largely profitless venture in the middle of the China Sea, is almost identical with a warning uttered by Guizot in 1844, as quoted by Cady, *op. cit.*, p. 60, and Albert Septans, *Les commencements de l'Indo-Chine française d'après les archives du ministère de la marine et des colonies*, Paris, 1887, p. 128. It is hard to decide whether Taboulet or Septans (Cady's source) is in error. Of Guizot's note Cady gives only an incomplete version, of Cintrat's (or Walewski's) only a brief report. Cady and Taboulet could of course both be right, if one assumed that the official of the Foreign Ministry who wrote the note in 1857 merely copied what Guizot had said in 1844. About the events of 1857 cf. also Cordier, "La politique coloniale," *T'oung Pao*, Vol. X, pp. 33-44.

51. See minutes of the session of the Special Commission on Cochinchina, May 18, 1857 (Arch. Aff. Etrang., *Mémoires et Documents, Chine*, Vol. 27 bis, fol. 1-31, published for the first time in abbreviated form by Taboulet, *op. cit.*, pp. 408f). The minutes contain the interesting statement that, if England had only one-tenth of the rights to Cochinchina that France could claim, Vietnam would already be an English possession. The reasons why Great Britain did not interfere with the French occupation of Cochinchina were (1) her troubles in India in 1857, (2) her recent alliance with France in the Crimean War, and (3) her need for French cooperation in China. Napoleon III was continually wary about England's position and sounded her out before

acting. As far back as May, 1856, Montigny informed Sir John Bowring, British commander-in-chief in the Far East, about "negotiations" with Cochinchina and received promises of "friendly and active cooperation" (Taboulet, *op. cit.*, pp. 395-397). Napoleon III even paid a personal visit to Queen Victoria in Osborne in August, 1857, before he ordered the attack. England did not object to French intervention in Vietnam, but at the same time refused to participate in it. Foreign Secretary Clarendon was far more concerned about denuding India of troops during the Indian crisis than about French designs on Indochina. About French-British diplomatic relations on the eve of the conquest of Vietnam, consult Cady, *op. cit.*, pp. 190ff.; Cordier, "La politique coloniale," *T'oung Pao*, X-XII (1909-1911), pp. 157-169; César Lecat Baron de Bazancourt, *Les expéditions de Chine et de Cochinchine d'après les documents officiels*, 2 vols., Paris 1861 and 1862; H. R. C. Cowley, *Secrets of the Second Empire*, New York, 1929.

52. In the middle of the nineteenth century, about the time Napoleon III became Emperor of the French, the development of capitalism and the "industrial revolution" in England and France had reached a degree at which the interior markets could no longer absorb the production. New outlets were needed, and this completely changed the foreign policies of these countries. The Asian policy of all the Occidental powers, after the beginning of the nineteenth century, reflected this vital necessity for more exports. Their aim was to create privileged markets for themselves. England had already assured herself of such a market in India. So had the Netherlands in Indonesia. China was opened to the European powers about the middle of the century. Other closed regions and potential markets lured Western capital: Japan, Korea, and Vietnam. French commercial and missionary interests combined here for further action. Cf. Devillers, *op. cit.*, p. 9. This distinguished author opens his story of the colonization of Vietnam by stressing the importance of economic motives along the lines of this reasoning. See also Jules Ferry, Premier of France from 1883-1885, "the first French statesman whose foreign policy has been dominated by the concern for colonial expansion" (Robert Delavignette and Ch. André Julien, *Les constructeurs de la France d'outre-mer*, Paris, 1946, p. 264), who wrote: "Colonial policy is the daughter of industrial policy." *Discours et opinions*, Vol. V, p. 557.

53. From the minutes of the session of the Special Commission on Cochinchina, May 18, 1857, cited in note 51 of this Chapter.

54. On July 15, 1857, Admiral Rigault de Genouilly, who recently had distinguished himself during the siege of Sebastopol in the Crimean War, was appointed commander-in-chief of the French forces in the Far East.

The instructions of November 25, 1857, reached him in January, 1858, shortly after the outbreak of the Franco-British hostilities against China. They were signed by the Minister of the Marine Admiral Hamelin, who himself had received instructions from Foreign Minister Count Walewski on the same day. Admiral Rigault de Genouilly was ordered to put an end to the persecution of the Christians in Vietnam by a "demonstration" to be executed without loss of time. He was to command the "demonstration" in person unless his presence was needed on the China coast. His forces were ordered to take Tourane and establish themselves firmly at that place. If the Admiral had to return to the Chinese theater of war, all measures were to be taken to guarantee the safety of the French garrison in Tourane. Walewski's instructions to Hamelin went further, but it seems that Rigault de Genouilly was not immediately informed about the future plans of the French government. It was left to his discretion to establish a protectorate over Cochinchina, if that were possible without too heavy sacrifices; otherwise he should conclude a treaty of friendship, commerce, and navigation, ask for compensation for the loss of the life of French missionaries, and seek guarantees for their future security. Walewski stressed that Admiral Rigault de Genouilly should have great latitude in deciding further steps after the conquest of Tourane. An expedition against Cochinchina must not distract from the Franco-British operations against China. Walewski's letter was published for the first time by Taboulet (*op. cit.*, p. 416f.) from Arch. Aff. Etrang., *Mémoires et Documents, Chine*, Vol. 27, fols. 330-341. Hamelin's instructions to Rigault de Genouilly were published previously by de Vaublanc, "La première campagne de Cochinchine, 1858-1859," in *Ecole de Guerre Navale*, 1935, pp. 34f. See also Paul Baudrit, "L'amiral Rigault de Genouilly," in *Bulletin de la Société des Etudes Indochinoises*, 1933, pp. 1516ff.

55. War had broken out between Great Britain and China in 1856. France joined a few months later, using as a pretext the execution of a French missionary, Father Chapdelaine. The war started with a common British-French attack on Canton, which was captured on January 5, 1858. The British and French now turned to the north, stormed the forts guarding the entrance to Tientsin, and threatened Peking. The Chinese emperor thereupon sued for peace. A treaty was negotiated, which provided for ratification in Peking. When the envoys of Britain and France arrived at the ceremony, they were treated like tribute-bearing ambassadors from dependent nations. To this the French and British ministers strongly objected. The war was resumed and Peking was taken. As a retaliation against the violation of a flag of truce, the beautiful summer

palace of the Manchu emperors was destroyed, sacked, and burned—an unwarranted, senseless, and barbarous act on the part of the European powers. In 1860 a peace treaty was finally signed in Peking. For the Anglo-French war against China, 1857-1860, see Cady, *op. cit.*, pp. 192-206; Cordier, *L'expédition de Chine, 1857-58*, Paris, 1905; Cordier, *L'expédition de Chine de 1860, histoire diplomatique, notes et documents*, Paris, 1906; Bazancourt, *Les expéditions de Chine et de Cochinchine d'après les documents officiels*, 2 vols., Paris, 1861-1862; Morse, *The International Relations of the Chinese Empire*, Vol. I.: *The Period of the Conflict, 1834-1860*, London, 1910.

56. One vessel and 450 men were supplied by Spain. About the Spanish participation in the action against Vietnam, see note 67 of this Chapter. The Spanish point of view is developed in Colonel Palanca's book *Reseña histórica de la expedición de Cochinchina*, Cartagena, 1869. Literature on pre-French Vietnamese history is scarce, but there is an abundance of books on the conquest itself, mostly by French authors. The most important sources are: Blet, *Histoire de la colonisation française*, 3 vols., Grenoble, 1946-1950; Boeuf, *Histoire de la conquête de la Cochinchine, 1858-1861*, Saigon, 1927; Chassigneux, *L'Indochine*, Paris, 1932; Chastel, *Un siècle d'épopée française en Indochine, 1774-1874*, Paris, 1947; Cultru, *Histoire de la Cochinchine française des origines à 1883*, Paris 1910; Roy, *La Chine et la Cochinchine*, Lille, 1862; Septans, *Les commencements de l'Indo-Chine française d'après les archives du ministère de la marine et des colonies*, Paris, 1887; Thomazi, *La conquête de l'Indochine*, Paris, 1934, Pallu de la Barrère, *Histoire de l'expédition de Cochinchine en 1861*, Paris, 1864; Vial, *Les premières années de la Cochinchine*, 2 vols. Paris, 1874. To these standard works eyewitness accounts and reports of participants have to be added: Rigault de Genouilly, *Expédition de Tourane* (no place and date of publication given); de la Grandière, *Les débuts de l'occupation française en Cochinchine*, Paris, 1864, 1888; de Pouchalon, *Indochine: Souvenirs de voyage et de campagne, 1858-60*, Tours, 1896. Furthermore, some publications in periodicals should be mentioned: Baulmont, "La prise de Tourane, Septembre 1858-9 et Mai 1859-Septembre 1859," in *Revue Indochinoise*, 1904 and 1905; Galos, "L'expédition de Cochinchine et la politique française en Extrême-Orient," in *Revue des Deux Mondes*, 1864; de Rosny, "La Cochinchine et l'occupation française du Port de Tourane," in *Revue Orientale et Américaine*, 1859; Sallet, "Campagne Franco-Espagnole du Centre-Annam: Prise de Tourane, 1858-1859," in *Bulletin des Amis du Vieux Hué*, 1928; Thomson, "The Diplomacy of Imperialism: France and Spain in Cochinchina, 1858-1863," in

Journal of Modern History, 1940; Le Thanh Canh, "Notes pour servir à l'histoire de l'établissement du protectorat français en Annam (1847-63)," in *Bulletin des Amis du Vieux Hué*. This is the only treatment of the conquest by a Vietnamese. Le Thanh Canh's notes were published in different issues of the *Bulletin*: 1928, nos. 3 and 4; 1929, no. 1; 1932, no. 2; 1937, no. 4. This bibliography lists works dealing with the whole French conquest of Vietnam or the first part of it. It omits books that are exclusively devoted to the later phases of the conquest: the actions against Tongking in the 1870's and 1880's.

57. Genouilly also complained that the missionaries had promised resources in the country that did not exist. They had given false reports about the disposition of the population, had characterized the power of the government as weakened by the mandarins—he found it strong. They had denied the existence of an army—the regular army, however, was very numerous and the militia comprised all able-bodied men of the country. They had boasted that the climate was healthy, but it was unhealthy. Genouilly furthermore complained that Vietnam had no highways and was cut up by innumerable flooded rice fields. Hué could be reached only by a shallow river, was well fortified in the European style, and was defended by an army well equipped with artillery. (See A. Thomazi, *La conquête de l'Indochine*, Paris, 1934, p. 32.)

58. Genouilly's utterances show that religious questions had little to do with the Franco-Spanish intervention. The decapitation of the Spanish bishop, Msgr. Díaz, by Tu Duc's orders is commonly given as one of the reasons for the Franco-Spanish intervention in Vietnam. But news of the execution reached Paris only in October, 1857, while the decision to attack Vietnam was made in July.

59. Colonel Henri de Ponchalon, a French officer who took part in the campaign, wrote an interesting diary, *Indochine: Souvenir de voyage et de campagne, 1858-60*, Tours, 1896, in which he records the conflict between Genouilly and Pellerin. He writes (*op. cit.*, pp. 133f.): "A lively debate has been taking place between the Admiral and Msgr. Pellerin, at the close of which the Bishop will be returned . . . to Hong Kong." Genouilly's strategic concept is explained in a letter to the Minister of Marine, in which he sets forth his reasons for attacking Saigon. This letter, reprinted in Thomazi, *op. cit.*, p. 33, again complains about the reports of the missionaries, which he calls "confused and contradictory." By taking Saigon, Genouilly intended to humiliate the king of Vietnam in the eyes of the neighboring kings of Siam and Cambodia. Another reason, not mentioned in his letter to the Minister but stressed by Thomazi, was his suspicion that the British planned to seize that

place. Genouilly's hostility toward the missionaries is also proved by a later report to the French government, dated September 21, 1859, in which he claimed that the principal barrier blocking his negotiations was the profound distrust felt by the Vietnamese for the French priests. (Quoted by Cady, *op. cit.*, p. 221, from the hitherto unpublished archives of the French Foreign Ministry, *China*, Vol. 28, fol. 249.)

60. See Thomazi, *op. cit.*, p. 37.

61. Quoted by Cady, *op. cit.*, p. 217.

62. The French Bishop of Saigon, Msgr. Lefèbvre, visited Genouilly on February 16, 1859, and subsequently influenced some of the Christian inhabitants of Cochinchina to seek French protection by assembling near Saigon. These Vietnamese Christians supplied the French troops with some food but did not assist them otherwise. Cf. Cady, *op. cit.*, p. 217; Bazancourt, *op. cit.*, Vol. I, pp. 300ff.; Ponchalon, *op. cit.*, diary entry for February 16, 1859. For an opposite opinion see Louvet, *La Cochinchine religieuse*, Vol. II, pp. 236-238. The author claims that the Vietnamese Christians assembled at Saigon later came to the aid of the French forces by forming a protective belt around the besieged city. Louvet does not give corroborating evidence for his statement.

63. British and French naval forces had been repulsed at the Taku forts in northern China on June 25, 1859. This called for French reinforcements in the Chinese war. At the same time Spain, France's ally in Indochina, lost interest in that campaign. Both these events had their influence on Genouilly's negotiations with Hué. The French admiral formulated three demands: (1) religious liberty for missionaries and native Christians; (2) freedom of commercial access to Vietnam; (3) cession of a point of land to serve as a guarantee. The Vietnamese delegate to the negotiations accepted these demands in principle but employed delaying tactics, while Genouilly's men died of cholera and typhus. On August 11, he dropped his territorial demand and substituted for it permission to establish a consulate and acknowledgement of France's right to protect the missionaries. As the Vietnamese plenipotentiary continued to stall, Genouilly issued an ultimatum, which expired on September 7, 1859. On that day he resumed hostilities under considerably worse conditions (Cady, *op. cit.*, pp. 230f.; Ponchalon, *op. cit.*, pp. 193-209; Bazancourt, *op. cit.*, Vol. I, pp. 347, 376).

64. While still a pretender to the throne, Napoleon had promised to unite Italy, but as soon as he became Emperor, he forgot his pledge. A member of the Italian secret society of the Carbonari, Orsini, reminded him by throwing a bomb at the Emperor. Now Napoleon III thought it wise to fulfill his promise. In alliance with Sardinia, he declared war

406

on Austria on May 3, 1859. After having been defeated in two battles, Austria signed the truce of Villafranca on June 11. The campaign lasted only thirty-nine days. Austria ceded the province of Lombardy to Sardinia. This gave the signal for a general uprising in Italy, which ended with the overthrow of all local dynasties and the creation of a kingdom of Italy. The Pope too was deprived of almost all his territory. This was one of the reasons why the Catholic party in France turned its back on the Emperor.

65. Genouilly departed for Paris on October 31, 1859. All during 1860 he pleaded with the French government to hold out in Saigon. In 1867 he became minister of marine. For the change of command during the campaign in Indochina cf. Thomazi, *op. cit.,* pp. 40-43, and Bazancourt, *op. cit.,* Vol. I, p. 364.

66. For the second phase of the Franco-British war against China, see also note 55 of this Chapter. The entire campaign was poisoned by rivalry and petty jealousy between the allies. It started with the first action of the war, the conquest of Canton, after which the British accused the French troops of having selected the most valuable articles of loot and of halting their thievery only after the British ambassador, Lord Elgin, intervened. The English, however, did not behave any better, so that the same Lord Elgin had to complain, "I have seen more to disgust me with my fellow countrymen . . . among populations too weak to resist and too ignorant to complain . . . than I saw during the whole course of my previous life." Cf. Cady, *op. cit.,* pp. 192-196; Laurence Oliphant, *Narrative of the Earl of Elgin's Mission to China and Japan in the years 1857-58-59,* Edinburgh, 1859, Vol. I, pp. 95f.; George M. Wrong, *The Earl of Elgin,* London, 1905, pp. 102-105, 109, 113; Bazancourt, *op. cit.,* Vol. I, pp. 158f.

67. With the 600 French soldiers under Jaureguiberry were about 230 Spaniards under Colonel Carlos Palanca, who wrote his own version of the war in Indochina (see note 56 of this Chapter). In addition to this small contingent of the Spanish army, four vessels of Spain's navy took part, but not all at one time. The Spanish contribution was rather modest and was viewed as such by the French. The Spanish government, however, stressed that Spain helped France to occupy Saigon and asked French assistance for the annexation of Tongking or a part of that province. When peace negotiations started in 1861, Palanca insisted on a Spanish foothold in northern Vietnam, preferably Hanoi. The French commander, Admiral Charner, was unable to spare the forces to aid any Spanish expedition against Hanoi and suggested a monetary contribution instead, which Spain finally accepted against the advice of Colonel Palanca. Spain was

accorded half of the indemnity collected from Vietnam: ten million francs. Cady (*op. cit.*, p. 273) calls Spanish participation in the Indochina campaign a "wholly unprofitable venture." See also Palanca, *op. cit.*, pp. 344ff.; R. Stanley Thomson, "The Diplomacy of Imperialism: France and Spain in Cochinchina, 1858-1863," in *Journal of Modern History*, 1940, pp. 334-356; Thomazi, *op. cit.*, pp. 41, 46f., 71-75.

68. The port of Saigon was opened to commerce on February 22, 1860, by initiative of Admiral Page. In the first year after its opening, 111 European vessels and 140 Chinese junks landed in Saigon, discharging 80,000 tons of cargo and leaving with rice for Hong Kong and Singapore. The Chinese of Cholon, Saigon's Chinatown, were the first to profit from the commerce with foreign countries. Thomazi (*op. cit.*, pp. 41f.), a strong advocate of French imperialism, summarizes the situation in a somewhat simplified form, saying that "Rumors spread over the country that our presence has become a source of wealth. One more reason for the mandarins to try to throw the 'barbarians' into the sea."

69. These ideas can be found especially in the writings of Francis Garnier, a navy lieutenant, author, explorer, and adventurer, who later played a prominent role in the first French attempt to conquer Tongking. See his *La Cochinchine française en 1864*, Paris, 1864, published under the pseudonym G. Francis, and *Voyage d'exploration en Indochine, effectué pendant les années 1866, 1867, et 1868*, 2 vols., Paris, 1873. In his writings Garnier takes a strong anti-British (and, by implication, also anti-American) stand. His argument held that if France was to avoid national decadence and world domination by the Anglo-Saxons, she must be present at all important points of the globe; France must not subordinate her Asian policy to the wishes of England. Garnier admired the Chinese but had not a very high opinion of the Vietnamese. France's civilizing mission must not be questioned in connection with the opening of countries like Annam, Cambodia, or Siam to French influence. In Indochina France should erect the empire of which Dupleix had dreamed in the eighteenth century. See Garnier, *Voyage d'exploration*, Vol. I., pp. 447f., 545-58; Albert de Pouvourville, *Francis Garnier*, Paris, 1931; Cady, *op. cit.*, pp. 275-93. About Garnier's role in the conquest of Tongking, see pages 370-74 of this Chapter.

70. Cady (*op. cit.*, pp. 276f.) analyzes the mood of France toward colonial questions in the 1860's. Two of the traditional roots of French imperialism in the Far East had lost their impact. The first was the personal and dynastic prestige of Napoleon III. In this respect the Mexican affair replaced interest in Vietnam. Saigon was now considered a prestige liability for the Emperor rather than an asset. Even the assump-

tion of the protectorate over the remainder of Cochinchina in 1867 aroused no enthusiasm in France. The second root of imperialistic motivation, interest in the fortunes of the Catholic missions, ceased to be a decisive element of French policy, especially after the appointment of Admiral Genouilly, a foe of the missionaries, to the post of minister of marine. Those interested in the continuation of French colonization in Indochina therefore felt it necessary to stress the "white man's burden" in the rich vocabulary of the French language. This is reflected in the works of French historians dealing with this period.

71. Like the Chinese who called the Europeans "foreign devils," the Vietnamese were shocked by the behavior of the French, especially by their shouting and losing of temper, by their white faces, the different color of their hair, and by their very different body odor. This disgust the Orientals felt toward the white man has been described by many travelers, authors, and scholars concerned with the East.

72. Vietnamese popular literature has produced many satirical songs against the mandarins. Some of these songs deal with very unpolitical subjects but suddenly take a turn against the mandarins. A good example is a love song quoted by Chesneaux (op. cit., pp. 100f.) in which a village youth woos a peasant girl. In proposing to her he warns her: "Never marry a literate man [a mandarin]; he has a long back which he likes to cover with beautiful material, he keeps combing his hair, and lets his nails grow [a sign that he does not have to perform manual work], and he leaves the table only to go to bed. . . ."

73. The most prolific French missionary author on this period was Henri Cordier, for many years editor of the magazine T'oung Pao, where most of his articles were published. He divided his interest between China and Vietnam. Cordier's most famous papers on Indochina, some of them already mentioned in previous notes, are: "Bordeaux et Cochinchine sous la Restauration," 1904; "Le Consulat de France à Hué sous la Restauration," 1884; "La France et la Cochinchine, 1857-8," 1905; "La France et la Cochinchine, 1852-58: la mission du Catinat à Tourane (1856)," 1906; " La France et l'Angleterre en Indochine et en Chine sous le Premier Empire (Indochine, 1852-58)," 1911; "La reprise des relations de la France avec l'Annam sous la Restauration," 1903. Other important French works on this period (some of them quoted in previous notes) are: Blet, Histoire de la colonisation française, 3 vols., Grenoble, 1946-1950; Boeuf, Histoire de la conquête de la Cochinchine, 1858-61, Saigon, 1927; Chassigneux, L'Indochine, Paris, 1932; Chastel, Un siècle d'épopée française en Indochine, 1774-1874, Paris, 1874; Cultru, Histoire de la Cochinchine française dès origines à 1883, Paris, 1910;

Gautier, *Les français au Tonkin, 1787-1883*, Paris, 1884; Hanotaux, *Histoire des colonies françaises*, Paris, 1905 (Vol. V deals with Vietnam); Meyniard, *Le Second Empire en Indochine*, Paris, 1891; Vial, *Les premières années de la Cochinchine française*, 2 vols., Paris, 1874. Typical of the missionary point of view is Abbé Louvet, *La Cochinchine religieuse*, 2 vols., Paris, 1885. The French authors base their accounts chiefly on official sources, most of them supplied by the Ministry of Marine and Colonies. Two Vietnamese authors also deserve mention in this bibliography: Cho Huan Lai, *Les origines du conflit franco-chinois à propos du Tonkin jusqu'en 1883*, Paris, 1935; Le Thanh Canh, "Notes pour servir à l'histoire de l'établissement du protectorat français en Annam (1847-63)," *Bulletin des Amis du Vieux Hué*, 1928, 1929, 1932, and 1937.

74. See Chapter V, note 27.

75. One of the reasons why France refused to support the revolution in the North was a tacit agreement with Spain, according to which Tongking was considered a Spanish sphere of influence. For the same reason the commander of the Spanish troops in Indochina, Colonel Palanca, pleaded for a common Franco-Spanish intervention in Tongking. When Bonard refused Palanca's demand for a campaign in support of the rebellion in the North, the Spanish commander had to give in, and with Bonard he signed the Treaty of Saigon on June 5, 1862. As soon as civil war broke out again in Tongking in August, 1862, Palanca renewed his demand. Bonard again refused. The court of Hué now tried to make use of the rift between the European powers by quoting alleged earlier statements of Palanca that Spain had no territorial aspirations and by appealing to the Spanish commander to help Vietnam in putting down the rebellion. This Tu Duc's mandarins even asked as a price for ratification of the Treaty of Saigon. That intrigue backfired, however. Bonard and Palanca joined hands once again and forced ratification of the treaty by an ultimatum. In April, 1863, Spain withdrew her contingent from Indochina, leaving France a free hand (Cady, *op. cit.*, pp. 272f.; Thomson, *op. cit.*, pp. 350-356; Blet, *op. cit.*, Vol. II, p. 223; Thomazi, *op. cit.*, pp. 71-75). Admiral Bonard, a sick man at that time, was replaced by Rear Admiral de la Grandière. Bonard died in 1867.

76. See Cady, *op. cit.*, p. 277.

77. "The persecution [of the Catholic faith] by the rulers of Annam was the pretext for our intervention and supplied us with the precious opportunity to establish ourselves in the Far East."—Gosselin, *op. cit.*, p. 89.

78. Thomazi, *op. cit.*, pp. 71f.

79. The rebellion broke out first on the island of Condore but was quickly suppressed there by a small French force under Ensign Richard. On December 12, 1862, an envoy of Tu Duc arrived at Saigon and handed the French authorities a note demanding an annulment of the peace treaty and restoration of the three provinces of Cochinchina to the sovereignty of Hué. The envoy departed immediately without awaiting a reply. On December 16 the revolt was in full swing in the whole of Cochinchina. The French were outnumbered but, owing to their superior armament, could hold their own. Bonard was obliged to call on Rear Admiral Jaurès, commanding French naval forces in the China Sea, for help. Jaurès sent what he could spare: half a battalion of Algerians from Shanghai, one battalion of light infantry from Tientsin, half a battery of artillery. He even "borrowed" eight hundred Spaniards from the captain-general of the Philippines. With these reinforcements Admiral Bonard started his counterattack on February 25, 1863. After a quick initial victory he presented an ultimatum to Tu Duc: If he did not ratify the treaty at once, Bonard would occupy the adjoining three provinces of Cochinchina and support the revolt against Hué in Tongking. Tu Duc accepted. Bonard and Palanca, guarded by more than a hundred soldiers, proceeded to Hué, where the ratification took place on April 14. On April 16, 1863, Tu Duc received Bonard and Palanca in solemn audience. The usual prostration of visitors to the Emperor of Annam was dispensed with. The two officers were even allowed to keep their swords during the ceremony. Cf. Thomazi, *op. cit.*, pp. 72-76.

80. Napoleon III's intervention in Mexico was probably his least realistic military adventure. It weakened France so much that she finally lost her decisive fight for supremacy on the continent of Europe against Prussia-Germany in 1870 and 1871. While the United States was paralyzed by the Civil War and therefore unable to enforce the Monroe Doctrine, Napoleon decided to intervene in Mexico, where an anti-clerical regime under Juárez had come to power. He forced upon the Mexicans a devoutly Catholic ruler, the Austrian Archduke Maximilian. In 1867 the Mexican revolution was victorious and Maximilian was executed at Querétaro, after the French army of occupation had been forced to leave the country under United States pressure with heavy loss of life, money, and prestige.

81. As a consequence of the Mexican venture, budget allocations for the war in Indochina were sharply cut (Cady, *op. cit.*, p. 274; Blet, *op. cit.*, Vol. II, p. 223).

82. Vietnamese law forbade the sale of opium under penalty of death. However, the province of Ha Tien in the South was exempted from this

draconic measure because its population was almost entirely Chinese. The Chinese were much addicted to this drug, and the Vietnamese emperors did not feel responsible for the welfare of their subjects of Chinese racial stock. Cf. Le Thanh Khoi, *op. cit.*, p. 369, note 76.

83. The price for a mandarinate of the ninth degree was one thousand *ligatures,* that for the sixth degree ten thousand. A comparison of the *ligature* with modern currency is difficult. According to Le Thanh Khoi (*op. cit.*, p. 369, note 76) the *ligature* was exchanged, at the time of the conquest, against one gold franc or about twenty United States cents. The purchasing power was probably much higher. The basic unit of the Vietnamese currency was a zinc coin, pierced in the middle, which the French called *sapèque* and the Indochinese *dong*. Sixty zinc coins were carried on a string, which unit was called a *tien*. Ten *tiens* formed the higher unit, named *ligature* by the French and *quan* by the Vietnamese.

84. Phan Than Giang was accompanied to France by a French naval lieutenant, Adrien Barthelemy Rieunier, who later became an admiral and minister of marine. Rieunier supplied a characterization of Phan Than Giang which Gosselin printed in his book (*op. cit.*, p. 141). Phan Than Giang was then seventy years old. According to Rieunier he was sweet and gentle. Under his fine and smiling features he hid an unusual energy. The old mandarin was ready to render a great service to his country: to persuade the French to leave Vietnam and restore the conquered provinces to their rightful ruler. He refused to believe that France had no intention of doing so. Le Thanh Khoi says that Phan Than Giang was "honest but incompetent" (*op. cit.*, p. 371). This contrasts sharply with the opinion of Cady, who calls him "venerable, able and persistent" (*op. cit.*, pp. 274, 280). After his mission had proven a failure and French penetration of Vietnam continued, Phan Than Giang committed suicide by poison (Thomazi, *op. cit.*, pp. 93ff.; Cordier, *Le conflit entre la France et la Chine,* Paris 1883, pp. 19f.; Blet, *op. cit.*, Vol. II, pp. 229f.; H. I. Priestley, *France Overseas,* New York, 1938, p. 116).

85. Up to that time, the French had used the name Cochinchina for the whole country. From then on Cochinchina referred to the protectorate in the south alone; the middle portion of Indochina became known as Annam; the northern part, adjoining China, was called Tongking. For the nomenclature and the frontiers between the three parts of Vietnam under French colonial rule, cf. the large, detailed map in Chassigneux, *op. cit.*, p. 546.

86. Albert Septans, *Les commencements de l'Indochine française d'après les archives du ministère de la marine et des colonies, les mémoires ou relations du temps,* Paris, 1887, p. 184, says about the

treaty: "We restored to Tu Duc all the territories drenched with the blood of our soldiers for an indemnity in money; we only reserved the right to have a consul in Hué." Septans was a captain on the general staff of the French marines. Another French author, M. du Hailly (*Souvenir d'une campagne dans l'Extrême-Orient,* published in 1866), shows how public opinion changed against a settlement in Indochina almost from one day to the next. The financiers especially used all their eloquence against it. The high cost of Napoleon's Mexican adventure had a decisive influence on the French taxpayer's unwillingness to subsidize a war against Vietnam. The Ministry of Finance was therefore very agreeable to an exchange of the conquered territory in Cochinchina against the payment of an indemnity. This made another navy man, Lieutenant Rieunier, complain (*Les premières années de la Cochinchine française*) that the sacrifices of France and "blood nobly shed" were to be bartered away against money. Napoleon III was not in favor of giving up the French conquest in Indochina. The Marquis de Chasseloup-Laubat and Admiral Rigault de Genouilly were the most ardent partisans of a colonization of Indochina. But a strong faction in parliament, and especially French public opinion, at that time were against continuing the conquest of Indochina. Chasseloup-Loubat fought this trend of public opinion in memoranda to the Emperor in which he claimed that Vietnam in French hands would prove as valuable to France as India was to the British and Java to the Dutch. Cf. Septans, *op. cit.,* pp. 184-187.

87. Quoted from the preface by M. de Bizemont to E. Luro's *Le pays d'Annam,* pp. 2 and 3, Paris, 1878.

88. The chief exponent of this navy policy was Francis Garnier, whose writings are dealt with in note 69 of this Chapter. Another was Admiral Rieunier (see notes 84 and 86 of this Chapter), who wrote under the pseudonym M. H. Abel. See e.g. his *Solution pratique de la question de Cochinchine, ou fondation de la politique française dans l'Extrême-Orient,* Paris, 1864. This book was distributed by the official agent of the Ministry of Marine and Colonies (Cady, *op. cit.,* p. 275, note 21).

89. For a recent well-documented treatment of this phase in Franco-Vietnamese relations, see K. Stanley Thomson, "France in Cochinchina: The Question of Retrocession 1862-65," in *The Far Eastern Quarterly,* Vol. VI, no. 4, August, 1947, pp. 364-378. The author shows Napoleon's continual wavering and how his hand was forced by the debates in the Corps Legislative and by the intervention of the Minister of Marine, Prosper de Chasseloup-Laubat. Thomson quotes a letter from Chasseloup-Laubat, reviewing the debates in parliament in the preceding months, which groups the legislators into three schools of thought: (1) those who

favored limiting France to a "factory" at Saigon; (2) those who would occupy certain strategic points like Saigon and others as a means of controlling the country and assuring France of the trade of Cochinchina; (3) those, with whom he associated himself, who would found a full-fledged colony in Cochinchina. Another strong partisan of conquest was Admiral Bonard, who predicted that if France made clear her firm determination to keep her colony, Cochinchina would pay its way within a few years. Admiral de la Grandière promised that the conquest would be easy, prompt, and not costly. The Ministry of Foreign Affairs was against continuation of the colonization of Indochina, and temporarily prevailed. The debate went on through 1864. By June, 1864, unrest in Vietnam became so threatening that Foreign Minister Drouhin de Lhuys was finally convinced that Grandière's suspicions of Annam were well founded, and he slowly gave in. If any one man was responsible for the momentous decision to retain the colony, that man seems to have been Chasseloup-Laubat, whose arguments finally prevailed upon Napoleon III. In a remarkable note of November 4, 1864, he put all the arguments in favor of conquest before the Emperor, and less than three months later the decision was taken to continue colonizing Indochina. Thomson summarizes the reasons for Napoleon's decision as follows: (1) desire for prestige in the Orient; (2) the conviction that France did have a true civilizing mission, a Christian mission which, once undertaken, she could not abandon; (3) a feeling of confidence that this most distant and most recent addition to "France overseas" was destined to enjoy a brilliant future.

90. During the first phase of the Mexican war Napoleon III was very anxious not to alienate Great Britain. The Mexican intervention had started as a common Franco-British debt-collecting action, and Napoleon was eager to retain England's good will. Therefore Cambodia was a very delicate problem, as it was under Siamese suzerainty and Siam itself was a British sphere of influence. Doudart de Lagrée, nevertheless, raised the French tricolor on the royal palace of Cambodia in Oudong, in March 1864, and declared in a letter to King Norodom that France will never tolerate Siam's interference in Cambodian affairs. However, he mitigated his harsh acts by sweet words. While Siam denied Cambodia's independence, he said, France recognized it absolutely. King Norodom tried to negotiate a new treaty with Siam in August 1864, was reprimanded by Admiral de la Grandière and travelled to Saigon in October 1864, accompanied by Doudard de Lagrée, to render his apologies. Thus, in effect, Siamese and Vietnamese suzerainty over Cambodia was replaced by that of the French. Cf. Septans, *op. cit.*, pp. 172-188.

91. The treaty was negotiated by Doudart de Lagrée with the assistance of Msgr. Miche in Phnom Penh between 1863 and 1867. It was signed in Paris on July 15, 1867. The most important provisions of the treaty were: (1) Siam recognized the French protectorate over Cambodia; (2) the existing treaty between Siam and Cambodia was declared null and void; (3) Siam renounced all tributes, presents, and other signs of Cambodian vassalage; (4) France promised not to incorporate the kingdom of Cambodia into her colony of Cochinchina; (5) Angkor and Battambang were definitely ceded to Siam. Other terms of the treaty included reciprocal freedom of travel and rights of property to exploit Cambodian forests and the right of the missionaries to preach and teach. Napoleon III first hesitated to ratify the treaty for fear it would offend the British, but was finally persuaded by Chasseloup-Laubat and de la Grandière to do so (Septans, *op. cit.*, p. 199; Cady, *op. cit.*, pp. 275f.; Blet, *op. cit.*, Vol. II, pp. 224-226; Thomazi, *op. cit.*, pp. 84-89; Antoine Cabatan, "Doudart de Lagrée et l'Indochine, 1828-1868," in *Revue de l'Histoire des Colonies Françaises*, 1933, pp. 205ff).

92. The exploration of the Mekong valley was a pet project of Chasseloup-Laubat, who was both minister of marine and president of the French Geographical Society. He obtained Napoleon's consent in 1865. The exploring team consisted of six men, five of them navy officers and one a representative of the Ministry of Foreign Affairs. Two of the participating naval officers were scientists, one a geologist, the other a botanist. Leader of the expedition was Doudart de Lagrée, second in command Francis Garnier. Lagrée died during the exploration through illness in the Yangtse valley in March, 1868. The five surviving members of the team returned, under the command of Garnier, via Hankow and Shanghai to France. At Hankow the historic meeting of Garnier and Jean Dupuis took place. To Francis Garnier now fell the task of writing and editing the report on the expedition. His book was published in 1873, in a two-volume folio-sized de luxe edition. Volume I contains a chronology of the exploration, while Volume II deals with meteorology, geology, mineralogy, anthropology, botany, the languages of the countries, and other subjects. Volume I is beautifully illustrated and contains excellent pictures of the ruins of Angkor. A one-volume edition of this book was later published by Garnier's brother. From the standpoint of French colonialism, the most important discovery of the Lagrée-Garnier expedition was the unsuitability of the Mekong River as a commercial route to southern China and the possibility of using the Red River for this purpose.

93. The author of this article was Louis Carné. The passage is quoted

by Renouvin, *op. cit.*, p. 69. A longer extract is given in Gosselin, *op. cit.*, pp. 157f.

94. Cady, *op. cit.*, p. 281.

95. Jean Dupuis, the energetic "empire builder" living in Shanghai, supplied the Chinese imperial army with weapons during an uprising of the Mohammedans in western China. He found it difficult to transport heavy pieces of artillery to the province of Yunnan by overland routes, and decided therefore to explore Francis Garnier's theory that it was possible to reach Yunnan from Hanoi by way of the Red River. In 1868, he tried for the first time to sail down the Red River from Yunnan, but was stopped by the Mohammedan insurgents. But in 1870 a second expedition succeeded. He crossed the mountain chain separating Yunnan from Vietnam, reached the Red River at Manghao, sailed up to Bacha, and discovered that it was possible to travel the whole country between Hanoi and Yunnan easily by boat. At the same time he established that these districts were rich in precious metals. He described his discovery in a book, *L'ouverture du fleuve rouge au commerce et les événements du Tonkin,* Paris, 1872 and 1873. He then went to France to obtain official sanction for the mission to open the Red River to French navigation. He received permission to go to Hué on a ship showing the French flag. The Paris government thought that Tu Duc would not dare refuse a vessel displaying the tricolor the right to enter the Red River. But he did. Dupuis, on the advice of the governor of Cochinchina, Admiral Dupré, undertook his voyage under the Chinese flag.

96. Taboulet, *op. cit.*, pp. 678-693. See also Dupuis' own accounts, *L'ouverture du fleuve rouge au commerce,* 1872-1877; *Journal de Voyage,* Paris, 1879; *Les origines de la question du Tonkin,* Paris, 1896; and see especially F. Romanet du Caillaud, *op. cit.*

97. In 1872 Dupuis solicited the help of the Ministry of Marine but did not succeed in extracting any other promise than that a French naval vessel would cruise near Haiphong and thus afford him a kind of moral support. It was furthermore stated that Dupuis had to bear the expenses of his undertaking and renounce any liability on the part of the government if he should encounter misfortune. Admiral Dupré supported Dupuis' plea, but the two men did not succeed in obtaining stronger government backing, mainly because the Minister of Foreign Affairs, the Duc de Broglie, was against any new colonial adventures. Cf. Cady, *op. cit.*, pp. 283ff.; Agnes Murphy, *The Ideology of French Imperialism, 1871-1880,* Washington, 1948, pp. 58-83.

98. Taboulet, *op. cit.*, p. 694.

99. Quoted by P. Boudet, "Francis Garnier," in *Cahiers de L'Ecole*

Française d'Extrême-Orient, nos. 20-21, (1939), p. 46. See also Taboulet, *op. cit.,* pp. 698-699.

100. See the letter of September 12, 1873 by Admiral d'Hornoy, Minister of Marine and Colonies, published for the first time by Taboulet, *op. cit.,* pp. 699-701.

101. About these Chinese pirates, Taboulet writes: "The remnants of the Taiping revolt, who had found refuge in the Tongking mountains, made the law [in Tongking]. Organized in the manner of the *Grandes Compagnies* of our Hundred Years' War, the Black and Yellow Flags lived off the country, blackmailing and terrorizing the population, with the representatives of the Hué government looking on helplessly. The Vietnamese officials were forced to let Chinese regulars penetrate the country in pursuit of the rebels, and if Chinese troops were lacking, they played along with the pirates and even took them into their service to limit the damage they did."—*op. cit.,* p. 679. See also Jean Dupuis, *Les origines de la question du Tonkin.*

102. About conditions in Tongking, see Msgr. Colomer, Apostolic Vicar of Eastern Tongking, letter of August 26, 1873, published by Romanet du Caillaud, *op. cit.,* pp. 410-12 and reproduced by Taboulet, *op. cit.,* pp. 680-682.

103. Cf. what Romanet du Caillaud, *op. cit.,* pp. 77-80 says in the Chapter "Projet de M. Senez." It is noteworthy that Taboulet pays little attention to Senez. Khoi and Cady do not mention him at all, nor Chesneaux, whose point of view would be strongly supported by a description of Senez' project.

104. Francis Garnier, born July 25, 1839, was only twenty-four when he became the administrator of the city of Cholon. Dupré first wanted to entrust his Tongking expedition to Captain Senez, who refused for reasons of health. See Romanet du Caillaud, *op. cit.,* p. 82.

105. See note 92 of this Chapter.

106. Romanet du Caillaud, an uncritical admirer of Garnier, says: "He directed a commercial enterprise and his geographical explorations at the same time. His aim was to penetrate into Tibet and decide the question, until then unsolved, of the origin of the great rivers that flood India and Indochina."—*op. cit.,* p. 84.

107. In addition to the works already mentioned, both on Garnier and on the conquest of Tongking, a number of biographies of Francis Garnier exist, of which the most important ones are by Leo Garnier, 1882; Edouard Petit, 1887; A. de Pouvoirville, 1931; Jacques Garnier, 1933; R. Vercel, 1946 and 1952.

108. Dupré's scheme was indeed unexpectedly promoted by the Viet-

namese themselves, when the court of Hué, in July, 1873, appealed to Saigon for assistance in expelling Dupuis from Hanoi. This encouraged Dupré to hasten his preparations and to start the action before a veto from Paris could reach him. It also underlined the military weakness of Tu Duc in Tongking. Romanet du Caillaud's frank story (the book is quoted little by later French authors) reveals that both Dupré and Garnier were consciously deceiving Hué.

109. In fighting the Vietnamese, Garnier used explosive projectiles, which were probably the main reason for his success against a numerically superior adversary. He himself described the use of these explosive projectiles in a letter to his brother, dated November 20, 1873. This letter and several others, as well as a complete description of this phase of the French conquest of Tongking, are to be found in *Tonkin, or France in the Far East*, by C. B. Norman, London, 1884.

110. "The cause of French imperialism in Tongking suffered a serious check in his death and acquired its most glorious martyr."—Cady, *op. cit.*, p. 286.

111. About the economic difficulties of Cochinchina and the colony's deficit, see in particular the letter of the Minister of Marine and Colonies d'Hornoy of September 12, 1873, to Admiral Dupré (Taboulet *op. cit.*, p. 699-701).

112. Taboulet, *op. cit.*, p. 738, telegram of the Minister of Marine to Admiral Dupré, of January 7, 1874. Also M. Dutreb, *op. cit.*, p. 98.

113. M. Luro was one of the first outstanding men in the administration of the colony. At the time he wrote to Garnier he was administrator of native affairs in Saigon. He later wrote one of the best early books on Vietnam (*Le pays d'Annam*, Paris, 1879). He had a high opinion of the Vietnamese nation, which he described as "strengthened by ten centuries of contact with Chinese civilization, and rejuvenated by the blood of the races it had subdued or pushed out of the way in its southward expansion."

114. Quoted from Romanet du Caillaud, *op. cit.*, p. 423, from a letter of December 21, 1873, by Luro to Garnier, who was killed the day the letter was written.

115. The expression Philastre used was "*baratier quelconque.*" This letter also reached Hanoi only after Garnier's death. Quoted by R. du Caillaud, *op. cit.*, pp. 421-422. Chesneaux quotes this passage on page 124, *op. cit.*, from H. Brunschwigg, *La colonisation française*, Paris, 1949.

116. The most plausible explanation of Philastre's nonaggressive attitude is threefold. As a longtime student of the Annamite language in close touch with the indigenous courts of law, he had come to look

upon such adventures as Garnier's through Annamite rather than French eyes. Furthermore, he was doubtless aware of the general nature of the previous instructions from Paris and the limitations as to both objectives and methods which these instructions had enjoined. Garnier had certainly exceeded those instructions. Finally, Philastre came to Hanoi directly from his conference with the court at Hué, before whom he had been unable to defend the tactics employed by Garnier. He apparently believed, therefore, that a flat disavowal of the French coup at Hanoi was the best means of facilitating the negotiations at Hué of the pending Cochinchina treaty."—Cady, *op. cit.*, pp. 287-288.

117. The treaty was signed by Hué on March 15, 1874. For the text of the treaty, see Gosselin, *op. cit.*, Appendices, Annexe no. 7, pp. 506-513.

118. J.-L. de Lanessan, *L'expansion coloniale de la France*, Paris, 1886, p. 527.

119. See his previously unpublished letter of Dec. 25, 1873, to Admiral Dupré, in Taboulet, *op. cit.*, pp. 731-733.

120. For details, see *La correspondance politique du commandant Rivière*, Hanoi, 1933. Rivière's views contrasted sharply with those of most Frenchmen who lived in Vietnam. They had on the whole a very high opinion of the Vietnamese, although they understood them little and indulged in much superficial psychological analysis. Even the French officers fighting in the colonial war in Indochina were captivated by the charm of the Vietnamese, both men and women. An example is the analysis of the Vietnamese character in *Notice sur la Basse-Cochinchine*, by L. L. de Grammont, Paris, 1864. The author took part in the Indochina campaign as an army captain. Here are a few of his observations: "The Annamites are naïve like children, subtle debaters, and cautious in the extreme. They are haughty by character but they are taught to hide this trait. They conceal, as the case may be, their spirit of cunning behind a mask of fear, or their pride behind a sweetish refinement. They are superstitious without fanaticism, slaves of their tradition, lacking political convictions. They are capable of loyalty and gratefulness. They are sometimes generous, full of respect for justice and veneration for the aged. They do not lack gaiety, though basically they are of an apathetic temper. They are less refined than the Chinese but have more moral strength. They are more intelligent than the Cambodians and the Siamese and more gifted for business. They are unimpressed by fits of rage but can be captivated by friendliness. They combine taste for luxury with personal modesty, glamorous feasts with a great simplicity of manners." And about Vietnamese women Grammont writes: "The

Annamite women in general are small but well built; the shape of their faces resembles the oval of the Europeans; their eyes are straight and not slit like the Chinese; their teeth are beautiful but, unfortunately, blackened by the use of betel. They wear their incomparably black hair on the back of their neck, bound together with a studied negligence not devoid of charm. Their complexion varies from brownish yellow to yellowish white. The latter is in highest esteem. The Annamite woman walks with her head high, her breasts pointing forward. She is gay, sweet, and likes to laugh. She is very prolific, an excellent mother to her children, and of indefatigable activity." Jean Baptiste Eliacin Luro, a friend of Francis Garnier, who came to Indochina with the French navy in 1864 and was from then on connected with the administration of the colony, wrote in his standard book on Vietnam, *Le pays d'Annam, Etude sur l'organisation politique et sociale des Annamites,* Paris, 1897: "Under a cool exterior the Annamite is mobile, easygoing, spirited, a talker, and a mocker. An admirer of knowledge, he is an ardent student. He possesses both memory and intelligence. Humble and polite in manner, he is in fact haughty and conceited. A passionate gambler, he is generous and lives from day to day. He does not possess the courage of other Occidental races; quite on the contrary, he is horrified by war but nevertheless despises death. His heroism is passive. Capable of accepting a general morality and even a positive religion, he imitates our vices rather than our virtues. The Annamite woman, as long as she is young, is coquettish, takes life easy, and is fond of luxury; as soon as she becomes a mother, she inspires respect for her domestic virtues."

121. Chesneaux, *op. cit.,* p. 129. Chesneaux seems to be the only French author who has pointed out this important fact.

122. These are the words of M. Rheinart, French resident at Hué at the time of Rivière's death, as quoted by Gosselin, *op. cit.,* p. 179.

123. "The New Motives for Imperialism which developed during the decade were the increasing concern for markets overseas and the intensification of international competition for colonies," Cady, *op. cit.,* pp. 289-294. See also Chesneaux, *op. cit.,* p. 127ff., and Taboulet, *op. cit.,* p. 675.

124. For the close relationship between these geographical societies and French imperialism, see in particular Agnes Murphy, *The Ideology of French Imperialism, 1871-1880,* Washington, 1948; and Donald Vernon McKay, "Colonialism in the French Geographical Movement, 1871-1881," in *Geographical Revue* XXXIII, 1943.

125. On May 15, 1883, the Chamber voted the credits for Tongking, 351 to 48, the opposition consisting mainly of conservative right-wingers. See Chesneaux, *op. cit.*, p. 129.

126. Quoted by Gosselin, *op. cit.*, p. 183.

127. The treaty of August 25, 1883, was replaced in June, 1884, by one somewhat modified in favor of Vietnam. However, the new treaty also gave to the French complete control of the Tongking administration, leaving the North of Vietnam a protectorate in name only. Annam was not subjected to the same degree of interference and control, but the French insisted on their right to put any number of troops at any place they chose. For full texts of the treaties see Gosselin, *op. cit.*, annexes 9 and 11; for brief descriptions, Hall, *op. cit.*, pages 573-574, and Le Thanh Khoi, *op. cit.*, p. 378.

128. See Hall, *op. cit.*, p. 573.

129. This was accompanied by a conflict with Thailand which led to a French naval demonstration before Bangkok. The French regarded themselves as the inheritors of the suzerainty that Vietnam had formerly exercised over Laos. However, the conquest of Laos was only completed and made permanent after China too had recognized France's new acquisition in a convention signed in June, 1895. England, which had been disturbed by French action against Thailand, finally also concluded a convention with France in January, 1896, in which the two powers agreed on their respective zones of influence in Indochina. Cf. Auguste Pavie, *A la conquête des coeurs,* re-edited by André Masson, Paris, 1947; P. Le Boulanger, *Histoire du Laos,* Paris, 1930.

130. This quotation is from the much neglected book by Joseph Chailley, entitled *Paul Bert au Tonkin,* Paris, 1887, pages 290, 291. Paul Bert, a former physician, professor of science at Bordeaux and Paris, entered public life after the 1870 revolution. He was prefect, deputy to the French Parliament, and Minister of Education. He was chosen for the difficult position in Indochina because of his great reputation as scientist, administrator, and man of public affairs.

131. Gosselin, *op. cit.*, p. 241. What Gosselin has to say on pp. 236-237 about the first installation by the French of a Vietnamese ruler sounds like a warning from the past—which, however, was not heeded by the leaders of France in 1947 when they first conceived the plan to send Bao Dai back to Vietnam as head of a French-sponsored government: "The installation of a new sovereign at Hué did not produce the expected results for the pacification of the country. Far from being resigned to accomplished facts, the whole of Annam rose from north to

south, in the name of its fugitive sovereign." The new French-appointed emperor Dong Khanh was commonly referred to by the Vietnamese as the "valet of the French."

132. Van Dinh Phung's revolt collapsed soon after his death late in 1895, and "all rebels who did not succeed in gaining Siam by crossing Laos were brought to Hué and put to death. The repression was terrible." Gosselin, *op. cit.*, p. 314.

133. De Tham, whose real name was Hoang Hoa Tham, was left undisturbed for many years and even tolerated as the head of a small region comprising twenty-two villages. Only after 1909 were his forces dispersed, after the roads that gave access to his retreat had been built. He himself was caught and killed in 1913. (See Le Thanh Khoi, *op. cit.*, p. 384.)

134. See J.-L. de Lanessan, *La colonisation française en Indochine*, Paris, 1895, p. 30. De Lanessan was particularly incensed by the practice of beheading village notables who either did not know or refused to say which way had been taken by a group of rebels that had gone through their village.

135. De Lanessan, *op. cit.*, p. 5. Canals had been built by the French in the South before this time, but it is again another French authority on Indochina who claims that they served strategic purposes only. They were built to facilitate access to the interior of the country, from which the many bands of guerillas operated. See Paul Bernard, *Nouveaux aspects du problème économique Indochinois*, Paris, 1937, p. 9.

136. Masson, *op. cit.*, p. 97.

Chronology

FOR the purpose of this brief summary, it will be useful to divide the history of Vietnam from the beginning of the twentieth century to the present time into five periods, each of which can be distinguished from the others by a definite trend of all major events.

First Period: 1900-1940

During these four decades, the French had to deal with numerous strong waves of Vietnamese resistance in various forms, but they remained always firmly in control of the whole country. This period was the only one during which Vietnam was not a burden to the French state. The economic development of Vietnam, which the French initiated but also kept strictly within definite limits, made Indochina France's "richest colony." It also produced great changes in the social structure of Vietnam. One result of these changes was the rise of new and Western-inspired movements of national liberation, among which, however, the Communists were not yet prominent when the fall of France brought this period to an end.

The main events and trends of this period can be associated with the following dates:

1900

Paul Doumer, Governor General of French Indochina, destroyed the old organization of the Vietnamese state and established French control on all levels of administration. "From this period dates Indochina as we know it today."—George Lamarre, in *L'Indochine,* edited by G. Maspéro, Vol. II, p. 18. The construction of large public works, such as the bridge over the Red River at Hanoi, the Trans-Indochinese railroad, and the new harbor installations at Saigon, was begun. Doumer's drastic fiscal reform was completed. The new taxes "hurt many private interests and went against century-old traditions, but the financial results were brilliant, and at the price of individual sacrifices, Indochina moved in a few years from the stage of a primitive economy on to the road of great modern achievements."—André Masson, *op. cit.,* pp. 98-99.

1901

An observant Frenchman, who became a prominent writer on French Indochina, visited Vietnam and noticed the price the Vietnamese people had to pay for Doumer's achievements: "The Public Works are empowered to requisition labor. This becomes an ill-disguised deportation. . . . [They] drain entire communities for public construction work, from which only a small fraction returns. . . . The mortality rate is frightening. Rice is furnished only irregularly. . . . There is a single physician over a distance of 120 kilometers."—Jean Ajalbert, *L'Indochine en péril,* Paris, 1906. The effect that the administration's monopoly of production and sale of salt had on the people was best described by one of the most eminent French authors on Indochina, the geographer and economist Pierre Gourou: "If the fisherman lacks salt, he had better discard his fish, which the sun will quickly ruin. . . . It is not rare to see a fisherman, with tears in his eyes, abandon the produce of a day's labor on the shore, simply because he did not save enough money to acquire, at its exorbitant price, the condiment he sees in abundance, a few hundred meters away, in the forbidden zone of the marshes."—*Les paysans du delta Ton-*

kinois, Paris, 1936. Self-production of salt or alcohol, common in precolonial Vietnam was severely punished after Doumer had made these products state monopolies. Together with the high customs tariffs, they became the main sources of income of the colonial administration.

1902

In October, Paul Beau took over as Governor General. Doumer had left Indochina in March. Beau's aim was the "moral conquest" of the Vietnamese people. He opened the lowest positions of the administration to Vietnamese aspirants, organized medical assistance, and abolished certain corporal punishments. Later (1907) he created the so-called "university" of Hanoi. But Beau's moral conquest failed. His promotion of education did not repair the damage done by the earlier governors, who "had unwittingly destroyed the traditional education" (Virginia Thompson, *French Indochina,* London, 1937, p. 285) and had re-established schools on paper only. The Vietnamese had become "more illiterate than their fathers had been before the French occupation."—Jules Harmand, *Domination et colonisation,* Paris, 1910, p. 264. A succession of bad harvests added to the existing discontent among the peasants and increased anticolonial sentiments among the educated; the former cheated the state by making their own salt and alcohol, and often opposed administrative action by force; the latter began to form secret nationalist societies.

1903

Phan Boi Chau, one of the great figures of the coming new Vietnamese resistance movement, directed his propaganda and underground work from his exile in China. With him, the old Confucianist opposition of the educated began to give way to a modern rationalist and antitraditionalist spirit.

425

1904

Chau went to Japan and conceived his plan to free Vietnam with Japanese help. This was also the year of the first rubber harvest, from trees planted eight years earlier.

1905

Japan's victory over Russia raised the hopes and intensified the resistance of the Vietnamese nationalists. Numerous secret societies were formed. Lacking a clear political goal, they all tended toward terroristic action. Phan Boi Chau returned clandestinely to Vietnam. Among his many new converts was Prince Cuong De, then only twenty-four, a direct descendant of Gia Long. He too turned toward Japan, where Count Okuma had begun to describe his country as the "soul that guides Asia."

1906

The pan-Indian national congress proclaimed the independence of India as its aim. Phan Boi Chau, who had returned to Japan followed by Prince Cuong De, published his rousing pamphlet *New Letters Written in Blood*. He founded the Association for the Modernization of Vietnam (Viet Nam Duy Tan Hoi, usually referred to as Duy Tan), Vietnamese students flocked to Tokyo; Vietnamese exiles in China read Rousseau, Voltaire, Diderot, and Montesquieu in Chinese translations, and smuggled these French authors and Chau's writings into Vietnam. Another great scholar, Phan Chau Trinh, who in 1905 had resigned his high post as Minister of Rites, also went to Japan, but returned firmly convinced that no help for the liberation of Vietnam would come from there. He submitted a boldly written memoir to Paul Beau requesting more education and fewer taxes for the Vietnamese people. Phan Chau Trinh rejected both Chau's revolutionary tactics and monarchist aim. He sought freedom through cooperation with France and wanted Vietnam to become a democratic republic.

1907

Paul Beau was recalled as Governor General in February. In March, nationalist intellectuals in Hanoi opened the Dong Kinh Nghia Thuc (Free School of Tongking), under the leadership of a young teacher, Nguyen Hien. The school, which was supported by all nationalist elements, became a center of anti-French agitation. It was suppressed in December. Nguyen Hien and his collaborators were arrested, tried, and condemned to death, but protests of the League of Human Rights prevented their execution. Instead, they were sent to Poulo Condore, which was turned into a French concentration camp for Vietnamese nationalists. In September, the French deposed the eccentric Emperor Than Thai, after declaring him insane. His seven-year-old son became Emperor under the name Duy Tan (New Reforms).

1908

Mass demonstrations at Faifo, Quang Nam, Thua Thien, and Bienh Dinh in March and April requested a reduction of the high taxes. As a symbol of their desire to turn from the old toward new ways of life, the demonstrators cut off their long hair. In Center Vietnam, a real mass movement of "hair cutters" with distinct political motives developed. The demonstrators were fired on without warning; many were arrested and deported to Poulo Condore, and some executed. During this time, the old leader De Tham resumed his active resistance in Tongking. An attempt to poison the French garrison at Hanoi on June 27 started a wave of ruthless repression against known nationalists all over the country. The "university" of Hanoi was dissolved, the importation of books from China was forbidden, and even nationalist "reformists" who preached co-operation with France, like Phan Chau Trinh, were deported to Poulo Condore. The new Governor General Klobukowsky (September, 1908-January, 1910) gradually restored order. His success was partly due to the fact that the nationalist movement had been dealt a serious blow by the Japanese government in July, 1907: Japan pledged to respect all French possessions in Asia, for a loan from France of 300,000,000 francs.

1909

The price of salt was now five times higher than in 1899, but because of fraud and underconsumption, the income from the sale of salt had only doubled during the same period. Klobukowsky failed in his efforts to reduce the high profits of the companies holding licenses for the production and sale of alcoholic beverages.

1910

Japan expelled Phan Boi Chau and Prince Cuong De.

1911

After the outbreak of the Chinese revolution in Canton, Chau went to China. He kept in close contact with all other Vietnamese exiles and with the Kuomintang, under whose influence he began to favor a Vietnamese republic, with Prince Cuong De as president. Albert Sarraut, "who tried to kill nationalism with kindness" (J. S. Furnivall, *Educational Progress in Southeast Asia*, New York, 1943, p. 87), began his first term as Governor General (November, 1911-January, 1914). Phan Chau Trinh was released from Poulo Condore and permitted to go to Paris.

428

1912

Chau succeeded in uniting most nationalist groups in a League for the Restoration of Vietnam (Viet Nam Phuc Quoc Dong Minh Hoi, usually referred to as Phuc Quoc). Under the presidency of Prince Cuong De, he organized in Canton a Vietnamese government in exile, but in spite of great propaganda efforts from abroad, the national movement remained weak, and active resistance was only sporadic during the next three years. Sarraut opened the French Lycée at Hanoi to Vietnamese pupils; but he also went to Canton, where he obtained the arrest of Vietnamese exiles in exchange for placing the French-owned Yunnan railway at the disposal of the Chinese authorities for their fight against the Kuomintang. Chau was thrown into a Chinese prison, where he wrote his autobiography.

1913

The Resident Superior of Annam at Hué broke into the tomb of Tu Duc to rob it of its treasures for the benefit of the colonial administration. Several terrorist attacks occurred at Hanoi and Thai Binh; an insurrection in the South, organized by Gilbert Chieu, was put down before it had a chance to develop.

1914

The main features in the economic and social development of Vietnam under the colonial regime were clearly perceptible before the outbreak of the First World War, and remained unchanged until the eve of the Second World War:

1) Capital came chiefly from abroad—until 1914 primarily from the French state, after 1920 largely from French private investors. "So successfully did the French resist the investment of non-French European capital in their close preserve that in

1938 they owned 95 per cent of the European capital invested in business enterprises and all the capital invested in government securities."—D. G. E. Hall, *A History of South-East Asia,* p. 657. The goal of all investments was not a systematic development of the country but immediate high returns. Only a small fraction of the high profits made in Vietnam by private companies was reinvested locally. The chief investors were large banks.

2) Economic policy was directed toward the exploitation of natural resources for direct export. The main exports were rice, coal, rubber, rare minerals, and other unfabricated goods. The development of indigenous industries was kept within narrow bounds. Apart from rice mills and cement works, they were restricted to the production of goods for immediate mass consumption—breweries, distilleries, match factories, sugar refineries, paper mills, and a few textile and glass factories. But all these industries employed only a total of about 90,000 workers in 1929. The aim of this restrictive economic policy was to preserve the colony as a market for overpriced, tariff-protected products of French industry. Between 1921 and 1938, Indochina's imports from France averaged 57.1 per cent of the total.—Hall, *op. cit.,* p. 657.

3) The development of Indochina as a market for French goods was obstructed by the brutal fiscal policy of the colonial regime, which took from the peasant the money he would need to purchase imported products. The exceptionally exploitive character of French colonialism, as K. Mitchel has pointed out in his *Industrialization of the Western Pacific,* thus contributed to the survival of many old village industries in Indochina. All public works—canals, railroads, harbors, and later highways—were paid for, either directly or indirectly, by the indigenous taxpayer, or as Pierre Gourou put it, "each piaster expended by the state has, directly or indirectly, been taken from the minute incomes of the peasants."—*Op cit.,* p. 224. The

great foreign concerns paid either no taxes or very little, and some were even subsidized by public funds.

4) Public works were not primarily undertaken for economic reasons, and although paid for by the Vietnamese, they were of benefit chiefly to the colonial regime and the French speculator, investor, and exporter. The Trans-Indochinese railroad, still uncompleted in 1940, duplicated the much cheaper water route; like the canals in the South, it was built mainly for strategic purposes, and under the pressure of profit-hungry financial groups in Paris. It had "no real economic justification," just like the much-advertised highways that "represent a political and touristic rather than an economic interest."—Paul Bernard, *op. cit.*, pp. 10 and 23. The peasant had no use for these highways and hated them. "The long lines of men and women carriers, trotting along barefoot at the side of the roads, among passing automobiles which they have learned to fear, is a familiar sight in the Annamite deltas."—Ch. Robequain, *The Economic Development of French Indochina*, London-New York, 1944, p. 105.

5) The area of rice land and rice production had enormously increased between 1880 and 1930, but the amount of rice for the individual peasant's consumption had decreased seriously and had not been compensated by the consumption of other foods. This was due to the rapid increase of the population, and to a social and economic policy that made the export of rice most profitable when the peasant had not enough to eat: The poorer the harvest, the less he was able to pay his debts, and the larger was the share of his crop he had to relinquish, in order not to lose his small plot of land to the large landowners and become a sharecropper. "French administration favored the establishment of large estates and European plantations. In Cochin-China concentration of land in this way went so far that the landed class came to control over 80 per cent of the rice-fields, with 200,000 families employed in share

431

cropping."—Hall, *op. cit.*, p. 655. This "landed class" consisted very largely of Vietnamese collaborators (but also of many Frenchmen) whom the colonial administration rewarded by letting them acquire the newly created land. They, and Chinese middlemen and French exporters, were the only ones who profited from the increase in the area of rice land. Again in Cochinchina, 71 per cent of the landowners had only 15 per cent of the land; the great landholders, no more than 2.5 per cent of all owners, had 45 per cent of the land. The number of peasant families in Vietnam without any land at all was estimated before the Second World War as comprising over 50 per cent of the population. The high profits of the large owners, who took at least 40 per cent of the tenants' crops, explained their total lack of interest in raising the output per hectare, which remained the lowest of all major rice-producing countries. And the French themselves, who "were more interested in commerce, in the export rather than the production of rice" (Devillers, *op. cit.*, p. 32), never did anything to improve the individual peasant's lot. While rice exports kept rising, many peasants "could not satisfy their hunger all year round."—Robequain, *L'Indochine*, p. 167.

6) In regard to medicine and public health, the main achievements of the French lay not in the social field but in the field of research. Infant mortality remained one of the highest in the world, hygienic conditions in mines and on plantations were appaling, hospitals and clinics were few and not primarily for the indigenous population. "The fact remains that the human cost of these first efforts to equip the country could have been greatly reduced with a better prepared, more modern and better financed medical organization."—Paul Mus, *Viet-Nam, sociologie d'une guerre*, p. 107. "All the justly famous work of the Pasteur Institute in Indochina did not alter the fact that medical assistance remained poorly organized and insufficient, particularly in the countryside, where the

432

mass of the people lived. In the Philippines there was one doctor for every 3,200 native inhabitants; in Indochina there was only one for every 38,000."—Lauriston Sharp, "Colonial Regimes in Southeast Asia," *Far Eastern Survey*, February 27, 1946, p. 49.

1915

The administration began to ship Vietnamese workers and soldiers to France, altogether about 100,000 during the whole war. Prince Cuong De was in Berlin to seek German military support against the French in Vietnam. Resistance revived with an attack by nationalists on a military post at Ta Lung (Langson), The French suppressed the triennial literary competitions in Tongking (later, in 1918, also in Annam).

1916

The eighteen-year-old Emperor Duy Tan led an unsuccessful revolt against the French. All participants were either executed or deported. Duy Tan was caught, deposed, and, like his father, exiled to Réunion Island in the Indian Ocean. The French installed Khai Dinh, father of Bao Dai, as the new Emperor.

1917

Return of Sarraut for his second term as Governor General (January, 1917-May, 1919). The success of the Chinese revolution in Canton freed Phan Boi Chau. A Vietnamese student of the military academy in Tokyo, Luong Ngoc Quyen, was arrested in Hong Kong and handed over to the French. His torture provoked an uprising of the indigenous garrison at Thai Nguyen, where he was kept. The town of Thai Nguyen was taken, but the Vietnamese were soon defeated by French troops from Hanoi.

1918

Sarraut reopened the university of Hanoi.

1919

The old revolutionary movement led by Chau declined rapidly.

1920

Cautious reforms were instituted under the Governor General Maurice Long (February, 1920-April, 1922). He created a consultative chamber for Annam and reorganized the Cochinchinese Colonial Council, admitting ten Vietnamese but raising the number of the French members to fourteen. A period of economic prosperity began. Many Vietnamese collaborators, in particular money-lending large landholders, became rich. They sent their sons to study in France and tried to obtain the additional privileges of those Vietnamese who had already received French citizenship. However, even among these elements, nationalist sentiments remained alive, and their children were likely to become revolutionaries.

1922

A new "bourgeois" type of nationalist leadership began to emerge — men like the gifted journalist Nguyen Van Vinh and the writer Pham Quynh, who both advocated Franco-Vietnamese collaboration, the former being republican, the latter monarchist.

1923

Bui Quang Chieu, one of the earliest to obtain French citizenship, and Nguyen Phan Long, both spokesmen of the

Vietnamese collaborationist bourgeoisie, founded the Constitutionalist Party of Cochinchina. Ho Chi Minh, whose name was still Nguyen Ai Quoc, went to Moscow. (He was born on May 19, 1890, according to Khoi, *op. cit.*, p. 440; Devillers, *op. cit.*, p. 57, gives 1892 as his year of birth. His real family name was Nguyen Van Cung, which he dropped when he left Vietnam in 1911. After long travels he settled in Paris in 1919 and became a member of the Socialist Party, but joined the Communist Party after the Congress of Tours in 1920.)

1924

The lack of success of the "reformist" movements led to a revival of clandestine groups. An attempt by a Vietnamese student in Canton to assassinate the visiting Governor General Merlin (August, 1922-April, 1925) failed.

1925

The Emperor Khai Dinh died. Bao Dai, twelve years old and studying in France, became Emperor. The interim governor used his youth and absence to arrogate to the French administration the remaining few royal prerogatives. Phan Boi Chau was led into a trap in the French concession in Shanghai and arrested. He was taken to Hanoi and condemned to death, but the sentence was commuted to confinement for life. Ho Chi Minh, who had returned from Moscow founded in Canton the Revolutionary Youth League (Viet Nam Thanh Nien), nucleus of the future Indochinese Communist Party. As a result of the election victory of the French Left in 1924, Alexandre Varenne, a Socialist, became Governor General (November, 1925-January, 1928). He granted an amnesty and a few civil liberties in Cochinchina, but brought no fundamental change in French colonial policy.

1926

The Cao Dai religion was founded in the South. Bao Dai was installed as Emperor but remained in France to complete his education. Ton That Han exercised the regency.

1927

Nguyen Thai Hoc, a young nationalist teacher, together with other nationalist intellectuals, created in Tongking the Vietnam Nationalist Party (Viet Nam Quoc Dan Dang, usually referred to as VNQDD), after the model of the Kuomintang.

1929

The Communist Party of Indochina was founded.

1930

This was a year of violent rebellion and cruel repression. In February the VNQDD started a general uprising, but only the garrison of Yen Bay was briefly successful. The movement was repressed "with heartless severity."—Hall, *op. cit.*, p. 646. For the first time, airplanes were used against villages. The VNQDD leaders were arrested and Nguyen Thai Hoc was executed. In March, Communist-inspired strikes broke out on plantations in Phu Gieng; in the summer, mass demonstrations of peasants started in northern Annam. Communist agitation and starvation led to a general uprising, to the establishment of local soviets, and to acts of peasant terror against landlords and notables. In August, the reorganized leadership of the VNQDD was arrested and executed. The Foreign Legion was let loose on the rebellious peasants. Airplanes against villages and the torture of prisoners were now common French methods of repression. A Committee for the Defense of Indochinese Nationals, under the French author Romain Rolland, listed 699 executions without trial during 1930, as well as 3000 arrests, 83 death sentences, and 546 sentences for life.

1931

Between January and April, 1500 more Vietnamese were arrested. Due to the "ferocity of the repression" (Hall, *op. cit.*, p. 647), both the nationalist and Communist wings of the revolutionary movement entered a period of decline.

1932

Bao Dai returned from France.

1933

After the failure of the revolutionary movements, the Vietnamese tried to advance the cause of national liberation through reforms from above. In the hope of forestalling a revival of revolutionary movements, the French promised substantial reforms. In May, the thirty-two-year-old governor of Phan Thiet, Ngo Dinh Diem, "known for his perfect integrity, his competence and intelligence" (Devillers, *op. cit.*, p. 63), was appointed Minister of the Interior and made secretary of a Commission of Reforms. All his efforts were sabotaged by the French and their Vietnamese tools at the court. Ngo Dinh Diem resigned in September.

1935

Under the leadership of Pham Cong Tac, the Cao Dai religious sect took on a political orientation and was henceforth a factor in the nationalist camp. The leaders favored Prince Cuong De and expected Japanese aid for the liberation of Vietnam. In 1938 the movement, restricted to the South, counted 300,000 members.

1936

The French Popular Front government extended some political freedom to the colonies. In Indochina, parties were permitted only in Cochinchina. The Communists in Saigon were temporarily put in the shade by a strong Trotskyite movement, which was victorious in a Saigon municipal election.

1938

Huynh Phu So, called by the French "the crazy bonze," began his preaching and founded the Hoa Hao sect in Lower Cochinchina. He predicted the war, the defeat of France, and the coming of the Japanese.

1939

The outbreak of the war led to the suppression of all political freedoms granted after 1936.

Second Period: 1940-1945

All during the Second World War, after the fall of France, Vietnam was occupied by the Japanese and economically exploited for the benefit of Japan—to the detriment of France and at the price of additional suffering for the Vietnamese people. The French colonial administration, which remained loyal to Vichy France and maintained a public order that was advantageous mainly for Japan, was removed by the Japanese only in March, 1945. The forceful removal of the French cleared the way for a Vietnamese national government, which was set up at Hué and was permitted by the Japanese to proclaim the independence of Vietnam. This government lacked both the means and the freedom of action to establish its authority over the whole country. However, the circumstances of its formation convinced the Vietnamese people that the end of the Second World War would also bring them the end of foreign rule. When Vietnamese exiles came back from China just before and after the collapse of Japan, another revolutionary government of independent Vietnam was formed in Hanoi. But unlike the one at Hué, the Hanoi government was dominated by the Communists, who during the war had succeeded in building up a paramilitary organization, and by successfully advertising their anti-Japanese activities in northern Vietnam had even gained Chinese and Allied support.

The main events of these years are:

1940

On June 19, three days after the fall of France, Japan demanded the end of all arms transports to the Chinese armies via Indochina, and the right to send a control commission to the Vietnamese-Chinese border. General Catroux, head of the colony since August, 1939, accepted the Japanese ultimatum on June 20. In July the government of Marshal Pétain replaced General Catroux with Admiral Decoux. A new ultimatum and a Japanese naval demonstration in the Gulf of Tongking led to the agreement of Haiphong, which permitted Japan to station troops in Indochina. A clash between French and Japanese troops at the Chinese border was the signal to the pro-Japanese nationalist group Phuc Quoc (founded by Chau in 1912) for a widespread uprising, which did not get the expected support of the Japanese, who preferred to cooperate with the Vichy French rather than support the Vietnamese nationalists. Mass executions by the French re-established order. When the Japanese moved into Vietnam in September, the Communists staged an uprising in the South (a counterorder of their leaders abroad did not reach them in time). It was suppressed through airplane bombardments, mass executions, and mass deportations. Vichy agreed to the use of all Indochinese cities, ports, and airfields by the Japanese army.

1941

Ho Chi Minh succeeded in persuading a few nationalist groups of exiles in China to join the Communists in a "united front," the Viet Nam Doc Lap Dong Minh. The Vietminh, as it was subsequently called, issued an appeal on September 8, asking the Vietnamese people to fight the "Japanese and French Fascists" on the side of the Allies, to which the Soviet Union had belonged since June, 1941. Under Japanese pressure, France was forced to cede Indochinese territory (parts of Cambodia and Laos) to Thailand. In July, Vichy and Tokyo signed a treaty of "joint defense," and on November 9 a convention that gave Japan economic control of Indochina. The Japanese maintained all the bad features of French colonialism, including the unchecked authority of the French administration to extract high taxes from the Vietnamese people.

1942

The Japanese army and political police began to "protect" Vietnamese nationalists from the French police. They gave "asylum" to the pro-Japanese leader of the Hoa Hao sect. In China, Ho Chi Minh was arrested by order of Chiang Kai-shek; Moscow-trained Vo Nguyen Giap, future Minister of Defense under Ho Chi Minh, began to organize guerilla groups for anti-Japanese activities in northern Tongking. Under the patronage of the Kuomintang, a new Vietnamese national front,

440

the Dong Minh Hoi (DMH), was founded and put under the leadership of an old exile—Nguyen Hai Than, in China since 1906. It remained ineffective, although it consisted of all important groups, such as the old VNQDD, the Phuc Quoc, and the Vietminh.

1943

Dissatisfied with the new Vietnamese national front, the Chinese released the Communist leader Nguyen Ai Quoc, who, in order to hide his identity, now took the name Ho Chi Minh. He was expected to put life into the Dong Minh Hoi, but worked only through and for his Vietminh. "Of all the members of the Dong Minh Hoi, only the Vietminh . . . was in a position to give needed information to the Allies on Japanese movements and installations; only the Vietminh had a network of cells throughout Vietnam, and it never placed this at the disposal of other members of the Dong Minh Hoi."—Ellen Hammer, "Parties and Politics in Viet Nam," *Foreign Affairs Reports,* Vol. II, No. 12, p. 149, December, 1943. Ho Chi Minh, as chief of all the nationalists grouped in the Dong Minh Hoi, now received from the Chinese Nationalist government 100,000 dollars per month, which he used to strengthen the Vietminh.

1944

This was the crucial year in the struggle among the Communist and non-Communist exiles in China for leadership of the Vietnamese national revolution. In March the Chinese organized the Congress of Lieu Tscheou, and again forced all Vietnamese groups to unite and to form a "provisional government." The Chinese Nationalists were opposed to a return of the French to Indochina. This Chiang Kai-shek had already told President Roosevelt in Cairo in November, 1943, saying of the French in Indochina "that for every dollar they have put in, they have taken out ten."—*The Public Papers and Addresses of Franklin D. Roosevelt,* 1944-45, Volume, "Victory and the Threshold of Peace," pp. 562-563. Roosevelt himself shared Chiang Kai-shek's sentiments. "France has had the country . . . for nearly one hundred years, and the people are worse off than at the beginning. . . . France has milked it for one hundred years. The people of Indochina are entitled to something better than this."—Cordell Hull, *Memoirs,* New York, 1948, p. 1597. Roosevelt favored an international trusteeship for Indochina, but in the Allied councils, the French, supported by the British, eventually won out. Although under heavy attack at the Lieu Tscheou Congress, Ho Chi Minh, thanks to his organization inside Vietnam, again emerged as the strongest Vietnamese leader in exile. In addition to financial support from the Chinese, his organization began to receive American weapons through the OSS (Office of Strategic Services) in southern China, in exchange for the information the Vietminh was able to give about the Japanese. "If the informations it supplied were frequently not very exact, they had the merit of being numerous, and this always makes an impression."—Devillers, *op. cit.,* p. 106. Inside Vietnam, the Vietminh groups began to apply their main weapon—terror—not only in their rather isolated attacks on the Japanese, but also to requisition rice and to eliminate their Vietnamese nationalist opponents. Ho Chi Minh was said to have left China for Vietnam in October.

1945

March 9: The Japanese disarmed and interned the French army, arrested most French administrators, and put an end to French rule in Vietnam. French military resistance was weak.

March 11: With Japanese permission, Emperor Bao Dai proclaimed the independence of Vietnam, but under Japanese pressure accepted the principles of the Japanese Greater East

Asia Manifesto. He asked Ngo Dinh Diem to form a Viet-namese national government, but the latter either chose not to answer the invitation or never received it through the Japanese-controlled communication service; Ngo Dinh Diem and the Japanese no longer trusted each other.

March 16: In Saigon the various nationalist groups came out into the open. The Cao Dai, Phuc Quoc, and other pro-Japanese leaders thanked Japan for having freed Vietnam from the "French pirates and assassins." In northern Annam anti-French sentiment crystalized in the founding of the Dai Viet party.

March 24: The French government (de Gaulle) announced a vague promise of more freedom for the Indochinese peoples in an Indochinese Federation. Vietnamese of every political orientation rejected this declaration, asserting that the inde-pendence of Vietnam had become a reality.

April 17: Bao Dai asked the scholar Tran Trong Kim to become Premier; Kim accepted and formed his government at Hué. All its members were French-educated but were also ardent Vietnamese patriots. Tran Van Chuong, later Ambas-sador of South Vietnam to Washington, was the moving spirit of this government.

May 8: Bao Dai, happy to be no longer a mere tool of the French, announced the preparation of a constitution for the reunited country, which would give the people full politi-cal and religious freedom. The slogan of the new regime would be "everything for the people."

May-June: The Tran Trong Kim government announced a fiscal reform, exempting all nonowners of property and all wage earners making less than twelve hundred piasters a year from personal income tax. Under a Ministry of Youth, the government began to organize a great youth movement. A

443

political amnesty was proclaimed, and political parties were officially permitted. French administrators were replaced by Vietnamese, and the French language was supplanted in all schools by the teaching of *"Quoc Ngu,"* the Vietnamese language in Latin transcription. But the presence of the Japanese army, the difficulties of communication due to Allied bombings, the lack of financial resources and of a minimum force to keep order, made the government of Tran Trong Kim ineffective. Everybody seemed to expect a decisive turn of events only after the collapse of Japan.

August 7: Hiroshima. Ho Chi Minh called his guerillas under Vo Nguyen Giap "Army of Liberation." The Vietminh also held a National Congress and announced the formation of a "Committee for the Liberation of the Vietnamese people."

August 10: Japan offered to capitulate. The Vietminh ordered a general uprising.

August 14: In the South, a United National Front was formed, consisting of the Cao Dai, the Hoa Hao, the Trotskyites, the Communists, who were still weak, and several other nationalist groups.

August 15: Japan capitulated.

August 16: The Japanese released all political prisoners. The United National Front took power in Saigon.

August 17: In a great demonstration in Hanoi, Vietminh leaders (and the Vietminh flag) appeared publicly for the first time, on the balcony of the Municipal Theater. There were more demonstrations on August 18, organized already and dominated by the Vietminh.

August 19: The nationalist groups who did not support the Vietminh were gradually driven from the streets of Hanoi: Vietminh storm troopers began to occupy all public buildings. Vietminh propaganda abstained from all attacks on the Japanese. The Japanese let the Vietminh take the arms of the "Indo-chinese Guards."

August 20: Without a fight, the Vietminh "Committee of Liberation" had achieved control of the administration in northern Vietnam. Discouraged, Tran Trong Kim offered to resign. Vietminh pressure grew stronger also in Hué and Saigon. The representative of the Hué government in Tongking sided with the Vietminh government in Hanoi.

August 21: Ho Chi Minh arrived in Hanoi but remained in hiding.

August 22: Bao Dai acepted Tran Trong Kim's resignation and asked the Vietminh leaders in Hanoi to form a new government of Vietnam. The Vietminh, after announcing in leaflets all over Saigon that their government in Hanoi had the support of the Allies, set up a "Committee of the South." The prestige of the Hanoi government and the mass support that the Vietminh were able to rally induced the United National Front to accept Vietminh leadership.

August 24: Bao Dai abdicated in favor of the Hanoi government, to whose representative he handed his insignia of power.

August 25: A "Provisional Executive Committee of South Vietnam," dominated by Communists, was installed in the Saigon government palace under the nominal authority of the Hanoi government. The Vietminh, ten days after the Japanese surrender, now dominated the whole country.

August 29: The formation of a "provisional government" with Ho Chi Minh as President was announced in Hanoi.

September 2: Ho Chi Minh solemnly proclaimed the independence of Vietnam and the establishment of a "Democratic Republic." His proclamation opened with a sentence from the American Declaration of Independence.

445

Third Period: 1945-1946

Contrary to Vietnamese expectations, and in spite of President Roosevelt's strong opposition, the Allies agreed to give Indochina back to France. The eighteen months from the surrender of Japan in August, 1945, to December, 1946, should be called the period of French reconquest of Indochina. Against heavy resistance, France succeeded in reinstalling her old colonial regime, although not in regaining control of the whole country. With English military help and tacit United States approval, the French first retook the South of Vietnam by force. To regain the North, they had to recognize and negotiate with the new Vietnamese national government that had been established, under the leadership of the Communist Ho Chi Minh, in August, 1945. This government had the blessing of Bao Dai, enjoyed the support of the Vietnamese people, was tolerated by the Chinese armies of occupation, and was also abroad widely regarded as the legitimate government of independent Vietnam. The military weakness of Ho Chi Minh's government and the political weakness of his party led him to give the French a foothold in the North. But when in a battle of ruse and force the French threatened to become strong enough to eliminate their adversaries, the Communist-led government had no choice but to capitulate or to make a desperate effort to break the tightening grip of the French. Rather than capitulate, the Vietminh leaders decided to fight. On December 19, 1946, the government called on all its forces to oust the French from Hanoi. This, however, was by no means the beginning of bloodshed in the postwar struggle for Indochina. Fighting had never entirely stopped since the returning French had started it by their forceful removal of the new regime in Saigon. Only through the subsequent refusal of the French to resume negotiations did the attack of December, 1946, become the official beginning of the Indochina war.

446

Here are the main events of this crucial short period in the modern history of Vietnam:

1945

September 12: British troops under General Gracey landed in South Vietnam to disarm the Japanese army south of the sixteenth parallel. Chinese armies of occupation begin to enter Tongking to disarm the Japanese north of the sixteenth parallel. With the British, a number of Frenchmen arrived. The VNQDD, Dong Minh Hoi, and other anti-Communist nationalist leaders returned to Vietnam with the Chinese, only to find that a revolutionary government claiming to represent all Vietnamese political groups was already firmly established in Hanoi, and was recognized as the government of reunited Vietnam in the Center and South.

September 21: The first French troops, arriving on British warships, landed in the South. General Gracey declared martial law in Saigon, where a clash between the Vietnamese and the French was feared. He forbade publication of all Vietnamese newspapers and all public meetings, but permitted the arming of some of the French soldiers who had been interned by the Japanese.

September 23: The French opened their historically fateful campaign to reconquer Vietnam by occupying all Vietnamese-held public buildings in Saigon, on which Allied flags were flying next to the Vietminh flag. The Vietnamese, taken by surprise, offered little resistance.

September 25: The ousted "Committee of the South," headed by the Communist Tran Van Giau, started an armed counteraction against the French. It turned into a general Vietnamese uprising in defense of their newly won independence. There was street fighting all over Saigon, and much violence was committed against French civilians. During the long fighting

447

in Saigon, General Gracey not only employed his Indian troops, but also ordered the Japanese to assist him in his actions against the Vietnamese.

End of September: French troops arrived in large numbers in an Anglo-French convoy.

October 3: General Leclerc arrived in Saigon, followed by the main body of the French troops on October 5.

October 11: After a brief truce, the fighting in Saigon was resumed. The common struggle against the French temporarily reunited all Vietnamese national and revolutionary elements behind the "Committee of the South," which had threatened to fall apart before the arrival of the British. The differences were sharpest between the strong group of Trotskyites and the Communists. The former wanted to oppose the landing of the British by force, and were supported in this position by the leaders of the Cao Dai and Hoa Hao sects. The Vietminh, however, pursued "peaceful tactics," because they believed in preventing the return of the French through negotiations and with Allied help—Russian, Chinese, and American. They also counted on the help they would find in France if a Communist-Socialist coalition came to power, which they expected to happen soon. Afraid that the popularity of the Trotskyite leader Ta Thu Thau might endanger their control of the "Committee of the South," the Communists took drastic action against their leftist rivals, in the course of which they assassinated Ta Thu Thau. (At a later period, after the Communists had clashed with the sects, they also murdered the Hoa Hao leader Huynh Phu So.)

October 25: General Leclerc started the military reconquest of Indochina. Supported by the British, the French took all important strategic points in Cochinchina within four weeks. The Vietnamese were reduced to guerilla activities. British action in Indochina aroused strong opposition in many parts

448

of the Empire. "In London, British liberals recoiled from reports of Royal Air Force attacks on Vietnamese in support of French troops." (Ellen Hammer, *The Struggle for Indochina*, p. 119), and in India, Pandit Nehru vigorously protested against the use of Indian troops by the British to do their "dirty work against our friends who are fighting the same battle as we."—New York *Times*, January 1, 1946. But British Foreign Minister Bevin on October 9 had formally recognized the French civil administration as the only government south of the sixteenth parallel, and General Gracey knew that his actions to restore French rule in the south of Vietnam were not contrary to British policy.

October 31: Admiral d'Argenlieu, de Gaulle-appointed High Commissioner of France for Indochina, arrived. His prepared conciliatory speech, which was said to have contained promises of more freedoms for the Vietnamese, was never delivered. D'Argenlieu turned into a hardheaded defender of colonialism after he assumed his post.

November 8: The Cao Dai forces surrendered after the French occupied their capital, Tay Ninh.

November 11: The Vietminh intensified their tactics to save a Communist-controlled Vietnam through negotiations, by playing the Chinese, who were opposed to a return of the French to Indochina, as well as other Allied sympathizers with Vietnamese independence, against the French. They dissolved the Communist Party of Indochina. They formed a new government in Hanoi and gave a number of ministries to the Chinese-sponsored VNQDD and Dong Minh Hoi leaders, the latter no longer a party coalition but a small Chinese-supported group. But while the Communists were taking their oaths to respect the democratic liberties and institutions of the new regime, their storm troopers were ordered to murder

449

anyone who tried to use these liberties and institutions against the Vietminh.

1946

January 6: The Ho Chi Minh government held and won the first Vietnamese elections for a National Assembly of the Democratic Republic of Vietnam. A number of seats that were guaranteed to the anti-Vietminh nationalists before the election remained empty: their holders were afraid to occupy them. The Assembly was soon adjourned and reconvened only once—in November—to vote for a constitution.

February 28: Conclusion of the Chinese-French agreement, through which France, at the heavy price of giving up all her possessions and prerogatives in China, prepared the way for the withdrawal of the Chinese troops from Vietnam and for eventual Chinese acceptance of France's return to Vietnam. Ho Chi Minh was now faced with the prospect of losing China's wavering but for Vietnam still crucial support against the French, for which he had spent much gold that went into the pockets of the Chinese generals in Vietnam. This prospect led Ho Chi Minh to consider temporary concessions to France. In order to avoid an armed French intervention, for which Vietnam was unprepared, the Hanoi government was now willing to let the French station small forces in Center and North Vietnam while negotiations for French recognition of Vietnamese independence continued. D'Argenlieu began at this time his own political maneuvers, in a hopeless attempt to win nationalist "moderates" for a Vietnamese government ready to cooperate with the French. He approached Ngo Dinh Diem, whose conditions he could never meet. Also, "there could be no question for the civil services and the French government of admitting a leader of a united Vietnam like Ngo Dinh Diem . . . whose nationalism frightened them."—

450

Devillers, *op. cit.*, p. 396. Earlier, Ngo Dinh Diem had been arrested by the Vietminh and "exposed to the perils of illness and hunger in the Tonkinese mountains."—Ellen Hammer, *op. cit.*, p. 149. He was then taken to Hanoi, where Ho Chi Minh tried to persuade him to enter his government. Although he refused, Ho Chi Minh thought it politically wiser to let Ngo Dinh Diem go free.

March 6: Ho Chi Minh and the Commissioner of France, Sainteny, signed a "preliminary convention"; the French were allowed to station a specified number of troops in Haiphong, Hanoi, and a few other towns. The Vietnamese gained French recognition of Vietnam as a "Free State" and a promise that Cochinchina would be reunited with Vietnam if the South voted for it in a referendum. The Chinese-oriented nationalists attacked the Vietminh strongly for having "surrendered" to the French.

March 18: French troops and tanks entered Hanoi. As they marched through the city, some Vietminh leaders became convinced that the March 6 agreement was a tactical error. After having served for six months as political advisor to Ho Chi Minh, Bao Dai left on a government mission to China, from which he did not return. He remained in exile in Hong Kong.

April 18: The first Franco-Vietnamese Conference opened at Dalat. It failed to solve any of the questions left open by the agreement of March 6. According to the Vietnamese, D'Argenlieu took a position contrary to both the spirit and the letter of the March agreement. The Hanoi government insisted on a conference in Paris.

May 27: In another move calculated to widen their popular basis, the Communists created the Vietnamese National Front (Lien Viet) comprising all parties and groups allied with the Vietminh, as well as all "mass" and other Communist-front organizations. "The Lien-Viet is a Government front which

451

was developed to include all patriotic, social and political organizations in the Republican area. The Viet-Minh was merged with the Lien-Viet in 1951 and thus technically disappeared; however, the term Viet-Minh has continued in general use both in Vietnam and elsewhere." (Bernard B. Fall, *The Viet-Minh Regime*, Cornell University, Ithaca, N. Y., 1954).

May 30: While Ho Chi Minh was on his way to France to negotiate the future status of Vietnam and in particular the status of Cochinchina within Vietnam, d'Argenlieu had prepared, and proclaimed on June 1, the Autonomous Republic of Cochinchina, headed by Dr. Nguyen Van Trinh. (When Dr Trinh realized a few months later he had only been used in an anti-Vietnamese political maneuver, he committed suicide.)

June 6: The decisive Franco-Vietnamese negotiations began at the Fontainbleau Conference. It soon became clear that the positions of the French and the Vietnamese were irreconcilable. The conference broke up on August 1.

September 14: In order to avoid a complete break, Ho Chi Minh and Marius Moutet, Socialist Minister of Overseas France, signed a *modus vivendi*. This, however, failed to stop the clashes between French troops and Vietnamese guerillas that had been going on in the south, with little interruption, ever since September, 1945.

October 15: The French exercised their customs and police control in Haiphong in a manner that the Vietnamese called contrary to the March agreement and the *modus vivendi* of September 14. The Ho Chi Minh government formed a Vietnamese army, headed by Vo Nguyen Giap.

November 8: The reconvened National Assembly, in voting the constitution, proclaimed the unity of North, Center, and South Vietnam.

November 20: Shooting broke out between French and Vietnamese soldiers in Haiphong, but the incident was settled by General Morlière and Undersecretary of State Hoang Huu Nam. D'Argenlieu, in Paris at the time, cabled to Saigon demanding that the Vietnamese be given a lesson. His deputy in Saigon, General Valluy, telegraphed to the French commander in Haiphong that "attempts at conciliation . . . are out of season. The moment has come to give a severe lesson to those who have treacherously attacked you. Use all the means at your disposal to make yourself complete master of Haiphong and so bring the Vietnamese army around to a better understanding of the situation." (Quoted in Ellen Hammer, *op. cit.,* p. 183, from Institut franco-suisse d'Étude coloniale, *France et Vietnam,* p. 42.)

November 23: After the expiration of a two-hour ultimatum demanding that the Vietnamese withdraw from the port, the Chinese quarter, and the French section of the city, the French army and navy went into action, subjecting Haiphong to heavy artillery fire and bombardment from the air. The Vietnamese quarters were completely destroyed. "No more than 6,000 killed, in so far as naval bombardment of fleeing civilians was concerned," the French naval commander, Admiral Battet, said later to Paul Mus (see *Témoignage Chrétien,* August 12, 1949). Other estimates of the number of Vietnamese killed on that day were as high as 20,000.

December 19: The Vietminh decided to attack and risk a long war of liberation rather than go under without a fight. Their attempt to overwhelm the French troops stationed at Hanoi opened the Indochina war.

December 20: A last appeal for negotiations by Ho Chi Minh to French premier Léon Blum was probably held up in Saigon. It remained unanswered. Ho Chi Minh called on the people to expel the French, predicting that Vietnam would not give up, even if the war should last ten years.

Fourth Period: 1946-1954

These eight years, during which Vietnam was devastated by the most frightful of all colonial wars, made up the worst period in the history of Vietnam since the West had come in contact with the East. But this time of misery and horror for the Vietnamese people was also a most harrowing period for the unenlightened men who ruled and exploited Vietnam in the name of France. And the cost to France of the Indochina war was infinitely higher than her expenses during the forty years it had taken to conquer and pacify Vietnam. In addition to being a unique chapter of modern military history, the Indochina war was probably also the most complicated and confusing chapter in the political history of our time: A colonial war that came to be regarded as a duel between world "communism" and "democracy"; a people's fight for freedom that produced a Communist dictatorship in a nation of peasants; a poorly disguised effort to perpetuate colonialism on which the United States, in spite of her open sympathy with the cause of the Vietnamese people, wasted four billion dollars—a sum with which it would now be able to transform South Vietnam into an Asian economic paradise within less than ten years; and a conflict in which everyone who stood up for peace and Vietnamese independence was in danger of promoting a Communist regime for Vietnam. Because the struggle for Indochina had been politically hopeless from the beginning, under no circumstances could the war have ended well for France. She lost all of Indochina, and only a political miracle prevented the Communists from gaining it all after the signing of the Geneva Agreement in July, 1954.

Although there was, characteristically, no foreign correspondent in Hanoi when the Indochina war broke out in December, 1946, the region at last began to attract the attention of people outside of France. This new "discovery" of Vietnam by the West led to a vast though frequently superficial journalistic production in America and England, which made articles and books in English on the events of this period more numerous than on any other in the modern history of Vietnam.

1947

January: After the French had made it clear that they would not consider resuming negotiations, military action suddenly became the only kind of contact between them and the Vietnamese. In a hard and protracted battle, the French army succeeded in evicting all Vietnamese troops from Hanoi, with the exception of a blockaded group of Tu Ve (Vietminh "self-defense" corps) in the Sino-Vietnamese quarters, which ceased resistance only on February 19. The road between Haiphong and Hanoi was cleared early in January; some of the encircled French garrisons in Tongking and Annam fought themselves free quickly, others only after the arrival of reinforcements from Cochinchina. Hué was taken on February 7, Nam Dinh only on March 11, by a mass descent of parachute troops. (The Vietminh, stopped on all fronts, resorted to guerilla tactics, which would be a main feature of the whole Indochina war.) (The description of these and the following events is based largely on Philippe Devillers: "Vietnamese Nationalism and French Politics," in *Asian Nationalism and the West*, edited by William L. Holland, New York, 1953; and Ellen Hammer: *The Struggle for Indochina*, Stanford, 1954,—still the two best studies in English of French policy in Indochina after the Second World War.)

February: Admiral d'Argenlieu anticipated later developments by trying to place the local conflict between French colonialism and Vietnamese nationalism on a high international level, presenting it as a struggle between world communism and anticommunism. Simultaneously, he tried to win "moder-

455

ate" Vietnamese nationalists to take an open position against the Vietminh and to cooperate with France. He was unsuccessful. "Failure to clarify French policies with regard to Indo-China, the encouragement given to Cochin-Chinese separatism, no less than the power still possessed by the Vietminh and the fear it inspired, all made these nationalists cautious."—Devillers, *op. cit.*, p. 202. They began to adopt the "policy of waiting" (*attentiste*), a position shared at this time by Bao Dai. The Admiral suffered setbacks also with the new Cochinchinese government under Le Van Hoach which had received extended though entirely theoretical powers on February 1. Under nationalist pressure, Le Van Hoach himself began to oppose separation of Cochinchina from Vietnam.

March: Under the new tripartite government of Socialists, Radical Socialists, and the Popular Republican Movement (M.R.P.) led by Ramadier, d'Argenlieu was recalled as High Commissioner for Indochina and replaced, on March 5, by Emile Bollaert, a member of the Radical Socialist group in the Council of the Republic. Communist propaganda became entirely nationalistic, and Vietminh policy was now dominated by the concern not to alienate middle-class elements. Vietminh political strategists were also no longer inhibited by the old pro-Chinese national groups, "of which with French help [they] had got rid in the summer of 1946."—Devillers, *op. cit.*, p. 214.

May 12: The new High Commissioner sent his political adviser Paul Mus to Ho Chi Minh, who indignantly rejected what amounted to a proposal of unconditional surrender as a prerequisite of reopening negotiations. (Paul Mus, a sincere friend of the Vietnamese people, has tried to explain why he accepted this mission doomed to failure in advance, in his curious, involved, but quite fascinating book, *Viet-Nam, Sociologie d'une guerre*, Paris, 1953.)

May 28: Anti-Communist "moderates," led by the Social

456

Democrat Nguyen Van Sam, founded a Front of National Union in Saigon.

August 22: The Front of National Union appealed to Bao Dai to return to Vietnam and head an anti-Communist national government. This conformed to Bollaert's concept of a "political solution" for the Indochina war. The effectiveness of the Front of National Union was undermined by the French veto against holding out hopes for independence, or even the use of the word, and by fear of the anti-Communist Vietnamese leaders of being "eliminated" by the Vietminh.

September 4: Bao Dai invited anti-Communist national leaders to a conference in Hong Kong.

September 10: Bollaert made a "key speech" at Ha Long, in which he offered the Vietnamese "liberty within the French Union." Both the Vietminh and the nationalist "moderates" pointed out that the French Union had been created by France without consultation with any of the three Indochinese states.

September 18: Bao Dai issued a cautious statement agreeing to "represent" Vietnam in negotiations with France. In a talk with Ambassador William Bullitt in Hong Kong on September 22, he was given to understand that the United States would support a non-Communist Vietnamese government

October: Violent Vietminh reaction to these French moves took place. The initiator of the Front of National Union, Nguyen Van Sam, who had also established contacts with resistance groups in the South, was assassinated, simultaneously with Dr. Truong Dinh Tri, a former minister of the Vietminh government and now Chairman of the Northern Administrative Committee. The latter was "an able and honest man who might have become the center of a nationalist rally in Tongking."—Devillers, *op. cit.*, p. 214. The head of the Hoa Hao sect, Huynh Pho So, another man whose influence the

457

Communists feared, had already been executed by the Vietminh in March.

October 8: Another French confirmation of Cochinchinese separatism added to the obstacles of an anti-Communist national rally. A politically ambitious Vietnamese colonel in the French army, Nguyen Van Xuan, became the third president of the separate state of Cochinchina. He was also chosen by the French as the first Vietnamese to become a general.

December 7: Against the advice of Ngo Dinh Diem and other nationalist leaders, Bao Dai signed a "preliminary agreement" with Bollaert.

December 22: Troubled by the lack of Vietnamese support in his negotiations with the French, Bao Dai invited Ngo Dinh Diem and other leaders to Hong Kong, to report on his talks with Bollaert. Ngo Dinh Diem told Bao Dai that he considerel the concessions the French were ready to make "absolutely insufficient."

1948

February 22: Nationalist leaders, including those of the "sects" and other religious groups, and representatives of the provincial governments in the South assembled in Saigon, at the initiative of Ngo Dinh Diem, to discuss the conditions for further negotiations with France.

· March 22: Bollaert, in a talk with Ngo Dinh Diem, categorically rejected the "dominion status" regarded by the latter as necessary for the success of an anti-Communist government of Vietnam. In the meantime, Bao Dai had tried to get better concessions in direct talks with French leaders in France. His demands were the unity of Vietnam and an autonomy even wider than that envisaged for the "Free State" of Vietnam in the convention of March 6, 1946. Bao Dai's demands were exactly the same as "those put forward by Ho Chi Minh at

Fontainebleau, a fact which goes to show that they were not those of only one of the parties but those of the whole nation."
—Devillers, *op. cit.*, p. 219.

June 5: Bao Dai and Bollaert signed the Ha Long agreement, stipulating the conditions for the formation of a Vietnamese government.

June 6: Tran Van Huu, governor of South Vietnam, announced the formation of a provisional central government of Vietnam. It was headed by General Nguyen Van Xuan. Bao Dai stayed aloof from it. "The Xuan government was neither representative nor popular and had little power; no Vietnamese of any stature, whatever his politics, would serve in it."
—Hammer, *op. cit.*, p. 222.

October: Bollaert was recalled. Leo Pignon, who as adviser to Admiral d'Argenlieu had been largely responsible for the latter's disastrous policy, was made High Commissioner. The new central government of Vietnam was in office but not permitted to govern. None of the important government services were transferred to it by the French. Under these conditions, Bao Dai, who had gone to France again, refused to return to Vietnam.

1949

January 23: The Chinese Communists took Peking.

March 8: In an exchange of letters with the President of France (Elysée Agreements) Bao Dai accepted the French conditions for his return to Vietnam to head the government, but did not return until the Cochinchina Assembly had voted (April 23) that Cochinchina should be reunited with Vietnam.

April 28: Bao Dai returned to Vietnam.

June 14: Bao Dai assumed his role as Chief of State, but his return did not produce the expected effect on the political situation in Vietnam. Ngo Dinh Diem rejected an offer to become Prime Minister, stating that "the national aspirations of the Vietnamese people will be satisfied only on the day when our nation obtains the same political status which India and Pakistan enjoy."

August 16: The French launched a great offensive in Tongking. The Vietminh, after two and a half years of war, held large territories in the North, the Center, and the South. French control was firm only in the larger cities.

December 16: After defeating the nationalist armies, the Chinese Communist troops arrived at the Vietnamese border.

1950

January 16: Peking recognized the Democratic Republic of Vietnam headed by Ho Chi Minh. Moscow followed suit on January 31.

February 2: First reports came of the arrival of Chinese equipment for the Vietminh. They started a general offensive.

February 7: Great Britain took the initiative in recognizing the State of Vietnam headed by Bao Dai. The United States followed closely.

May 6: Bao Dai formed a new government under Tran Van Huu—his first government he had headed himself, his second had been formed by Nguyen Phan Long—but no new support for him was forthcoming from the ranks of the anti-Communist nationalists.

May 8: The United States announced a decision to give aid to France for the war in Indochina.

May 30: A United States Economic Mission arrived in Saigon.

July 15: An American military mission arrived in Vietnam.

July-August: The Korean war and United States fear of the consequences of a Vietminh victory for Southeast Asia led

460

to a readiness in Washington to increase American aid to the French in Indochina. United States aid, however, did not change French policy in Vietnam. United States officials in Saigon who disagreed with French policy in Indochina were transferred at the insistence of the French.

September-October: The French suffered severe defeats in the North and had to abandon several strong points near the Chinese border.

December 6: General De Lattre de Tassigny was appointed High Commissioner and commander of the French troops.

December 8: The State of Vietnam created its own army.

1951

January - March: De Lattre succeeded in halting the Communist advance. The Vietminh was forced to return to guerilla tactics. The troops at the disposal of the French now numbered 391,000.

September 20: De Lattre went to Washington to plead for more American aid, in particular for new planes and other modern equipment, of which more and more began to arrive in Vietnam.

December: A speech by the Radical Socialist Deputy Daladier revealed a growing French opposition to the Indochina war. Daladier demanded that France seek peace through the United Nations.

1952

January 11: De Lattre died. The Communists started a new offensive. With Chinese equipment, including artillery, they were now able to reduce de Lattre's gains and to eliminate many smaller positions between the cities held by the French.

461

June 3: Under the new High Commissioner Letourneau, the French again provoked all "moderate" nationalists by naming Nguyen Van Tam as Premier of the central government. Nguyen Van Tam, father of the Nguyen Van Hinh who was later made chief of the Vietnamese army, was hated for the part he had played earlier in the cruel suppression of Vietnamese resistance movements.

September 21: The Vietminh staged an attack near Saigon.

October 16: A new Vietminh offensive started in Tongking and was followed by a French counteroffensive that brought no decisive results. French military and political policy in Vietnam was attacked more and more vigorously in France under the leadership of the Radical Socialist deputy Mendès-France. Bao Dai retired more and more from Vietnamese affairs. Disgusted by the political situation he himself had done much to bring about, he gave in to his penchant for comfort and pleasure, and becomes known as the "emperor playboy" at the Riviera.

1953

Opening of the year: The state of Vietnam was still independent only in name. Only a few disreputable politicians and the politico-religious sects supported the French and the Bao Dai regime during the final phase of the Indochina war. The support of the sects, however, was conditional and required substantial subsidies by the French, and noninterference with their provincial autonomy, which was defended by the sects' armies. The Binh Xuyen, a group of former river pirates who at one time cooperated with the Vietminh, were given the right to run Saigon's lucrative gambling houses and vice rackets, and later even put in control of the Saigon police. But the loyalty of all these groups to France remained doubtful.

May 8: General Navarre became commander of the French forces.

July 27: After the Korean armistice, United States aid for the French in Vietnam grew in volume.

November 20: French troops occupied Dien Bien Phu in order to forestall a Vietminh march through Laos.

November 26: Ho Chi Minh, in an interview for a Swedish newspaper, declared himself ready to talk peace.

December 17: Prince Buu Loc replaced Nguyen Van Tan as Premier in Saigon.

December 21-26: A Vietminh offensive cut Vietnam in two by taking the town of Thakhek on the Mekong River.

1954

February 18: The "Big Four" agreed at Berlin to hold a conference at Geneva in order to seek a solution for Korea and the Indochina war.

March-April: The battle of Dien Bien Phu raged.

April 26: The Conference of Geneva opened.

April 28: A joint Franco-Vietnamese declaration stated that Vietnam, (the independence of which the French had proclaimed half a dozen times), was now fully independent.

May 6: Dien Bien Phu fell.

June 3: General Paul Ely was appointed French High Commissioner for Indochina.

June 6: The French agreed to the appointment of Ngo Dinh Diem as Premier of South Vietnam.

June 15: Ngo Dinh Diem assumed his office as government head in Saigon.

June 29: The French began to evacuate the southern parts of the Red River delta.

July 21: The signing of the Geneva Agreement took place.

Fifth Period: 1954-1957

Vietnam, in gaining full national independence, lost its unity together with the hope that the end of colonialism would bring also an end to oppression of all Vietnamese. More than one-half of the nation had to accept a Communist dictatorship that was regarded as powerful enough to extend its rule also over the other half soon. But the emergence of a strong anti-Communist leadership in the South changed these prospects as radically as it had dashed all hopes of the French to remain in control in the non-Communist part of the country. With United States financial assistance, the government of South Vietnam settled half a million refugees from the North, built up a new national army and administration, eliminated all pro-colonial and pro-Communist elements from positions of influence, broke the disruptive power of the armed politico-religious sects, deposed the "Chief of State" and former Emperor Bao Dai, and made clear, through the holding of two elections, that it intended to move in the direction of more freedom and toward the establishment of viable democratic institutions. To what degree and for how long these endeavors will be successful will again depend largely on the United States. To make South Vietnam securely democratic, American foreign aid will have to become as effective in developing Vietnam's economy as it has been in creating Vietnam's national army, because this army and people will be strong enough and determined enough to defeat Communist aggression only if South Vietnam progresses economically to a point that makes the attraction of communism for the suffering masses of Asia a thing of the past.

The events following the Conference of Geneva are too familiar to most readers to require elaboration. The main dates are:

464

1954

July 23: Mendès-France stated in the French National Assembly: "We have asked that anyone in the zone in which he now resides be enabled to reach the other zone if he deems it safer. It is the first time that such a provision for transfer —important in a country divided among many races and sects and where reprisals are to be feared—has been accepted by a Communist state."—Quoted from *Terror in Vietnam*, published by the National Catholic Welfare Conference, Washington, D. C. Refugees started streaming toward ports and the seashore to flee south. The number of people who left North Vietnam eventually came close to one million.

August: The government of Premier Ngo Dinh Diem did not control the army, lacked a competent administration, had no authority over the territories ruled for many years by the "sects," and struggled desperately to house and feed the growing masses of refugees.

September: Open conflict began with the French-appointed chief of the army, General Nguyen Van Hinh, whom Ngo Dinh Diem soon dismissed. When Bao Dai became aware that it might be advantageous for him to please the United States, he ordered General Nguyen Van Hinh to go to France. On September 25, Ngo Dinh Diem reorganized his cabinet with the aim of winning the cooperation of some leaders of the "sects."

October: On the ninth, the Vietminh occupied Hanoi. The French intensified their campaign against Ngo Dinh Diem. They wanted to replace him with a man under whom they would be able to maintain control in the South and freedom of action in regard to the North. "Ever since the military collapse of Tongking," wrote the London *Economist* on January 8, 1955, "the French have in fact been ready to write off

465

the Saigon government, and particularly since it has been led by a strong anti-French Prime Minister."

November: General Collins, President Eisenhower's special Ambassador to South Vietnam, arrived in Saigon on November 8; this strengthened Ngo Dinh Diem's position against the French. United States aid enabled the government to start a large-scale program of refugee resettlement. But the general conviction that the South could not hold out against the Communist pressure remained unbroken throughout the world. "The odds were considered at least eight to one against Diem and the free world."—Carl T. Rowan, *The Pitiful and the Proud.* New York, 1956, p. 350.

December: A Franco-Vietnamese convention removed the major economic privileges of the French in Vietnam.

1955

January: The United States agreed on aid to Vietnam directly to the Vietnamese instead of indirectly through the French. The press of the United States began to adopt a positive attitude toward Ngo Dinh Diem.

February: The United States Army mission took over the training of the Vietnamese army from the French. Clashes occurred between the national army and troops of the Hoa Hao sect. The government insisted on and succeeded in taking away control of the Vietnamese armed forces from the French.

March 29: In the name of a "National Front" of the sects and other dissident groups, the Binh Xuyen, after first issuing an ultimatum, attacked the national government by firing at the presidential palace. The national army reacted vigorously. The French interfered, and with Ambassador Collins' support imposed an armistice on the government.

April 28: Bao Dai ordered Ngo Dinh Diem to France and

466

appointed General Van Vy head of the national army. Ngo Dinh Diem refused to comply with Bao Dai's orders. Backed by a "Revolutionary Committee" at Saigon that mobilized support of his government, the Premier resumed the struggle to oust the Binh Xuyen. The Revolutionary Committee demanded the removal of Bao Dai as Chief of State and the withdrawal of all French troops. The Binh Xuyen was routed during the month of May. The Saigon police, which had been controlled by the Binh Xuyen for many years, was now as firmly in the hands of the national government as the army. The United States government and press were at last convinced of Ngo Dinh Diem's staying power.

May 9-11: French Premier Faure and Secretary Dulles discussed Franco-American differences of policy toward Vietnam. The French agreed to withdraw their troops toward the coast, and to go along with the United States policy of support for Ngo Dinh Diem.

May 13: In accordance with the armistice agreements, the French evacuated Haiphong.

June 3: The national army attacked and pursued the remnants of the Hoa Hao forces.

June 6: The Vietminh government demanded talks, in accordance with the Geneva Agreement, to prepare the elections in July, 1956, to unify Vietnam.

July 16: Ngo Dinh Diem declared that South Vietnam, not having signed the Geneva Agreement, would not take part in general elections unless they were guaranteed to be free in the North as well as in the South.

July 18: After an announcement of aid by the People's Republic of China to the Democratic Republic of Vietnam (North Vietnam) on July 7, Moscow also concluded an aid agreement with Hanoi.

467

October 23: In a popular referendum held to elect the Chief of State, Ngo Dinh Diem received 5,721,735 votes, against 63,017 for Bao Dai.

October 26: The President proclaimed South Vietnam a republic.

1956

January 23: Government decrees fixed the procedures for the elections of a Constituent National Assembly.

March 4: General elections for the Constituent National Assembly were held.

March 15: The opening session of the Assembly, consisting of 123 deputies, took place.

July: The crucial month during which the elections to unify Vietnam should have been held as provided in the Geneva Agreement passed without incident.

October 26: The Republic of South Vietnam received a Constitution.

November: The land reform program in South Vietnam received a new impetus through a decree issued in October, which aimed at breaking up the large landholdings created during the colonial period. In regard to land reform, things were quite different in the North. "The northern agrarian reform program degenerated into an instrument of terror devoid of any economic justification and the indiscriminate purge directed against groups of people who by no definition could legitimately be regarded as big landowners, had such a demoralizing effect on the population that sporadic risings broke out in November 1956 north of the seventeenth parallel; and the D.R.V.N. finally had to admit publicly the breakdown of its agrarian reform program."— Ellen Hammer, "Progress Report on Southern Viet Nam," *Pacific Affairs*, Vol. XXX, No. 3, September, 1957.

1957

January: It was estimated that South Vietnam had received in the two-year period 1955 and 1956 American aid to the amount of half a billion dollars, of which 340,000,000 went into building up and maintaining the armed forces. No French troops remained in Vietnam.

March: The government of President Ngo Dinh Diem announced a series of regulations intended to encourage foreign investments.

Former critics as well as early supporters of President Ngo Dinh Diem are still disturbed over the new Republic's slow progress in the sphere of civil liberties, but at least in the United States little doubt is left as to the viability of the regime. To many it seems not unreasonable to hope "that unity, when it comes, will be established on nationalist and not on Communist terms."—Ellen Hammer, *ibid.*, p. 235. However that may be, it is now certain that the great majority of the Vietnamese people, whether they live in the South or in the North, share the hope that unity will be established on other than Communist terms, and that it will be established without the use of force. The world no doubt will be a safer place and the Vietnamese a happier people once these hopes are fulfilled.

Bibliography

THE FOLLOWING bibliography, although by no means complete, lists all important works on the subject of this book. They are mostly in French, and consist to a large extent of contributions to periodicals, as many studies on Indochina history and civilization were published only in scholarly reviews, such as the *Bulletin de l'Ecole Française d'Extrême-Orient* (BEFEO). The reviews and periodicals containing studies quoted in this book are listed at the head of this bibliography; those containing studies that are mentioned only in the bibliography are listed separately.

This bibliography departs from a common practice which consists in dividing large bibliographies into half a dozen or more separate alphabetical lists, grouping works either according to different periods of history or in an order that separates specific studies by subject matter. Here all works are listed in two groups, one called History, the other Civilization.

Under I, History, the reader will find the books and articles a) on Vietnamese history proper, whether ancient or modern; b) on prehistory, including relevant archeological studies; c) on the history of the Catholic missions in Vietnam; d) on France during the period of her conquest of Vietnam; e) on the history of countries that have had an influence on Vietnamese history, such as China, Champa, Cambodia, and Thailand; and f) a few books and articles on the problems of contemporary Vietnam. In addition, group I contains also books of historical significance by travelers in Vietnam, as well as memoirs by and biographies of participants in historical events.

470

BIBLIOGRAPHY

Under II, Civilization, are listed the books and publications in periodicals dealing with specific aspects of Vietnamese and Indochinese civilization at different periods, such as social organization, religion, law, education, philosophy popular customs and beliefs, language, literature, and art, both in respect to the Vietnamese people and to the minority populations of Vietnam and former French Indochina.

Most authors on Vietnamese history and civilization are French, and although some are outstanding scholars in their fields, they are relatively unknown outside of France. The reader who would like to know more about the authors whose works are either frequently quoted in, or have otherwise left their mark on *The Smaller Dragon* may find it useful to consult the following biographical and critical notes:

AUBARET, Louis Gabriel Galdéric. Naval officer, administrator, diplomat, and linguist. Aubaret took part in the campaigns in China and Vietnam in 1858, during which he acquired a great mastery of the Chinese and Vietnamese languages. He was interpreter in the treaty negotiations with Hué in 1863. (See note 84, Chapter VI.) Because he favored the return to Vietnam of the three Conchinchinese provinces ceded by Hué in 1862, he became suspect to de la Grandière and other colonial leaders, but his administrative and linguistic abilities made it possible for him to hold several high positions before he was transferred from Indochina to Albania, as consul in Scutari. Aubaret's main works are his French-Vietnamese dictionary (1861) and his translations from the Chinese original of the Gia Dinh Thong Gi (*History and Description of Lower Cochinchina*, 1863) and of the Hoang Luat Le (*Code annamite. Lois et règlements du royaume d'Annam*, 1865). He published also two Vietnamese grammars.

CADIERE, Leopold Michel. Born 1869; missionary, ethnographer, linguist, corresponding member of the BEFEO and the *Review Indochinoise*. Cadière is probably the most prolific author on Indochina. His works cover almost every aspect of Indochinese history, culture, and civilization. The two lists of his studies in this bibliography represent only a small fraction of his total work.

CADY, John F. Professor of history at Ohio University, formerly lecturer in history at the University of Rangoon. His *Roots of French Imperialism in Eastern Asia* is a thorough and up-to-date study of French policy in the Far East during the two decades prior to military intervention in Vietnam, and during the first decade of French rule in Indochina. Cady not only produced hitherto unknown data but also threw new light on the complex motivations behind French colonial action in Asia. For further details and some critical remarks about Professor Cady's book, see notes 1, 16, 17, 34, 50, and 70, Chapter VI.

COEDES, George. Born 1886; an internationally renowned French Orientalist. From 1910 on, Coedès worked at the Ecole Française d'Extrême-Orient (EFEO), of which he later became director. His main contribution to Indochinese history is the study of Funan and other early "Hinduized" Indochinese states. See notes 8, Chapter II, and 58, Chapter III.

CORDIER, Henri. Born in New Orleans in 1849, died in Paris in 1925; one of the many prominant French orientalists. Cordier went to China in 1869. After his return to France in 1876, he soon became the leading French scholar in Chinese and Indochinese history of his time. He was also one of the two or three most productive authors on colonial history, in particular on the history of European intervention in the Far East during the nineteenth century. Cordier was a member of many French and international societies concerned with Oriental studies. For a survey of his main works, see also note 73, Chapter VI.

CHASSIGNEUX, E. Born 1875; professor of history and geography at Orléans and Paris. Chassigneux was connected with the EFEO in Hanoi from 1908 to 1910, and later with the Ecole Coloniale in Paris. His brief history of Vietnam (in Gabriel Hanotaux, *Histoire des colonies françaises et de l'expansion de la France dans le monde*, Vol. V, *L'Indochine*, Paris, 1932) is one of the saddest examples of history distorted by colonial propaganda. But because Chassigneux established himself as an authority on the irrigation of the Tongking delta, he is also frequently quoted as an authority on Vietnamese history. It is his view that Dutch, Portuguese, and

English colonial rule was a great evil, in contrast to French colonial rule, which he regards as a blessing for the peoples of Indochina. See notes 46, 58, 68, Chapter IV.

CHESNEAUX, Jean. A contemporary French author with a Marxist approach to history and strong pro-Communist political opinions. Chesneaux's recent book on Vietnam is nevertheless a valuable contribution, although it deteriorates in the later chapters into a Communist propaganda pamphlet. The main merit of this author lies in the emphasis he puts on the much neglected social and economic aspects of the precolonial history of Vietnam and in his successful effort to uncover the views of earlier French authors who were critical of French policy in Vietnam from the beginning of intervention. Unfortunately, Chesneaux seldom mentions the page and often not even the book from which he takes his interesting quotations. For a more detailed appraisal of his book, see notes 38, 48, Chapter I; 2, Chapter II; 13, 32, and 47, Chapter III; and 121, Chapter VI.

DES MICHELS, Abel. Born 1865 in Java. Des Michels studied medicine and law, but changed later to oriental languages. He is the author of many studies on the language and literature of Vietnam, and he translated from the Chinese original the Imperial Annals of Annam, published in two volumes in Paris, 1889-1892. See note 10, Chapter III.

DEVILLERS, Philippe. A French journalist who spent the years from 1945 to 1952 in Saigon. He is the author of the most important book on French policy in Indochina, in particular after the Second World War, and on the Indochina war. However, the introductory chapters of Devillers' *Histoire du Viet-Nam de 1940 à 1952* are not on the same high level as his treatment of twentieth-century Vietnam. See notes 2, Chapter V; 52, Chapter VI, and pages 432, 455, and 456 of Chronology.

GOSSELIN, Captain Ch. An officer in the French army who fought the Vietnamese resistance movements after 1883 and later held high administrative posts in Indochina. He is the author of *L'empire d'Annam,* which is probably the most widely read book on Vietnam. Gosselin's sketches of ancient Vietnamese history are now quite out of date, but his description of the conquest of Indochina, although firmly partisan, is still among the best and most readable of all works by the authors who wrote about the military and political events after 1883. The direct source material of Gosselin's books remains indispensable for any new study on the period of conquest and pacification. For details, see notes 43, Chapter I; 31, 50, 57, Chapter IV; and 131, Chapter VI.

GOUROU, Pierre. A leading authority on the subject that the French call "human geography." His *Le paysan du delta tonkinois* is a classic among the studies of this school, which believes that geographical factors are decisive in determining social conditions. Unfortunately, this theory tends to exculpate the colonial regime from responsibility for the misery of the Vietnamese peasants by pointing out that under the given geographic limitations no other regime could have substantially improved their lot. See note 43, Chapter I, and pages 425 and 430 of Chronology.

HALL, D. G. E. Although his *History of South-East Asia* is a difficult book to read and a controversial one in many respects, it is nevertheless the main work of a modern author on Southeast Asia as a whole. For details see Foreword and notes 29, 30, Chapter I; 2, 58, 61, Chapter III; 17, Chapter IV; 21, 26, Chapter VI; and pages 429-432 of Chronology.

HAMMER, Ellen. One of the foremost American students of French colonial policy, whose *Struggle for Indochina* is an indispensable book for anyone who wants to acquaint himself with French and Vietnamese policies during the Indochina war. See pages 455 and 469 of Chronology.

LAUNAY, Adrien. Born 1853; a missionary who came to Vietnam in 1877. He returned to Paris in 1882 to teach at the seminary of the Society of Foreign Missions. Launay first wrote a history of ancient and modern Vietnam and then settled down for the rest of his life to write a history of the Catholic missions in Cochinchina in three volumes, a history of the Tongking mission and a general history of the Society of Foreign Missions from its foundation to his own time. Launay must be regarded as the greatest authority on the history of the French Catholic missions in the Far East.

474

LE THAN KHOI. This is the leading contemporary Vietnamese historian. For a brief analysis of his work, see the Foreword and many of the notes in this book, especially the following: 11, 64, 68, Chapter II; 36, 46, Chapter III; 41, Chapter IV; 22, 48 Chapter V; 16, 44, Chapter VI.

LURO, Jean Baptiste. Born 1837. He died, at the age of forty, in 1877, after serving from 1865 on as one of the group of young and talented early administrators in Saigon. Navy lieutenant, Inspector of Native Affairs, friend of Francis Garnier. Luro wrote two of the best early studies of Vietnamese society. See notes 113, 114, and 120, Chapter VI.

MASPERO, Georges. Born 1872. Son of an Egyptologist, he studied Oriental languages, entered the colonial administration (Cambodia in 1894, became Resident Superior in Laos, and served in high administrative posts in Cochinchina and also as Resident Mayor of Haiphong. Georges Maspéro was collaborator and correspondent of the EFEO. As an author he is known chiefly for his histories of Champa and of the Cambodian empire. He published several smaller studies on Angkor and on the history of Vietnam. Maspéro is also one of the authors who wrote French propaganda versions of Vietnamese history. His version appeared in an illustrated, two-volume work on Indochina, published under his direction in Paris and Brussels in 1929.

MASPERO, Henri. Born 1883. Brother of Georges Maspéro. A scholar in Oriental languages, history, and geography. Professor of Chinese at the EFEO. Henri Maspéro wrote several studies dealing with the Vietnamese language and with Vietnamese history. See notes 3, 4, 11, 13, and 64, Chapter VI.

MASSON, André. A contemporary author of a brief and well-written modern history of Vietnam and the other countries of French Indochina. Masson is somewhat less biased than most pro-colonial French historians of Indochina. See page 424 of Chronology.

MAYBON, Charles B. A much neglected older French historian of Vietnam. Maybon wrote one of the best, though now also dated, histories of Vietnam up to 1820. See notes 46, 59, Chapter III.

MUS, Paul. Born in Hanoi, now professor at Yale. Mus is the author of a remarkable book on Vietnam and the Indochina war, and of several smaller studies through which he tried to create a better understanding between the French and the Vietnamese, and a basis for peace between France and Ho Chi Minh's Democratic Republic of Vietnam. See note 62, Chapter III, and pages 432 and 456 of Chronology.

ROBEQUAIN, Charles. An economist and prominent author on contemporary Vietnam. His *Economic Development of French Indo-China*, although uncritical of the priniciples underlying French economic policy in Indochina, is the most informative and factually most reliable book on the subject. Robequain is also the author of an excellent small book on the geography and the populations of French Indochina, as well as of several studies of various minorities and different regions of Vietnam. As an exponent of the school of human geography (see Pierre Gourou) Robequain believed that the misery of the Vietnamese people had "natural," not essentially social causes. See notes 1, 5, Chapter I, and page 331 of Chronology.

SILVESTRE, Pierre Jules. Born 1841. Silvestre came to Vietnam as a young lieutenant of the marines in 1863, entered the colonial administration in 1867, and soon became head of the Department of Indigenous Justice. "Through his fairness and integrity he acquired such a reputation among the indigenous people that plaques were put up in all pagodas of the province for 'Silvestre, the Just.'" Quoted from A. Brebion, *Dictionnaire de bio-bibliographie générale ancienne et moderne de l'Indochine française*, Paris, 1935.

TABOULET, Georges. A contemporary author on French colonial history who wrote several smaller studies devoted to the first years of French rule in Cochinchina, as well as biographical studies of missionaries (Lefèbvre, Pigneau). In 1955 and 1956, Taboulet published two large volumes of documents, many of them never published before, to which he added a wealth of additional source material in his annotations and his historical and biographical introductions. This material makes his two volumes, next to Le Thanh Khoi's *Viet-Nam*, the most important books on Vietnamese history.

476

BIBLIOGRAPHY

See Foreword and notes 20, Chapter V, and 1, 21, 34, Chapter VI.

VIAL, P. F. A. Born 1831, died 1907. A naval officer and colonial administrator, Vial came to Vietnam in 1860. He was Director of Native Affairs from 1864 to 1871. After Paul Bert's sudden death in 1886, Vial was interim Resident Superior of Indochina. He was one of the remarkable young administrators that the navy developed during the first decade of French rule in Saigon (Garnier, Luro, Philastre, Silvestre, and Vial, all of whom were also prominent authors on Vietnam). Apart from several studies on the colonial administration, Vial wrote an important two-volume work on this period.

Several prominent authors on Indochina and Vietnam, such as Alexander of Rhodes, Francis Garnier, and Jean Dupuis, need no introduction because of the part they themselves play in *The Smaller Dragon*. The works of another group of authors are discussed in the notes. To some of them the reader will find references in this bibliography. Among these authors, the following should be singled out: Aurousseau, Briffaut, Chavannes, Cultru, De Bazancourt, De Lanessan, Diguet, Durand, Gaspardone, Gaultier, Goloubew, Grousset, Heine-Geldern, Huard, Latourette, Nguyen Van Huyen, Pasquier, Pham Quynh, Philastre, Schreiner, Tran Van Giap, and Tran Van Trai.

The notes to *The Smaller Dragon* contain references to and quotations from the following periodicals and publications:

Annuaire statistique de l'Indochine

Annuaire statistique de l'Union française

Archives du Ministère des Affaires Etrangères (Arch. Aff. Etrang.)

Archives du Ministère de la Marine—Service Historique (Arch. Min. Mar. S. H.)

Archives de la Société des Missions Etrangères (Arch. Miss. Etrang.)

Bulletin de l'Ecole Française d' Extrême-Orient (BEFEO), Hanoi and Paris

Bulletin des Amis du Vieux Hué (Bul. Amis Hué), Hanoi
Bulletin de la Société des Etudes Indochinoises, Saigon
Bulletin de la Société de Géographie de Rochefort
Bulletin des Outre-Mer
Bulletin et Travaux de l'Institut Indochinois pour l'Etude de l'Homme (IIEH), Hanoi
Bulletin Général de l'Instruction Publique (Bul. Gén. Instr. Publ.), Hanoi
Cahiers Internationaux, Paris
Cahiers de la Société de Géographie de Hanoi (Cahiers Soc. Géog. Hanoi)
Cahiers de l'Ecole Française d'Extrême-Orient (CEFEO), Hanoi
Dan Viet Nam
Far Eastern Quarterly (FEQ), Ithaca, N. Y.
Geographical Revue, New York
Indochine, Hanoi, (an illustrated bi-weekly)
Journal Asiatique, Paris
Journal of Modern History, Chicago
Journal of Siam Society, Bangkok
La Patrie Annamite
Pacific Affairs, New York, published by the Institute for Pacific Relations
Revue des Arts Asiatiques (Rev. Arts Asiatiques), Paris (now called Arts Asiatiques)
Revue Coloniale, Paris
Revue de Paris
Revue des Deux Mondes, Paris
Revue de l'Extrême-Orient (Rev. Ext.-Or.), Paris
Revue Indochinoise, Hanoi
Revue Indochinoise Juridique et Economique (Rev. Indoch. Jurid. Econ.) Hanoi
Revue Orientale et Américaine, Paris
T'oung Pao, Leiden (Archives dealing with history, geography, ethnography and the languages and arts of East Asia.)
Times of Vietnam, Saigon (a weekly English-language newspaper)

478

The following periodicals either contain studies listed in the bibliography or are generally of importance to the subject of this book:

Annales de l'Extrême-Orient et de l'Afrique (Ann. Ext.-Or. et Afr.), Paris

Annales de la Société des Mission Etrangères (Ann. Soc. Miss. Etr.) Paris

Archives du Ministère de la France Outre-Mer (Arch. France Outre-mer)

Arts et Archéologie Khmers (Arts Arch. Khmers), Paris

Asiatic Quarterly Review, London (title for Asiatic Review from 1886-1890)

Asiatic Review, London (see above; called Asiatic Quarterly Review from 1886-1890 and Imperial and Asiatic Quarterly Review from 1891-1912)

Asie Française (Asie Fran.), Paris

Bulletin du Foyer des Etudiants Annamites, Viet Nam Thanh Nien, Hanoi

Bulletin de la Société des Missions Etrangères (Bul. Soc. Miss. Etr.), Paris

Bulletin de la Société Académique Indochinoise de France, Paris

Bulletin Economique de l'Indochine (Bul. Econ. Indoch.), Saigon

Bulletin of the School of Oriental and African Studies (Bul. Sch. Or. and Afr. Studies) University of London, London

Cahiers de l'Institut d' Etudes de l'Orient Contemporaire, Paris

Etudes Asiatiques, Paris

Extrême-Asie, Saigon (an illustrated monthly)

Far Eastern Review (FE Rev.), Manila and Shanghai

Far Eastern Survey (FES), New York

France-Asie, Saigon

Harvard Journal of Asiatic Studies (Harvard Jl. As. Studies), Cambridge, Mass.

Imperial and Asiatic Quarterly Review (Imp. As. Q. Rev.), London, (now called Asiatic Review)

L'Asie Française, Paris

Missions Catholiques (Miss. Cath.), Lyons

Mitteilungen der Geographischen Gesellschaft in Wien (Mitt. Geog. Ges. Wien)

Revue Française de l'Etranger et des Colonies (Rev. Fran. Etr. et Col.), Paris

Revue de l'Histoire des Colonies Françaises (Rev. Hist. Col.), Paris

Revue d'Histoire des Missions (Rev. Hist. Miss.), Paris

Wiener Beitraege zur Kunst und Kulturgeschichte Asiens (Wiener Beit. Kunst Kult. Asiens)

The bibliographies listed below, published either as such or contained in books dealing with Southeast Asia, French Indochina or Vietnam, are specially mentioned for their extensive selection of titles not listed in the bibliography to *The Smaller Dragon* and for the many valuable annotations they contain.

BOUDET, Paul, and BOURGEOIS, Remy. *Bibliography de l'Indochine Française, 1913-1926: Supplement for 1927-1929*, 2 vols., Hanoi, 929.

BREBION, A. (publ. after the author's death by CABATON, A.). *Dictionnaire de bio-bibliographie générale, ancienne et moderne de l'Indochine française*, Paris, 1935.

CADY, John F. *The Roots of French Imperialism in Eastern Asia*, Ithaka, N. Y., 1954. Contains a brief but well selected bibliography with instructive annotations.

CORDIER, Henri. *Biblioteca Indosinica*, 4 vols., Paris, 1912-1915.

EMBREE, J. F., and DOTSON, L. O. *Bibliography of the Peoples and Cultures of Mainland South-East Asia*, New Haven, Conn., 1950.

HALL, D. G. E. *A History of South-East Asia*, New York, 1955. Hall has a long, select bibliography for every country of Southeast Asia and on the region as a whole.

HUARD, Pierre, and DURAND, Maurice. *Connaissance du Vietnam*, Paris and Hanoi, 1954. This outstanding scholarly book has the most extensive bibliography of works by Vietnamese authors in any French publication.

BIBLIOGRAPHY

LE THANH KHOI. *Le Vietnam,* Paris, 1955. Contains a brief but well organized bibliography (Orientation bibliographique).

THOMPSON, Virginia. *French Indochina,* London, 1937. The 600 items listed in this volume add up to the most extensive bibliography in any English book on the subject.

With a few exceptions and for obvious reasons the following bibliography lists only works concerned with Vietnam and Indochina up to 1900. A number of titles are listed both under I, History, and under II, Civilization.

I. HISTORY

Abel, M. H. *Solution pratique de la question de Cochinchine, ou fondation de la politique française dans l'extrême-orient,* Paris, 1864.

Agard, A. *L'Union Indochinoise française ou l'Indochine Oriental,* Hanoi, 1935.

Ajalbert, Jean. *L'Indochine en péril,* Paris, 1906.

Allison, J. M. S. *Church and State in the Reign of Louis Philippe,* Princeton, 1916.

Anonymous. "Création de deux villages de colonisation en Cochinchine (village de Ha-tien et village de Rach-gia)," *Bul. Econ. Indoch.* No. 704 (Sept. 20, 1931).

———. *La Cochinchine, ce qu'elle est, ce qu'elle sera,* Perigueux, 1865.

———. *Relation des missions des évêques français aux royaumes de Siam, de la Cochinchine, de Cambodge, et du Tonkin,* Paris, Pierre le Petit, 1674.

———. "Traduction de l'inscription du tombeau de Mgr. d'Adran." BSEI (1903), 63-65.

———. *Vie du vénérable Jean-Louis Bonnard,* Lyon, 1876.

Antonini, Paul. *L'Annam, le Tonkin et l'intervention de la France en Extrême-Orient; coup d'oeil sur l'histoire nationale de l'Empire d'Annam; l'Indochine physique; le Foyer annamite; les chrétiens: les persécuteurs et les martyrs, Mgr. de Béhaine et le futur empereur Gialong, Mgr. Puginier, guerre de Chine, conquêtes de l'Indochine,* Paris, Bloud, c. 1889.

Aubaret, G., tr. *Histoire et description de la basse Cochinchine (pays de Giadinh) traduites pour la première fois, d'après le texte original,* Paris, Impr. Impériale, 1863. (See introduction to Bibliography; see also under Civilization.

Aurosseau, Léonard. "Exposé de géographie historique du pays d'Annam, traduit du 'Cu'o'ng mu'c,'" BEFEO 22 (1922), pp. 143-160.

————. "La première conquête chinoise des pays annamites; origine du people annamite," BEFEO 23 (1932), pp. 137-264.

————. "Notes sur les origines du people annamite," *Bulletin de l'Ecole Française d'Extrême-Orient,* Vol XXIII, pp. 263f.

————. "Sur le nom de Cochinchine," BEFEO 24 (1924), pp. 563-579. English translation in *Indian Antiquary* 55 (1926), pp. 134-140. (See notes 24, Chapter I, 4, 10, Chapter II.)

Aymonier, E. *Le Cambodge,* Vol. III, Le groupe d'Angkor et l'histoire, Paris, 1904.

Baldinotti, G. "La relation sur le Tonkin du P. Baldinotti," BEFEO 3 (1903), 71-78. (Baldinotti was one of the first missionaries to visit Tongking, early in the seventeenth century. In Italian, with French translation.)

Baldwin, J. R. "England and the French Seizure of the Society Islands," *Journal of Modern History,* Vol. X (1938).

Baron, Samuel. *Description du royaume de Tonquin,* published in 1685 and reprinted in *Revue Indochinoise,* 1914-1915.

Baudrit, Paul. "L'amiral Rigault de Genouilly," *Bulletin de la Société des Etudes Indochinoises,* 1933.

Baulmont, Lieut. M. G. R. "La prise de Tourane, Sept. 1858-9 et Mai 1859-Sept. 1859," *Revue Indochinoise,* 1904, 1905.

Berland, Henri, tr. "Les papiers du Dr. Crawfurd, envoyé spécial au Siam et en Cochinchine par le Gouvernement des Indes en 1821," BSEI n. s., 16 (1941), No. 4, pp. 7-134.

Bernard, Henri. "Le conflit de la religion annamite avec la religion d'Occident à la Cour de Gia-long," CEFEO, No. 25 (1940), pp. 17-30. (Also *Bul. Gen. Instr. Publ.,* January, 1941.)

Bernard, Paul. *Nouveaux aspects du problème économique Indochinois*, Paris, 1937.

Bezacier, Louis. *L'ancienne armée annamite*. Hanoi, Taupin, 1941. (From *Bulletin de l'Association professionnelle des fonctionnaires français do la garde indigène de l'Indochine*, 1940-1941.)

Blet, Henri. *L'histoire de la colonisation française*, three vols., Grenoble and Paris, 1946, 1948, 1950.

Bodde, D. *China's First Unifier: A Study of the Ch'in Dynasty as Seen in the Life of Li Ssu*, Leiden, 1938.

Boeuf, Abel. *Histoire de la conquête de la Cochinchine, 1858-1861*, Saigon, 1927.

Bois, Georges. "Les débuts du christianisme en Annam," BSEI n.s., 8 (1933) No. 3, pp. 23-41. (A reply to Bonifacy's study on the same subject. See below.)

Bonifacy, A. *Les débuts du christianisme en Annam des origines au début du XVIIIe siècle*, Hanoi, 1930.

Borri, Cristoforo. "Relation de la nouvelle mission des Pères de la Compagnie de Jésus au royaume de la Cochinchine." Translated and annotated by Lt. Col. Bonifacy. *Bul. Amis Hué* 18 (1931), 277-405. (See note 38, Chapter IV.)

Bouchot, Jean. *Documents pour servir à l'histoire de Saigon, 1859 à 1868*, Saigon, 1927.

———. "Note historique sur Cholon," *Extrême Asie*, No. 23 (1928).

Boudet, Paul. "Chasseloup-Laubat, et la politique coloniale du Second Empire—Le Traité de 1864, entre la France et l'Annam," BSEI 22 (1947), No. 2, pp. 17-75.

———. "La conquête de la Cochinchine par les Nguyen et le rôle des émigrés chinois," CEFEO, No. 26 (1941), pp. 20-21; also BEFEO 42 (1942), pp. 115-132.

———. "Le marquis de Chasseloup-Laubat et la politique coloniale du second empire," CEFEO, No. 34 (1934), pp. 27-29.

Bougainville, Henry, Baron de. *Journal de la Navigation autour du monde de la frigate La Thétis et de la Corvette l'Espérance pendant les années 1824-25-26*, Paris, 1837, 2 vols.

Bouvier, René. *Richesse et misère du delta tonkinois*, Paris, Impr. Tournon, 1937.

Brebion, A. *Bibliographie des voyages dans l'Indochine française du IXe au XIXe siècle,* Saigon, 1910.

——. *Dictionnaire de bio-bibliographie générale ancienne et moderne de l'Indochine française,* Paris, 1935.

Briggs, Lawrence P. *The Ancient Khmer Empire,* Philadelphia, 1951.

Buch, Wilhelm J. M. "La Compagnie des Indes néerlandaises et l'Indochine," BEFEO 36 (1936), pp. 97-196. 1. La Compagnie des Indes Orientales. 2. Les premières relations avec l'Annam jusqu'en 1635. 3. Le commerce avec l'Annam et le Tonkin, 1636-1639. 4. Le Tonkin contre l'Annam, 1639-1651.

——. "La Compagnie des Indes néerlandaises et l'Indochine," BEFEO 37 (1937), pp. 121-237. Illus. 5. Le commerce au Tonkin de 1644 à la chute de Formose en 1662. 6. Relation avec l'Annam depuis le traité de 1651 jusqu'au milieu du XVIIIe siècle. 7. Le commerce avec le Tonkin de 1662 à 1700. 8. Le commerce au Cambodge jusqu'en 1641 et l'expédition du Laos. 9. Les relations avec le Cambodge depuis 1641.

Cabaton, A. "Doudart de Lagrée et l'Indochine, 1828-1868," *Revue de l'Histoire des Colonies Françaises,* 1933.

Cadière, L. "Alexandre de Rhodes." *Extrême-Asie,* Nos. 15-16 (1927), pp. 113-126.

——. "L'Annam: histoire: le Champa, la dynastie des Nguyen," *Bul. Amis Hué,* No. 18 (1931), pp. 92-108.

——. "Les Français au service de Gia-Long. III. Leurs noms, titres et appelations annamites," *Bul. Amis Hué,* (1920), pp. 137-176.

——. "Les Français au service de Gia-Long. VII. Les diplômes et ordres de service de Vannier et de Chaigneau," *Bul. Amis Hué,* No. 9 (1922), 139-180.

——. "Les Français au service de Gia-Long. IX. Despiau commerçant," *Bul. Amis Hue,* No. 12 (1925), pp. 183-186.

——. "Les Français au service de Gia-Long. XII. Leur correspondance," *Bul. Amis Hué,* No. 13 (1926), pp. 359-447.

——. "Le mur de Dong-Hoi; étude sur l'établissement des Nguyen en Cochinchine," BEFEO, No. 6 (1906), pp. 87-254.

——. "Les résidences des rois de Cochinchine (Annam) avant Gia-Long." *Bul. Comm. Arch. Indoch.* (1914-16), pp. 103-185.

———. Résumé de l'histoire d'Annam. Quinhon, Libr.-Impr. Quinhon, 1911, p. 103.

———. "Tableau chronologique des dynasties annamites," BEFEO, No. 5 (1905), pp. 77-145. (See introduction to Bibliography; see also Civilization.)

Cadière, L., and Pelliot, P. "Première étude sur les sources annamites de l'histoire d'Annam," BEFEO, No. 4 (1904), pp. 617-671.

Cadière, L., and Cosserat, H. "Les Français au service de Gia-Long. VI. La maison de J. B. Chaigneau, consul de France à Hué." *Bul. Amis Hué,* No. 9 (1922), pp. 1-32.

Cady, John T. *The Roots of French Imperialism in Eastern Asia.* Ithaca, N. Y. 1954 (See introduction to Bibliography.)

Caillaud, Romanet du. *Essai sur les origines du christianisme au Tonkin et dans les pays annamites,* Paris, 1915.

———. *Histoire de l'intervention française au Tong King de 1872 à 1874,* Paris, Challamel, 1880.

Callery, J. M. *Journal des opérations diplomatiques de la légation française en Chine,* Macao, 1845.

Castonnet-Desfosses, H. "L'Annam au moyen âge," *Revue Libérale,* December, 1883, pp. 417-448.

Chaigneau, J. B. *Le mémoire sur la Cochinchine de Jean-Baptiste Chaigneau,* Hanoi and Haiphong, Impr. d'Extr.-Or., 1923.

Chaigneau, Michel Duc. *Souvenirs de Hué (Cochinchine),* Paris, 1867, 271 pp.; Shanghai, Editions Typhon, 1941.

Chailley, Joseph. *Paul Bert au Tonkin,* Paris, G. Charpentier, 1887. (See note 130, Chapter VI.)

Chappoulié, Henri. *Aux origines d'une église: Rome et les missions d'Indochine au XVIIe siècle,* Paris, 2 vols., Bloud and Gay, 1943-1947.

———. This is the latest work on the early history of the Catholic missions in Indochina. The first volume covers the period up to 1678, the second the years from 1679-1696.

Chassigneux, E. "Histoire," in Vol. V, *L'Indochine*; Hanotaux and Martineau, eds., *Histoire des colonies françaises et de l'expansion de la France dans le monde,* Paris, 1932. (See introduction to Bibliography; see also under Civilization.)

Chastel, Guy. *Un siècle d'épopée française en Indochine, 1774-1874*, Paris, 1947.

Chavannes, Ed. *Mémoires historiques de Se-ma T'sien*, 6 vols., Paris, 1895-1905. (See also notes 26, Chapter I; 4, 40, Chapter II; introduction to Bibliography.)

Chesneaux, J. *Contribution à l'histoire de la nation vietnamienne*, Paris, 1955. (See introduction to Bibliography.)

Cho Huan Lai. *Les origines du conflit franco-chinois à propos du Tonkin jusqu'en 1883*, Paris, 1935.

Claeys, Jean, Y. "Introduction à l'étude de l'Annam et du Champa: les chams; les annamites," Preface by Victor Goloubew, *Bul. Amis Hué*, No. 21 (1934), pp. 1-144.

Claeys, J. Y., and Huet, M. *Angkor*, Paris, 1948.

Clifford, Sir Hugh. *Further India*, London, 1904.

Coedès, G. *Les états hindouisés d'Indochine et d'Indonesie*, Paris, 1948.

———. *Pour mieux comprendre Angkor*, Paris, 1947.

———. *Textes d'auteurs grecs et latins relatifs à l'Extrême-Orient depuis le IVe siècle av. J.-C. jusqu'au XIVe siècle*, Paris, 1910. (See introduction to Bibliography; see also under Civilization.)

Colani, M. "Recherches sur le préhistoriquee indochinois," BEFEO, XXX, pp. 299-422.

Colenbrander, H. T. *Koloniale Geschiedenis*, 3 vols., The Hague, 1925.

Collins, Ross W. *Catholicism in the Second French Republic, 1848-1852*, New York, 1923.

Coral Remusat, Gilberte de. *L'art khmer/Les grandes étapes de son évolution*, Paris, 1951.

Cordier, H. *Histoire générale de la Chine et de ses relations avec les pays étrangers depuis les plus ancien jusqu'à la chute de la dynastie Mandchoue*, Paris, 1920.

———. "La politique coloniale de la France au début du Second Empire (Indo-Chine, 1852-1858)," *T'oung Pao*, 2nd ser., X-XII (1909-1911).

———. "L'arrivée des Portugais en Chine," *T'oung Pao*, 1911.

———. "Le consulat de France à Hué sous la Restauration," *Rev. Extr.-Or.*, No. 2 (1883), pp. 139-267.

———. "La reprise des relations de la France avec l'Annam sous la Restauration," *T'oung Pao*, 2nd ser., 4 (1903), pp. 285-315. (See also introduction to Bibliography; see also under Civilization.)

Cothonay, M. P. *Vies de quatre missionnaires morts martyrs à Hanoi*. Tours, Cattier, n.d.

Courcy, Marquis R. de. *Souvenirs*, 3 vols., Paris, 1900.

Cowley, H. R. C. *Secrets of the Second Empire*, New York, 1929.

Crawfurd, John. *Journal of an embassy from the governor-general of India to the courts of Siam and Cochin China; exhibiting a view of the actual state of those kingdoms*, 2nd ed., 2 vols., London, Colburn and Bentley,1830.

Creel, H. G. *The Birth of China*, London, 1936.

———. *Confucius, the Man and the Myth*, New York, 1949.

Cremieux, Max. "Les origines de l'Annam," *Rev. Troupes Col.* 1 (1905), pp. 563-573; No. 2 (1905), pp. 93-101.

Crochet, L. *Vie du vénérable François Jaccard*, Paris, 1879.

Cultru, P. "Conférence sur l'occupation de la Cochinchine," BSEI (1909) 1st sem., pp. 45-62.

———. *Histoire de la Cochinchine française, des origines à 1883* Paris, 1910. (See notes 4, 15, 29 56, 73, Chapter VI; see also introduction to Bibliography.)

Cunningham, Alfred. *The French in Tonkin and South China*. *Hongkong*, Hongkong Daily Press, 1902; 2nd rev. ed., 203 pp. London, Sampson Low, 1902.

Dao-Dang-Vy. "Page historique: Nguyen Truong To et son temps," *La Patrie Annamite*, No. 221.

Dao-Thai-Hanh. "Son Excellence Phan-Thanh-Gian," *Bul. Amis Hué*, April-June, 1915, pp. 211-224.

Daudin, Pierre, and Le-Van-Phuc. "Phan-Thanh-Gian (1796-1867) et sa famille d'après quelques documents annamites," BSEI n.s., No. 16 (1941), No. 2, pp. 153.

De Bazancourt, César L. *Les expéditions de Chine et de Cochinchine; d'après les documents officiels*, 2 vols., pp. 413 and 426, Paris, Amyot, 1861-1862. (See notes 51, 55, 63, Chapter VI; see also introduction to Bibliography.)

Debidour, Antonin. *Histoire des rapports de l'église et de l'état en France de 1789 à 1870*, Paris, 1898.

De Frondeville, Henri. "Un prélat normand évangélisateur et précurseur de l'influence française en Extrême-Orient: Pierre Lambert de la Motte, évêque de Beryte (1624-1679)," *Rev. Hist. Miss.*, No. 1 (1924), pp. 350-407.

De Grammont, Capt. Lucien. *Onze mois de sous-préfecture en Basse-Cochinchine; contenant en outre une notice sur la langue cochinchinoise, des phrases usuelles françaises-annamites, des notes nombreuses et des pièces justificatives, avec une grande carte de la Basse-Cochinchine*, 502 pp., Napoleon-Vendée, J. Sory, 1863. "Geography, ethnography, history of French conquest, organization of the country under the mandarins and French administration and colonization." (*Bibliography of the Peoples and Cultures of Mainland Southeast Asia*, by John F. Embree and Lillian Ola Dotson, Yale University, New Haven, 1950.)

———. *Notice sur la Basse-Cochinchine*, Paris, 1864. For an interesting description of the Vietnamese people by De Grammont, see note 120, Chapter VI.

De Larclause, Savin. "Compagnes de Chine et de Cochinchine et les premières années de la Cochinchine française (1856-1866)," BSEI n.s., 14 (1939), nos. 3-4.

De la Loubère, Simon. *Du royaume de Siam*, 2 vols., Paris, 1691.

De Lanessan, J. L. *L'expansion coloniale de la France*, Paris, 1886. (See also notes 10, Chapter I; 134, 135, Chapter VI; introduction to Bibliography.)

———. *La colonisation française en Indo-Chine*, Paris, 1895

Deloustal, Raymond. "Ressources financières et économiques de l'état dans l'ancien Annam; Quoc dung chi; traduction annotée des livres xxix-xxxii du Lich trieu hien chuong loai chi," *Rev. Indoch.* n.s., 13, Sept.-Dec., 1924, pp. 193-228, 381-414; Jan.-April, 1925, pp. 59-78, 281-303.

———. "Ressources économiques et financières de l'état dans l'ancien Annam," *Bul. Amis Hué*, 1932.

———. "Ressources financières et économiques de l'état dans l'ancien Annam; Impôts des monopoles et règles en matière de perception." *Bul. Amis Hué* 19 (1932), pp. 157-218. (Continuation of above.)

BIBLIOGRAPHY

Delvaux, (R. P.) Adolphe. "L'ambassade de Minh-Mang à Louis-Philippe, 1839 à 1841," *Bul. Amis Hué* 15 (1928), pp. 257-264.

———. "L'ambassade de Phan-thanh-Gian en 1863, d'après les documents français," *Bul. Amis Hué* 13 (1926), pp. 69-80.

———. *Lettres des missionnaires de la Cochinchine et du Tonkin au commencement du XVIIIe siècle; traduites de l'allemand; préface de L. Cadière et H. Cosserat,* n.p., n.d.

Demartinecourt, Capt. "La cour d'Annam sous les dernières années du règne de Tu-Duc." *Mém. Soc. Bourguignonne Géog.,* 4 (1886), pp. 185-202; 6 (1888), pp. 97-116.

De Pouchalon. *Indochine: Souvenirs de voyage et de campagne, 1858-60,* Tours, 1896.

De Pouvourville, A. *L'annamite,* 107 pp., Paris, Larose, 1932.

———. *L'Indochine française,* Paris, Ed. de l'Encyclopédie coloniale et maritime, 1937.

De Rosny. "La Cochinchine et l'occupation française du Port de Tourane," *Revue Orientale et Américaine,* 1859.

Deschanel, Paul E. L. *La question du Tonkin,* Paris, Berger-Levrault, 1883.

Des Michels, Abel, tr. *Les annales impériales de l'Annam; traduites en entier pour la première fois du texte chinois,* 2 vols. Paris, Leroux, 1889-1892. (See introduction to Bibliography; see also under Civilization.)

De Vaublanc. *La première campagne de Cochinchine, 1858-1859,* Ecole de Guerre Navale, 1935.

Deveria, Gabriel, ed. and tr. *Histoire des relations de la Chine avec l'Annam-Vietnam du XVIe au XIXe siècle; d'après des documents chinois traduits pour la première fois,* Paris, Leroux, 1880.

Devillers, Philippe. "Vietnamese Nationalism and French Politics," in *Asian Nationalism and the West,* ed. by William L. Holland, New York, 1953.

———. *Histoire du Viet-Nam de 1940 à 1952,* Paris, 1952 (See also introduction to Bibliography.)

D'Hervey de Saint Denys. "L'Annam ou Tong-King et la Cochinchine, au point de vue historique et philologique," CR Acad. Inscr. Belles-Let., 1885, pp. 360-367.

Dickenson, J. T. "Chronology of the kings of Tong King," *Chin.*

Reposit. 8 (1839), pp. 205-212. (Translated from the *Nouvelles Lettres Edifiantes.*)

Diguet, E. *Annam et Indo-Chine française,* Paris, Challamel, 1908. (See notes 22, 29, Chapter V; see also introduction to Bibliography and under Civilization.)

Dobby, D. H. G. *Southeast Asia,* London, 1950.

D'Ornano. *La vie passionante du comte Walewski,* Paris, 1853.

Dubois, Adolphe. *Les accords Franco-Chinois,* Paris, 1928.

Duerrwell, George. "Notice historique sur la conquête des provinces de la Basse-Cochinchine," BSEI, 1902, pp. 43-60.

Dumarest, André. *La formation des classes sociales en pays annamite; préface de Henri Gourdon,* Thesis, Paris; Lyon, Impr. Ferreol, 1935.

Dumoutier, Gustave. "Etude historique sur Trieu-vo-de et sa dynastie (206-109 av. J.-C.), fondation du royaume de Nam-viet, après la destruction de Van-Lang," *T'oung Pao,* 2nd ser., 7 (1906), 413-436.

———. "Etude historique et archéologique sur Co-loa capitale de l'ancien royaume de Au-lac," *Cah. Soc. Géogr.,* Hanoi, 1940.

———. "Etude historique et archéologique sur Hoa-lu, première capitale de l'Annam independant, dynasties Dinh et Le (antérieure) 968 à 1010 de notre ère," *Bul. Géog., Hist., Descr.,* 8 (1893), pp. 38-174.

———. "Le Comptoir hollandais de Pho-hien," *Bull. Géogr. Hist. Desc.,* 1895.

———. "Notes ethnographiques et historiques sur les Giao-chi," *L'Anthr.,* 1 (1890), pp. 651-655.

Duong-Quang-Ham. *Leçons d'histoire d'Annam,* Hanoi, 1936.

———. "Une grande figure de l'histoire d'Annam: Nguyen-van-Hué," *Bul. Gén. Instr. Publ.,* Nov.-Dec., 1923, pp. 116-119, 192-198.

Dupont de Nemours. "Notice sur la vie de M. Poivre (avec une introduction et des notes par Louis Malleret)," BSEI, 1932, No. 3.

Dupuis, Jean. *Les origines de la question du Tong-Kin,* xxxvi, 240 pp. Paris, Challamel, 1896.

———. *L'ouverture du fleuve rouge au commerce et les événements du Tonkin,* Paris, 1872 and 1873.

————. *Le Tonkin de 1872 à 1886; histoire et politique,* Paris, Challamel, 1910.
About the role Dupuis played in the first French attempt to conquer Tongking, see pages 367-75, and notes 95, 96, 97, Chapter VI.

Durand, E. M. "Evêque et patriote: Mgr. Pigneau de Béhaine, évêque d'Adran," *Rev. Hist. Miss.,* 1926, pp. 353-369, 549-580.

Duyvendak, J. L. "The True Dates of the Chinese Maritime Expeditions in the Early 15th Century," *T'oung Pao,* Vol. XXXIV (1938).

————. *Chinese Discovery of Africa,* London, 1950.

Eckel, Paul E. *The Far East since 1500,* London 1948.

Embree, J. F., and Dotson, L. O. *Bibliography of the Peoples and Cultures of Mainland South-East Asia,* New Haven, Conn., Yale Univ., 1950.

Emerson, R., Mills, L. A., and Thompson, V. *Government and Nationalism in Southeast Asia,* New York, 1942.

Fall, Bernard. *The Viet-Minh Regime,* Ithaca, N. Y., Cornell U., 1954.

Faure, Alexis. *Les Français en Cochinchine au XVIIIe siècle: Mgr. Pigneau de Béhaine, évêque d'Adran,* Paris, Challamel, 1891.

Ferrand, G. *Relations de voyages et textes géographiques arabes, persans et turcs relatives à l'Extrême-Orient du VIII au XVIII siècles,* 2 vols., Paris, 1913-1914.

Ferrière le Vayer, Th. de. *Une embassade française en Chine, Journal de voyage,* Paris, 1854.

Ferry, Jules F. C. *Le Tonkin et la mère patrie; témoignages et documents,* Paris, Victor-Harvard, 1890.

Finlayson, George. *The mission to Siam, and Hué, the capital of Cochin-China, in the years 1821-2. From the journal of the late George Finlayson,* London, Murray, 1826.

Finot, L. *Un martyr lorrain en Extrême-Orient, La vie et la mort du bienheureux Aug. Schoeffler,* Metz, 1900.

Fitzgerald, C. P. *China: A Short Cultural History,* 3rd rev. ed., New York, 1950.

Fontanier, Henri, tr. "Une mission chinoise en Annam (1840-1841)," *T'oung Pao,* 2nd ser., 4 (1903), pp. 127-145.

Francastel, Paul. "Origines du Viet-Nam," *France-Asie,* No. 13 (April, 1947), pp. 336-342; No. 14 (May, 1947), pp. 430-442; No. 15 (June, 1947) pp. 571-584.

Franke, O. *Geschichte des chinesischen Reiches,* 5 vols., Berlin, 1930-1952.

Furnivall, J. S. *Educational Progress in Southeast Asia,* New York, 1943.

Galos, Henri. "L'expédition de Cochinchine et la politique française en Extrême-Orient," *Revue des Deux Mondes,* 1864.

Garnier, F. "Chronique royal du Cambodge," *Journal Asiatique,* 1871-1872.

——. *La Cochinchine française en 1864,* Paris, 1864. (Published under pseudonym of G. Francis.)

——. *De la colonisation de la Cochinchine,* 1865.

——. *Voyage d'exploration de l'Indochine,* Paris, 1885, 2 vols. About Francis Garnier, and for a description of his role in the abortive attempt to conquer Tongking in 1873, see pages 370-75, and notes 99, 104, 106, 107, 108, 109, 110, 114, 115, 116, Chapter VI.

Gaspardone, Emile. "Annamite et thai au XVe siècle," *Jl. Asiatique,* 1939.

——. "Matériaux pour servir à l'histoire d'Annam. I. La géographie de Li Wen-fong," BEFEO 29 (1929), pp. 63-105.

——. "Les pays du Sud et la Chine des derniers Han et des Trois Royaumes," Cours 1950-1951 of the College of France. (See notes 48, 57, Chapter II; 53, Chapter III; 73, Chapter IV; see also introduction to Bibliography.)

Gaultier, Marcel. *Gia-Long, préface de M. Pierre Pasquier, gouverneur général de l'Indochine,* Saigon, Ardin, 1933.

——. *Minh-Mang,* Paris, Larose, 1935. (See notes 11, 13, 16, 17, Chapter V; see also introduction to Bibliography.)

Gautier, Albert H. *Les Français au Tonkin, 1787-1883,* Paris, Challamel, 1884.

Goloubew, Victor. "Le peuple de Dong-son et les Muong," CEFEO, No. 10 (1937), pp. 19-23. Also TIA 2 (1937) pp. 16-18. (See notes 17, 31, Chapter II.)

————. "L'âge du bronze au Tonkin et dans le Nord-Annam," BEFEO, 29 (1929), pp. 1-46.

————. *L'archéologie du Tonkin et les fouilles du Dong-Son,* Hanoi, 1937. (See introduction to Bibliography.)

Geddie, John. "The French in Tonquin," *Scot. Geog. Mag.,* 1 (1885), pp. 170-174.

Gosselin, C. *L'empire d'Annam; préface de Pierre Baudin.* xxvi, 560 pp. Paris, Perrin, 1904. (See introduction to Bibliography.)

Gourou, P. *The Future of Indochina,* Paris, 1947. (See introduction to Bibliography; see also under Civilization.)

Grandjean, G. *L'épopée jaune, missionnaires et marins en Indo-Chine, 1765-1885,* Ed. Malfere, 1938.

Granet, Paul Marcel. *La civilisation chinoise,* Paris, 1929.

Gros, Jules. *Origines de la conquête du Tong-Kin depuis l'expédition de Jean Dupuis jusqu'à la mort de Henri Rivière,* Paris, Picard, 1887.

Grosse-Aschhoff, Angelos. *The negotiations between Ch'i-Ying and Lagrené, 1844-1848,* Allegany, N. Y., 1950.

Grousset, René. *Histoire de l'Extrême-Orient,* Paris, 1929.

————. *The Rise and Splendor of the Chinese Empire,* Berkeley, 1953.

————. *China,* New York, 1934. (See notes 26, 36, 38, Chapter II; 7, Chapter III; see also introduction to Bibliography.)

Hall, D. G. E. *A History of South-East Asia,* New York, 1955.

————. "From Mergui to Singapore, 1686-1819," *Journal of Siam Society,* Bangkok, Vol. XLI, No. 1, July, 1953. (See Foreword and introduction to Bibliography.)

Hall, J. R. *The Bourbon Restoration,* London, 1909.

Hammer, Ellen. "Parties and Politics in Viet Nam," *Foreign Affairs Reports,* Vol. II, No. 12, Dec., 1943.

————. *The Struggle for Indochina,* Stamford, 1954.

————. "Progress Report on Southern Viet Nam," *Pacific Affairs,* Vol. XXX, No. 3, Sept., 1957. (See also introduction to Bibliography.)

Harmand, Jules. *Domination et colonisation,* Paris, 1910.

Harrison, Brian. *South-East Asia,* London, 1954. (See Foreword and notes 7, 11, 19, 21, Chapter I.)

Haussmann, A. *Voyage en Chine, Cochinchine, Inde et Malaisie,* Paris, 1848

Heine-Geldern, Robert. "Suedostasien," Vol. 2, pp. 689-968. in G. Buschan, ed., *Illustrierte Voelkerkunde,* Stuttgart, 1923. (See note 17, Chapter II; see also introduction to Bibliography and under Civilization.)

Hirth, F. *China and the Roman Orient,* Leipzig, 1885.

Hobbs, Cecil C., and Assocs. *Indochina: a bibliography of land and people,"* Washington, 1950.

Howarth, H. H. *History of the Mongols from the Ninth to the Nineteenth Century,* London, 1876-1888.

Huard, Pierre, and Durand, Maurice. *Connaissance du Vietnam,* Paris and Hanoi, 1954. This is the most up to date and most comprehensive study of Vietnamese civilization, with brief chapters also on pre-history and history. This book contains almost complete lists of works on these subjects by Vietnamese authors. (See also under Civilization.)

Huard, P. "Les Portugais et l'Indochine," IIEH 3 (1940), pp. 47-65. (See introduction to Bibliography; also under Civilization.)

Hull, Cordell. *Memoirs,* New York, 1948.

Hutchinson, E. W. *Adventures in Siam in the Seventeenth Century,* London, 1940.

Indochine, Gouvernement Général. *Contributions à l'Histoire des Mouvements Politiques de l'Indochine Française,* 7 vols. of documents, Hanoi, 1933-1934.

Itier, J. *Journal d'un voyage en Chine en 1843-44-45-46,* Paris, 1848.

Janse, Olov R. T. *Archaeological Research in Indo-China: The District of Chiu-Chen During the Han Dynasty,* 2 vols., Cambridge Mass., 1947, 1949.

Jaquenet, J. B. S. *La vie de l'abbé Gagelin,* Paris, 1850.

Joinville, P. de. *La mission de la Cybèle en Extrême-Orient,* Paris, 1914.

Kaeppelin, P. *La Compagnie des Indes Orientales et François Martin,* Paris, 1908.

Kaltenmark, M. "Le Dompteur des Flots," *Han Hiue*, Vol. III, (1948), fasc. 1-2.

Kammerer, A. *La découverte de la Chine par les Portugais au XVIe siècle et la cartographie des Portulans*, supplement to *T'oung Pao*, Vol. 1944.

Kherian, G. "Le problème démographique en Indochine," *Revue Indochinoise Juridique et Economique*, 1937, Vol. I, pp. 6-8.

King, John Kerry. *Southeast Asia in Perspective*, New York, 1956.

Koeffler, John. "Historica Cochinchinae Descriptio," translated and reprinted in *Rev. Indoch.*, 1911.

Labarthe, Charles. "Ha-noi, capitale du Tong-king en 1883," *Rev. Géog.*, 13 (1883), pp. 91-103.

———. "Le Tong-king: esquisse historique et ethnographique," *Rev. Géog.*, 14 (1884), pp. 268-284.

Lamarre, Georges. "L'organisation administrative," Vol. II, *L'Indochine*, pub. under the direction of Georges Maspéro, Paris, 1930.

Landes, A. "La commune annamite," *Journal Officiel Cochinchine*, July, 1880, pp. 446-447; 451-454, 458, 469-473; also *Exc. et Rec. 2*, 1880, pp. 213-242.

Lanoue, H. "Activités économiques américaines en Indochine," *Cahiers Internationaux*, No. 36, May 1952, p. 86.

Latourette, K. S. *History of the Christian Missions in China*, New York, 1929. (See notes 23, 25, 41, Chapter II; 7, Chapter IV.)

———. *The Chinese. Their History and Culture*, New York, 1945.

———. *A Short History of the Far East*, New York, 1951. (See introduction to Bibliography.)

Lattimore, O. *Inner Asian Frontiers of China*, London, 1940.

Launay, A. *Mémorial de la Société des Missions Etrangères*, 2 vols., Paris, 1912-1916.

———. *Histoire ancienne et moderne de l'Annam: Tong-King et Cochinchine; depuis l'an 2700 avant l'ère chrétienne jusqu'à nos jours*, Paris, Challamel, 1884.

———. *Histoire de la mission de Cochinchine, 1658-1823; documents historiques* 3 vols.: I, 1658-1728; II, 1728-1771; III, 1771-1823, Paris, Douniol and Retaux, 1923-1925.

———. *Histoire de la mission du Tonkin: documents historiques*, Vol. I, 1658-1717, Paris, Maisonneuve, 1927.

495

———. *Histoire général de la Société des Missions Etrangères de-puis sa fondation jusqu'à nos jours,"* 3 vols., Paris 1894 (1920). (See also introduction to Bibliography.)

Le Boulanger, Paul. *Histoire du Laos français,* Paris, 1931.

Leclerc, Adhemere. *Histoire du Cambodge,* Paris, 1914.

Lehault, P. *La France et L'Angleterre en Asia, Vol. I, Indochine, les derniers jours de la dynastie des rois d'Ava,* Paris, 1892.

Lemaitre, Capt. *Religions, cultes, rites et superstitions en terre d'Annam; influence de l'idée philosophique sur la vie politique et sociale du peuple annamite; conférence faite aux officiers de la garnison de Saigon, le 16 septembre 1932,* Saigon, Impr. de l'Union, 1932.

Lemire, Ch. *Les cinq pays de l'Indochine française,* Paris, 1899.

Le-Quang-Nhut. "Les origines du peuple annamite," *Rev. Indoch.,* Sept., 1906, pp. 1390-1395.

Le-Thanh-Canh. "Notes pour servir à l'histoire de l'établissement du protectorat français en Annam (1847-63)," *Bull. Amis Hué,* 1928, 1929, 1932, 1937.

Le-Thanh-Khoi. *Le Viet-Nam,* Paris, 1955. For a critical analysis of this important work, see Foreword, p. 9, and introduction to Bibliography.

Le-Thanh-Tuong. *Un patriote annamite admirateur de la France: essai sur la vie de Phan-Thanh-Giang, Vice-Roi de Cochinchine,* Hanoi, Nam-Ky, 1938.

Leuba, J. *Un royaume disparu: Les Chams et leur art,* Paris, 1923.

Levy, Roger. *Recherches préhistoriques dans la région de Mlu Prei, accompagnées des comparaisons archéologiques,* Hanoi, 1943.

———. *Regards sur l'Asie,* Paris, 1952.

Linh-Nam. "Dai-Viet? Dai-Nam? Annam? Viet-Nam?" *Sud-Est,* No. 6 (Nov., 1949), pp. 29-32. (A study of the names under which Vietnam was known throughout history.)

Louvet, Abbé L. E. *La Cochinchine religieuse,* 2 vols., Paris, Le-roux, 1885. (See notes 37, Chapter III; 74, 97, Chapter IV; 29, Chapter VI.)

———. *Monseigneur d'Adran, notice biographique,* Saigon, Impr. de la Mission, 1896.

Louzon, Robert. *La Chine: Ses trois millénaires d'histoire, ses cinquante ans de révolution,* Paris, 1954. (A Marxist interpretation by an anti-Communist.)

Luro, E. *Le pays d'Annam. Etude sur l'organisation politique et sociale des Annamites,* Paris, Leroux, 1878; 2nd ed., 1897. (See introduction to Bibliography.)

Lyautey, L. H. G. *Lettres du Tonkin et de Madagascar (1893-9),* 2 vols., Paris, 1920.

Madrolle, Claude. "Annam et Vietnam," *France-Asie,* No. 31 (Oct., 1948).

———. Le Tonkin ancien, BEFEO, 37 (1937), pp. 263-332.

Maitre, E. "Documents sur Pigneau de Béhaine," *Rev. Indoch.,* 1913.

Majumdar, R. C. *Ancient Indian Colonies in the Far East: I, Champa,* Lahore, 1927.

Makepiece, Brooke, and Bradell. *One Hundred Years of Singapore,* London, 1921.

Malleret, Louis. "Une tentative ignorée d'établissement français en Indochine au XVIIIe siècle; les vues de l'Amiral d'Estaing," CEFEO, No. 29 (1941), pp. 10-16.

Mangenot, E. *Le Bienheureux Augustin Schoeffler,* Nancy, 1900.

Mansuy, H. *La préhistoire en Indochine,* Paris, 1931.

Marquet, J. and Norel, Jean. "L'occupation de Tonkin par la France, (1873-1874), d'après des documents inédits," BSEI, 1936, No. 1, pp. 5-199.

Maspéro, Georges. "Luoc bien Nam-Viet su Ky lich tsieu nien-Ky tableau chronologique des souverains de l'Annam," *T'oung Pao* 5 (1894), pp. 43-62.

———. *Le royaume de Champa,* Paris, 1928.

———. *L'empire Khmer,* Phnom Penh, 1904. (See introduction to Bibliography.)

Maspéro, Henri. "Etudes d'histoire d'Annam: 1. La dynastie des Li antérieurs; 2. La géographie politique de l'empire d'Annam sous les Li; 3. La commanderie de Siang," BEFEO, 16 (1916), No. 1, pp. 1-55.

———. "Etudes d'histoire d'Annam: 4. Le royaume de Van-Lang; 5. L'expédition de Ma-Yuan; 6. La frontière de l'Annam et du

Cambodge du VIIIe au XIVe siècle," BEFEO, 18 (1918), No. 3, pp. 1-36.

———. "Etudes d'histoire du Viet-Nam: le royaume de Van-Lang," *Dan Viet Nam*, No. 1 (May, 1948), pp. 1-12.

———. "Le Protectorat général d'Annam sous les T'ang; essai de géographie historique," BEFEO, 10 (1910), pp. 539-584, 665-682.

———. "L'expédition de Ma Yuan," BEFEO, 3, 11. (See introduction to Bibliography; see also under Civilization.)

Masson, André. *Hanoi pendant la période héroique (1873-1888),* Paris, Geuthner, 1929.

———. *Histoire de l'Indochine,* Paris, 1950. (See introduction to Bibliography.)

Masson, Capt. J. *Souvenirs de l'Annam et du Tonkin,* Paris, Lavauzelle, 1892.

Maury, A. P. *Mes campagnes au Tong-King,* 2nd ed. Lyon, Vitte Y Perrussel, c. 1890.

Maybon, Charles B. *Histoire moderne du pays d'Annam (1592-1820) étude sur les premier rapports des européens et des annamites et sur l'établissement de la dynastie,* Paris, 1920. (Pref. by Henri Cordier.)

———. *Les marchands européens en Cochinchine et au Tonkin (1600-1775),* Hanoi, Ed. *Revue Indochinoise,* 1916.

———. "Nguyen-Anh, empereur et fondateur de dynastie: Gia-Long (1802-1820)," *Rev. Hist. Col.,* 1919, pp. 47-126.

———. "Quelques documents inédits concernant Pierre Poivre," *Etudes Asiatiques,* 1925, Vol. 2, pp. 143-157.

———, ed. *La relation sur le Tonkin et la Cochinchine de M. de la Bissachère, missionaire français (1807), publiée d'après le manuscrit des Archives Affaires étrangères, avec une introduction et des notes,* Paris, Champion, 1920. (Pierre Jacques Lemounier de la Bissachère, 1764-1830.)

Maybon, Charles B., and Russier, Henri. *Notions d'histoire d'Annam,* 2 vols., 173 and 225 pp., Hanoi-Haiphong, Impr. d'Ext.-Or., 1909. (Reviewed by L. Finot in *Jl Asiatique,* May-June, 1910, pp. 555-557. About Maybon, see introduction to Bibliography.)

McKay, D. V. "Colonialism in the French Geographical Movement, 1871-1881," *Geographical Revue,* XXXIII, 1943.

Mesny, William. *Tungking,* London, Sampson Low, 1884; Hong Kong, Noronha, 1884.

Meyniard, Ch. *Le second empire en Indochine,* Paris, 1891.

Montezon and Estève. *Mission de la Cochinchine et du Tonkin,* 1858.

Moura, J. *Le royaume du Cambodge,* 2 vols. Paris, 1883.

Munier, Paul *Gia-Long, la vie prodigieuse d'un grand roi,* Hanoi, Imp. d'Ext.-Or., 1932 (*Cahiers Soc. Géogr.* Hanoi, 23).

Murphy, Agnes. *The Ideology of French Imperialism, 1871-1880,* Washington, 1948.

Mus, Paul. "Au Vietnam: ni guerre civile ni réaction; alors peut-être . . . ," *Le Monde,* March 25, 1949.

———. "The role of the village in Vietnamese politics," *Pac. Aff.,* 23, 1949, pp. 265-272.

———. *Le Vietnam chez lui,* Paris, Hartmann, 1947.

———. *Vietnam: Sociologie d'une guerre,* Paris, 1952. (See introduction to Bibliography, see also under Civilization.)

Needham, J. *Science and Civilization in China,* Cambridge, 1954. See notes 42, Chapter II; 25, 66, Chapter III.

Ner, M. *Les musulmans de l'Indochine française,* Paris 1941.

Nguyen Lan. *Nguyen Truong To,* Hué, 1941.

Nguyen-Thieu-Lau. "Le port et la ville de Faifo au XVIIe siècle," CEFEO, No. 30 (1942).

Nguyen-Van-Nhan. "An introduction to Viet-Nam," *Asian Horizon,* 2, (1949), No. 1, pp. 48-55.

Nguyen-Van-To. "Les Chinois ont-ils conservé les rapports de leurs premiers ambassadeurs en Annam?" *Bul. Soc. Ens. Tonkin,* 13 (1933), pp. 65-67.

———. "Origine des noms de Faifo, Tourane et Cochinchine," *Bul. Soc. Ens. Tonkin,* 14 (1934), pp. 70-71.

Nguyen-Van-Truyet. *Essai historique sur les relations du royaume d'Annam avec l'empire chinoise d'autrefois,* thesis, Montpellier, Impr. l'Abeille, 1924.

Noir, L. S. *Les français au Siam et au Cambodge,* Paris, 1894.

Norman, C. B. *Le Tonkin ou la France dans l'Extrême-Orient,* Paris, 1884.

———. *Tonkin; or France in the Far East,* London, Chapman and Hall, 1884.

Oliphant, L. *La Chine et le Japon, la mission du comte Elgin pendant les années 1857, 1858, 1859,* Paris, 1860.

Pallu, L. de la Barrière. *Histoire de l'expédition de Cochinchine,* Paris, 1864.

Pallu, François. *Relation abrégé des missions et des voyages des évêques français, envoys aux royaumes de la Chine, Cochinchine, Tonquin & Siam,* Paris, Denys Bechet, 1668.

Papinot, E. "Un martyr français au XIXe siècle: le bienheureux Théophane Vénard (1829-1861), prêtre de la Ste. des Missions étrangères de Paris," *Rev. Hist. Miss.,* 1929, pp. 385-406.

Paris, C. *Abrégé de l'histoire d'Annam de 2874 avant J. C. à 1890 ère chrétienne; avec un essai de carte historique et plusieurs tableaux,* Hanoi, Schneider, 1890.

Parker, E. H. "Annamese and Chinese," *China Rev.,* 16 (1887-1888), pp. 270-273.

Pasquier, Pierre. *L'Annam d'autrefois: Essai sur la constitution de l'Annam avant l'intervention française,* Paris, 1930. (See introduction to Bibliography; see also under Civilization.)

Patris, Charles. *Essai d'histoire d'Annam: Première partie, l'antiquité et le haut moyen âge,* Hué, Impr. Dac-lap, 1923.

———. "Le peuple d'Annam dans l'antiquité et le haut moyen âge; essai d'étude historique," *Rev. Indoch.* n. s. 35, March-April, 1921, pp. 115-150; May-June, 1921, pp. 305-344; 36, July-Aug., 1921, pp. 31-76; Sept.-Oct, 1921, pp. 231-274.

Pavie, A. *A la conquête des coeurs,* Paris, 1921.

Pelliot, Paul. "Deux itinéraires de Chine en Inde, à la fin du VIII siècle," BEFEO, 4 (1904), pp. 130-413.

Perennes, H. *Un grand coeur, Mgr. François-Marie Pellerin,* Brest, 1938.

Perez, Lorenzo. "Los Españoles en el imperio de Annam," Archivo Ibero-Americano 18 (1922), pp. 293-340; 19 (1923), pp. 5-24; 24 (1925), pp. 289-324; 26 (1926), pp. 145-178, 289-326; 27 (1927), pp. 5-41, 145-195, 289-325; 28 (1927), pp. 5-37, 145-196; 29 (1928), pp. 187-227; 30 (1928), pp. 179-240; 35 (1932), pp. 161-

204, 321-365; 36 (1933), pp. 49-93. (Spanish Franciscan missionary activities, eighteenth century.)

Perin, J. "La vie et l'oeuvre de Luro," BSEI, n. s., 15 (1940), Nos. 1-2, pp. 13-26.

Petit, E. *Francis Garnier, sa vie, ses voyages, ses oeuvres,* Paris, 1885.

Peyssonnaux, H. and Bui-Van-Cung. "Journal de l'ambassade envoyée en France et en Espagne par S. M. Tu-Duc (août 1877 à septembre 1878)." *Bul. Amis Hué,* 7 (1920), pp. 407-444.

———. "Le traité de 1874; journal du secrétaire de l'ambassade annamite," *Bul. Amis Hué,* 7 (1920), pp. 365-384.

Pham-Huy-Thong. *L'esprit public vietnamien hier et aujourd'hui,* Paris. Van-hoa Lien-hiep Union culturelle des Vietnamiens de France, 1949.

Pham-Phu-Thu. "L'ambassade de Phan-thanh-Gian (1863-1864)," translated by Ngo Dinh Diem and Tran Xuan Toan, *Bul. Amis Hué,* 6 (1919), pp. 161-261; (1921), pp. 147-187, 243-381.

Pham Quynh. *L'évolution intellectuelle et morale des Annamites depuis l'établissement du protectorat français,* Paris, 1922.

———. *Essais franco-annamites,* 2 vol., Hué, 1929-1938. (See page 434 of Chronology; see also introduction to Bibliography; also under Civilization.)

Phillips, C. S. *The Church in France, 1848-1907,* New York, 1936.

———, ed. *Handbook of Oriental History,* London, 1951. This small volume contains mainly lists of Oriental dynasties. It has a complete list of all legendary, semi-historical and historically verified Vietnamese rulers.

Ponchalon, Colonel Henri de. *Indochine: Souvenir de voyage et de campagne, 1858-60,* Tours, 1896.

Priestley, H. I. *France Overseas,* New York, 1938.

Przyluski, J. "Kôl and Munda: a New Aspect of the Austro-Asiatic Problem," JGIS, IV, Pt. 1 (Jan. 1937).

Purcell, V. W. W. S. *The Chinese in Southeast Asia,* London, 1951.

Raindre, Gaston. "Papiers inédits du comte Walewski," *Revue Française,* March 1, 1925.

Retours, R. des. *Nouvelle histoire des Tang,* Paris, 1932.

Rey, L. "Voyage from France to Cochin-China, in the ship *Henry*, Captain Rey, of Bordeaux, in the years 1819 and 1820," in *New voyages and travels published by* Sir R. Phillips, London, 1821. Vol. 4, No. 5, pp. 103-128.

Rhodes, Alexandre. *Divers voyages et missions*, Paris, 1653.

————. *Relations des heureux succès de la foi au royaume de Tonkin*, 1650.

————. *Histoire du Tonkin*, 1652.

————. *Carts du royaume humaniste*, 1650. About Alexander of Rhodes and his role in the history of the Vietnamese Catholic missions, see pages 214-217, and notes 39, 41, 42, 43, Chapter IV.

Richard, Abbé. *Histoire naturelle, civile et politique du Tonkin*, 2 vols., Paris, 1778.

Rivière, Henri. *Correspondance politique du commandant Rivière au Tonkin, avril 1882-mai 1883; publiée avec une introduction et des notes par André Masson; préface de Paul Boudet*, Paris, Editions d'art et d'histoire, 1933. About Henri Rivière and his role in the conquest of Tongking in 1883, see pages 376-77, and notes 120, 122, Chapter VI.

Robequain, Ch. *The Economic Development of French Indochina*, London and New York, 1944. (See introduction to Bibliography; see also under Civilization.)

Roberts, S. H. *History of French Colonial Policy, 1870-1925*, 2 vols., London, 1929.

Robertson, Daniel Brooke. *Report by Sir B. Robertson respecting his visit to Haiphong and Hanoi, in Tonquin*, 10 pp. London, Harrison, 1876. (China No. 2., 1876.)

Roosevelt, Franklin D. *The Public Papers and Addresses of Franklin D. Roosevelt, 1944-45*, New York.

Rouger, C. E. *Histoire militaire et politique de L'Annam et du Tonkin depuis 1799*, Paris, 1906.

Rowan, Carl D. *The Pitiful and the Proud*, New York, 1956. (See page 466 of Chronology.)

Roy, J. J. E. *La Chine et la Cochinchine*, Lille, 1862.

Ruch, W. J. M. "La Compagnie des Indes Néerlandaises et l'Indochine," BEFEO, Vols. XXXVI and XXXVII.

Sacks, I. Milton. "Communism and Regional Integration," in *South*

Asia in the World Today, edited by Phillips Talbot, Chicago, 1950.

Sainson, Camille. *Histoire particulière du Nan Tchao,* Paris, 1904.

——, tr. *Ngann-nann-tche-luo; mémoires sur l'Annam; traduction accompagnée d'un lexique géographique et historique,* Peking, Impr. Lazaristes au Pe-tang, 1896.

Sallet, Albert. "Campagne Franco-Espagnole du Centre-Annam: Prise de Tourane, 1858-1859," *Bul. Amis Hué.*

——. "Le vieux Faifo: I. Souvenirs chams; II. Souvenirs japonais; III. Les tombes européennes," *Bul. Amis Hué,* 6 (1919), pp. 501-519, illus.

Sansom, G. B. *Japan: A Short Cultural History,* London, 1952.

——. *Japan and the Western World,* London, 1950.

Schneider, Reinhold. *Iberisches Erbe,* First Part, *Das Leiden des Camoes,* Olten, 1949.

Schreiner Alfred. *Abrégé de l'histoire d'Annam,* 2nd ed., revised and enlarged for the period between 1858-1889, Saigon, 1906 (See introduction to Bibliography; see also under Civilization.)

Scott, James G. *France and Tongking; a narrative of the campaign of 1884 and the occupation of Further India,* London, Unwin, 1885.

Sellet, A. "Le vieux Faifo," *Bul. Amis Hué,* 1919.

Septans, A. *Les commencements de l'Indo-Chine française d'après les archives du ministère de la marine et des colonies,* Paris, 1887.

Sharp, Lauriston. "Colonial Regimes in Southeast Asia," *Far Eastern Survey,* Feb. 27, 1946.

Silvestre, J. "Etude sur l'Indo-Chine," *Bul. Soc. Géog. Rochefort,* 1 (1879-80), pp. 57-74, 107-140. (See introduction to Bibliography; and also under Civilization.)

Société des Etudes Indochinoises. *Inscription de la montagne de Vinh-te,* Saigon, Impr. Saigonnaise, 1905. (Translation of inscription ordered by Emperor Minh Mang in honor of the mandarin Thoai Ngoc Han.)

Stapel, F. W., ed. *Geschiedenis van Nederlandsch-Indie,* 4 vols., Amsterdam, 1939.

Staunton, Sidney A. *The war in Tong-king. Why the French are in Tong-king, and what they are doing there,* Boston, Cupples, Upham and Co., 1884; Cambridge, Hodges, 1884.

Stewart, H. F., and Desjardines, Paul. *French Patriotism in the Nineteenth Century, 1814-1833,* Cambridge, 1933.

Taboulet, Georges. "Les débuts de l'Amiral Bonard en Cochinchine," CEFEO, No. 33 (1942), pp. 14-16.

———. "Emile et Clement Luro, colons en Cochinchine," BSEI, n. s., 15 (1940), Nos. 1-2, pp. 113-128.

———. "J. B. Eliacin Luro, Inspecteur des Affairs Indigènes en Cochinchine," BSEI, n. s., 15 (1940), Nos. 1-2, pp. 27-112.

———. "La première évocation de la question de Cochinchine du Conseil des Ministres (juillet 1857)," BSEI, n. s., 18 (1943), Nos. 1-2, pp. 69-77.

———. "Quelques lettres de Mgr. Lefèbvre, premier évêque de Saigon français (1862-1865)," BSEI, n. s., 18 (1943), No. 4, pp. 9-26.

———. "La vie tourmentée de l'évêque de l'Adran," BSEI, n. s., 15 (1940), Nos. 3-4, pp. 9-41.

———. *La geste française en Indochine,* Two volumes, Paris, 1955 and 1956. (See Foreword and introduction to Bibliography.)

Tavernier, Emile. *Le déclin de l'apogée du règne des Tay-son: les batailles de Qui-nhon (jan-fev. 1801),* Hanoi, Impr. Trung-bac Tan-van, 1934. (From *Bul. Gen. Instr. Publ.,* June-Aug. 1934.)

———. *Monseigneur Pigneau de Béhaine, évêque d' Adran (quelques aspects de sa vie politique et religieuse),* Hanoi, Le-Van-Tan, 1934. (From *Bul. Soc. Ens. Tonkin,* 14, 1934, pp. 345-390.)

Than Luong. *Histoire resumée du Viet-Nam,* Hanoi, 1955.

Thompson, Virginia, *French Indochina,* London, 1937.

Thomson, J. O. *History of Ancient Geography,* Cambridge, 1948.

Thomson,, K. Stanley. "France in Cochinchina: The Question of Retrocession, 1862-65," *Far Eastern Quarterly,* Vol. VI, No. 4, Aug., 1947.

Tinh, Michel, "La vie et le martyre du Bienheureux Le-van-Gam," BSEI, 1903, pp. 91-102.

Trinh-Hoi-Duc. *Histoire et description de la Basse-Cochinchine,* Paris, 1863.

Tran-Van-Trai. *L'enseignement traditionnel en Annam,* thesis, Paris, Lapagesse, 1942. (See under Civilization; see also introduction to Bibliography.)

Tsae, Tin-Lang. *Mémoires d'un voyageur chinois sur l'empire d'Annam*, Publications de l'Ecole des langues orientales vivantes, Ser. 1, Vol. 7, Paris, 1878.

Veuillot, Eugène. *Le Tonkin et la Cochinchine; le pays, l'histoire et les missions*, new ed., Paris, Société générale de librairie catholique, 1883.

Villa, Marguerite. "Les Espagnols dans l'Empire d'Annam; table succincte de la série des articles du Père Lorenzo Perez, Archives Ibéro-Américaines, 1922-1933," BSEI, n. s., 15 (1940), Nos. 3-4, pp. 105-106.

————, tr. "La révolte et la guerre des Tayson d'après les franciscains espagnols de Cochinchine; les espagnols dans l'empire d'Annam, Archives Ibéro-Américaines, juillet-septembre 1932, Nos. 107, quatorzième article," BSEI, n. s., 15 (1940), Nos. 3-4, pp. 65-106.

Villars, P. "Les Anglais au Tonkin," *Revue de Paris*, 1903.

Villemerevil, A. B. de. "Les voyages des européens des côtes d'Annam à la Vallée du Mekong," *Bul. Soc. Géog. Rochefort*, ii, 1880-1881.

Wales, H.G. Quaritch. *Ancient South-East Asian Warfare*, London, 1952.

————. *The Making of Greater India*, London, 1951.

Ward, W. A. R. *A History of Siam*, Bangkok, 1933.

White, John. *History of a Voyage to the China Sea*, Boston, 1823. (See notes 8 and 15, Chapter V.)

Winckel. *Cochinchine française; les relations de la Hollande avec le Cambodge et la Cochinchine au XVIIe siècle*, Saigon, Impr. Nationale, 1882.

————. "Les relations de la Hollande avec le Cambodge et la Cochinchine au XVIIe siècle," *Rev. Indoch.*, Nov. 1906, pp. 1761-1777, also *Exc. et Rec.* No. 12 (1882), pp. 492-514.

Wittfogel, Karl A. *Oriental Despotism, A Comparative Study of Total Power*, New Haven, Yale University Press, 1957. (See also notes 42, Chapter II; 25, 66, Chapter III.)

Wittfogel, and Fang Chia-Sheng. *History of Chinese Society*, Philadelphia, 1949.

Yule, H. *Cathay and the Way Thither,* London, 1913.
——. *The Book of Ser Marco Polo,* London, 1921.

II. CIVILIZATION

Abadie, Maurice. *Les races du Haut Tonkin de Phong-Tho à Lang-Son, Préface de Paul Pelliot,* Paris, Challamel, 1924.
——. "Les Man du Haut Tonkin," *Rev. Ethnog. et des Trad. Pop.,* 3 (1922), pp. 81-110, 205-214.
Agat. "Le bouddhisme en Annam," *L'Avenir du Tonkin,* June 9, 1934.
Anonymous. "Les races pré-chinoises du Haut-Tonkin," *Rev. Troupes Col.,* 1907.
——. *Variétés sur les Moïs: recueil de relations anciennes de divers voyages accomplis par Gautier (1882), Nouot (1882), Humann (1884), Yersin (1893) chez les Moï et les Stieng,* Saigon, Ouvrage édition du Gouvernement de la Cochinchine, Impr. Ardin, 1935. (Documents on the Moi, 1861-1935.)
——. "De la puissance paternelle en droit français et en droit annamite," *Bul. Gén. Instr. Publ.,* Nov., 1924, pp. 123-127.
——. "Les droits des villages (du Tonkin)," *Asie Fran.,* 6 (1906), pp. 253-254.
——. "Les examens triennaux des lettres au Tonkin," *Rev. Indoch.* Oct., 1894, pp. 176-197.
——. "Le mariage annamite," *France-Asie,* No. 5 (Aug., 1946), pp. 222-225.
——. "L'organisation sociale des Annamites," *Rev. Indoch.* Sept., 1893, pp. 127-155.
——. "La police des villages, Tonkin," *Asie Fran.,* 11 (1911), p. 371.
——. *Annuaire statistique de l'Indochine, 1937-1938.*
——. *Annuaire statistique de l'Union française outre-mer, B-91.*
Ardant du Picq, Lt. Col. "Monographie du pays moï (Indochine, province de Kontum et de Banmethuot)," *Rev. Troupes Col.,* 19 (1925), pp. 389-404, 550-565; 20 (1926), pp. 25-45, 137-156, 205-231.

BIBLIOGRAPHY

Aubaret, G., tr. *Code annamite; lois et règlements du royaume d'Annam; traduits du texte chinois original,* 2 vols. Paris, Impr. impériale, 1865. (See introduction to Bibliography; see also under History.)

Auboyer, Jeannine. "Les religions de l'Indochine et de l'Insulinde," Vol. 4, pp. 385-433, photog. Vietnam: pp. 426-433, in M. Gorce and R. Mortier, *Histoire générale des religions,* Libr. Aristide Quillet, 1947.

Aurillac, H. *Cochinchine: Annamites, Moïs, Cambodgiens,* Paris, Challamel, 1870.

Baudesson, Henri. "Deux ans chez les Moïs (une section d'études du Transinochinois)," *Tour du Monde,* 1906, pp. 37-384.

———. *Indochina and its primitive peoples,* translated by E. Appleby Holt, London, Hutchinson, New York, Dutton, 1919.

Beerski, P. Jeanerat de. *Angkor/Ruins in Cambodia,* London, 1923.

Benedict, Paul K. *Selected list of materials for the study of the Annamese language,* New York, Southeast Asia Institute, Language Series No. 3, 1947. (Annotated.)

———. "Tonal systems in Southeast Asia," *Jl. Am. Or. Soc.,* 68 (1948), pp. 184-191.

Bernard, (R. P.) Henri. "Le conflit de la religion annamite avec la religion d'Occident à la cour de Gia-Long," CEFEO, No. 25 (1940), pp. 17-30; also *Bul. Gén. Instr. Publ.,* Jan. 1941.

Bonifacy, A. "Les débuts du christianisme en Annam," *L'Avenir du Tonkin,* April 23-Nov. 15, 1929, also Hanoi, Impr. Tonkinoise, 1930.

———. "Les génies du temple de Thê-loc," BEFEO, 10 (1910), pp. 683-694.

———. "Les populations montagnards du Tonkin," *Rev. Troupes. Col.,* 1906, 2nd sem., pp. 335-363, 431-459.

Bouinais, A. and Paulus, A. *Le culte des morts dans le Céleste Empire et l'Annam, comparé au culte des ancêtres dans l'antiquité occidentale,* Musée Guimet, Bibliothèque de vulgarisation, Vol. 6, Paris, Leroux, 1893.

Bouyanne, A. A. *L'hydraulique agricole au Tonkin,* 2 vols., Hanoi, 1931.

Boyer, Gabriel. *Le régime des successions en droit annamite,* thesis, Paris, 1920.

Briffaut, Camille. *La cité annamite,* A major scholarly study, essential for an understanding of Vietnamese society before its transformation under colonial rule.

——. *Droit civil sino-annamite,* Hanoi, Impr. d'Ext.-Or., 1921. (Historical notes on the Sino-Annamite family, marriage, succession, etc.)

——. "L'esclavage et l'engagement pour dettes dans le droit sino-annamite," *Revue des Questions pratiques de legislation industrielle,* 1906 and 1907; also Lyon, Storck, 1907.

——. *Principes de la loi pénale annamite,* Hanoi, Impr. Tonkinoise, 1918. (Commentary on the royal ordinance, July 16, 1917. See introduction to Bibliography.)

Brodrick, Alan H. "The son of Heaven, an emperor in French Indo-China," *Geog. Mag.,* 11 (1940), pp. 428-442.

——. *Little China; The Annamese Lands,* Oxford University Press, London-New York, 1942.

Brunhes, Jean. "Chez les primitifs de l'Indochine centrale," *Jl. Marine Marchande,* April 12, 19, 1923.

Bui-Thi-Cam. *Etude sur la condition privée de la femme en droit annamite,* thesis, Paris, Loviton, 1940.

Bui-Tuong-Chieu. *La polygamie dans le droit annamite.* Etudes théoriques et pratiques du droit étranger, Paris, Rousseau, 1933.

Cadière, Leopold. *Croyances et pratiques religieuses des Annamites,* (Publications de la Société de Géographie.) Hanoi, Imp. d'Ext.-Or., 1944.

——. "La famille et la religion en pays annamite," *Bul. Amis Hué,* 17 (1930), pp. 353-413.

——. "Philosophie populaire annamite," *Anthropos,* 2 (1907), pp. 116-127, 955-969; 3 (1908), pp. 248-271; also *Rev. Indoch.* Sept.-Dec. 909, pp. 835-847, 947-989, 1189-1216.

——. "Puériculture magique en Annam," *Annali Lateranensi,* 1 (1937), pp. 153-167.

——. "Les religions de l'Annam," *Recherches de science religieuse,* 1913, Nos. 1-3, 6. (See introduction to Bibliography; see also under History.)

BIBLIOGRAPHY

Canivey, Jules. "Notice sur les moeurs et coutumes des Moï de la région de Dalat, plateau du Lang-Biang, province de Phanrang, Annam," *Rev. Ethnog. et de Sociol.*, 4 (1913), pp. 1-30.

Chappoulié, H. *Rome et les missions d'Indochine au XVIIe siècle*, 2 vols., Paris, 1943-1947.

Chapuis, (R.P.) A. "La maison annamite au point de vue religieux," *Bul. Amis Hué*, 1937, pp. 1-50.

Chassigneux, E. *L'irrigation dans le delta du Tonkin*, Paris, 1912. (See introduction to Bibliography; see also under History.)

Chatterji, Bijan Raj. *Indian Cultural Influence in Cambodia*, University of Calcutta, 1928.

Coedès, G. *Pour mieux comprendre Angkor*, Paris, 1924. (See introduction to Bibliography; see also under History.)

Cordier, Henri. "Les Lolos (état actuel de la question)," *T'oung Pao* 2nd ser., 8 (1907), pp. 597-687. (See introduction to Bibliography; see also under History.)

Cottes, A. "Sur les populations Thai du Tonkin," *Premier Congr. Intern. Etudes Ext.-Or.*, Hanoi, 1902, pp. 118-119.

Coué, André. Doctrines et cérémonies religieuses du pays d'Annam, BSEI, 1933, No. 3, pp. 85-194, also Saigon, Testelin, 1933.

Coulet, Georges. *Cultes et religions de l'Indochine annamite*, Saigon, Ardin, 1929.

Courtois, E. "La famille annamite: mariages, naissances, décès, cérémonies auxquelles ils donnent lieu," *Rev. Indoch.* 1900, 1st sem., pp. 509-511.

Cremazy, L. *Le culte des ancêtres en Chine et dans l'Annam*," *Rev. Indoch.*, Nov., 1900, pp. 1066-1068, 1088-1089.

Cuisinier, Jeanne. *Les Muong. Géographie humaine et sociologie*, Paris, Institut d'Ethnologie, Musée de l'Homme, 1948. (Travaux et Mémoires de l'Institut d'Ethnologie, Université de Paris, 45.) An ethnographic monograph. The standard work on the Muong.

Cupet, Capt. "Chez les populations sauvages du Sud de l'Annam 1887-1891," *Tour du Monde*, 1 (1893), pp. 177-256.

Cury, L. *La société annamite; les lettres, les mandarins, le peuple*, thesis, Paris, 1910.

Dang-Ngoc-Oanh. "La collation des titres nobiliaires à la cour d'Annam," *Bul. Amis Hué*, 5 (1918), pp. 79-98.

——. "Les distinctions honorifiques annamites," *Bul. Amis Hué,* 2 (1915), pp. 391-406.

Dang-Phuc-Thong. *La femme dans la société annamite,* Hanoi, Impr. Tan-Dan, 1931.

D'Arbois, Jean. "La commune et le régime de propriété dans l'ancien Annam," *L'Avenir du Tonkin,* April 18, 1931, p. 1; supplement of April 25, p. 2; supplement of May 4, p. 4; supplement of May 26, p. 2.

Dartiguenave, Henri. "De quelques principes fondamentaux de la loi pénale annamite," *Rev. Indoch.,* Dec., 1909, pp. 1153-1170.

De Barthelemy, P. *Au pays moï,* Paris, Plon, 1904. (Moï of Hué region; Stiengs and Moï of Djambra.)

——. "Au pays des Moïs," *Bul. Soc. Géog.* Paris, 7th ser., 20 (1899), pp. 330-343.

Deloustal, Raymond. "La justice dans l'ancien Annam; traduction et commentaire du Code des Lê," BEFEO 8 (1908), pp. 177-220; 9 (1909), pp. 92-122, 471-491, 765-796; 10 (1910), pp. 1-60, 349-392, 461-505; 11 (1911), pp. 25-66, 313-337; 12 (1912), No. 6, pp. 1-33; 15 (1913), No. 5, pp. 1-59; 19 (1919), No. 4, pp. 1-86; 22 (1922), pp. 1-35.

Des Michels, Abel. "Mémoire sur les origines et le caractère de la langue annamite et sur l'influence que la littérature chinoise a exercé sur le mouvement intellectuel en Cochinchine et au Tonkin," Mémoires presentés par divers savants à l'Académie des inscriptions et belles-lettres, Ser. 1, 10 (1893), Pt. 1, pp. 1-31.

——. "Quelques observations au sujet des mots chinois Giao chi, nom des ancêtres du peuple annamite," Vol. I, pp. 281-297. In *Recueil de l'Ecole des Langues Orientales,* 1889. (See introduction to Bibliography; see also under History.)

D'Enjoy, Paul. "Du droit successoral en Annam; institution d'hérédité: biens du culte familial; fêtes rituelles," *Bul. Mem. Soc. Anthr.* 5th ser., 4 (1903), pp. 498-504.

De Pouvourville, A. *L'annamite.* (Vietnamese culture and French influences on Vietnamese character and society.) Paris, Larose, 1932.

——. "Le village annamite," *Monde Col. Illus.,* 16 (1939), pp. 148-149.

510

De Rozario, E. "Le Tonkin: groupes ethniques indigènes," *Bul. Soc. Ens. Tonkin,* 15 (1935), pp. 187-215.

Desbois, Jean. "Rituel funéraire annamite," *France-Asie,* No. 8 (Nov. 1946), pp. 459-467.

Diguet, Edouard J. J. *Les Annamites; société, coutumes, religions,* Paris, Challamel, 1906. (A good general study.)

———. *Etude de la langue tai précédée d'une notice sur les races des hautes régions du Tonkin, comprenant grammaire, méthode d'écriture tai et vocabulaire,* Hanoi, Schneider, 1895.

———. *Les montagnards du Tonkin. Preface de A. Pavie,* Paris Challamel, 1908; also 1926. (See introduction to Bibliography; see also under History.)

Dodd, William C. *The Tai race, elder brother of the Chinese, results of experience, exploration and research,* Cedar Rapids Torch Press, 1923. (An account of the distributioon of Thai populations in South China and Southeast Asia.)

Dorgelès, Roland. "Twentieth century 'savages'; The 'Mois' of Indo-China suddenly assaulted by the white man's civilization (translated by Gertrude Emerson)," *Extrême-Asie,* 7 (1933), pp. 317-325.

Dubois, M. *Quoc-ngu et mécanisme des sons de la langue annamite; étude phonétique pratique,* Hanoi, Impr. d'Ext.-Or., 1909; also *Rev. Indoch.,* Sept.-Dec. 1908, pp. 383-393, 531-542, 642-649, 721-733, 821-826, 861-883.

Duerrwell, George. "La famille annamite et le culte des ancêtres," BSEI, No. 55 (1908), 2nd sem., pp. 1-16.

Dumarest, André. *La formation des classes sociales en pays annamite; préface de Henri Gourdon,* thesis, Paris, Lyon, 1935.

Dumoutier, G. "Une fête religieuse annamite au village de Phu-dong (Tonkin)," *Rev. Hist. Relig.,* 28 (1893), pp. 67-75.

Eickstedt, Egon von. "Forschungen in Sued- und Ostasien: II. Siam und Laos, das Tai Problem und die Chinoisants," *Z. Rass.,* 10 (1939), pp. 67.

———. "Forschungen in Sued- und Ostasien: III. Im Rotflussdelta und bei den obertonkinesischen Bergvoelkern." *Z. Rass,* 10 (1939), pp. 120-162.

Escalere, Lucien. *Le bouddhisme et cultes d'Annam*, Shanghai, Impr. T'ou-Se-We, 1937.

Fournier-Wailly, C. "Les institutions traditionnelles et la justice indigène en Annam et au Tonkin," *Asie Fran.* 9 (1909), pp. 328-339.

———. "La justice annamite et le milieu social indigène en Annam et au Tonkin," *Asie Fran.*, 9 (1909), pp. 375-387.

Fung, Y. L. *History of Chinese Philosophy*, Peiping, 1937.

Furnivall, J. S. *Educational Progress in Southeast Asia*, New York, 1943.

Garcin, F. *Au Tonkin: un an chez les Muongs*, Paris, Plon, 1891. (By an army officer.)

Gautier, Amédée. "Les Moï," *Bul. Soc. Géog. Rochefort*, 6 (1884-1885), pp. 139-149.

Giran, Paul. *Magie et religion annamites: introduction à une philosophie de la civilisation du peuple d'Annam*, Paris, Challamel, 1912. (Reviewed by J. Przyluski in BEFEO, 1913, No. 7.)

Girard, Henri. "Les tribus sauvages du Haut-Tonkin, Mans et Meos: notes anthropométriques et ethnographiques," *Bul. Géog. Hist. Descr.*, 18 (1903), pp. 421-497; also separately published, Paris, Impr. Nationale, 1904.

Gourou, Pierre. *L'utilisation du sol en Indochine française*, Paris, 1940.

———. *Les paysans du delta tonkinois; étude de géographie humaine*, Paris, 1936. (See introduction to Bibliography; see also under History.)

Grivaz, Raymond. *Aspects sociaux et économiques du sentiment religieux en pays annamite*, thesis, Paris, Domat-Montchrestien, 1942. (Etudes de Sociologie et d'Ethnologie juridiques, Vol. 34.)

Groslier, Georges. *The Art and Civilization of Angkor*, Frederick A. Praeger, New York 1957. ". . . this book is one of the first full-scale accounts of (Angkor Wat's) structure and its history to be issued for the general reader . . . The book is written with an obviously deep love for the subject, and in any case, the illustrations are its real charm."—*The New Yorker*, Nov., 7, 1957. (For a long list of works on Angkor, see note 34, Chapter I.)

Heine-Geldern, R. von. "L'art prébouddhique de la Chine et de l'Asie du Sud-Est et son influence en Océanie," *Revue des Arts*

Asiatiques, XI (1937), No. 4. (See introduction to Bibliography; see also under History.)

———. "Suedostasien," in G. Buschan, ed., *Illustrierte Voelkerkunde,* Stuttgart, 1923. (See note 17, Chapter II.)

Hobbs, Cecil C. and assocs. *Indochina: a bibliography of land and people,* Washington, 1950.

Ho-Dac-Diem. *La puissance paternelle dans le droit annamite,* thesis, Paris, Jouve, 1928.

Huard, Capt. Paul. "Les Muongs (contribution à l'étude des groupes ethniques du noeud des trois frontières: Annam, Cochinchine, Cambodge)." TIA, 3 (1938), pp. 261-268.

Huard, P. "Le noircissement des dents au Tonkin," *Indochine* (March 25, 1943).

Huard and Bigot. "Les caracteristiques anthropo-biologiques des Indochinois," *Tr. Inst. Anat. V.,* Hanoi, 1938.

Huard, Pierre, and Durand, Maurice. *Connaissance du Vietnam,* Paris and Hanoi, 1954. This is the most up-to-date and most comprehensive study of Vietnamese civilization, with brief chapters on geography, pre-history, law, literature, music, medicine, etc. as well as almost complete lists of works on these subjects by Vietnamese authors. See also under History.

Hughes, E. R. *Chinese Philosophy in Classical Times,* London, 1942.

Jammes, L. "Quelle est la religion des annamites," BSEI, 1895, 2nd sem., pp. 31-36.

Janneau, G. "Essai sur l'origine de la langue annamite," BSEI, 1883, Trim. 3-4, pp. 187-200.

Jobbe-Duval, E. *La commune annamite d'après de récents travaux,* Paris, Larose, 1896. (From the *Nouvelle Revue historique de droit français et étranger.*)

Kherian, G. "Le problème démographique en Indochine," *Revue Indochinoise Juridique et Economique,* 1937.

Kresser, P. *La commune annamite en Cochinchine; le recrutement des notables,* thesis, Paris, Domat-Montchrestien, 1935.

La Giang. "La polygamie," *Indochine,* March 16, 1944.

Lajonquiere, E. Lunet du. *Inventaire descriptif des monuments du Cambodge,* 4 vols., Paris, 1902-1911.

Lan, J. "Le riz: législation, culte, croyances," *Bul. Amis Hué,* 6 (1919), pp. 389-452.

Landes, A., tr. *Les pruniers refleuris, poème tonquinois; transcrit par M. Phan-Duc-Hoa, lettré de la municipalité de Cholon, traduit et accompagné de notes par A. Landes,* Saigon, Impr. du Gouvernement, 1884; also *Exc. et Rec.,* No. 17 (1884), pp. 225-229; No. 18 (1884), pp. 301-383; No. 19 (1884), pp. 43-146. (Introductory chapter entitled "Notes sur la langue et la littérature annamites.")

——. "Notes sur les moeurs et les superstitions populaires des Annamites," *Exc. et Rec.,* 6 (1880), pp. 447-464; 7 (1881), pp. 137-148; 8 (1881), pp. 351-370; 11 (1882), pp. 267-279; 14 (1882), pp. 250-269; 15 (1883), pp. 580-593.

Lasker, B. *Peoples of Southeast Asia,* New York, 1944.

Lavallée, A. "Notes ethnographiques sur diverses tribus du Sud-Est de l'Indo-Chine," BEFEO, 1 (1901), pp. 291-311.

Lechesne, P. *L'Indo-Chine seconde; régions moïs (Kontoum-Darlac),* Quinhon, Annam, Impr. de Quinhon, 1924.

Le Dantec. "Les peuples de la Rivière-Noire," *Ann. Géog.,* 1892, pp. 249-259.

Legendre, A. F. "Les Lolos (étude anthropologique)," *Bul. Mém. Soc. Anthr.,* 6th ser., 1 (1910), pp. 77-94.

Lemonier, Lt. Col. "L'éducation militaire de Gia-Long," *Rev. Troupes Col.,* 28 (1934), pp. 561-600.

Leuba, J. *Un royaume disparu: Les chams et leur art,* Paris, 1923.

Leuret le Ferron. "L'assistance sociale dans l'Annam d'autrefois et sa renaissance sous l'action de la puissance protectrice," Annales Univ. Hanoi, 1 (1933), pp. 149-164.

Le-Van-Dinh. *Le culte des ancêtres en droit annamite,* Paris, 1934.

Maître, Henri. *Les jungle moï (exploration et histoire des hinterlands moï du Cambodge, de la Cochinchine, de l'Annam et du Bas-Laos),* Paris, Larose, 1912.

Malleret, L. *Groupes ethniques de l'Indochine,* Saigon, 1937.

Malot, Fernand. *La commune annamite; sa formation, sa constitution, ses rapports avec l'état,* Paris, Jouve, 1903.

Marcel, Henri. "Le role des maîtres indigènes dans l'enseignement, l'application et la vulgarisation des règles de l'hygiène," *Bul. Gén. Instr. Publ.*, April, 1928, pp. 117-215.

Maspéro, Henri. "Moeurs et coutumes des population sauvages," in G. Maspéro, ed., *Un empire colonial français, l'Indochine*, Paris, 1929, Vol. 1, pp. 233-255.

———. *Les religions chinoises*, Vol. I.

———. "Quelques mots annamites d'origine chinoise," BEFEO, 16 1916), No. 3, pp. 35-39. (See introduction to Bibliography; see also under History.)

Ma Touan Lin. "Ethnographie des peuples étrangers à la Chine," Geneva, 1876-1883.

Maunier, R., Chauffard, E., Boulloche, L., Prêtre, C., and Finot, L. *Les populations indigènes de l'Annam; étude de sociologie coloniale*, Paris, 1910.

Maurice, A. "Recherches sur les Muongs (2e serie)," TIA, 6 (1939), pp. 1-20.

Meillet and Cohen. *Les langues du monde*, 2nd ed., Paris, 1953, articles by H. Maspéro and J. Przyluski.

Migot, O. "Le bouddhisme en Indochine (pénétration, développement, diverses formes actuelles)," BSEI, n. s., 21 (1946), 2nd sem., pp. 23-38.

Monfleur, A. *Indochine française: Annam: monographie de la province du Darlac* (1930), Hanoi, Impr. d'Ext.-Or., 1931, also Exposition coloniale internationale, Paris, 1931.

Mus, Paul. "The role of the village in Vietnamese politics," *Pac. Aff.*, 23 (1949), pp. 265-272. (See introduction to Bibliography; see also under History.)

Nguyen-Huu-Khang. *La commune annamite, étude historique, juridique et économique; préface de M. Pierre Lampul*, Paris, Sirey, 1946.

Nguyen-Huy-Lai. *Les régimes matrimoniaux en droit annamite*, thesis, Paris, Domat-Montchrestien, 1934, *(Etudes de Sociologie et d'Ethnologie juridiques)*.

Nguyen-Manh-Tuong. *L'individu dans la vieille cité annamite; essai de synthèse sur le code des Lê*, thesis, Montpellier, Impr. de la presse, 1932.

Nguyen-Van-Huyen. *La communauté villageoise et le culte des génies tutélaires,* Hanoi, Taupin, 1940. (From *Indochine,* No. 9, Nov. 7, 1940.)

———. *La civilisation annamite,* Hanoi, Impr. d'Ext.-Or., 1944. (Summary review by E. Seidenfaden in JSS, 36, Pt. 2 (1947), pp. 151-169.)

———. "Le culte des immortels en Annam," CEFEO, No. 30 (1942), pp. 15-16.

———. *Le culte des immortels en Annam,* Hanoi, Impr. d'Ext.-Or., 1944.

———. "Les Man du Tonkin et leur habitation," CEFEO, No. 34 (1943), p. 29. (See introduction to Bibliography.)

Nguyen-Van-To. "Origine du quoc-ngu," *Bul. Soc. Ens. Tonkin,* 13 (1933), pp. 290-292.

Ory, P. *La commune annamite au Tonkin,* Paris, Challamel, 1894. (Organization, particularly political.)

Parker, E. H. "The Muong language," *China Rev.,* 19 (1891), pp. 267-280.

Parmentier, H. *Les sculptures chames au Musée de Tourane,* Paris, 1922.

———. *L'art khmer classique,* 2 vols., Paris, 1939.

———. *La religion ancienne de l'Annam, d'après les dernières découvertes archéologiques de l'Ecole Française d'Extrême-Orient,* Paris, Leroux, 1906. (Annales du Musée Guimet, Bibliothèque de Vulgarisation, Vol. 20, pp. 1-14.)

Pasquier, Pierre. *L'Annam autrefois; essai sur la constitution de l'Annam avant l'intervention française,* Paris, Société des Editions Géographiques, Maritimes et Coloniales, 1907, reissued 1930. (See notes 57, Chapter I; 18, 36, Chapter III; 22, 35, Chapter V; see introduction to Bibliography; see also under History.)

Petit, Robert. *La monarchie annamite,* Paris, Domat-Montchrestien and Loviton, 1931. (*Etudes de Sociologie et d'Ethnologie Juridiques,* Vol. 5.)

Pham-Quang-Bach. *Essai sur l'idée de la loi dans le code Gia-Long,* Paris, Picart, 1935.

Pham Quynh. *L'idéal du sage dans la philosophie confucéenne,*

Hanoi, 1928. (See introduction to Bibliography; see also under History.)

Pham-Van-Luu. "Le mariage annamite," *Bul. Soc. Géog. Col.* Marseille, 1906, pp. 265-274.

Pham-Van-Truong. *Essai sur le code Gia-Long,* thesis, Paris, Sago, 1922.

Philastre, P. L. F. *Etudes sur le droit annamite et chinois; le code annamite; Art. 84 vérification sur place des partes de l'impôt en grain des rizières causées par des calamités naturelles,* Saigon, 1871.

———. *Etudes sur le droit annamite et chinois; le code annamite; Art. 86, terres et rizières des sujets méritants,* Saigon, 1871.

———. *Etudes sur le droit annamite et chinois; le code annamite; nouvelle traduction complète comprenant les commentaires officiels du Code, traduits pour la première fois; de nombreuses annotations extraites des commentaires du code chinois; des renseignements relatifs à l'histoire du droit, tirés de plusieurs ouvrages chinois; des explications et des renvois,* 2 vols., Paris, Leroux, 1876; 2nd ed., 2 vols., Paris, Leroux, 1909. (See notes 115, 116, Chapter VI; see also introduction to Bibliography.)

Przyluski, J. "Moeurs et coutumes de l'ancien An-nam," in G. Maspéro, *Un empire colonial français, l'Indochine,* Paris, 1929. Vol. 1, pp. 205-213.

Robequain, Charles. *L'Indochine,* 3rd ed., Paris, 1952.

———. *The Economic Development of French Indochina,* London, New York, 1944.

———. *Les races montagnardes de l'Indochine,* Paris, 1947. (*Problèmes de l'Indochine contemporaine, Collège libre des sciences sociales et économiques, Section d'Outre-Mer,* No. 6.)

———. *Le Than Hoa, étude géographique d'une province annamite,* thesis, 2 vols., Université de Grenoble, Paris, 1929. ("Human geography" of an important Vietnamese province. See introduction to Bibliography and under History.)

Robert, G. "Notes d'ethnographie indochinoise," *Rev. Ethnog. et de Sociol.,* 5 (1914), pp. 223-226.

517

Rosset, C. W. "Die hinterindischen Volksstaemme," *Mitt. Geog. Ges. Wien,* 39 (1896), pp. 113-139.

———. "The wild peoples of Farther India," *Jl. Am. Geog. Soc.,* 25 (1893), pp. 289-303.

Rouilly, Marcel. *La commune annamite,* thesis. Paris, Presses Modernes, 1929.

Roux, Jules. *Le triomphe définitif en Indochine du mode de transcription de la langue annamite à l'aide des caractères romains ou "Quoc ngu,"* Paris, 1912. (Conférence faite le 6 juillet 1912, à la Mairie du VIe arrondissement de Paris sous les auspices de l'Association philotechnique de Paris.)

Savina, F. M. *Histoire des Miao,* Hongkong, Impr. Soc. Miss. Etr., 1924. (Study of Miao history and culture.)

Schmidt, Wilhelm. *Grundzuege einer Lautlehre der Mon-Khmer-Sprachen,* Wien, Gerold, 1905. (Denkschriften der Kaiserlichen Akademie der Wissenschaften in Wien. Philosophisch-Historische Klasse, V. 51, No. 3.)

Schreiner, Alfred. *Etude sur la constitution de la propriété foncière en Cochinchine.* Saigon, Menard, 1902; also BSEI, No. 43 (1902), 1st sem., pp. 3-303.

———. *Les institutions annamites en Basse-Cochinchine avant la conquête française,* 3 vols., Saigon, Claude, 1900-1902. (See introduction to Bibliography; see also under History.)

Scott, James G. "Annamese ancestral worship," JRASS, No. 15 (1885), pp. 164-171.

Securani, M. "L'ancienne armée annamite," *Rev. Troupes Col.,* Nos. 245-248 (Dec. 1937-March 1938).

Seton, Grace T. *Poison arrows,* London, Travel Book Club, 1938. (Popular travel book about the Moï.)

Silvestre, J. *Considérations sur l'étude du droit annamite, par le Commandant J. Silvestre, ancien chef de la justice indigène en Cochinchine, professeur a l'Ecole des Sciences politiques,* Paris, Bureaux du Recueil général de Jurisprudence; also Saigon, Portail, 1923.

———. "Introduction a l'étude du droit annamite." *Ann. de l'Ecole des Sciences Politiques,* July 15, 1889, pp. 385-404. (See introduction to Bibliography.)

518

Soothill, W. E. *The Analects of Confucius,* Yokohama, 1910.

Tavernier, Emile. "Comptes-rendus critiques de 'Le culte des ancêtres en droit annamite' de M. Le-van-Dinh et de 'La polygamie dans le droit annamite' de M. Bui-tuong-Chieu," *Bul. Soc. Ens. Tonkin,* 14 (1934), pp. 222-228, 207 239

———. *La famille annamite.* Saigon, Editions Nguyen-Van Cua, 1927. *(Publication de la Commission Luro faite sous le patronage de la Société des études indochinoises.)*

Thomas, Winburn T., and Manikam Rajah B. *The Church in South East Asia,* New York, 1956.

Tran-Ba-Tho, tr. "La piété filiale: préceptes de la morale confucéenne," BSEI, No. 54 (1908), 1st sem., pp. 55-156. (Tr. in Quoc Ngu and in French; also Chinese text.)

Tran-Van-Giap. "Le bouddhisme en Annam, dès origines au XIIIe siècle; Introduction. I. Les origines. II. Les pèlerins. III. Bodhidharma et ses successeurs. IV. Vinitaruci et ses successeurs. V. Vo-ngon-thong et ses successeurs. VI. Thao-duong et ses successeurs. Conclusion. Appendice," BEFEO, 32 (1932), pp. 191-268.

———. "La vie d'un mandarin annamite du XVIe siècle d'après une stèle funéraire découverte dans la région de Dong-Son à Thanh-Hoa," CEFEO, No. 26 (1941), pp. 24-25. (See introduction to Bibliography.)

Tran-Van-Trai. *La famille patriarcale annamite,* thesis, Paris, 1942. (One of the major works on Vietnamese society by a Vietnamese scholar. See also notes 57, Chapter III; 34, Chapter V and introduction to Bibliography; see also under History.)

Truong-Vinh-Ky, Petrus J-B. *Cours d'histoire annamite à l'usage des écoles de la Basse-Cochinchine,* 2 vols., Saigon, Impr. du Gouvernement, 1875-1905.

Vallot, P. G. *Origine de la langue annamite et du cuoc ngu,* Hanoi, Schneider, 1903.

Villard, E. "Etude sur le droit administratif annamite," *Exc. et Rec.,* No. 11 (1882), pp. 306-357; also Saigon, Impr. Coloniale, 1882; also Saigon, 1892.

———. "Etude sur le droit civil annamite," *Exc. et Rec.,* No. 5 (1880), pp. 321-372.

———. "Etude sur le droit pénal annamite," *Exc. et Rec.*, No. 13 (1882), pp. 73-167.

Vu-Van-Hien. *La propriété communale au Tonkin (contribution a l'étude historique, juridique et économique des Cong-dien et Cong-tho en pays d'Annam)*, thesis, Paris, Presses modernes, 1939; also Hanoi, Impr. d'Ext.-Or., 1939.

Waley, Arthur. *Three Ways of Thought in Ancient China*, New York, Doubleday (Anchor Book).

———. *The Analects of Confucius*, New York, 1939.

Wickizer, V. D., and Bennett, M. K. *Rice Economy of Monsoon Asia*, San Francisco, 1941.

Wittfogel, Karl A. *Oriental Despotism, A Comparative Study of Total Power*, New Haven, Yale University Press, 1957. (See notes 42, Chapter II; 25, 66, Chapter III.)

Index